# THE CAMBRIDGE HISTORY OF
## LATIN AMERICA

VOLUME X

*Latin America since 1930:*
*Ideas, culture and society*

# THE CAMBRIDGE HISTORY OF
# LATIN AMERICA

# THE CAMBRIDGE
# HISTORY OF
# LATIN AMERICA

VOLUME X

*Latin America since 1930*
*Ideas, Culture and Society*

*edited by*

## LESLIE BETHELL

*Emeritus Professor of Latin American History*
*University of London*
*and*
*Senior Research Fellow*
*St. Antony's College, Oxford*

 CAMBRIDGE
UNIVERSITY PRESS

Published by the Press Syndicate of the University of Cambridge
The Pitt Building, Trumpington Street, Cambridge CB2 1RP
40 West 20th Street, New York, NY 10011-4211, USA
10 Stamford Road, Oakleigh, Melbourne 3166, Australia

© Cambridge University Press 1995

First published 1995

Printed in the United States of America

Library of Congress Cataloging-in-Publication Data

Latin America since 1930. Ideas, culture and society / edited by
Leslie Bethell.
p.    cm.  – (The Cambridge history of Latin America : v. 10)
Includes bibliographical references and index.
ISBN 0-521-49594-6 (hc)
1.Latin America – Civilization – 20th century.    I. Bethell,
Leslie.    II. Series.
F1410.C1834 1984 vol. 10
[F1414]
980.03'3 – dc20                                              95-19365
                                                                CIP

A catalog record for this book is available from the British Library

ISBN 0-521-49594-6 hardback

# CONTENTS

vi                          *Contents*

# GENERAL PREFACE

Since *The Cambridge Modern History*, edited by Lord Acton, appeared in sixteen volumes between 1902 and 1912 multi-volume Cambridge Histories, planned and edited by historians of established reputation, with individual chapters written by leading specialists in their fields, have set the highest standards of collaborative international scholarship. *The Cambridge Modern History* was followed by *The Cambridge Ancient History, The Cambridge Medieval History* and others. The *Modern History* has been replaced by *The New Cambridge Modern History* in fourteen volumes. *The Cambridge Economic History of Europe* and Cambridge Histories of Iran, of Southeast Asia and of Africa have been published; in progress are Histories of China, of Japan, of India and of Latin America.

Cambridge University Press decided the time was ripe to embark on a Cambridge History of Latin America early in the 1970s. Since the Second World War and particularly since 1960 research and writing on Latin American history had been developing, and have continued to develop, at an unprecedented rate – in the United States (by American historians in particular, but also by British, European and Latin American historians resident in the United States), in Britain and continental Europe, and increasingly in Latin America itself (where a new generation of young professional historians, many of them trained in the United States, Britain or continental Europe, had begun to emerge). Perspectives had changed as political, economic and social realities in Latin America – and Latin America's role in the world – had changed. Methodological innovations and new conceptual models drawn from the social sciences (economics, political science, historical demography, sociology, anthropology) as well as from other fields of historical research were increasingly being adopted by historians of Latin America. The Latin American Studies monograph series and the *Journal of Latin American Studies* had already been established by the Press and were beginning to publish the results of this new historical thinking and research.

Dr. Leslie Bethell, then Reader in Hispanic American and Brazilian History at University College London, accepted an invitation to edit *The Cambridge History of Latin America*. He was given sole responsibility for the planning, co-ordination and editing of the entire History and began work on the project in the late 1970s.

*The Cambridge History of Latin America,* to be published in ten volumes, is the first large-scale, authoritative survey of Latin America's unique historical experience during the five centuries since the first contacts between the native American Indians and Europeans (and the beginnings of the African slave trade) in the late fifteenth and early sixteenth centuries. (The Press will publish separately a three-volume Cambridge History of the Native Peoples of the Americas – North, Middle and South – which will give proper consideration to the evolution of the region's peoples, societies and civilizations, in isolation from the rest of the world, during several millennia before the arrival of the Europeans, as well as a fuller treatment than will be found here of the history of the indigenous peoples of Latin America under European colonial rule and during the national period to the present day.) Latin America is taken to comprise the predominantly Spanish- and Portuguese-speaking areas of continental America south of the United States – Mexico, Central America and South America – together with the Spanish-speaking Carribean – Cuba, Puerto Rico, the Dominican Republic – and, by convention, Haiti. (The vast territories in North America lost to the United States by treaty and by war, first by Spain, then by Mexico, during the first half of the nineteenth century are for the most part excluded. Neither the British, French and Dutch Caribbean islands nor the Guianas are included, even though Jamaica and Trinidad, for example, have early Hispanic antecedents and are now members of the Organization of American States.) The aim is to produce a high-level synthesis of existing knowledge which will provide historians of Latin America with a solid base for future research, which students of Latin American history will find useful and which will be of interest to historians of other areas of the world. It is also hoped that the *History* will contribute more generally to a deeper understanding of Latin America through its history in the United States, Europe and elsewhere and, not least, to a greater awareness of its own history in Latin America.

The volumes of *The Cambridge History of Latin America* have been published in chronological order: Volumes I and II (Colonial Latin Amer-

ica, with an introductory section on the native American peoples and
civilizations on the eve of the European invasion) were published in
1984; Volume III (From Independence to *c.* 1870) in 1985; Volumes IV
and V (*c.* 1870 to 1930) in 1986. The publication of volumes VI–X
(1930 to the present) began in 1990. Each volume or set of volumes
examines a period in the economic, social, political, intellectual and
cultural history of Latin America.

While recognizing the decisive impact on Latin America of external
forces, of developments within the world system, and the fundamental
importance of its economic, political and cultural ties first with Spain and
Portugal, then with Britain, France and Germany and finally with the
United States, *The Cambridge History of Latin America* emphasizes the evolution of internal structures. Furthermore, the emphasis is clearly on the
modern period, that is to say, the period since the establishment of all but
two (Cuba and Panama) of the independent Latin American states during
the first decades of the nineteenth century. The eight volumes of the
*History* devoted to the nineteenth and twentieth centuries consist of a
mixture of general, comparative chapters built around major themes in
Latin American history and chapters on the individual histories of the
twenty independent Latin American countries (plus Puerto Rico).

An important feature of the *History* is the bibliographical essays which
accompany each chapter. These give special emphasis to books and articles
which have appeared since Charles C. Griffin (ed.), *Latin America: A Guide
to the Historical Literature* (published for the Conference on Latin American
History by the University of Texas Press in 1971). Griffin's *Guide* was
prepared between 1962 and 1969 and included few works published after
1966. All the essays from Volumes I–X of *The Cambridge History of Latin
America* – where necessary revised, expanded and updated (to *c.* 1992) –
are brought together in a single bibliographical volume, Volume XI,
published in 1995.

# PREFACE TO VOLUME X

*The Cambridge History of Latin America* Volumes I and II began with a survey of native American peoples and civilizations on the eve of the European 'discovery', conquest and settlement of the 'New World' in the late fifteenth and early sixteenth centuries, but were largely devoted to the economic, social, political, intellectual and cultural history of Latin America under Spanish and (in the case of Brazil) Portuguese colonial rule from the sixteenth to the eighteenth centuries. Volume III examined the breakdown and overthrow of colonial rule throughout Latin America (except Cuba and Puerto Rico) at the beginning of the nineteenth century and the economic, social and political history of the independent Spanish American republics and the independent Empire of Brazil during the half century from *c.* 1820 to *c.* 1870/80. Volumes IV and V concentrated on the half century from *c.* 1870/80 to 1930 – for most of Latin America a 'Golden Age' of predominantly export-led economic growth as the region became more fully incorporated into the expanding international economy and a period of material prosperity (at least for the dominant classes), significant social change (both rural and urban), political stability (with some notable exceptions such as Mexico during the revolution), ideological consensus (at least until the 1920s), and notable achievements in intellectual and cultural life.

Volumes VI–X of *The Cambridge History of Latin America* are devoted to Latin America during the six decades from 1930 to *c.* 1990. Volume VI (published in 1994 – in two Parts) brings together general essays on major themes in the economic, social and political history of the region as a whole: the fourfold increase in population (from 110 to 450 million); the impact of the 1929 Depression and the Second World War on the Latin American economies; the second 'Golden Age' of economic growth (1950–80), this time largely ISI (import substitution industrialization)-

led, followed, however, by the so-called 'lost decade' of the 1980s; rapid
urbanization (less than 20 per cent of Latin America's population was
classified as urban in 1930, almost 70 per cent in 1990) and urban social
change; the transformation of agrarian structures; the development of
state organization and, in the 1980s, the beginnings of 'state shrinkage';
the advance of (as well as the setbacks suffered by) democracy in Latin
America; the (few) successes and (many) failures of the Latin American
left, both democratic and non-democratic; the military in Latin American
politics: military interventions and coups, military regimes, and the
problem of transition to civilian rule; the urban working class and urban
labour movements; rural mobilizations and rural violence; changes in the
economic, social and political role of women; and, finally, the persistence
of the Catholic church as a major force in political as well as religious and
social life throughout the region, and the rapidly growing Protestant
churches. Volume VII (published in 1990) is a history of Mexico, the five
Central American republics (Guatemala, Honduras, El Salvador, Nicaragua and Costa Rica), Panama and the Panama Canal Zone, the Hispanic
Caribbean (Cuba, Puerto Rico and the Dominican Republic) and Haiti.
Volume VII (published in 1991) is a history of the nine republics of
Spanish South America (Argentina, Uruguay, Paraguay, Chile, Peru,
Bolivia, Ecuador, Colombia and Venezuela). Volume IX (now the only
volume still in progress) will be a history of Brazil and of Latin America's
international relations – predominantly relations with Britain, continental Europe (in particular Germany), and above all the United States.
Volume X is devoted to the history of ideas and culture in Latin America
since *c.* 1920 (which is for this volume a more appropriate starting point
than 1930).

*The Cambridge History of Latin America* Volume X, *Latin America since
1930: Ideas, Culture and Society* opens with a long chapter – the longest of
any in the entire *History* – by Richard Morse that explores the 'multiverse
of identity' (both national and regional identity) in Latin America from
the 1920s to the 1960s through the writings of novelists, essayists,
philosophers, historians and sociologists. It should be read alongside the
chapters on economic ideas and ideologies in Latin America since 1930
(by Joseph Love) and science and society in twentieth century Latin America (by Thomas Glick) already published in *CHLA* Volume VI Part 1, as
well as the chapters that immediately follow it in this volume, those by
Gerald Martin on Latin American narrative, by Jaime Concha and by
Jason Wilson on Latin American poetry, and by Gordon Brotherston on

indigenous literatures and cultures. The volume also includes chapters on Latin American music (for the most part 'art music', but with a note on popular music) by Gerard Béhague, on Latin American architecture by Damián Bayón, and on Latin American art also by Damián Bayón. It concludes with chapters on the history of the Latin American cinema by John King and on the history of radio and television (the mass media) in Latin America by Elizabeth Fox. The early sections of some of the chapters in this volume to some extent overlap with the later sections of Gerald Martin's chapter on the literature, music and art (and early cinema) of Latin America from 1870 to 1930 in *CHLA* Volume IV.

Like Volume VI, this volume was an unusually long time in the writing and editing. Some chapters were commissioned more than a decade and a half ago. Many have been extensively revised and rewritten over the years. I am grateful to the authors of these chapters for their patience, especially Richard Morse. His chapter was one of the first ever to be discussed (on the beach at Leblon in Rio de Janeiro sometime in the late 1970s, as he cruelly likes to remind me) and is one of the last to be published. Gordon Brotherston, on the other hand, accepted an invitiation to contribute a chapter when the rest of the volume was already largely written. John King generously agreed to write the chapter on cinema when Julianne Burton was forced to withdraw. Jason Wilson at a late stage agreed not only to contribute a chapter on poetry after 1950 (to complement Jaime Concha's chapter on poetry in the first half of the twentieth century) but also to supply the bibliographical essay that accompanies both. Sadly, Damián Bayón died during the final stages of the editing of the volume.

A conference held at the Woodrow Wilson International Center for Scholars, Washington, D.C. in May 1986 offered an early opportunity for a number of contributors to *CHLA* Volume X to present preliminary drafts of their chapters to each other and to a group of distinguished non-contributors. I am grateful to Richard Morse, Director of the Wilson Center's Latin American Program at the time and himself a contributor to the volume, for the support he gave in the organization of this conference. It was, like the conference on *CHLA* Volume VI held at the University of California, San Diego earlier in the same year, in part funded by the Tinker Foundation.

Several contributors to this volume – four British (two resident in the United States), three North American, one Chilean (resident in the United States) and one Argentine (resident in France) – commented on the chapters of their colleagues. I am especially grateful in this respect to Richard

Morse, Gerald Martin and John King. James Dunkerley, who served as an associate editor on *CHLA* Volumes VII and VIII, offered support and encouragement in the editing of Volume X as well as Volume VI.

Secretarial assistance was provided by Hazel Aitken at the Institute of Latin American Studies, University of London (in the period 1987–1992) and Linnea Cameron at the Department of History, University of Chicago (in 1992–93).

# 1

## THE MULTIVERSE OF LATIN AMERICAN IDENTITY, *c.*1920–*c.*1970

### INTRODUCTION: CONTEXTS FOR IDENTITY

In the twentieth century the term 'identity' has been heavily worked to denote linkage between culture and society. Although the word keeps losing its edge, new generations periodically resharpen it. The term is so loose that one can apply it to anything from mankind at large[1] to a single person seeking self-knowledge via psychotherapy. Artists, poets, historians, anthropologists, philosophers and politicians entertain versions of identity even when not consciously in quest of it or not confident of the term's utility. This chapter will consider identity primarily with reference to national societies, to aggregations of national societies (Latin America), and to sub-national societies or groups. Two distinctions are important. First, identity, which implies linkage to or manifestation of collective conscience, is not the same as 'reality', a word widely used in Latin America to mean historical, socio-geographic factors that might be recognized as creating a circumambient reality. Both terms fluctuate between a descriptive, empirical meaning and a prospective or promissory one. 'Reality' may signify what 'really' exists or else, in a quasi-Hegelian sense, a 'higher' reality to be ascertained as a *sine qua non* for pursuit of the historic vocation of a people or nation (e.g., essays of interpretation of the 'Peruvian reality'). Identity is not 'national character' as diagnosed by detached socio-psychiatry but collective awareness of historic vocation. Reality starts with environment, identity with tacit self-recognition.

Identity, a human universal, assumed special accents with the rise of modern nations. Germany was a strategic case. As its leaders, thinkers,

---

[1] See Ernst Cassirer, *An Essay on Man: An Introduction to a Philosophy of Human Culture* (New Haven, Conn., 1944), Part II, ch. 6.

musicians and artists began to envision a German 'nation', they were driven to explore wellsprings of identity in ethnicity, folk culture and philosophic premises of history and religious faith. Germany has been called the first 'underdeveloped' country, implying that its advent on the world stage required not merely political *sagesse,* military prowess, and economic weight but affirmation of collective selfhood. Because England and France became (somewhat unwittingly) the first 'developed' countries as the industrial age dawned, their intelligentsias were more at home with political and economic matters than with the portentous metaphysical interests of Germans. In philosophizing, moreover, the English and French tended to conflate their national ideals with recipes for mankind at large. This produced a body of Enlightenment thought which in its more glib and self-serving aspects encountered head-on challenge from German romanticism. By the early nineteenth century this German rejoinder was a powerful solvent on mind and sensibility in England and France.

The lessons that the German analogy holds for Latin America and, more concretely, the ultimate influences of German ideas upon the region are examined later in the chapter. For the moment an illustration will show how present-day thinking on identity still falls under the shadow of the Enlightenment versus romanticism construction or, as in the case at hand, empiricism versus holism. In a collective work published in 1987, eight historians addressed the topic of colonial identity in the Atlantic world using six case studies (three of which were Brazil, Spanish America and the British Caribbean) to compare the formation of distinctive patterns in the period 1500 to 1800.[2] This comparative project required divorcing identity as 'self-definition and self-image' from the story of political independence and asking why some colonies had more 'success' at achieving psychological as well as political autonomy. The authors pursued their inquiry in a detached Anglo-empirical spirit rather than the empathic, holistic tradition of romanticism. The introductory chapter for example endorsed a quest for positive indicators of the 'process of identity formation' and cited such possible deterrents as the lack of printing presses in Brazil for three centuries or the absence of universities in the British West Indies until the 1950s. Identity is thus seen, as it was in the Enlightenment, as manipulable by technological and institutional innovation.

Scholars from the region itself had already addressed two of these cases

[2] Nicholas Canny and Anthony Pagden (eds.), *Colonial Identity in the Atlantic World, 1500–1800* (Princeton, N.J., 1987).

with different premises and purposes. Antônio Cândido, one of Brazil's foremost literary historians and critics, sees the absence of presses and gazettes in colonial Brazil not as inhibiting collective identity but as shaping it. Given an illiterate society, sacred oratory with its spoken word adapted to baroque arabesques and symbolism, was an ideal genre.[3] The Barbadian poet and historian Edward K. Brathwaite believes the distinctive spoken language of the present-day West Indies to be an emergent *nation language*, a form of 'total expression' that provides the keystone for regional identity. His colleagues at the School of Education, University of the West Indies, Brathwaite finds, have set out the grammar and syntax of the nation language but cannot connect it to literary expression. The whole school system, he holds, imposes a Victorian set of literary attitudes and responses that block creativity. The crux of the matter lies still deeper. The language issue lies not simply in lexicon, phonetics and subject matter but is rooted, Brathwaite argues, in the English capitulation since Chaucer to iambic pentameter. Caribbean life – the African legacy; the oral, communal expression of the people – is alien to the English language as parochially practised in England. 'The hurricane does not roar in pentameter.' Nor do the drums pulse to it. What the storm *does* roar in and what people *do* dance to – the young literati of the 1940s found out from their traditional calypsos – is a dactylic beat. This discovery provides academic nomenclature to legitimate everyday facts of life. Until then the disinherited must use the emergent nation language as a 'forced poetics' that perpetuates their culture while disguising self and personality. For literati and universities, one might venture, identity is not their invention but their belated recognition of social circumstance.[4]

The critical significance of language, or discourse, cannot receive central attention in this chapter.[5] Enough has been said, however, to suggest that the nature of our eight historians' concern with publication and universities (a reflection perhaps of modern academic anxiety) may not be wholly consistent with the understandings of this chapter. More germane to present purposes is the 'existential' commitment expressed as follows by W. H. Auden: 'In contrast to those philosophers who begin by considering the *objects* of human knowledge, essences and relations, the existential

---

[3] Antônio Cândido, 'Oswald viajante', in *Vários escritos* (São Paulo, 1970), pp. 51–6.
[4] Antônio Cândido, *Literatura e sociedade* (São Paulo, 1965), pp. 110–11; Edward Kamau Brathwaite, 'English in the Caribbean', in L. A. Fiedler and H. A. Baker, Jr. (eds.), *English Literature: Opening Up the Canon* (Baltimore, Md., 1981), pp. 15–53, and *Roots* (Havana, 1986).
[5] For a general treatment, see Richard M. Morse, 'Language in America', in *New World Soundings* (Baltimore, Md., 1989), pp. 11–60.

philosopher begins with man's immediate experience as a *subject*, i.e., as a being in *need*, an *interested* being whose existence is at stake.'[6] This 'existential' gambit is inviting, for it treats collective experience as a project or adventure. This informal inquiry can be launched in such a spirit, by placing Latin America alongside two other civilizations that confronted the industrial West in the nineteenth century – namely, Japan and Russia. This is not done in the empirical vein of meticulous 'comparative history' but simply to help sketch out a set of questions more useful for present purposes than the ones more frequently posed in academic circles.

Japan had for centuries acquired civilizational ways from the Chinese. Fruitful adaptation brought self-knowledge and, when the time came, an impressive capacity to select what was needed from the West with few confusions of purpose. The germ of Tokyo University was an institute of 'barbarian learning' designed to translate Western texts that seemed useful for the Japanese national project. This project was preceded by a scholarly movement to free Japan from the formalism and pedantry of the Chinese Confucian tradition (although not at the expense of the tradition itself) attended by evocations of Japanese spirit and esthetic. Such evocations have been likened to the quest by German romantics of the same period for an unbridled release of domestic tradition.[7]

In the case of Russia there had been longer direct exposure to the West than in Japan, notably via the construction of St Petersburg in 1703–12. As in Japan there was awareness of a domestic civilization that required decisions on what was to be 'protected'. The Russian generation of Slavophiles and Westernizers defined the dichotomy, with the former dreaming of an ideal pre-Petrine Russia and the latter of an ideal West. Westernizers complicated matters with their 'Russian rehash' of Western ideas, however, while Russian nationalists sent for study to Germany succumbed to a crypto-Francophilism more fanatical than even the chauvinism of the Parisian boulevards.[8] In any case the dialectic was established as clearly in Russia, allowing for clandestine cross-overs, as in Japan.

How Latin America fits into our summary comparison hinges on how the notion of an original culture is handled. The Japanese recognized a domestic culture to which exogenous elements were to be selectively

---

[6] Quoted in Mitzi Berger Hamovitch (ed.), *The Hound and Horn Letters* (Athens, Ga., 1982), p. xiv.
[7] See Marius B. Jansen, *Japan and its World, Two Centuries of Change* (Princeton, 1980), ch. 1.
[8] Nicolas Berdyaev, *The Origin of Russian Communism*, trans. R. M. French, new ed. (Ann Arbor, Mich., 1960), ch. 1; Isaiah Berlin, *Russian Thinkers* (Harmondsworth, 1979), pp. 114–49.

assimilated, while Russian nationalists envisioned recovery of pre-Petrine rural communalism and non-Western Christianity. Nineteenth-century Latin America, in contrast, was not a single nation, while its fragmented parts shared the culture and religion of the Iberian peninsula, by then a 'backward' region of western Europe. For Russian critics the societies of England and France may have represented soulless atomism, but for modernizing elites in Latin America these European leaders were paragons. And, if such elites regarded their Ibero-Catholic heritage as déclassé, all the more so were the hundreds of Afro-American and Amerindian communities that were stigmatized by past or present bondage. Whatever opposed the progress of the urban, Europeanized world was to be effaced. Consider the military campaigns against 'natives' and backlanders under General Roca in Argentina and under the Mexican dictator Porfirio Díaz in Sonora and Yucatan and the Canudos war in Brazil. Even 'judicious sociologists' like Carlos Octavio Bunge and Alcides Arguedas were agreed that 'nothing could be expected of the degraded aboriginal people'.[9]

Japanese engagement with Western science and culture was controlled and methodical, as instanced by the institute for 'barbarian books', the 'learning missions' sent abroad in the 1870s to identify 'realistic' national models for selective emulation, and the temperate enthusiasm for European institutions and manners during the 1880s that led to a permissive if not uncritical 'new Japanism'. On the other hand, many Russians, whether Europeanizers or Slavophiles, felt after 1848 that socialism would never regenerate bourgeois 'equilibrium' in the West and that Russia's 'primitive' collectivism offered possibilities for direct transition to modern socialism. Latin American elites, in contrast, apart from intransigent conservative factions or occasional free spirits, were prepared neither to question the implications of Western technology, rationalization and imperialism nor to promote broad consensus on matters of national culture and tradition. In his early writings, the Mexican philosopher Leopoldo Zea held that for Latin America the nineteenth century was in effect a 'lost century'.[10]

There were of course Latin Americans, individual *pensadores* and occasionally a national 'generation', who made signal contributions toward devising an agenda for their country or their continent. The point is that they were often adrift when it came to identifying *domestic* ingredients to be

[9] See José Luis Romero, *Latinoamérica: las ciudades y las ideas* (Buenos Aires, 1976), p. 311.
[10] See Leopoldo Zea, *The Latin-American Mind,* trans. J. H. Abbott and L. Dunham (Norman, Okla., 1963).

appropriated and adapted. The classic example is Domingo Faustino
Sarmiento (Argentina, 1811–88), whose reflections on the life and times of
the Argentine caudillo Facundo in *Civilización y barbarie* (1845) seemed to
pit liberal Europe as filtered through Buenos Aires against the 'barbarism' of
the pampas.[11] Read searchingly, Sarmiento's essay goes well beyond this
formula, especially when combined with the notes on his 1846–7 travels to
Europe and the United States when he discovered Europeans themselves to
be barbarous if compared to American frontiersmen. The general point,
however, is that well-to-do classes throughout Latin America, including
their 'enlightened' and reformist spokesmen, freely applied the term 'barbarian' not, as did the Japanese, to foreigners but to groups within their own
countries who were assignably 'native': Indians, mestizos, Afro-Americans,
or dirt farmers of Iberian descent.

The decisive rebuttal to Sarmiento came from José Martí (Cuba, 1853–
95) who, if he did not excel Sarmiento in his gift for social portraiture, was
a more adept analyst of social process and the exigencies of nationhood. In
an incisive passage in 'Nuestra América' (1891) he challenged those who
mistook the struggle between 'false erudition and Nature' as one between
'civilization and barbarity'.[12] 'The native halfbreed has conquered the
exotic Creole . . . The natural man is good, and he respects and rewards
superior intelligence as long as his humility is not turned against him.'
The tyrants of Latin America climb to power by appealing to disdained
native elements and fall by betraying them. 'Republics have paid with
oppression for their inability to recognize the true elements of their countries, to derive from them the right kind of government, and to govern
accordingly.' 'To govern well, one must see things as they are.'

Martí's contribution to defining the identity issue was to democratize
it. Nationalism had taken hold in Latin America but without the romanticist implication of rootedness in the people. Until the early twentieth
century, pensadores, essayists and historians seemed agreed that cultural
questions were a province of diagnosis and prescription reserved for intellectuals. The idea that people at large were the bedrock of national
identity was incongruous in default of sustained, pluricentric, multi-
ideological popular movements such as had shaped political awareness

[11] Domingo F. Sarmiento, *Life in the Argentine Republic in the Days of the Tyrants*, trans. Mrs Horace
Mann (New York, 1961); and see Joseph T. Criscenti (ed.), *Sarmiento and his Argentina* (Boulder,
Co., 1992) and Tulio Halperín Donghi et al. (eds.) *Sarmiento, Author of a Nation* (Berkeley, 1994).
[12] José Martí, *Our America*, Philip S. Foner (ed.) (New York, 1977), pp. 86–7.

and political process in Western Europe, most significantly the Protestant Reformation and the proletarian revolution. Thinkers, theologians, ideologues and politicians might supply doctrine and tactics for these diversely composed movements, but their roots were in widespread feelings and aspiration. Save for its African population, the United States was settled by émigrés from the two 'revolutions', thus internalizing them. Latin America, however, resisted them. The mother countries barred Protestantism at the gates, along with its messages concerning modern individualism. Europe's later proletarian 'revolution', which took forms from government paternalism through a gamut of socialisms all the way to anarchism, syndicalism and terrorism, made only tentative incursions because of the limited scope of industrialization in Latin America, the lasting efficacy of elite 'conciliations', and a permanent reserve army of workers. However much the pensadores may have kept abreast of progressive thought in Europe, the people whom they claimed to 'think for' were blocked from forming coherent movements that might have given inspiration, definition and support to the critiques made by the intelligentsia.

The identity question therefore consists not entirely of a consensual act of portraiture by sensitive observers but also of a popular voice, featuring the disinherited, that pursues outlet in the generalized discourse of society. For two reasons the identity search came later in Latin America than in Western Europe and the modernizing world, achieving full momentum only in the twentieth century. First, it was only by the 1910s and 1920s that there occurred a conflation of intellectual and popular outlooks as exemplified in letters and visual arts in Mexico, modernist manifestoes in Brazil, socio-political dialogues in Peru, ethno-literary pronouncements in Haiti and diverse manifestations elsewhere. Secondly, with regard specifically to the pensadores, we have argued that their assurances of prior European identity were in the last century too problematic, and their confidence for sustaining critical exchange with ideologies of the industrial West too insecure, to favour a coming-to-terms with world currents. They acquiesced in regnant prescriptions for 'progress' and ruefully confessed their domestic retardation. Here again the early twentieth century was a renovative moment. For suddenly the vanguard voices of Europe, attuned to earlier prophetic cries of the Baudelaires and Nietzsches, were raised in cacophonous condemnation (or even condemnatory exaltation) of the rationalist, scientific and menacingly dehumanizing premises of the Western enterprise.

In Europe vanguardism, or modernism[13] had antecedents as an attitude both critical and celebratory of 'modernization'. One might call modernism a cognitive assault on the contradictions of modernity. In its golden age (1910–30) modernism, particularly from its Parisian arena, finally made its impact on Latin America, but not in a merely tutorial role. For Europe now experienced the crisis of nerve associated with technification, commodification, alienation and rampant violence as these found expression in Marxian contradictions, Spenglerian decadence, Freudian invasions of the subconscious, and of course, industrialism and the First World War. This seeming collapse of evolutionary assumptions gave Latin Americans leverage for dismissing presumed determinisms of their past and for inventing a new 'reality' and a new future. Europe now offered pathologies and not simply models. Disenchantment at the centre gave grounds for rehabilitation at the rim. Latin America had to produce its own Rousseaus and Herders at the same time that it was keeping up with the Picassos and Joyces.

Over the years many have claimed that Latin American high culture was derivative from metropolitan sources in the nineteenth century and suddenly responsive to indigenous or *indigenista* leads after 1920. Almost the reverse is true. What made the Latin American *prise de conscience* of the 1920s possible was not the artists' and intellectuals' stubborn appropriation of 'native' subject matter but their bold acrobatics to retain intellectual footing amid the disintegration of Western rationales and received understandings. With the centre now unstrung, views from the periphery earned respect. Alejo Carpentier (1904–80) was to discover the world as polycentric and Jorge Luis Borges (1899–1986) to find that it has no centre at all. As the Mexican novelist Carlos Fuentes puts it, 'the Western writer can be central only in recognizing that today he is ex-centric, and the Latin American writer only in recognizing that his eccentricity is today centered in a world without cultural axes.'[14]

A newspaper article of 1925 by José Carlos Mariátegui, 'Is There a Hispanic American Thought?', illustrates how his generation had begun to dissolve the polarities of intellectual life on the 'periphery'.[15] During three and a half years of exile in Italy (1919–23), Mariátegui directly

13 I use 'modernism' in the European, North American (and Brazilian) meaning to designate twentieth-century vanguardism, not the Spanish American *modernismo* that was akin to symbolism and Parnassianism.
14 Carlos Fuentes, *La nueva novela hispanoamericana,* 6th ed. (Mexico, D.F., 1980), p. 32.
15 José Carlos Mariátegui, '¿Existe un pensamiento hispano-americano?' in *Temas de nuestra América,* 2nd ed. (Lima, 1970), pp. 22–6.

experienced both the decadence and the promise of Europe. Here he found Marxist analysis of social and economic domination an eye-opener and learned to admire how modernism, especially surrealism, could shatter the solid bourgeois world into absurd fragments. It was to a degree the modernist impulse that led him to extract Marxism itself from positivist armature giving its scientific message mythic force, translating its categories into praxis and relativizing its pretension to universal evolutionism.

In 1925 Mariátegui sensed that his query about Hispanic American thought was germinating in the 'nerve centers of the continent', although he felt that the true question was whether there existed a *characteristically* Hispanic American thought. He chided the Argentine socialist Alfredo Palacios, who had proclaimed the hour at hand for 'radical emancipation' from European culture. Europe had been the lodestar, wrote Palacios, but the Great War showed its culture to contain the seeds of its own decay. Palacios, Mariátegui felt, had led youthful tropical temperaments to exaggerate the prospects for Latin American thought. It was a tonic, he said, to call 'our America' the future cradle of civilization or to proclaim, as José Vasconcelos had in his motto for the National University of Mexico, that: 'Through my race the spirit will speak.' But it was an error to predict the imminent demise of European hegemony. The West was in crisis but far from collapse; Europe was not, 'as is absurdly said, exhausted and paralytic'. 'Our America' continued importing ideas, books, machines and fashions. Capitalist civilization was dying, not Europe. Greco-Roman civilization had long since perished, but Europe went on. Who could deny, Mariátegui asked, that the society of the future was being shaped in Europe or that the finest artists and thinkers of the age were European? He therefore acknowledged a French or German thought but not yet a Hispanic American one, which instead was a 'rhapsody' of European motifs. One might in the countries of the Río de la Plata speak of a spirit of 'Latinity', but it awoke no recognition from autocthonous peoples of the continent.

The purpose of this chapter is not to provide an inventory of trends and genres but to review and selectively illustrate various tactics, whether deliberate or unwitting, for establishing recognition of shared identity. An impressionistic glance from the 1920s to the 1960s suggests three distinctive categories of expression or analysis that carry forward the lines of inquiry set forth by Mariátegui, presented here as modernism, the 'neo-naturalist' novel in conjunction with the 'identity' essay, and philosophy plus history of ideas. Cultural history in an academic vein would assign Latin American modernism to the 1920s, the identity essay to the 1930s and 1940s, and history of ideas to the 1940s and 1950s. Such pigeon-holing, however, omits the tangled antecedents, both New World and European, of these expressive forms and forecloses appreciation of their persistence after the assigned decades.[16] The narratives of the Latin American literary 'boom' of the 1960s, for example, clearly bear the mark of these antecedents. In the twentieth century, cultural expression in Latin America has acquired a heavier retrospective concern, and the logic of exposition requires overrunning the designated decades. The chronological ladders of literary history matter less than the cumulative impact of self-recognition.

First, then, we sketch the career of modernism in three locations during the 1920s and 1930s. The first two of these locales are not countries – the usual reference point for literary histories – but cities. This is because modernism found its Latin American crucibles in urban settings just as it did in Europe (Paris, Vienna, Milan, Berlin). Unlike, say, romanticism or realism, which managed a broad geographic palette, modernism required the arena where mind and sensibility awoke to specifically *modern* features of the Western world view: velocity, simultaneity, collage, inversion, free association, catachresis, the cult of machines and rationality – but not to the exclusion of 'primitive' evocations. The two cities chosen are São Paulo, the burgeoning financial and industrial capital of South America, and Buenos Aires, its earlier commercial and cultural capital.[17]

In São Paulo, founded in 1554, a city whose colonial traces had vanished, whose population had leaped from 65,000 to 580,000 in thirty years, whose streets were thronged by Italians, Syrians and Japanese, whose sky was perforated overnight by smokestacks, the imagination was challenged not to understand but to see, not explain but apprehend. It was assigned an act of *cognition*.[18] Buenos Aires in contrast entered the post–First World War era of national and cultural assertion precisely as its citification and

---

[16] Stabb traces the identity essay from 1890 and could certainly have dropped at least as far back as Sarmiento's *Facundo,* while Abellán traces the history of the American 'idea' back to 1492. Martin S. Stabb, *In Quest of Identity: Patterns in the Spanish American Essay of Ideas, 1890–1960* (Chapel Hill, N.C., 1967); J. L. Abellán, *La idea de América, origen y evolución* (Madrid, 1972).

[17] Jorge Schwartz compares Paulista and Porteño avant-gardism in *Vanguarda e cosmopolitismo: Oliverio Girondo e Oswald de Andrade* (São Paulo, 1983), while Raúl Antelo examines the Paulistas' reception of Spanish American vanguardism in *Na ilha de Marapatá (Mário de Andrade lê os hispano-americanos)* (São Paulo, 1986).

[18] See Nicolau Sevcenko, *Orfeu extático na metrópole: São Paulo, sociedade e cultura nos fremantes anos 20* (São Paulo, 1992).

Europeanization had come under question. A note of decadence, of ominous warning was sounding in both high and popular culture. So accepted was the cosmopolitan ethos that commonplaces of domestic history and culture assumed a mythic cast, as in the nostalgic Argentine *gauchismo*. Brazilians might exalt their *bandeirantes*, or colonial path-finders, as did modernist poet Cassiano Ricardo in a dithyrambic account of their exploits or modernist sculptor Victor Brecheret in a monumental public statue; yet the *bandeirante*, historically quite as venerable as the gaucho, had not faded into a mythic past but was exemplary for pioneers of a dynamic future. He was a flesh-and-blood hero, unlike Ricardo Güiraldes's oneiric, 'shadowy' gaucho in *Don Segundo Sombra* (1926), who concludes the most renowned work of Argentine fiction of the 1920s by fading from sight as a man, leaving the observer's meditation cut off from its source, his lifeblood flowing away. Here inquiry probes beyond 'reality' to a domain of enigma or paradox. The challenge is not cognition but *decipherment*. If the Brazilian 'anti-hero' of Mário de Andrade's *Macunaíma* (1928) finally goes off to muse alone as a star in the vast firmament, it is not because the old life has evanesced but precisely because it is all too tenacious, too real, in a land 'sem saúde e com muita saúva' – with no health and lots of ants.[19]

Mexico, our third instance, is a case of modernism manqué because the putative modernist moment coincided with a revolution. Although in retrospect the Mexican Revolution seems not to have been a full-dress socio-political *renversement*, it did at least convert Mexico City into a radiant, innovative centre by what was then interpreted as a collective act of vision and volition. The revolution itself became a 'modernist' event by working lightning reversals and expansions of sense and sensibility. Under its inspiration the painterly imagination fused Aztec deities, the late-medieval *danse macabre* (rediscovered by José Guadalupe Posada), German expressionism, and Montparnasse cubism, not to mention Renaissance muralism and Spanish ecclesial baroque. The *revolution*, Octavio Paz has said, had no programme. It was a gigantic subterranean revolt, a *revelation* that restored our eyes to see Mexico. Thus Mexicans in the modernist age such as Paz's representative list of painters and writers (Rivera, Orozco, López Velarde, Azuela, Guzmán and Vasconcelos) were less concerned with inversion, collage, or geometric reduction than with retrieval. Diego Rivera, after a dozen years in Paris (where he won stardom as a cubist)

---

[19] Ricardo Güiraldes, *Don Segundo Sombra*, trans. Harriet de Onís (New York, 1966); Mário de Andrade, *Macunaíma*, trans. E. A. Goodland (New York, 1984).

returned to Mexico, adopted a dynamic, even orgiastic fauvist manner, and, at his best, escaped the clutch of official ideology to capture the germination and sheer materiality of plants, people and machines. Orozco and Siqueiros developed a home-grown expressionism, in Siqueiros's case with ideological baggage similar to Rivera's, in Orozco's with moral and personal accents. In Mexico, the modernist agenda was not the *cognition* of São Paulo or the *decipherment* of Buenos Aires but a task of *propaganda* in the original sense of a duty to spread the 'good tidings'.[20]

Historically, the modernists seem a focal point of the 1920s. However, the interpretation of their early messages (Oswald de Andrade) or the cumulative influence of their unfolding work (Borges) took time, even decades. Only the quasi-modernist Mexican muralists won instant fame. Years later, in 1942, Mário de Andrade, playfully known as the pope of Brazilian modernism, poignantly recounted the fate of avant-gardism.[21] He recalled the exaltation of the 1920s, the infatuating rediscovery of Europe and Brazil, the festive impulse to demolition, the dance on the volcanoes: 'Doctrinaire, intoxicated by a thousand and one theories, saving Brazil . . . we consumed everything including ourselves in the bitter, almost delirious cultivation of pleasure.' Yet looking back from Brazil's Estado Novo (1937–45) and a second global war he felt that while joyously trying to serve his time and country he had succumbed to a vast illusion. More was needed than to break windows, joggle the eternal verities, or quench cultural curiosity: not mere political activism, not explosive manifestoes, but greater anxiety about the epoch, fiercer revolt against life as it is.

This statement, while highly personal, betokens a general Latin American transition. For reasons related to the collapse of the international economy, to authoritarian threats at home and abroad, to ominous murmurs of the dispossessed, and to ennui with hermetic or meretricious features of vanguardism, the modernist flame was wavering, to reassert its inspiration only a generation or more later. If fiction, poetry and the arts were exemplary vehicles of modernism, a shift in primacy occurs in the 1930s and 1940s as conspicuous novelists leaned toward a world of commonsensical yet menacing phenomena while essayists derived cues from

---

[20] See Dawn Ades, *Art in Latin America: The Modern Era, 1820–1980* (New Haven, Conn., 1989), chs. 6–7; Octavio Paz, *Sombras de obras* (Mexico, D.F., 1983), pp. 163–79; Olivier Debroise, *Diego de Montparnasse* (Mexico, D.F., 1979).

[21] Mário de Andrade, 'O movimento modernista', in *Aspectos da literatura brasileira*, 4th ed. (São Paulo, 1972), pp. 231–55.

philosophy, history, ethnography and psychology to solidify their grounds for speculation. One might pair them as neo-naturalists (such as Rómulo Gallegos, José Américo de Almeida or Ciro Alegría) and neo-pensadores (such as Mariátegui, Price-Mars or Samuel Ramos). The former, however, moved beyond Zolaesque canons and even, paradoxically, anticipated the 'marvellous realism' of the 1960s while the latter laid partial claim to empirical science, but a science leavened by post-positivist philosophy and modernist wit.

The late 1940s and 1950s created fresh context for intellectual endeavour, now conducted with an eye to such external circumstances as the aftermath of the Spanish Civil War, the Second World War, and the incipient Cold War and to such domestic trends as the advent of populist politics and the developmentalist alliance between the state and new industrial groups. The mid-1940s saw the appearance of reformist, constitutional regimes, while rapid urbanization, the growth of middle sectors with a supposed stake in a stable order, and the by now canonical imperative of development 'from within' seemed to brighten possibilities for revolutionary change. Modernist extravagance seemed whimsical and dated save for monumental products like Mexican murals or Brazilian architecture, absorbable to the purposes of mushrooming bureaucracies. Imaginative writers tended private gardens unless they found occasions for political statement (Pablo Neruda, Miguel Angel Asturias) or enticed the growing audience for 'best sellers' (Manuel Gálvez, Erico Veríssimo, Jorge Amado) or consolidated their careers around research and institutional service (Jorge Basadre, Sérgio Buarque de Holanda).

Various circumstances contributed to endow the identity question with a less nationalistic, more speculative dimension: the effect of the Spanish Civil War in incorporating the Hispanic world to global politics; the modernization of Spanish academe and the transatlantic migration of many of its finest scholars; the effect of the Second World War in assimilating Latin American countries to a purported democratic partnership and in subsequently prescribing their global economic role. Just as modernism had played its part in shaping sensibilities in the 1920s, so in the late 1940s and 1950s philosophy, and particularly the schools of phenomenology and existentialism, played a part – inconspicuously for a general public – in rehabilitating the intellectual image of the American continents. Latin American philosophers anticipated social scientists by two decades in professionalizing their discipline with a vocabulary that made explicit certain promptings of the modernists and raised to higher planes of generalization the reconnoitering of indigenists, novelists, and essay-ists. What is more, the Germanic style that caught on gave cachet to Latin American philosophizing while slighting the Anglo American analytic vein in favour of a holism more consonant with Iberian precedents.

The next three sections of this chapter, then, examine modernism, the novel and essay, and philosophy as moments of a *prise de conscience* that took shape in Latin America in the 1920s and, in shifting modes and guises, still continues. These three moments are not strictly consecutive nor confined to specific decades, nor are they the sole intellectual beacons of their periods, nor are they walled off like 'disciplines' (some writers are identified with more than one of them: Vasconcelos, Mariátegui, Martínez Estrada, Mário de Andrade). The point is that activity in these areas made distinctive contributions to the identity quest broadly defined. Moreover, they have heuristic uses, for if we liken them to Whitehead's three stages of mental growth they suggest ways of understanding how minds, from many angles and suppositions, may reach tacit recognition of shared experi-ence.[22] Whitehead's initial stage of 'romance' – here, Latin American modernism – is a first apprehension when subject matter has the vividness of novelty, and its possibilities are 'half-disclosed by glimpses and half-concealed by the wealth of material'. Knowledge is *ad hoc* and piecemeal. Emotion flares up in the transition from bare facts to awareness of unex-plored relationships. The stage of 'precision' – here the novelists and essayists – subordinates breadth of relationship to exactness of formula-tion. It provides grammars of language and science along with a mode of analysis that digests facts as they accumulate. Finally comes the stage of generalization – analogous to the philosophic contribution – which rekin-dles romanticism but now with benefit of orderly ideas and apposite technique. Whitehead's stages are familiar in common experience where, however, they forever spin in cycles and nested minicycles. For present purposes the three stages are applied not as a grand evolutionary scheme but to treat cultural history on the 'periphery' less as an importation of models than as domestic gestation.

In what follows certain outcomes of our three 'stages' will be traced up to the 1970s, and the envoi will briefly consider two notable develop-ments from the late 1950s to the 1970s, namely, the invasion of academic social science and the literary 'boom'. The simultaneity of these occur-rences rescues us from what might have seemed an evolutionary process. By the 1960s social scientists had recognized the determinative effects of

---

[22] Alfred North Whitehead, *The Aims of Education* (New York, 1949), pp. 28–52.

international economic and political forces and were producing a body of 'dependency' theory that assimilated Latin American to modern Western history, assigning it lugubrious prospects. (More 'radical' exponents preached a doctrine of revolutionary voluntarism to upset the logic of economic domination they had so persuasively set forth.) The literary imagination, on the other hand, was not so much appalled by forces of *domination* as it was captivated by the *resistance* of local societies to the dictates of 'development', whether of foreign or domestic origin. Hence its fascination with the colonial or aboriginal past, with mythic recurrence or 'eternal return', and with an ethos of 'marvellous realism'. What Antonio Gramsci was for the sociologist, Mircea Eliade represented for the novelist. The social science and literary 'booms' formed a new generational *prise*. But while the scientists distantly echoed nineteenth-century positivism (though with a self-conscious modernization of language), artists and writers were captivated by tensions and contradictions of a new baroque age, often mediated by modernist mentors who were now accorded belated or posthumous acknowledgement. Without Borges, Fuentes claims, 'there simply would have been no modern Hispanic American novel'[23] – and indeed Borges himself both inspired and helped to shepherd the whole transition from the 1920s to the 1980s.

This dichotomy arose clearly in the 1960s, when social scientists, whatever the provisos and shadings of their analyses, *rationally* perceived Latin America as 'inserted into' schemes of metropolitan domination, manipulation and desacralization. The writers for their part, however 'leftist' their political sympathies might in some cases be, *instinctively* 'marvelled at' the intransigence of their societies to the invasion of Western rationalism, capitalism, and political mandates. How do we bridge these divergent visions? One might suppose the possibility, the multiple possibilities, for dialectical engagement if not, in any facile sense, for 'synthesis'.

## MODERNISM

### *São Paulo: Modernism as Cognition*

The opening salvo of modernism in Brazil was Modern Art Week, occurring in São Paulo city from 11 to 17 February 1922.[24] This was in fact the

---

[23] Fuentes, *La nueva novela*, p. 26.
[24] General treatments include Wilson Martins, *The Modernist Idea: A Critical Survey of Brazilian Writing in the Twentieth Century*, trans. Jack E. Tomlins (New York, 1970) and John Nist, *The Modernist Movement in Brazil* (Austin, Tex., 1967).

only self-styled modernist movement in Latin America, the analogue in Spanish America being vanguardism. Modern Art Week was celebrated by young writers and artists in the Parisian-style municipal theatre as if mocking the stale Europhilism for which it stood. The event – eight days of public exhibits and three days of 'festivals' (lectures, readings, concerts) – was calculated to scandalize the public, and in this it fully succeeded. Although the participants included a few from Rio de Janeiro – such as Ronald de Carvalho, Manuel Bandeira, and the elder statesman Graça Aranha, author of *Canaã* (1902) – most were Paulistas including, to cite names that have lasted, the sculptor Brecheret, painters Anita Malfatti and Di Cavalcanti, writers Guilherme de Almeida and Menotti del Picchia, and the two stars to be discussed shortly, Oswald de Andrade and Mário de Andrade.

Because Modern Art Week was taunting, carnivalesque and outrageously vanguard, the sessions provoked catcalls, even fistfights. Years later Mário de Andrade wrote of this moment that: 'Given its character as a risky game, its extreme spirit of adventure, its modernist internationalism, its raging nationalism, its gratuitous antipopulism, its overbearing dogmatism – it revealed an aristocracy of the spirit.'[25] The initial impression of Paulista modernism as a prank or *boutade* obscured recognition of the decade preceding Modern Art Week when modernist notions took shape, from foreign examples and domestic messages, within a small cenacle as instanced by Oswald's tidings from his first Parisian visit of 1912, the 1913 exhibit of the young Lithuanian expressionist Lasar Segall (destined to be one of Brazil's finest artists), daily meetings of a coterie in the bookstore O Livro, and the controversial expressionist show of Anita Malfatti in 1917. In other words, Paulista modernism did not capitulate in mimetic fashion to Parisian dada, cubism and the like. Marinetti's futurism, originating in industrial, 'unpoetic' Milan, did have a vogue on the eve of Modern Art Week, perhaps because its gospel of automation and sheer movement was congenial to São Paulo. But Paulista cognoscenti were sceptical, and Marinetti, whom Mário de Andrade disliked, alienated Brazilians on a later visit, not the least for his fascist sympathies.

Modern Art Week, then, was not an eye-opener for initiates and in this differed from the New York Armory Show of 1913. Although two-thirds of the latter was given to pioneering American trends, the Europeans received the acclaim, especially cubists and fauvists, who caused shock,

[25] Mário de Andrade, 'O movimento modernista', p. 236.

bemusement and awe.[26] In São Paulo the purpose of the Week was not to mystify a parochial bourgeoisie with Europe's latest *divertissements* but to use these as explosives to demystify the foundations of a class-based system of literary production and to achieve artistic expression of national scope. São Paulo's modernists were concerned less with stylistic novelty than with mastery of the artistic media. The Brazilian musicians, Guiomar Novais and Villa-Lobos, may have performed European composers, but the music of Villa-Lobos himself swept all before it. As Mário de Andrade later wrote, beneath the *blague* and raillery lay three central objectives: permanent freedom for esthetic research, renovation of the Brazilian artistic intelligence and stabilization of a national creative consciousness on a collective rather than individualist base. To oversimplify: the Armory Show helped American artists catch up to Europe; Modern Art Week helped art itself catch up to the idea of Brazil.

One may ask why upstart industrial São Paulo hatched this sophisticated movement rather than Rio, Brazil's cultural and publishing headquarters. Mário's answer was that while Rio, as seaport and political capital, had an inborn vocation for internationalism, coffee and industry had given São Paulo a more modern spirit and more vibrant foreign connection. Rio retained a dose of folkloric 'exoticism' with an interfusion of urban and rural cultures. São Paulo was a burgeoning metropolis perched on its plateau with a large hinterland that was more *caipira* (bumpkin) than exotic. Rio, successively the seat of a viceroyalty, an empire and a republic, immured by fanciful mountains that left it facing toward Europe, was an *imperial* city. São Paulo had from the start turned its back on the sea and followed an inland vocation, first *bandeirismo*, then the westward march of coffee, and finally industry in quest of markets. São Paulo is an *imperialist* city. Its very modernity betokened a certain innocence. In 'malicious' Rio, wrote Mário de Andrade, an exhibit like Anita Malfatti's 'might have caused a public stir but no one would have been carried away. In ingenuous São Paulo it created a religion.'[27]

Modern Art Week was one of four events in 1922, centennial year of Brazilian independence, that denounced the status quo from quite different angles. The other three, all based in Rio, were: the Copacabana revolt of the *tenentes*, young officers claiming national renovation and social

[26] See Milton W. Brown, *The Story of the Armory Show*, 2nd ed. (New York, 1988); Eliane Bastos, *Entre o escândalo e o sucesso: a Semana de 22 e o Armory Show* (Campinas, 1991).
[27] Mário de Andrade, 'O movimento modernista', p. 236.

justice; the creation of the Centro Dom Vital and the review *A Ordem* to mobilize the church's programmes of indoctrination and political action; and the founding of the Communist Party. Modernism, particularly in its iconoclastic, heroic years of 1922–30, seems removed from the social and political *engagement* of these initiatives unless we abandon the narrowly avant-gardist meaning of Brazilian modernism, as Lafetá does, and prolong the movement to the early 1940s.[28] Lafetá divides modernism into an aesthetic project, which seeks to renovate the means of expression and break with traditional language, and an ideological project, which delves into national consciousness seeking specifically Brazilian expression. These projects are not mutually exclusive. Single writers might pursue both in shifting combinations; or single works might bridge the two. As collective expressions, however, the aesthetic project was foremost at the outset, began yielding to the ideological in the late 1920s, and lost primacy in the 1930s.

The early phase, with a cast of Paulistas and Cariocas including Antônio de Alcântara Machado, Sérgio Milliet, Sérgio Buarque de Holanda and Di Cavalcanti, was marked by Mário de Andrade's esthetic orientations, the irreverence and audacity of the review *Klaxon* (1922), and a pilgrimage to Minas Gerais as a preamble to a collective discovery of Brazil. Soon Oswald de Andrade showed his genius for composing verbal *affiches* with the Brazilwood Manifesto of 1924, a charge that Europe had profited long enough from Brazilian exports of sugar, coffee and rubber and that now Brazilian poetry must go on the list. His Anthropophagic Manifesto of 1928 along with an anthropophagic review co-edited with Alcântara Machado and Raul Bopp radicalized and primitivized the Brazil-wood thesis. To be sure, Oswald took cues from fauvism, futurism, and above all dadaism. In 1920 Francis Picabia had even published a 'Manifeste Cannibale Dada' in Paris and co-founded the review *Cannibale* with Tristan Tzara. But Oswald's Anthropophagy was far from imitative. For Brazilians cannibals were a historical reality, not a *divertissement*. That is, once one accepts the Tupi as the original Brazilian, his cannibalism is no longer savage, exotic, or an anthropological curiosity. It now becomes the Indian ritual *ingesting* of the strength and power of enemies and eventually of European invaders. The modernists needed precisely this lesson to handle the cultural relation between Brazil and Europe (hence Oswald's *bon mot*, 'Tupi or not Tupi'). They could now repudiate the clumsy binomial be-

---

[28] João Luiz Lafetá, *1930: A crítica e o modernismo* (São Paulo, 1974).

tween mimicry of Europe and a 'native' culture cut from whole cloth. Cannibalism recognized both the nutritive property of European culture and a transformative process of appropriation. Brazilians might chuckle at the *boutades* of French modernism; but for guidance on 'primitivism', language, and culture they turned to sixteenth-century mentors such as Montaigne, Rabelais and the Pleiad poets, who had been at a point to forge French culture rather than cleverly embellish it.[29]

Brazil-wood and anthropophagy show points of mutual reinforcement between the esthetic and ideological projects. If Oswald moved toward 'ideological' issues in the late 1920s, Mário de Andrade remained true to his linguistic-literary priority, for he was obsessed by the search for a 'de-geographized' Brazilian language (i.e., not compiled of picturesque regionalisms) adequate for expressing the cosmos of the Brazilian people.[30] He went beyond 'aesthetics' in the narrow usage, however, when he rejected naturalist technique, which merely ratified a vision of Brazil that was implicit in cultural preferences of the oligarchy. Although closely attentive to politics, Mário was not an activist, because he accepted as the precondition for action not a grand design but new grammar and lexicon. The success of modernism in stripping discourse to its elements therefore made the arts a testing-ground for reinventing politics.

The early benchmarks for Lafetá's 'ideological' project were almost coincident with those of Oswald's manifestoes. The two movements that passed, in Antonio Candido's terms, from 'aesthetic to political nationalism' were Verdeamarelismo or Green-and-yellowism (the national colours) in 1925 and Anta, named for the Brazilian tapir, in 1927. Key players in both groups were Cassiano Ricardo, Guilherme de Almeida, Menotti del Picchia and the notorious Plínio Salgado. Salgado joined the modernists from the start bringing with him an addiction to nationalism and a conservative familial Catholicism refreshed by the Catholic revival in Rio. He wrote two creditable political novels (*O èstrangeiro*, 1926, and *O esperado*, 1931), but the quality of his literary efforts declined as his political interests took focus. A trip to the Near East and Europe in 1930

---

29 Erdmute Wenzel White, *Les années vingt au Brésil: Le modernisme et l'avant-garde internationale* (Paris, 1977); Michael Palencia-Roth, 'Cannibalism and the New Man of Latin America in the 15th- and 16th-century European imagination', *Comparative Civilizations Review*, 12 (1985): 1–27. Maggie Kilgour examines the cannibal theme in Western literature from Homer and Ovid to Coleridge and Melville in *From Communion to Cannibalism: An Anatomy of Metaphors of Incorporation* (Princeton, 1990).

30 Edith Pimentel Pinto assembles the notes Mário gathered throughout his life for a 'modest grammar' of Brazilian speech in *A Gramatiquinha de Mário de Andrade: texto e contexto* (São Paulo, 1990).

gave him sympathetic awareness of fascism, and by 1932 he was leading Brazil's Integralist party.[31]

After 1925 modernism spread elsewhere from the São Paulo–Rio axis. In places the Paulistas' example was overshadowed, as in Recife where Joaquim Inojosa shepherded a nascent modernist movement that soon yielded to a northeast school of regionalism inaugurated by a manifesto in 1926. Its members found a sociological expositor in Gilberto Freyre (see below) and produced a crop of novelists in the 1930s who won renown immediately in Brazil and more gradually overseas. In later years, specifically in *Região e tradição* (1941), Freyre perhaps magnified the significance of regionalism just as in the early years he had been dismissive of Paulista modernism. In any case the northeast novelists, discussed in the next section, richly exemplify the 'ideological' option of the period, with one of them, Graciliano Ramos, mastering the 'rare equilibrium' needed to imbue familiar schemes for representing reality with the conquests of the avant-garde.[32]

Of the mainstream modernists the two who have best stood the test of time are Oswald de Andrade (1890–1954) and Mário de Andrade (1893–1945). Unrelated by family, they were comrades in the heroic years of modernism, then drew apart but continued respecting and finding sustenance in each other's example.

Oswald's public self was iconoclastic and Rabelaisian. He was the dandy, the enfant terrible, the self-styled 'clown of the bourgeoisie'.[33] Save for an excursion to Amazonian Peru, Mário never left Brazil, while Oswald plunged into modernist Paris as early as 1912. He was impatient with Mário's professorial inclinations and his devotion to cultural intricacies. Oswald rendered his poems and narratives, his perceptions and prescriptions, in a telegraphic style of explosive vignettes. His life and works, Antônio Cândido observes, betoken an eternal voyager, 'the transitive esthetic of the traveller' who composed a divinatory vision from swiftly seized fragments. His conformist bourgeois casing is stripped off by the search for plenitude through a ceaseless redemptive journey. Oswald's Pau-Brasil poems of 1925 open with a series of poetic

[31] Hélgio Trindade treats Salgado's career from modernism to politics in *Integralismo (o fascismo brasileiro na década de 30)* (São Paulo, 1974), parts 1, 2.
[32] Laferá, 1930, p. 156; Joaquim Inojosa, 'O movimento modernista no Norte', in *Os Andrades e outros aspectos do modernismo* (Rio de Janeiro, 1975), pp. 218–39.
[33] For interpretations of Oswald, see Antônio Cândido, *Vários escritos* (São Paulo, 1970), chs. 2–4 and prefaces by Haroldo de Campos and Benedito Nunes in Vols. 2, 6, and 7 of Oswald's *Obras completas* (Rio de Janeiro, 1972).

abstracts of the colonial chroniclers, retrieving their direct language and Kodak vision. In one of his telescoped poems, 'Mistake of the Portuguese', Oswald echoes Montaigne to show the arbitrariness of opposing roles: A pity it was raining when the Portuguese arrived, making him clothe the Indian! – On a sunny day the Indian would have disrobed the Portuguese.

Other poems were quite as synoptic. The recruit who swore to his sweetheart that even if he died he would return to hear her play the piano, but he stayed in Paraguay forever. Or the slave who leaped into the Paraíba river with her daughter so the baby wouldn't suffer. Or the 'feudal lord': 'If Pedro II / Comes around / With a big story / I'll lock him up.' The poems and manifestoes address several historical themes: the church–state apparatus that moulded Brazilian civilization, patriarchal society and its moral standards, messianic dreams, the rhetoric of Europhile intellectuals, an indianism that camouflaged the outlook of the colonizer and the frustrations of the colonized. Not only did Oswald posthumously inspire Brazil's internationally known Tropicália movement of the late 1960s, but he also anticipated the motifs that were, at that same moment, to attract academic historians. Of Oswald's fiction his two most notable books were *Memórias sentimentais de João Miramar,* published in 1924 (where prose and poetry merge in a cinematic technique that renders the routines and vapidities of the coffee bourgeoisie on transatlantic tour) and *Serafim Ponte Grande* (1933).[34] The latter, an even more radical text, has been called a non-book, an anti-book, a fragment of a great book, and finally 'a great non-book of book fragments'.

Antônio Cândido observes that *Serafim* is the counterpart to Mário de Andrade's *Macunaíma* (considered below). Each narrative takes the reader on a 'mythological' journey into acute cultural trauma, with the parochial Paulista bourgeois immersed in sophisticated Europe on one hand and the Amazonian 'native' in industrial São Paulo on the other. Both situations required grotesque, erotic and obscene language of Rabelaisian gusto to smash the literary equilibrium of Brazil's *fin de siècle,* the universe of Machado de Assis where stylistic excess took the chastened forms of sentimentality, pathos and grandiloquence. Facing the asynchronous collision of what the world took as civilization versus primitivism, Oswald and Mário put their anthropophagic principles to the test in an act of

---

[34] 'Sentimental Memoirs of John Seaborne', trans. Ralph Niebuhr and Albert Bork, *Texas Quarterly,* 15/4 (1972), 112–60; *Seraphim Grosse Pointe,* trans. Kenneth D. Jackson and Albert Bork (Austin, Tex., 1979).

devoration. This meant that the noble savage of Indianist novels must yield to the bad savage whose need for marrow and protein required expropriation of the enemy's cultural past.[35] For Oswald, however, *Serafim* was another turning-point. Written from 1925 to 1929, it reached print only in 1933. By then he had discovered that intellectuals had been playing ring-around-the-rosy. Short of cash, ignorant of Marx, yet anti-bourgeois, he had become a bohemian. But he was now ready to join the Proletarian Revolution. Happily he did not succumb. He broke with Marxism in 1945 and returned to anthropophagy, the base for a new career in philosophy which might reveal, he hoped, why the recent war had done little to solve the world's abiding problems.

Mário de Andrade's first book of verse in the modernist vein was *Paulicea desvairada* (1922), or 'hallucinated city' (São Paulo).[36] Although he had abjured his early 'metrical' poems, his verse, while now 'free', was suffused with assonance, internal rhymes, and classic metrical effects. He rejoices in the splintered vision of modernism but is on some counts a willing hostage to tradition. He is, for example, unabashedly lyrical about São Paulo; his point of reference is not the inhuman urban dynamism of the futurists but explicitly his own 'self'. Mário dedicates the book to his 'beloved master', Mário de Andrade, and his 'Most Interesting Preface' insists that he sings in his own way. In the book's first line São Paulo is the 'commotion of my life'. Even with its physical identity effaced by business and industry, São Paulo sweeps the observer into an age-old carnivalesque setting of grey and gold, ashes and money, repentance and greed. The poet's world is not one that *he* has decomposed as an imagist or surrealist might; nor is it one that has fallen into pieces *on its own*. It is rather a self-given mystery that he feels challenged to apprehend through fused vision, objective and private, and through a harlequin figure symbolizing ancient myth and lonely self, revelry and sorrow, foolery and wisdom. Hence a strong hint of romanticism in his verse.

Mário de Andrade confessed that in the chit-chat of his 'interesting' preface one scarcely knew where *blague* left off and sobriety began. He even parodied his own avant-garde by founding a school of 'Hallucinism' at the start of the preface and disbanding it at the end. He confessed to being

---

[35] Antônio Cândido, *Vários escritos,* pp. 84–7; Haroldo de Campos, 'The Rule of Anthropophagy: Europe under the Sign of Devoration', *Latin American Literary Review,* 14/27 (1986), 42–60.

[36] Mário de Andrade, *Hallucinated City,* bilingual ed., trans. Jack E. Tomlins (Kingsport, Tenn., 1968). Telê Porto Ancona Lopez traces Mário's intellectual development in *Mário de Andrade: ramais e caminho* (São Paulo, 1972).

old-fashioned and scolded those who poked fun at Rodin or Debussy only to kneel before Bach and African sculpture or even cold squares and cubes. Being placed in Brazil, 'outside' history, offered Mário a more serene vantage point to contemplate the art of all epochs than was enjoyed by those at the 'centre', who felt appointed to dethrone and remake. He felt no call to denigrate Parnassians and other immediate predecessors, for he was constructing a past, not merely a future, which helps explain his refusal of futurism. His challenge was that of the Indian church builders of colonial Mexico who in the space of a generation had to retrace the logic of European architectural development since primitive romanesque. We marvel at how far Mário travelled when we learn that as late as 1916 this young man of middle-class Catholic upbringing was asking his archbishop's permission to read the indexed Balzac, Flaubert and the Larousse dictionary.

Narrowly ideological accounts of Mário's intellectual journey portray a somewhat artless mind groping among incongruous influences – family Catholicism, positivism, Jules Romains's unanimism, liberalism, nationalism, Freudianism and several strains of Marxism – without finding a prescription for more than political reformism. Gilda de Mello e Souza warns, however, that Mário's intellectual positions, taken at face value, do little to explain his creative power. In his mythopoeic 'rhapsody' *Macunaíma* (1928) she discovers two obsessions that permeated and unified his life work: to understand the nature of music (he was a trained musicologist) and to analyse the creative process of the common people.[37] Musical analogies gave access to a 'reality' that mocked the intellective faculty, while fascination with the mind, culture and expressive resources of common folk not only helped stitch together his Catholicism, unanimism, and Marxism but foretold the recognition in Brazil, decades later, of 'conscientization' as therapy for a 'pre-political' citizenry.

In *Macunaíma*, Mário created a Brazilian folk hero (without precisely intending to), a persona of shifting ethnic identity who meanders throughout Brazil and across the centuries. Morally, he was a representative man, holding to neither a heroic code nor a diabolic anti-code. A conspicuous trait was his indolence (*preguiça*), an impediment to economic 'progress' but, by affording leisure for creativity, a prerequisite for 'civilization'. The text draws on Mário's vast knowledge of lore, culture, psychology, language and books without becoming a whimsical bricolage. He controlled

[37] Gilda de Mello e Souza, *O Tupi e o alaúde* (São Paulo, 1979).

his materials by principles of musical composition derived from close knowledge of the intricate process by which a popular talent without viable traditions appropriates and ingeniously reworks Iberian, Indian and African ingredients to find a voice of its own. By Aristotelian 'imitation of action' the author hoped to elucidate the task of the Brazilian artist or intellectual. Thus *Macunaíma* entwines scholarly and popular sources in leading the hero through a fanciful geography that 'corrects' shifting historical disparities between penury and affluence, archaism and technology, to produce 'co-existence'.

As founding director of São Paulo's municipal Department of Culture (1934–7) Mário had a brief chance to translate his understanding of education, Brazilian traditions and the permeations between popular and highbrow culture into a public programme.[38] This experience exemplified how Mário navigated the transition from the esthetic to the ideological years, always keeping his concern with language and art as a context and source of coherence for his concern with 'politics', that is, the polis. Oswald in contrast had no way to organize his vision, to convert lightning into a steady glow, to cultivate the delicate filaments between art and politics. With the advent of the bureaucratic Vargas era he could not, like Mário, find a platform, however cramped, from which to pursue tasks *pro bono publico* of administration, pedagogy and research. He finally took refuge by writing two remarkable messianic theses in a vain attempt to obtain a professorship.

In an interview of 1974 Antônio Cândido spoke of this genial pair as two dialectical forces – Mário the 'revolutionary' and Oswald the 'terrorist' – and as two outstanding sources for contemporary Brazilian literature.[39] Who was the more important? Oswald if one seeks language that breaks with traditional mimesis, but Mário if one seeks language for a Brazilian view of the world. In time of existential trouble as in the late 1960s and early 1970s Oswald plays a more agglutinative role, finding a climate wherein to survive culturally. At a moment offering constructive socialist possibilities Oswald's example suffers eclipse because Mário more clearly embodies the notions of service, collectivity, and search for the people. The historical moment continues to determine the reputation of each.

[38] See Carlos Sandroni, *Mário contra 'Macunaíma'* (São Paulo, 1988), pp. 69–128; Joan Dassin, *Política e poesia em Mário de Andrade* (São Paulo, 1978).
[39] Antônio Cândido, 'Entrevista', *Trans/formação*, 1 (1974), 20–22.

*Buenos Aires: Modernism as Decipherment*

The modernist agenda for Argentina was different from that for Brazil. Here was a country without the sprawling tropical geography and 'primitive' ethnicity of Brazil. It was a flat, traversable territory with nearly a quarter of its population corralled in an Anglo-French capital city. Even though industrialism had taken only preliminary hold, Argentina alone in Latin America – save perhaps for its miniature replica Uruguay and its western neighbour Chile – seemed to have crossed the threshold of Western modernization. 'Rich as an Argentine' was a byword in Paris. There were tensions and predatory forces in Buenos Aires as in any Western city; but the south European provenance of much of its proletariat and petty bourgeoisie did not pose such problems of assimilation as plagued Mexico, Peru, and even Brazil. Argentina's formative era seemed to have passed, as had been acknowledged in the second part of the national epic by José Hernández, the *Vuelta* ['Return'] *de Martín Fierro* (1879), when the defiant gaucho resignedly accepts the encroachment of 'civilization'. In this setting Marxism could take a conciliatory cast in the revisionist version of Juan B. Justo (1865–1928), the acknowledged Marxist pioneer of Latin America who translated volume one of *Kapital* and edited the socialist daily *La Vanguardia*. Argentine writers were not more 'cosmopolitan' than their Paulista counterparts, but their sense of a completed phase of history, their acceptance of Buenos Aires as a sub-equatorial Paris or London, the lack of challenge from 'exoticism' and problems of survival, allowed them to cast their inquiry in more familiar Western terms.[40] Borges went so far as to dismiss the passionate identity question in saying that 'being Argentine is either a fatality, in which case we cannot avoid it, or else a mere affectation, a mask'.[41] His first book of verse (*Fervor de Buenos Aires*, 1923) was, like Mário de Andrade's *Hallucinated City* of the previous year, an urban paean; yet while Mário's city was the 'commotion of my life' – or, a force not yet appropriated – for Borges the streets of Buenos Aires were in his opening lines simply 'mi entraña' (my entrails).

[40] For Buenos Aires in the 1920s: Christopher Towne Leland, *The Last Happy Men: The Generation of 1922, Fiction and the Argentine Reality* (Syracuse, 1986); Beatriz Sarlo, *Una modernidad periférica: Buenos Aires, 1920 y 1930* (Buenos Aires, 1988); Francis Korn, *Buenos Aires, los huéspedes del 20* (Buenos Aires, 1974).
[41] Jorge Luis Borges, 'El escritor argentino y la tradición', in *Discusión* (Buenos Aires, 1969), pp. 151–62.

To savour directly the ethos of urban Argentina in the 1920s and 1930s – a haunting sense of creole-immigrant identity fused with assurance of having entered the Western mainstream, yet darkened by hints of impending *débâcle* – one turns to the tango culture. The tango was not, save when packaged for export, a 'ballroom' dance. Nor was it a samba that suspended social hierarchy and engulfed onlookers in a shared world, where 'schools' and *blocos* are communal and incorporative, and whose cues come from social reference points, not the private psyche.[42] The musical origins of tango culture may have been African or creole while its social origins were along the river and in the outskirts (*arrabales*) of Buenos Aires. As a child Borges had known the *arrabal* poet Evaristo Carriego and his tango lyrics, and he devoted an early book to this modest bard of the urban poor. Later he renounced the tango as it entered its international phase of 'sentimentality' with Enrique Discépolo and Carlos Gardel. For him, vicariously perhaps, the tango was the vivacious, erotic dance of the harbour's brothels. Yet despite Borges it found its unique destiny only in the mid-1920s, not as a dance but as a lyrical, generally male outpouring of private fantasies that offsets an elusive social reality. This version neither adjusts to the world nor creates surrogate *communitas* but exalts interior images. As a confessional act it resists collectivization; it is not sung in chorus nor danced by groups. The singer yearns for a mythic past, for childhood, a mother, a *barrio,* and for a time that was loving and luminous. Composers from proletarian, anarchist backgrounds strike an occasional note of social protest, but generally an overriding fatalism precludes coming to grips with society. The singer is moved not by war but by the bereaved mother, not by the desecration of rural life but by the bird that sings no more. Instead of seeing vagabonds and delinquents as a social product, he bemoans a private destiny. Usually unmarried and without fixed employment, the narrator lacks the elemental ties that yield social knowledge by involvement. His stereotyped women abandon or betray him, and the dance itself, which had once exalted carnality, becomes a mechanical exercise that levels the sexes in dispirited routine.

In *Radiografía de la pampa* (1933) the poet Ezequiel Martínez Estrada (see below) analysed the dissociation between private imagination and public reality that the tango so compellingly rendered as 'pseudo-structures' pervading the whole of city culture and society. The literary

---

[42] Compare Julio Mafud, *Sociología del tango* (Buenos Aires, 1966) and Roberto DaMatta, *Carnavais, malandros e heróis* (Rio de Janeiro, 1979; Eng. trans., Notre Dame, Ind., 1991).

world exemplifies his theme in the somewhat mythicized antagonism between the Florida and Boedo groups. Their differences were couched as a rarefied debate over pure versus engaged art that did little to illuminate the situation of writers struggling for expression in Argentina. If we believe Borges the whole episode was a sham literary feud cooked up between the chic downtown set of Calle Florida and the 'proletarian' set of Boedo.[43] Disingenuously, Borges claimed he would have preferred Boedo affiliation, 'since I was writing about the old Northside and slums, sadness, and sunsets'. But he learned that he was a Florida warrior and it was too late to change, although a few, like Roberto Arlt, managed dual alliance. 'This sham,' Borges continued, 'is now taken into serious consideration by "credulous universities".'

Leónidas Barletta, a loyal Boedista, claims that the split was fundamental and would serve for decades to distinguish between the 'asphalt' writers and the *poetas de gabinete,* between those who understood the Russian Revolution and those who refused to, between those pledged to art for revolution's sake and those to revolution for art's sake. From the other camp Córdova Iturburu recalls that many Boedistas, like Barletta himself, were apolitical in the early years and that what divided the groups was at first not politics but the commitment of one to Russian and French naturalist novels and of the other to 'the task of achieving an expression in tune with the times'.[44] The Florida or *Martín Fierro* group insisted that a literary review should no more deal with politics than it does with horse races and women's fashions, and that if literature is not taken as a profession, it will remain mired in superannuated naturalism.

The critical point is not the historical importance of the feud but the disembodied nature of the debate. It lacked the engagement with circumstances of the esthetic and ideological projects in São Paulo. Suffice it to compare the *Martín Fierro* manifesto (1924) with the Paulista Pau Brasil manifesto of the same year. The former inveighed against the 'hippopotamic impermeability of the honourable public', the professor's 'funereal solemnity', the mimetism of Argentine high culture, the fear of equivocation that causes desperate reliance on libraries. New sensibility was needed. The Hispano-Suizo was finer art than a Louis Quinze chair. One could find a lesson of synthesis in a marconigram without throwing out the family

[43] Jorge Luis Borges, 'An Autobiographical Essay', in *The Aleph and Other Stories, 1933–1969* (New York, 1971), pp. 164–5.
[44] Leónidas Barletta, *Boedo y Florida, una versión distinta* (Buenos Aires, 1967); Córdova Iturburu, *La revolución martinfierrista* (Buenos Aires, 1962).

album. The emancipation of language begun by Rubén Dario did not preclude using Swiss toothpaste. '*Martín Fierro* has faith in our phonetics, our vision, our ways, our hearing, our capacity to digest and assimilate.'[45] In the Pau Brasil manifesto Oswald de Andrade did not state the issue; he rendered it: 'Carnival in Rio is the religious event of the race. Brazilwood. Wagner submerges before the Botafogo samba schools. Barbarous and ours. Rich ethnic formation. Vegetable wealth . . . Poetry still hidden in the malicious lianas of knowledge . . . Yet the lessons exploded. Men who knew everything were deformed like inflated balloons . . . There'd been inversion of everything, invasion of everything . . . The agile theatre, son of the mountebank. Agile and illogical. The agile novel, born of invention. Agile poetry . . . Let's divide: Imported poetry. And Brazilwood poetry. Exported.'[46]

The point is not that Argentine writers were blasé or deracinated but rather that the world, above all the urban world wherein they lived, instilled a curious set of ambivalences: a sense of irrecoverable or mythic past and a sense of a present in disarray or decadence; a sense of national achievement, whether cultural or economic, that was eminently 'respectable' for South America yet a haunting sense that the success was illusory; a groping for local identity and destiny that seemed condemned to find issue in international discourse and imagery. While such tensions did not lend themselves to public manifestoes, their very indeterminacy might elicit shafts of vision from the gifted writer. The Spanish surrealist Ramón Gómez de la Serna, conspicuous in the tertulia life of Madrid, marveled at the dedication of literary life in Buenos Aires.[47] The writer, he found, lived in absolute solitude; he might venture out for a testimonial or a new exhibition but immediately returned to his handsome estancia or his rented room. As a prime example of such a 'writerly' writer he singles out Macedonio Fernández (1874–1952) 'who has lived sixty years without being seen, feigning to be an old man to justify his retirement – which began when he was sixteen – when he's the precursor of everyone'. In his 'Autobiographical Essay' Borges later claimed that Macedonio impressed him more deeply than any other man. His philosophic bent, his belief that our world is a dream world and that truth is incommunicable, his vision

[45] Reprinted in María Raquel Llagostera (ed.), *Boedo y Florida* (Buenos Aires, 1980), pp. 7–9.
[46] Oswald de Andrade, 'Manifesto of Pau-Brasil poetry', *Latin American Literary Review*, 14/27 (1986), 184–7.
[47] Ramón Gómez de la Serna, *Retratos contemporáneos escogidos* (Buenos Aires, 1968), pp. 59–83, 189–212.

both splintered and radiographic – such traits made him a home-grown modernist before his time and an alleged influence on Borges, Bioy Casares, Marechal, Cortázar, and others. Some wonder, however, whether he was a true 'precursor' or simply a native son, inexplicably attuned to the wavelength of marconigrams, who never crossed the charmed circle of irremediably private imagination.

One might select any of several writers as illuminating the Argentine outlook and *mise-en-scène* of the 1920s and 1930s: the mystical dialectic of redemption that hovers in Güiraldes's *Don Segundo Sombra* (1926); the poetry of Oliverio Girondo, tracing a sure flight from the absurd domain of quotidian objects in *Veinte poemas para ser leídos en la tranvía* (1922) to *En la masmédula* (1954), a book said to penetrate the vertigo of interior space; the obstinate counterpoint of Eduardo Mallea (1903–82) between the prevarications and philistinism of 'visible' Argentina and a subterranean promise of selfhood and moral commitment in the 'invisible' one; or *Adán Buenosayres* (published in 1948 but begun in the 1920s) by Leopoldo Marechal which follows classical and Joycean models to render Buenos Aires as the arena for an Odyssean spiritual quest starting among the Martinfierristas of the 1920s and including a Dantean descent to the infernal Cacodelphia, a probable spoof on Mallea's 'invisible' Argentina. As with São Paulo we will juxtapose two representative if arbitrarily chosen figures as a shorthand device: Jorge Luis Borges (1899–1986) and Roberto Arlt (1900–42). The fact that they are clumsily accorded Florida and Boedo affiliation respectively spices the contrast; it doubles the counterpoint as it were.

The phasing of Borges's early travels deeply affected his mental development and his influence on the Porteño literary scene of the 1920s.[48] At fifteen he went to Europe with his family; here the war trapped them, and he returned only at age twenty-one. That is, he was uprooted precisely as he was asserting intellectual control and experiencing the disenchantment of late adolescence. Hence the identity of Argentine culture, and above all Buenos Aires, remained for him an almost mythic premise. He could even wonder in later years whether he had really left the English books and walled garden of his early home. What had he ever done but 'weave and unweave imaginings derived from them?' The European sojourn was important in two ways. First, it placed 'Georgie' (his nickname) in Switzerland, a wartime sanctuary where he could calmly ponder the harbingers of

[48] Emir Rodríguez Monegal, *Jorge Luis Borges: A Literary Biography* (New York, 1978), parts 2, 3.

the modern condition: De Quincey, Heine, the French symbolists, Whitman, Schopenhauer, Nietzsche. When he came to German expressionism he was prepared to read its revolutionary messages in context and to appreciate its advantages over other modernisms like cubism, futurism, surrealism and dadaism. Second, the family's move to Spain in 1919 initiated him to an active, inventive literary community via the tertulias of Gómez de la Serna and Rafael Cansinos-Asséns. 'Georgie' began publishing essays and poems and became identified with ultraism, a movement with international linkage. It drew from Mallarmé and French modernism but also from creationism, launched in 1914 by the precocious Chilean Vicente Huidobro (1893–1948) and epitomized in his lines: 'Why do you sing of the rose, oh poets? / Make it bloom in the poem! / The poet is a little god.' In a Borges pronouncement of 1921, ultraism was to reduce the lyric to primordial metaphor; suppress connective or redundant language; eliminate ornament, confession proof and sermonizing; and fuse images to enhance their suggestive power.

By the time he returned to Buenos Aires in 1921 Borges had, from inside the whale, assimilated the unfolding designs of Western literature and, as a poet, begun to contribute to immediate outcomes. Barely more than a youth, he had the experience and serenity to assume leadership in the renovation of Argentine letters. His poems in *Fervor de Buenos Aires* (1923) showed, however, that the return to origins was a litmus test for what might be artificial in the tertulias of Madrid. Borges, said his French translator, ceased being an ultraist with his first ultraist poem. So deep are the personal meanings of *Fervor* that Borges much later confessed to feeling that throughout his life he had been rewriting that one book. Emblematic of such meanings was his poem 'Fundación mitológica de Buenos Aires' wherein he 'discovers' that the city actually had a beginning, for he had judged it to be eternal like water and air. The poem suspends history, leaving space for private mind and collective memory to take hold. The primeval setting of monsters, mermaids, and magnets that bedevilled ships' compasses, where the explorer Solís was devoured by Indians before his own men, co-exists with the immigrant grinding out a *habanera* on the first hand-organ and with a political claque for Yrigoyen. A solitary tobacco shop perfumes the desert like a rose, and a whole block of Borges's *barrio*, Palermo, materialized beneath dawns and rains. This vision is startlingly akin to Freud's treatment of Rome when a year later, in *Civilization and its Discontents* (1930), he likened the mind itself to the Eternal City, conceived as a psychic entity with a copious past where 'nothing that has come into existence will have passed away and all the earlier phases of development continue to exist alongside the latest one'. Taking Buenos Aires as a microcosm and not a fragment, finding it haunted by dark and timeless omens, Borges was to rise above schools and manifestoes to accept vocation as a master cryptographer and theoretician of enigma.

If Borges, born in the last year of the old century, linked the strenuous present to a mythicized past, Roberto Arlt, born the first year of the new one, epitomized in his life and writings the dissolution of both history and community. Borges traced his forebears to the conquistadors, a lineage bolstered by the solid Victorian stock of his English grandmother. Arlt's home was one of ethnic improvisation. His father came from Prussia, spoke German, was bohemian, improvident, and authoritarian with his son. His mother was from Trieste, spoke Italian, read Dante, Tasso, Nietzsche and romantic novels, and was drawn to occult sciences. From this household Arlt became the first Argentine to write of the immigrants and lumpen from within, to render them fit subjects of literature. His subject-matter and his appeal to a mass public made Arlt an ideal candidate for Boedo. His caustic *aguafuertes,* or chronicles of daily life, in *El Mundo* delighted hundreds of thousands of readers, while Borges's bi-weekly book page in the women's magazine *El Hogar* was squeezed aside and finally dropped. Yet Arlt was taken up by the patrician Güiraldes, who corrected his chaotic Spanish, introduced him to Proust's work, made him his secretary, and published chapters of his first novel in *Proa.*

Arlt like Borges entertained fixations that led him into a universe of his own, possessing its inner logic and not submissive to fads in style or ideology. For Borges, as he matured as a poet and spinner of tales, a (perhaps *the*) central preoccupation shone forth as the philosophic challenge of distinguishing appearance from reality. To pursue this obsession required finely honed language and abstractions; yet his very success at imposing linguistic and conceptual control, at achieving what David Todd calls 'semantic ascent' above commonplace reality, led to a realm of inherent contradiction where the subject-matter of paradox displaces the subject-matter of consensual 'experience'. This of course generates a paradox regarding the persona of Borges himself. For once he addresses ultimate reality in an epistemological or ontological sense he lies open to charges of estheticism, elitism, and effete cosmopolitanism launched by persons whose own grasp of 'reality' is, on philosophic grounds, unexamined and sheerly tactical.

Arlt's reality consisted only of the urban society of his time and place, and specifically those reaches wherein he moved. Yet so intense was his rendering of it that he transcended the premises of naturalist fiction to arrive, like Borges, at a domain of paradox. Arlt divided his social universe into three parts – the lumpen, the petty bourgeoisie, and 'los ricos' – with class identification determined not by wealth, power and prestige but by the disposition for humiliation. An avid reader of Dostoevsky, Arlt was captivated by the underground man, overwhelmed and isolated by a society he cannot understand. Diana Guerrero observes that to the extent he lives out this abasement as guilt because it keeps him from being an effective social being he accepts it, but without renouncing the conviction of his superiority.[49] The victim is cynical and derisive; he flaunts his precious humiliation, precious because it alone yields reference points in a society from which he is isolated. The petty bourgeoisie suffers this degradation in its most excruciating form. The lumpen (vendors of newspapers and Bibles, brothel attendants, thieves, murderers and the like), caged in a world of boredom and ferocity, head irreversibly down the path to dehumanization. 'Los ricos', like the lumpen, live beyond the pale of petty-bourgeois legality but also beyond reach of humiliation. Their life therefore becomes unimaginable, and Arlt's fiction discloses only the elegant façades of their mansions. So remote is this world that the petty bourgeois has no more hope of reaching it than does the lumpen, which means that proletarian ennui and terror are in fact the repressed truth of petty bourgeois existence.

The petty bourgeois situation is therefore defined by an impressive hypocrisy, that is, the impossibility of being non-hypocritical, of recognizing, publicizing and suffering the torture of one's degradation. To acknowledge the contradiction between their situation and their professed values would mean slipping down the class ladder. Reflecting on his novel *Los siete locos* (1929), Arlt described his characters as *canaille* and as sad, vile and dreamy. They are interconnected by a desperation sprung not from poverty but from the bankruptcy of civilization. They move ghostlike in a world of shadows and cruel moral choices. 'If they were less cowardly they'd commit suicide; with a bit more character they'd be saints. In truth they seek the light but do so wholly immersed in mud. They besmirch what they touch.'[50] Marriage is the classic defeat in the Arltian world because it sentences one to daily petty-bourgeois routine. Hence such

---

[49]  Diana Guerrero, *Roberto Arlt, el habitante solitario* (Buenos Aires, 1972).
[50]  Roberto Arlt, *The Seven Madmen*, trans. Naomi Lindstrom (Boston, 1984). See also David Maldavsky, *Las crisis en la narrativa de Roberto Arlt* (Buenos Aires, 1968).

incidents of resistance as the groom who betrays his wife on their wedding day or the man who resorts to homicide during coitus to forestall violence by the partner. It is a world pervaded by fearful symmetries. The prostitute who goes home to her man wipes off her make-up; the 'honest' housewife who welcomes her man home applies it before he arrives. Throughout his narratives runs the theme of betrayal, as in the popular culture of the tango and *sainete*. The immigrant world reinforces it. Children of immigrants pose another symmetry; they not only betray the new *patria* by assuming the ideals of their parents but betray those same ideals in accepting the new *patria*. Arlt's writing thus throws a bridge from Porteño tango culture to the Dostoevskyan alienation of urban man in the West. His paradoxes and labyrinths, sprung from the lives of Buenos Aires, taken with those of Borges, sprung from frontiers of epistemology, form a fearful symmetry.

### Mexico: Modernism Manqué

Mexico forces us into a more permissive approach to modernism than we have so far used. Because Brazil and Argentina experienced no 'revolution' in the 1920s, and entertained no revolutionary expectations, we have until now considered writers whose visibility was at the time modest. Only hindsight shows Borges or Oswald de Andrade to have been framing messages for future times of trouble. Once revolution occurs, however, it too becomes a 'modernist' event by working lightning reversals and expansions of sense and sensibility. In Mexico, furthermore, revolutionary discourse and imagery brought forth indigenous elements that European modernism prized as 'exotic'. Yet by chronological accident, Mexico's modernist generation was somewhat young to assume cultural leadership. The immediate seniors who did assume it might experience fresh illuminations (José Vasconcelos, Alfonso Reyes). Or else, like the novelists, they might *seem* to innovate by sensitively reporting private versions of the 'happenings' which had swept them up. We thus face three considerations: first, cultural manifestations of the Revolution (notably novels, chronicles, and mural painting); second, the reception of Western modernism in the 1920s; third, transactions between the revolutionary impulse and the modernist temper.

To orientate our reflections it may help to contrast the nearly contemporaneous Mexican and Russian Revolutions. Modernist innovation in the arts chronologically bracketed the Russian Revolution, lasting from the 1880s to the Stalinist 'great change' after 1928. Marked by such liberative, partly mystical movements as Prometheanism, sensualism and apocalypticism, this 'profound cultural upheaval' was neither initiated nor immediately curtailed by Bolshevism.[51] It lent an aura of mixed apprehension and spiritual fulfillment to the dream of social transformation that had flickered in urban circles since the 1860s. Once the political whirlwind struck, apocalyptic spirits sensed the onset of final catastrophe while cubo-futurists accepted the Revolution without demur. As early as 1920, Zamiatin's novel, *We,* chillingly anatomized the imminent society by demonstrating the implications of wholly rationalized social life. In contrast, Mexico's first generation of 'revolutionary' novelists, imbued from youth with liberalism, positivism and naturalism, spent their mature lifetimes readjusting their ideological blinders in simply trying to glimpse the facts and ironies of the case at hand.

Russia had a thirty-year modernist flowering of world importance that withered after 1928 under a regime obsessively concerned to control thought and expression. In Mexico, newly hatched modernist impulses of the 1920s in literature, if not in painting, showed ambivalence to the Revolution; their fruition still lay ahead. The golden age of the Revolution under Cárdenas (1934–40) coincided with the Stalinist great purges, but while the Soviet Union was smothering intellectual inquiry and esthetic experiment, Mexico averted relapse into caudillist rule. Writers exiled in the 1920s returned to publish critical memoirs. Socialist education was prescribed for public schools, and the vocabulary of pre-Leninist Marxism was popularized, in this case expanding rather than shrinking the realm of public discourse. The rise of a 'triumphalist' state in the post-Cárdenas decades did not inhibit arts and letters from steady growth in maturity, diversity and imagination. The central challenge to Soviet artists was not to create culture for a new society, whose programme was officially defined, but to find a place for the arts of the past.[52] In Mexico, however much the state has promoted an official culture, the intellectual is challenged to appropriate a cultural past as the precondition for national 'identity'.

For post-revolutionary Mexico Enrique Krauze has identified three intellectual generations that overlapped in the 1910s. Two were Porfirian. The

[51] James H. Billington, *The Icon and the Axe* (New York, 1970), pp. 474–532.
[52] Boris Thompson, *The Premature Revolution: Russian Literature and Society, 1917–1946* (London, 1972), p. 76.

younger of these centred on the Ateneo group, a motley assortment of artists, literati and intellectuals who began meeting in 1910. While noted for humanism, spiritualism, anti-positivism and reverence for the classical tradition, their intellectual break with the previous century was by no means decisive. The ateneístas were dispersed in the early revolutionary period and when they reappeared it was rarely in leadership roles, Vasconcelos being the outstanding exception. The recipes for institutional change in the 1917 Constitution are less traceable to the ateneístas than to political economists of the positivist generation that preceded them.

Krauze's 'revolutionary' Generation of 1915 (born 1891–1905) came of age when the Revolution was a *fait accompli*.[53] They arrived without mentors or bookish vocations, obedient to the call of action and of imposing order. They included Vicente Lombardo Toledano, labour leader and eclectic socialist; Daniel Cosío Villegas, editor, historian, economist, publisher; Samuel Ramos, philosopher, essayist, public functionary. In the 1930s this generation found solidarity with exiled intellectuals from Spain whose professionalism greatly advanced the institutionalization of academic life. The poet and essayist Ramón López Velarde (1888–1921), who was navigating *con brio* the transition from Spanish American Modernism to Western modernism, was cut off in mid-career and required posthumous resurrection.[54]

Instead of dispersing this generation as it had the ateneístas, the Revolution kneaded it in a common effort to build what the Porfiriato had denied or the violent years had destroyed. Many who might have been complacent office holders or 'pure' intellectuals or alienated reformers were thrust into public roles of improvisation and reconstruction. Talent was commandeered to overhaul legal codes, establish banks, devise economic policy, found publishing houses and vanguard reviews, rebuild education from rural cultural missions to the university, create research centres, or excavate Indian cities. Within this kaleidoscopic endeavour the vanguard message was muted. *Estridentistas* led by Manuel Maples Arce introduced the new esthetics (dadaism, creationism, futurism) but left no monuments. The *agoristas* were perhaps more experimental but even less memorable.

Of greater esthetic projection than the groups mentioned were the *contemporáneos*. Considered slightly junior to Krauze's 'revolutionary' generation, they included among others Jaime Torres Bodet, Carlos Pellicer, José

[53] Enrique Krauze, 'Cuatro estaciones de la cultura mexicana', in *Caras de la historia* (Mexico, D.F., 1983), pp. 124–68; see also his *Caudillos culturales de la Revolución Mexicana* (Mexico, D.F., 1976).
[54] See Guillermo Sheridan, *Un corazón adicto: la vida de Ramón López Velarde* (Mexico, D.F., 1989).

Gorostiza, Salvador Novo, Xavier Villaurrutia and the acerbic essayist Jorge Cuesta.[55] As they matured they found bureaucratic or diplomatic niches, with Torres Bodet eventually becoming Mexican secretary of education and director general of UNESCO. While still students the future *contemporáneos* reinvented the Ateneo de la Juventud under its original name but fell short of their predecessors' idealism. Isolated in private worlds, they became a generation rather than a functional group. They left their mark on the narrative, essays and theatre, but their special achievement was poetry drawn from personal realms populated, in Paz's phrase, 'by the ghosts of erotism, sleep and death'. Gorostiza, perhaps the most striking of the poets, has been likened to Rilke, Valéry and Eliot in the quality of his inspiration. The *contemporáneos* loosely corresponded to the 'aesthetic' current in São Paulo or to Florida in Buenos Aires; but in Mexico the 'ideological' or Boedista position was commandeered by a culturally triumphant state, with the paradoxical result that the enthusiasm of Europeans and Americans for Mexican muralism, novels and folk art gave foreigners a hand in defining Mexican identity (*lo mexicano*). 'One of the greatest tragedies of the Revolution,' writes Luis Villoro, 'perhaps lies in the fact that the moment of greatest revolutionary advance failed to coincide with the moment of generosity and optimism of its intelligentsia.'[56]

The crowning irony, Guillermo Sheridan reminds us, was that because bureaucratic nationalists regarded the *contemporáneos* as elitist, Europeanizing and sometimes even 'effeminate', one of the latters' 'most eloquent displays of patriotism would be the careful, energetic, and of course futile battle against these restrictive and anecdotal conventions.' The moment when the group (or *grupo sin grupo*) founded their review *Contemporáneos* (1928–31) was precisely when they drifted apart. The journal suffered from indecisive eclecticism, wavering between European avant-gardism and Mexican nationalism. Its great merit, Sheridan comments, derived 'more from the quality of its collaborators than from the journal's ability to amalgamate them'. The nationalists had the universalists at a clear disadvantage. The latter found it more difficult to ignore being publicly caricatured by Rivera and Orozco than it was for the Florida clique to dismiss the taunts of Boedo. In 1932 a published interview with the

[55] Oscar Collazos (ed.), *Los vanguardismos en la América Latina* (Barcelona, 1977), pp. 105–22; Guillermo Sheridan, *Los Contemporáneos ayer* (Mexico, D.F., 1985); Paz's essays on Pellicer, Gorostiza and Villaurrutia in Luis Mario Schneider (ed.), *México en la obra de Octavio Paz* (Mexico, D.F., 1979), pp. 242–77.

[56] Luis Villoro, 'La cultura mexicana de 1910 a 1960', *Historia Mexicana* 10/2 (1960), 206.

'ambiguous and inscrutable' Gorostiza ignited a polemic by manipulating his words into a seeming 'act of contrition' aimed at 'rectifying' his alleged Europhilism. It took time for the *contemporáneos* to win the recognition that a protégé, Octavio Paz, accorded in 1966 when he stated that 'in a strictly intellectual sense nearly all that's being done now in Mexico owes something to the Contemporáneos, to their example, their rigor, their zeal for perfection'.[57]

The challenge here was not, for the moment, to parse meanings of modernity and to surmise their import for a recalcitrant 'colonial' ethos. For in Mexico the dikes of tradition had cracked and rapid change had set in. The times required not the vatic cries and cryptic images of vanguardism but keen reportage and diagnosis for which an earlier generation from the naturalist tradition was trained. The future was to be inferred from leaders and events, not gleaned from random clues of private imagination. The two writers to receive special attention here were both born before 1890. The first, Martín Luis Guzmán, was plunged into the Revolution from the start, and its subsequent course yielded his prism on the world. The second, Alfonso Reyes, by his loyalty to Western humanism and his aloofness from quotidian events adopted a macrocosmic view that assimilated Mexican to Western culture rather than a prismatic one that probed particulars of time and place. Both were sympathetic to modernism. In his travel chronicles of 1916–18 Guzmán wrote of his entrancement by vorticism, imagism and Rivera's Parisian cubism, and Reyes, while ambassador to Argentina and Brazil in 1927–38, was early to recognize Borges's genius and became an *aficionado* of Brazilian Anthropophagy. They learned lessons from modernism without adopting its tactics.

Martín Luis Guzmán (1887–1976) grew up in a rural town near Mexico City where he occasionally glimpsed Porfirio Díaz moving at the summit of greatness, resplendent in ceremonial uniform or else mysteriously garbed in black.[58] When he was eleven Guzmán's family moved to Veracruz, cradle of the Reform laws. There he read Rousseau, Hugo, and Pérez Galdós and in school succumbed to liberalism and the Mexican civic ideal personified in Juárez. Later as a student in Mexico City he repudiated the positivist apologia for the regime and began to frequent the Ateneo. In May 1911 he demonstrated for Madero, baptizing his political career. By now the guidelines for Guzmán's life as a writer and publicist were in

---

[57] Paz cited in Sheridan, *Contemporáneos*, p. 21.
[58] Guzmán recalled his life in 'Apunte sobre una personalidad', in *Academia: Tradición, independencia, libertad* (Mexico, D.F., 1959), pp. 11–51.

place: classic liberal principles, a vague but committed vision of an emergent Mexico, and fascination with the thoughts and instincts of great leaders. Since the age of fourteen, moreover, he had shown a journalist's vocation. His intellectual shortcomings were offset by his passion, grasp of human character and reportorial skill.

The diagnosis that would inform his future writings Guzmán set forth from exile in Spain in *La querella de México* (1915).[59] Here he offered no such pathology of economic institutions as those of Wistano Luis Orozco, Andrés Molina Enríquez, or Luis Cabrera. The deeper cause of Mexico's distress, he assumed, was a 'penury of spirit' reflected, first, in the mimicry and dilettantism of intellectuals who had never cultivated philosophy and science, studied national history, or analysed social problems and, second, in the apathy and moral obtuseness of the Indians, whose spiritual desperation pre-dated the trauma of Spanish conquest and stemmed from the superstition, terror and cannibalism of Aztec society. Two impulses to renovation, national independence and the Reform, were extinguished under the Porfiriato when the creoles turned away from history and the work of construction. The country lived in 'the shadow of the caudillo', a phrase that became the title of Guzmán's novel *La sombra del caudillo* (1929). When revolution came the creoles sacrificed their own hero, Madero, and renewed the chaos of warring factions, each clamouring for foreign recognition instead of cultivating morality for leadership. How could one redeem the Indian while the creole was unregenerate? 'We seem to have intelligence in surfeit. What lacks is virtue.'

His journalist's eye, his friendship with revolutionary leaders, and above all his moral vision explain Guzmán's fascination with single actors and lend his writings a Thucydidean accent. *La sombra del caudillo* is in part a roman à clef based on events and figures of the mid-1920s. *El águila y la serpiente* (1928) is a memoir of Guzmán's own experience from Madero's death in 1913 to his exile in 1915, yet composed with such dramatic craft and illumination of character that it assumes imaginative force in the tradition of Sarmiento and da Cunha.[60] On the surface the camera's eye of authorial narration links the book's kaleidoscopic episodes. Deeper unity arises from the tension between Villa and Carranza projected against the mute, anonymous mass of peasant soldiery. Ideologies, lofty political aims, the claims of history fade before primordial instinct and

[59] *La querella* was extended in newspaper articles from New York (1916–18): Martín Luis Guzmán, *La querella de México: A orillas del Hudson; otras páginas* (Mexico, D.F., 1958).
[60] *The Eagle and the Serpent*, trans. Harriet de Onís (Garden City, N.Y., 1965).

fugitive passion. The collective soul is only dimly sensed. The human mass moves as one body, swaying, weaving, stumbling, murmuring, fused by a secret filament – a huge reptile crawling drunk and sluggish along the cavernous street of an empty city. The observer must jerk free to escape a crushing sense of physical and moral oppression.

Actors are stripped to psychic essentials. In confronting Carranza, Villa opposes the amoral instincts of a child to the picayune, selfish scheming of an old man. Villa is half-tamed and feline. His pistol is an extension of his hand; bullets spurt from the man, not the gun. He is incapable of etiquette, yet tenderness may at times dim his glittering eyes. He marvels at such simple life processes as the mystery of sleep. When in a paroxysm of wrath Villa orders 170 prisoners slaughtered, Guzmán risks his own life to argue why it is wrong. As to a child he explains that he who surrenders renounces the chance of killing others. Villa leaps up, issues the counter-order, and when it arrives in time, wipes the sweat from his brow. Later he mumbles thanks 'for that thing this morning, that business of the prisoners'. Carranza, a Porfirian-style figure whom Guzmán recalls with ambivalence, assumes a benign, patriarchal air. In an ancient tradition he has mastered the art of village politics, of pitting opponents against followers, of premeditated corruption, of fanning passions, intrigues and bad faith. Impervious to noble ideals, bereft of magnanimity, he prizes flattery over actions, servility over talent in his subordinates. He is in short a stubborn old man with all the ruses and pettiness of senility.

With Guzmán as with Mariano Azuela, 'father' of the revolutionary novel, the point of interest is not the author's disenchantment or pessimism but the fact that he painfully sets aside ideology and reduces his subject to directly experienced elements. While Guzmán's prose therefore has some of the naturalist power of a Zola, his feat of psychic reduction is akin to the vanguardist pulverization of received forms. To seize the meanings and possibilities of the Revolution Guzmán gradually ceased fitting it to his early political categories. Villa became for him emblematic as an amoral or pre-moral figure, arisen from the disinherited masses and unshaped by fancy ideological or moral codes. 'Primitive' instinct and his elemental, sometimes contradictory convictions informed his future society.[61] In search of the essential Villa, Guzmán went on to write the five-volume *Memorias de Pancho Villa* (1938–40) using an autobiographical first

---

[61] Larry M. Grimes, *The Revolutionary Cycle in the Literary Production of Martín Luis Guzmán* (Cuernavaca, 1969), p. 72.

person and Villa's own pungent language in a valiant effort to suspend judgement and recreate the psyche and self-vindication of the subject himself.[62]

Alfonso Reyes (1889–1959), barely twenty when the Ateneo was founded, was Guzmán's colleague in the group. But while Guzmán sought to recover an eclipsed liberal tradition and to penetrate a discrete Mexican 'reality', Reyes addressed the general case of a society that had 'arrived late at the banquet of civilization'. The challenge he took on was not redemption from the authoritarian uses of positivism but the placement of Mexico within occidental culture. Of the four Ateneo luminaries it has been said that Vasconcelos was driven to rebuild the world, Antonio Caso to contemplate it, Henríquez Ureña (the 'Socrates' of the group) to explain it, and Reyes to illuminate it. These missions may at later moments, particularly during the flight of the ateneístas after the outbreak of revolution, have seemed diaphanous. Yet in the long run they offer co-ordinates for the *derniers cris* of vanguardism. Reyes at an early age began to trace paths for the 'moralization' of Mexican society and culture relying on classical studies and the Spanish *siglo de oro,* with reinforcement from French and English letters, current strains of philosophy and literary theory, and fresh appreciation of Mexican culture itself. The agenda did not centre on local 'problems' of race, politics and poverty. The issue was to assimilate thinking in Mexico to the canons and experience of the West. His generation, his temperament, his upbringing did not seduce Reyes toward the short-circuits of vanguardism. He addressed not outcomes but premises of Western civilization, in particular the branch that included Mexico.

Guzmán, we saw, entered the political maelstrom as a *maderista* in 1911. Reyes, however, was the son of General Bernardo Reyes, the entrepreneurial governor of Nuevo León and a loyal, if reformist, Díaz supporter. On 9 February 1913, the general was killed before the National Palace leading a counter-revolution that soon brought death to Madero. Refusing the offer of Provisional President Huerta to become his secretary, Alfonso left Mexico in poverty and remained abroad until 1938. Years later Alfonso recalled his father as a hero who was amused by tempests and displayed such sterling virtues as vitality, loyalty, moderation and a prudence matched by bravura. His death, 'an obscure equivocation in the

---

[62] *Memoirs of Pancho Villa,* trans. Virginia H. Taylor (Austin, Tex., 1965); see also Christopher Domínguez, 'Martín Luis Guzmán: El Teatro de la política,' *Vuelta, Revista Mensual,* 11/131 (1987): 22–31.

moral clockwork of our world', was a spilling of aging wine.[63] This libation gave Alfonso a quarter century of Wanderjahre and with it the life and outlook of a universal writer. While Guzmán looked for nobility in the cadres of new leadership, Reyes found it in the old. Although he saw Don Porfirio and his coterie as insulated from the democratic era by a wall of glass, an abyss of time, filial piety allowed him to discern heroism in the old order and, by extension, the more distant past.

The treatment of philosophy later in this chapter examines the notion of 'anabatic recovery', that is, an 'upstream' expedition from local circumstances to outlooks of the contemporary West and thence, against the current of time, to the sources of Western thought. The clench of immediacy impels and shapes the campaign making it, in Ortega's term, a 'perspectival' assault on the citadel of Western culture. Reyes did not conduct an 'anabasis'. He began his journey with a genealogy already in mind; his mission was to illuminate, not assault and reinterpret. As a penniless expatriate in 1913 his brief stay in the Paris of Picasso and Gertrude Stein did not yield him, as it had Oswald de Andrade a year earlier, a foothold within dissolving ideas and images. Reyes soon moved to Spain where he joined the cenacle of the proto-surrealist Ramón Gómez de la Serna, as would Borges a few years later. But Ramón's catachrestic *greguerías* (shocking oxymoronic one-liners) were for him less a symptom of modernism than a reprise of Quevedo, Goya and the history of Spanish alienation. Spain's ambivalent relation with the Rest of the West from its own version of the classical, Christian tradition drew Reyes to Menéndez Pidal, Unamuno, Ortega, Juan Ramón Jiménez and the Generation of 1898 and its successors, who had revived the eighteenth-century debate between Hispanism and modernity. Reyes required this context not to 'invent' a Mexican identity but to discover Mexico's presumptive place in the scheme of things. Just as he rejected vanguard reversals of the rules, so later would he chide the phenomenologists for their claim to have given philosophy a fresh start.

In Spain, freed of constraints of his homeland, Reyes laid the foundations for his life work. He assembled his impressions of contemporary Spain in *Cartones de Madrid* and recreated the Spaniards' pristine view of Tenochtitlán in *Visión de Anahuac;* he secured scholarly command of the ancient and the Spanish classics; he wrote *El suicida* to develop a diffuse

[63] Emmanuel Carballo, 'Alfonso Reyes a la luz de una fecha', in Margarita Vera Cuspinera (ed.), *Alfonso Reyes, homenaje de la Facultad de Filosofía y Letras* (Mexico, D.F., 1981), pp. 383–7; Barbara Bockus Aponte, *Alfonso Reyes and Spain* (Austin, Tex., 1972), p. 11.

humanist's credo from the mystery of the suicidal impulse; he composed a dramatic poem, *Ifigenia cruel,* of autobiographical inspiration whose protagonist rejects the rancour and persecutions of her homeland in favour of freedom and autonomy. What remained was to round out his American experience.

After serving the Mexican legation in Paris, Reyes regained a diplomatic post in Spain in 1920. Then in 1927 he was named ambassador to Argentina, serving there until 1930, in Brazil until 1936, and in Argentina again until 1938. Reyes has been scolded for not publicizing these national literatures throughout Hispanic America. He did, however, publish penetrating commentary on the Argentine temperament and was thanked by Borges for having rescued him from being simply the son of Leonor Azevedo. In the case of unknown Brazil, Ruedas argues that even so keen a mind as Reyes's was unprepared to orchestrate the memory of Machado de Assis, the cacophonic modernism of São Paulo, and the telluric fiction of the northeast. Nor indeed was Brazilian literature ripe for exportation despite the war whoops of the Brazil-wood manifesto. What Reyes did do was to reflect on nuances of Brazilian social life, learn an unaccented Portuguese, and publish a literary newsletter named *Monterrey* after his native city (1930–7), which tried neither to introduce Mexicans to Brazilian literature nor vice versa.[64] As in all his writings Reyes was concerned with neither expository journalism nor intellectual formulas but with luminous understandings.

When Reyes finally returned to Mexico in 1938, his connections with the Spanish intelligentsia and his sympathy with Spanish culture equipped him ideally – given the Republican sympathy of the Cárdenas government – to create a mecca for émigré Spanish intellectuals. He became president of the Casa de España, and when it became the Colegio de México in 1940 he continued as its director until his death in 1959. However much the Colegio itself may later have succumbed to bureaucratization and government co-optation, here was a moment when, after a long interregnum, the humanist, Americanist messages of the best Spanish thought could find transatlantic assimilation.

Reyes was a prolific, multifarious writer like Andrés Bello or Sarmiento or Martí or Eugenio María de Hostos whose life work evades easy synthesis. Others, like Machado de Assis or Mariátegui or Borges or Octavio Paz,

---

[64] Jorge Ruedas de la Serna, 'La misión brasileña de Alfonso Reyes', in Cuspinera, *Alfonso Reyes,* pp. 195–210; Manuel Ulacia, 'A antropofagia de Alfonso Reyes', *O Estado de São Paulo* (literary supplement), 10 June 1989.

are perhaps more layered and complex than the first group, but their psychic obsessions flash more clearly; they drop conspicuous, though never facile, clues to the enigmas that await deciphering. If there is a key to Reyes, it lies embedded in his passion for Greek culture, traceable from his early Ateneo years through the classical studies of his last two decades in Mexico. The Roman example of juridical uniformity and use of urban centres for spreading 'civilization' had been prominent for Spanish colonial jurists. The ateneístas rejected this outlook of privilege in favour of Greek *sophrosyne:* search for an inclusive Mexican culture, thought unfolding without dogmatisms, freedom for creativity, disciplined love of reason and beauty, and a dynamic equilibrium of contrasting views.[65] Throughout his life Reyes held true to the Greek precedent, in part as inspiration for a Mexican ideal, in part as the source for an outlook transmitted to Mexico in a version less distorted than it had been in northern Europe by the religious and scientific revolutions. In a sense Reyes was an *arielista,* but one whose classical, Mediterranean understandings delved to origins, not tinctured as were Rodó's by the fears and forebodings of *fin de siècle* Paris.

## FICTION AND THE ESSAY

### Naturalism and its Pathetic Fallacies

The foregoing treatments of Brazil, Argentina and Mexico in the 1920s reveal tension between two ways of appropriating experience. Of the writers discussed, Borges pursues a covert search for epistemological foundations while at the other extreme Martín Luis Guzmán conducts a frontal assault on phenomena as directly presented. The rest flourish in zones of transaction: Mário de Andrade, caught between nostalgia and iconoclasm, lucid visions and patient research; Oswald de Andrade, who employs oxymorons of the vanguard esthetic to overturn hallowed verities of Brazilian history; Roberto Arlt, who chronicles petty bourgeois life while alert to Dostoevskyan reversals; and Alfonso Reyes, who explores the Iberian and classical past to fix co-ordinates for the here and now of a 'new world'. Yet for reasons suggested earlier the aesthetic emphasis of the heroic modernist years was shifting toward an ideological or broadly explicative emphasis in the late 1920s. This makes the identity essay an obvious

[65]  Ernesto Mejía Sánchez, 'Alfonso Reyes y el mundo clásico', and Paola Vianello de Córdova, 'Alfonso Reyes y el estudio de las culturas clásicas', in Cuspinera, *Alfonso Reyes,* pp. 105–46.

attraction, not simply because of its diagnostic uses but because its authors were more critical of the status quo and more respectful of aspirations of the disinherited than had been the earlier pensadores.

First, however, let us consider the novelists of the mid-1920s to mid-1940s. Of these, a significant number became recognized by their stylistic taste for naturalism or their penchant for the land, regionalism or indigenism. To call them 'neo-naturalists', however, is misleading insofar as this implies reprise of a literary mode of the 1880s and 1890s that had in turn reflected European fashion. For while European naturalism was a step in a logical sequence from romanticism and realism to symbolism and modernism, in Latin America it offered fresh tools for an ancient inquiry. French and English authors, that is, were less concerned with local 'identity' than with credible versions of the social universe at a moment when scientific ratification was a *sine qua non*. Naturalism was for them a transitory phenomenon. Latin American literature, however, was heralded at the era of European conquest by an early brand of naturalism ('natural history') or – in that dawning age of science, imperialism, journalism, censuses and bureaucratic reports – the attempt to decode a strange environment from self-given phenomena. By the eighteenth century the broad question of 'American' identity was voiced and, after independence, preoccupation with the attributes of discrete nationhood. In the 1880s these concerns meshed with the European vogue of naturalism, but as something more than a mimetic episode or an ephemeral response to the procession of 'styles' at the centre.

The 'eternal return' of naturalism is illustrated below for Brazil. But first, the relation of transatlantic naturalism to realism deserves attention. In Europe realism avoided 'romantic' subjectivity and idealism but stopped short of the determinism that gave naturalism its reputation for moral aloofness. Martín Luis Guzmán fits the looser category. If he failed to adopt the shock methods of modernism or count on historic precepts of Western humanism, neither did he choose clinical naturalism for organizing his world. Trusting what he saw and knew, he took his chances along the frontiers between documentation and fiction, psychological portraiture and moral judgement, the journalistic and the empathic eye. Much the same could be said of Mariano Azuela, whose *Los de abajo* (1915), originally subtitled 'Views and Scenes from the Present Revolution', established him as the founder of the Mexican revolutionary novel. Although he admired Zola for books as 'chaste as any treatise on medicine', Azuela called not him but Balzac the 'greatest novelist of all times' for having raised testimony on popular life to the realm of high art.[66]

As the 1930s drew near, a new wave of fiction came into sight: the Colombian José Eustasio Rivera's *La vorágine* (1924), the Brazilian José Américo de Almeida's *A bagaceira* (1928), and the Venezuelan Rómulo Gallegos's *Doña Bárbara* (1929) followed by the Ecuadorian Jorge Icaza's *Huasipongo* (1934) and the Peruvian Ciro Alegría's *El mundo es ancho y ajeno* (1941). While these newer authors remained faithful to the hallowed domestic tradition of 'natural history' they also, in part unwittingly, encouraged subversion of the original aim of naturalism. Characterized as *novelas de la tierra* (novels of the earth or land), their narratives became criticized for allowing geographic space to cancel interior space. 'Wild nature came to the fore', wrote Emir Rodríguez Monegal, 'and to such a degree dominated the human actor, moulding and determining him, that his individual character nearly disappeared, or was reduced . . . to the role of an archetype: the sign or symbol of something, but not a person. Only in the 1960s and 1970s, with the acceptance of 'marvellous realism' in Latin American fiction, he continued, could we appreciate that 'these works establish deep linkage between the marvelled narratives of the first explorations and discoveries of America and the novel (frankly mythic) of a Rulfo, a García Márquez, a Vargas Llosa'.[67] One example among many is *Don Goyo* (1933) by the Ecuadorian novelist Aguilera Malta.[68] The folk hero Don Goyo predicts the ruin of his community of mangrove cutters by the invasion of whites. In this confrontation the actors are mechanized and unmotivated, propelled by lust, fear and a quest for idyllic pleasure. Humans are likened to objects (a woman's hips become a canoe on the river) while human behaviour is projected onto an angry, muttering nature (the mangroves overhear human lovers; trees have intercourse with the river). Don Goyo is finally killed by a mangrove tree, as though by intention, and only then does he achieve vitality as his corpse topples from

---

[66] Eliud Martínez, *The Art of Mariano Azuela* (Pittsburgh, Pa., 1980), pp. 88–9; Stanley L. Robe, *Azuela and the Mexican Underdogs* (includes bilingual text) (Berkeley, 1979); Adalbert Dessau offers ideological analysis in *La novela de la Revolución Mexicana*, trans. Juan José Utrilla (Mexico, D.F., 1972).

[67] Emir Rodríguez Monegal, *El boom de la novela latinoamericana* (Caracas, 1972), pp. 49–50. For up-to-date treatises on 'regional' novels, see Carlos J. Alonso, *The Spanish American Regional Novel* (Cambridge, Eng., 1990) and Doris Sommer, *Foundational Fictions: The National Romances of Latin America* (Berkeley, 1991).

[68] Demetrio Aguilera Malta, 'Don Goyo', trans. E. E. Perkins, in Angel Flores and Dudley Poore (eds.), *Fiesta in November: Stories from Latin America* (Boston, 1942), pp. 120–228.

a canoe and descends the current, laughing in triumph over the now submissive river and its sharks. Yet as John Brushwood has pointed out, the author avoids full surrender to the naturalist 'pathetic fallacy' by stylizing and distilling the course of events and by 'persistent intercalation of the nonliteral' to sustain Don Goyo's movement between man and legend.[69]

For the moment, then, we are left with a paradox. The discussion above of Guzmán and Azuela suggests that their personal, open-ended 'realism' was an *ipso facto* renunciation of modernist experimentalism and iconoclasm.[70] Yet it now appears that 'naturalism', a clinical and methodical brand of realism, opens the door to what is inexplicable and mythic. Thus realism appears pragmatic and commonsensical with naturalism being prescriptive and mythopoeic. This would mean that Latin American neo-naturalism of the 1930s deviated from the Zolaesque prototype and became instead an episode on the path from modernism to the complex narratives of the 1950s during a brief interval when the need for social description and political protest loomed large. By the beginning of the 1940s naturalist ideological protest loses primacy. Social and political malfeasance is now traced to an urban point of origin, not to the feudal periphery, and ascribed to human nature rather than to regional geography. 'For this new line,' wrote Rodríguez Monegal, 'Manichaeism is a political charge more than a virtue; protest becomes a burden; true denunciation is presented as a narrative, not in emotionally charged speeches; the supernatural blends intimately with the quotidian.'[71] For him the emblematic figure of the post-naturalist transition was Ciro Alegría, who published his best book in 1941 and then nothing of note before his death a quarter century later. A contemporary of Onetti and Lezama Lima, Alegría felt himself trapped, his critic surmised, between his rich thematic repertoire and a solid, two-dimensional technique before a literature about to move from, as it were, *Uncle Tom's Cabin* to *The Sound and the Fury*.[72]

[69] John S. Brushwood, *The Spanish American Novel: A Twentieth-Century Survey* (Austin, Tex., 1978), pp. 96–101. See also Roberto González Echevarría's treatment of *Doña Bárbara* in *The Voice of the Masters: Writing and Authority in Modern Latin American Literature* (Austin, Tex., 1988), ch. 2, and for Brazil José H. Decanal, *O romance dos 30* (Porto Alegre, 1982).

[70] For Azuela's mannered attempts to adopt a modernist esthetic in his later career see Martínez, *Art of Mariano Azuela*.

[71] Emir Rodríguez Monegal, *Narradores de esta América*, Vol. 1 (Buenos Aires, 1976), p. 172; 'The New Novelists', *Encounter*, 25/3 (1965), 97–109.

[72] Rodríguez Monegal, *Narradores*, pp. 166–74; also Antonio Cornejo Polar, 'La novela indigenista: una desgarrada conciencia de la historia', *Revista Lexis*, 4/1 (1980): 88; Julio Rodríguez-Luis, *Hermenéutica y praxis del indigenismo: la novela indigenista de Clorinda Matto a José María Arguedas* (Mexico, D.F., 1980).

Naturalism as reportage or as 'scientific' interpretation clarifies aspects of the identity question that concern us. Our clues thus far proffered as to the historical role of naturalism in Latin America, however, are somewhat disparate. For example: (1) because the Americas have been a 'new world' for half a millennium they are of permanent interest as an arena for 'novelties' to be meticulously reported; (2) Latin American writers of the 1880s and 1890s were influenced by the rationale and technique of Zolaesque naturalism; (3) political and ideological pressures of the 1930s opened a space propitious for neo-naturalist fiction, often in the form of novels of the land that might retrieve the foundation myths implied in (1) above; and (4) while naturalism claimed clinical authority more strict than that of realism, this gave its narratives a transhuman scientific warrant which paradoxically resembled the *deus ex machina* of the marvellous realism that won literary cachet in the 1940s.

Various authors wove these strands into patterns; an obvious example is Alejo Carpentier, who often expatiated on the matter. His key books for present purposes are his first novel, *¡Ecue-Yamba-O!* (written 1928, published 1933), and his *El reino de este mundo* (1949).[73] The former, featuring themes of social justice and Afro Cuban culture (the book's title means 'Lord, Praised Be Thou' in ñáñigo dialect), was a product of time and place for its elements of social realism and 'indigenism', seasoned however by modernist hints of cubism, futurism and especially surrealism. Citing Juan Marinello, González Echevarría remarks that in *¡Ecue-Yamba-O!* Carpentier portrays Afro Cubans from the inside and outside simultaneously, causing a 'crack' at the centre of the novel, or cleavage between the black world and a white perception of it. Carpentier experienced his curative revelation on a trip to Haiti with Louis Jouvet's theatre company in 1943. Here direct contact with Afro-Caribbean religion and with the monuments erected by Henri Christophe inspired him to break with cosmopolitan sur*realism* in favour of a 'marvellous *realism*' (or magic *realism* from the Afro viewpoint) having roots in communal faith, myth and identity. *El reino de este mundo,* a story immersed in the ordeal of Haitian independence, was the initial fruit of this conversion. In later novels he expanded and emancipated his American theatre to develop, wrote Rodríguez Monegal, 'the contrast between the magic of the American topography or the "marvellous" quality of its history and the products of a European superculture that pursues and even oppresses its human actors'.

---

[73] *The Kingdom of this World,* trans. Harriet de Onís (New York, 1957).

Carpentier's successive discussions of his ideas did less to dissolve his original contradictions than to orchestrate his several realities – socialist realism, surrealism, magic realism (which discredits causation), and marvellous realism (which celebrates the unwonted, or *lo insólito*) – to yield a 'real' matrix for imaginative reconnaissance.[74]

Carpentier's fiction and pronouncements help place realism and naturalism in literary context. It remains, however, to demonstrate that naturalism *tout court* has had its own career and that it is known to appear in relatively unadulterated form. In her *Tal Brasil, qual romance?* [If such is Brazil, what is its novel?] Flora Süssekind makes this case for Brazil, which witnessed three flowerings of naturalism in the 1880s/1890s, the 1930s and the 1970s.[75] Her premise is that the naturalist aesthetic flings the cloak of science across the abiding quest for New World identity. In representing a national reality it seeks mimesis that admits no doubts or divisions, even to the point of sacrificing stylistic felicity. Insofar as it grows from a sense of uprootedness and orphanhood, however, the mimetic fixation may be of emotive origin. A writer's goal is therefore not necessarily 'tal Brasil, qual romance?' but may be 'tal Brasil, tal romance' ('as is Brazil so *must* be its novel'). Carried to its logical conclusion, the argument leaves us to assume that the great nay-sayers of Brazilian identity – who like Machado de Assis or Oswald de Andrade or Guimarães Rosa accept the fragmentation of Brazil on the one hand and its universal attunements on the other – become literary foundlings without progenitors or disciples.

Examining three successive moments of naturalism allows underlying premises to be distinguished from shifting technique and sensibility. Thus to explicate the 1930s requires knowledge of the other two moments, for each shares the photographic imperative. The 'photographer' assumes that he faces a coherent subject and must perform as a mere lens, even though he himself is part of the subject portrayed. In all three periods writers vow to report without distortion or preconception and perform a 'visually' mimetic act. Their critical verbs are see, examine, discern and portray. They propose to cancel the reader's role as interpreter by connecting the reader directly to the evidence. Science and literature merge in a linear vision. Comparing the three moments of naturalism, however, reveals that three disparate political diagnoses have been smuggled in under the pretense of objectivity. In the

---

74 Emir Rodríguez Monegal, 'Lo real y lo maravilloso en *El reino de este mundo*', in Klaus Müller-Bergh (ed.), *Asedios a Carpentier* (Santiago, Chile, 1972), pp. 101–32; Roberto González Echevarría, *Alejo Carpentier: The Pilgrim at Home* (Ithaca, N.Y., 1977), ch. 2.
75 Flora Süssekind, *Tal Brasil, qual romance?* (Rio de Janeiro, 1984).

1880s the things that are 'seen' yield a deterministic view of biological heredity and a presumption against socialism as a political remedy. In the 1930s they dismiss heredity, posit social dialectic and predict structural change or revolution. In the 1970s our informant is no longer the white-coated physician of the early period nor the decadent patriarchal heir of the middle one but the heroic, marginalized news reporter with his hopes pinned to democratic insurgence via denunciation.

While remaining faithful to direct reportage and the quest for nationality, the regionalist novels of the 1930s, especially the novels of the northeast (Jorge Amado, José Lins do Rego, and with qualifications, Graciliano Ramos), abandon the pathology of individuals in favour of the fortunes of economic enterprises. Interest turns from individuals and their genes to the self-made man and his manipulation of factors of production. Titles that once identified persons (*Bom crioulo, A normalista*) now feature crops and enterprises (*Cacao, Usina, São Bernardo*). Romans-fleuves are favoured for handling inter-generational socio-economic forces, while 'cycles' of novels echo the economists' new cyclical version of Brazil's economic development. The nostalgic sociologist Gilberto Freyre and the Marxist economic historian Caio Prado Junior (scion of Paulista entrepreneurs) both published influential works in the 1930s – *Casa Grande e Senzala* (Eng. trans. *The Masters and the Slaves*) and *Formação do Brasil Contemporâneo, Colônia* (Eng. trans. *The Colonial Background of Modern Brazil*) respectively – that gave academic support for the transition from the patriarchal fazenda to the industrial *usina* that the novelists identified (see below).

From the three successive episodes – the 1880s/90s, the 1930s and the 1970s – the limits and confusions of Brazilian naturalism become clear. 'Tal Brasil, tal romance' contains a fatal ambivalence. Does naturalism truly enjoin unmediated replication of Brazil? Or does it, unlike open-ended realism, imply replication and imposition of Zola, European literature, or Western science? Does it reproduce a recognized foreign model or an unrecognized Brazil? If we assume that the naturalist intention is to replicate Brazil, we must ask whether Brazil is truly unitary or whether it is fractured by race, class, power, wealth and group outlooks, as indeed Euclides da Cunha found it to be. Naturalism admittedly draws energy from these divisions and is far from the genre of static national-character portraiture. Where it finds 'unity' is in a future condition (aryanization, economic development, revolution, or democratic consensus) and in the patterned forces at work to produce it. Naturalism finds redemption over the generations in precisely those fractures within its own diagnosis that yield spiralling self-correction and fresh openings instead of circularity and frozen identity. In each period, moreover, an occasional writer, classed as a naturalist on formal grounds, makes a private breakthrough to broader currents of sensibility. The obvious case in the 1930s is Graciliano Ramos, who called his diverse writings an unfolding series rather than a cycle, who was not driven to anchor his writerly instincts in documentary form, who refused to taxonomize his fictional characters, and who never sacrificed his art to political circumstance.

### The Search for Causality: Mariátegui, Price-Mars, Prado

The term 'identity essay' usually implies compact, eclectic, interpretive texts that characterize aspects of a people's history and outlook.[76] It may further imply a piece of writing that is opinionated, impressionistic, aphoristic, or simply an exercise in literary charm. From the proper pen, however, one essay is more persuasive than a treatise. Octavio Paz instances Ortega y Gasset, whom he calls a true essayist, perhaps the best in Spanish and master of a genre that resists easy synopsis. The example is apropos because Ortega's probings into Hispanic identity were a beacon for New World essayists of the 1920s, 1930s and beyond. The essayist, writes Paz, needs the art of suspension points. When he becomes categorical, as Ortega often does, he must add a pinch of salt. He does not systematize but explores. His prose flows fresh, never in a straight channel, always equidistant from the treatise and the aphorism, two forms of congealment. The essayist should bring us treasures and trophies but never a map. He does not colonize, he discovers.[77]

The essayists to be discussed here, successors in a sense to the pensadores, were freer than their forerunners to challenge the social outlook and political convictions of elites and less encumbered in making overtures to modernized philosophy and social science. Moreover, all were in various ways responsive to the modernist climate in literature and the arts, which helped season the new social sciences with expressive concerns. In fact, it is precisely the blend of instrumental and expressive orientations

---

[76] For the Spanish American essay: Stabb, *In Quest of Identity;* Peter Earle and Robert Mead, *Historia del essayo hispanoamericano* (Mexico, D.F., 1973). In *O caráter nacional brasileiro,* 4th ed. (São Paulo, 1983) Dante Moreira Leite examines national character in Brazilian writings using social-science rather than literary criteria.

[77] Octavio Paz, 'José Ortega y Gasset: el cómo y el para qué', in *Hombres en su siglo* (Barcelona, 1984), pp. 97–110.

(or to use José Lezama Lima's more elegant pairing: the search for causality versus search for imaginative or mythic form) that guides the three group-ings offered.

First comes a trio of differing ages though each published his most famous book in the same year, 1928. They are: José Carlos Mariátegui (Peru, 1894–1930), Jean Price-Mars (Haiti, 1876–1969), and Paulo Prado (Brazil, 1869–1943). All three started with a view of countries whose beginnings had been exploitative and sanguinary and whose 'eman-cipatory' nineteenth century had been largely a mirage. Their nations were not yet nations. They shared an evolutionary view of history but feeling that their own societies were blocked at inception by the incongruent forces unleashed by European conquest. They therefore look to problems and causes, urging more productive, egalitarian societies equipped to rejoin history. While each writer had comparable diagnostic intentions, they identified central blockages differently for each country. Mariátegui found his central target in Peru's economic exploitation and the land question, Price-Mars in Haiti's racial intolerance, and Prado in the abulia or, in the medieval term, 'spiritual dryness' of all classes of Brazilians.

Both Mariátegui and Price-Mars achieved their reputations with books of seven essays: *Siete ensayos de interpretación de la realidad peruana* and *Ainsi parla l'oncle*.[78] Both helped to launch, or were later invoked by, interna-tional movements, respectively Third World Marxism and negritude, although as the latter movement took shape, Price-Mars hoped that Black people would be absorbed to, not differentiated within, mankind. Thus he argued the assimilation of Haitians to the human condition while Ma-riátegui demonstrated the peculiar historical conditioning of Andean America. The paradox was that Price-Mars required cultural specificity to clinch his universalist argument, while Mariátegui invoked universal prin-ciples to show the uniqueness of his case.

When their books appeared Price-Mars, a generation older than Ma-riátegui, was a pillar of the Haitian establishment. A physician, former inspector general of public instruction, and minister to Paris, he had published an indictment of the Haitian elite (*La vocation de l'élite*, 1919) for having provoked the U.S. occupation of 1915 and for being guilty of

---

[78] José Carlos Mariátegui, *Seven Interpretive Essays on Peruvian Reality*, trans. Marjory Urquidi (Austin, Tex., 1971); see also Jesús Chavarría, *José Carlos Mariátegui and the Rise of Modern Peru, 1890–1930* (Albuquerque, 1979); José Aricó (ed.), *Mariátegui y los orígenes del Marxismo latinoamericano*, 2nd ed. (Mexico, D.F., 1980). Jean Price-Mars, *So Spoke the Uncle*, trans. Magdalin W. Shannon (Washing-ton, D.C., 1983); see also Jacques C. Antoine, *Jean Price-Mars and Haiti* (Washington, D.C., 1981); *Témoignages sur la vie et l'oeuvre du Dr. Jean Price Mars 1876–1956* (Port-au-Prince, 1956).

*bovarysme collectif* at a time when Mariátegui, at the threshold of his 'radical-ization', had been reporting the doings of Lima's high society under the sobriquet 'Juan Croniqueur'. The latter's political activity and his Euro-pean interlude would soon form his socialist explanation of why the Peru-vian elite had not, in four centuries, assumed its appointed economic function. Price-Mars had attributed his country's woes to the 'puerile vanity' of his elitist peers in promoting the 'rancid' idea that 'the Gauls are our ancestors'. As for his country's heritage, he wrote, 'eight-tenths of it is a gift from Africa'. For Peru, Mariátegui came to see the 'Indian problem' as a false issue.

Born to an impoverished family, crippled in childhood and forced to work at fourteen, Mariátegui knew the belly of the Peruvian monster, and during his European exile (1919–23) he moved into the larger belly of the Western one. The secret of his intellectual *prise* lies in his Italian sojourn. He had arrived thinking of Marxism as 'confused, heavy, and cold'; only in Italy did he have the 'revelation'. A clue to the fragmentation of his opinions in Europe is his fascination with modernist art. Surrealism par-ticularly intrigued him for splintering the solid bourgeois world to expose its meretricious ideals.

Mariátegui's changed outlook owed much to the vitalist Marxism that he absorbed under Croce, whose denial that Marxism had laid bare the iron laws of history inspired the young Peruvian; for Croce, Marxism was persuasive as praxis but not as science. Mariátegui then proceeded to Croce's own teacher, Labriola; to Sorel and Pareto; and to Marxist sympa-thizers like Gramsci, Gobetti and the Russian revolutionaries. Post-war socialist journals and congresses steered Mariátegui toward revolutionary communism rather than revisionism. His choice was braced by the fascist march on Rome (1922), which symbolized for him the political bank-ruptcy of capitalism and recalled the attitudes of South American elites. The task, he saw, was no longer to 'catch up' with Europe but to expose the crepuscular spirit of bourgeois life and to embrace the cause of *el hombre matinal,* of peoples receptive to a 'multitudinous myth' wherever it could be found.

Mariátegui thus questioned whether Peru had really experienced a na-tional history as a sequential transcending of stages. What aggravated the problem was that 'progressive' spokesmen construed the unassimilability of the vast indigenous population as a challenge for educational policy, humanitarianism, or 'human rights'. By suspending the ethnic definition of the 'Indian problem' he linked it directly to the 'land question', shifting it from a problem of tutelage to a revolutionary agenda. The solution did not lie, he felt, in a mystical 'Zionism' of servile races, Indian or black. Although Indian militants might win leadership over their fellows, an autonomous Indian state would not be a classless society but one with all the contradictions of a bourgeois state. Only the struggle of Indians, workers and peasants, he wrote, allied with the mestizo and white proletariat against the feudal, capitalist regime could permit the unfolding of indigenous racial characteristics, and institutions with collective tendencies. This might eventually unite Indians of different countries across present boundaries that divided ancient racial groups and lead to political autonomy for their race. Meanwhile, as long as vindication of the Indian is kept on a philosophical or cultural plane, he felt, or idly discussed in the pseudo-idealistic verbiage of a liberal bourgeois education, the economic base of the problem would be disguised.

The starting point of Price-Mars was not the 'land question', for impoverished though the Haitian masses might be, the country had experienced its 'agrarian revolution' with the expulsion of the French and become a nation of peasants. The economic issue was not land but fiscal and social exploitation and cultural oppression. *Ainsi parla l'oncle* opens with the question, 'What is folklore?'. For Price-Mars the term 'folklore' (coined in 1846) had less innocuous connotations than it may for modern readers; for him it referred to the realm of belief, not to exotic practices and colorful artifacts. His insistence on folklore reflected his conviction that the root cause of Haitian stagnation was that its heritage was a broken mirror yielding a 'reduced image of human nature'. His argument responded in part to the cultural nationalism provoked by the U.S. occupation, but in larger measure to the general Western view, shared by the Haitian elite, that African and Afro-American culture was primitive and barbarous. *Ainsi parla l'oncle* was in part occasioned by Price-Mars's 1915 encounter in Paris with Gustave Le Bon, whose books had for years influenced Latin American intellectuals who deplored race mixing. Price-Mars took him to task and Le Bon challenged him to write the book. For Mariátegui not only did the ethnic argument offer no foothold for political diagnosis but, when it came to the Afro-Peruvian, he felt he had brought fetishistic sensualism to Catholic worship, 'exuding from every pore the primitivism of his African tribe', while he corrupted the Indians with his 'false servility and exhibitionist, morbid psychology'.

For Price-Mars, Haitian rehabilitation must find its ethnic premise. Because the elite 'donned the old frock of Western civilization' after 1804, ignoring or suppressing the African transplants and syncretisms of the people, Price-Mars accused them of denying their country the binding force of shared symbolism so conspicuous in the Greco-Roman world and in modern Africa. Hence the importance of Haitian creole, that promised to be the vehicle for a national literature. Or of voodoo – ridiculed by sensationalist travellers as fetishism or even cannibalism – which Price-Mars defended as a religion that reached no less mystical heights than did Christianity. Language and faith betokened a new social form arising from confused mores and beliefs. At the moment it was a mere chrysalis, yet to which 'philosophers and brave men pay heed'. Price-Mars traced Haitian culture to the highest African civilizations. If one were to compare Africans with Europeans and Americans, he wrote, one would not find the former to be the closest to barbarism or the farthest from a higher social ideal. Mariátegui, in all the sufferings of his short life, perhaps never experienced the humiliation of Price-Mars when, as a Black intellectual heading the Haitian mission to the St Louis World's Fair of 1904, he visited the Deep South of the United States. *Ainsi parla l'oncle* expresses visceral emotion in closing with the ancient adage: 'There is nothing ugly in the house of my father.'

Mariátegui and Price-Mars built from reputable contemporary sources: neo-Marxist thought and racial anthropology respectively. The inspiration for Paulo Prado's *Retrato do Brasil, ensaio sobre a tristeza brasileira*[79] (Portrait of Brazil, Essay on Brazilian Sadness), the third of the 1928 landmarks, is more diffuse. Scion of a Paulista family of planters, politicians, and entrepreneurs, Prado was drawn to life in Europe and exhibited, contemporaries remarked, traits of dilettantism and neurasthenia. He won credentials as a historian, however, under the tutelage of João Capistrano de Abreu and was a discerning patron of São Paulo's vanguardist movement of 1922. Prado's *Portrait of Brazil* reveals little of the modernity of Mariátegui and Price-Mars and little of the modernism of the Paulista avant-garde. His text requires two readings, both linking it to less fashionable modes of enquiry. On the first, it shows affinity to late-positivist essays that deplored the anaemia and languor of mixed-race populations. A closer reading brings to light a more venerable, Catholic frame of reference.

The first chapter, 'Luxúria' (lust), describes tropical seductiveness and scenes of 'pure animality'. Documents told Prado that one-third or more of

---

[79] Paulo Prado, *Retrato do Brasil*, 5th ed. (São Paulo, 1944). Darrell E. Levi gives a family history in *The Prados of São Paulo, Brazil: An Elite Family and Social Change, 1840–1930* (Athens, Ga, 1987), esp. pp. 130–37 for Paulo.

the cases brought to the Holy Office in Bahia in 1591–2 featured shame-less sins of 'sexual hyperesthesia'. The second chapter addresses the more tyrannical passion of 'Cobiça' (covetousness). Here Prado evokes visions of El Dorado and Potosí that 'volatilized' the social instincts and anarchic individualism of deportees, castaways and mutineers. Emblematic were the *bandeirantes,* he felt, whose energy and ambition lacked mental or moral basis. 'What wealth, holy Lord, is that' – in Prado's quote from Pombal – 'whose possession brings on the ruin of the State?'

The third chapter, 'Tristeza' (sadness), is the hinge of the book and will detain us again later. It opens with the classic contrast of the morally hygienic spirit of the New England and Virginia colonists with the des-potic, demoralized life of the Portuguese in Brazil. Sexual excess (*post coitum animal triste*) and the mirage of easy wealth stamped the Brazilian psyche with abulia and melancholia. A chapter on Romanticism claims that in the era of independence Brazil's 'sickness' was displaced to the new ruling and intellectual classes as a pathological *mal romântico* that found central loci in the new law schools of Recife and São Paulo. In Europe, Prado felt, romanticism was a passing fashion, while in Brazil it created *tristeza* by its 'concern with human misery, the contingency of events, and above all . . . the desire for happiness in an imaginary world'. In a 'Post-scriptum' Prado confesses that he disregarded the *bovarysme* of São Paulo (a key term for Price-Mars as well) and composed his book (in contrast to Mariátegui) as an impressionist version of the forces of history without cubic masses of data and chronology. Only mental images were to remain. His national history was rooted not in the ubiquitous racial conflict of the Americas but in the intimacy of miscegenation. While denying Gobi-neau's presumption of racial inequality, however, he saw the 'hybrid vigour' of race-crossing as limited to the early generations.[80] The closing off of social opportunities condemned the population to somatic deficiency and congenital indolence – qualities that, ironically, preserved the unity of Brazil's vast territory. For the four republican decades after 1889, Prado concludes, politicians had danced on this bloated and atrophied body. The two solutions he envisioned were war, which might bring a 'providential hero', or revolution, which might banish the chimeras of the colonial past.

Thus far Prado's argument has been presented *ad literam*. What follows is perhaps a reading more adequate to the text and to the author's subja-cent intentions. We may start by comparing the first sentence of Prado's

---

80 See Georges Raeders, *O inimigo cordial do Brasil: o Conde de Gobineau no Brasil* (São Paulo, 1988).

book with that of Mariátegui's *Siete ensayos* (which affirms that the schism
in Peruvian history is best seen as economic, thus demolishing at a stroke
the specious *indigenismo* of the elite) and with Price-Mars's *Ainsi parla
l'oncle* (whose 'What is Folklore?' was to be answered by a critical inventory
of Haitian oral traditions, legends, songs, riddles, customs, ceremonies
and beliefs – thus ripping off the *masque blanc* from the *peau noire* long
before the terms were coined). Here is Paulo Prado's initial sentence: 'In a
radiant land lives a sad people.' First, note that he speaks of 'a sad people'
and not 'three sad races', the phrase from the Brazilian poet Olavo Bilac
used as a title of a book on racial identity and national consensus in
Brazilian literature by the U.S. literary historian of Brazil, David
Haberly.[81] Prado sees Brazil not as an ethnic mosaic but as a nation that
collectively experiences, as we have noted, a state of spiritual dryness.
Second, Prado's sentence implicitly refers us to the first salvo of Rousseau's
*Social Contract:* 'Man was born free, and he is everywhere in chains.'
Rousseau addressed a state of external oppression, Prado a state of soul.
From these clues we recognize that Prado's first two chapters, 'Lust' and
'Covetousness' – two of the deadly sins – point toward theological and
moral issues that transcend the fixation of commentators on genes, race,
heredity, sanitation and scientific determinism.

As the book's subtitle indicates, Prado's third chapter, 'Sadness', is his
pivot. Sadness does not figure in the modern repertory of the seven capital
sins; its nearest equivalent is sloth. Yet the genealogy of sloth shows that it
merges with medieval acedia, which once counted as a 'deadly' sin and
included both mental or spiritual states (listlessness, loathing, slackness of
mind) and qualities of behaviour (torpor, negligence, idleness).[82] By the
late Middle Ages, with the spread of moral theology to the common folk,
acedia lost its theological force, yielding primacy in the roster of capital
vices to sloth and to an emphasis on 'external' manifestations of indolence.
By the time of the Renaissance, acedia and its theological component of
*tristitia* were secularized under the atmospheric term 'melancholy'.

Prado's attempt to recover the moral premises of Brazil's Catholic society, inspired by his reading of sixteenth-century Inquisition documents,
was part of a project of fellow Paulista modernists who had recognized the
significance for Brazil of Europe's transition from the late Middle Ages to

---

[81] David T. Haberly, *Three Sad Races: Racial Identity and National Consciousness in Brazilian Literature*
   (Cambridge, Eng., 1983).
[82] See Siegfried Wenzel, *The Sin of Sloth: Acedia in Medieval Thought and Literature* (Chapel Hill, N.C.,
   1967), pp. 60–63, 164–5 for 'spiritual dryness'.

early modernity. The difference was that while Prado sought, perhaps subconsciously, the medieval therapy for *tristitia,* his younger cohorts Mário de Andrade and Oswald de Andrade looked ahead to Montaigne, Rabelais and a Renaissance therapy. Prado, that is, held to *tristitia* as a theological, 'internal' aspect of acedia while Mário and Oswald addressed 'external' or behavioural aspects. Thus Mário adopted the Portuguese word *preguiça* (from the Latin *pigritia*) or 'indolence' to designate a Brazilian lack of firm character or aptitude for modern, disciplined life, but also praised it as idleness propitious for cultivating the arts and as a tropical antidote to a technified, consumerized society.[83] Oswald gave an even more positive accent to *ócio* ('leisure', from the Latin *otium*), stressing its denials in the forms of *negócio* ('business', from *nec-otium* or *not-leisure*) and *sacerdócio* (from *sacerdotium* or 'priesthood'). Oswald's 'way out' was the transition from technical to natural life, or from civilization to culture.[84]

Paulo Prado's 'way out' returns us to historical origins and to the corrective for acedia. His therapy was perhaps confusedly expressed. But surely it prefigures the contribution of his compatriot Paulo Freire, whose conscientization would, a generation later, challenge the passive *tristitia* of the people with psychological and even theological empowerment, presenting a culturally and sociologically rooted version of 'education' in contrast to the utilitarian and manipulative 'schooling' of the industrial West. Freire's starting point was surely one sad people, not three sad races.

*Balancing Myth and Evidence ( 1 ): Martínez Estrada, Paz, Ortiz,*
*González*

The next group of four essayists (who have, or had, many other literary roles) entertain hopes for their homelands comparable to those of the first group but are driven less to cope or remake than to contemplate the self-givenness of identity itself. Identity becomes as much a processual structure as a goal. Two of the writers, Ezequiel Martínez Estrada (Argentina, 1895–1964) and Octavio Paz (Mexico, 1914– ), display rich literary, philosophic and historical understandings, and a prose that leads them on voyages of interior discovery and to private acts of communion. No less

---

[83] Mário de Andrade, 'A divina preguiça' (1918), in M. R. Batista et al., *Brasil: I° tempo modernista – 1917/29* (São Paulo, 1972), pp. 181–3. Mário's *Macunaíma* was published in 1928, the year of the three books under discussion. The first utterance of the hero as a tot appears on the first page as 'Ai! que preguiça!' – 'Ay, what laziness!' or 'Aw, what a drag!'

[84] Oswald de Andrade, *Do Pau-Brasil à antropofagia e às utopias* (Rio de Janeiro, 1972), pp. 157–64.

than Paz's Mexican pilgrimage, Martínez Estrada's Argentine X-ray draws him into a labyrinth of solitude. Fernando Ortiz (Cuba, 1881–1969) and José Luis González (Dominican Republic, b.1926) are more sociable guides (as befits Antilleans). They welcome us to the tour, point out the everyday environment of objects, vegetation, crops and people of diverse colours and professions. But as these objects or persons take on symbolic or mythic force we see patterned dimensions and movements that had escaped us. Here as in the labyrinths lie mysteries. Cuba's two main export crops take on the persona of a man and woman; the *ajiaco* or stew pot becomes a symbol of Cuba and a four-storeyed house the image of Puerto Rico: or we suddenly discover that the voices of a very modern Cuba are implicated in meanings, still audible, of a fourteenth-century Spanish poet. Problems and causes and certainly 'solutions' are more evident on these sunny isles than in the labyrinths of solitude. But as we squint into the sunlight we sense a move from linear to recurrent time.

In 1933 the Argentine poet Ezequiel Martínez Estrada published *Radiografía de la pampa*, claiming new territory for the identity essay.[85] Here the Indo- and Afro-American components of society were absorbed or inconspicuous; they could not, as in Peru or Haiti, dictate agendas for national therapy, such as agrarian reform or racial tolerance. Indeed, for several decades Argentina had seemed to be solving the chronic regional problems of poverty, social oppression and educational neglect. It was reckoned as prosperous, modern, or in a later term, developed. Yet by the 1920s premonitions were afloat in cosmopolitan Buenos Aires, as seen in the discussion of Borges and Arlt. For Martínez Estrada, who had published six books of poetry by 1929, the calamitous political and economic events of 1929–32 forced him from evocations to diagnosis. Yet even though Argentina might be moving toward exclusion from the club of Western nations, neither was it germinating an exotic identity as an arrested enclave. Martínez Estrada had come to see Argentine history to be static and not evolutionary and to feel that the country had never come to terms with that history nor even with its prehistory ('the Pleistocene still held fully sway'). At the same time he felt that Nietzsche, the voice for a new civilization in the West, spoke directly to Argentine society with his notions of collective resentment, will to power, and society's fear of the individual.

[85] EzequielMartínezEstrada, *X-Ray of the Pampa*, trans. Alain Swietlicki (Austin, Tex., 1971). See Peter G. Earle, *Prophet in the Wilderness. The Works of Ezequiel Martínez Estrada* (Austin, Tex., 1971).

To translate Nietzschean premonitions for the Argentine setting Martínez Estrada turned to domestic history and to those who could help him read it.[86] Important cues came from the French-born, humanely sceptic director of the National Library Paul Groussac. For a year and a half the poet browsed through some 400 books but accumulating them as lived experience, not as data. Later he would devote strategic volumes to three Argentines whose lives and writings he found emblematic: Sarmiento, José Hernández and W. H. Hudson. This trio was balanced by three Europeans who taught him to interpret collective life: Spengler by his symbolic readings, the Freud of *Totem and Tabu* as a diagnostician of tumult in the social psyche, and Simmel, whose *Sociology* was his 'control book' for the configurationist method. Another European mentor – perhaps even more important than these three, for Martínez Estrada devoted a 900-page book to him – was Balzac, who saw history as the morphology of the facts and learned, as Martínez Estrada would later do, from J. K. Lavater (1741–1801), a Swiss poet, mystic, physiognomist, and influence on Stendhal who claimed to divine the soul's imprint on the human face.

In his commemorative interview Martínez Estrada provided 'exegeses' of the six parts of his book. The first deals with Trapalanda, the Indians' promised land that became the Argentines' illusory, 'impossible' country from the conquest to the present. The deceived intruder invents a false Arcadia to expunge the traces of his failure. 'He wants what he has not and wants it as what was denied.' Part two is a study in solitude, a term that harks back to the *soledades* of classic Spanish poetry. Martínez Estrada feels solitude to emanate from space and time: from space because here was a ' "new" world petrified in its fossils, savagery, panoramas of an astral scale', and villages strewn like aerolites; and an emanation from time because here time worked in reverse in that Spain's mission was to conquer a relic, the emblematic sepulchre of Christ, rather than to confer life on a *new* world. In 1500 the Spaniards reverted to existence as of the year 700. The German, Gallic, Italian and Saxon peoples saw them sclerotic and rupestrine, a true 'American' people because no other race was so qualified for maintaining the primordial barbarism of America.

In 1950 Octavio Paz closed his *Labyrinth of Solitude* with a 'dialectic of solitude': the 'nostalgic longing for the body from which we were cast out', an evocation of purification rites, spiritual combat and finally grace

---

[86] See Martínez Estrada's reflections on the silver anniversary of *Radiografía* in his *Leer y escribir* (Mexico, D.F., 1969), pp. 131–6.

or communion. Martínez Estrada's 'solitude' lacks this theological accent and refers to dismemberment by isolation and the chimerical boundaries of empire. America for him was without historicity. Unlike Napoleon on Saint Helena, its caudillos could not record the history they had made but wrote only autobiographies. Common to both Argentine and Mexican solitudes was passivity or disillusionment before history. In *Children of the Mire* Paz contrasts the Spanish with a 'modern' poet, to remind us that the aesthetic revolution of Góngora's *Soledades* reflected his refusal of commerce, industry and the conquest of America. Góngora *reorients poetry because he cannot change life.* Rimbaud's poetry, on the other hand, spills over into action. His verbal alchemy urges human nature to 'multiply the future'. He aims to provoke new psychic states (religions, drugs), liberate nations (revolutions), transform erotic relations, throw a bridge to utopia. Rimbaud *changes poetry so as to change human nature.*[87]

The third part of *X-Ray* deals with 'primitive forces', divisible into telluric, mechanical and psychic. To a degree Martínez Estrada sees them as energies that for Sarmiento produced the face-off between barbarity and civilization. He admired his mentor's telluric sense of the scout and trail guide of the pampas but failed to share his conviction that encroachment by the state brought tidings of civilization. For Martínez Estrada civilization and barbarity were centrifugal and centripetal forces in equilibrium. Barbarity found refuge in the new regime to await its opportunities during economic crisis or episodes of ruffianism. Europe's troops, ships, diplomats and gold were impotent against Rosas but all-powerful against Sarmiento and the new presidents. The nationality that Rosas achieved with land the new presidents built with bricks and iron. Gauchos became day labourers and public life was formally organized; but the nation did not exist. The telluric provinces of the caudillos became suburbs of the national capital. As the sum of public powers the state became the arsenal of violent impulses retired from circulation. It kept huge armies of employees and soldiers, producing university graduates like paper money – without control or solvency. The strength of the state lay in its having weakened all else. The country became a dumping ground for the detritus of civilization: telephones and journalism, cars and movies, books and textiles. Man, a passive vegetable, confronts a world of objects that is born, multiplies and dies.

[87] Octavio Paz, *Children of the Mire,* trans. Rachel Phillips (Cambridge, Mass., 1974), p. 113. Paz rehearsed his treatment of solitude in 'Poesía de soledad y poesía de comunión' (*El Hijo Pródigo,* 1943) reprinted in his *Primeras letras (1931–1943)* (Mexico, D.F., 1988), pp. 291–303.

For its author Buenos Aires, successor to metropolitan Spain, was the book's keystone: the enemy in the house who devours, subverts, corrupts. Here and in *La cabeza de Goliat* (1940) he portrays Buenos Aires as Argentina's oneiric fantasy that became the capital not of the nation but only of itself, like the teratological creature that does not live for the species. Originally caudillos divided the land around cabildos as points of control and settlement. Later the railroads divided it into tariff zones, not to create a circulatory system but to irrigate a phantasmal body. For Porteños, who felt they lived on Europe's periphery, to look at their 'interior' or heartland meant not the pampas but Europe. Argentine railway cars placed in motion from London were pounds sterling producing pounds sterling, not vehicles producing wealth.

Such musings led Martínez Estrada to adopt 'pseudo-structures' for diagnosing the national malady. These he saw as false forms not in accord with environment, life, or national mission. Lacking inborn instincts Argentines took on a borrowed crust. Thus, religion became a formula and not a faith, a private belief and not a social force, a public cult and not a source of freedom. Or, if laws are not inscribed on a people's soul, a state based on force of law is a false one. Or, Argentina adopted cars and planes merely for touring with no constructive function; they became problems, not solutions. Or, some countries 'make history, some live it, and others falsify it; we write it'. Or, Argentine women now appear worldly with their short hair, exposed thighs and pencilled eyes; yet beyond the aphrodisiac shell lies an incorruptible vestal. And finally, the tango could not escape the author: a narcotic performance bereft of flirtation, resistance and possession, and emptied of directing will.

The device of pseudo-structures goes beyond familiar explanations of evolutionary blockage or mimesis on the periphery. It aims toward psychology and therapy, that is, toward converting the immediate objects, characters, and *mise-en-scène* dear to historians, essayists and anthropologists into symbolic markers. Thus while the book appears on the surface to be steeped in minutiae of national culture, it is indeed an X-ray that lights up common structures. As the author put it, one consults the radiologist, not the photographer, when the problem is glandular, not cutaneous. Instead, then, of treating Argentina as a breakaway success story, he absorbed it into a common American history. There was, he surmised, an 'ethnic, somatic and mental South American commonality that lends a similar atmosphere to half a continent'. Nothing binds these nations, which share no high ideals of confraternity. The supremacy of nature over the inhabitants and of environment over will isolates human events, forcing them to float unrelated in a halo of irresponsibility. The southern countries submit to northern centres of economic energy ruled by the unknown lender and calibrated to profit, not public need. South America served as Europe's suburban real estate: 'we are all defending the owner's possessions while intoxicating ourselves with the clandestine liquors he sends us: gold, magazines, movies, weapons'. A generation later 'dependency theory' would be removed from the cultural armature where Martínez Estrada had placed it, causing appreciable restriction of its cognitive scope.

X-Ray delivered a powerful message to the next Argentine generation as instanced in a tribute by H. A. Murena, who in 1954 praised it as the 'exact and dramatic description of the illness by the patient himself', who as a physician relates without concessions the genesis, growth and prognosis of a cancer in his own body. Placing Martínez Estrada in the company of three other prophetic Argentine writers (Borges, Mallea and Leopoldo Marechal), Murena accords him the extra tribute of heralding the rise of a new conscience in the Americas at large.[88] At the end of his life (he died embittered in 1964) Martínez Estrada, released from a bleak job in the post office, tested his hemispheric vocation (1959–62) by giving seminars on Latin America at the National University of Mexico and spending two years in Cuba, where he composed a lengthy study of Martí as a revolutionary but where, despite his admiration for Fidel Castro, he was never invited to meet him.

Save perhaps for Mariátegui's *Seven Essays* the best known Latin American essay in the twentieth century may well be Octavio Paz's '*El labirinto de la soledad*', published in 1950 and revised in 1959. *The Labyrinth of Solitude* has similarities to X-Ray (for one thing both authors were poets), although Paz stated in an interview of 1975 that he had not yet read X-Ray in 1950.[89] An explicit link is their Nietzschean inspiration. Martínez Estrada was influenced by his theory of collective resentment, as discussed above, while Paz claimed he could not have written *The Labyrinth of Solitude* without Nietzsche's guidance, especially *The Genealogy of Morals*. 'Nietzsche taught me to see what was behind words like virtue, goodness,

[88] H. A. Murena, 'La lección a los desposeídos: Martínez Estrada', in *El pecado original de América*, 2nd ed. (Buenos Aires, 1965), pp. 95–119.

[89] The expanded edition of the English translation, *The Labyrinth of Solitude* (New York, 1985), contains three complementary writings and one interview by Paz: 'The Other Mexico', 'Return to the Labyrinth of Solitude', 'Mexico and the United States', and 'The Philanthropic Ogre' (trans. L. Kemp, Y. Miles and R. P. Belash). The reference to Martínez Estrada is on p. 331.

evil. He guided me in exploring the Mexican idiom: If words are masks, what is behind them?'[90] More broadly, both authors drew deeply from history, philosophy, sociology and literature. On the matter of history, Martínez Estrada felt that Spain at the conquest reverted to an early medieval phase that gave it no purchase for taming the American environment, whereas Paz reminded readers that Spain was not simply a caste-ridden society but had adopted a universalist tradition before the Counter Reformation, synthesizing the strands at least in the realm of art. As for literature, the lesson of Balzac was critical for Martínez Estrada while Paz, who used poets widely, gave a sketch of Sor Juana Inés de la Cruz as an emblematic figure that would eventually inform his masterful *Sor Juana or, The Traps of Faith* (1982). Both men were fully cognizant of psychology, Martínez Estrada as an admirer of Freud's *Totem and Tabu* and Paz as a critical reader of the Mexican philosopher Samuel Ramos, who in 1934 had published an influential study of Adlerian derivation to explain the Mexican 'inferiority complex' and the Frenchification of Mexican elite culture. Ramos, Paz declared, 'dwells on psychology; in my case psychology is but a way of reaching moral and historical criticism'.[91]

As discussed earlier, Martínez Estrada and Paz both gave prominence to the solitude theme with its implications of expulsion and pilgrimage. Paz develops it with reference to the myth of the Fisher King – as found in Sir James Frazer and in T. S. Eliot's *Waste Land* – and to the search for grace through jungles, deserts, or underground mazes. While Martínez Estrada exempts 'Saxon' Americans from this ordeal – for they defied and conquered environment – Paz finds all Americans to be prisoners of solitude. 'If the solitude of the Mexican is like a stagnant pool', he writes, 'that of the North American is like a mirror. We have ceased to be living springs of water.' A dimension available to the Mexican and not to the Argentine was Aztec civilization. In Mexico Paz feels, 'the ancient beliefs and customs are still in existence beneath Western forms'. Modern man, he observes, was exiled from eternity, where all times are one, to chronometric time that lacks all particularity. The Mexican fiesta, whether Indian or Catholic, suspends clock and calendar time for a moment so as to reproduce an event, not celebrate it. Myth permits man to emerge from solitude and rejoin creation. In Mexico, myth reappears in human acts and

---

[90] Earle, *Prophet*, pp. 106–9; Paz, *Labyrinth*, p. 351.
[91] Samuel Ramos, *Profile of Man and Culture in Mexico*, trans. Peter G. Earle (New York, 1963); Paz, *Labyrinth*, pp. 330–32. For Ramos and his antecedents, see Henry C. Schmidt, *The Roots of Lo Mexicano: Self and Society in Mexican Thought, 1900–1934* (College Station, Tex., 1978).

intervenes in its history, opening doors of communion. If North Americans see the world as something to be perfected, Mexicans see it as something to be redeemed.

Other parallels might be traced. Martínez Estrada's pseudo-structures, meaning a false form over natural environment and declared missions, correspond to the recurrent masks in *Labyrinth* that must be torn off if Mexicans are to live and think in an 'open' solitude where transcendence awaits; they are not simply to reach out to fellows but become 'contemporaries of all mankind'. Or, the two writers shared a similar sense of the immersion of their lands in the Americas. Martínez Estrada saw Argentina as still captive of the primitive, telluric forces of the southern Americas that undermined the futile incursions of civilization from without, whether Europe or North America. While Paz also feels Mexico to be symptomatic of Spanish America, his meditation starts by directly comparing Mexico with the United States. He takes the latter not loosely as a northern industrial country but as a specifically New World country with a version of solitude that helped him pose questions to ask of Mexico.

These two works move the identity essay from the realm of national 'problems', assumed to be curable by enlightened intervention, to a search for national psyche whose continuous disclosure lies in the inscrutable realm of historical process.

A book of a style and spirit quite different from the two just examined is *Contrapunteo cubano del tabaco y azúcar* published in 1940 by Fernando Ortiz.[92] It contains a general statement of his thesis on the counterpoint of tobacco and sugar with a lengthy appendix on the 'ethnography and transculturation' of the two crops that expanded with each edition. Again we have a book that needs two readings. On the first reading, we recognize that the starting point is not Caribbean history conceived as a political and cultural invasion of an exotic periphery. Instead, Ortiz features two crops (one indigenous, one transplanted) that define the native landscape of every Cuban. He starts with an experienced Cuban 'reality' still to be specified rather than with conflictive impositions upon it. He deduces his story of Cuba not from ideologies of control and exploitation but from biotic requirements of two forms of vegetation. Tobacco and sugar are defined not as the currency of capitalist exchange but as products of Cuban

92 Fernando Ortiz, *Cuban Counterpoint, Tobacco and Sugar* (New York, 1970). See Gustavo Pérez Firmat, *The Cuban Condition: Translation and Identity in Modern Cuban Literature* (Cambridge, 1989); Antonio Benítez-Rojo, *The Repeating Island: The Caribbean and the Postmodern Perspective*, trans. James E. Maraniss (Durham, 1992), ch. 4.

soil that in themselves dictate institutional arrangements and ways of life. Ortiz builds from the land and its fruits (as did the early Marx and Engels in the *German Ideology*), not with human contrivances.

There is, then, a lucid and poetic ingredient in Ortiz's counterpoint because it originates in nature and not from maleficent forces. From germination to human consumption, he observes, tobacco and sugar are radically opposed. One grows from cuttings, the other from seeds; one is needed for its stalk, the other for its foliage; sugar is ground for juice, tobacco is dried out; one is white and odourless, the other dark and aromatic. This duet rested on a foundation that Mariátegui would have called economic infrastructure. Ortiz was aware that for tobacco and sugar the same four factors are present: land, machinery, labour, and money. He saw the implications of skilled immigrants versus slaves; small holdings versus plantations; a universal market for tobacco and a single one for sugar; national sovereignty against colonialism. In short, sugar passed into distant, corporate, all-powerful hands while tobacco 'created a middle class, a free bourgeoisie' without the extremes of slaves and masters, proletariat and rich.

Structural-economic determination was not, however, fundamental for Ortiz. In fact there was perhaps *no* 'foundation' to his argument. And here begins the second reading of *Cuban Counterpoint,* taking a clue once more from opening sentences. If Mariátegui dismissed any plane save the economic for interpreting the schism caused by the Spanish conquest, Ortiz drew on a jovial Spanish poet of the Middle Ages, the Archpriest of Hita (c.1283–c.1350), who personified Carnival and Lent in unforgettable verses, cleverly imbuing the assertions and rebuttals of their satirical contest with the 'ills and benefits that each has conferred on mankind'. Like Paulo Prado he had recourse to the Iberian tradition. But unlike Prado, who found clues in persistent 'sinful' categories of moral behaviour, he called to mind the 'mocking verse' of the *Libro de Buen Amor* (1343) with its Battle of the Lord Flesh-Season and the Lady Lent serving as his precedent 'to personify dark tobacco and "high yellow" sugar.' Lacking authority as a poet or priest to conjure up creatures of fantasy, wrote the disingenuous Ortiz, he had merely set down 'in drab prose, the amazing contrasts I have observed in the two agricultural products on which the economic history of Cuba rests'.[93]

[93] Juan Ruiz (Archpriest of Hita), *The Book of True Love,* trans. Saralyn R. Daly (bilingual ed.) (University Park, Pa., 1978).

In his examination of Ortiz's thought and sensibility Gustavo Pérez Firmat attempts to show that his appreciation of Cuban culture and society depends less on historical ingredients and stages than on the processual formation of the nation's vernacular underpinning. His key notion is 'the fermentation and turmoil that *precedes* synthesis', his two key terms being 'transculturation' (translational displacements that generate vernacular culture) and *ajiaco* (a metaphor for the outcome of displacements). The word *ajiaco* itself – a simmering stew – is onomastic, for it combines the African name for an Indian condiment (*ají* or green pepper) with the Spanish suffix *-aco*. The *ajiaco* is never finished, changes incessantly with fresh ingredients, has no core of flavour and substance, and changes in taste and consistency depending on whether one dips from the bottom or the top. It is not the *crisol* or 'melting pot' of North America, taken from the metaphor of metal foundries, with its outcome of fusion. Here the image is unending *cocción* (literally concoction), implying indefinite deferral or a 'no-ser-*siempre-todavía*' (a state of always not yet). The idea is caught in the difference between the words *cubanidad,* implying defined civil status, and *cubanía,* an open-ended spiritual condition of desire which is given even to those who simply want it. Indeed Ortiz's own work is a prime example of his metaphor, a vast body of texts all falling short of finality and synthesis, creating doubt whether one is reading *about* Cuba or *experiencing* Cuban culture first hand. *Cuban Counterpoint* with its proliferating appendices is an outstanding case. All this, Pérez Firmat suggests, refers back to Ortiz's original counterpoint between the European *contrapunto,* or initial 'point', furnished by the debate between Carnival and Lent in the *Libro de Buen Amor* and the *contrapunteo,* or '*counter*point', of Cuba. As he sensed it, history itself is thus a constant simmer, not an itinerary, nor even a dialectic.

Ortiz's engaging manner of pictorializing invisible forces at play in a complex and changing society (national identity in motion we might call the effect) invites comparative reference to a similar use of technique forty years later by the Dominican-born Puerto Rican, José Luis González in his essay 'El país de cuatro pisos' (1980).[94] He in effect arrives at the simmering *ajiaco* of Ortiz, but in Puerto Rico the succession of Spanish and varied forms of U.S. domination since the nineteenth century has been too asphyxiating to allow the blossoming of a spirit equivalent to *cubanía.* González therefore addresses prevalent versions of Puerto Rican 'national

[94] José Luis González, *Puerto Rico: The Four-Storeyed Country,* trans. G. Guinness (Princeton, 1993), ch. 1.

culture' in the traditional Hispanic and modernizing American interpretations as masks for elite ideologies.[95] The reason is that in the absence of a popular independence movement the formation of a nation was left to political and juridical arrangements that produced a national culture dichotomously defined by the dominant class. Popular culture was disparaged as 'folklore' while the group González sees as culturally most important, the Afro-Puerto Ricans, were held to be virtually insignificant.

The stratification of cultural vision leads González to the corrective metaphor of Puerto Rico as a house of four storeys. This device suspends the search for a static national identity by presenting four socio-cultural ingredients in historical order, with a popular, mestizo and above all Afro-Antillean society at the bottom. Above it lies a stratum of expatriates from the Spanish American independence wars enlarged by Europeans and a subsequent 'mezzanine' of Corsicans, Majorcans and Catalans. Next comes the U.S. occupation that provides, especially in the 1930s to 1950s, an alternative to the classic Spanish model for 'guided identity'. And finally comes the fourth floor, constructed from late-blooming U.S. capitalism welded to the opportunist populism of contemporary Puerto Rico. At first this architectonic structure may seem to elaborate the basic dualism of oppressors and oppressed. The question however is not who is on top but what upholds the structure. In addition, these 'floors' do not compose a fixed portrait but represent forces of living history that have operated, some in neglected or clandestine fashion, through the centuries. For González a critical point came in recent years when pseudo-industrialization and the pseudo-autonomous political formula reached a dead end, with marginalization of citizens, the demoralizing false beneficence of the colonial power, the rise of delinquency and criminality and institutionalized demagogy.

Here the structural metaphor of González takes on some of the fluidity of Ortiz's *ajiaco*. He feels that the dismantled culture of the Puerto Ricans 'on top' is replaced not by a somewhat discredited Americanization but by the rise of and permeation by the ever more visible culture of Puerto Ricans 'from below'. Similarly, the elitist myth of the stalwart Hispanic peasant (*jíbaro*) yields to the reality of the Afro-Antillean populace. Puerto Rico's 'special relationship' with the United States having lost its mys-

---

[95] The Puerto Rican identity controversy was shaped for a generation by Antonio S. Pedreira's *Insularismo* of 1934 (3rd ed.; San Juan, 1946), who cast the antagonism of Hispanophiles and Americanizers in Spenglerian and Orteguian terms of culture versus civilization. In lieu of their insular oscillation between Madrid and Washington he urged his countrymen to set out to fish in deep waters even though, as in the faraway past, a Dutch pirate might lurk there. Juan Flores offers a 'new reading' in: *Insularismo e ideología burguesa* (Río Piedras, 1979).

tique, the 'simmering' process extends outward to the neighbouring Antilles as well as vertically in the island society. French and English can be seen not simply as imperial languages but as Antillean or creolized ones that serve the needs of decolonization. Recovery of its popular culture implies a re-Caribbeanization of Puerto Rico, to give it a custom-made regional identity rather than a 'Latin' or 'Anglo' American one that is ready-made.[96]

### Balancing Myth and Evidence (2): Freyre, Buarque de Holanda

In his preface to the fifth Brazilian edition of Sérgio Buarque de Holanda's *Raízes do Brasil* the distinguished critic Antônio Cândido names three books that awakened his generation to the 'gust of intellectual radicalism and social analysis' created by the 1930 Revolution and not wholly snuffed out by the Estado Novo (1937–45). They were *Casa-Grande e Senzala* (1933) by Gilberto Freyre, *Raízes do Brasil* (1936), and *Formação do Brasil contemporâneo* (1942) by Caio Prado Júnior, appearing successively when Cândido's group were students in the *ginásio*, *curso complementar* and *escola superior*.[97] The first two books are discussed here as being in the essayist vein of this section (despite the immense length of Freyre's major works).[98]

Gilberto Freyre (1900–87) embeds complex and controversial meanings in his writings. Some of the intricacy derives from the biographic fact that he left his ancestral home in Pernambuco at eighteen to enter Baylor University in Waco, Texas. In 1920 he made a leap nearly as bold to enter the Master of Arts programme at Columbia University, which removed him from a stronghold of primitive Baptism, Jim Crowism and lynching to a sophisticated intellectual environment (with its nearby Harlem, of course). Recognized as a precocious *litterateur*, Freyre was soon familiarizing Brazilian readers with Mencken, Sandburg, O'Neill, Dreiser, Sinclair Lewis, Amy Lowell, Charles Beard, and more. It was a post-Whitman, post-W. D. Howells cast that stopped short of Eliot, Pound and the modernists. This youngster from a traditional region was thus immersed

---

[96] Historical and ideological critiques of 'El país de cuatro pisos' include Juan Flores, 'The Puerto Rico that José Luis González built', *Latin American Perspectives*, 11/3 (1984), 173–84, and Manuel Maldonado Denis, 'En torno a "El país de cuatro pisos": Aproximación crítica a la obra sociológica de José Luis González', *Casa de las Américas*, 23, 135 (1982), 151–9.

[97] Antônio Cândido's preface to *Raízes* is reprinted in his *Teresina etc.* (Rio de Janeiro, 1980), pp. 135–52.

[98] For a collective study of Prado, see Maria Angela d'Incao (ed.), *Historia e ideal: ensaios sobre Caio Prado Júnior* (São Paulo, 1989).

in the non-traditional but racist society of Texas, then exposed to a cosmopolitan city, a taste of literary life, and a world-class university that inculcated Deweyan social thought and fine points of bibliography and documentation. Although in New York his mentor, Franz Boas, assured him that innate racial differences did not exist, he was perplexed, after a three-year absence from Brazil, why some mulatto Brazilian sailors he ran into on Brooklyn Bridge seemed 'caricatures of men'.[99] He completed his education by reconnoitering Europe. By now, however, his American years had stamped his mind.[100]

José Lins do Rego described Freyre's return to Recife in 1923 after nearly six years of absence. It seemed a 'marriage' with his native land in a fiesta of light and colour; his first chronicles were carnivalesque, reflecting certain tension between the down-to-earth American culture that had shaped his mind and the tantalizing Brazilian one that now beckoned him to his origins. Such ambivalence was to mark his career as he wavered between intuition and research, between literary and scientific readings of history. His profuse writings, while usually informed, intelligent and provocative (even his clichés are in a way his own), do not always fulfill his intellectual claims. He spends hundreds of pages to demarcate his academic territory and justify his procedural mannerisms, showing less concern with the searching European debates since the Enlightenment over art versus science than with the bureaucratization of knowledge in American curricula as he experienced it. His book *Como e porque sou e não sou sociólogo* (*How and Why I am and am not a Sociologist*) (1968) is a self-justifying autobiography rather than an intellectual voyage, with such chapters as 'Why I'm More Anthropologist than Sociologist' or 'Why I'm a Writer without Ceasing to be Somewhat Sociological'.[101]

Ineluctably Freyre deleted his frontier between social science and literature, which he regarded as curricular categories rather than distinct modes of sensibility. He produced two novels, or 'seminovels', to assure dual control of his enlarged domain (*Dona Sinhá e o filho padre*, 1964, and *O outro amor do doutor Paulo*, 1977) followed by a study of 'heroes and villains' in Brazilian novels as 'socio-anthropological' types.[102] His boosters call

[99] Gilberto Freyre, *The Masters and the Slaves*, trans. Samuel Putnam, 2nd Eng. ed. (Berkeley, 1986); pp. xxvi–xxvii.
[100] *Gilberto Freyre: sua ciência, sua filosofia, sua arte* (Rio de Janeiro, 1962).
[101] Gilberto Freyre, *Como e porque sou e não sou sociólogo* (Brasília, 1968).
[102] Gilberto Freyre, *Heróis e vilões no romance brasileiro* (São Paulo, 1979). The 'seminovel' *Dona Sinhá* is translated as *Mother and Son* (New York, 1967). See Edilberto Coutinho, *A imaginação do real: uma leitura da ficção de Gilberto Freyre* (Rio de Janeiro, 1983).

Freyre's oeuvre an *histoire-fleuve;* liken him to Tolstoy, Balzac and Joyce; call him a poet; and hail him as a founder of meta-literature. Such plaudits are less explicable by his not inconsiderable literary gifts than by the remarkable self-invention and projection of his persona. The secret of Freyre's distinction lies beyond squabbles over his scholarship, his complex politics, his paeans to Brazilian civilization, his insouciant view of historical process, or his ambiguous portrayal of paternalism, slavery, race, sex and women. He commits the cardinal academic sin of enjoying his vocation.

On cognitive grounds an obvious starting point is Freyre's preference for an empathic 'Proustian' sociology of Brazil as against an 'objective' Durkheimian one rooted in 'social facts'.[103] Freyre adapts the two names to his own ends. Having little affinity with either writer, he misunderstands them. Proust's process of recollection was more sensitive than Freyre's, for it brought back experience as a whole rather than cataloguing it. (Proust's world of memory was released by a single *petite madeleine* soaked in tea. Freyre would have described sixty Pernambucan sweetmeats and a dozen types of maté.) If Proust penetrates far beyond mere atmospheric musings, Durkheim casts off gracefully from the realm of data. Freyre confesses that the latter's 'Israelite' background may add a Cleopatra's nose to his work but with no hint of the implications. He overlooks Durkheim's contributions to morals and the nature of civilizations; or his constructs of mechanical and organic solidarity, critical for elucidating Freyre's loose notions of social structure; or his clues to 'abnormal' social organization in pre-industrial societies set forth in his preface to the second edition (1902) of *Division of Labor.*[104]

If Freyre has such blind spots, what accounts for his influence and acclaim? A kindred spirit is perhaps Edmund Burke, whose conservatism, historical idealism and style give him lasting appeal. Despite Marx's charge that Burke was a cant-monger and sycophant in the pay of oligarchs, Burke's message that England is a partnership between the living, the dead and those to be born still stirs hearts in a manner that *Capital* cannot.[105] Freyre in his turn was attacked by progressives of the 1960s and pseudo-progressives of the 1980s. Yet his national vision is one that many Brazilians endorse in their (increasingly rare) self-conceited moments: 'The

[103] Gilberto Freyre, *Sociologia,* 4th ed.; 2 vols. (Rio de Janeiro, 1967), Vol. 1, pp. 70–72.
[104] See Durkheim and Marcel Mauss, 'Note on the notion of civilization', *Social Research,* 38/4 (1971), 808–13.
[105] M. M. Bober, *Karl Marx's Interpretation of History* (New York, 1965), pp. 83–4.

secret of Brazil's success in building a humane, Christian and modern civilization in tropical America has been her genius for compromise.' While the British, as no other people, have had this genius in the political sphere, Brazilians extend it, Freyre adds for good measure, to the cultural and social realms. [106]

Freyre touches imaginations in Brazil and elsewhere by eschewing academic sobriety in favour of long-winded, ingratiatory, often saucy inventories of contraband information. When in 1969 he recalled Freyre's impact on his teenage generation of the mid-1930s, Antonio Candido suspended his later political misgivings to recapture the non-conformist intent that infused 'the uninhibited composition of *Casa-Grande e Senzala* with its candor in treating the sex life of patriarchalism and the decisive importance ascribed to the slave in forming our most intimate mode of being'. Future generations, he imagined, might not understand 'the revolutionary force, the liberating shock of this great book'. [107]

Later on as a 'participant observer' Cândido defined concisely the two poles between which Freyre's reputation has swung ever since. As a young professor and critic in the early 1940s he gave an interview that confessed distaste for the cultural sociology practiced by 'our master', whose recent works had fallen 'into the most lamentable social and cultural sentimentalism, into conservatism and traditionalism'. [108] This prescient critique took fifteen or more years to be widely endorsed, although Cândido himself was never perplexed in reconciling the 'liberating' with the 'patriarchal' Gilberto, while his nuanced appreciation of Gilberto's work goes well beyond these two succinct opinions. Now that Gilberto has departed, leaving a still-charismatic oeuvre, it remains to sift political considerations, which (justifiably) irritated many contemporaries, from qualities that account for his esprit and power to captivate and for the predictable longevity of his major works. The enigma lies in Freyre's fascination with antagonisms and transformations that yield no solidary historical pattern. The *saudosismo* (nostalgia, longing) he is accused of may not be mere longing for a past beyond retrieval, but also recognition that the past was not, within its cultural tradition, what it might have been. Otherwise it would not have suffered the entropy he describes. Freyre saw the evil of colonial Brazil —

---

[106] Gilberto Freyre, *New World in the Tropics* (New York, 1963), p. 7. In a lively post-modern essay Vasconcelos urges that Freyre's readers rise above criticism polarized in the purely ethical terms of 'well written perverse sociology' versus 'badly written subversive sociology'. Gilberto Felisberto Vasconcelos, *O xará de Apipucos* (São Paulo, 1987).

[107] Cândido, *Teresina etc.*, p. 136.

[108] Mário Neme (ed.), *Plataforma da nova geração* (Porto Alegre, 1945), p. 39.

flogging, mutilation, tyranny – conveying it with more force than he did the putative good. Yet while he calmly documents the planter's wife serving her husband the gouged eyeballs of his *mulata* mistress in a desert dish of blood, he elsewhere claims that Brazil's secret for building a humane, Christian civilization had been a genius for compromise. For him the Brazilian monarchical example corrected excesses of the patriarchal plantation tradition.[109]

In *The Waning of the Middle Ages* Huizinga had set himself precisely Freyre's problem of a culture that was drifting without guideposts toward modernity, in his case northeast Europe in the early Renaissance where the chivalric code still prevailed.[110] Modern scholars, wrote Huizinga, fix on new forms of political and economic life that emerged in the fifteenth century. Chroniclers of the time, however, had focused on superannuated feudal habits with their 'heroic rules'. Huizinga was more concerned with this inertial mind-set than with the Renaissance awakening. The contemporary actors, he felt, were drawn to a 'symbolistic attitude' rather than to a causal or genetic one. He wrote of course about a European society 500 years before his own and, as a Dutchman, knew what was to happen. Freyre described a society bearing pre-modern traits that was not five centuries behind him but only two. Like Huizinga he was a historian, but vicariously an actor as well. Neither he nor his society had completed the transition from the symbolist to the causal attitude. He proudly confessed having used symbolic figures such as the plantation boy or the upwardly mobile law student.[111] The third book of his main trilogy finishes by mythicizing past, present and future. 'The period recalled in this essay', he wrote, speaking of the 1860s–1910s, 'represented in Brazil the supersession of the myth of the King by the myth of a Republic founded on an abstractly Positivist motto: Order and Progress.'[112]

If Gilberto Freyre suggests one of Huizinga's medieval chroniclers, his contemporary, Sérgio Buarque de Holanda (1902–82), takes the path of Huizinga himself. Both pursue the secret of Brazil, but Gilberto evokes its image while Sérgio inserts the nation into Western historical process and prescribes for its extrication from traditional politics. One, in an American spirit of anthropological pluralism, celebrates Brazilian patriarchal

[109] Freyre, *New World*, p. 205.
[110] Johan Huizinga, *The Waning of the Middle Ages* (Garden City, N.Y., 1954), chs 3, 4, 15.
[111] Freyre, *Como e porque*, pp. 68–9.
[112] Gilberto Freyre, *Order and Progress: Brazil from Monarchy to Republic*, trans. Rod W. Horton (Berkeley, 1986), p. 405.

culture; the other uses his European training to explore the tension between patriarchalism and the encroachment of Western liberalism. In the categories of art historian Heinrich Wölfflin, Freyre's was a baroque or painterly mentality that explored variations on a central theme while Sérgio Buarque followed a classical or linear search for tectonic strength.

Sérgio's interest in history was kindled in secondary school by his prolific mentor Afonso d'E. Taunay. Yet his early inclinations were more cultural than historiographical. In São Paulo and after 1921 in Rio he joined the modernists' iconoclastic rediscovery of Brazil. He plunged into literature and journalism with only perfunctory attention to his law studies. In 1929 he went to Germany for *O Jornal* of Rio where he interviewed writers, including Mann, and composed Portuguese subtitles for *The Blue Angel* and other films. Rio had prepared him well for what he called the 'worldly bohemian euphoria' of late Weimar.[113] Now, however, he was ready to absorb history and sociology from Meinecke (whose lectures he attended), Kantorowicz, Sombart and particularly the example of the departed Weber. As it did for Mariátegui in Italy a few years earlier, the European sojourn orientated his life work. He came home in 1931 with a 400-page manuscript bearing the alternative titles 'Teoria da América' and 'Corpo e alma do Brasil' that would yield two chapters for his seminal *Raízes do Brasil* (1936). Evincing a shift in priorities from literature to history, *Raízes* was the cornerstone for his career as a historian.[114] In *Os monções* (1945) and *Caminhos e fronteiras* (1957) he counterpoises the image of penurious, expansionist, *mameluco* Brazil to that of Freyre's coastal, seigneurial society. His magisterial *Visão do paraíso* (1959) examines the 'baroque' mind-set of Portuguese explorers and settlers subtly contrasting it with the Spaniards. His introduction to the *Obras* of Azeredo Coutinho (1966) reviews economic antecedents to Brazilian independence. As editor of the first seven volumes of the *História geral da civilização brasileira* (1960–72) he assembled a composite history of Brazil from Iberian and Amerindian origins to the advent of the Republic, writing Volume 7 on the late Empire himself. Because *Raízes* so concisely set out theoretical

---

[113] Francisco de Assis Barbosa collected Sérgio Buarque's European dispatches of 1929–30 in *Raízes de Sérgio Buarque de Holanda* (Rio de Janeiro, 1989); see also Assis Barbosa's 'Formación de Sérgio Buarque de Holanda', prologue to the Spanish version of Sérgio's *Visão do paraíso*, trans. Estela dos Santos (Caracas, 1987).

[114] Buarque de Holanda, *Tentativas de mitologia* (São Paulo, 1979), pp. 29–30, and 'Corpo e alma do Brasil', *Espelho* (Rio de Janeiro), March 1935 (reprinted in *Revista do Brasil*, 3/6 (1987): 32–42). Sérgio's literary criticism of 1940–41 appears in *Cobra de vidro*, 2nd ed (1978) and his studies from the 1950s of colonial literature in Antônio Cândido (ed.), *Capítulos de literatura colonial* (São Paulo, 1991).

formulations that anticipate his future interests, it claims attention in what follows.[115]

Sérgio Buarque's *Raízes* like the books by Mariátegui and Price-Mars consists of seven essays. Although *Casa-Grande* had appeared three years earlier, Sérgio seldom refers to Freyre in his text. The first two chapters of *Raízes* actually fit with many of Gilberto's ideas, although 'influence' is difficult to attribute given the hefty manuscript that Sérgio brought from Germany in 1931. As for personal relations, Gilberto recalled in 1982 that he and Sérgio had been 'bohemian' comrades in Rio of the 1920s and that as editor of the classic José Olympio series of 'Brazilian Documents' his maiden introduction in 1936 to Volume 1, Sérgio's *Raízes,* praised the author's analytic skill, interpretive flair and glee in shedding intellectual light.[116] It may well be that the two budding intellectuals' search for Brazilian identity from afar, in the United States and Germany, led to certain triangulations.

A few reflections from *Raízes* may be cited that mesh with, though come to a finer point than, Gilberto's diffuse vignettes. Sérgio starts with hierarchy and social organization. In colonial Brazil both were nebulous. Hierarchy was imported not as a rigid principle but as a ceaseless calculus of privileges, which paradoxically made Iberians pioneers of the 'modern mentality'. Long before the advent of 'revolutionary ideas' they were sensitive to irrationality and social injustice. 'Everyone knows', writes Sérgio, 'that Portuguese nobility was never rigorous and impermeable.' Porous hierarchies went with a weak capacity for social organization. Solidarity grew from sentimental bonds, not from calculated interests, while routinized labour was unacceptable because it prized achievement external to the person of the worker. Brazilian life accented the affective and passionate at the expense of discipline, to which African slaves added a honied, insinuating tone. The *senzala* morality penetrated administration, the economy and religious belief. The very creation of the world seemed understood as an 'abandonment, a languishing (*languescimento*) of God'. Such traits were the opposite needed for a people on the path to political modernization. Lacking discipline and organization on one hand and the hallowed principle of feudal loyalty on the other, the only recourse was to

[115] Maria Odila Leite da Silva Dias presents an introduction to Sérgio's historiography with representative texts in *Sérgio Buarque de Holanda* (São Paulo, 1985). Assis Barbosa gathered evocations of his career, including texts by Sérgio, in a special number of *Revista do Brasil*, 3/6 (1987).

[116] Gilberto Freyre, 'Sérgio, mestre de mestres', *Folha de São Paulo,* 11 May 1982 (reprinted in *Revista do Brasil*, 3/6 (1987): 117).

sheer obedience as notably imposed by Jesuit schooling. 'Today,' wrote Sérgio in 1936, 'simple obedience as a principle of discipline seems an outworn, ineffective remedy and thence, inevitably, the constant instability of our social life.'

The chapter 'Trabalho e aventura' treats the Portuguese adoption of 'adventure' in preference to 'work'; yet, implicitly challenging Freyre's long-term cultural determinism, Sérgio describes Englishmen of the early modern period as being no less given than Iberians to indolence, prodigality, and the good life. It was the Dutch occupation of northeast Brazil that revealed the historic rupture between Brazil and the 'new' North Atlantic. Yet, Sérgio asks, could Dutch Protestants found a society on the dissolvent principles they encountered? What they lacked in plasticity they had to excess in entrepreneurial spirit, capacity for work and social cohesion. As adventurers weary of persecutions, however, they sought impossible fortunes without striking roots in the land. The Portuguese achievement had been to efface, wittingly or not, the distinction between themselves and their new world. 'Their weakness was their strength.'

Sérgio's analysis is thus far roughly compatible with Gilberto's save that he relies on political sociology in a broad European sense and Freyre on anthropology in the condescending, atheoretical American one. The former looks for exit from political tradition, the latter for celebration of cultural tradition. They divide at the nineteenth century, where Gilberto's *Mansions and Shanties* traces vegetative change from patriarchalism to semi-patriarchalism while Sérgio treats the mid-century as a missed opportunity to liquidate the colonial heritage of servile labour and exploitation of the land. The 1850s, Sérgio shows, might have been a benchmark with the incursion of corporations, banks, telegraphs and railroads. Yet two mentalities lingered, traditional versus rational, corporeal versus abstract, parochial versus cosmopolitan. Patriarchalism formed an indivisible whole whose members were linked by sentiments and duties, never by interests and ideas, whereas in political theory, Sérgio held, the birth of the state requires suppressing the family order and producing citizens responsible to public laws. Here he recalls Antigone representing the family and Creon the abstract, impersonal polis, noting that in Brazil Antigone was still alive and obstinate. 'New' elites, transplanted from fazendas to cities, favoured 'intelligence' and 'talent' – love of sonorous phrases and ostentatious erudition – over the concerns of James Madison (whom Sérgio cites from Charles A. Beard) who disparaged moral and religious motives in favour of reconciling divergent economic interests. The forced improvisation of an urban bourgeoisie meant that attitudes once peculiar to the rural patriciate now extended to all classes. Modernization gave fresh impetus, as it were, to patriarchal culture.[117]

To define the human substrate of Brazilian society Sérgio advanced his disputed notion of the 'cordial man'. By cordiality he meant neither the calculated leniency of patrons soothing their workers nor elaborate rituals of politeness (e.g., English or Japanese) that disguised or repressed private feelings. Brazilians, Sérgio felt, were averse to ritualism. Social life liberates the cordial man from rationalizing his world and from fearing to live with his own self. Cordiality, he argues, dictates preferences whereas democratic benevolence aims to balance off and neutralize egoisms. While the 'humanitarian' ideal of greatest welfare for the greatest number subordinates quality to quantity, cordiality loses force beyond a narrow circle and fails to cement extended forms of social organization. Nor is cordiality per se a source of good principles, for 'social crystallization' requires an innate normative element. Thus does Sérgio define Brazil's challenge of political organization.

Gilberto and Sérgio both started from a loosely defined premise of patriarchalism. For Freyre this was the subject of his trilogy, 'History of Patriarchal Society in Brazil', that demonstrates the extraordinary assimilative capacity of Brazilian society while tracing the decadence of its once-vigorous patriarchal substructure. Freyre's entropic treatment of social change was redeemed in part by his futuristic vision of 'messianic' cities such as Brasília and Goiânia (*cidades-esperança*); or his multi-ethnic image of modern Brazil (anticipating by decades the U.S. shift from the melting-pot myth to that of cultural pluralism, or from *e pluribus unum* to *ex uno plures*); or his 'tropicology' theory that shifts 'development' calculus from an industrial-non-industrial binomial to one that juxtaposes Western rationalism and tropical functionalism.[118] What Gilberto never managed was to visualize historical process that would connect his account of the past with his luminous hopes for the future.

If Gilberto was an imagist, Sérgio was an architect. While he too relished the savour of time and place, his forte was the X-ray that probes from historicism to history, from empathy to analysis. Thus in carrying Brazil's

---

[117] Sérgio's theory of elite 'intelligence' perhaps draws from the *medalhão* of Machado de Assis in 'Education of a Stuffed Shirt' (*The Psychiatrist and Other Stories* (Berkeley, 1963), pp. 113–22). For a later treatment of Sérgio's 'improvised' bourgeoisie, see Roberto Schwarz, *Ao vencedor as batatas* (São Paulo, 1977), especially his discussion (pp. 42–43) of the novelist José de Alencar and the 'fables that owe their symbolic force to a world wherein Brazil found no place'.

[118] For example, Freyre's *Brasis, Brasil, Brasília* (Lisbon, 1960).

story to the nineteenth century he stripped the obsolescent *casa-grande* image to the category of 'cordiality', subsuming patriarchalism to a general case of interpersonal relations.[119] Similarly with democratic liberalism, he did not linger over political niceties of the *Federalist* papers but went straight to Bentham for a statement of utilitarian individualism.[120] Instead of leaving him with a moribund culture that faced a modern one powerless to be born, this strategy allowed Sérgio a dialectic construction. His conclusion fits Spengler's notion of 'historical pseudomorphosis', designating cases where an old culture blankets the land so heavily that a young culture cannot achieve expressive form or even self-consciousness.[121] The young soul is cramped in former moulds; its feelings stifle in senile works and, lacking creativity, it can only hate the distant power. For Sérgio the old soul was embedded in the national psyche and the young one was an inevitable part of the immediate future. Rather than composing a linear transition, they were both by the nineteenth century fully present and engaged.

Sérgio's historiography was of a piece with his political commitment. In his closing essay of *Raízes* on 'Our Revolution', he neither forecast the tropical utopia of Freyre nor did he, in the cavalier manner of Paulo Prado, propose War or Revolution as solutions. As a historian he accepted processes at work. The options of fascism or domestic Integralism were dubious. He was attracted to features of Marxism but in the spirit of a Brazilian 'anarchist mentality', not of Muscovite discipline. Rapid urbanization was converting rural Brazil into colonies without the climate for industrial liberalism. At times, he ventured, political personalism might be more salutary that the declamatory slogans of liberal democracy. On the other hand, *casa-grande* patriarchalism was evaporating to leave behind the culture of *cordialismo* as possible articulation between natural sentiment and dogmatic liberalism. Sérgio refused to discount the positive example of Brazil's second empire (1840–89) wherein the mechanism of the state functioned 'with a certain harmony and stateliness (*garbo*)'. This nuanced analysis – true to history, open to possibility – did not inhibit decisive political commitment. He formally protested against the Vargas dictatorship (1945); was a founder of Esquerda Democrática, soon the Partido Socialista Brasileira (1946); resigned his professorship at the University of

---

[119] For the 'modernization' of cordiality, see Roberto DaMatta, *A casa e a rua* (São Paulo, 1985), pp. 55–80, and *Carnivals, Rogues, and Heroes*, ch. 4.

[120] For the persistent blockage of liberalism in Brazil, see Wanderley G. dos Santos, 'Liberalism in Brazil: Ideology and Praxis', in M. J. Blachmann and R. G. Hellman (eds.), *Terms of Conflict: Ideology in Latin American Politics* (Philadelphia, Pa., 1977), pp. 1–38.

[121] Oswald Spengler, *The Decline of the West*, 2 vols. (New York, 1939), Vol. 2, ch. 7.

São Paulo to protest against the military government's dismissal of faculty members (1969); was a founder of the Centro Brasileiro Democrático (1978) and at the end of his life the Partido dos Trabalhadores (1980). Rarely are creative intellect and coherent political stance so securely matched.

### Lezama Lima: History as image

Although of the essayists so far discussed only three were primarily literary figures, all were attuned to literature and expressive arts, and all were adept with metaphor and analogy. At the same time the group were versed in or conversant with history, philosophy, social thought and theory, and even social science, the literati no less than the others. Far from being 'impressionists' they were deeply informed eclectics, aware of pitfalls in exploring terrain that was vaguely or unwarrantably mapped and of the idées reçues of presumptive readers schooled under the sign of positivism. Cognizant of history, they tried to balance the lessons of vanguardism in the arts against new European cues for the study of society. But neither arts nor sciences were yet institutionalized or commodified in Latin America. The intellectual enjoyed a private pasture. For the three writers first examined, the balance of their enquiries tipped toward the challenge of explaining history, not rendering it, and therefore toward the problem of causality, not reconstruction through images. For the next six the scales were closer to equilibrium. And for the one to be considered now the balance tipped sharply toward an imagistic strategy.

In 1957 the Cuban poet, novelist and essayist José Lezama Lima (1910–76) gave five lectures in Havana, published as *La expresión americana,* in which he suspended the search for causes so as to convey more directly the historic meanings of hemispheric America.[122] Lezama had founded several influential literary reviews; he was an established poet who wrote with hermetic density, reviving without replicating the Spanish baroque; and he was germinating his masterpiece *Paradiso* (1966; Eng. trans. 1974) where in the words of Mario Vargas Llosa, 'the history of humanity and of traditional European culture appears summarized, deformed into carica-ture, but at the same time poetically enriched and assimilated within a

---

[122] The edition used here is that of 1969 published in Santiago, Chile. The only critical edition, however, is the Portuguese translation by Irlemar Chiampi (*A expressão americana,* São Paulo, 1988), which contains a valuable introduction and notes that are freely utilized here.

great American narrative'.[123] Lezama's literary genius was complemented by a vast repertoire of history, metaphysics and esoterica, always subordinate, however, to the expressive purpose of his account. *La expresión americana* appeared in 1957 at the critical threshold of Latin America's (misnamed) literary boom and its (precipitate) social science boom. A fork in the path, reconciled or glossed over by previous essayists, was coming into evidence. Instinctively, Lezama made his choice for imagistic (though not impressionistic) historiography.

With this said, the starting point is not the philosophic reach of Lezama's miniature New World symphony but, as Julio Cortázar wrote in a luminous chapter on Lezama, his innocence, an American innocence, insular in both literal and extended senses.[124] Lezama was integrally Cuban. He found foreign names to be unspellable, while his foreign quotations were 'orthographic fantasies'. Argentine intellectuals thought he lacked formal correctness as did Cuban sophisticates with their deodorant style. Between Lezama and a Europeanized writer, Cortázar continues, lies 'the difference between innocence and guilt'. The latter carries a frightening tradition as a succubus. 'Why write, if everything has, in a way, already been said?' If a new slice of the invisible appears – symbolism, surrealism, or the *nouveau roman* – Europeans put aside their guilt for a moment. But slowly they feel European again and each writer retains the albatross around his neck. Meanwhile, Cortázar continues, 'Lezama wakes up on his island with a pre-adamite happiness, without a fig leaf, innocent of any direct tradition. He assumes them all, from the Etruscan interpreting entrails to Leopold Bloom blowing his nose in a dirty handkerchief, but without historical compromise . . . ; he is a Cuban with only a handful of his own culture behind him and the rest is knowledge, pure and free, not a career responsibility.'

Because of his agile command of European ideas one might be tempted to call Lezama derivative. But that would explode his whole notion of what America is about and cancel his innocence. From intimate experience Lezama knew what he wanted when, at the start of *La expresión americana*, he avoided the search for causality to accept the contrapuntal historical vision offered 'by the *imago*, by the image participating in history'. Then

---

[123] Cited in D. W. and V. R. Foster (eds.), *Modern Latin American Literature*, 2 vols. (New York, 1975) I, 479.

[124] Julio Cortázar, *Around the Day in Eighty Worlds* (San Francisco, 1986), pp. 82–108. The English edition reproduces the selection of the French edition (1980) which in turn draws from texts published in *La vuelta del día en ochenta mundos* and *Ultimo round* (Mexico, D.F. and Madrid, 1967 and 1969).

came the choice of how to identify his images or myths. One guide might have been T. S. Eliot, save that he was neo-classic *à outrance,* unconcerned with new myths as a pessimistic critic of what he took to be a crepuscular era. An alternative was the German literary critic E. R. Curtius, who surmised that old myths must all be reinvented (if indeed they deserved it) to offer their enigmas in a new guise. Lezama chose the latter as the European who liberated him. 'If a culture cannot create an imaginative form . . .', he wrote, 'when it suffers the quantitative burden of the millennia it will be grossly indecipherable.'

This leads Lezama in his opening chapter 'Myths and Classic Fatigue' to a distinction between two forms of recall: recollection and memory. Recollection is a product of the spirit while memory is plasma of the soul, ever creative and spermatic; with it we *memorize* from the roots of the species. 'Even the plant harbours the memory that allows it to acquire its plenitude of form.' Citing Ludwig Klages he recalls that the year of Goethe's death (1832), whose last words were 'More light!', was the year the phosphorous match was invented. 'It is difficult,' wrote Lezama, 'to disregard the wee chronological tribute of the discovery of the match. Not in vain did Germans consider routines of memorization [e.g., of dates] as forms of *Witz,* of ingenuity.' Faulty memory accounts, he felt, for the terrible American complex involving belief that expression is not an immanent form but a problématique to be resolved, forgetting that the plasma of his own autochthony fills a space equal to Europe's.

Having set the terms for his evocations, Lezama moves toward three historic phases of American expression: 'baroque curiosity', 'romanticism and the fact of America', and 'birth of creole expression'. These were conceived in historical sequence for ease of exposition, with 'history' making them interactive. Drawing on scholars of the baroque, Lezama defined American baroque as 'counter-conquest' rather than 'counter-Reformation'.[125] Its three components were internal *tension, plutonism* (an original fire that breaks fragments to recompose them), and a plenary, not degenerative, style that acquires new tongues, furnishings, forms of life and curiosity, a mysticism in new modes of prayer, and taste in food that all give off a way of life, refined and mysterious, theocratic and self-

---

[125] For the twentieth-century revival and 'modernization' of the 'American' baroque see: José Lezama Lima, *Esferaimagen / Sierpe de Don Luis de Góngora / Las imágenes posibles* (Barcelona, 1970); Haroldo de Campos, *O sequestro do barroco na formação da literatura brasileira* (Salvador, Bahia, 1989) and 'Lezama e a plenitud pelo excesso', *O Estado de São Paulo,* Caderno 2, 10 July 1988; Severo Sarduy, *Nueva instabilidad* (Mexico, D.F., 1987); Alejo Carpentier, *Concierto barroco* (Havana, 1987).

absorbed, vagrant yet entrenched in essences. American baroque was not frustrated or doctrinaire or self-censored but an outlook of the late seventeenth and eighteenth centuries that became 'a firm friend of the Enlightenment', even drawing on antecedent Cartesianism. Lezama adduces two eighteenth-century artists of popular origin as examples of the vitality and metamorphoses of baroque: First is the Indian or mestizo José Kondori from the Peruvian lowlands and purported sculptor of the genial portal of San Lorenzo church (1728–44) in Potosí. Lezama takes his art to represent a Hispano-Indian synthesis in 'an occult and hieratic form' that betokens a 'pact of equality'. Second is the Brazilian sculptor Aleijadinho (Antônio Francisco Lisboa, 1738–1814) whose art culminates 'the American baroque, uniting in grandiose form the union of Hispanic and African cultures'.

For his central figure Lezama calls up Sor Juana Inés de la Cruz (1651–95), who turned her baroque vision toward a quest for universal science that approximates the Enlightenment. She was the first American poet, he believed, to achieve primacy in the Hispanophone world, and even though she apologized that her remarkable poem 'First Dream' imitated the *culteranista* Spanish poet Góngora, Lezama calls this 'a charming act of humility more than a literary truth'. Octavio Paz, whose biography of Sor Juana appeared a quarter century after Lezama's essay, concurs in his praise of 'First Dream' but is less euphoric about the baroque, particularly if seen as a wellspring of American culture. He feels that its 'plethoric and inflated forms . . . faded at their frenetic peak, attracted by the void. The baroque festival is an *ars moriendi.*' Sor Juana's ideal of multi-faceted yet connected knowledge, Paz argues, was unattainable in New Spain, where she was unaware of the intellectual revolution that was transforming Europe. Even so, her baroque poem negates the baroque and 'prefigures the most modern modernity'.[126] Here the two interpretations join. Whether by her intuition of the vitalities of her immediate culture (Lezama) or by her prophetic sense of how to leap beyond the constrictions that bound her (Paz), both poets acclaim Sor Juana as a 'modern' poet who anticipated Rilke, Valéry, Gorostiza, and, Paz insists, Mallarmé.

Because his essays are not a textbook Lezama jumps from baroque to romanticism, omitting the Enlightenment and classicism. The obvious messages of liberalism, rationalism, guided education, empiricism, anti-

[126] Octavio Paz, *Sor Juana or, The Traps of Faith*, trans. Margaret Sayers Peden (Cambridge, 1988), pp. 147, 381, 419; 'First Dream' in *A Sor Juana Anthology*, trans. Alan S. Trueblood (Cambridge, Eng., 1988), pp. 166–95.

mysticism, and 'development' did not concern him. These would all float into the Latin American ideological *ajiaco* and receive lip service and intermittent acquiescence from those in power. What concerned Lezama was the Americanization of a culture that New World baroque foreshadowed. This would necessarily happen in the nineteenth century with romanticism as the mainspring but not the romanticism of literati, nor even the romantic figure of Bolívar, who 'is marginalized once he draws near the promised land and pulls back at naming a reality'. Lezama's romantics were not in the mould of Napoleon or Rousseau or Victor Hugo. He resolved to see the era as decisively formative yet represented by heroes whose lives were decisive failures, and not as with Bolívar contingent ones. He needed to encapsulate history as lived out and of course found romanticism suffused with tensions between individual and society, private vision and academic 'reality', the beauty of forests and ugliness of trains that invade them. Lezama wished to capture the grand romantic tradition of 'the dungeon, of absence, of the image, and of death'. From this he points to an American reality 'whose destiny is composed more of possible absences than of impossible presences', a tradition wherein lay 'the achieved historical fact' with José Martí as its grand master.

For the romantic moment Lezama selected three figures: Fray Servando Teresa de Mier, Simón Rodríguez, and Francisco de Miranda, all of them 'romantic by frustration', all of them embittered and one killed by the events of national independence and all of them actors on the vast transatlantic stage. Fray Servando embellished the American political tradition with: the conjecture that the Virgin of Guadalupe appeared not on the cape of the humble Indian Juan Diego but on that of Quetzalcóatl who was in fact the apostle St Thomas; a sweeping condemnation of the achievement in America of a backward and ignorant Spain; an assertion that the Laws of the Indies contained a Magna Carta for governance in the Americas; his shift from the English to the U.S. political model but always envisioning a constitution derived from norms of behaviour and not doctrinal law. Fray Servando's travels and exiles (to Spain, France, Italy, Portugal, England and the United States) and his detentions, imprisonments, and escapes resist enumeration. So fantastic were his perambulations that a parodic novelist was needed to catch the flavour of his life. In *El mundo alucinante* (1969) the Cuban writer Reinaldo Arenas alleged that between prison terms Fray Servando met Simón Rodríguez, Bolívar, Napoleon, Humboldt, Lady Hamilton, Chateaubriand and Madame de Stael;

that he escaped prison off the Veracruz coast by gnawing open his iron chains; that he reported seeing twenty-nine carloads of black people fed into a train furnace in the United States (a country where every breath of air was taxed) as they were 'the closest thing to coal'. At the end Fray Servando's portrait of Mexican president Guadalupe Victoria becomes entangled in a vignette of Fidel Castro.[127]

Lezama likens Fray Servando to Fabrice del Dongo in Stendhal's *The Charterhouse of Parma* who was forever in headlong flight during the Napoleonic wars. But the comparison goes deeper. Lezama makes much of *paisaje* (landscape) as space wherein a new destiny unfolds and a native romantic spirit takes root in American soil. Stendhal too, Brombert tells us, gave landscapes a prime role as concrete figurations of his lyricism, notably at the unique site of the Dongo castle with its sublime lake and rolling hills: not a picture-book setting but transfigured into 'a world of revery and energy'. As fugitives both heroes needed space to secure freedom and vision for enriching themselves and reconstructing their world. Persecution thus brings liberation.[128] The Mexican baroque world had deteriorated so slowly, writes Lezama, that few were aware of it. 'Fray Servando is the first who decides to be persecuted, for he has sensed that another emerging landscape is seeking him out, one that no longer relies on the great arch that united Hispanic baroque and its enrichment in American baroque.' The new one intuits the opulence of a new destiny, an image or island, arising from portolanos of the unknown to foster the freedoms of the native landscape, now liberated from dialogue with a ghost. In Fray Servando's transition from baroque to romanticism Lezama finds occult American surprises. 'He thinks he breaks with tradition when he in fact exalts it. Thus when he believes he has departed from what is Hispanic he rediscovers it within himself, now enhanced. To reform within the old order, not breaking but retaking the thread, is what is Hispanic.'

Lezama's second paragon is Simón Rodríguez (1771–1854) – not, significantly, Bolívar, but his tutor. Bolívar called Rodríguez his 'only universal teacher', who shaped him toward 'freedom, justice, the great and the

---

[127] Edmundo O'Gorman's prologue and chronology in *Fray Servando Teresa de Mier* (Mexico, D.F., 1945), pp. vii–lix; Seymour Menton, *Prose Fiction of the Cuban Revolution* (Austin, Tex., 1975), pp. 100–4.

[128] The Stendhalian prison restores heroes to their own selves, or allows them to discover and even create them. 'The prison thus assumes a protective and dynamic role. It liberates one from the captivity of social existence.' See Victor Brombert, *Stendhal: Fiction and the Themes of Freedom* (Chicago, Ill., 1976), pp. 152, 173.

beautiful'. Lezama attributed the influence of Rodríguez on Bolívar not to historical accident but to what both shared of a 'demonic and primigenial' spirit. Rodríguez's era may have led him to a disguised Rousseauan notion of pedagogy, 'but his virus was essentially Socratic' and carried him from the daimon of idea or logic to the passionate Eros of understanding. He contained something of the pedagogic Aleijadinho, being 'ugly, excessive and itinerant'; something of Swedenborg without his prophecies and theocracy; and something of Blake without his lyricism. He spent his old age wandering in poverty amid the Andes founding schools, opening shops for gunpowder, candles, or groceries, but never rediscovering his one great dialogue with the adolescent Bolívar. At the end he admitted: 'I, who wanted to make of the world a paradise for all, have made it a hell for myself.'

Of Lezama's three subjects he calls Francisco de Miranda (1750–1816) the first great American who constructed in Europe and the United States a frame appropriate to his life work. Yet his reversals of fortune, and his eventual demise indirectly caused by Bolívar, accorded him the destiny of Fray Servando in his dungeon and 'the fatal flight of Simón Rodríguez to the centre of the earth toward the lakes of protohistory'. Miranda's case was complex, for he became a friend of Washington and Hamilton, moved as a performer across the Europe of the French Revolution, of Pitt and Catherine the Great, and whom in 1795 the young Napoleon called 'a Don Quixote excepting that he is not crazy. That man has a sacred fire in his soul.' Then came the encounter with the young Bolívar, who 'attached his name to the first great calamity of Venezuelan independence'. More facile with pen than with sword, Miranda remained what he had always been, a plotter and conspirator rather than a man of action. 'Ruckus (*bochinche*), ruckus!' he exclaimed on his arrest by Bolívar, 'These people can only raise a ruckus.' Wherewith he departed for his final imprisonment. Like the others of Lezama's romantic trio, his ambitions exceeded his gifts – which is why Lezama found them exemplary.

Following his private version of the romantic moment Lezama addresses the birth of creole expression. Having written of illustrious prisoners, brave exiles, fugitive misanthropes and untamable heroes, he counterposes a submerged current that raises verbal altars for fresh lustre and smashes the gloomy mansion of the metropolis. Here he introduces another trio composed of Martí, Rubén Darío and César Vallejo, who plunge verbal shafts into the detritus of inefficacy and dead lexicon. These true Americans compose their words to acknowledge the new *paisaje* and its need for expression in vivid molecules (*corpúsculos coloreados*). 'Every American contains always a quiet Gongorism that explodes his discourse, yet in comfort, not tragically like the Spaniard.' From the literary stars Lezama turns to the people, whose role as architects of America was finding recognition. For the birth of America 'the stoicism of Quevedo and the scintillation of Góngora find popular roots. They engender a creole culture of superb resistance in ethical matters and a keen sense for language and for discriminating the sources of independence.'

The anonymous *corrido* now becomes an exemplary expression of creole culture. Whereas the European *romance* celebrated Carolingian or Mozarabic historical feats, the informal *corrido* of America limits itself, as in Mexico, to the defence of the city plaza, the shadow of execution, and most notably the broadsides and the tears of love in the provinces, or, as in Argentina, reaches a plenitude of tenderness in the maternal image of the ombu tree on the boundless pampas. Goya had symbolized weapons as a theology wherein defeat was accompanied by clouts of a sulfurous broom. To combat that tragicomic world in collapse, he reached beyond his prancing genius toward the rays of Enlightenment. The Mexican engraver, who always accompanies the *corrido,* has no theological world but only the dictates of circumstance. If he should say, with Paul Valéry, that events had no interest for him, he would be lost. In America the reaction to degenerescence was offset by a new *paisaje* that resisted concentration on death. José Guadalupe Posada converts uproar and bare facts into a skeleton that smiles. Finally, Lezama pays his delicate tribute to Martí, whose *versos sencillos* acquired tenderness in the *corrido*'s designs and spirals that intervened between *copla* and *romance*.

Lezama's final chapter unites his argument in his own allusive way. He starts off concerned less with American expression than with expression *per se*. Modernism, he says, begins with attention to 'something else': *faire autre chose, faire le contraire*. But after a decade the links to the past emerge. For Joyce, neo-Thomism was not late scholasticism but it revealed a creative medieval world. Stravinsky's voyage via Rimsky-Korsakov, ragtime and jazz back to Pergolesi was not a neo-classical discovery but a thread of tradition leading to the secret of music. The grand exceptions were Leonardo and Goethe, who are lessons for our age in requiring 'swift and intuitive knowledge of past styles, countenances of what remained creative after so many shipwrecks, and adequate placement in contemporary polemics'. Then came their successor, Picasso: 'No painter taught so many occult things, revived so many styles, projected on dead eras so many possibilities of re-encounters and beginnings.'

As Chiampi summarizes Lezama's 'parabolic' argument inspired by Picasso, 'the wealth of a culture depends on its capacity to assimilate, synthesize and renovate potential forms of other cultures. The American "summa", conceived via the paradigmatic modernity of Picasso, now requires, with the example of the Greeks facing the Egyptians and Persians, critical vision and precaution for selectivity in starting to incorporate influences.' This leads to Lezama's emphatic anti-Hegelian argument attacking the European view that nature is reducible to man, omitting *paisaje*. Accepting Schelling's dictum that 'nature is the visible spirit and the spirit is invisible nature', Lezama assumes that the 'spirit that reveals nature and man is *paisaje*'. He continues with vignettes from his earlier text of Havana Bay, the Andean baroque of Cuzco, the pampa of *Martín Fierro* (*paisaje* or nature?, he queries), and the line connecting Miranda's dungeon to Martí's death scene. All are forms of *paisaje* where the struggle of nature and man creates a cultural *paisaje* as man triumphs over nature. Thus Sor Juana's dream is night over the valley of Mexico when sleep converts scholastic dialectic into clues to secrets of *paisaje*. Lezama adds some reflections on three North Americans – Melville, Whitman and Gershwin – who each in his own way won emancipation from Hegelian historicism, thus placing Anglo America squarely into his hemispheric argument.

From what precedes Lezama extracts his idea of 'gnostic space', a space of and for knowledge. The notion is rooted in post-Kantian Romantic idealism, interpreted by Lezama as a challenge to Hegel's lectures on *The Philosophy of History* and Ortega's commentary thereon. The question is whether space passively awaits insemination by a world-historical Idea or Spirit without collaboration or whether it contributes to the intrusion of the Spirit. In Lezama's answer: 'In the American influence what predominates is what I dare to call open, gnostic space, where insertion of the invading spirit is recognized by immediate visual comprehension. The frozen forms of European baroque and every explicit manifestation of a damaged body dissolve in America in that gnostic space identified by its own breadth of *paisaje*, its surplus of gifts.' He continues: 'Why could the western spirit not penetrate Asia and Africa but did so totally in America? Because that gnostic space was awaiting a form of vegetative fecundation . . . the blessing of a temperature adequate to receive the generative particles.' What Lezama rejected in Hegel were his pronouncements that: 'Nature, as contrasted with Spirit, is a quantitative mass, whose power must not be so great as to make its single force omnipotent.' Or that, 'North America will be comparable with Europe only after the immeasurable space which that country presents to its inhabitants shall have been occupied, and the members of the political body shall have begun to be pressed back on each other.'[129] For Lezama the critical pressure was not between the spirit and nature or among communities of an imported civilization, but between people and nature to produce *paisajes*.

## IDENTITY IN THE SHADOW OF PHILOSOPHY

In the 1940s and early 1950s the Latin American *prise de conscience* of the twentieth century leads to the realm of philosophy. For the historian this yields the opportunity not simply to pursue his usual assignment of relating cultural expression to large trends and events but also to ask how expressive crafts or academic disciplines come, by internal maturation, to artistic or intellectual control. With this last question in mind the Peruvian philosopher Francisco Miró Quesada traces the origins and fruition of the Latin American 'philosophizing project'.[130] He does so, not unmindful of historical context, but without giving primary focus to the political enthusiasms or class 'bias' of his subjects. His concern is not with philosophy as justificatory *response to* circumstance but with how, in Whitehead's sense, philosophy gained in precision for generalization as it became *immersed in* circumstance. He shows the intellectual quest for 'reality' or 'identity' to be not merely a matter of will-power or chance illumination but a technical enterprise as well.

The professionalization of philosophy in Latin America preceded that of the social sciences, which got fully under way only in the 1960s. Ironically, colonial Spanish America had produced reputable philosophers who sometimes attained metropolitan standards. The neo-scholasticism of the universities was an Iberian transplant; it began to yield to Enlightenment influences after 1760 and was discredited after independence. Overnight Latin America shifted from colonial status within the Ibero-Atlantic world, where its thinkers shared intellectual premises, to neo-colonial status in the modern Western world where they were to adapt maxims and methods derived from quite different understandings. This produced what Miró Quesada calls a *vivencia del desenfoque,* or 'bifocal coexistence'. The Ibero-Atlantic world, that is, had not internalized the Western 'revolution of values' that Louis Dumont, stressing its British version, traces from

129 G. W. F. Hegel, *Lectures on the Philosophy of History,* trans. J. Sibree (London, 1894), pp. 84, 90.
130 Francisco Miró Quesada, *Despertar y proyecto del filosofar latinoamericano* (Mexico D.F., 1974) and *Proyecto y realización del filosofar latinoamericano* (Mexico, D.F., 1981).

Mandeville to Adam Smith, or from Locke to Bentham.[131] When Latin Americans finally tried to join this 'revolution', its philosophic origins in the great religious and scientific revolutions had become veiled. By the early nineteenth century, Anglo-French definitions of individual, state and nation, of freedom, democracy and economic principles, of science, rationality and empirical demonstration were serenely argued without reference to the turbulent social and ideological contexts from which they had arisen. A new universalism had replaced that of the Roman Catholic Church. But unlike the Catholic order, the 'Enlightened' one failed to transplant its philosophic assumptions, insofar as these were culturally and historically rooted, to new host countries.

As we turn toward Latin America's philosophic renaissance in the 1940s, this background helps to keep three considerations in mind. First, when we recall the importance of philosophy as the foundation for ideology in Europe, we may assume that philosophic speculation would come to the fore in Latin America once it was recognized that here ideology was to answer conditions that were *sui generis.* Secondly, the scarcity of informed, systematic philosophic thought in Latin America for a century after independence is only partly attributable to the inadequacy or narrow professionalism of its institutions of higher learning. More importantly, it reflected the *pensador*'s inability to philosophize without clear, self-consistent knowledge of his society and without having recovered the logic of European philosophic thought since its Greek origins. That is, he could not simply 'join in' the flowing current of contemporary European philosophy. What would ultimately be required was, in Miró Quesada's term, an 'anabatic recovery' (*recuperación anabásica*) of that philosophy, a heroic upstream campaign or anabasis, to its sources. Thirdly, even though Latin American adaptations of European thought, notably positivism, might serve the purposes of dominant groups, one cannot conclude that intellectual activity was a reflex response to class interest. Whatever the political sympathies of a Latin American positivist or *científico,* the imported discourse of political or moral philosophy did not effectively serve domestic purposes of diagnosis and therapy. The multiple formulations in the 1970s of what is significantly called 'liberation philosophy' has required not so much a softening of the heart – the human heart is always a bit obdurate – as rigorous domestication of the philosophic enterprise and a less blinkered vision of the social facts of the case.

[131] Louis Dumont, *From Mandeville to Marx* (Chicago, Ill., 1977).

Miró Quesada gauges the renaissance of philosophy in Latin America by the contributions of three generations: the patriarchs, the shapers (*forjadores*), and a third wave of technically equipped thinkers who inherit a ready-made 'philosophical project'. To these a fourth generation that matured in the 1940s can be added; it has moved from what Francisco Romero called a 'normal' situation where academic conditions were in place for true philosophizing to a 'natural' one where both the activity and the conditions for pursuing it could be routinely assumed.

Save for Alejandro Deústua (Peru, 1849–1945) and Enrique José Varona (Cuba, 1849–1933), the patriarchs were born between 1860 and 1883: José Vasconcelos (Mexico, 1882–1959), Alfonso Caso (Mexico, 1883–1948), Alejandro Korn (Argentina, 1860–1936), Carlos Vaz Ferreira (Uruguay, 1872–1958), Enrique Molina (Chile, 1871–1964) and Raimundo de Farias Brito (Brazil, 1862–1917). This generation initiated the 'anabatic recovery' of the Western tradition, although their notions of how philosophy might be acclimated to the American scene were vague or, as with Vasconcelos, more declaratory than analytic. Miró Quesada ascribes two qualities to the patriarchs: first, they were enamoured of Western ideas to the extent that they might accept the Bergsonian critique of positivism without understanding Bergson's reasoning; second, they were necessarily confined to spontaneous and isolated expressions of the philosophic enterprise.

While these features may loosely characterize the generation as a whole, they lose force when applied to leaders. As early as 1908, for example, Vaz Ferreira made a searching critique of William James' pragmatism in a series of six lectures.[132] And while he never brought his thought into a coherent 'system', his richly aphoristic *Fermentario* (1938) is a self-secure reconnaissance of many realms – society and psychology, science and metaphysics, religion and immortality – that holds the analytic, the speculative and the confessional in careful balance to place him, Alejandro Arias has said, in the tradition of Marcus Aurelius, Nietzsche and Unamuno. Of all Latin American thinkers, writes Francisco Larroyo, 'perhaps Vaz Ferreira has attained *l'esprit de finesse* in highest measure'.[133] Vasconcelos was quite different. In book-length treatises he dashed off a metaphysics

---

132 Carlos Vaz Ferreira, *El pragmatismo, exposición y crítica* (Montevideo, 1909). In Chile, Enrique Molina produced a simultaneous critique of James; see Solomon Lipp, *Three Chilean Thinkers* (Waterloo, Ont., 1975), p. 107.
133 Alejandro C. Arias, *Vaz Ferreira* (Mexico D.F., 1948); Francisco Larroyo, *La filosofía iberomericana*, 2nd ed. (Mexico, D.F., 1978), p. 124.

(1929), an ethics (1932), an esthetics (1935) and an organic logic (1945). As early as 1918 he had laid the basis for his 'system' in *Monismo estético* (Esthetic Monism). His most famous book was *La raza cósmica* (*The Cosmic Race,* 1925) which predicted that a 'fifth race' would produce ethnic fusion of scientific, spiritual, and aesthetic capacities permitting civilization to reclaim the tropics as its land of promise. Four 'races' – black, Indian, Mongol and white – had thus far forged world history in isolation. Because the white race had resisted miscegenation while taming nature, it was left to Ibero-Americans, with all the 'defects' of their civilization, to provide the cradle for a fifth race. 'The inferior races', wrote Vasconcelos, 'would become less prolific with education, and the best specimens will keep ascending an ethnic scale whose ideal type is not precisely the white but the new race to which the white himself must aspire so as to dominate the synthesis.' Aesthetic mating of the 'black Apollo' with the 'blond Venus' rather than brutal struggle for survival, Vasconcelos claimed (ignoring Darwin's attention to sexual selection), would determine a eugenic outcome, preserving the gifts of mestizos, Indians, and 'even the Negro', who 'surpasses the white in an infinity of spiritual attitudes'.

If this summary suggests a latter-day *pensador* clumsily navigating from social Darwinism to Bergsonian idealism, it is only a fragment of the truth. Vasconcelos by no means merely accompanied European fashions. His vocation led toward contact with the divine through sensual passion. Yoga and theosophy captivated him. Nietzschean exaltation took him to Hinduism, Buddhism to Pythagoras. Plotinus became his lodestar. Without being bookish, as he accused the *ateneístas* of being, Vasconcelos still felt that encounter with books could be redemptive, not benign or critical books but revelatory or prophetic ones. As secretary of education in the early 1920s he distributed Homer, Plato, Dante, Cervantes, Goethe and a dozen more classics in tens of thousands of copies to Mexican schools. In his turbulent public life he sought to incarnate his own mystical ideal, not to project it intellectually. He called himself a Tolstoyan Christian; Krauze calls him a creole Plotinus.[134]

---

[134] Enrique Krauze, 'Pasión y contemplación de Vasconcelos', *Vuelta,* 78 (1983), 12–19 and 79 (1983), 16–26; see also John H. Haddox, *Vasconcelos of Mexico: Philosopher and Prophet* (Austin, Tex., 1967). For other patriarchs, see Jack Himelblau, *Alejandro O. Deústua: Philosophy in Defense of Man* (Gainesville, Fla., 1979); Medardo Vitier on Varona in *La filosofía en Cuba* (Mexico, D.F., 1948), ch. 11; Enrique Krauze, 'Antonio Caso: el filósofo como héroe', *Revista de la Universidad de México,* 39 (nueva época), 29 (1983), 2–10; Solomon Lipp on Korn in *Three Argentine Thinkers* (New York, 1969), ch. 3; Lipp on Molina in *Three Chilean Thinkers,* pp. 101–41; Sylvio Rabello, *Farias Brito, ou uma aventura do espírito,* 2nd ed. (Rio de Janeiro, 1967).

The transition from the patriarchs, who devised personal versions of the philosophic enterprise, to the shapers, who erected consciously American foundations for it, was orientated by trends of largely Germanic origin, particularly phenomenology and existentialism, often filtered via France or via Ortega y Gasset and the Spaniards. German thought might from the start have been a source of creative energy for Latin America when we recall that Germany was in a sense, as we have said, the world's first 'underdeveloped' country, that its intelligentsia rejected the brittle pansophism of the Enlightenment, and that German thought was, by the dawn of the nineteenth century, probing more deeply than French and English into nationhood, ethnicity, culture, religion and historical process.[135] Latin America, however, received only echoes of this tradition through the eclecticism of Cousin, the anti-positivism of Krausism that caught hold in Spain, the Hegelian precepts that appealed to Cubans for justifying self-rule, the 'Germanist' school of Recife and Sergipe in Brazil, or finally, by the century's end, retailed versions of revisionist Marxism.[136]

The reception of Spengler's *Decline of the West* (1918–22) signalized the Germanizing of Latin American thought. Proof of European 'decadence' was precisely what Latin Americans needed to break loose from intellectual mimicry and to explore what cultural assertion at the periphery might now involve. By treating Europe as a world culture in decline, Spengler legitimized newly emergent cultures. Yet while his historical pronouncements might illuminate discrete New World situations, such as the Argentina of Martínez Estrada or the Andean realm of Victor Raúl Haya de la Torre, they failed to yield foundations for comprehensive, self-consistent philosophy. These larger guideposts arrived in two stages. First came the neo-Kantian, idealist reaction to positivism of the Marburg school, which began in Germany in the 1870s and reached Latin America in the early twentieth century. The second, decisive influence made swifter transit, arriving by the end of the First World War. This was a return to metaphysics featuring the philosophy of culture, the theory of values, and existentialism, all grouped around phenomenology, taken less as a philosophy than a movement.

Phenomenology poses large challenges to the historian of ideas in Latin America. On one hand, it was a shaping influence on existentialism and

---

[135] Cf. Marshall Berman, *All That is Solid Melts into Air* (New York, 1982), part I.
[136] See Leopoldo Zea, 'Alemania en la cultura hispanoamericana', in *Esquema para una historia de las ideas en Iberoamérica* (Mexico, D.F., 1956), pp. 59–89; João Cruz Costa, *Contribuição á história das idéias no Brasil* (Rio de Janeiro, 1956), pp. 296–330.

on the perspectivism of Ortega y Gasset which by the 1940s were in wide ascendency in Latin America. On the other hand, phenomenology, both in the seminal writings of Edmund Husserl (1859–1938) and in extensive commentaries, is abstract, technical and almost bereft of illustration and analogies. Yet despite its eclipse by Marxism by the 1960s there were signs that phenomenology had influenced the case of Latin American thought. What follows is an attempt to suggest how the phenomenological outlook met ingrained habits of thought and conjunctural needs of the moment. [137]

First of all, phenomenology does not deal with concrete 'phenomena' or sheer facts but with the essence of things conceived apart from their existence. For the phenomenologist empiricism is not a philosophical pursuit, nor does he draw on the special sciences. He is no more concerned to marshall evidence for his findings than is the geometer to demonstrate the reality of a triangle. To non-philosophical sciences phenomenology ascribes a 'natural' or naive attitude that assumes an explainable world existing outside the consciousness of the subject. The mind roams at will through the world, dividing it into fields of inquiry, extracting laws or regularities. This naive attitude rests on canonical postulates while philosophy, Husserl insisted, requires a 'radical' attitude that dismisses all presuppositions. Philosophy is, in this sense, more rigorous than science. Descartes was a persuasive mentor becuase he had deduced scientific method from the single postulate of the *cogito*. Husserl eliminated even this postulate by assimilating the mind to its *cogitata* from the start (his *Cartesian Meditations* appeared in 1931). Husserl demanded special intuition: not the emotional intuitionism of Bergson but a disciplined, 'eidetic' intuition that 'brackets' the world as naively seen, reduces it to essences (*eidos* — essence), and culminates in the *epoché,* or suspension of judgement.

Thus phenomenology fights on several fronts: against empiricism and scientism, against scepticism and relativism, against mysticism and traditional metaphysics. What it proposes is appropriation of pure consciousness, the living stream of experiences: a primal apperception that suspends

---

[137] A concise introduction to phenomenology is the article, 'Phenomenology', by Husserl himself in the fourteenth edition of the *Encyclopaedia Britannica* (1929). A good anthology is Joseph J. Kockelmans (ed.), *Phenomenology: The Philosophy of Edmund Husserl and its Interpretation* (Garden City, N.Y., 1967); it provides keys to Husserl's thought, shows implications for human sciences, and traces the transition to existential phenomenology in writings by and about Heidegger, Sartre, and Merleau-Ponty. For phenomenology in Latin American legal thought, see Josef L. Kunz, *La filosofía del derecho latinoamericano en el siglo XX* (Buenos Aires, 1951), ch. 8 and Luis Recaséns Siches et al., *Latin American Legal Philosophy* (Cambridge, Eng., 1948).

the categories of subjective and objective and must undergird common sense and scientific inquiry. Four aspects of this 'radical' attitude concern the cultural historian. First, fusion of mind and object means that consciousness is consciousness-of-something: not a relation between mind and object but an act that confers meaning. In other words, consciousness is governed by intentionality, a neo-scholastic term that Husserl took from his mentor, Franz Brentano. The conscious process already harbours an intentional correspondence to objects. A second corollary is intersubjectivity. Because the world is available to everyone, the possibility of solipsism vanishes. Cultural objects, for example, refer back to the intentions that comprise them. Representations of the world cohere in mutual participation; the world coalesces where experiences intersect. Minds are thus unified, making subjectivity inseparable from inter-subjectivity.

In the third place, phenomenology neither pursues preexisting truths nor aspires to construct a system. Rather, the epoché immerses the conscious ego in the flux of experience. That is to say, it suspends awareness of what does or does not exist to reveal the world as a correlate of consciousness. Like art, philosophy thus conceived brings truth into being through attentiveness and wonder. Its task is not progressive construction but ever-renewed parturition or experiment, given that complete 'reduction' or epoché is unattainable. Finally, there are implications for history. There is, for phenomenology, no Hegelian Idea or evolutionary law to be unveiled. Instead, an ego renders the social world as a circumference of alter egos — past, present, and future — for whom living space is not a geographical notion but a home, and language not a grammatical system but a vehicle of intentions. Human situations are not resultants of ideological or economic forces but constellations of shared, intentional behaviour toward nature, time and death. If Marx said that history does not walk on its head, neither, Merleau-Ponty reminds us, does it think with its feet. Phenomenology addressed the body *in toto,* not its extremities. From this follows a concern with historicity, or the ceaseless interplay between cultural tradition and the activity of participants that yields its sediment.

We may assess the significance of phenomenological thought for Latin America on two planes. First, it is in some respects consistent with the venerable neo-scholastic heritage of the Iberian world. The notion of intentionality, derived from Aristotle, softens the hard, self-sufficient world of science, while the comprehensive reach of phenomenology, from a self-given or presuppositionless foundation, echoes the claim of Catholic thought to universalism and self-legitimation. Positivism too had appealed as an inclusive system: yet phenomenology, while claiming even greater procedural rigour, lacks the evolutionary implication that classed Latin America at an inferior stage of 'development'. In the second place, phenomenology met conjunctural needs. Its historicism legitimized the *pensadores'* search for identity and supported the vague but persistent notion of a Latin American civilization. Moreover, its 'aestheticism' struck a chord with an important domestic concern (cf. José Vasconcelos, *Monismo estético*, 1918; Brazil's J. P. da Graça Aranha, *A estética da vida*, 1921; Alejandro Deústua, *Estética general*, 1923; Antonio Caso, *Principios de estética*, 1925; Samuel Ramos, *Filosofía de la vida artística,*1950). The conception of art or constant parturition relieved the sense of unilateral dependence on metropolitan intellectual authority.

The brand of existentialism that spread in Latin America derived from phenomenology through the early Heidegger, Sartre and Merleau-Ponty. Although there are affinities between the two, distinctions are possible. Existentialism has no pretension to systematic rigour; its subject matter is human existence, not consciousness; it rejects Husserl's eidetic reduction that suspends the naive attitudes of the special sciences; and, instead of justifying beliefs by intuitive perception, it aspires to awaken adherents to a special way of life or 'authentic existence'.[138] For the cultural historian, however, the significance of both modes of thought for Latin America bears strong similarities.

For understanding how and why existential phenomenology was internalized in the Ibero Atlantic world and not simply received as an 'influence', the pivotal figure is José Ortega y Gasset (1883–1955).[139] His importance has little to do with his pronouncements on Latin America, which were relatively few, nor with the controversial question of his originality as a philosopher. Partisans of Unamuno scored their point in likening him to Charles, the Spanish ruler who was First of Spain and Fifth of Germany. Our interest in Ortega here is that at the outset of his career he saw Spain's ambivalence toward European modernization to require philosophic explication, not economic or political recipes. His use of German thought was crafted to this end. His sources and findings were diffused in his *Meditaciones del Quijote* (1914) and later via the *Revista de Occidente* (1923–

---

[138] Herbert Spiegelberg, 'Husserl's Phenomenology and Sartre's Existentialism', in Kockelmans, *Phenomenology*, pp. 252–66.

[139] For the formation of Ortega's thought: Julian Marías, *José Ortega y Gasset: Circumstance and Vocation*, trans. Frances M. López-Morillas (Norman, Okla. 1979); Philip W. Silver, *Ortega as Phenomenologist: The Genesis of 'Meditations on Quixote'* (New York, 1978); Fernando Salmerón, *Las mocedades de Ortega y Gasset,* 3rd ed. (Mexico, D.F., 1983).

36) and his disciples who emigrated to Latin America after 1936. For Latin Americans who recognized their situation as analogous to that of the Iberian peninsula, Ortega demonstrated uses of philosophic thought which, at face value, seemed amorphous and unanchorable. What he attempted was, in effect, to link the psycho-historical specificity of a Martín Luis Guzmán to the inclusive Western humanism of an Alfonso Reyes.

It is loosely said that while Miguel de Unamuno (1864–1936) urged the Hispanization of Europe, Ortega preached the Europeanization of Spain. The simplification is considerable. Ortega felt that to become truly a Spaniard, to understand Spain, meant becoming a technical philosopher. This would produce a fresh European philosophy with unexpected Spanish accents. To shut the windows, to resort to Spanish mysticism, could only prolong the 'Tibetanization' of Spain. The country would remain a cistern, a repository of European flotsam, and not become a spring, or source of interpretation. Assimilating European *ciencia* (science) was not to 'catch up' but to overcome *inconsciencia,* or unconsciousness of one's own history.

Ortega was aware of the implications of his thought for Latin America and once told Alfonso Reyes that he would enjoy being known as Ortega 'the American' in the style of Scipio 'Africanus'. Ortega visited only Argentina, however, and resisted involvement with the rest of America. His essays on that country assimilated it to the hemispheric case and to the Hegelian notion that the Americas as a whole, Argentina and the United States alike, were primitive and immature.[140] When it came to the New World he spoke not as a Spaniard but also as a European. He was Ortega Americanus *malgré lui,* not because of his American writings (which were not without insight) but in spite of them. Ortega's lesson for America lay in his 'perspectivism' or 'circumstantial thinking' which bore traces of phenomenology but was far from a replica. Indeed, Ortega's German education had been at Marburg under the influence of Hermann Cohen, Paul Natorp, and pre-Husserlian neo-Kantianism. It was only in 1913, three years after his return to Madrid, that two disparate books were published to wrench him into intellectual maturity. One was Husserl's *Ideas,* which struck him by its innovative method but straightaway impelled him to go farther. He later wrote that he emerged from phenomenology without having entered it and that 'phenomenology was not a philoso-

[140] Zea, 'Ortega el americano' in *Esquema,* pp. 93–120. See Ortega's essays, 'Hégel y América', 'La pampa . . . promesas', and 'El hombre a la defensiva' in Vol. 7 of *El espectador* (Madrid, 1929), pp. 11–21, 193–264. Also Peter G. Earle, 'Ortega y Gasset in Argentina: The exasperating colony', *Hispania,* 70, 3 (1987), 475–86.

phy for us' but 'a piece of good luck'. The other book was Unamuno's *Tragic Sense of Life*, whose shocking imagery and 'palpable hits' in demonstrating the opposition between reason and life disclosed still vital mainsprings of Spanish thought. Ortega now accepted to strike out alone without support from his own generation.

Discussion of Ortega's perspectivism commences with his pronouncement that 'I am I and my circumstance, and if I do not save it, I do not save myself.' The two initial I's are the clue. The first designates a personal, internal reality that is not of the senses. The second 'I' is a dynamic part of circumstance. In contrast to Husserl's 'surrounding world' (*Unwelt*), Ortega's 'circumstance' contains the human organism as an ingredient. He thus disallows both subjectivism, which leads to the sceptical position that truth cannot exist if the only viewpoint is individual, and rationalism, which holds that because truth exists it requires a supra-individual viewpoint. Nor does Ortega accept Husserl's reduction, for by bracketing reality it suspends the 'natural attitude', or *living* perception, and turns to contemplate perception itself. Ortega asks that each person contribute his own irreplaceable truth, that he not adopt an imaginary retina. There *is* a reality, but a profound one from which appearances spring, not the 'laminated' reality of positivism that reflects surfaces. The latent, true reality is offered only in perspectives. The issue, then, is not the 'destiny of man' but concrete destinies requiring reabsorption of circumstance, humanization of life and conversion of the world 'out there' into a true, personal world. Later Ortega was to deride the existentialism of Parisian boulevards for the 'gratuitous' choice it imposed. One's fate, one's tragic fate – he believed – was proposed, not imposed. One cannot choose one's fate; one chooses whether to be faithful to it.

While the generation of the patriarchs might acknowledge the new Husserlian and Orteguian currents, they were not positioned to give them understanding reception. In 1934 Alfonso Caso bravely produced a book on the philosophy of Husserl, whom he praised for vindicating the role of intuition in apprehending essences. The book was perhaps his weakest effort, for 'it is really Bergson whom he understands, not Husserl'.[141] In 1939 Alfonso Reyes, who bore something of the relation to contemporary Europe that a Renaissance humanist bore to seventeenth-century philosophy, wrote an appreciative essay on Alejandro Korn and his disciple, Francisco Romero, yet disparaged the German sources that shaped the

---

[141] Patrick Romanell, *Making of the Mexican Mind* (Lincoln, Nebr., 1952), p. 83.

passage between the two. From his humanist outlook he dismissed Scheler and Heidegger and regarded Husserl's phenomenology as a flickering spark that cast no light.[142] What follows starts with the transition from Korn (an exemplary patriarch) to Romero (an exemplary *forjador*), then examines the pedagogic and philosophic contributions of the Spanish *transterrado*, José Gaos, and his Mexican disciple Leopoldo Zea. These representative cases illustrate – far from exhaustively – the disciplinary ripening and mutual engagement of intellectual abstraction and self-given *realidad*.

Alejandro Korn (1860–1936) was a 'patriarch' not so much for his writings, which never reached achieved form, as for his public life, teaching and example of a mind at work.[143] His gift was wholeness of understanding. He saw no split between technical philosophy and social conscience or between foreign influence and domestic intelligence. For him philosophy was not airy speculation nor assimilation of exotic theories but congruent expression of mental attitude. Korn is often lumped with Latin American anti-positivists, but as Francisco Romero has said, he experienced on his own the European philosophic renovation: 'not an echo but a correspondence'. Nor did he accept conventional charts of periods and influences. The *Bases* (1852) of Juan Bautista Alberdi, if they came with English utilitarianism and economic determinism, he affirmed to provide a sturdy positivist foundation that anticipated Comte, Spencer and even elements of Marx while being consonant with the needs of Argentina. Alberdi's synthesis served three generations. The task at hand, Korn felt, was not to discredit Alberdi's argument but to imitate his genius in identifying durable bases for synthesis under changed conditions. If, for example, creation of wealth had preoccupied Alberdi, the current challenge was distribution. But unlike the facile interpreters of 'national character', he did not mechanically apply world thinkers to the national case. He conflated the particular and the general. The chairs he held were ethics, metaphysics, gnosiology and history of philosophy, while his centre, founded in 1929, was not a 'centre for studying Argentine Reality' but the Kantian Society of Buenos Aires. Faithful to Miró Quesada's 'recuperación anabásica', he recapitulated European philosophy since the Greeks.

[142] Alfonso Reyes, 'Korn y la filosofía argentina', in *Obras completas*, Vol. 9 (Mexico, D.F., 1959), pp. 166–71.

[143] Alejandro Korn, *El pensamiento argentino* (Buenos Aires, 1961), pp. 233–60. (The 1983 edition bears the original 1936 title, *Influencias filosóficas en la evolución nacional*.) See also Francisco Romero et al., *Alejandro Korn* (Buenos Aires, 1940); Lipp, *Argentine Thinkers*, ch. 3.

Korn's concern was that the scientific pretension of positivism was too restrictive for current needs. He thought science to be an ordering of partial and abstract features of reality. Philosophy on the other hand should address how values are distilled, in biological, social and cultural clusters, from the promptings of single persons. The cornerstone of philosophy is axiology, opposing subjectivity to the objectivity of science. Because universal values are illusory, they must be rooted in the autonomy of human personality which, unlike science, can assess the circumstantial value of real objects; they must bend before the normative conscience. Metaphysics, traditionally linked to philosophy, becomes an independent exploration of the unknown, a necessary but impossible venture that is never satisfied but can reveal contradictory aspects of reality and make us conscious of our power and impotence. Korn, in sum, orchestrates science and metaphysics to axiology, freedom, and ultimate arbitration by human beings.

These premises, rooted both in Argentine needs and in the course of Western philosophy, gave Korn his Ockham's razor for testing winds of change from wherever they might blow. As for his compatriots, José Ingenieros (1877–1925), he felt, fought to rescue positivism by intellectual fireworks without abandoning scientistic dogmatism, while Ricardo Rojas (1882–1957) urged a 'nationalist restoration' considered not as nostalgia for past glories but as palingenesis of peoples' inborn energies. For him, a more coherent contribution was that of Juan B. Justo (1865–1928), who translated Marx and founded the Socialist Party. Argentine socialists recognized, Korn believed, that the social problem was less economic than ethical, while beneath their profession of Marxism lay the influence of Le Play, Schmoller and Leo XIII. This outlook was therapy for the pragmatic persuasion that converted conscience to a biological function, excluded *telos* from the cosmic process, and gave ethics a utilitarian cast.

Korn's Argentine concerns shaped his views on Western philosophic currents and made him impatient with mere fads. He deplored Spengler's *payasadas* (clowning) that allowed positivists to give a mystical cast to scientific determinism. Without denigrating the psychiatric research of Freud, he charged him with having reinvented the wheel of sexuality, constructed long ago by Plato, Pascal and Darwin. He mistrusted Keyserling's introduction of the oriental comparison with its 'esoteric penumbra'. 'The voyage to the Orient is fruitful providing one returns.'

He was more dismissive of Jamesian pragmatism than were his contemporaries Enrique Molina (Chile) and Carlos Vaz Ferreira (Uruguay). Yet the country of Emerson, Josiah Royce and Dewey was certain to chart a lofty path: 'For now it's imperative to find philosophic inspiration there.' Bergson was a decisive influence for having opened free space within determinism; yet Korn was disappointed that he had neither implanted a theoretical base nor produced an ethics. Croce was appealing mainly for his spirited attacks on scientism and rationalism.

The German tradition Korn spoke of with more deference and less assurance. His contemporaries, he wrote, paid homage to Kant, still regarded as 'influential', supposing him to be a nebulous metaphysician (even though Kant had demolished rational metaphysics) and unaware that German philosophy was a string of revolts against Kant. We have not heard, Korn remonstrated, that the up-to-date philosophy in Germany is the latest attack against the great thinker; we do not know what, after all this, is left standing. As of 1927 it was hard to detect a dominant German trend or genial figure. Dilthey appealed most to Korn but was still 'an unknown savant.' He liked Rickert's work on the limits of science but not his theory of values. He was attracted to the German Catholic tradition that challenged the dominant Protestant culture but felt unprepared to navigate the waters of modern German philosophy: 'only my friend Francisco Romero I feel can move with ease in this labyrinth.' As for himself, he found academic philosophy insipid. To commune with high German culture still meant turning to Kant and Goethe. 'The last German philosopher is Nietzsche', wrote Korn. 'He gave philosophy its axiological orientation.'[144]

Francisco Romero (1891–1962), who met Korn in 1923 and became an informal disciple, fulfilled the mentor's expectation that he would master the abstruse German contribution. Like Korn he addressed the state of philosophy in Latin America, the task of *recuperación anabásica,* and his duties as teacher and intellectual publicist but also managed to make contributions, notably his *Teoría del hombre* (1952), that were fully ripened. If Korn won continental recognition as an exemplary foe of positivism, Romero won acclaim as the dean of Latin American philosophers or, in Miró Quesada's view, the leader of the *generación forjadora.* His reputation rests on his having advanced and unified the explorations of Korn,

---

[144] Risieri Frondizi, Korn's compatriot, reexamined axiology in *What is Value?, An Introduction to Axiology,* trans. Solomon Lipp (Lasalle, Ill., 1963).

with firmer grounding in contemporary, especially German, thought and greater aptitude for synthesis.[145]

Romero assumes from the start that a Latin American contemplates European philosophy from a vast amphitheatre; whatever his intellectual limitations, they do not include the blinkers of regionalism and dogmatism. Here time lies open no less than space. The certainties of the positivist, Darwinist, nationalist age had crumbled. The modern age was one of psychological insecurity at both the centre and the rim of 'civilization'. For all alike, the future stretches indiscernibly ahead. To penetrate that future takes us to history, not as deterministic schema nor as blind flux nor as haphazard relativism but via 'ontological historicism' that assumes consciousness of the past for reconceiving the present. To demonstrate historicity Romero offers the metaphor of a river whose waters may flow peaceably along its bed or nearly dry up or overflow into adjacent canals or flood to convert the whole valley into its bed; or finally its surface may freeze leaving the liquid mass to flow silently beneath. Similarly history, although channelled by the inner nature of man, may at times seem to flow of its own accord. Microvisions supplement the panoramic one. 'Man seems wrapped in a subtle medium that is his conception of the world', not as conscious knowledge but as something lived, immediate, or almost unconscious.[146] A race, an epoch, a people each has a world view, as do social classes, human types, single persons; and these are often juxtaposed and blended. From this premise Latin Americans can claim partnership in the work of philosophic reconstruction.

A key to Romero's thinking, as for Husserl's, is intentionality. In its modern use this scholastic term has two general meanings: first, it designates ascent from the animal level, where the world is experienced passively as engulfing the subject, to an intentional level where man converts his amorphous milieu into defined objects that provoke reaction. Secondly, it designates the transition from associationist psychology, which explains mental life as a mix of impressions derived from sense experience, to consciousness of a subject-object relationship that involves the ego with the world as participant. To this Romero adds a further division. First is the self-centred intentionality of the *psyche* prevailing over the *individual;* sec-

---

[145] Born in Spain, Romero came to Argentina in 1904. Important here are his *Filosofía contemporánea*, 3rd ed. (Buenos Aires, 1953), *Papeles para una filosofía* (Buenos Aires, 1945), *El hombre y la cultura* (Buenos Aires, 1950), *Sobre la filosofía en América* (Buenos Aires, 1952), and *Teoría del hombre*, 2nd ed. (Buenos Aires, 1958) (*Theory of Man*, trans. William F. Cooper (Berkeley, 1964)). For discussions see Lipp, *Argentine Thinkers*, ch. 4, and Miró Quesada, *Despertar*, chs. 5, 6.

[146] Romero, *Filosofía contemporánea*, pp. 130–31.

ond is the 'disinterested' interest (or *spirit*) that seeks correspondence between human energy (the *person*) and value itself, thus projecting intentionality toward the objective and universal. This signifies a distinction
between immanence, or enclosure in a particular reality, and transcendence,
a spilling over of the self yet without abandoning the original centre. For
Romero, the early modern religio-philosophic revolution (Luther, Descartes, Hobbes) implanted immanentism by making the individual the sole
depository of knowledge, belief, and sovereignty. This atomizing of the
medieval heritage was arrested by the romanticist inspiration of the nineteenth century, a corrective renewal for philosophy in the early decades of
the twentieth. In the socio-political realm, however, Romero felt the crisis
still to be acute, as evidenced by his pathology of the leading traits of
Western culture: intellectualism, activism and individualism.[147]

Romero closed *Teoría del hombre* by applying intentionality and transcendence to what he considered the three major world cultures which above
all others possess dignity and universality and confer on man a sense of
destiny: India, China and the West. (Jewish culture he regarded as inseparable from Western.) The substrate of Indian culture he took as the
undivided whole from which all beings arise, making private existence a
passing instance that finds meaning only as it merges with the universal.
Indian culture is non-temporal, disvaluing time. Central to classical Chinese culture is the social complex, a family with infinite predecessors,
governed by ancestors and sanctified as the nexus with the supernatural.
This culture is 'eternalist', paralysing time in the shadow of an ancestral
past. Alone of the three, Western culture possesses historicity and allies
with time in its 'throbbing consecutiveness' to achieve demands of the
spirit. Whatever it may learn from others, it alone rescues the individual
from realities that surpass him and seem to overflow with meaning. If
citizens of other cultures abandon theirs to join ours, it is because the
West, whatever its stains and crimes, alone acknowledges what is genuine
in single beings. The others deny the historicity of man as a self that is
strengthened and purified in the spiritual quest for universality. Man is
born when he confers objectivity on the world through judgement; other
cultures disparage and even annul the privilege of judging.[148]

One of Romero's uses for philosophy, then, particularly its modern

---

[147] Romero, *Teoría del hombre*, chs. 6, 7; Lipp, *Argentine Thinkers*, pp. 114–16, 122–25, 138–45;
Miró Quesada, *Despertar*, pp. 147–53.

[148] Romero, *Teoría del hombre*, ch. 12; also his chapter 'Temporalismo', in *Filosofía contemporánea*, pp.
25–49.

German variants, was to map the broad lineaments of world cultures. In so doing he smoothly assimilated the Latin American tradition (as he had the Jewish) to Western culture, and although he kept abreast of Latin American currents, he made no heroic attempt to develop a cultural category for them. Or perhaps he did so by implication when, as discussed above, he praised the philosophic achievement of contemporary Europe but detected crisis in the socio-political realm, where he found intellect unsupportive of values, activism lacking a mission, and individualism frustrated by inadequate political organization. In addressing Latin America one surmises that instead of enquiring into local 'identity' he was asking how a subculture might, from unique resources, contribute to therapy for the whole.

There were literati of Romero's approximate generation who addressed directly the question of Argentine 'identity', sometimes in the context of a larger America, such as Ricardo Rojas or Eduardo Mallea, and sometimes taking cues from contemporary philosophy, such as Martínez Estrada, Carlos Alberto Erro, or the Spanish maestro himself, Ortega y Gasset, in a few casual sketches. Yet conditions were not propitious for assimilating identity to a canon of philosophic interpretation. First, Argentine identity swung within a multi-ideological political arena among the disparate poles of Amerindian origins, the Hispanic heritage and the diluvial immigration of modern times. Second, although there was no local dearth of philosophic talent, it lacked a roof under which to assemble for common endeavour (Romero in fact resigned all his academic positions in the Peronist years, 1946–55).

In Mexico circumstances were more favourable for Miró Quesada's awakening of the Latin American philosophic 'project'. Here the Revolution had struck roots, matured and seemingly translated the disparate hopes of the 1920s into a domestic cultural agenda. The muralists had apotheosized the Indian substrate of national culture, whose architectural monuments and ethnic descent were everywhere visible, while the influx of Italians, Central Europeans and Japanese to the South Atlantic zone had no parallel here. Doubts as to whether a 'revolution' had indeed occurred lay ahead. Two further factors enhanced philosophic receptivity in Mexico. The first was that the Revolution was premature to have absorbed the modernist élan. Older hands retained intellectual mentorship (Reyes, Caso, Vasconcelos and the slightly younger Samuel Ramos) and could adapt to new situations within the large philosophic vistas of an earlier period. The second was the exodus of Spanish intellectuals to Mexico in the late 1930s. They came with professional competence in arts, letters and sciences as well as sports and the mass media. Of the 20,000, or perhaps many more, exiles who arrived in Mexico, 650 appear in a roster of those with high professional accomplishment.[149] The anti-dictatorial politics of humanists and social scientists placed them to relegitimize the central Iberian component of Spanish American culture that had been so problematical, above all in Mexico, since independence. As Europeans, moreover, they could expand the question of transatlantic identity to its hemispheric dimension.

Although Spanish intellectuals and professionals were received throughout Spanish America, a critical mass came to Mexico, generally because of President Lázaro Cárdenas's policy of offering asylum to Spanish republicans and specifically through the efforts of Mexican scholars, conspicuously Alfonso Reyes and Daniel Cosío Villegas (1898–1976), to arrange accommodation for their Spanish colleagues. The Casa de España, founded in 1938, provided a base, transformed two years later into El Colegio de México. Here we limit ourselves to the consequences for philosophy in Mexico of the Spanish *hegira,* and, of the fifteen or twenty philosophers among the 650 professionals, we will focus on José Gaos, whose pedagogical genius and mentorship of the Hiperión group made him responsible, or at least a catalyst, for opening a new chapter in the exploration of 'identity'.

José Gaos y González Pola (1900–69) was born in Gijón, Spain. Unlike Francisco Romero, who came to Argentina as a youth and absorbed New World flexibilities, Gaos arrived in Mexico in 1938 with the full baggage of his European career. A disciple of Ortega and a militant in the Socialist Party, he became professor of philosophy at the Central University of Madrid in 1932 and rector in 1936. Memoirs by Mexican disciples and his own 'confesiones' convey something of his enigmatic character.[150] To start with an outrageous epithet, Uranga calls him, in the slang term from North American English, a 'jerk'. Far from a slur on Gaos's mental acuteness, this is an affectionate judgement by a salacious creole of his gachupín professor who had assumed the full weight of tradition and ancestral formal structures and had accepted his lot as condemnation. Gaos's father, he once told Uranga, had wished him to be a notary. 'And now you see me here as a professor. Am I in any way better off?' Resigned

[149] Salvador Reyes Nevares (ed.), *El exilio español en México, 1939–1982* (Mexico, D.F., 1982); José Luis Abellán, *Filosofía española en América (1936–1966)* (Madrid, 1967).
[150] José Gaos, *Confesiones personales* (Mexico, D.F., 1959); Emilio Uranga, *¿De quién es la filosofía?* (Mexico, D.F., 1977), pp. 177–223; Oswaldo Díaz Ruanova, *Los existencialistas mexicanos* (Mexico, D.F., 1982), pp. 103–54.

and sceptical, he seemed like a cameraman in the historical morgue of philosophers, empathizing with the specimens. He enviously congratulated anyone who abandoned philosophy, as when Marx boxed up Hegel's books and forgot them forever. A victim of congenital nihilism, his life was governed by regimen in his teaching, his voluminous writing and translating, his exercise (swimming), eating, loving and drinking. He much preferred Heidegger to Husserl but studied the latter assiduously to master the secrets of phenomenology. He had neither the spark of an original philosopher nor the literary fluency of a master essayist. He died as he had lived, in harness, presiding over a doctoral examination.

Wherein then lay the genius of Gaos? First, he was a magisterial lecturer. Second, he commanded every important philosopher and philosophic system since the Greeks. Third, he was implacable in his exegesis of philosophic texts. Fourth, his easy familiarity with Western philosophy, including contemporary versions, and his having wrestled with the Orteguian circumstances of a marginalized, 'retarded' Spain equipped him to fathom Mexican and American dilemmas at first glance. It was he who called the Spanish newcomers *transterrados* instead of refugees or exiles (*desterrados*) – i.e., transplaced, not displaced – for this 'morphological extension, this transcendence of Spain in America made him think that he had not been exiled but simply transported to another place in the same land that had watched him suffer'.[151] Finally, his scepticism and avoidance of systemic philosophizing left his disciples space for free speculation. They did not form a school (some rejected their mentor's German existentialism in favour of the French brand), but they *were* a group, who might consort with neo-Kantians but raised the hackles of neo-Thomists and neo-Marxists. Gaos's proselytes included such soon-to-be recognized Mexican philosophers and intellectual historians as Luis Villoro, Rafael Moreno, Pablo González Casanova, Francisco López Cámara, Edmundo O'Gorman, Bernabé Navarro and José Luis Martínez; the Peruvian philosopher Augusto Salazar Bondy and the Puerto Rican historian Monelisa Lina Pérez-Marchand. In striving to meet the interests of his students Gaos desisted in seminars from directly addressing Mexican autognosis or identity but dropped back to the eighteenth century, to the critical moment of the Enlightenment impingement, when foreign ideas no longer came from without in the heads of immigrants or visitors but from within in the

---

151 Uranga, *¿De quién?*, p. 190; also José Gaos, 'Los "transterrados" españoles de la filosofía en México', in his *Filosofía mexicana de nuestros días* (Mexico, D.F., 1954), pp. 287–323.

heads of native importers. One case favoured a colonial outlook, the other an impulse of independence and national personality.[152] Some years later economists would propose an analogous contrast, for a subsequent period, between development from without and development from within.

The purpose of this section has not been to review the discipline of philosophy as practised in Latin America but to highlight practitioners whose training assisted them to lay foundations and shape an agenda for the 'identity' question, whether in national or in continental terms. At this point the achievement of Leopoldo Zea (1912– ) deserves special attention as the favoured disciple of Gaos, who remarked that if Zea had not existed Gaos would have had to invent him to justify himself as a professor.[153] Others of Zea's peers may have made more ingenious speculative flights, but it is Zea who devoted his life to developing underpinnings for the ideological and political quest for Latin American self-awareness and autonomy. Because of his unpretentious, often didactic language, his largely tactical use of philosophic luminaries, and his concern with historical matrix, philosophers on the 'cutting edge' tend to belittle his conceptual acumen. On the other hand, North American historians, as *soi-disant* empiricists, chide him for not being exhaustive and even-handed in tracing intellectual trends of the last century and for allowing his vision of the future to skew his account of the past. Finally, activists who commend his argument for 'liberation' (mental, political, economic) fault him for lacking engagement and specificity. Zea can be accused, that is, of failing to see the forest for the trees, of failing to see the trees for the forest, and of failing to convert the forest into ridgepoles and rafters. To the purists he would respond that he uses Hegel as a source of ideas, not a text for exegesis. He reminds the historians that empirical dismemberment of history impedes (sometimes purposely) ideological reconstruction. To activists the answer is that the task of recovering half a millennium of hemispheric history differs from crafting instrumental prescriptions for time and place.

Zea staked his claims with his influential books on Mexican positivism (1943–4), which provided scaffolding for his subsequent study (1949) of the 'two stages' of nineteenth-century Spanish American thought. In them he formulated premises for extending his analysis to the Americas, to the

---

[152] 'Lo mexicano en filosofía', in Gaos, 'Los "transterrados" ', pp. 325–57.

[153] See Miró Quesada, *Proyecto y realización del filosofar latino-americano,* pp. 141–83; Tzvi Medin, *Leopoldo Zea: ideología, historia y filosofía de América Latina* (Mexico, D.F., 1983); Solomon Lipp, *Leopoldo Zea: From Mexicanidad to a Philosophy of History* (Waterloo, Ont., 1980).

West, and finally to the world. Despite later shifts in perspective and intellectual sources, Zea has been in Isaiah Berlin's terms a hedgehog, not a fox. The two points of departure for his unified mission are interlocked. First was his general attraction to the themes of historicism and liberation, for which he found elements in his highly selective use of Hegel, Ortega, Scheler, and Mannheim as well as Vico and Croce, with an early, somewhat fortuitous existentialist (largely Sartrian) parenthesis. Hegel and his notion of a *reality* to be *realized* remained important although with Zea's proviso that 'I back off from Hegel the moment he deifies the spirit'. The ancillary point was his division of Latin American thought into the two stages of romanticism and positivism. For Europeans this was a natural split, but it had not yet been applied systematically to Latin America. Moreover, the point of Zea's transplacement of the 'two stages' from Europe to America was not to certify the 'mental emancipation' of Latin America (a term he used somewhat ironically) from the scholastic and authoritarian proclivities of the colonial centuries but to demonstrate that Latin Americans could not, by faddish importations, deny their unassimilated past. Here was his Hegelian inspiration: a dialectical capacity to assimilate and not deny or eliminate the past, without which history becomes serial repetition. These two points – historicism, or recognition of a given people's inescapable immersion in history, and liberation, or the assimilation or 'digestion' of history – laid a foundation for his global adventures in ideology.

Because Zea's ideas had structure, breadth and flexibility, and reflected the temper of the times, he was able to mount a series of undertakings in the late 1940s and early 1950s having hemispheric projection. He founded the Hiperión group dedicated to identifying the logic of Mexican history from the premises of existential phenomenology and including such promising figures as Emilio Uranga, Jorge Portilla, Joaquín Sánchez MacGregor and Luis Villoro. This initiative led Zea to organize a series of short, widely read books on *México y lo mexicano* whose authors included mentors such as Alfonso Reyes, José Gaos, Silvio Zavala and Samuel Ramos and other Spanish Americans such as Mariano Picón Salas (1901–65) and Rafael Heliodoro Valle (1891–1959). Beyond this Zea began identifying intellectual historians throughout Latin America whose contributions would expand the search for authentic history to continental scope. Published in the Tierra Firme collection of the Fondo de Cultura Económica, the volumes he solicited created a lasting benchmark for the history of ideas in America. Later came the founding of the

Co-ordinating Centre at the National University of Mexico for interconnecting Latin American studies programmes throughout the region. Such programmes, Zea recognized, were routine in metropolitan curricula but not in the region itself, thus denying it elements for a comprehensive view of the subject.

In the 1960s the configuration of Zea's ideas shifted somewhat. On the surface it seemed that he was accepting a 'Third World' diagnosis lifting the notions of dependency and liberation from a rejuvenated Marxism and from writings of Marcuse, Fanon and even Che Guevara. He was not, however, echoing the *dernier cri*. The two now consecrated watchwords he had already treated explicitly in the introduction ('Sentimiento de dependencia') and first section ('La emancipación mental') of *Dos etapas del pensamiento en Hispanoamérica* (1949). He in fact held close to his original course, although conflating his search for Latin American identity with that for a philosophy pure and simple of man wherever he exists. In this his trajectory was close to that of Brazil's Mário de Andrade who, from grounding in folklore, popular music, ethnology, psychology and literature, had worked toward the universal from knowledge of Brazil and its regional fragments. Zea's base, in contrast, was philosophical, extending far beyond the purview of technical concerns but with little attention to the gambits of the burgeoning social sciences, to the visions of 'boom' novelists, or – as his critics insist – to details of microhistory.

Politically, Zea has held to a loose, relatively non-combative position that Medin calls 'nationalist, social, anti-imperialist neo-liberalism' in the most idealistic tradition of the Mexican Revolution. Any radicalism he may seem to endorse is tempered by humanism. His socialism means social justice, not abolition of private property. His liberty implies solidarity, a balance of sacrifice and benefit, radicalism within reformism. On one hand, he adheres to the finest flowering of Mexico's revolution. On the other hand, he remains alert to the grand dialectics of Hegel and Marx. If Hegel's history as dialectical liberation informs his analysis, however, he criticizes Hegel's Eurocentrism in defining the trajectory and beneficiaries of the Spirit. Similarly, in discussing Marxism he distinguishes between liberation of workers by their own promptings and effort, as a subject of history, and their external liberation by leaders and parties, as an object of history. This subject-object split applies also to his analysis of relations between the United States and Latin America or between the industrial world and the Third World. By Western calculus Latin America is still, as Hegel long ago declared it to be, prehistoric. For Zea, its only entry into history is by its own *toma de conciencia* a moral ideal and not a convergence of 'objective' interests. To be prisoner of the facts means to accept them. Because the will to change them is subjective, objectivity means for Zea the identification of subjective projects that converted history into 'reality'. Thus, paradoxically, objectivity creates a metahistory to supersede a 'real' history that can no longer continue and is therefore 'unreal'.

Why Zea runs afoul of orthodox historians is obvious. With fellow philosophers there are also problems, although again related to norms of a discipline. He has been charged, for example, with being a preacher and not a philosopher, with accepting the technically impoverished tradition of Caso, Vasconcelos and Ramos, and for not seeing that the force of philosophy lies in a neutrality that allows it to exercise the fierce weapon of Socratic criticism to unmask mystification. This professional critique focuses, however, on methods rather than on objectives. It seems excessive to demand that Zea practice Socratic deconstruction when his aim is to identify bases for nationhood in the tradition of Vico, Rousseau, Herder and Michelet.

In 1968–9 Zea began an exchange with the Peruvian philosopher Augusto Salazar Bondy (1927–74) that Cerutti calls 'one of the central links of current philosophic thought in Latin America'.[154] Both paid homage to their common mentor, José Gaos, and to his agenda for philosophy in Latin America.[155] Their arguments even overlap: both agreed that underdevelopment and external oppression had inhibited the flowering of philosophy in America. Both agreed on the derivative nature of domestic philosophizing, with Salazar Bondy however claiming that political and economic conditions were not suitable for 'originality' (fresh ideas and formulations) or for 'authenticity' (fidelity to circumstances at hand) – although he wavered on the second point. Zea replied that authentic philosophy is not a function of development. Developed and 'over-developed' countries, he argued, produce unauthentic philosophy in abundance when they universalize a vision of men who cannot recognize humanity in others, of liberty understood to apply only to a minority, and of a licence for violence justified by security and self-protection. 'Authenticity' can appear in any

[154] Augusto Salazar Bondy, *¿Existe una filosofía de nuestra América?*, 1968; 6th ed. (Mexico, D.F., 1979); Leopoldo Zea, *La filosofía americana como filosofía sin más*, 1969; 8th ed. (Mexico, D.F., 1980). Horacio Cerutti Guldberg traces the subsequent course of the debate in *Filosofía de la liberación latinoamericana* (Mexico, D.F., 1983), pp. 161–8.

[155] Cf. Gaos, *Pensamiento de lengua española* and *En torno a la filosofía mexicana*, 2 vols. (Mexico, D.F., 1952–3).

setting. As for 'originality', Zea insists that his previous explorations into *lo mexicano* and *lo americano* were not attempts to regionalize the philosophic enterprise but to use a favourable vantage point, given the narcissism of 'developed' countries, for constructing a philosophy 'for man wherever he be found.' He now advocated a philosophy of liberation that approached the universal via the Third World rather than in direct confrontation of *lo americano* with Europe.

In 1978 Zea gave his more recent formulations context by calling to mind three discredited historical projecs: the autochthonous *proyecto libertario* of Bolívar for a free union of American peoples, which soon collapsed with the unleashing of local power struggles; the conservative project, which sought to remedy chaos by restoring the colonial regime of order and social hierarchy; and the civilizing project, endorsed by Mora, Lastarria, Bilbao, Montalvo, Sarmiento and Alberdi, which pinned its hopes to positivist education, immigration and foreign investment, creating a pseudo-bourgeoisie subordinate to the West and rejecting historical roots and culture. Drawing on his personal brand of Hegelianism, Zea now asserts that the time has come for a new *proyecto asuntivo*, recognizing that the past can no longer be rejected but must be taken up or *assumed*.[156] Once assumed, or absorbed, it is then transcended and can be selectively negated in dialectical fashion, or affirmative negation. For this project Zea's disparate precursors include Bello, Simón Rodríguez, Bilbao, Rodó, Vasconcelos, González Prada, Reyes and Ugarte, but above all Martí, who most clearly defines a project of liberation to reinvigorate the Bolivarian ideal.

Throughout the period of the Cold War, Zea strongly resisted accepting the ideological dichotomization of the world. Whatever the perils and perplexities of the post-Cold War era that has dawned, it at least strengthens the basis for the ecumenical outlook that he has so fervently advocated across the decades. Moreover, the less structured, less predictable character of the current world scene may offer richer possibilities for intellectual transactions between the realms of speculative philosophy and political engagement.

## TWO REALITIES: SOCIOLOGICAL AND MARVELLOUS

The deceptively sequential treatment of modernism → naturalism/essayism → philosophy now leads to the apotheosis of social science in

---

[156] Leopoldo Zea, *Filosofía de la historia americana* (Mexico, D.F., 1978), pp. 269–94. Also Zea, *The Role of the Americas in History*, trans. Sonja Karsen (Lanham, MD, 1991).

university curricula and of the Latin American novel (or more cautiously,
narrative) for international readership. These coincident phenomena of the
late 1950s and 1960s objectified a tension detectable in writings of an
earlier period. Mariátegui, for example, was, in his own way, a Marxist
and economic determinist yet took inspiration from surrealism and even
the young Borges; Price-Mars, schooled in Paris in medicine and social
science, became the apostle of myth and voodoo as the substrate of Haitian
culture; the poet Martínez Estrada was deeply versed in historiography;
Fernando Ortiz, a painstaking ethnographer, found his mentor in a medieval Spanish poet-priest. What follows investigates the branching apart of
scientific and literary endeavour that was in some respects loosely joined.

The social science story centres on the career of sociology, social anthropology and aspects of history. (In the 1950s and 1960s São Paulo's so-called
'school of sociology' pioneered or rewrote whole sectors of the socio-
economic and political history of Brazil.) Just as philosophy had its 'patriarchs' so sociology had exemplary pioneers, such as Andrés Molina Enríquez
(Mexico, 1866–1940), Juan Agustín García (Argentina, 1862–1923), or
Alberto Torres (Brazil, 1865–1917). They were succeeded by a generation
of 'shapers' who as institution- and curriculum-builders tackled the chal-
lenges of theory and empiricism, pure and applied science, value-free sci-
ence and ideology, European derivation and Latin American innovation.[157]
The three names often identified as outstanding shapers are José Medina
Echavarría (1903–77), Gino Germani (1911–79), and Florestan Fernandes
(Brazil, b. 1920).[158] Two were, like Gaos, acculturated foreigners: Medina
Echavarría, who came from Spain to Mexico (1939–46), then went to
Puerto Rico (1946–52), and thereafter crowned his career in Chile; and
Germani from Italy who became head of the Institute of Sociology at the
University of Buenos Aires in 1955 and proceeded to put his stamp on the
modernization of sociology in Argentina with influence throughout the
Americas before capping his career at Harvard. Florestan Fernandes is ac-

[157] For case studies of the intellectual and institutional development of sociology since the mid-
nineteenth century, see José Joaquín Brunner, *El caso de la sociología en Chile: formación de una
disciplina* (Santiago, 1988); Juan Francisco Marsal, *La sociología en la Argentina* (Buenos Aires,
1963), and El Colegio de México, *Ciencias sociales en México* (Mexico, D.F., 1979). A special
number of *Revista Paraguaya de Sociología*, 11/30 (1974) includes four critical studies of sociology
in Latin America from c.1950 to the mid-1970s: Rolando Franco, 'Veinticinco años de sociología
latinoamericana', (pp. 57–92) and country studies by Manuel Villa Aguilera (Mexico), Eliseo
Verón (Argentina), and Carlos H. Filgueira (Uruguay).
[158] Joseph A. Kahl's study of Latin America's 'new sociology' focuses on Germani, Pablo González
Casanova (Mexico), and Fernando Henrique Cardoso (Brazil): *Modernization, Exploitation and Dependency in Latin America* (New Brunswick, N.J., 1976).

claimed as the founder of the 'Paulista school of sociology' (a term he disowns) which produced a loosely Marxist counter-statement (with functionalist accents) to the previously conservative tenor of Brazilian social analysis and opened the way to a fresh historiography. Fernandes's disciple, Fernando Henrique Cardoso, was important in linking the work of the Paulistas to the continent-wide enquiries sponsored under Medina Echavarría at the UN Latin American Institute of Economic and Social Planning (ILPES) in Santiago, a collaboration notably realized in *Dependencia y desarrollo en América Latina* (1968) by Cardoso and Chilean sociologist Enzo Faletto.[159]

Among Medina's abundant contributions, not so much to modernizing as to intellectualizing sociology in Latin America, are his two broad but concise synopses of the foundations of sociology and its role in Latin America: one on the theory and technique of sociology (1941) at the threshold of his Latin American career and the other on the sociology of Latin America economic development (1964) after he had edited the path-breaking sociology collection of the Fondo de Cultura Económica, directed the Centro de Estudios Sociales at the Colegio de México in the 1940s, and thereafter, in Chile, acquired a comprehensive vision of Latin America, thanks to his leadership role in the UN programme (CEPAL and ILPES) and the Latin American Social Sciences Faculty (FLACSO).[160] Grounded in wide knowledge of European, American and Latin American social thought and science against a mature philosophic background, Medina wrote in a spirit of critical sympathy without sectarian rancour, with respect for adjoining fields of inquiry, affirming sociology as an autonomous yet interdependent domain. However divergent the starting-points of Comte and Weber in physical science and in neo-Kantian historicism, they coincided, Medina held, in endorsing empirical science and method as applied to social data. A philosopher's destiny, Medina believed, was *concentration,* or addressing the integral social realm (*lo social*); the sociologist's was to handle *dispersion,* or the 'most fiercely concrete phenomena'. Yet if division of labour was proper for the sciences, any given problem should be examined as a whole. He even felt that subtle and complex 'secrets of the age' were best fathomed by Picasso, Miró or Klee.

Gino Germani sharply tilted the balance of influences and intellectual commitments that composed Medina's hopes for a scientific sociology.

[159] *Dependency and Development in Latin America*, trans. Marjory M. Urquidi (Berkeley, 1979).
[160] José Medina Echavarría, *Sociología: teoría y técnica,* 1941; 3rd ed. (Mexico, D.F., 1982); *Consideraciones sobre el desarrollo económico en América Latina* (Montevideo, 1964).

Although versed in German philosophy, he found its 'culturalist' or 'spiritualist' character that had flourished in Latin America earlier in the century to be quite indefensible. Former controversies over the discipline he dismissed as obsolete. By now, he argued, sociology was accepted as a 'positive' discipline, with empirical research conjoined with theory in a relationship expressible in concrete, operational terms. The social scientist no longer need rely on pre-existent data but could for certain purposes use experimental methods, given the technification, standardization, routinization and specialization of his profession. As befitted an industrial world, social research had graduated from artisanal to industrial methods, while schools of sociology were replacing occasional chairs of *cátedras* isolated in law faculties.[161]

Like Medina, Germani was attracted to U.S. contributions that had raised sociology to 'the highest level in the field of methodology and research techniques' and had infused Durkheim, Weber and Simmel with 'the vigorous Saxon empirical tradition'. Medina, however, (whom Germani admired) had seen the United States as a unique case marked by a fluid social structure, a frontier tradition, a prosperous economy, and massive immigration. He saw it not so much as a comprehensive model but as a source of discrete instruments such as the social survey, community study, case method, interview and life history, and he cautioned against the fetishism of quantification. Germani, unlike Medina, spoke for a 'scientific sociology' of judgemental neutrality that might have roots in discrepant ideologies but would be self-corrective given the renovative action of a scientific community. It was not the 'scientism' *per se* of Latin America that explained current weaknesses, he felt, but the incomplete institutionalization of science itself. Germani, who from his youth in Italy had opposed fascism (in both its left and right forms) and professed a strong political liberalism, was charged by the right for challenging their mystique of social solidarity and by the left for advocating an 'American' sociology without exploring the 'imperialist' messages it concealed. His 'second exile' to Harvard in 1966 coincided with the appearance of a re-Europeanized 'critical sociology' under diverse neo- and post-Marxian influences carried forward by Pablo González Casanova, Orlando Fals Borda, Fernando Henrique Cardoso, Aníbal Quijano, John Saxe-Fernández and others.

[161] Gino Germani, *La sociología en la América Latina,* 2nd ed. (Buenos Aires, 1965); *La sociología científica,* 2nd ed. (Mexico, D.F., 1962); *Argentina: sociedad de masas,* 2nd ed. (Buenos Aires, 1966).

Although his direct and innovative influence on the profession was largely limited to Brazil until the 1960s, Florestan Fernandes was, through his reputation, writings, or disciples, possibly the foremost preceptor of 'critical sociology' on a continental scale. If Medina was the *problematizador* of the new sociology and Germani the pilot from scientism to functionalist science, Fernandes – the only Latin American of the three – aimed to re-theorize the field from grass roots rather than from foreign paradigms wherein he too was thoroughly schooled. In his autobiography Fernandes attributes the shaping of his sociological vocation to an 'apprenticeship' when, at age six, he was forced to find employment at the lumpen fringe of an urban society composed of sharks and sardines.[162] When eventually he found his way to the Faculty of Philosophy of the University of São Paulo, he found no secure foothold, as Medina and Germani had, in the received wisdom of international social science. Occasional foreign professors were true mentors, such as Jean Maugüé who deepened his understanding of Hegel and Marx, or Roger Bastide who guided his early research on race relations, or Herbert Baldus who introduced him to ethnology and became a lifelong friend, or Donald Pierson who encouraged him to take São Paulo as a sociological laboratory. But for the most part foreign professors made unfulfillable cultural demands and presented an eclectic panorama of ideas that seemed unrelated to Brazil, a training that required random ingestion and tended to substitute 'intellectual artificiality' for 'cultural parochialism'. To Fernandes they seemed 'less concerned with the organism of the patient than with the brilliance of the operation'.[163] Still, there were advantages to an academic bill of fare that was too heterogeneous to be copied and forced consumers to make their own syntheses. It became apparent to Fernandes that while the Faculty could not offer the 'right' system one might at least learn architectonic principles for building one and recognize that Marx, Durkheim, and Weber were not reconcilable in simple additive fashion.

Fernandes formulated his politico-scientific position carefully during his formative years and asks those who read his writings of the 1940s and 1950s to see behind his apparent empirical critique or 'experimentalist' sociologism a firm, gradual intention to dissolve the inhibitions of 'a

---

[162] Florestan Fernandes, 'Em busca de uma sociologia crítica e militante', in *A sociologia no Brasil* (Petrópolis, 1977), pp. 140–212. Many facets of Fernandes's personal, academic and intellectual career are examined in Maria Angela D'Incao (ed.), *O saber militante: ensaios sobre Florestan Fernandes* (Rio de Janeiro and São Paulo, 1987).

[163] For a complementary reminiscence by Claude Lévi-Strauss of his period as a young visiting professor at the University of São Paulo, see his *Tristes Tropiques* (New York, 1964), pp. 106–8.

society as oppressive and repressive as the Brazilian'. To have linked his socialist tenets to his position as a sociologist at this time would have exceeded the bounds of the 'scientific sociology' that was accepted by the power elite as a misunderstood positivist sociologism. Meanwhile he cultivated his private determination to bind Engelsian materialist sociology to a pathology of present society and to the collapse of capitalism as foretold by Rosa Luxemburg. Instead of devoting his initial research to this agenda, however, he selected two themes that led to the human bedrock of Brazil: the Tupinambá Indians on the eve of European conquest and black–white relations since slavery. The Tupinambá taught him the 'folk philosophy' of their society where those who had nothing to divide shared their own persons with others. Here Fernandez acquired his primary 'wisdom about man, life, and the world'. His second understanding arose from his work with Bastide on blacks and whites in São Paulo. In the early 1950 few would have selected racism to spearhead an inquiry into industrializing São Paulo, where blacks were a small fraction of the population and race a subsidiary issue. Yet Fernandes's project forced him to reconstruct the region's economic history and its transition to capitalism; to interpret abolition as a revolution of 'whites for whites' that hastened consolidation of the urban, industrial economy; to juxtapose racial and social stratification, yielding the hypothesis of a transition from a society of 'estates' (*sociedade estamental*) to one of classes that created a 'bourgeois revolution'; and to identify mechanisms of control applied to all disinherited groups irrespective of race.[164] If his studies of the Tupinambá celebrated the sardines, his analysis of estates and classes indicted the sharks.

As substitute in 1952 for Roger Bastide in his sociology chair at the University of São Paulo and its occupant in 1955, Fernandes resolved to create a 'greenhouse' as a counter-institution within the establishment. The intent was to nurture a sociology 'made in Brazil' (as distinct from a 'Brazilian sociology') and to open 'political space' from which to influence the seat of academic power. While Fernandes's co-workers over the years were not united on doctrinal grounds, they shared a commitment to construct a sociology for developing lands from 'a descriptive, comparative, or historico-differential perspective'. They would not compete with

---

[164] See Roger Bastide and Florestan Fernandes (eds.), *Relações raciais entre negros e brancos em São Paulo* (São Paulo, 1955) and Florestan Fernandes, *The Negro in Brazilian Society,* trans. J. D. Skiles et al. (New York, 1969). Fernandes's disciples, Fernando Henrique Cardoso and Otávio Ianni, extended the research on São Paulo to the southern states of Paraná, Santa Catarina and Rio Grande do Sul. See also Florestan Fernandes, *A revolução burguesa no Brasil: ensaio de interpretação sociológica* (Rio de Janeiro, 1975).

sociologists from metropolitan nations, yet would break with the eclecticism of foreign mentors. Although he enjoyed theoretical sociology and never abjured his faith in science, Fernandes felt obliged to descend from the Olympian heights of 'scholarship' and face the blind alley of dependent capitalism in a society that with no militant socialist movement could never duplicate the classic bourgeois revolution of Europe. The task was to revisit old questions but isolating Marxian 'specific differences' and demystifying a 'bourgeois conscience' that was 'dependent, ultraconservative, and profoundly pro-imperialist'. With a strong foundation in his earlier work he turned directly toward research themes that were at the crux of Brazil's impending crisis: entrepreneurship, labour, education, the state, political participation and internal relations.[165]

To trace Latin American sociology since the 1940s wholly through the careers and writings of eminent scholars would be to highlight theoretical concerns and to neglect the pragmatic, reductionist uses of their speculations by university communities. In the late 1950s universities began to expand at a dizzying rate. The professional curricula that for generations had validated the status and careers of upper-class sons as lawyers, doctors and engineers (or dentists and veterinarians for the less fortunate) were hopelessly inadequate for training the leadership and middle-management cadres needed to inflate and modernize public and private-sector bureaucracies at a time when 'development' was the order of the day. The academic solution was to create departments and faculties of social science on an emergency schedule. In the 1930s a few institutions, such as El Colegio de México and, despite the reservations of Fernandes, the University of São Paulo, had been well placed to adapt curricula to domestic society and culture. But the perceived need to apply 'science' to human affairs was now so urgent, and funding for academic staff and infrastructure so abundant after 1960s, that there was little time for judicious redesigning of foreign (notably U.S.) curricular models, much less for creative innovation *in situ*.[166] During the 1970s, the poet-economist Gabriel Zaid tells us, the caloric intake of Mexicans declined by 5 per cent; yet the budget for the National University increased by 600 per cent and that for regional universities by 1,400 per cent. For Zaid the implication was that the mere presence of a marginal population feeds the growth of bureaucratic pyra-

---

[165] Along with many colleagues Fernandes was removed from his university position by the military government in 1969, and regained it only in 1986. That same year he was elected to Brazil's congress/constituent assembly as a candidate of the Partido dos Trabalhadores (PT).

[166] See Florestan Fernandes, *Universidade brasileira: reforma ou revolução?* (São Paulo, 1975).

mids at the centre; simply by existing, destitute villages create a 'need' for contractors, tax collectors, amiable and well-informed tour guides, to say nothing of Mexican anthropologists holding foreign doctorates and expensively trained to document at grass roots level the nation's grievous socio-economic asymmetries.[167]

Funding for academic expansion came largely from Latin American governments, often externally financed, that saw universities as a source of planners and technocrats and as a means of co-opting the allegiance of the new middle classes. Secondarily, support came directly from foreign governments and private foundations anxious to assist the 'evolutionary' progress of the region. Whereas previously the Kellogg and Rockefeller Foundations had tackled the generally non-controversial fields of medicine and agriculture, the younger Ford Foundation now moved into the social sciences while attempting to maintain the applied or practical intentions of its predecessors. Mounting campaigns against malaria or infertile soil, however, was not the same as devising remedies for school desertion, income concentration, and authoritarianism. Issues of culture and ideology caused the grantors to loosen their criterion of direct empirical relevance. The Ford Foundation won distinction by its strategic, hand-crafted programme of fellowships, research support, curriculum development and concern for human rights and its success at selling a pluralistic, or at least permissive, but essentially U.S. version of the social science enterprise to intellectual elites in Latin America.

The apparent paradox was that the North Americanization of the new social science establishments (with generous European and domestic accents to be sure) occurred precisely when large sectors of them were drawn to one or another brand of activist or intellectual Marxism, or else simply to the idea of Marxism. After its transplantation in the revisionist version of Juan B. Justo and the 'indigenous' version of Mariátegui, Marxism had fallen into disrepute as a result of disenchantment with Stalinism in the 1930s, the Allied war against fascism in the 1940s, and developmentalist hopes of the 1950s. Apart from the party apparatus, only such intellectual stalwarts as Caio Prado Júnior and Aníbal Ponce, along with the Cuban journal *Dialéctica,* kept alive its intellectual promise. Suddenly, with the economic polarization of national societies, the loss of faith in developmentalism and in the 'benevolence' of international capitalism and the stirring example of a 'fresh start' in Cuba, Marxism regained its initiative.

---

[167] Gabriel Zaid, *El progreso improductivo* (Mexico, D.F., 1979).

The joint hegemony of U.S. methods and Marxist interpretations in the social sciences was paradoxical but not illogical. According to Rolando Franco, 'Latin America had national schools for teaching sociology directed by Marxist socialists that, before the second half of the 1960s, differed in no way from the "functionalist" orientation professed at similar places with other objectives.'[168] As Dumont and Foucault have both held, Marxism did not represent an 'epistemic break' with Ricardian economics but was its logical culmination. Economics took priority for Smith and Ricardo, then assumed hegemony for Marx and Engels.[169] Both liberal empiricism and Marxian 'science' strove to unmask a social reality more concrete and definitive than the quasi-Hegelian Latin American 'reality' evoked by essayists and philosophers. Empiricists and Marxists alike arrayed the branches of inquiry in a hierarchy – whether a 'priapic' scale from hard to soft disciplines (i.e., economics to literature) or a Marxian ladder from infrastructure to superstructure. Because the essayists disregarded this scalar construction – or else like Lezama reversed it to favour an 'imagistic' strategy; or like Gabriel Zaid contrasted the voracity of economics with the veracity of poetry – Latin American and particularly U.S. social scientists found them 'soft' and 'subjective'. It is no surprise, then, to find fluent traffic between liberal empiricists and Marxists, for while their *politics* were poles apart their *ideologies,* in Dumont's sense of the term, were similar.[170] However much their therapies differed, both outlooks fixed on instrumental goals and both accepted a vision of Latin America as penetrated from above, for better or for worse, by a structure of capitalist domination that was reaching the taproots of society. A vision of the region as a family of nations created during centuries and even millennia by those at its taproots was more difficult to come by. Such a picture has begun to emerge since 1970, although more often as a jigsaw puzzle, given academic specialization and tribal narcissism, than as a vision.

This account of the professionalization of social science is selective and designed to assist contrast with the simultaneous literary 'boom' of the

168 Franco, 'Veinticinco años de sociología latinoamericana', p. 83.
169 Louis Dumont, *From Mandeville to Marx* (Chicago, Ill., 1983), pp. 147–8; Michel Foucault, *Power/Knowledge*, trans. C. Gordon et al. (New York, 1980), p. 76; Alan Sheridan, *Michel Foucault: The Will to Truth* (London, 1980), pp. 70–3.
170 In his chapter, 'A Comparative Approach to Modern Ideology and to the Place within it of Economic Thought' (in *From Mandeville to Marx*, pp. 3–30), Dumont defines ideology not in the derogatory sense but as 'the totality of ideas and values – or "representations" – common to a society or current in a given group'. In this, he means that England, France and Germany have held a common ideology since the seventeenth century in comparison to India, China or Japan.

late 1950s and 1960s. The pairing is devised not so as to characterize academic and literary phenomena as such but to probe their respective premises, or ideologies in Dumont's sense, and suggest their relation to broader Western context. The social scientists, for all their internal quarrels, drew energies from new or newly modernized universities; from unprecedented salaries, fellowships abroad and research grants; and from a common project of demystifying the colonial past, the pseudo-science of positivism and the slackness of belletrism and of blazing the paths for national development. Although the social sciences created a more sudden and compact explosion than did the literature of the period, it was not seen as a 'boom', given its rationality of purpose and its matter-of-fact management by governmental and philanthropic agencies.

The literary 'boom' was so called because of factors external to literature itself, such as the availability of expert translators for an international audience and campaigns by publishers to enrich the often lacklustre metropolitan literary menu of the period with exotic narratives. Rodríguez Monegal decorated his incisive account of the 'boom' with wittily chosen epigraphs to document ancient uses of the term and to trace the origins of the 'boom' itself to the late nineteenth century.[171] Authors like Borges and Asturias who began writing in the 1920s were now swept into visibility along with Mario Vargas Llosa, born in 1936. Although by now there exist elegant treatments of the literary generation born in the 1920s and 1930s, they often deal with 'influences' and 'idiosyncrasies'. Actually, to categorize a 'group project' is more difficult with novelists than with social scientists. 'Boom' yields no such generational handle as romanticism or naturalism. This becomes clear from leafing through any collection of mutually critical interviews with writers – for example, that of Rita Guibert.[172]

Since interviews offer few solid clues, two handles will be used in what follows but with no pretense of literary exegesis: marvellous realism and, in a non-technical sense, deconstruction. Magic realism and marvellous realism, which acquired currency during the boom, should be distinguished from each other, and both of them from surrealism and the fantastic, which date from modernism. Although surrealism might be called a modern invention, all have antecedents in past centuries of European arts and literature. At a still earlier period, when people 'believed in'

[171] Emir Rodríguez Monegal, *El Boom de la novela latinoamericana* (Caracas, 1972).
[172] Rita Guibert, *Seven Voices* (New York, 1973).

God and the devil, the supernatural and magic, such 'realisms' would not have had today's oxymoronic connotations. To define them loosely: magic realism refers to causality that is contrary to 'natural laws'. Marvellous realism refers to the extraordinary or unaccustomed (*lo insólito*) but is consonant with 'reality' and induces enchantment without the dread or presentiments of the fantastic. The fantastic evokes anxiety (fear) through intellectual anxiety (doubt). Surrealism projects spontaneous thought or images from the subconscious, free of convention and rational control.[173] None, not even magic or marvellous realism, was a Latin American creation. In its modernist guise the 'marvellous' appeared as an aesthetic category in André Breton's *Manifesto* of 1924, while in 1925 magic realism was the subject of a book by Franz Roh, a German; Pierre Mabille published *Le miroir du merveilleux* in 1940. In Latin America meanwhile Borges wrote a graceful landmark essay, 'Narrative Art and Magic' (1932),[174] and a few years later explored the fantastic vein. Preliminary but somewhat inconsistent formulations of magic realism were offered by Arturo Uslar Pietri in 1948 and Angel Flores in 1954. But the Latin American 'authority' became Alejo Carpentier (1904–80), starting with his 1948 statement and continuing to his collected interpretations in the early 1960s.[175] In retrospect it turned out that earlier fiction by Borges, Asturias and Arguedas or subsequent works by Rulfo, Roa Bastos, Vargas Llosa, Onetti and above all García Márquez had broken with the discourse of realism, infusing it in various manners with *lo maravilloso,* but it was Carpentier, with his highly readable texts, analytic essays and explicit concern with Caribbean or Latin American 'identity' who championed the cause.

Carpentier's trip to Haiti in 1943 led to the pivotal prologue to his novel *The Kingdom of this World* (1949) where he announced his discovery that 'the history of all America is but a chronicle of marvellous realism'.[176] After leaving Paris, where he had lived from 1927 to 1939, he lived till 1945 in

---

[173] See Irlemar Chiampi, *O realismo maravilhoso: forma e ideologia no romance hispano-americano* (São Paulo, 1980).

[174] Jorge Luis Borges, 'El arte narrativo y la magia', *Obras completas* (Buenos Aires, 1974). pp. 226–32.

[175] For Mabille's influence on Carpentier, see Irlemar Chiampi. 'Carpentier y el surrealismo', *Revista Língua e Literatura,* 9 (1980), 155–74.

[176] The prologue appeared separately in 1948 and then only in the novel's first edition; it was reprinted in Carpentier's *Tientos y diferencias* (Havana, 1966), pp. 95–9. See Emma Susana Speratti-Piñero, *Pasos hallados en El reino de este mundo* (Mexico, D.F., 1981); Alejo Carpentier, *Entrevistas,* ed. Virgilio López Lemus (Havana, 1985); González Echevarría, *Alejo Carpentier,* pp. 107–29; Alexis Márquez Rodríguez, *Lo barroco y lo real-maravilloso en la obra de Alejo Carpentier* (Mexico, D.F., 1982); Rodríguez Monegal, 'Lo Real y lo maravilloso'.

Cuba, then moved to Venezuela as a voluntary exile. On coming home to America he had plunged into colonial texts spending eight years in a passionate search to fathom the American world. In 1964 he observed that 'America seemed to me an enormous nebula that I tried to understand because I had the obscure intention that my work would unfold here, would become deeply American.' In what some call Carpentier's fullest definition of the 'marvellous' he relates how 'it arises from an unexpected alteration of reality (the miracle), from a privileged revelation of reality, . . . from a widening of the scales and categories of reality, as perceived with particular intensity by an exaltation of the spirit that leads it to an "ultimate state" (*estado límite*)'. Chiampi, who cites this interview, notes that Carpentier uses two sets of verbs: those like 'alter' and 'widen' denoting a modification of reality, and those like 'reveal' and 'perceive' that imply a mimetic function. This oscillation appears to be intentional, rendering the marvellous as both a perception that deforms the object and as a component of reality. Phenomenological and ontological positions are thus joined to resolve the apparent contradiction of 'deform' and 'exhibit'.[177]

Carpentier's famous 'prologue' criticized the emptiness of European modernism (although it had put him on his track). And if Europeans were also searching for alternatives to the formulae of 'Western' culture in primitivism, realm of the unconscious, Nietzsche or Bergsonian vitalism, for Carpentier these led only to general abstractions. The notable case was surrealism, which was for him never more than an artifice like certain oneiric writings or praises of folly of which he had tired. He felt the marvellous presupposed a faith. Those who are not Quixotes, he wrote, cannot throw themselves into the world of Amadís de Gaula. Unlike collective dance in America, that in Western Europe had lost magic or invocatory power. In Haiti thousands of men yearning for freedom had believed in the lycanthropic powers of Mackandal, a collective faith that produced a miracle at his execution. What Carpentier yearned for was to connect the realities of America to marvellous elements of the culture and not, as he felt surrealism did, to a universal logic. On all this he differs greatly from Borges, who dismissed Argentine identity as an unavoidable fatality or else mere affectation, and for whom magic and the fantastic were universals (as in his 1932 essay on magic). Indeed Borges could write a story of eleven lines, '*La trama*', which is universal, Argentine, realistic, magic, marvellous, fantastic, and – why not? – surrealist all at once. In

---

[177] Chiampi, *Realismo maravilhoso*, pp. 32–4.

the first paragraph Caesar, surrounded by assassins, sees Brutus among them and exclaims, '*Tú también, hijo mío!*' Nineteen centuries later a gaucho in southern Buenos Aires, attacked by other gauchos, sees his godchild among them and says quietly, '*¡Pero, che!*' 'They kill him and he doesn't know that he dies so that a scene may reoccur.'

Carpentier's commentaries are useful because he wrote from his French experience and with Gallic clarity (though not without contradiction and ambivalence) in reappropriating his Latin American origins. He created sophisticated publicity for the 'boom' of the sixties and the vitality of Latin American culture, much as writers and artists had done for Mexico half a century earlier. His pronouncements, however, do not yield direct access to such diverse texts, even if 'marvellous', as those of Rulfo, Guimarães Rosa and García Márquez. Indeed, his personal 'truth' lies in his novels, not his essays. Looking beyond technical literary analysis, however, Carpentier and others who joined him deserve their role in the arena of cultural history. For one thing, his case for marvellous realism lends vivid, non-intellectualized vocabulary and imagery to the abstracted identity quest and the balancing of localism and universalism discussed above for philosophers and sociologists. We can now relate Borges and Carpentier to the philosophic part of the inquiry by classifying the former as one who posits the 'defining qualities of man and history in a universal sense' and identifies magic, hallucination, and narrative not as embedded in specific cultures but as 'superficially dissimilar although homologous manifestations of being'. Carpentier on the other hand, like most Latin American artists and intellectuals, González Echevarría holds, adopted a polycentric Spenglerian and Orteguian view of world history that accommodates magic and the marvellous to cultural specificity.[178]

A further point is that marvellous realism translates into the sociological terms of enchantment and disenchantment. As originally proposed this Weberian polarity implied gradual intrusion, with modernization and industrialism, of an ethos of rationalization affecting all realms of personal and institutional behaviour. This is what Carpentier deplored in Europe and found therapy for in America. Here, despite poverty and caudillism, one still found cultural plurality, myth, eternal return, spontaneity and human rapport. In societies that had not since independence managed to universalize rationalization, where large countries seemed permanent Belgiums inserted into Indias, human communities that evinced aptitude for

[178] González Echevarría, *Alejo Carpentier*, p. 122.

the marvellous seemed fated to be permanent fixtures. They would not turn into the vanishing gypsy dancers of romantic Europe. When young Haitian modernists published a literary *Revue Indigène* in 1927, the title 'indigenous' did not mean 'native' American but referred to an alternative, non-rationalized culture, once called 'barbaric' or primitive. Moreover, because nations so constructed are anomalies in the West, they at times fall under the sway of homebred caudillos who confront the invasion of 'rational' commercialism and imperialism in 'marvellous' ways. Their careers became special narrative projects for Asturias, Carpentier, Roa Bastos, García Márquez, Fuentes and others.[179] If novelists accepted a permanent indigenous presence, developmental or Marxian social scientists found this premise difficult to reconcile with their evolutionary faith. But since the 1960s – while economics, political science and sociology remain ensconced for their instrumental importance (despite their grievous errors of diagnosis) – it would seem that social anthropology, ethnohistory, literary criticism, psychology, sociology of ideas and kindred fields have moved to the cutting edge of social studies. It seems also that the profession of the essayist, who knows how to synthesize gracefully without perspiring, has not fallen from fashion. Meanwhile, who knows what the poets and novelists have in store?

An important strategy that literary criticism offers for the study of Latin America remains to be mentioned. Marvellous realism, one must grant, has become shopworn and acquired too many connotations, from the empirical to the imaginative, for it to do much more than call attention or set a mood or inspire private visions. Like social science, however, literary study may offer schemas rather than themes, whose purpose is not to describe or savour phenomena but to demonstrate fresh ways of arranging them. The goal is not investigation or evocation but reconceptualization. As we saw, social scientists were bent on reconceiving society or, in a significant term used by some, demystifying it. Yet, irrespective of their political ideologies, they accepted (or at least pledged fealty to) the ground rules of science and empiricism. Their diagnoses, built on Western maxims and ideas, were certainly in commonsensical ways *critical,* but their prescriptions seemed drawn from a familiar Western armory, with whatever seasoning from local historical and cultural accents.

For all its looseness and heterogeneity, what marvellous realism suggested was that here were *different* societies, even though nestled in the

<hr />

[179] Angel Rama, *La novela latinoamericana, 1920–80* (Bogotá, 1982), pp. 361–419.

bosom of the West. Once a novelist suspects that his job may not be primarily to *demystify*, which most serious writers can manage, but to *deconstruct* vocabulary and categories, then the game becomes a free-for-all. When available discourse fails to capture circumstances, artists sometimes excel at opening paths to recognition. To demystify is to draw aside a veil from a scene known to exist. To deconstruct is to examine elements of a bogus scene so as to recombine them in a cognitively more satisfying pattern. Although lacking the instrumental imperative of demystification, deconstruction enjoys more imaginative scope.

Here we may borrow five cases offered by the Peruvian critic Julio Ortega that illustrates ways in which talented authors, with different aims and tactics, succeed in dissolving familiar worlds.[180] He starts with the 'critical writing' of Borges whereby literature examines the functions of language so as to question its own function. Borges, in Ortega's view, approaches culture not as a monument but as a text. As did Joyce and Picasso he deconstructs the idea of a stable culture, 'the idea of information as a museum, as a hierarchical, exemplary, hegemonic monumentality . . . Within culture, the notion of "truth" thus becomes a formal operation that is no less fantastic than the literary act itself.' To abbreviate Ortega's other cases: The 'mythical writing' of Rulfo deconstructs a social life while constructing the ideological space of a social hell; in his 'colloquial writing' Cortázar deconstructs the genre of the novel itself and establishes a code for fresh dialogue; Lezama Lima uses 'poetic writing' to deconstruct the notion of referentiality in favour of the text as 'abundance of meaning'; and finally García Márquez using 'fictional writing' deconstructs history by shifting it to the 'critical consensus of popular culture'.

Examples now crop up to show that even the iron laws of liberal/Marxist economics are vulnerable to deconstruction which, if practised with high critical skills, is more persuasive and constructive than blunt academic refutation. Poet-economist Zaid relegates statistics to a bristling appendix and deconstructs them in the text with a 'biblical' parable that compares the indigent potter's six sons, who work hard from childhood and marry only when they can afford it, with the economist's six sons, who acquire tuition bills and mortgaged houses long before parasitic jobs are created for them in the 'pyramids'. Anthropologist Stephen Gudeman shows that

---

[180] Julio Ortega, *Poetics of Change: The New Spanish-American Narrative* (Austin, Tex., 1984), pp. 3–119.

the language of Colombian peasants is serviceable for their economic life, even though it contains no liberal/Marxist vocabulary (which would require deconstruction for them) to designate 'profit', 'capital', 'interest', or 'investment'. Anthropologist Michael Taussig shows how Andean peasants and tin miners instead of surrendering to commodity fetishism resist economic 'laws' by anthropomorphizing (or *re*constructing) their domination in the form of contracts with the devil, thus re-enacting the first historical moment of subjection. Finally, the Brazilian anthropologist Muniz Sodré confronts the premises of Western economics with a 'seduced truth' of African inspiration that, being symbolic, is also reversible. Once ritualized, truth is purged of univocal doctrinal meaning. Afro-Brazilian ritual arenas therefore expose reversibilities of the global society to replace, for example, the Western axiom 'exchange creates surplus' with the more venerable axiom that 'exchange is reciprocal' and requires restitution.[181]

### CONCLUSION

We now come to a point where, in framing a conclusion, it is possible to suggest how the half century treated in these pages bears a relationship to developments in Europe since the Enlightenment, specifically the co-existence of literary and scientific establishments. While Latin America has accompanied these developments for two centuries thanks to individual *pensadores* or generational coteries or bookstores and newspapers or foreign travel by the privileged or somewhat problematic academic institutions (Mexico and Brazil even lacked universities in the nineteenth century), it has only since the 1920s boasted literary establishments of international calibre and linkage, and only since the 1950s has it groomed its cadres of social scientists. In *Between Literature and Science: the Rise of Sociology* Wolf Lepenies uses France, England and Germany to show that in the late eighteenth century no sharp division of literary and scientific works had yet occurred.[182] He identifies Buffon, whose *Histoire naturelle* attained 250 popular editions, as the last scholar whose reputation rested on stylistic presentation and the first to lose it because his research was

---

[181] Zaid, *Progreso improductivo;* Stephen F. Gudeman, *Economics as Culture: Models and Metaphors of Livelihood* (London, 1986); Michael T. Taussig, *The Devil and Commodity Fetishism in South America* (Chapel Hill, 1980); Muniz Sodré, *A verdade seduzida: por um conceito de cultura no Brasil* (Rio de Janeiro, 1983).

[182] Wolf Lapenies, *Between Literature and Science: The Rise of Sociology,* trans. R. J. Hollingdale (Cambridge, Eng., 1988).

erratic.[183] He was a prototype for Latin American *pensadores* of a century later whose world had not yet split into the 'two cultures'.

The encroachment of science, such as encyclopaedism or English economics, was countered by the romantic reaction, emphasizing the sanctity of the self and Wordsworthian lyricism in England, and in Germany historicity, community and the spirit. The tension between literature and science has lasted for generations, in England through such notable paired champions as Coleridge and Bentham, then Matthew Arnold and T. H. Huxley, then F. R. Leavis and C. P. Snow.[184] The German case is of special interest for Latin America. Dumont contrasts post-Enlightenment individualist or 'nominalist' England and France with the 'holistic' countries in the rest of the world.[185] His critical case is Germany, which offered the example of a peripheral culture making ideological adjustment to modernity as 'the first underdeveloped country'. Yet if German culture was 'holistic', it was early to accept Lutheran individualism, a pietist or internal individualism, however, that left intact the sentiment of global community unlike the modern nominalist brand. German culture was therefore favourable for mediation. Without referring to Latin America, Dumont opens conceptual space wherein to treat it alongside other world regions. His categories of nominalism and holism remind us, on one hand, of the shift in affiliation of Latin American elites after 1760 from Iberian to Anglo-French intellectual outlooks and, on the other, to the increasing 'visibility' of indigenous and African elements in the twentieth century. The 'premature' Latin American embrace of nominalism postponed a coming to terms with issues raised by the German critique of Enlightenment universalism until the reception of early twentieth-century German philosophy.

Octavio Paz has his own controversial interpretation of why the literature-science split failed to occur in Latin America after independence.[186] (In Europe the 'two cultures' were of course permeated by crossovers. The 'artist' Balzac took Buffon at face value as a 'scientist' and tried to do for human society what Buffon had done for zoology. Later, the 'scientists' Marx and Engels claimed to have learned more from Balzac

---

[183] Buffon, a man of imposing size, thought large mammals far more admirable than insects, a prejudice reinforced by his inability to use a microscope because he was short-sighted. Antonello Gerbi, *The Dispute of the New World*, trans. Jeremy Moyle, rev. ed. (Pittsburgh, Pa., 1973), pp. 15–20.

[184] John Stuart Mill, *On Bentham and Coleridge*, ed. F. R. Leavis (New York, 1962); Lionel Trilling, 'The Leavis-Snow Controversy', in *Beyond Culture* (New York, 1979), pp. 126–54.

[185] Dumont, *From Mandeville to Marx*, pp. 3–30, and *Essays on Individualism* (Chicago, Ill., 1986), pp. 76–132.

[186] Octavio Paz, *Children of the Mire*, chs. 5, 6.

than from economists and historians.) Paz's point, however, is that the Iberian world could not incubate modern literature because it had no modern age, 'neither critical reason nor bourgeois revolution', to provoke the process. Spanish romanticism was therefore superficial and sentimental, and Spanish America could only imitate Spain. The romantic 'urge to change reality' or 'unite life and art', Paz argues, was postponed in Latin America until the modernist age whose branching impulses were much the same as romantic ones: into magic or politics, into religious or revolutionary temptation. Because Paz feels that positivism in nineteenth-century Latin America was not the outlook of a liberal bourgeoisie interested in industrial and social progress, it was therefore 'an ideology and a belief', not a culture of science. He concludes that Europe's science-romantic binomial was postponed there for a century: 'Positivism is the Spanish American equivalent of the European Enlightenment, and modernism was our Romantic reaction.'

Antônio Cândido criticized Paz's argument *avant la lettre* when in his magisterial *Formation of Brazilian Literature* he pointed out the importance of the individual and of history in Brazilian romanticism, not wholly as a European imposition but as part of a domestic 'invention' of nationhood, identity and literature. Cândido confirms Paz, however, in noting that the possibilities opened by Brazilian romanticism were later 'carried to the extreme, as in Symbolism and various modernist currents'. González Echevarría explicitly criticizes Paz in holding that, while Latin America may not have produced romantics of German or English stature, the issues of modernity were vital dilemmas there too, and one must study their spokesmen in thought no less than in action. Through an analysis of Carpentier's *Explosion in the Cathedral* he shows how a modern-(ist) writer may project an analogy between the modernism of the eighteenth century and that of his own time, or 'a counterpoint between self-conscious modernities'.[187]

The two positions on romanticism just examined are not wholly antithetical, for both recognize affinities between romanticism and modernism; but for Paz the romantic impulse of Latin American modernists is a discovery

---

[187] Antônio Cândido, *Formação da literatura brasileira (momentos decisivos)*, 2nd ed.; 2 vols. (São Paulo, 1964), Vol. II, pp. 23–34; González Echevarría, *Voice of the Masters*, pp. 33–6, 171–72n. and *Alejo Carpentier*, pp. 226, 234. In *Sources of the Self: The Making of the Modern Identity* (Cambridge, Mass., 1989), chs. 21–4, Charles Taylor emphasizes the persistent engagement, far into the modernist age, of Enlightenment and romanticism: not as two 'styles' of sensibility but as an evolving contention between instrumental reason and the emergent freedom of the self-determining subject.

while for Cândido and González Echevarría it is a recovery. The critical point is that irrespective of the judgement on romanticism, the culture of science, which fuelled European romanticism in positive as well as hostile ways, was not yet available in Latin America to energize the dialectic. The Olympian Machado de Assis turned his back on the whole romantic-scientistic-naturalist farrago and went his way with Dante and Menippean satire. What this chapter has attempted is to characterize the (re)birth of romanticism in modernism, then the provisional rapprochement, in Charles Taylor's terms, between the 'emergent freedom of the self-determining subject' and 'instrumental reason', culminating in the Latin American version of the literature-science split that Lapenies documents for Europe. This is not a case of delayed replication of the metropolis. The Latin American setting makes a world of difference. What matters are analogies, which illuminate and assist interpretation of both arenas of the phenomenon. Earlier it was suggested that the instrumental guideposts of Latin American social science in the 1960s are no longer seen as determinative and are slowly yielding to recognition that peoples, not policies, determine outcomes. As for literature, Antônio Cândido speculates that the romantic agenda of regionalism, still a heavy influence on modernism (as evinced above by the three discrete urban locales of São Paulo, Buenos Aires and Mexico City) and on the novels of the 1930s and 1940s, has now given way to a 'super-regionalism' that absorbs cultural specificity into the discourse of universalism. Guimarães Rosa was the pioneer, followed by Rulfo, García Márquez, Vargas Llosa and many others.[188] The intellectual hegemony of scientism and romanticism may have drawn to a close – to create, *ça va sans dire,* new challenges.

[188] Antônio Cândido, 'Literatura, espelho da América?', paper for the conference 'Reflections on Culture and Ideology in the Americas', Oliveira Lima Library, Washington, D.C., 19–21 March 1993.

# 2

# LATIN AMERICAN NARRATIVE
## SINCE *c.* 1920

## INTRODUCTION

There are many ways in which one can try to encapsulate the process of Latin American fiction, but no point of departure is ultimately more persuasive, given the material conditions of Latin America's historical experience, than the distinction between an Americanist and a 'universalist', or 'cosmopolitan', orientation. The Americanist impulse can be traced from the earliest days of Latin American independence, when it took on both a nationalist and an anti-colonial ideology and rhetoric. The cosmopolitan impulse, equally strong, corresponds to a permanent desire to know and understand the global culture within which and against which the Latin American nations have had to define themselves. At the present time, in an era of 'pluralism', when even the existence of a recognizable and reasonably homogeneous 'Latin American' entity is questioned, such generalizations are not infrequently challenged, but this distinction remains profoundly persuasive as a conceptual tool. It applies within and between periods, and it applies within and between the forms and contents of literary works. To explain why one tendency or the other predominates at any particular time is not easy, but the phenomena themselves are not difficult to identify.

Similarly, although there is little agreement among critics and historians as to the detailed periodization of Latin American narrative in the twentieth century, the task inevitably becomes easier the more broadly the picture is focused. For the purposes of this history within a history, therefore, it seems appropriate to identify two literary eras, separated by the Second World War.[1] The first, from approximately 1915 to 1945, the

---

[1] This chapter continues the review of Latin American fiction by Gerald Martin in *CHLA* Volumes III and IV, where it appeared as part of a wider treatment of Latin American artistic culture between

period between the two world wars, is that of the Latin American social novel (extending the earlier traditions of *costumbrismo, realismo* and *naturalismo,* and embracing *regionalismo,* the *novela de la tierra, indigenismo* and other similar trends). Within this period, 1930 sees a transitional moment, when patterns and options established in the 1920s become temporarily hardened as the social congeals into the political and the merely playful slides into the fantastic and the metaphysical. The second era, from the late 1940s to the present, is the age of the Latin American 'New Novel' (extending the discoveries of the international avant-garde, including Anglo-American 'Modernism', and incorporating *realismo mágico, literatura fantástica* and other experimental currents). Unmistakable signs of the 'New Novel' can be detected as early as the 1920s (Mário de Andrade, Asturias, Carpentier, Borges), whilst respectable versions of the social realist novel continue to be written to the present day. Fusions and hybridizations are equally frequent. In general, however, the historical dividing line – the mid-forties – is quite clear both in Spanish America and in Brazil.

The realist mode had been manifested in historical novels and in what critics call *costumbrista* fiction during the romantic period (the early and middle decades of the nineteenth century) and in naturalism à la Zola after the 1880s. In neither case was there any great sense of a continental dimension in the works produced. On the contrary, in the first period – after a brief Americanist moment following independence – the essential thrust in most countries was national, if not nationalist, and from the 1870s the rather scientific and positivistic naturalist movement viewed national problems from an essentially objective, although progressive universal perspective – an internationalism without politics, so to speak. Paradoxically, it was Darío's *modernista* movement, usually accused of 'cosmopolitanism' and of psychological enslavement to France, which transformed the linguistic culture of Spanish America (the Brazilian case was somewhat different) and gave it a unifying cultural identity which has

1800 and 1930. Since the chapter on 'The literature, music and art of Latin America, 1870–1930' in *CHLA* IV could offer only an outline of developments in narrative in the first three decades of this century, and given that the 1920s is by common assent the first important moment of Latin American narrative on a continental plane, this chapter begins with a brief re-assessment of the early decades of the century, and especially the 1920s. Given its editorial context in a global history of Latin America, it seemed appropriate to emphasize particularly the theme of the relation of texts to contexts, of literature to history. For a much fuller treatment of the subject, see Gerald Martin, *Journeys through the Labyrinth: Latin American Fiction in the Twentieth Century* (London, 1989). All translations are the author's unless otherwise noted. For this reason it has not been thought appropriate or necessary to reference the – very brief – quotations from the texts themselves.

persisted until the present time. It was this sense of identity which, after the humiliation of Spain in 1898 and the affirmation of Mexican nationalism after 1917, allowed the social realists of the 1920s to produce works which may not have attained 'universality' but which unmistakably offered versions of the national and the continental combined in unified literary discourses and images. (The same phenomenon would be seen in Brazil in the 1930s.) This achievement, evidently the product of important philosophical and ideological shifts, could not of course have come about without equally important shifts in the class character of those who wrote and those who read fiction, not to mention their respective attitudes to those of their compatriots who could do neither but who were increasingly the subject matter of those works.

Much of the momentum was external. Latin America's integration into the world economic system after 1870 had not only brought about significant alterations in the continent's economic, social and political condition but had also brought the region closer to the attention of Europe and North America than at any time since the independence era; and outsiders invariably saw Latin Americans, as they do to this day, as one large international group of cultures rather than as the separate cluster of nationalities which Latin Americans tend themselves to perceive. The very concept of 'Latin' America – a French invention, for reasons which are obvious – was only fully asserted in the early years of the twentieth century, at a time when so many members of the Latin American ruling class were spending long sojourns in the French capital, with occasional sorties to Madrid. Once Spain's gender had changed after 1898 – from patriarchal conqueror and oppressor to defeated mother country – it became possible to view cultural questions rather more coolly and the occasional upsurges of 'Hispanidad' were usually temporary symptoms of resistance to French culture rather than the conservative enthusiasms they seemed at first sight to signify.

Spain's historic surrender and expulsion had liberated Cuba and Puerto Rico, and to that extent was welcomed in the sub-continent. Certainly it removed a heavy emotional burden from the Spanish American psychology, and matters were in a rather brutal way simplified when the United States moved to fill Spain's traditional role as imperialist oppressor. The 'Hispanic' became accessible again as Spain (and, for Brazil, Portugal) now represented Latin America's European source of tradition and history (Iberian America), whilst France continued to act as a more modern and plural version (Latin America) and the United States stepped in to provide a much more genuinely alien, genuinely external enemy, both objectively and subjectively (the Other America rather than Pan-America). The way was clear for Spanish Americans to search anew for their cultural identity, as they had between about 1780 and 1830, and as the Spaniards were already doing through the introspective meditations of the Generation of 1898. The greatest precursor of this quest was undoubtedly the Cuban revolutionary poet José Martí (1853–1895), the 'Apostle' (of Cuban independence, obviously, but also of cultural nationalism and, above all, of the cultural unity of 'Our America').

The most influential expression of such a quest, however, was that of José Enrique Rodó (1871–1917), whose essay *Ariel* (1900), elitist and Hellenistic as it was, nevertheless questioned the cultural value of North American civilization almost at the very moment that the United States began its irresistible rise, first to hemispheric, then global supremacy. Rodó's rhetoric influenced a whole generation of Spanish American students and intellectuals and acted as a unifying force which put an end to Positivism and ranged the whole of Latin America as one cultural and spiritual entity against the Anglo-Saxon colossus of the north. Over the next two decades numerous other thinkers developed these themes in an increasingly less abstract way than had Rodó, and although it would be many years before the force of nineteenth-century positivism and biologism – with their racial interpretations of Latin American identity – were finally swept aside, the ideological impact of the social sciences and the political impact of the embryonic workers' movements exerted an increasing influence on the democratic tenor of narrative itself.

The Spanish American independence centenaries clustered around 1910, coinciding in Mexico with the start of the Revolution, provided the clearest possible focus for such debates, and it became apparent as each new anniversary was celebrated that nationalist affirmation was being asserted against a continental dimension, each national identity viewed within a family context (Brazil, which had declared its independence in 1822, of course being the most problematical member of such a family group). Especially noteworthy was the work by the great Argentine literary historian Ricardo Rojas, *La restauración nacionalista* (1910), but there were numerous other works in the same vein such as Manuel Ugarte's *El porvenir de América Latina* (1910) and Francisco García Calderón's *Les Démocraties latines de l'Amérique* (1912). More negative positivist-inspired works such as Alcides Arguedas's *Pueblo enfermo* (1909), whilst also influential, were gradually losing their conviction, and Spengler's *Decline of the West*

(1918), coinciding with the end of a futile war in Europe, effectively liquidated the problem of Latin America's racial inferiority and cultural backwardness almost at a stroke – at least in theory. Henceforth, the principal problems to be confronted by Latin American fiction, which had never had to consider the historically specific moral dilemmas which consumed the nineteenth-century European 'realist' novel, were social, economic and political in character, not biological and psychological. Thus within the general perspectives of nationalism and Americanism, the avenues of anti-imperialism, socialism and even communism began to open up, though communist ideology and politics would only become both widely attractive and apparently feasible after 1945 when Latin American writers became capable of also attaining 'universality'.

## REGIONALISM: LATIN AMERICAN NARRATIVE BETWEEN THE WARS

The story of the Latin American novel in the early decades of the twentieth century appears, in retrospect, as the story of a mapping, a narrative of fields, paths and horizons, in which knowledge, progress and development were seemingly no longer problematical, the only frontier the line between present and future, the known and the knowable, the developed and the as yet undeveloped. They were often written by men and women who originated in the provinces and moved to their national capital. And if, as frequently occurred, such novels and stories were records of failures, they tended to be confirmed only on the last page as if to emphasize their imminent resolution. They abound with images of open doors and open books, deeds waiting to be done and histories waiting to be written.

The classic expression of a savage, untamed America is to be found in the works of the Uruguayan Horacio Quiroga (1878–1937). His short stories, bridging the gulf between *modernismo* and *telurismo*, between Poe, Kipling and Conrad, provided an image of the struggle of man against nature and – though to a lesser extent – against his fellow man which fused the gothic and the epic, fantasy and realism, in a mix which foreshadowed not only his more direct successors in the 1920s and 1930s but also the so-called 'magical realists' of later generations. Quiroga, whose own life was marked by a succession of tragedies, had visited Paris at the height of *modernismo* at the turn of the century, but had been unable to 'triumph' there, felt out of place and exiled himself to Misiones, the wild frontier area in northern Argentina. His tales of horror and savagery, in such collections as *Cuentos de amor, de locura y de muerte* (1917), *Cuentos de la selva* (1918), *El salvaje* (1920), *Anaconda* (1921), *El desierto* (1924) and *Los desterrados* (1926), are more natural than social, more individual than collective, but provide the earliest and most authoritative example of a modernization of the genre which opened up entirely new paths in the Latin American short story and in fiction as a whole.

The best known of all Latin American novels about the jungle is *La vorágine* (1924) by the Colombian writer José Eustasio Rivera (1888–1928), whose only other major work was a collection of *modernista* poems entitled – somewhat ironically in view of the tenor of his later novel – *Tierra de promisión* (1921). *La vorágine* is a complex and heterogeneous work, which critics have traditionally called contradictory, though the passage of time has shown that its contradictions were only too well understood by the author and are those of Latin America itself (or, rather, its intellectuals), torn between the 'backward', autochthonous world of primitive nature and the apparently unattainable models of metropolitan development. Rivera's hero Arturo Cova is an anachronistic romantic idealist ('Ah, jungle, mistress of silence, mother of solitude and mist! What evil spirit left me a prisoner in your green dungeons?'), who feels the call of a wild nature of which he has no knowledge or understanding, in an age of capitalist development. His absurd, overblown rhetoric, like a Latin popular song of betrayal and despair, pervades the entire narrative ('Before I fell in love with any woman, I gambled my heart with Destiny and it was won by Violence'); but it soon becomes clear that the desired space of Cova's imagination has already been occupied by the most brutal realities, to which he is fatally slow to adapt. The vortex of the title, which represents the heart of darkness, the vast Amazon forest, is itself a partly romantic concept (the wilds of nature), but one negated by the realities of the Darwinian struggle for survival in a jungle conceived as a barbarous world of free competition in the age of primitive accumulation. Rivera put his experience as a boundary commissioner for the Colombian government to good effect and produced a novel whose denunciation of the brutal labour practices on the rubber plantations caused a national outcry after the book's publication. His insights showed the land as not merely a remote and mysterious natural landscape but as an economic and political arena, the workers as real people rather than biological impulses, and woman as a creature potentially equal to the males who made the grand gestures of history and wrote the idealized novels. The last line of *La vorágine* is possibly the most quoted in Latin American literature: 'Los devoró la selva!' ('The jungle devoured them.')

There is a traditional (primordial?) kind of logic in beginning with those writers who evoked the mystery and romance – or horror – of the American forests. But few critics would dispute that the true point of departure of twentieth-century narrative is the so-called 'Novel of the Mexican Revolution', a fictional sub-genre which inaugurates the new wave of social and regionalist fiction of the 1920s, just as the Mexican Revolution itself set the political agenda for much of Latin America after 1917. *Los de abajo* by Mariano Azuela (1872–1952) was the first important novel of the Mexican Revolution and, indeed, the greatest of them all. Its implicit project – political liberation opening the path to modernity – although frustrated, dominated the entire 'regionalist' wave of the 1920s and the 1930s. (Azuela had in fact also composed the very first narrative of the Revolution itself in 1911, with *Andrés Pérez, maderista,* an embittered fictional account of his own early experiences in the conflict.) Although written and serialized in 1915 while the Revolution was still under way, *Los de abajo* was not widely read or acknowledged until 1925, at precisely the moment where other major social novels were coming to critical attention across the Latin American continent.

Ironically enough, Azuela never truly understood the real political issues at stake in the Revolution but he viewed it with a sincere and critical eye. He did not pretend to narrate from the peasant point of view and was careful only to enter the consciousness of middle-class characters like himself; still his title emphasized that the peasant was the principal protagonist of the novel as he was of a historical rebellion expropriated by the rising agrarian and industrial middle sectors. The narrative shows the brief triumph of the primitive revolutionaries – 'A whirlwind of dust, swirling along the highway, suddenly broke into violent hazy masses, swelling chests, tangled manes, dilated nostrils, wild eyes, flying legs and pounding hoofs. Bronze-faced men, with ivory teeth and flashing eyes, brandished rifles or held them across their saddles' – and their tragic defeat – 'At the foot of the carved rock face, huge and sumptuous as the portico of an old cathedral, Demetrio Macías, his eyes fixed in an eternal gaze, keeps on pointing with the barrel of his gun.' Through the intense, almost cinematographic dynamism of its prose, the candid acknowledgment of the gulf between city and country, mental and manual labour, intellectuals and peasants, *Los de abajo* was in many respects more 'modern' than many of the regionalist narratives which followed it in subsequent decades. However, in later life Azuela himself, although a prolific novelist, never came close to matching, at leisure, what he had achieved in the heat of battle.

Azuela's principal literary competitor was Martín Luis Guzmán (1887–1976), a general's son who joined the revolution and sided, like Azuela, with Pancho Villa. *El águila y la serpiente* (1926) is a compelling documentary narrative inspired by Guzmán's personal experience of the leading protagonists of the insurrection. His unforgettable portraits have given permanent shape to the historical image of the conflict. Villa approximated most closely to the Mexican national self-conception at the time, and his legendary exploits dominate the fiction of the Revolution. Zapata's more mythical, Indian presence was slower to evolve, and the only major novel to convey his story was *Tierra* (1932) by Gregorio López y Fuentes (1891–1966), which thereby helped to mould the tragic persona of another national hero ('The news, like a hungry dog, goes diligently from door to door. It is passed on in whispers, in huddled groups, by men at the plough and women at the well. He has been seen. So it's true, he's not dead . . . ').

If the jungle provides the most dramatic and intense version of the natural world which is the context of American social and economic reality, the Indian is America's original autochthonous inhabitant. Azuela's protagonist, Demetrio Macías, is himself a 'full-blooded Indian' whose endeavour is, however, precisely to become something more than a mere extension of the landscape. Nineteenth-century literature had seen numerous noble but exotic savages safely consigned to the forests of the past, most notably Alencar's *O Guarani* (Brazil, 1857), Mera's *Cumandá* (Ecuador, 1879) and Zorilla's *Tabaré* (Uruguay, 1879). These were romantic, 'Indianist' works. Even the best known novel about the Indians of the Andean sierras and the acknowledged precursor of twentieth-century 'Indigenism', Clorinda Matto de Turner's *Aves sin nido* (Peru, 1889), betrays through its cloying title the fact that the work remained profoundly romantic despite its militant intentions.

The most important work of early twentieth-century *indigenismo* is *Raza de bronce* (1919), by the Bolivian Alcides Arguedas (1879–1946), whose pathbreaking status seems all the more extraordinary when it is recalled that an early version entitled *Wata Wara* appeared in 1904, five years before his apocalyptic socio-historical essay *Pueblo enfermo*. As a member of a powerful landowning family from the Bolivian *altiplano* who was also an assiduous traveller to Paris, Arguedas registered in his novel the horrifying brutality on Bolivian haciéndas, which nevertheless continued up to the Revolution of 1952 (and even longer in Peru). Like Quiroga and Rivera, Arguedas had taken part in the *modernista* movement and was now recanting the errors of his own escapist past. Thus *Raza de bronce* not only conveyed the plight of the *pongos* but also satirised the merely self-indulgent efforts by so many 'modernist' writers to exalt Latin American landscapes. His own striking descriptions of the unforgettable panoramas of the Bolivian Andes were based on extensive personal experience. The combination provided one of the earliest examples of the portrayal of the Indians as 'beggars on golden stools'.

This historical moment also saw the golden age of Latin American equivalents of the 'western': tales of Mexican *vaqueros*, Venezuelan *llaneros*, Chilean *huasos*, Argentine, Uruguayan and Brazilian *gauchos*. The man on horseback is an ambivalent but uniquely potent figure in Hispanic culture, given the long tradition of knight errantry and aristocracy, crusades and conquests, hunting and cattle herding, not to mention more elemental associations between taming and mounting horses and the physical domination of nature and even of women. The horse, in other words, focuses a complex network of symbols – power over the land, social status and privileged mobility – whose force is far from spent.

In 1926 yet another former *modernista*, the Argentine landowner Ricardo Güiraldes (1885–1927), who, like Arguedas, had spent much of his life in Paris, published what for many critics is the greatest regionalist work of the century, *Don Segundo Sombra*. Alone among the exalted works of the period, this bittersweet novel about the gaucho spirit of the pampas looks back unashamedly to the golden past rather than the beckoning future, to a time when there was no immigration and little urbanization, when the pampa was unfenced and the gauchos rode free like knights of the purple plain (to interphrase W. H. Hudson and Zane Grey). Since the novel's nostalgic vision communicates the essential structure of feeling of Güiraldes's entire oligarchical generation, it is not surprising that this great land of the future should have become the land that never was. The novel is narrated through a screen of nostalgia, artfully combining the Parisian forms of symbolism and impressionism with the epic spontaneity of life on the endless pampas. The story is told by Fabio Cáceres, a once poor and illegitimate country boy who through the whim of fate is educated by a legendary gaucho figure, the eponymous Don Segundo, from the age of fourteen to twenty-one, until he discovers, like Argentina, that he is, after all, heir to great wealth and responsibility (and, accordingly, not really illegitimate at all). He resigns himself to his new station but longs for the life he has lost with Don Segundo, one of the first heroes in the Americas to ride off into a cosmic twilight in the last scene of the text. The novel gazes back on spontaneity from reluctant immobility, innocence from knowingness, beginnings from a premonition of the end (Güiraldes died soon after its publication), and its conclusion is suitably elegiac: 'Concentrating my will on carrying out the smallest acts, I turned my horse and, slowly, rode back to the houses. I went as one whose life-blood was ebbing away.' The work became an instant classic, fit for every school-boy, and far less discouraging ideologically than José Hernández's more sober epic poem *Martín Fierro* (1872) a half century before. To that extent it may be considered one of the most troubling art works in Latin American history.

In 1929 the Venezuelan Rómulo Gallegos (1884–1969) produced what seemed to be exactly the novel Latin American fiction had been crying out for in that new era of progress and enterprise after the First World War: *Doña Bárbara*. Güiraldes had exalted stoicism and fatalism in the face of Life, since History was no more than illusion. The trail was for riding, life being a river that flows inexorably into the sea of death, but the horizon for Don Segundo and Fabio, rather like Fitzgeralds's *The Great Gatsby* from the same era, is a mere pampa mirage. Not so for the Venezuelan, who wrote about his own country's plains, the *llanos* or savannahs. Although not remotely as sophisticated as Güiraldes, with his Paris-constructed aesthetic consciousness, Gallegos must still be counted the greatest regionalist novelist in Spanish America taking his oeuvre as a whole. Güiraldes longed for the past, so he mendaciously idealized one of the working classes, Don Segundo Sombra (whose description was based on one of the family's hired hands). Gallegos, from the aspiring middle classes, looked to the future, so the hero of *Doña Bárbara* is a compromise figure, a member of the ruling landowning class but invested with the characteristics of the rising professional and industrial bourgeoisie and also capable of inspiring the masses through his personal charisma and educating them through his enlightened knowledge and passion for 'cultivation'.

*Doña Bárbara*'s characterization was wooden and its action somewhat stiffly narrated, but the novel's importance lies in its breadth of vision and the infinitely layered symbolism inspired by Sarmiento's earlier epoch-making *Facundo: civilización y barbarie* (Argentina, 1845). Although short on psychological realism (he had almost no personal experience of the Llanos or their inhabitants), Gallegos updated Sarmiento's problematic to see it in terms of development, one of the grand themes of Latin American history. Moreover, he set it in the context of a Latin American cultural process viewed in terms of the great debates of Western history (spirit, matter), Latin American history (Spaniards, Indians) and universal history (male, female). He was undoubtedly the first novelist in the continent to perceive the full importance of this – now standard – Americanist conceptual framework, however simplistically dramatized in the struggle between the progressive landowner Santos Luzardo and his ruthless adversary the female caudillo Doña Bárbara (a covert symbol for the regime of Juan Vicente Gómez, effective dictator of Venezuela from 1908 to 1935 and himself the heir to a whole century of 'barbarous' caudillo figures). Interestingly enough, Santos discovers that what is needed is not so much an enlightened democracy as a somewhat steelier 'good *caudillismo*'; but Gallegos himself did not put this into practice when he became President in the last months of the post-war democratic *trienio* (1945–8).

For Gallegos, at any rate, as for Santos Luzardo, the *llano*, symbol of Venezuela's future, is a field for action, not for aesthetic or nostalgic contemplation, and his image of it stands as a symbol of the perspective of an entire generation of optimistic, democratic Americanist politicians: 'Plains of the *llano*, one and a thousand trails . . . Great land lying open and outstretched, made for work and grand deeds: all horizons, like hope; all paths, like will.' Fifty years ago this was the most admired novel in Latin American history. Then, twenty-five years ago, as the flood-tide of the 1960s 'Boom' washed all else away, it fell into disrepute and Gallegos was deemed to be less the novelist of underdevelopment than an embarrassingly underdeveloped novelist, whose work was as devoid of real people as the vast empty savannahs he depicted. Yet the visionary Gallegos was always more subtle than his detractors would allow. Few of the other novelists shared so confidently in his belief in capitalist development and incorporatist politics, but it is this, precisely, which makes him the most significant representative in literature of the dominant economic and political ideologies of the coming era: developmentalism and populism. Yet Gallegos also learned and changed. Míster Danger, the North American who longs to rape nubile Venezuela (Marisela) in *Doña Bárbara*, simply makes a run for it when confronted by Santos Luzardo's heroic resolution. Such later works as *Sobre la misma tierra* (1943) would take imperialism more seriously. And whereas in *Doña Bárbara* a repressed and repressive Santos prohibits the erotic antics of Venezuelan folklore when his peons dance around the camp fire, the almost Homeric *Cantaclaro* (1934) is notable for its tolerant and indeed exultant response to Llano traditions. Similarly, whereas Doña Bárbara's original sin was her Mestizo origin, the protagonist of *Canaima* (1935), Marcos Vargas, is a young man of great promise who immerses himself in an Indian jungle community in order to create a new, mixed culture. By this means Marcos, and his creator, were pointing the way beyond the regionalist novel to the more complex – indeed, labyrinthine – fiction which was to give Latin American narrative its worldwide reputation and focus.

It should be repeated that these 'novels of the land', as they came to be called, at first approvingly and later deprecatingly, were by no means the only fiction written in Latin America in the period from 1915 to 1945. There was a good deal of urban fiction, both within and outside the social realist genre, and there were avant-garde works by writers like Macedonio Fernández, Borges, Onetti and others, along with numerous other trends. But 'Americanism' was the banner of the era and the novel of the land gave the image of the continent – still undiscovered, uncompleted, largely unknown, but now aggressively emergent – that most foreign readers and indeed most Latin Americans wished to see. Like the earlier *costumbrista* fiction, it was a special form of knowledge, but also now a form of political assertion as incipient industrial capitalism brought new classes to the scene and the problem of the land and agrarian reform signalled vast social transformations and forms of class conflict previously unknown in the continent. In poetry also, Pablo Neruda, by far the best known poet of the era, took this politically motivated Americanist theme to its highest and literally its most monumental point with his epic *Canto General* (1950), whose best known section, 'Alturas de Macchu Picchu', was composed in 1945.

## The 1930s

By the early 1930s a new wave of disillusionment was sweeping the subcontinent, against an international background as sombre as the modern world would ever know. Writers now gave less attention to grand historical symbols and focused more closely on their characters, albeit from a sociological and economic rather than a psychological standpoint. In every Latin American republic the triumphalist faith in development and modernization typical of the years after 1918 had evaporated, and political ideologies now began to separate intellectuals and artists in new and painful ways.

Under the influence of international movements like communism and fascism, literature, like politics and economics, became more programmatic. The pseudo-scientific, objectivist realism of late nineteenth-century naturalist writing now became transmuted into a more sociologically critical form of realism, as writers incorporated the perspectives of socialism and, though much more gradually, of psychoanalysis. The somewhat vague and idealistic humanist slogans of the 1920s, typical of the great symbolic narratives discussed above, were transformed with revolutionary force into the more ideologically explicit forms of commitment characteristic of the 1930s. In sharp contrast to this politically overdetermined 'realism', non-socialist writers withdrew into 'philosophy', fantasy or the new Catholic existentialism, as the aftermath of 1929 and the collapse of international trade turned the 1930s into another moment of relative isolation in Latin America.

Both in politics and literature, then, the main story of the 1930s was one of radical assaults on a conservative status quo whose response was authoritarian retaliation; and the outward-looking Americanist works of the 1920s were succeeded in each republic – paradoxically, given the growing internationalist influence of world communism – by another period of national introspection. At the same time the committed, ideologically explicit works which now appeared in most countries were matched by a growing tendency towards essays written by *pensadores* consumed, in the wake of Spengler and visits by other foreign luminaries like Keyserling, Waldo Frank and Ortega y Gasset, with national character and the metaphysics of the Mexican, Argentinian or Brazilian 'mode of being in the world'. The early phases of this process were marked by the influential Argentine magazine *Sur* (1931–76), many of whose pages were devoted to such continental self-analysis. These metaphysical tendencies were prolonged well into the mid-1950s, by which time the rising middle sectors had begun to forge their own more specific cultural identity, with new university systems, the growth and influence of the social sciences, and a redefined insertion of the professions into the life of the continent.

In tracing these conflicting trends, it is important to keep in mind that regionalism is in essence merely the other face of literary nationalism. During this specific period, in fact, it signalled the need for national integration. Nowhere was this more true than in Brazil, the huge Portuguese-speaking republic, almost a continent in itself, which is separated from Spanish America by language, a distinct historical experience, and the special influence of African culture. The regionalist impulse was uniquely important in Brazil for the very reason that national synthesis was still so far from being achieved. Rio de Janeiro's elegantly classical nineteenth-century movements had been predictably superseded in the early decades of the twentieth century by São Paulo's various forms of modernism, but it was much more of a shock to the literary system when, in the 1930s and 1940s, the centre of gravity was once more displaced to the apparently decaying Northeastern periphery to produce one of the golden eras of Brazilian narrative.

The great precursor of this historic shift was *A bagaceira* (1928) by José Américo de Almeida (1887–1980). Like *Doña Bárbara*, Almeida's novel portrays the modernization of the hacienda (*fazenda*) system, in this case that of the Brazilian sugar plantation or *engenho*. Almeida, who had trained as a lawyer, shared other attributes with the Venezuelan writer, including a lifelong commitment to represent the image of the people and to campaign on their behalf. He was closely associated with the *tenentes* movement of the 1920s, a leader of the 1930 Revolution and a minister of public works under Getúlio Vargas between 1930 and 1934. Later writers would have less comfortable relations with state power. *A bagaceira* was set in the sugar belt between the droughts of 1898 and 1915, depicting not only the permanent menace of nature but also the transition from labour-intensive to machine-based cultivation. It was characteristic of an entire sociological line in Brazilian fiction – still heavily influenced by Comtian Positivism and Zola's Naturalism – and its very title recalls those of other famous narrative works of the late nineteenth century. The somewhat melodramatic story follows the relationship between a beautiful refugee from the drought, Soledade, and an idealistic young student, Lúcio; and between Lúcio and his father the sugar baron, who eventually robs him of both his woman and his dreams of social progress. For all its self-evident imperfections, *A bagaceira* undeniably inaugurated a new complex of subjects such as the sugar mill, the drought, the *retirante* (migrant refugee) and the bandit. After 1930 these became stock themes to which a whole generation of younger Brazilian writers would turn.

A redoubtable woman, Raquel de Queirós (b. 1910), was the first writer to profit from Almeida's pioneering example. She was a judge's daughter, and a qualified teacher by the age of fifteen. Her first novel *O quinze* (1930) began precisely where *A bagaceira* had ended, with the horrific *sêca* (drought) of 1915 which had devastated the entire Northeastern territory and had thrown countless desperate refugees into a hopeless search for food, water and work. Queirós's novel was strikingly sober, almost neo-realist (like many novels written by Latin American women), made effective use of everyday language and gave sympathetic insight into the individual aspects of social situations, above all the condition of women. *O quinze* was followed by three further novels before the young writer was twenty-eight, after which she turned her back on narrative fiction and opted for the theatre and for documentary endeavours of various kinds. It was at this time that she became, first, a Communist Party activist, and then, in 1937, a Trotskyist, for which she was rewarded with three months in prison around the time her third novel, *Caminho de pedras,* appeared. In later years she became something of a national institution and, like her mentor Gilberto Freyre, a much more conservative figure preoccupied with semi-eternal folkloric and popular traditions rather than with more immediate social concerns.

Another prodigy, similar to Queirós both in his equally precocious literary career and in his political militancy, was Jorge Amado (b. 1912), the son of a merchant turned coffee planter, who was educated in Salvador and Rio. Amado was to become Brazil's best known twentieth-century novelist, and in 1931, at the age of nineteen, produced his first novel *O país do carnaval,* the expression of a lost generation looking for some nationalist ideal in the midst of stagnation and moral despair. After this polemical start he produced a series of more overtly committed novels, with a carefully calculated combination of socialist and populist ingredients. The first of them, *Cacau* (1933), exposed the inhuman condition of workers on the cocoa plantations of Ilhéus, and was followed by a sequence of urban novels set in Salvador, including *Suor* (1934) and *Jubiabá* (1935). Amado's political odyssey during these years obeyed a complicated and sometimes contradictory itinerary, and he was jailed on several occasions between 1937 and 1942. He had used the 1930s to travel the length and breadth of his own vast country and much of Latin America besides, and he soon began to win an international reputation. Perhaps his greatest novel, *Terras do sem-fim,* appeared in 1943 a work of great conviction and uncharacteristic sobriety which develops themes and characters first outlined in *Cacau* and paints the decline of the old rural *coronéis* on a vast temporal and geographical canvas. It is the most profoundly historical of all the Brazilian novels of this most notable era, to which, in a sense, it puts an end. Amado subsequently joined the Brazilian Communist Party and went into exile when the party was banned in 1947. He travelled extensively through Eastern Europe and elsewhere and produced books which rather crudely followed the party line with titles like *O mundo da paz* (1950) and *Os subterráneos da liberdade* (1954). After the 1956 Soviet thaw he turned to a different kind of writing, composing a series of works calculated to appeal to a much wider popular audience in the capitalist West, the first of which was *Gabriela, cravo e canela* (1958), a worldwide bestseller. It would be difficult to deny that his almost embarrassingly sexual female protagonists have offered a more independent image of Latin American women than most traditional novels, though it could be argued that they merely substitute one form of exploitation for another. This later phase, which for some readers shows the real Amado – more sentimental than ideological, more voluptuous than passionate, and inherently colourful and picturesque – has made him as successful in the capitalist world since the 1960s as he was in the Communist world in the 1950s, and by far the most marketable Brazilian novelist of all time.

A rather different case was José Lins do Rego (1901–57). He had spent his childhood in the big house of one of his maternal grandfather's sugar plantations in the state of Paraíba, and he built a narrative world around this early experience. He studied law in Recife, where he was part of a literary circle including Gilberto Freyre and José Américo de Almeida. He remains identified above all with his *Sugar-Cane Cycle* of 1932–36, which effectively provided a literary illustration of Freyre's influential historical essay *Casa-grande e senzala* (1933). *Menino de engenho* (1932), *Doidinho* (1933), *Bangüê* (1934), *O moleque Ricardo* (1935) and *Usina* (1936), inspired by the plantation of his legendary grandfather Coronel Zé Paulino, mark out the successive phases in a Brazilian quest for lost time as the young central character, Carlos, is educated and socialized during a period in which slavery and plantation life are giving way to the mechanized practices of the sugar mill. In these works Lins do Rego effects an unforgettable fusion of emotional memoir and historical document, at one and the same time tragic and dispassionate, bearing witness to an era and a culture, albeit from the standpoint of the declining ruling class. Some years later *Fogo morto* appeared (1943) and provided a still more historically distanced appraisal of the decadent old order. It proved not only a delayed culmination of the literary sugar cycle but also Lins do Rego's greatest novel.

Another writer from the region was to achieve even greater acclaim than Lins do Rego: indeed Graciliano Ramos (1892–1953) was to be recognized, in due course, as Brazil's most outstanding literary stylist since Machado de Assis half a century before him. Ramos's father, a storekeeper, took the family to live in Palmeira dos Indios, Alagoas in 1910 and much later became its prefect from 1928–30. Graciliano, the eldest of fifteen children, began writing his first novel, *Caetés*, in 1925, but did not complete it for publication until 1933, by which time he was living in Maceió (Alagoas) and meeting other writers such as Queirós, Amado and Lins do Rego. He published a second novel, *São Bernardo,* in 1934. Its outstanding technical achievement made it one of the first novels from Latin America to convey through a first-person narrative the world view of an uneducated anti-heroic protagonist. A self-made landowner, Paulo Honório, narrates with economic starkness the violent story of his disastrous marriage to a schoolteacher. Ramos was imprisoned in 1936 for alleged subversion, was subjected to brutal maltreatment, and spent a year inside, adding to his inherently pessimistic cast of mind. (*Memórias do cárcere,* a bitter and unforgiving memoir of his stay in prison, was published in 1953.) His masterpiece *Vidas sêcas* appeared in 1938, conveying the bitter experience of a family of illiterate refugees fighting to survive almost impossible odds in the natural and social desert of the Northeast. With its almost matchless linguistic and conceptual austerity reflecting the barren lives of its repeatedly humiliated *sertanejo* protagonists, this novel remains one of the most affecting literary works to have come out of Latin America. *Vidas sêcas* is an early Third World classic, one of only a few works to have found original solutions to the challenge of communicating illiteracy and inarticulateness with sensitivity, tact and precision. Eventually the desperate trekkers decide to abandon the hopeless conditions of the countryside and migrate to a new – though possibly equally hopeless – life in the city ('They would come to an unknown and civilized land, and there they'd be imprisoned . . . The Sertão would keep on sending strong, ignorant people, like Fabiano, Missy Vitória and the two boys'). (Many years later, in his depressing novel *Essa terra,* 1976, Antônio Torres would show that things had not changed much.)

   After the novel of the Mexican Revolution, the novel of the Brazilian Northeast is one of the most important regional sub-genres in Latin America. More surprisingly, perhaps, a similar wave of socially and politically committed works appeared in Ecuador during the same period. After Alcides Arguedas's *Raza de bronce* in 1919, Indian-orientated social realist works appeared in many Spanish American republics in the 1920s; yet most writers, like the rural judge Enrique López Albújar (1872–1965) in Peru, for example, despite the vehemence of his portrayals, still saw the Indians as inherently inferior, irrational and superstitious (*Cuentos andinos,* 1920). In that sense his work may be compared directly with that of his Bolivian contemporary. Indian integration seemed unlikely, if not impossible, to such people, then as now. In Ecuador, however, a generation of young writers with different perceptions, known as the Grupo de Guayaquil, appeared. They included Joaquín Gallegos Lara (1911–47), in whose garret they assembled, Enrique Gil Gilbert (1912–74), Demetrio Aguilera Malta (1909–81), whose work would later take on a 'magical realist' orientation, José de la Cuadra (1903–41), a short story writer of a power to match Horacio Quiroga, and Alfredo Pareja Diezcanseco (b. 1908): 'five in one fist', as Gil Gilbert would later say at Cuadra's funeral. In 1930 the first three published an epoch-making joint work, *Los que se van*, subtitled 'Cuentos del cholo y del montuvio'. It caused a sensation because of its violent subject matter and shocking, popular language.

In 1934, inspired in part by his colleagues from the tropical coast, the highlander Jorge Icaza (1906–76) launched a literary missile entitled *Huasipungo*, one of the most hotly debated works in the history of Latin American narrative. He had worked as an actor and playwright in a theatre company during the 1920s and published his first narrative work, *Cuentos de barro*, in 1933. His definitive claim to fame, however, was established in the following year and coincided, fittingly, with Zdhanov's intervention in the writers' congress in the USSR and the subsequent imposition of 'socialist realism' in the Communist world. The novel's title refers to the *huasipungos* or plots of land farmed by the Indians on feudal estates until the Liberal reforms of 1918. It is perhaps the most brutally laconic and deliberately offensive novel ever published about the condition of the Latin American Indians and the shameful realities of the hacienda system which prevailed from the colonial period to the present century. The question it raises perennially in the mind and conscience of each reader is: what exactly are we offended by as we read it? Icaza interprets everything according to the base-superstructure distinction of vulgar Marxism and traces the implacable logic of the semi-feudal socio-economic system on the basis of one case study, the building of a road through the hacienda by a North American lumber company. Icaza's position is that it is difficult to be human when subjected to inhuman treatment. The higher one's social class, the more 'worlds' one has available. His Indians have only one available world, as the Ecuadorean novelist is at pains to show us ('He searched for some mental support but found everything around him elusive and alien. For the others – mestizos, gentlemen and bosses – an Indian's woes are a matter for scorn, contempt and disgust. What could his anguish over the illness of his wife possibly signify in the face of the complex and delicate tragedies of the whites? Nothing!').

Viewed across the decades, it may seem almost incredible that at the same time that Icaza and his contemporaries were writing such works in Ecuador and elsewhere, Jorge Luis Borges and his circle in Argentina were, as we shall see, writing their complex and labyrinthine literary inquisitions. There could hardly be a clearer example of what the concept of uneven development might mean as applied to cultural expression. Of course there is nowhere in Latin America where the relation between literature and society has been more direct, or more turbulent, than in the Andean republics of Peru, Bolivia and Ecuador, mainly due to the unavoidable connection between three great historical problematics: the national question, the agrarian question and the ethnic question. Peruvian cultural expression, in particular, often has a raw and unmistakably bitter flavour unlike that of any other country. There in the 1920s Víctor Raúl Haya de la Torre and José Carlos Mariátegui elaborated the two ideological alternatives to conservative or liberal rule in the continent: populism (Aprismo) and communism.

Aprismo was the creed of Ciro Alegría (1909–67), the most important Peruvian indigenist novelist of the entire regionalist era. He had spent much of his childhood on his grandfather's hacienda close to the River Marañón in Huanachuco. Living in Lima, years later, Alegría reneged on his background, joined Apra and was imprisoned during the events of 1932. After escaping from jail and being rearrested, he went into exile in Chile in 1934, where he fell ill with tuberculosis, became paralysed and lost the faculty of speech, before writing two episodic novels *La serpiente de oro* (1935), about the boatmen of the Marañón, and *Los perros hambrientos* (1938), about the Indian and Cholo peasants of the high cordilleras and their struggle against both nature in all its cruel indifference and Peruvian society in all its brutal hostility. However it was his next novel, *El mundo es ancho y ajeno,* which gave him his continental reputation. It was written in four months in 1940 for a Pan-American competition announced by the New York publishers Farrar and Rinehart. Like *Los perros hambrientos* it has a tone of classical authority and a simple grandeur reminiscent of Gallegos's best work and with a similar nineteenth-century conception. Using a vast historical, geographical and social canvas, this later work portrays a free community of Indians in northern Peru between 1912 and the 1930s, focusing on their mayor, Rosendo Maqui, once considered one of the great character creations of Latin American fiction ('The Indian Rosendo Maqui crouched there like some ancient idol, his body dark and gnarled like the *lloque* with its knotted, iron-hard trunk, for he was part plant, part man, and part rock. It was as if Rosendo Maqui were cast in the image of his geography; as if the turbulent forces of the earth had fashioned him and his people in the likeness of their mountains'). The novel ends like almost all indigenist novels: the Indians are robbed of their land by a cruel and unscrupulous landowner and obliged to wander the earth, only to discover with increasing desperation that although Peru is broad it has become alien, and that neither pacificism, banditry nor socialist insurrection seem likely to modify their historical destiny. Alegría won the New York competition, and was warmly lauded by John Dos Passos, a member of the jury, making the Peruvian novelist one of the two or three best-known Latin American writers of this period.

*El mundo es ancho y ajeno* is ambitious, panoramic and the only one of the great regionalist works to have a genuine historical framework, as we follow the epic quest for land and justice to the jungles and the rivers, the mines and the cities, among the bandits and the trade unionists. The book will endure as a great, if sometimes clumsy monument to the indigenist doctrine of an entire epoch. It is majestic despite its unevenness and moving despite its sentimentality, and it does provide the reader with a means by which to imagine the experience of the Andean Indians.

## Urban Themes

No simple formula can illuminate the relation between country and city in Western history. Whatever our desires, no society has ever been free to choose between these two political and economic alternative realities nor between the different lifestyles which they have conditioned – although artists and intellectuals have often liked to imagine that they could – because it is precisely in the historical dynamic between the two milieux that social meaning has existed. From the very beginning writers from Latin American city environments were acutely conscious of the provincial and possibly caricatural status of their own neo-colonial and dependent cities compared to the world's great metropoli of past and present: theirs were parasitic enclaves, comprador corridors between city and country. Life in those increasingly ugly conurbations seemed somehow even more absurd than in European cities, whose existence was justified by the whole weight and authority of European history, however alienating the urban experience as such might seem to any given inhabitant of those places.

It was the Cuban writer Alejo Carpentier who in a memorable essay asserted that it was the mission of Latin American artists to do for their cities what Balzac had done for Paris, Dickens for London and Joyce for Dublin. He acknowledged that he and his contemporaries had an especially difficult problem, since not only were their readers ignorant of the context of their literary recreations but these were in any case cities 'without style' or, perhaps, with 'a third style, the style of things that have no style'.[2] Ironically enough, at the very time that Carpentier was writing, around 1960, the urban novel was finally beginning to prevail. However, given the subcontinent's involuntary role in Western mythologies, it seems likely that Latin America's fate may be always to represent the 'country' to Europe's 'city', and that, given its landscapes and state of development, novels of the land may continue to be important for longer than we think – or, perhaps, for as long as we can imagine.

In fact urban novels like those which had been written by Balzac and Dickens did not appear in Latin America until late in the nineteenth century, by which time Zola was the dominant influence, though few of his imitators at that time had his grasp of detail or social motivation. Latin American capitals were very small and largely provincial in character until well into the present century. The most notable exception to the general picture was Brazil, where the mulatto writer Joaquim Maria Machado de Assis (1839–1908) became Latin America's only truly great novelist in the century after independence and one of the undoubted masters of the genre in the Western world. The key to his achievement lay in finding a humorous, parodic, iconoclastic form with which to negotiate the difficulties of living in an intranscendent semi-colonial city, long before the similar twentieth-century solutions improvised by such 'post-colonial' writers as Borges or Naipaul.

Between the two world wars, however, there were few such humorous responses to the experience of Latin American cities. An early protest novel about the woes and injustices of urban existence was *Triste fim de Policarpo Quaresma* (1915) by Alfonso Henriques de Lima Barreto (1881–1922), another Brazilian mulatto who was in many respects the successor to Machado de Assis. In 1917 the Chilean Eduardo Barrios (1884–1963) followed this example with another novel of urban alienation and despair, *Un perdido*, in which the hopeless loser of the title is unable to discover meaning or satisfaction in life in twentieth-century Santiago. In the 1920s the Argentinian novelist Roberto Arlt (1900–42), now belatedly considered one of the most significant writers of the continent, gave an early indication of the

---

[2] Alejo Carpentier, 'Problemática de la actual novela latinoamericana', in *Tientos y diferencias* (Havana, 1966), p. 15.

extent to which Latin American fiction, particularly in Buenos Aires and Montevideo, would be able to echo or even anticipate European currents of nihilism and absurdism. This was because for writers or protagonists with a European mentality and European nostalgias, Latin America was either a nowhere land or a caricature. Arlt produced a remarkable sequence of urban horror tales, *El juguete rabioso* (1926), *Los siete locos* (1929) and *Los lanzallamas* (1931). Like the rural Quiroga before him, Arlt constructed his reality somewhere between alienation, madness, depravity and criminality, with neither the author nor the characters able to distinguish satisfactorily between these elements of the existential analysis. His is a world without transcendence, in which the bourgeoisie's official ideology of honour, hard work and decency is contradicted everywhere by reality and the only means of self-affirmation are crime or madness. The tradition is that of Dostoyevsky and originates in Argentina with Eugenio Cambaceres (1843–88), and goes on through Onetti, Marechal, Sábato and many others. It was somehow fitting though also ironic that Arlt was for a time Ricardo Güiraldes's secretary, for it was Güiraldes whose *Don Segundo Sombra* bade a sorrowful farewell to the gaucho era and indeed to literary concentration on the rural sector as a whole, whilst the clearest sign that in Argentina at least the age of urban fiction had definitely arrived was the appearance of Arlt's literary provocations.

It has become a commonplace of Latin American historical criticism to say that the New York prize awarded to *El mundo es ancho y ajeno* in 1941 should have gone to another competitor, the Uruguayan Juan Carlos Onetti (1909–94). Ciro Alegría was the last of the old-style 'regionalist' authors, rooted in the land, whilst Onetti was the first and perhaps the most important of a quite new generation of novelists routed through the cities. His first novel, *El pozo,* appeared in 1939, and shows that writers in Montevideo or Buenos Aires had no need to read Céline, Sartre or Camus to know that they were alienated or anguished. Onetti's fiction begins where Arlt left off, though Onetti always achieves the necessary distance from his materials to be able to impose the delicacy and coherence of art on even the most sordid and contradictory reality. *El pozo* tells the story of Eladio Linacero, a university-educated journalist frustrated but also mediocre, who shares a room like a prison cell with an ignorant Communist militant ironically called Lazarus, and vainly longs to become a writer. Outside the drab and depressing city which Montevideo has become lies a Uruguay without history: 'Behind us, there is nothing: one gaucho, two gauchos, thirty-three gauchos.' This is sacrilege: these 'thirty-three gauchos' were the symbolic heroes of Uruguay's liberation struggle. Clearly we have travelled very far from Gallegos and the other Americanists by this point. Latin America is a continent with nothing worth writing about beyond the writer's own anguish, and Onetti ends his work with a statement of existential bankruptcy: 'This is the night. I am a solitary man smoking somewhere in the city; the night surrounds me, as in a ritual, gradually, and I have no part in it.' Despite the gloom, Onetti is always more concerned to communicate a vision than to make a point, elaborating a picture not only of city life (Montevideo, Buenos Aires and his invented community of 'Santa María') but also of reality and consciousness themselves as labyrinthine, a tissue of perceptions and motives impossible to disentangle and clarify, with the effort to do so ending always in weariness, boredom, frustration and defeat. Later works by Onetti include *Tierra de nadie* (1941), *La vida breve* (1950), *Los adioses* (1954), *El astillero* (1961), generally considered his masterpiece, *Juntacadáveres* (1964), *Dejemos hablar al viento* (1979) and *Cuando entonces* (1987).

Undoubtedly, Onetti inaugurates the mature phase of Latin American urban fiction with his disturbing, world-weary narratives. As mentioned, this is a line of fiction particularly common in the River Plate, where the Argentine Eduardo Mallea (1903–82) gave it a somewhat portentous philosophical orientation from the 1930s to the 1950s (see especially *Todo verdor perecerá*, 1941), whilst the Uruguayan Mario Benedetti (b. 1920) concentrated more closely on the social and historical determinants of that same grey, heavy despair during the 1960s and 1970s. His best known works include *Quién de nosotros* (1953), *Montevideanos* (stories, 1959), *La tregua* (1960), *Gracias por el fuego* (1965) and *Primavera con una esquina rota* (1982). One of the most apocalyptic of such writers was Ernesto Sábato (Argentina, b. 1911), author of *Sobre héroes y tumbas* (1961). Even Onetti lacks the nightmarish note characteristic of Sábato's fiction, which also includes *El túnel* (1948) and *Abaddón el exterminador* (1977). Sábato's almost Dostoyevskyan work is at once a meditation on the condition of mankind in the twentieth century and on the development of Argentina from the time of Rosas to the time of Perón, viewed as a family history of criminal depravity. For him Buenos Aires is a home to nightmares, built on a vast sewer: 'Everything floated towards the Nothingness of the ocean through secret underground tunnels, as if those above were trying to forget, affecting to know nothing of this part of their truth. As if heroes in reverse, like me, were destined to the infernal and accursed task of bearing witness to that reality.'

Thus from the time of Roberto Arlt fiction was gradually moving to the metropolitan realm and away from the rural, though the latter continued to dominate until the late 1950s. In the cities, symbolic prisons, writers often found themselves in trouble with the authorities and much narrative fiction was devoted to prison themes in the 1930s and 1940s (whereas in the 1970s and 1980s themes of exile or 'disappearance' tended to be more frequent). There is indeed a sense in which for all Latin American writers, regardless of ideology, the literary act is always also a political one.

This traditionally strong emphasis on social and political themes only added to the difficulty which women writers, already condemned as second-class citizens to confrontation with a virulently patriarchal society, experienced in the early decades of the century. Interestingly enough, most of the women writers well known to the twentieth century, like Sor Juana Inés de la Cruz (Mexico, 1648–95), Gertrudis Gómez de Avellaneda (Cuba, 1814–73), or Clorinda Matto de Turner (Peru, 1854–1909), were involved in some form of literature of protest. But in the early twentieth century conditions were not favourable to this kind of activity by women, though there were notable exceptions such as Raquel de Queirós, discussed above, or Chile's valiant regionalist novelist Marta Brunet (1897–1967), whose career began as early as 1923 with *Montaña adentro*. Normally, however, women novelists were limited both by experience and by expectation to more domestic varieties of writing (and, of course, to the short story, a form particularly accessible to minority and disadvantaged writers of all kinds). Thus, for example, even though the delightful *Las memorias de Mamá Blanca* (1929) by Teresa de la Parra (Venezuela, 1891–1936), is set on an hacienda in the countryside, it has a light and intimate tone quite different from the kinds of regionalist writing then in vogue. (Her *Ifigenia. Diario de una señorita que escribió porque se fastidiaba*, 1924, is an excellent example of the nascent feminist consciousness emerging in those years.)

The gradual shift of emphasis to the cities, which has marked the whole of the twentieth century, has undoubtedly favoured the equally gradual emergence of women writers, above all perhaps in the River Plate area. In Argentina the wealthy Victoria Ocampo (1890–1979), through her literary salon, her patronage and her magazine *Sur*, brought together and encouraged a whole generation of Argentine literati, as well as putting them in touch with writers and developments from abroad. Her series of ten volumes of *Testimonios* (1935–77) are her most widely read works. Silvina Ocampo (1906–93), Victoria's sister, was married to the writer

Adolfo Bioy Casares but was also one of Argentina's best known short story writers in her own right, with collections including *Viaje olvidado* (1937), *Autobiografía de Irene* (1948), *La furia* (1959) and several others. All were marked by a delicate but insistent sense of the perverse and the fantastic. Meanwhile in Chile María Luisa Bombal (1910–80) wrote two novels not much noticed at the time but which have since been recognized as milestones in the development of women's writing in Latin America, *La última niebla* (1934) and *La amortajada* (1938), both suffused by an intensely subjective mode of perception, a tormented vision from within. For women, too, the theme of imprisonment was a constant referent, though not at the hands of the state but by courtesy of their own fathers and husbands.

## MODERNISM: FROM THE NEW NOVEL TO THE 'BOOM'

*El mundo es ancho y ajeno* (1940) was the last great regionalist work, though similar novels continued to be written and the social realist mode has persisted through a whole series of formal and ideological transformations up to the present day. Our task now is to travel back again in time to the 1920s to search for the origins of the 'Latin American New Novel', usually associated with the 1950s or even considered synonymous with the 'Boom' of the 1960s. Closer analysis will reveal that Latin America has taken a far more important part in twentieth-century Modernism (and Postmodernism) than even the most nationalistic Latin American critics tend to assert. The truth is that the only really persuasive description for Latin America's most distinctive line of fiction since the 1920s is, precisely, 'Modernism' in the European and North American sense, and it is important to ask why it has been more persistent in the new continent than in either Europe or the United States. Clearly, despite the technical fertility of Joyce, Proust, Woolf or Faulkner, European and North American Modernism has no system, no theory, except as a 'sign of the times'. Latin American writers, however, regardless of their politics, were always pulled in two directions and learned to balance different realities and different orders of experience and thereby to find their way into history as well as myth. Indeed, the essence of what has been called 'magical realism' (itself a form of Modernist discourse), is the juxtaposition and fusion, on equal terms, of the literate and pre-literate world, future and past, modern and traditional, the city and the country: or, to put it another way, the fusion of *modernista* and *naturalista* elements, radically updated, in one unifying discourse. This requires the application of indirect narration and the treatment of folk beliefs, superstitions and myths with absolute literalness. Joyce and Faulkner showed the way, and both were from marginal regions with something of the bi-culturalism required, but neither of them needed to formulate this as an explicit part of their system or project; whereas in Latin America all narratives, inevitably, bear the imprint of their origins in their structure, because all Latin American writers are from the 'periphery'.

As we have seen, most novels about Latin American cities concentrate on the negative, repressive aspects of the urban experience and rather few celebrate it as any kind of liberation from nature. In that sense the romantic impulse remains very strong in the subcontinent. The city is a world of alienation, reification, exchange values, consumption and exhaustion, contrasted negatively with the cosmic fertilization and global significance of the indigenous world which preceded it. Yet the great regionalist novels of the 1920s and 1930s also go well beyond the romantic obsession with mere landscape or mere spirituality, and so terms like 'novel of the land' or 'regionalist novel' are unsatisfactory and perhaps even misleading. These works were 'regional' not in the sense that they were 'sub-national' but precisely because, from this moment, Latin America was conceived as one large though not yet integrated nation made up of numerous 'regions' (the twenty republics). Put another way, it is not so much a regionalist spirit as a nationalist and Americanist ideology which conditions and structures the novels of Latin America's first important narrative moment, integrating the country and the city within one nationhood and connecting each of these within an Americanist supra-nationhood or continental vision. (Of course this is not the same as identifying Latin America's place within world culture, a process which the *modernistas* had tentatively initiated, albeit on unequal and semi-colonial terms: that more global literary-historical achievement – one which ended an entire cultural era – began at the same time as the novels studied thus far were being written, but was undertaken by a different kind of writer and, although likewise initiated in the 1920s, was only completed in the 1960s and early 1970s.) Regionalism and Americanism, then, are two sides of the same impulse and the concept 'novel of the land' was actually a symbolic designation: the 'land' is not so much the telluric earth as the American continent itself as a field of endeavour and object of meditation, with individual works alternating within the semantic field marked out by these two poles: region and continent.

Seeing this, we can understand why the capital cities depicted in the novels mentioned above are not usually imagined as capitals of that regional, American interior. Instead, they are European enclaves, treacherously conspiring or weakly collaborating in the exploitation of natural raw materials, or — like Lima, Rio de Janeiro and Buenos Aires — with their backs turned on the regions and gazing out longingly over the ocean that leads back to Europe. Naturally some writers have always argued that cosmopolitanism is an unavoidable and in any case desirable reaching out to the world, a wish to integrate Latin America into the universal order of things, to take its place among the cultures, recognizing and being recognized. This is a process of discussion whose end is not in sight.

Thus each of the regionalist works takes up the debate initiated by Domingo Faustino Sarmiento and Euclides da Cunha on the national question. Are these territorial entities really nations? What sort of community is a nation? How do regions smaller and larger than the nations relate to them? If these countries are not yet nations but nationhood is the project, how is it to be achieved? And to what extent might Latin America be conceived as a unified plurality which only makes sense at the level of the continent and therefore only makes unified writing possible from a continental perspective? The narrative fiction of the nineteenth century had symbolically founded nations and established the identity of the governing classes. Naturalist novels had examined the pathology of the lower classes and been disappointed by what they saw. In the 1920s 'regionalist' fiction looked again and took a more positive view, not only of the lower classes, but of the possibilities for a constructive relationship between the rulers and the ruled. The interior now was not only a field for imagination and romance, but for epic and social exploration, for knowledge and definition. Thus writers embarked on the journey from capital to interior, only to realize that the future was not after all clear: first, because everything was more complicated than had been thought, not least because alliances with the workers involved commitments which might not always suit the interests of the volatile petty bourgeoisie; and secondly, because the road still appeared to lie through Europe, whether capitalist or socialist. Thus to the chain from capital to village is added the journey from there back again to the capital and across the seas to Europe — and then back again to the village, with all those newly assimilated experiences within the writer's consciousness. This indeed is the fundamental explanation of what I have called elsewhere the 'Ulyssean' writer and the growth of the 'Ulyssean' novel,[3] inaugurated and given definitive form by perhaps the greatest of all twentieth century Modernist writers, James Joyce. He was not, at first sight, what young Latin American artists ought to have been looking for in the 1920s, and yet, avant-garde seductions aside, the Irishman and his Latin American admirers had a number of things in common which facilitated his influence: for example migrations and exile; Catholicism, its traditions and repressions; and the counter-conquest of an alien, imperial language.

None of these factors apply in the same way to the other great model, William Faulkner. Of course there would have been no Faulkner without Joyce, and we will recall that Faulkner learned from the Joyce who had written *Ulysses* and not from the one who went on to write *Finnegans Wake*. Still, Faulkner and his compatriot John Dos Passos were more accessible models in the Latin America of the thirties, forties, and fifties, whilst Joyce would finally exert his full impact only in the 1960s and 1970s. This is not really so surprising: what Faulkner, and to a lesser extent, Dos Passos, actually permitted, was the renovation and restructuring of the Latin American social novel through the next thirty years, whereas, de-spite the admiration he inspired in a generation of young Americans in Paris, Joyce's impact on most authors – if not, crucially, on the most important of them – remained largely fragmentary or superficial except in poetry and was only generally assimilable in the 1960s, the age, indeed, of the final flowering of Latin American Modernism in the form of the 'Boom' novel.

The bridge to Modernist developments in narrative was, indeed, avant-garde poetry. In that, at least, the continent was already fully modern, in the sense that many poets – Vicente Huidobro, Jorge Luis Borges, Oswald de Andrade, Manuel Bandeira, César Vallejo and Pablo Neruda – were writing poetry as 'up to date', innovative and recognizably twentieth-century as anything being produced in Europe, the Soviet Union or the United States.

The novel, however, is always slower to mature (in the end it is always a historical, retrospective genre, which needs time to focus) and in the 1920s there emerged in literature, broadly speaking, a contrast between a poetic expression whose dominant mode was cosmopolitan, produced by international experience and orientated in the same direction, and the various forms of 'nativist' fiction – regionalist, Creolist, telluric, indi-

<hr/>

[3] See Martin, *Journeys through the Labyrinth*, passim.

genist, etc. – examined above, which, because they lay somewhere between realism and naturalism, we are calling social realism. Its impetus had been both shaped and accelerated by the Mexican Revolution, and at that time was thought, not entirely paradoxically, to be the most innovative as well as the most typical current in Latin American literature, at a moment when few would have imagined that Latin Americans might participate in cultural discoveries and developments on equal terms. Equally strikingly, the novelists who were closest to the poets were young avant-garde writers like the Brazilian Mário de Andrade with his pathbreaking novel about the Brazilian culture hero *Macunaíma* (1928), the Guatemalan Miguel Angel Asturias, author of the quasi-ethnological *Leyendas de Guatemala* (1930), the Argentine Jorge Luis Borges, who was already intermingling literature with criticism in quite new ways, and the Cuban Alejo Carpentier, with his Afro-American *Ecué-Yamba-O* (1933). It was these writers who would lead the way into the future. Joyce had mapped the route to the great labyrinth of modernity and had effectively ordained the literary systematization of Modernism. Once seen, this labyrinth could not be ignored and had to be traversed. In the case of the Spanish American trio just cited, the full dimensions of their talents would not become apparent until the 1930s and – due to the nature of the 1930s and the intervention of the Second World War – would only become visible after 1945; and even then, only relatively so, because it was not until the 1960s that the complex interaction between Latin American and international conditions of education, readership and publishing combined to produce a situation in which the achievements of Latin American art could be relatively quickly and generally recognized.

In the 1920s, many young Latin American intellectuals and artists were in Paris at the same time as Joyce (and Picasso and Stravinsky). At the moment when the pre-war *modernista* movement, already fading autumnally in the last years of the *belle époque,* was giving way to the avant-garde of the *années folles,* these young writers, who had made the pilgrimage to Paris aided by the plunge of the franc, began to found and participate in a succession of new and exciting magazines with futuristic titles – *Proa* ('Prow': in his 1925 review of *Ulysses* in that same magazine Borges said that Joyce himself was 'audacious as a prow', in other words, an avant-garde explorer and adventurer) in Buenos Aires; *Revista de Avance* in Havana; *Contemporáneos* in Mexico; *Imán* in Paris itself – in all of which the name of Joyce would appear, usually as a rather distant, almost mythological referent.

Astonishingly, in view of his later trajectory, it was Borges who first appreciated the true significance of Joyce, and who became not only the pioneer translator of the famous last page of *Ulysses* but also saw that work as a 'wild and entangled land' into which only the most foolhardy would venture.[4] Borges's initial enthusiasm was soon renounced, just as he would in due course also dismiss his own avant-garde moment – *ultraísmo* – , his localist *Fervor de Buenos Aires,* his 'too vulgar' story 'El hombre de la esquina rosada', all plots requiring social or psychological realism, all wilful obscurity and linguistic experimentalism. He would later describe *Ulysses* itself as 'a failure', a work of microscopic naturalism with, paradoxically, 'no real characters'. Yet whenever Borges wished to explore the nature of literary language, he turned to Joyce's example, just as he did whenever he wished to discuss translation, comparativism, literary purity, artistic devotion, or totality. Moreover Borges, one of the writers who made possible the concept of 'intertextuality', frequently named Joyce as a key innovator of the phenomenon.

Many young Latin American poets sought to make use of Joyce's example in the 1920s, but were mostly unprepared for the task. It has not been much noticed that the reason for this is that Joyce was on his way past Modernism to what is now called Postmodernism. Thus in the 1930s it was Faulkner and Dos Passos who more clearly showed how to apply the new Modernist techniques to narrative fiction and thereby provided the means for updating the social or regionalist novel. The point, however, is that Joyce's influence began before either, was more widespread if not more powerful, and grew slowly but surely to a crescendo in the 1960s and 1970s. Moreover, in a few literary milestones of the following era – Asturias' *El señor Presidente* (1946) (see below), *Al filo del agua* (1947) by Agustín Yáñez (1904–80), considered by critics one of the great transitional works of Latin American fiction and a precursor of the 'New Novel', and Leopoldo Marechal's *Adán Buenosayres* (1948) (see below), the particular combination of interior monologue and stream-of-consciousness techniques with other devices, especially wordplay and myth, made critics correctly conclude that these historically fundamental works were more Joycean than Faulknerian. Not until 1945, four years after Joyce's death, was *Ulysses* available at last to those who could read neither French or English, when the first translation appeared in Buenos Aires.

Many years later the great 'Boom' of Latin American fiction – itself

---

[4] Jorge Luis Borges, 'El *Ulises* de Joyce', in *Proa* (Buenos Aires), 6 (January 1925), 3.

now mythologized, its writers living legends – produced an emphatic shift of gravity to the urban realm, with the emergence and consolidation of its 'big four' – Cortázar, Fuentes, García Márquez and Vargas Llosa – followed by others like Lezama Lima, Cabrera Infante and Donoso. In an article on these new Latin American novelists in 1977, Emir Rodríguez Monegal, the influential Uruguayan critic, made a striking retrospective assessment of the Irish writer's influence: 'Joyce's achievement was to be imitated in many languages. Slowly, and through many successful works . . . *Ulysses* became the invisible but central model of the new Latin American narrative. From this point of view, Cortázar's *Hopscotch*, Lezama Lima's *Paradiso*, Fuentes's *Change of Skin* and Cabrera Infante's *Three Trapped Tigers*, are Joycean books. Whether or not they are obviously Joycean, they do share the same secret code. That is, they agree in conceiving of the novel as both a parody and a myth, a structure which in its topoi, as much as in its private symbols, reveals the unity of a complete system of signification.'[5] An equally decisive accolade was later paid to Joyce by the Mexican novelist Fernando del Paso, author of the Ulyssean novel *Palinuro de México* (1977): 'I consider that *Ulysses* is a sort of sun installed at the centre of the Gutenberg Galaxy, which illuminates not only all the works which followed it but all of universal literature that preceded it. Its influence is definitive and unique in modern Western literature . . . *Finnegans Wake* is a comet of great magnitude moving away from us at the speed of light, in danger of becoming lost for ever. But there is also the possibility that it will return one day and be better understood.'[6] This explains convincingly why the Joycean paradigm has been so attractive in Latin America. Viewed from this long perspective, however, it becomes obvious that Latin America as a whole, despite its post-colonial status, took less time to assimilate Joycean writing than a number of the English-speaking literatures for which such assimilation was easier and, moreover, assimilated it more completely. The same cultural factors which have made Latin America a hospitable environment for Joycean or 'Ulyssean' novels to flower are factors which, in turn, have allowed Latin American narrative to return the favour and influence a whole succession of European and North American works in the postmodern period since the 1960s.

---

[5] Emir Rodríguez Monegal, 'The New Latin American novelists', *Partisan Review*, 44 1 (1977), 41.
[6] Quoted by R. Fiddian in his 'James Joyce y Fernando del Paso', *Insula* (Madrid), 455 (October 1984), p. 10.

*Myth and Magic: The Origins of the Latin American New Novel*

After the social realism of the 1920s and 1930s, much of the narrative fiction of the 1950s, 1960s and 1970s has been given a more seductive name: 'Magical Realism'. When the label was given above all to Miguel Angel Asturias and Alejo Carpentier, as it used to be, together with one or two like-minded writers like Venezuela's Arturo Uslar Pietri and Ecuador's Demetrio Aguilera Malta, the term, although problematical, was in some ways attractive and acceptable. Now that, like the concept 'baroque', it has become an almost universal description of the 'Latin American style' –exotic and tropical, overblown and unrestrained, phantasmagorical and hallucinatory – it may seem so ideologically dangerous that it should really be rejected. And yet writers as influential and prestigious as Italo Calvino, Salman Rushdie, Umberto Eco and even John Updike have acknowledged its influence and allure, and so it seems possible that it has been at least partly 'decolonized'.

It has not been sufficiently understood that its origins lie in the surrealist movement of the 1920s, the most important avant-garde system coinciding historically with Modernism. Surrealism was never a significant influence in either Britain or the United States, both of which were far too empirical for such schemas at that time. Its emphasis upon the unconscious, and therefore the primitive, its insistence that there was a world more real than the visible 'reality' of commonsense and positivism, the idea that art is a journey of discovery involving free association and the liberation of the repressed, were all tailor-made for Third World interpretations and applications, and therefore for cementing the growing cultural relationship between France and Latin America following independence and the declaration that what the British persist in calling 'South' America was actually 'Latin'. Moreover, this relationship in which, instead of superordinate to subordinate, imperialist to colonial, France exchanged her rational civilization on equal terms (she had no large colonial axe to grind in Latin America) with the New World's supposed instinctual barbarism, was ideally suited to the interests of both sides.

The more convincing and less ideological justification for this most controversial of literary terms – magical realism – is that the 'magic' derives from the cultural sparks which fly from the juxtaposition and clash of different cultures at different levels of development, but this seems not to be the explanation for its attraction. In the era of Hollywood stars, Coca

Cola and the intensifying fetishism of commodity exchange, it ought not to be too difficult to understand why 'magic' realism would give us pleasure and conciliate a number of painful contradictions. However in the end it is myth, the universal currency of communication through translation and transformation, which is the only unifying factor between, say, Andrade, Asturias, Borges, Carpentier and García Márquez, who, in other terms, are quite different kinds of novelist. To that extent, it would have been more logical to go for the concept of 'mythical realism'. Either way, one of the crucial features insufficiently stressed in most discussions is the question of the collective dimension characteristic of all magical realist writers, in contrast to the almost inveterate individualism of most kinds of fantastic writing.

Although rarely acknowledged as such, it is almost certainly the case that Mário de Andrade (1893–1945) was the first example, together with Miguel Angel Asturias, of this phenomenon in Latin American literature – thanks largely to his fertile relationship with Brazil's own 1920s *Modernista* movement. Interestingly enough, Andrade had never been abroad when he wrote *Macunaíma* (1928), a key text of the famous 'anthropophagous' movement, and most of what he knew about Brazil had come from books. Certainly what followers of Bakhtin would now call the 'carnivalization' of Latin American literature and the development of the 'polyphonic novel' began with *Macunaíma,* as is indicated by Mário's humorous explanation of his work: 'The Brazilian has no character because he has neither a civilization of his own nor a traditional consciousness . . . He is just like a twenty year old boy.' The eponymous hero travels around Brazil, from the primitive to the modern and back again, as Andrade whimsically confronts such previously unexplored themes as tribalism, totemism, sacrifice, cannibalism and – of course – magic. Oswald de Andrade, challenging the incomprehension with which the novel was greeted, said: 'Mário has written our *Odyssey* and with one blow with his club has created the cyclical hero and the national poetic style for the next fifty years.'[7] Towards the end of the novel there is an intriguing incident as the hero loses consciousness in a battle with a giant, and the narrator announces: 'Macunaíma got into the canoe, took a trip to the mouth of the Rio Negro to look for his consciousness, left behind on the island of Marapatá. And do you think he found it? Not a hope! So then our hero grabbed the consciousness of a Spanish American,

---

[7] Quoted by Haroldo de Campos, '*Macunaíma:* la fantasía estructural', in Mário de Andrade, *Macunaíma* (Barcelona, 1976), p. 11.

stuffed it in his head, and got on just as well.' Perhaps this was the moment when Brazil began to become part of Latin America. At any rate, Mário de Andrade was one of the first writers in the Third World to dare to take not only myth but also magic seriously and unapologetically, as a system of ideas and practices for working on the natural world as an alternative to Western science and technology.

The young Alejo Carpentier's brief novel *Ecue-Yamba-O* ('Praise be to Ecue') was published in 1933, though its first version was signed 'Havana Prison, 1–9 August 1927'. He was later reluctant to see the work republished. He felt that although it was based partly on people he had known as a child, he had failed to grasp either the essence of their psychology and way of life or the linguistic medium needed to convey it. He only relented at the very end of his life, when a clumsily produced pirate edition appeared. While it is undoubtedly true that Carpentier's novel on the culture of Cuba's Black population was more interesting for what it promised than for what it achieved, its project was similar to *Macunaíma* and to Asturias's *Leyendas de Guatemala*. Of course he and Asturias were both from small countries with large ethnic populations which made the question of a unified national identity more than usually problematical. Both were closely associated with the Surrealists in Paris in the 1920s; both knew of Joyce, both believed in the power of myth, metaphor, language and symbol, both were Freudian in orientation, Marxisant and revolutionary by instinct. They would each, from that moment, through the dark hibernatory age of the 1930s and 1940s – a fertile, global unconscious for both of them – gestate these ideas and in due course, around 1948, each would start to talk of 'magical realism' (Asturias) or 'the marvellous real' (Carpentier).

As an active member of Cuba's 1923 Generation, Alejo Carpentier (1904–80) was involved in efforts to revolutionize national culture and to confront the dictatorship of Gerardo Machado. The guiding thread of the search for identity was Afro-Cubanism, the quest to integrate the Black experience into Cuba's national self-expression, underpinned by the pathbreaking folkloric and ethnological work of Fernando Ortiz (1881–1969), one of Latin America's most original thinkers. Stories by Carpentier inspired compositions by the Mulatto composer Amadeo Roldán, and Carpentier subsequently became a leading authority on Cuban music in his own right. *Ecue-Yamba-O* includes several attempts to recreate the intense experience of Afro-Cuban music; and although it would be effortlessly surpassed by Carpentier's own *El reino de este mundo* (1949) almost two decades later, it was undoubtedly one of the first important attempts to characterize the Black presence in narrative.

By 1928 Miguel Angel Asturias (1899–1974) had almost completed his first major book in Paris, where he was studying ethnology at the Sorbonne. Early public readings took place in the year that *Macunaíma* was published. These *Leyendas de Guatemala* (1930), still virtually unstudied to the present day, are one of the first anthropological contributions to Spanish American literature. Like Andrade, who called for an American 'cannibalization' of European culture, Asturias thought attack the best form of defence and communicated a radically different vision, revealing a Latin American world as yet unimagined. Asturias's small country had behind it what Andrade's huge one lacked: a great native civilization. Thus the second part of his integrative strategy was to relate the 'primitive' (we were all 'Indians' once upon a time, in the tribal era) to the classical maize-based civilizations of the Pre-Columbian era: Mayas, Aztecs, Incas. All were earth, maize, sun and star worshippers, space men. In Asturias's fiction the pre-human forces and creatures of native myth are given new life, and the Indians themselves are inserted into that landscape: the Spaniards here are very late arrivals.

Asturias's next major work was one of the landmarks of Latin American narrative, which, in the post-Second World War period, confirmed the rise of urban fiction which had already been signalled in Argentina and Uruguay. Ironically enough, the novel in question, *El señor Presidente* (1946), was about a very small capital city, that of his native Guatemala, and it was set in the period of the First World War, before the process of Latin American modernization had become generally visible. Asturias's entire life until the age of twenty-one had been overshadowed by the fearsome dictatorship of Manuel Estrada Cabrera (1898–1920), and his own father's legal career was ruined by the tyrant. This novel, in which every action and every thought is in some way conditioned by the real dictator and his mythological aura, reflects the horizons of Asturias's own childhood and adolescence ('A monstrous forest separated the President from his enemies, a forest of trees with ears which at the slightest sound began to turn as though whipped up by the hurricane wind . . . A web of invisible threads, more invisible than the telegraph wires, linked each leaf to the President, alert to all that went on in the most secret fibres of his citizens.'). From that darkness, that imprisonment (not only the dictatorship, but also Hispanic traditionalism, semi-colonial provincialism, Catholicism and the Family), Asturias travelled to Paris, 'City of Light', to undertake his cultural apprenticeship to the twentieth century, in a capital which offered perhaps the most remarkable array of ideas, schools and personalities gathered in one Western city since the Renaissance. The contrast between that light and the earlier darkness, perceived retrospectively and at first unconsciously, gives the novel its peculiar dramatic dynamism. Many readers have also found something characteristically Latin American in its contrast between imprisonment and freedom, reality and utopia. It was in the 1920s and 1930s, then, in the transition between the 'novels of the land' and the new 'labyrinthine' fiction, between 'social realism' and 'magical realism', that the liberation of Latin American fiction began.

In 1967 Asturias would become the first Latin American novelist to win the Nobel Prize. Yet even he was not to be the most influential narrator from the continent. That honour goes, undoubtedly, to Jorge Luis Borges (1899–1986), one of those rare literary phenomena, a writer who literally changed the way in which people see literature and, accordingly, the world. An almost indispensable point of reference in the era of Postmodernism, Borges – whose mature work is, effectively, a critique of Modernism – has influenced even the most influential of contemporary thinkers, like Michel Foucault and Jacques Derrida, as well as almost all his literary successors in Latin America. Yet although he had been a leading avant-garde poet in the 1920s, Borges was never any kind of revolutionary in the usual meaning of the word. He was never interested in magic, nor in the primitive, nor in Freud, and certainly not in Marx. Joyce was an early fascination, but not a model to be imitated. Yet if Andrade, Asturias and Carpentier brought about the opening to myth, oral expression and popular experience which was to allow the exploration of Latin American culture from the 1920s and thus to provide the essential basis for the 'New Novel', it is Borges, unmistakably, who supplied the sense of precision and structure which permitted the inter-textual systematization of that culture and the creation of the Latin American literature in which, ironically, he never believed. He was, indeed, universal, but in a uniquely Latin American way.

Borges had been a leading participant in the youthful Hispanic avant-garde, prominent in the 'Ultraist' movement in the 1920s and a tireless cultural animator and contributor to little magazines. At the same time his early poems entitled *Fervor de Buenos Aires* (1923) demonstrate that he too was at that time torn between the cosmopolitan lure of Europe and travel, on the one hand, and nostalgia for the local and the picturesque on the other. Needless to say, the pleasures and pains of both are heightened, for the 'Ulyssean' writer, by the contrast between them, which can only be fully experienced in the labyrinth of time, space and memory. But in the 1930s the still young writer renounced both nativism and the avant-garde as infantile disorders and began to effect a long, slow revolution, first in Latin American fiction and eventually in Western literature as a whole. For some critics the publication of his *Historia universal de la infamia* in 1935 marks the birth of 'magical realism' in Latin America. But this honour, as we have seen, must go to Andrade, Asturias and Carpentier, all writers with more convincingly 'native' cultures than that of Borges's disappearing gauchos. Indeed, the attraction of the gaucho for Borges was that of the Western gunslinger for certain North American ideologies: his insistent individualism. Nevertheless Borges's *Historia universal,* a distant relative of Kafka's work, does mark the birth of Latin America's distinctive tradition of 'fantastic literature', a tradition most firmly rooted precisely in Argentina and Uruguay. For example, *Museo de la novela de la eterna* by Argentine Macedonio Fernández (1874–1952), an influence on the artistically dehumanized writings of both Borges and Cortázar, though not published until 1967, was conceived in the 1920s and written in the 1930s. And Adolfo Bioy Casares (b. 1914), Borges's close friend and collaborator, was himself an outstanding narrator of both short stories and novels such as *La invención de Morel* (1940) or *El sueño de los héroes* (1954).

The two styles – 'magical realism' and 'fantastic literature' – were by no means the same, but certainly overlapped and both took on characteristically Latin American features, not least in their obsessive dualism. The tropical magical realism, centered on the Caribbean and Brazil, specifically set out to fuse an elemental but 'fertile' native culture with the more – but also less – knowing gaze of European consciousness; whereas the labyrinthine metaphysic of fantasy emanating from the River Plate, in the absence of such an alternative culture, fused the local reality, perceived as drab and second-rate, with a fantastic dimension which was really, perhaps, a sign for the superior 'meta-consciousness' of the Europe by which Argentinians and Uruguayans felt they were inevitably defined and to which they hopelessly aspired. Borges's whole endeavour would be to resolve this tension through a strategy of relativization and redefinition. Through this endeavour he quite literally changed the world.

At the end of the 1930s Borges prepared a landmark collection, the *Antología de la literatura fantástica* (1940), in collaboration with Bioy Casares and Silvina Ocampo; and then came his two incomparable collections of stories *Ficciones* (1944) and *El Aleph* (1949). After that, and once he had collected his essays in *Otras inquisiciones* (1952), rather like some precocious scientific experimenter, Borges's work was effectively at an end. He continued of course to write poems, stories and essays, despite increasing blindness, but never again with the revolutionary force of his work in the 1940s. Later writers like Carlos Fuentes came to suggest that without Borges there would not even have been a 'modern' Latin American novel, which is clearly untrue but nevertheless a remarkable claim given his years as a political outcast and the fact that he never felt remotely tempted to write anything as vulgar as a full-length novel. He did, however, compile his own eccentric catalogue of books, writers and ideas in order to chart his own course through Western literature, demonstrate that its central themes are really no different from those of the Orient, and thereby justify his fundamental belief that 'universal history is the history of a few metaphors.'[8] For this purpose he invoked the spirits of Poe, Croce, Shelley, Schopenhauer, Kafka and Hawthorne, among others, to support Carlyle's belief that 'history is an infinite sacred book that all men write and read and try to understand and in which they too are written'.[9] Borges then deduced what may be the key to an appreciation of his influence, namely the idea that all writers are many writers and that 'each writer creates his precursors' – that is, 'each writer's work modifies our conception of the past as it will modify the future'.[10] This approach in the brilliantly inventive essays of *Otras inquisiciones* allowed him to make such provoking statements as that Chesterton 'restrained himself from being Edgar Allen Poe or Franz Kafka', or that, regarding two versions of a certain tragic history, 'the original is unfaithful to the translation'.[11]

Borges has, almost single-handed, revolutionized our ability to think about reading and writing. In real respects he has demystified these processes and even more profoundly the concepts of authorship and originality by emphasizing the artifice of art. This is the more extraordinary when one considers that reading and writing is what writers and critics are supposed to be meditating on all the time, yet it took a sceptic like Borges to see through the myths which have prevailed since romanticism. Almost equally as important is his approach to influences and his demonstration –

---

[8] Jorge Luis Borges, 'Pascal's Sphere', in *Other Inquisitions, 1937–52* (London, 1973), pp. 73–4.
[9] Borges, 'Partial Enchantments of the *Quijote*', in *Other Inquisitions*, p. 46.
[10] Borges, 'Kafka and his Precursors', in *Other Inquisitions*, p. 108.
[11] Borges, 'On Chesterton', in *Other Inquisitions*, p. 84; 'About William Beckford's *Vathek*', in *Other Inquisitions*, p. 140.

despite himself – of the materiality of thought, language, literature and culture. The implications for a post-colonial literature are far-reaching. Moreover, since he was, despite everything, a Latin American, his revolutionary effect on literature and criticism has enormously advanced the international image and reputation of Latin America and its participation in Western culture. A whole swathe of twentieth-century writing from Kafka, Pirandello and Unamuno to Calvino, Kundera and Eco (not to mention Cortázar and García Márquez) only makes the kind of unified sense it currently does thanks to the meaning which Borges's way of seeing retrospectively confers on these writers whilst also linking them backwards to their great distant 'precursors', as mentioned above. In Latin America itself this gives confirmatory legitimacy to a certain form of cosmopolitanism, which has been necessary for cultural communication and even survival, a certain way of being in and out of, part of and separate from Western civilization, and at the same time a global approach to culture, knowledge and other people and other nations which is somehow wholly appropriate to the continent which completed humanity's knowledge of the world.

Andrade, Asturias, Borges and Carpentier made these decisive contributions to Latin American culture in this century, in the transition between a traditional and a modern world, and between Europe and Latin America. They were the great cultural bridges, effective intermediaries between two worlds, and thus the first 'Ulyssean' narrators, travellers through both time and space. When Andrade, Asturias, Borges and Carpentier began to write, in the mid-1920s, Latin America had barely begun to experience modernity, whereas the writers who attained celebrity and wrote their greatest works in the mid-1960s had grown up with it all their lives and absorbed the new pace and variety of contemporary urban experience without even thinking about it. For them, indeed, the city and its inhabitants were the primary reality and it was the countryside which was abnormal. For the earlier generation the motor car, airplane, gramophone, cinema and radio were all new experiences to be absorbed after childhood, but modernity as a whole and life in a great modern conurbation were recent enough in origin to be perceived as essentially non-American experiences. In that sense, indeed, 1920 was really the last moment where the divorce between modernity and underdevelopment could ever be quite so visible and quite so culturally shocking in the Latin American environment.

## The New Novel

The 'New Novel', which in retrospect began its trajectory at the end of the Second World War, followed the different paths marked out by the writers who had undergone the 'Ulyssean' experience in the 1920s, above all Asturias, Borges and Carpentier. It is perhaps surprising, at first sight, that the most important novels to emerge during this period, following another great war, should again have been 'regional' or even 'telluric' in orientation. Not until the 'Boom' itself in the 1960s were Latin American writers able regularly to produce great works of urban fiction in response to the growth of a well-educated, middle-class audience and the increasing concentration of the population in large cities. One might say, oversimplifying inevitably, that the post-war era was the moment in which the Faulknerian impulse predominated in Latin American fiction and that the Joycean mode would only fully crystallize in the 1960s, after the publication of Cortázar's *Rayuela* in 1963.

Of course even William Faulkner was a 'Ulyssean' writer in both senses of the word. Longing for adventure he had travelled the world – first in his imagination and then, briefly, in reality – and had returned, 'weary of wonders', as Borges would put it (in his poem 'Ars Poetica'), to perceive that 'Art is that Ithaca, of green eternity, not of wonders', and thus to make a new world, Yoknapatawpha County, Mississippi, out of his original world. And he was also a Modernist, Joycean writer, who was inspired by the Irishman's unrivalled exercise of formal freedom and adapted the interior monologue and stream-of-consciousness to his own historical purpose.

Yet again it was Borges, never a lover of long fiction, who made the most ironic but also the most significant contribution to Spanish American consciousness of Faulkner by translating *The Wild Palms* in 1940, the year after its first publication, just as he had translated the last page of *Ulysses* in 1925. *The Wild Palms*, with its juxtaposition of distinct realities, is the precursor of a narrative line which would culminate in Vargas Llosa's *La Casa Verde* in 1966. Faulkner's domain is the unfinished, traumatized rural environment of the American South, an accursed land like the lands of Juan Rulfo, João Guimaraes Rosa and Gabriel García Márquez. Faulkner's characters are Black, Red and White, rich and poor (though usually the former declining into the latter), portrayed over 300 years but particularly since the early nineteenth century, all struggling to discover a destiny and assert an identity which can never be forged collectively against a

bitter and tragic history of violation, extermination, slavery and civil war,
and a legacy of guilt, despair and solitude. It is this nexus of themes and
techniques – miscegenation and its contrasts and juxtapositions foremost
among them – which makes Faulkner such a formidable influence on the
Latin American New Novel. Like Faulkner, then, the leading Latin American writers were by the 1940s citizens not only of their own lands but of
the world, and they looked on their continent and its culture with a
radically transformed gaze, mapping the cultural landscape through their
geographical, social and historical explorations. It was, in short, a process
of internalization of Latin American history.

Many critics would agree that the first page of the New Novel –
indeed, for one critic the first page of the 'Boom',[12] was the magical,
incantatory opening of Asturias's *El señor Presidente:* 'Boom, bloom, alum-
bright, Lucifer of alunite! The sound of the prayer bells droned on, hum-
ming in the ears, uneasily tolling from light to gloom, gloom to light'.
And the first work which decisively united the concept of the New Novel
with that of magical realism was the same author's *Hombres de maíz* (1949).
Ariel Dorfman perceived its importance as early as 1968: 'Although its
origins fade into remote regions and its socio-cultural coordinates are still
disputed, the contemporary Spanish American novel has a quite precise
date of birth. It is the year 1949, when Alejo Carpentier's *El reino de este
mundo* and Miguel Angel Asturias's *Hombres de maíz* saw the light of day.
The latter, both the fountainhead and the backbone of all that is being
written in our continent today, has met with a strange destiny, like so
many works that open an era and close off the past.'[13]

The opening of the later novel was as strange and dramatic as that of *El
señor Presidente*. Asturias was trying to imagine the world of Maya culture
through his sleeping indigenous protagonist, Gaspar Ilóm, 'buried with his
dead ones and his umbilicus, unable to free himself from a serpent of six
hundred thousand coils of mud, moon, forests, rainstorms, mountains,
birds and echoes he could feel around his body'. No novel has more profoundly explored the hidden labyrinths of Latin American cultural history.
Asturias even has an unconcealed affection for – and much more direct
knowledge of – the peasant, Mestizo culture which helped create him but
which, as part of the Western heritage, he questions and even deplores, so

[12] William Gass, 'The First Seven Pages of the Boom', *Latin American Literary Review,* 29 (Pittsburgh, PA., 1987), 33–56.
[13] See Ariel Dorfman, '*Hombres de maíz:* el mito como tiempo y palabra', in his *Imaginación y violencia en América* (Santiago, Chile, 1970), p. 71.

that folk culture from the European side is as well represented as the myths and legends of the contemporary Indians and their pre-Alvaradian ancestors. The narrative's point of departure, the resistance of Gaspar Ilóm at the beginning of the century, is based on a real historical incident. This was itself representative of a historical process which still continues both in Guatemala and Latin America generally – a process whose chain-like structure is also visible in *Raza de bronce, Huasipungo, El mundo es ancho y ajeno,* José María Arguedas's *Todas las sangres* (see below) and Vargas Llosa's *La Casa Verde* (see below), namely that of the native Indian, uprooted from his culture and ejected from his homeland by the typical processes of Western capitalism and culture, who either rebels or sets out defeated on the road to loneliness and alienation. Clearly, in that sense this is a retrospective, assimilative work, a panoramic examination of a historical landscape, a meditation by a city man on the origins of a national and continental culture and on the theme of cultural loss ('Who has never called, never shouted the name of that woman lost in his yesterdays? Who has not pursued like a blind man that being who went away from his being, when he came to himself . . . ?'). Other authors who have written about the contemporary Maya Indians are the Guatemalan Mario Monteforte Toledo (b. 1911), with *Anaité* (1940) and *Entre la piedra y la cruz* (1948), and, above all, the outstanding Mexican writer Rosario Castellanos (1925–74), with *Balún Canán* (1957) and *Oficio de tinieblas* (1962). *Balún Canán* is indeed the most important novel from the Maya region after Asturias's *Hombres de maíz,* though it is only one of a number of varied works by Castellanos, whose pioneering feminist approach to Latin American social relations gives all her work, fiction, poetry and theatre, a truly radical cutting edge.

The year of *Hombres de maíz,* 1949, was also the year when Alejo Carpentier, in the prologue to *El reino de este mundo,* wrote what is effectively the great magical realist manifesto, his essay on 'Lo real maravilloso'. This novel, a small literary jewel, deals with the slave revolts in eighteenth-century Haiti and ends with a classic meditation: 'In the Kingdom of Heaven there is no grandeur to be won, inasmuch as there all is an established hierarchy, the unknown is revealed, existence is infinite, there is no possibility or sacrifice, all is rest and joy. For this reason, bowed down by suffering and duties, beautiful in the midst of his misery, capable of loving in the face of afflictions and trials, man finds his greatness, his fullest measure, only in the Kingdom of this World.'[14] French-speaking

---

[14] Alejo Carpentier, *The Kingdom of this World,* trans. Harriet de Onís (London, 1967), p. 149.

Haiti itself has produced a number of novels which might conveniently be placed within a broadly magical realist definition. They would include *Gouverneurs de la Rosée* (1944) by Jacques Roumain (1907–44), *La Bête de musseau* (1946) and *Le Crayon de Dieu* (1952), both written jointly by the brothers Philippe-Thoby and Pierre Marcelin, and *Compère Général Soleil* (1955) and *Les Arbres musiciens* by Jacques Stephen Alexis (1922–61).

Other Spanish American writers often considered magical realist are the Venezuelan Arturo Uslar Pietri (b.1905), a close friend of both Asturias and Carpentier in Paris in the 1920s and one of the theoreticians of the movement, author of *El camino del Dorado* (1947) and *Oficio de difuntos* (1976); and the Ecuadorean Demetrio Aguilera Malta (1909–81), author of *Don Goyo* (1933) and *Siete lunas y siete serpientes* (1970). In the 1950s there were a number of variations on these magical realist models. By far the most successful was *Pedro Páramo* (1955) by the Mexican Juan Rulfo (1918–86). Rulfo has the extraordinary distinction of having written not only this, the most widely admired Mexican novel of the century, but also *El llano en llamas* (1953), some of the continent's most compelling short stories. His work gives him a close literary kinship with the Brazilian Graciliano Ramos. *Pedro Páramo* is a novel in which recognizable European motifs like the Oedipal, Thesean and Dantean quests are perfectly subordinated to the requirements of a metaphorical presentation of the colonized, feudal heritage of a whole country, a whole continent, unified by the power of myth ('I came to Comala because they told me my father lived here, one Pedro Páramo. My mother said so. And I promised her I'd come to see him as soon as she died. I squeezed her hands as a sign that I would do it; because she was about to die and I was in a mood to promise anything'). Rulfo's novel operates on both the national (Mexican/Latin American) and individual (universal) planes, and once again a critical vision compatible with the new Marx and the new Freud underpins the entire narrative. Without such a framework it becomes indecipherable and spirals away into labyrinths of 'magic' and 'mystery' ('This town is full of echoes. You would think they were trapped in the hollow walls or beneath the stones'). As the design for his novel, Rulfo – who, mysteriously, never managed to write another – dreamed up a brilliantly simple conception, worthy of Kafka: all the characters in the novel are dead when it begins and the town they inhabit, Comala, is a dead town where the air is full of tormented souls wandering in search of a redemption which, to judge from their terrestrial experience, is unlikely ever to come. Yet, as in all true magical realist works, it is social relationships which govern this apparently most ethereal of novels. This is of great importance, since *Pedro Páramo*, perhaps even more than García Márquez's *Cien años de soledad*, has been used time and again to justify the belief that Latin America is magical, mysterious and irrational – this is precisely what magical realism is *not* about – and that its literature celebrates this strange 'reality'; whereas for half a century most important writers have been attempting to carry out deconstruction of the myths elaborated over the previous 450 years. It has been said that this novel is pessimistic. Certainly Rulfo himself was, and it is difficult to see any other conclusion for a book reflecting the experience of the Mexican peasants in the past century. Yet Pedro himself is finally murdered: the Revolution may be shown – as in Azuela – to be confused, cynical or opportunistic, but in however indirect a way one of the landowner's illegitimate sons does take his revenge and the pile of barren rocks which is Pedro's regime does finally come crashing down: 'Pedro . . . leaned on Damiana Cisneros's arms and tried to walk. After a few paces he fell, pleading inside. He hit the earth and began to crumble like a pile of stones.' Two other writers who have examined the rural landscapes of post-revolutionary Mexico are his fellow Jaliscan Juan José Arreola (b. 1918), author of *La feria* (1963) and Elena Garro (b.1920), author of the novel *Los recuerdos del porvenir* (1963), a startlingly original revisionary work about the aftermath of the Mexican Revolution.

At this moment in literary history Brazil was, for once, quite closely in step with events in Spanish America. In 1956 the Brazilian João Guimarães Rosa (1908–67) produced *Grande sertão: veredas* (*The Devil to Pay in the Backlands*), one of Brazil's most important novels, again set in the unyielding, mysterious, exasperating and apparently eternal barren wastes of the Sertão, in this case that of Minas Gerais. The work has been compared with *Gargantua and Pantagruel*, *Don Quijote*, *Ulysses* and *Cien años de soledad*. Rosa was the writer who in 1946 turned Brazilian fiction away from social realism (as Asturias and Carpentier were doing in Spanish America), with his first collection of stories, *Sagarana*. In 1956, the same year as *Grande sertão*, the even more challenging narratives of *Corpo de baile* appeared. Later collections were *Primeiras estórias* (1962), *Trifle* (*Terceiras estórias*) (1967), and *Estas estórias* (1969). The Portuguese title of *Grande sertão* suggests the same concept of the field and the paths as in Gallegos's *Doña Bárbara*, that great telluric labyrinth in which the plain may represent both life itself (individual and universal) and the book which recreates it. In conception, however, it is much closer to another novel by Gallegos *Cantaclaro* (1934) – though the difference in sheer erudition and literary panache is evident – or to the Argentine Leopoldo Lugones's *El payador* (1916), a treatise on the gaucho 'minstrels'. Rosa makes no allowances for the reader in terms of the novel's hermeticism and reliance upon dense layerings of imagery, symbolism and regional vocabulary. The story is narrated by one Riobaldo ('dry river'), a former cowboy and bandit from the Sertão, now a landowner, who addresses some unknown interlocutor – the writer? the reader? the devil? – as he recalls his adventures and perplexities over a long and passionate life riding the great plains at the end of the last century: 'You, sir, knew nothing about me. Do you now know much or little? A person's life, all the paths into its past: is it a story that touches upon your own life at all, sir?'[15] If the novel is about Brazil, then it underscores the impossibility, recognized by so many Brazilian writers, of ever going beyond the concept of the nation as an irreconcilable plurality; if about man's condition in the world, then it underlines that Western man's destiny is to arrive forever at a crossroads, torn always between impossible choices and dualities, good and evil, male and female, objective and subjective, history and myth, in a world which, like fictional stories, is ultimately impossible to interpret. More clearly than other writers, Rosa shows just how much the Latin American novel of its era was forced to reconcile the requirements of the twentieth-century Modernist text with the impulse of romance, a medieval genre which is still surprisingly relevant in a world of loose ends, a still unwoven social and historical reality where more things are unresolved than identified, and where messianic movements promising transcendent meaning, the triumph of good over evil and imminent or eventual salvation are still invested with immense force.

A reading of this remarkable Brazilian novel prompts the reader to reflect again that this vast country – Lévi-Strauss's 'sad tropics' – remains dominated in its own consciousness by the 'three sad races' – the Portuguese, with their *saudade,* still missing Europe; the Africans, liberated from slavery only a century ago, longing for their magical past; and the Indians, staring into space, pining for their long-lost cultural universe. Thus far the combination has failed to produce a successful democratic society, but capitalism has taken firm root through the efforts of outsiders, including optimistic immigrants from all over the world. Little wonder that the largest republic in the region offers the perplexing image of a

---

[15] J. Guimarães Rosa, *The Devil to Pay in the Backlands,* trans. J.L. Taylor and H. de Onís (New York, 1971), p. 482.

country with a national identity that strikes outsiders as unusually distinctive, whilst Brazilian artists and intellectuals themselves continue to insist that this most extraordinary of nations somehow remains a mystery unto itself.

An equally unique literary phenomenon was Peru's José María Arguedas (1913–69) whose early indigenist works, *Agua* (1935, stories) and *Yawar Fiesta* (1941), were contemporaneous with the works of Ciro Alegría. He is now considered perhaps the greatest indigenist novelist of the continent, mainly due to *Los ríos profundos* (1958) and *Todas las sangres* (1964). Although the interest of his works is in some respects circumscribed by their strictly Americanist orientation and, it must be said, by some limitations of technique, Arguedas is today counted among the most important Latin American novelists this century. *Los ríos profundos* is largely autobiographical. Arguedas lost his mother early and suffered rejection from his own family, living for much of his childhood among Quechua Indians. Quechua, indeed, was his first language and one of the fascinations of his writing is the relationship between the Spanish in which it is mainly written and the Quechua thought patterns and structures which lie beneath. Arguedas's classic explanation of his literary endeavour was as follows: 'I tried to convert into written language what I was as an individual: a link, strong and capable of universalizing itself, between the great imprisoned nation and the generous, human section of the oppressors.'[16] Angel Rama concluded that Arguedas's paradoxical solution was to make himself 'a white acculturated by the Indians',[17] and this is the problematic worked through by *Los ríos profundos* ('Fleeing from cruel relatives I threw myself upon the mercy of an *ayllu* where they grew maize in the smallest and most delightful valley I have known. Thorn bushes with blazing flowers and the song of doves lit up the maizefields. The family heads and the ladies, *mamakunas* of the community, looked after me and imbued me with the priceless tenderness which fills my life.'). The strength of *Los ríos profundos* lies in its juxtaposition of two worlds, its uniquely poetic approach to the realm of nature, and its innovative conception of language and myth in a narrative tradition previously dominated by the conventions of the European bourgeois novel.

Arguedas's longest work, *Todas las sangres,* is probably the last of the great indigenist narratives (though the novels of another Peruvian, Manuel

---

[16] J.M. Arguedas, 'No soy un acculturado' (1968), from the appendix to his posthumous novel *El zorro de arriba y el zorro de abajo*.

[17] Angel Rama, *Transculturación narrativa en América Latina* (Mexico, D.F., 1982), p. 207.

Scorza, are also remarkable – see below). It is an appropriate sequel to *El mundo es ancho y ajeno* (though published, ironically enough, in the midst of the 'Boom'). If *Huasipungo* is the classic of vulgar Marxism, *Todas las sangres* is the classic of dialectical materialism. It would appear to be set in the 1950s, in the period shortly before the Cuban Revolution and, in Peru, the foundation of the Apra Rebelde led by Luis de la Puente Uceda and the peasant upheavals in the valley of La Convención and Lares led by Hugo Blanco. It presents a kind of microcosm of Peruvian history by detailing the social transformations taking place around the small town of San Pedro when the old patriarchal landowner Don Andrés dies and curses his two sons, Bruno, a reactionary religious fanatic who wishes to maintain the feudal system yet eventually assists the Indians in their uprising, and Fermín, a ruthless modernizing capitalist, a member of the new nationalist bourgeoisie, who owns the local wolfram mine and is involved in a desperate struggle with a foreign multinational company. Bruno's hacienda and Fermín's mine dominate the otherwise decaying local economy, where the gentry are in decline and the Cholos scrape to make a living. Nearby are two free Indian communities, the prosperous Lahuaymarca and the poor Paraybamba. Within these social sectors the widest possible range of ethnic groups, classes and fractions of Peru is represented. This is a story which has been told many times in Latin American social realist literature, but never with such a sense of contradiction, mastery of detail and dynamic movement. The principal protagonist is Rendón Willka, an Indian who was exiled from the community as an adolescent for standing up for his rights at school. On his return eight years later Willka is an indigenist militant, a kind of Christ figure, one of the most complex and attractive character creations in Latin American fiction, a man who knows both of Peru's component social parts and thus has insight beyond that of the other characters. When Willka cries out shortly before the end of the novel that the Indians have 'found their country at last', he is not talking about the neo-colonial, capitalist state which has been developed – or, rather, underdeveloped – since Peru gained its formal independence in the early nineteenth century. Rather he looks forward to a new, genuinely plural society when 'the Peruvian' has finally managed to emerge from the ethnic labyrinth of blood and cultural conflict.

All the novels discussed thus far have left the novelist himself, and his natural habitat – the city – out of the frame. That is why consideration of another novel by Alejo Carpentier, *Los pasos perdidos,* has been delayed until now, although it was published in 1953. It remains his most important work despite the attractions of the even more ambitious *El siglo de las luces* (1962), a great historical novel about the independence movements of the Caribbean in the eighteenth century, *El recurso del método* (1975) and *Consagración de la primavera,* his celebration of the Cuban Revolution (1978). *Los pasos perdidos* is the most programmatic of all novels about the relationship between Latin America (above all the Caribbean and Venezuela) and 'Europe' (above all Spain and France), and between Latin America and 'modernity' as represented by the United States. In that sense it is an indispensable cultural document of Latin America's twentieth century. The title echoes Breton's Surrealist project, though the search for lost time and primitive roots actually takes place against a later Gallic background, that of post-war existentialism, in which a sometime Latin American, living in self-inflicted exile in New York, is nevertheless imbued with the absurdist ideas of Camus, though with none of the rebellious voluntarism of Sartre. The anonymous protagonist is a musician, a scholar and artist living an existence of utter alienation from both true values and from his Latin American cultural origins, selling his art in the capitalist market place by writing the music for advertising films. Once the narrator arrives in the jungle he falls in love with a Latin American Mestizo woman, a mixture of the continent's three great ethnic groupings, and forgets his North American wife and French mistress, giving himself over to a spontaneous eroticism which is also a cosmic ritual. This return to the maternal realm of nature stimulates him to write a long-cherished symphony based on Shelley's *Prometheus Unbound,* only to find that in order to obtain the materials to complete it – not to mention seeing it performed – he must return to the alienating civilization from which he has so recently escaped ('Today Sisyphus's vacation came to an end'). When, after a frustrating time in New York, he tries to journey back once more to the little jungle community, he finds that the waters of the river have symbolically risen and he cannot find the way through the labyrinth of trees and water. The conclusion is that there is no turning back because artists and intellectuals are, first and last, the antennae of the race: their realm is the present and the future.

## The 'Boom'

Between the Second World War and the 1960s, as we now see, the 'New Novel' was beginning its remarkable rise to world attention, virtually unnoticed at first, with each new achievement in some part of Latin America remaining unrelated by either writers or critics to what was going on elsewhere. Economically and politically a different age seemed to be dawning and in the post-war years and again in the late 1950s there was much optimism that the Latin American middle classes, with liberal democratic regimes to represent them, might be on the verge of some new era of political stability as well as real economic expansion. The book which first reflected this changing and essentially urban reality was *La región más transparente* (1958) by Carlos Fuentes (b.1928), a novel about Mexico City and Mexican identity which now, with the benefit of history, appears clearly as the first novel of the 'Boom' and thus the signal of the developments that were shortly to occur in Latin American narrative. Paradoxically, of course, these developments became visible at the very moment that the Cuban Revolution was about to transform the whole perspective of Latin American history by proclaiming a Third World, anti-urban and anti-bourgeois ideology.

  *La región más transparente* may have provided the early signs, but no one doubts which work effectively inaugurated the new movement by continuing the interrogation of Latin American identity which Carpentier had pursued in *Los pasos perdidos*. That novel was *Rayuela* (1963) by the Argentine Julio Cortázar (1914–83). Cortázar's achievement lies, first, in having updated and synthesized the twin traditions or 'Joycism' and Surrealism which were the legacy bequeathed by Andrade, Asturias and Carpentier from the 1920s; and second, in having fused them through an intense reading of the ideas and forms explored before him by his compatriot Borges. No other novelist and no other work so comprehensively embody this triple heritage. Cortázar's first novel, *Los premios* (1960), about an allegorical journey on a European cruise liner – tickets won by lottery and going nowhere – was already a rather timid fusion of Joyce (in structure and linguistic texture), Kafka (in theme and symbolic design), Borges and other Modernist currents. Its culminating moment, when the passengers capture the bridge, only to discover that no one is navigating the ship, is one of the great defining moments of Latin American literature, anticipating not only the vision of Postmodernism as a whole – of which the Argentine writer's own story 'Blow-Up' ('Las babas del diablo') was an early path-finder – but also the 'Boom' writers' overwhelming sense of cultural emancipation from 'Europe' ('It was true, now he came to think about it: the bridge was entirely empty but . . . it didn't matter, it hadn't the slightest importance because what mattered was something else, something that couldn't be grasped but was trying to show itself and define itself in the sensation that was exciting him more and more.'). Cortázar's emphasis upon sensation, spontaneity, imminence and the primacy of experience over conceptualization is one which characterizes Latin American fiction from its romantic origins in the early nineteenth century to its Surrealist designs in the early twentieth century.

It has been argued that *Rayuela* was to Spanish American fiction in 1963 what *Ulysses* had been for European and North American literature as a whole in 1922. Certainly it was a major point of crystallization and particularly significant for its timing – published early in the sixties. Moreover, its very structure is a comparison of two cities, moving from an exploration of art and its media and institutions in the first part, 'Over There', to an analysis of consciousness and language themselves in the second 'Over Here'. There are many quite tangible Joycean influences, but Cortázar's work also invokes Surrealist concepts not present in Joyce and existentialist considerations which post-dated him. Much of *Rayuela* also explores, tragicomically, the obscure and often sinister motives which lie behind the most frivolous or inconsequential behaviour, in a way reminiscent of Borges in stories like 'El Aleph'. Most of all, though, Cortázar's unique place in contemporary narrative is due to his simultaneous exploration and incarnation of the international avant-garde and its special concerns.

*Rayuela,* unmistakably, was the novel most admired by the other writers of the 'Boom', the one which made it visible and recognizable, the work situated at the other pole from *Cien años de soledad,* with which the literary firework show reached its grand crescendo in 1967. Yet despite first impressions to the contrary, *Rayuela* is really a variant of the conceptual model underpinning *Hombres de maíz, Pedro Páramo,* the later *La Casa Verde* and, indeed, *Cien años de soledad* itself, a work which rejects the rationalistic logocentrism of European civilization and posits a return to the natural, authentic world of America. Whether America – least of all Argentina, least of all Buenos Aires – can convincingly be considered in any sense spontaneous or natural is a questionable point, but the essential thrust of this position is that it is by definition newer, younger and more spontaneous than Europe or North America (which has on the whole – jazz apart – sacrificed spontaneity for mechanization), no matter how unspontaneous it may actually be on its own terms. This posture turns Europe's constant use of Latin America for catharsis to America's advantage, inverting the Surrealism which so influenced Asturias, Carpentier, Neruda, Paz and Cortázar himself, as if to suggest that Europeans irremediably approach Surrealism from the wrong side, whereas the Latin Americans can always come from the fertile maternal darkness of autochthonous America into the dazzling light of rational knowledge, and then, with their new knowledge aboard, can plunge back into the night and the underworld once more, as the earth itself does, growing, changing, advancing dialectically to the rhythm of the whole universe.

Cortázar, despite his age and his subsequent decision to take French citizenship, was the key writer of the youthful 1960s, though, in the climax to the 'Boom', what actually happened was something quite complicated. The Argentinian writer marks the moment where Joyce rules, but the other major novelists who seized that particular historic opportunity – Fuentes, Vargas Llosa and García Márquez – were all already Faulknerian writers, and their greatest works, written during the 'Boom', are recognizably in Faulknerian vein. Nevertheless, each of them also has an unmistakable additional element, and this is the labyrinthine, historical-mythological national quest motif which Joyce initiated in the 1920s and which Asturias, Carpentier, Guimarães Rosa and Cortázar had been elaborating progressively since the 1920s. Nothing written since has yet superseded those great works, the culmination – for the time being – of 400 years of Latin American cultural development and – possibly false – consciousness. Like Joyce in the First World, they seem for the moment to have put an end to the possibility of further developing the novel as we know it. The current moment seems to be one of assimilation at best, exhaustion at worst.

At any rate, the overtly Modernist works of the 1960s were swiftly perceived as a 'Boom', which moved rapidly towards a climax with *Cien años de soledad* and then shattered into the twinkling fragments of the 'Post-Boom' – or perhaps Postmodernist – novels of the 1970s. It was a confused and contradictory moment, marked deeply by the Cuban Revolution, which at first was itself so pluralist that writers like Cabrera Infante were able to publish extracts from Joyce as well as Trotsky – both were later effectively proscribed – in revolutionary arts journals like *Lunes de Revolución*. The sense of diverse ideological alternatives offered by Cuba and the various social democratic experiments of the day, combined with the new cosmopolitanism bred by a consumption-orientated capitalist boom and an expansion of the Latin American middle classes – buyers and consumers of novels – created a period of intense artistic activity throughout the sub-continent. If there was an overall shape to it in literature, however, that shape was for several years to come a Joycean and 'Ulyssean' one, but a Joycean one which wished not only to superimpose history over myth as abstract categories, but a specifically Latin American history involving the quest for identity and cultural liberation.

Speaking in the 1980s of the 1960s, which he compared explicitly with the 1920s, Perry Anderson identified the perspective for artists and intellectuals as an 'ambiguity – an openness of horizon, where the shapes of the future could alternatively assume the shifting forms of either a new type of capital or of the eruption of socialism – which was constitutive of so much of the original sensibility of what had come to be called Modernism'. After asserting that Modernism lost its creative thrust after 1930, Anderson continued: 'This is not true, manifestly, of the Third World. It is significant that so many of . . . the great Modernist achievements of our time should be taken from Latin American literature. For in the Third World generally, a kind of shadow configuration of what once prevailed in the First World does exist today.'[18] *Ulysses* was the supreme literary product of a peculiarly fertile, highly charged conjuncture, at the moment where the old European regime really was – or so it seemed – finally about to be laid to rest, and where some new modern world – which might be either communist or capitalist – was imposing itself with a speed and vigour the mind could barely encompass, due to a confluence of forms which Anderson summarizes as follows: 'European Modernism in the first [thirty] years of this century thus flowered in the space between a still usable classical past, a still indeterminate technical present, and a still unpredictable political future. Or, put another way, it arose at the intersection between a semi-aristocratic ruling order, a semi-industrialized capitalist economy, and a semi-emergent or insurgent, labour movement.'[19] Suddenly, Latin American writers of the period, above all in the 1920s, were able to take a step back, gain perspective and write works which were no longer, in their one-dimensional 'realist' historicity, secret metaphors for their own terminal lifespan, but metaphors for the whole of human experience since the earliest times. It was of course the development of the social sciences, especially ethnology, which had made such a development possible, viewed from the standpoint of a Western civilization whose own belief systems were in a state of disarray, at once underlining the relativity of culture and making mythology and mystification ever more alluring to the – reluctantly – profane mind of capitalist consciousness. Only in La-

[18] Perry Anderson, 'Modernity and Revolution', *New Left Review*, 144 (1984), p.109.
[19] *Ibid.*

tin America, however, due to its specific bi-cultural circumstance, was the magical reconciliation of myth and history regularly performed.

*La región más transparente* remains perhaps the single most evocative novel about twentieth-century Mexico City. For many people, however, *La muerte de Artemio Cruz* (1962), written partly in Havana at the very beginning of the 'Boom', is probably Carlos Fuentes's outstanding literary achievement. It is also, appropriately enough, seen as the work which effectively puts an end to the cycle of novels of the Revolution (for some critics they ended in 1917, when the Revolution itself ended; for others in 1940, when Cárdenas left office; for others after the Tlatelolco massacre of 1968; whilst for others, ironically enough, they will only come to an end when the ruling Partido Revolucionario Institucional (PRI) ceases to hold power). It is, intriguingly, a vision of the legacy of the Mexican Revolution seen from the standpoint of the then still youthful Cuban Revolution, at a moment when writers like Fuentes and even Vargas Llosa supported it more or less unequivocally. Possibly more than any other Latin American novelist, Fuentes has pursued the theme of identity, which in Mexico since the Revolution has at times taken on the proportions, among intellectuals at least, of a national obsession. (The paradigm is Octavio Paz's *El laberinto de la soledad*, first published in 1950.) *La muerte de Artemio Cruz*, like most of the novels of this era, is retrospective (the character, on his death bed, looks back over his own life and over the history of Mexico and its Revolution: these are the same and the book is their story), and of course labyrinthine. Men quest into the future and then into the past, and novels shadow those quests in ways which, in the twentieth century, are increasingly complex. Fuentes's novel is the most straightforwardly labyrinthine of all ('Chaos: it has no plural.'). We see this most clearly when the author confronts his character overtly half-way through the novel: 'you will decide, you will choose one of those paths, you will sacrifice the rest; you will sacrifice yourself as you choose, ceasing to be all the other men you might have been'. Artemio Cruz, to the extent that can be imagined outside of the novel, is, like Rulfo's Pedro Páramo, a cynical and callous man, though in his heart of hearts he has the same sentimentality and even the same beautiful dreams as his predecessor. As Cruz is finally wheeled into the operating theatre for heart surgery, the novel seems to exonerate him, rather surprisingly, by beginning its ending on a note of absolute fatalism: 'On your head will fall, as if returning from a long journey through time, without beginning or end, all the promises of love and solitude, of hatred and endeavour, violence and tenderness, love and disenchantment, time and oblivion, innocence and surprise . . . In your heart, open to life, tonight.' It is important nevertheless to do justice to the audacity and complexity of this novel, its often brilliant writing, its superb evocation – precisely in and because of its contradictions – of contemporary Mexico, and its ability to give the reader the opportunity to meditate on the Revolution, the meaning of power and the difficulty of making choices in the actually existing world. Like Azuela's, Fuentes's negative judgement on Mexican history merges with a hymn to his turbulent and contradictory country, creating a curious bitter-sweet tension all its own: 'your land . . . you will think there is a second discovery of the land in that warrior quest, that first step upon mountains and gorges which are like a defiant fist raised against the painfully slow advance of road, dam, rail and telegraph pole . . . you will inherit the earth'.

Fuentes, it is worth remarking, was the most clubbable of the 'Boom' writers. Not only did he launch the entire bandwagon and then do everything possible to publicize it; he also associated the Spaniard Juan Goytisolo with the movement and effectively invited in the novelist generally agreed to be the fifth member of the 'Boom', the Chilean Jose Donoso (b. 1924). Donoso's first novel, *Coronación* (1955), had been social realist, but the 'Boom' encouraged him to branch out and he produced a series of works like *Este domingo* (1966), *El lugar sin límites* (1967), and then, in 1970, his *El obsceno pájaro del noche,* at once gothic and surreal, one of the outstanding literary creations of the era. Subsequent works by Donoso include *Casa de campo* (1978), *La misteriosa desaparición de la marquesita de Loria* (1980), *El jardín de al lado* (1981) and *La desesperanza* (1986), which takes a critical look at the Pinochet period.

Despite the critical success of *El obsceno pájaro,* Donoso never quite managed to turn the Boom's big four into a big five. Mario Vargas Llosa (b. 1936) was a member from the very beginning and has remained one of Latin America's most widely admired and controversial novelists up to the present. With the passage of time *La Casa Verde* (1966) seems to become an ever more compelling representation of the lives, dreams and illusions of ordinary Latin Americans, and the fact that its author wrote it at the age of thirty, and – following the success of the also admirable *La ciudad y los perros* (1963) – under pressure of immense audience expectation, makes the achievement all the more remarkable. Nevertheless, despite the acclaim with which it was greeted, it has not been as popular with readers and critics as other novels by Vargas Llosa. The book is effectively in two halves, the once corresponding to events which take place in the jungle, around the mission and garrison of Santa María de Nieva, and the other to the city of Piura on the edge of the northern desert, near the coast, which happens to be the first city founded by the Spaniards on their arrival.

Vargas Llosa's achievement is all the more astonishing since the Amazon, apart from its sensationalist possibilities – so difficult to realize in fiction – does not at first sight appear to be ideal material for his complex Faulknerian techniques. The world he depicts is a male one, and the most cherished fantasies are masculine: the realm of nature is seen only too clearly as an ideological construction which provides both a justification of masculine domination and an ever available means of escape from the class hierarchies of an unjust social order. Bonifacia, the Indian teenager, is known as 'Jungle Girl'; Lalita the jungle sex slave is obviously related to Nabokov's Lolita; and the theme reaches its climactic moment with the musician Anselmo's passion for Toñita, the Latin American dream girl, beautiful, adolescent, blind and mute, but capable of feeling and hearing, and therefore a receptive instrument – like a harp – in the hands of the male, who can use her for any kind of fantasy and therefore as an effective aid to his own masturbatory desires. The vision of Anselmo in his tower – explorer, conquerer, exploiter, creator of fantasies and fountainhead of myth (from epic hero to popular street singer) – is one of the most complete and radical presentations of the patriarchal complex, presented by Vargas Llosa with an almost perfect blend of ambiguities which at once holds, recreates, exposes and subverts. This is an unusual achievement in Latin America where, on the whole, the partisan character of narrative psychology – based on a largely unmediated and none too subtle real history of violence and repression – leads most novelists into presenting villains as villains even unto themselves. Like Rulfo, Vargas Llosa shows us a far more human and thus tenacious social and psychological reality, without in any way underplaying its lamentable and despicable aspects.

After *La Casa Verde* Vargas Llosa brought us, in *Conversación en la Catedral* (1969), Latin America's most complete and desolate picture of one of its great cities, with their penthouses and shanty towns, beggars and plutocrats, and the injustices, squalor and almost incredible contradictions which link them together: 'from the doorway of the *Crónica* Santiago looks down Avenida Tacna, without love: cars, uneven and faded buildings, the skeletons of neon signs floating in the mist of a grey noon. At what precise moment had Peru fucked up? . . . Peru fucked up, Carlitos fucked up, everyone fucked up. He thinks: there is no solution'. Six hundred pages later, as the novel ends after an unceasing stream of sordid and violent events, passing frequently through brothels and prisons, the reader realises that the author agrees with his character about 'Lima the horrible': there is no solution. By now, however, for all this novel's mesmeric brilliance, it was becoming clear that Vargas Llosa was really lamenting the human and social condition rather than specific societies, and that like Borges and so many others before them he was saying that society was everywhere corrupt, but even worse – hopeless – in the place he had been cursed to be born in. For this reason, ironically, his most successful works in the future would not be his ideologically overwritten political fiction but his humorous and satirical works like *Pantaleón y las visitadoras* (1973), about a military operation to organize a brothel in the Amazon, and the uproarious *La tía Julia y el escribidor* (1977), about the writer's own early marriage to his aunt, conceived as one among many Latin American soap operas.

The 'Boom' reached its climax in 1967 with the publication of its most famous literary manifestation, *Cien años de soledad* by the Colombian novelist Gabriel García Márquez (b. 1927). If the opening to Asturias' *El señor Presidente* is the boom-blooming first page of the 'New Novel', it is arguable that García Márquez's first sentence retrospectively provides the first page of Latin American narrative as a whole: 'Many years later, as he faced the firing squad, Colonel Aureliano Buendía was to remember that distant afternoon when his father took him to discover ice. Macondo at that time was a village of twenty adobe houses, built on the banks of a river of transparent water that ran along a bed of polished stones, which were white and enormous like prehistoric eggs. The world was so recent that many things lacked names, and in order to mention them it was necessary to point one's finger'. This innocent, fairy-tale beginning has the transparency of the great works of childhood, like *Robinson Crusoe, Gulliver's Travels* or *Treasure Island*. Almost anyone can understand it and yet this remarkable book, despite its limpidity, is also one of the most deceptive and impenetrable works of contemporary literature, a worthy successor to those other children's works for adults, *Don Quixote, Gargantua and Pantagruel, Tristram Shandy* and *Alice through the Looking Glass*. It is of course the novel which, more than any other, was taken to confirm the historical demise, not only of social realism, but of the kinds of Modernist works which, despite their experimental aspects, nevertheless sought to produce what sceptical post-structuralist critics sometimes call 'cultural knowledge', and therefore to herald the arrival of the linguistically inclined, experimental or Postmodernist novel. Yet *Cien años de soledad* contains a greater variety of carefully encoded material relating to the positivistic orders of social psychology, political economy and the history of ideas than almost any other Latin American novel that comes to mind. Thus Angel Rama's verdict on García Márquez's early works is equally applicable to *Cien años de soledad:* 'I do not believe any other novelist has so acutely, so truthfully seen the intimate relationship between the socio-political structure of a given country and the behaviour of his characters.'[20]

This crucial question – how magical and how realist is García Már-quez's writing? – is relevant to all his fictional production. In *La hojarasca* (1955), *La mala hora* (1962), most of the stories of *Los funerales de la Mamá Grande* (1962) or, quintessentially, *El coronel no tiene quien le escriba* (1958), the basic narrative conventions are those of critical realism, with implicit but perfectly straightforward economic, social and political – that is, historical – explanations for the psychological motivations of each of the characters (Angel Rama speaks of 'a pronounced social determinism'). By contrast the later *El otoño del patriarca* (1975), an extraordinary linguistic achievement, is nevertheless characterized by a weakness for hyperbole and the grotesque (though one should add, in justice, that for a number of critics – and for García Márquez himself – this is the Colombian's su-preme achievement).

In *Cien años de soledad,* as in most of García Márquez's work, Latin America is a home of futility and lost illusions. Nothing ever turns out as its characters expect; almost everything surprises them; almost all of them fail; few achieve communion with others for more than a fleeting moment, and most not at all. The majority of their actions, like the structure of the novel as a whole (and of course its first chapter), are circular. Ploughers of the sea, they are unable to make their lives purposive, achieve productive-ness, break out of the vicious circle of fate. In short, they fail to become agents of history for themselves; rather, they are the echoes of someone else's history, the last link in the centre–periphery chain. The only explana-tion possible is that these characters are living out their lives in the name of someone else's values or someone else's dreams. Hence the solitude and distance, those recurrent themes of Latin American history: it is their abandonment in an empty continent, a vast cultural vacuum, marooned thousands of miles away from their true home. Conceived by Spain in the sixteenth century (the stranded galleon, the buried suit of armour), the

[20] A. Rama, 'Un novelista de la violencia americana', in P.S. Martínez (ed.), *Recopilación de textos sobre García Márquez* (Havana, 1969), pp. 58–71 (p. 64).

characters awaken in the late eighteenth-century Enlightenment (magnet and telescope are symbols of the two pillars of Newtonian physics), but are entirely unable to bring themselves into focus in a world they have not made.

A number of critics have recognized the strike against the Banana Company and the ensuing massacre as the central shaping episode of the entire novel. The memory of this event is the secret thread which leads the reader, if not the characters, out into the light at the end of the labyrinth. García Márquez was born in 1927, eighteen months before the historic massacre took place. In the novel the Banana Company has brought temporary prosperity around the time of the First World War, but as profits are threatened in the mid-1920s the workers begin strike action, and the authorities respond with brutal violence, which they then deny: 'In Macondo nothing has happened, nor is anything happening now, nor will it ever.' All history and all memory are comprehensively blotted out by the rain which lasts four years, eleven months and two days, and which recalls the previous 'plague of insomnia' in chapter 3, significantly provoked on that occasion by the suppression of Colombian Indian history. Now proletarian history was to be erased. In this instance, however, despite assiduous efforts by Colombia's official historians to make even the memory of the murdered strikers 'disappear', it was not to be so easy. The massacre was perpetrated by troops under General Carlos Cortés Vargas at the Ciénaga (Magdalena) railway station on 5 December 1928, in direct connivance with the United Fruit Company. The conservative government of Miguel Abadía Méndez (1926–30) reported that a mere nine strikers were killed and, like all succeeding regimes, set about suppressing the true story. After some tempestuous parliamentary debates in September 1929, almost nothing of importance concerning these events appeared in Colombia in the forty years up to the publication of *Cien años de soledad*.

García Márquez shows us that the true history of Colombia and of Latin America is to be established not by the great patriarchs but by members of the younger generation, that of the writer himself (through the two characters called Aureliano Babilonia and Gabriel), who finally come to read and write the real history of the continent. They do so by deciphering the magical reality and labyrinthine fantasies of the previous one hundred years of solitude, this very novel, which is their world, and in which so many other characters have been bewitched and bewildered. Hence the mirror/ mirage ambiguity on the last page. There we find the apocalyptically named

Aureliano Babilonia 'deciphering the instant he was living, deciphering it as he lived it', or, as the Mexican philosopher Leopoldo Zea would no doubt argue, negating the past dialectically in order to become, in Octavio Paz's phrase, 'contemporary with all men'. Thus Aureliano breaks out of false circularities, meaningless repetitions, the prehistory before the dawn of true historical consciousness. His reading literally puts an end to one hundred years of solitude, to *Cien años de soledad,* and turns the reader who is reading about him back into the history outside the book. How, one wonders, can critics argue that the 'Boom' writers wilfully detached themselves and their works from Latin American history?

Thus the 'Boom' of the Latin American novel that was heralded by *La región más transparente* in 1958 and announced by *Rayuela* in 1963 climaxed with *Cien años de soledad* in 1967; and the latter, as text, is perfectly aware of its own literary-historical significance, one whose implicit claim is that the 'Boom' itself is proof of the impending transformation of Latin America, of the end of neo-colonialism and the beginning of true liberation. The inter-textual references to Alejo Carpentier's *El siglo de las luces, La muerte de Artemio Cruz, Rayuela* itself and *La Casa Verde* are clear signs of this, in contrast with the work of a writer like Borges, whose textual references are either to Argentina itself, or, much more often, to literatures outside Latin America. The sense of euphoria in the novel, and particularly in its final pages, is palpable. García Márquez had even, momentarily, found a means of reconciling his underlying intellectual pessimism about the human condition with his wilfully optimistic conception of the march of history. Truly he appeared to have liberated the Latin American literary labyrinth. And this, surely, is one of the grandest of historical illusions.

## POSTMODERNISM: FROM 'BOOM' TO 'POST-BOOM'

Each of the great 'Boom' novels of the 1960s was about some kind of quest and about the nature of Latin American identity; each also provided a metaphor for the course of Latin American history; they were also linguistically exploratory and structurally mythological: labyrinthine, preoccupied with consciousness, obsessed with the woman both as muse and materiality. In short, they were Joycean, Ulyssean works, products of patriarchal idealism inspired by and dedicated (though only rarely addressed) to Penelope, the Other, the world of matter, the female, the people, the nation, Mother America. The true story of the 'New Novel', then, is of a moment in Latin American history when the Joycean narrative became both generally writable and also unavoidable.

Then politics took a decisive role in developments. In Europe in the 1920s the key contradiction had been that which existed between the bourgeois liberal democratic systems of the advanced capitalist world and the communist ideology made feasible as a historical threat or promise by the October Revolution. These movements seemed to many writers at first to be going in roughly the same direction but at different speeds and with different priorities, and between them they allowed for the extraordinary explosion of the avant-garde in the period after the First World War. At the same time the spectre of the dictatorship of the proletariat produced a rapid tactical extension of the franchise, especially to women, in the more advanced and stable capitalist states, such as Britain, the United States and France, and the rise and triumph of fascism in Italy, Germany and Spain. As the 1929 Depression began to bite and with Soviet attitudes hardening, choices came to seem less free and literature was forced to divide into two camps, to the artistic detriment of both. In Latin America the economic expansion of the 1950s and 1960s, combined with the threat and lure of the Cuban Revolution – at first hastily matched, just as in Europe in the 1920s, with a promised extension of bourgeois democracy (the Alliance for Progress, Frei and Belaúnde et al.) – created for bourgeois liberal writers, in a new cosmopolitan era of consumer capitalism, a perspective of change, progress and apparently infinite choice – a benevolent labyrinth – which dazzled them and produced the fertile contradictions so characteristic of Latin American novels of the 1960s. Then, as the true intentions of Cuban socialism gradually took shape out of the mists of ideology and propaganda (Castro's declaration that he was a Communist, the USSR connection, the guerrilla struggles on the mainland, the Cabrera Infante and Padilla affairs), conflicts began to emerge and the stream of protest letters from Latin American writers on the subject of intellectual conscience were merely the outward sign of the fact that writers were no longer 'free' to imagine and to create whatever they liked, because reality was closing in on them once again. And once again they were forced, as writers had been in the 1930s, to choose, like Fuentes's Artemio Cruz. After the death of Che Guevara in the mountains of Bolivia in 1967 and other setbacks for guerrilla struggle in Latin America, Cuba began to batten down the revolutionary hatches and the – probably inevitable – trajectory between Castro's *Words to the Intellectuals* (1961) and the 'Padilla Affair' (1971) was completed. Elsewhere, a more overtly violent repression swept a continent in which film was able to record much more immediately than literature the horror of all that was going on, particularly in Argentina, Chile and Bolivia. In the face of this situation, some writers spoke left and wrote right, sustaining the contradictions of their situation ever more acutely, well into the new era. That era itself, however, belongs to yet another 'new novel' (à la française), none other than the 'Post-Boom' novel, which we should probably call late-Modernist or even Postmodernist. In the transition between the representative works of the 'Boom', and the developments of the 1970s, lies the moment where Latin America (meaning of course its novel-writing middle sectors) 'caught up' with Europe and finally produced equivalent, if still specifically Latin American, narrative forms to those being produced contemporaneously in Europe and the United States.

Paradoxically enough, it was in Cuba, always open to the lure of the baroque, broadly conceived – it was in Havana that the 1920s Góngora revival was most enthusiastically celebrated – and at the same time especially vulnerable to North American popular culture, that Joyce's specifically linguistic lessons seem to have been easiest to learn. The *Orígenes* group, organized around the large figure of José Lezama Lima and younger men like Cabrera Infante, had been experimenting long before the 1960s with language, parody, satire and other forms of humour. Thus Lezama Lima's *Paradiso* (1966) and Cabrera Infante's *Tres tristes tigres* (1967) were by no means surprising products of the Caribbean island, and both were specifically applauded by Cortázar himself. Other important Cuban proponents of the new vogue were Severo Sarduy, later a member of the *Tel Quel* circle, and Reinaldo Arenas. It must be said at this point, however, as the Cuban cultural commissars were soon to say from their own more dogmatic standpoint, that while the technical focus of the new fiction appeared immeasurably widened, its social relevance, with some notable exceptions, was becoming inexorably narrower. The Joyce of *Dubliners* and *Ulysses* was, when all is said and done, *also* a social observer applying new techniques to traditional everyday materials and by that means revolutionizing the realist novel. Many of the younger Spanish American writers of the sixties and seventies were interested only in selected aspects of the Joycean 'package', or in the somewhat whimsical works published by Cortázar after 1963, such as *Vuelta al día en ochenta mundos* (1967), *62/Modelo para armar* (1968) and *Ultimo round* (1969). *Libro de Manuel* (1973), which decisively marks Cortázar's turn to commitment, was far less influential.

Typical of the new mood were the young Mexicans of the *Onda*, or 'new wave', for whom Joyce was the great experimentalist of the twentieth century, not its exemplary craftsman. Some of them tended to use him and Cortázar less as an influence or an inspiration than as a pretext for engaging in 'semi-automatic' experiments that in reality had more to do with Surrealism or psychedelia. A reluctant precursor of such young writers is Salvador Elizondo (b.1932), author of the pathbreaking French-style *Farabeuf* (1965), similar in conception to Cortázar's 'Blow-up'. Elizondo has written a number of articles on and around both Joyce and Borges, in addition to his pioneering translation and commentary of the first page of *Finnegans Wake. La Princesa del Palacio de Hierro* (1974) by Gustavo Sainz (b.1940) may be construed as one long homage to the Molly Bloom soliloquy, whilst in his *Obsesivos días circulares* (1969 and 1978) the narrator is trying to read *Ulysses* itself throughout his narrative, failing ever actually to achieve this objective because life – in its most incoherent and absurd contemporary forms – keeps getting in the way. What such works implicitly question, in the age of pop and television advertising, is whether 'Literature' can have any meaning or function for us now: Joyce brought the novel to an end, perhaps, but this was only the sign of a wider cultural and social malaise – we would like to be his equals, but civilization itself appears to be saying that the gesture would be futile. This dilemma is at the heart of the postmodern conundrum.

The potential confusion, complexity and bitterness of these conflicts in the Latin American situation was exemplified by the lamentable debate in 1969 between two emblematic figures, Julio Cortázar himself, the cosmopolitan icon, and José María Arguedas, perhaps the greatest nativist novelist this century and the last of the great regionalist writers. Cortázar was at that time in self-imposed exile from Latin America, working in Paris as a translator for international organizations, whereas Arguedas, as we have seen, was a Quechua-speaking novelist, brought up among and for a time by the Indians of the Peruvian sierras. He never resolved his traumas and inner conflicts, which were those of Peru as a whole, but in 1964 had produced his own supreme achievement, *Todas las sangres,* at the very moment when such writing appeared to have been definitively superseded by the new novel. Cortázar's reply to Arguedas's critique of the 'Boom' as a cosmopolitan betrayal of the real Latin America was published in *Life* magazine. Arguedas reprinted his views in the 'First Diary', corresponding to May 1968, of his posthumously published novel, *El zorro de arriba y el zorro de abajo* (1971) – generally considered, ironically enough, Arguedas's first effort at self-referential fiction. Arguedas, genuinely shocked by Cortázar's self-conscious sophistication and pretensions to professionalism, exclaimed that 'writing novels and poems is not a profession'. Arguedas presented himself as indigenist, provincial, Peruvian and American, deriding Cortázar's 'brilliance, his solemn conviction that one can understand the essence of one's own nation from the exalted spheres of some supranational perspective'. As his erratic diatribe developed, Arguedas linked Joyce, Cortázar and Lezama Lima together as purveyors of an elitist literature born of the corrupt cities, and declared himself proud to be among those 'marginalized' by the new writing. Cortázar's reply to his adversary's comments was typically dazzling, and he made some telling points; but to accuse a writer from Arguedas's background of a bad case of inferiority complex was not one of the better ones.[21] It has to be said also that Cortázar, like other defenders of the 'New Novel', offered no strategy for reconciling the demands of the regional and the national, still less of the regional and the supranational, while the concept of class was not mentioned once in twenty pages of discourse. In the most brutal of ironies, Cortázar later managed to maintain his support for the Cuban Revolution (sorely tested but decisively reasserted in May 1971), wrote *Libro de Manuel* in the early 1970s, and became one of the most active and effective campaigners for the Allende regime in Chile after 1970 and for the Nicaraguan Revolution after 1979; whilst Arguedas, for his part, committed suicide in November 1969, shortly after their bitter polemic.

After Arguedas's death, the other great representative of the regionalist current still alive at the time was Augusto Roas Bastos (Paraguay, b.1918), with whom he had much else in common. Roa had written one of the most interesting novels of the late 1950s, *Hijo de Hombre* (1959), which was almost a premonition of the literary and political future. The work is all the more interesting in retrospect, since it was one of the very last of the recognizably pre-'Boom' novels by an author who was in due course to write one of the most remarkable 'Post-Boom' works, *Yo el Supremo* (1974). His first novel, like that of Arguedas, dealt with a bi-cultural and indeed bi-lingual society; and also, like Arguedas's, it painted a moving picture of oppression and suffering, matched by heroic powers of resistance on the part of the usually anonymous poor, and raised the question of commitment in a form which pointedly confronted the reader himself with inescapable dilemmas. Whilst never committing abso-

---

[21] J. Cortázar, 'Un gran escritor y su soledad: Julio Cortázar', *Life en Español*, 33/7 (Mexico, D.F., 1969), 43–55.

lutely to any specific ideology, Roa's concerns are uniquely those of the
Latin American Left as a whole during the period from the 1950s to the
1980s. A long-time supporter of the Cuban Revolution, Roa took his
novels closer than those of any other major writer to the debates of Fanon,
Mao, Castro, Guevara and Liberation Theology. *Hijo de hombre* tells the
dramatic story of two Paraguayan communities, lost in the outback, over a
period of three decades from the early 1900s to the time of the Chaco War
with Bolivia and its aftermath in the 1930s. The novel juxtaposes two
views of Christianity, that of the official Church and that of the Indian
peasants who interpret Christ's torment as a reflection of their own agony:
'This was the ceremony which gave us villagers of Itapé the name of
fanatics and heretics. The people of those times came year after year to
unnail Christ and carry him through the town like a victim they wished to
avenge rather than a God who had wanted to die for men's sakes.'

Roa has often said that the people have a capacity for heroism and self-
sacrifice which is in itself utopian and carries the seeds of the future. Their
concrete experience and beliefs should be the first, if not the last, concern
of the Latin American novelist. Thus although he does not share the
messianic Christianity of his desperate peasant characters, he presents it
with respect and indeed underlines its socio-economic content. In this
regard, as Roa himself modestly pointed out, he anticipated the development of the Church militant which was to be such a force in Latin America
in the coming years. His insistence in *Hijo de hombre* on his old kind of
'zero degree writing' – the writing of hunger – makes his work the logical culmination of a Marxist, and hence internationalist focus, which had
been developing from Icaza's vulgar and Arguedas's dialectical 'Old Left'
perspectives to the kind of Third-Worldist 'New Left' vision we glimpse in
*Hijo de hombre* itself. At the same time, however, Roa recognized the
inevitability of taking up the challenge of the new whilst resisting its
temptations, and the result was *Yo el Supremo* (1974, see below), as fear-
somely complex, self-referential and meta-textual as anyone could require
whilst reaffirming the previous collective tradition in new ways in the face
of a much more complex world.

After *Cien años de soledad* and the high-point of the 'Boom', the hardening
of the Cuban Revolution, the Chilean coup of 1973 and other such revolutionary reverses coincided with a sense of voluntarism and surfeit on the
part of authors who were now in many cases wanting to write big novels
rather than proving able to write great ones. Needless to say, Latin Ameri-

can fiction has continued to produce large numbers of outstanding works, and remains perhaps the most fertile body of narrative in the world today, whilst publicity and sales have continued on an ever upward trend. Nevertheless, most readers would agree that the works of the past two decades do not quite match the old ones in scale and perspective, and the genre has not developed very far beyond its state in the mid-seventies. What we have seen has been more of a repositioning than an advance.

Curiously, most of the novels to be examined in this section are exclusively urban, with cities viewed as Dantean infernos (this was Asturias's original conception for *El señor Presidente*). The more usual approach is parody, though mixed often enough with a tragic vein; when this becomes extreme, as it has towards the century's end, then an apocalyptic note becomes increasingly apparent. The first, and in some ways the most impressive, of Latin America's wilfully wayward blockbusters, was published at the end of the 1940s, when Asturias, Carpentier and Borges were at the peak of their creativity. *Adán Buenosayres* (1948) by the Argentine Leopoldo Marechal (1900–70), was a monstrous construction of almost 800 pages set, significantly enough, in the 1920s, and specifically addressed to readers in the Argentine capital itself. It is undoubtedly one of the great neglected works of Latin American Modernism, partly due to its Catholic framework and partly due to Marechal's fervent support for Peronism at a time when most other artists and intellectuals – such as his close associate of the 1920s, Borges – were in opposition. It is also the most obviously Dantesque of all Latin American novels, since the Inferno itself appears to be situated not far below the streets of Buenos Aires, and it was the first Latin American novel to attempt a close approximation to what Joyce had done for Dublin. Such a project, however, did not emerge naturally from Latin America's historical experience and Marechal lacked the lightness of touch to compensate for the novel's structural weaknesses.

In Brazil, Erico Veríssimo (1951–75) also set out to produce grand novels on the scale, and with some of the characteristics, of Tolstoy, Joyce and Proust, though legibility was always a primordial objective of his work. Nevertheless, he was also concerned with self-referentiality, the role of the writer and the function of fiction. His best known works are *O resto é silencio* (1942) and his largest project, the three-volume *O tempo e o vento* (1949, 1951, 1962), a historical epic about the people of his home state of Rio Grande do Sul. In this novel also the city predominates, both in subject matter and in structural presentation, and Veríssimo has little interest in the world which lies outside. Nevertheless, his experiments with simultaneity and multiplicity on the lines of Dos Passos, Huxley and Woolf – so well suited to Latin America's pluralist realities – predate those of Fuentes and Vargas Llosa by many years.

In 1966, at the height of the 'Boom', José Lezama Lima (1910–76) produced his astonishing novel with the Dantean title of *Paradiso* (1966), mixing both classical and Catholic imagery and achieving the remarkable double coup of offending both the Catholic Church and the Cuban Revolution through its approach to eroticism in general and homosexuality in particular. Lezama had been writing the work since 1949, just as Marechal had been composing his novel since the 1920s (indeed, both are set mainly in that decisive decade). Where Dante's patriarchal vision implies that the ideal woman can never be found on earth, and not finding her will always cause torment, Lezama's very title opts for unambiguous fulfilment, and it may be that sexual inversion and its consequent democratization of gender relations is here proposed as one key to future social transformation. The initials of the undoubtedly autobiographical protagonist José Cemí give the clue to the novel's conception of the child as holy infant constituted through sensuality and language within the trinity completed by his mother and father. For a Cuba undergoing the seemingly unavoidable puritanical backlash consequent on revolutionary consolidation, with its historically masculine gestures, Lezama's book appeared a somewhat provocative way of celebrating the city of Havana, whose traditions of sinfulness the authorities were keen to put behind them. The book has now been thoroughly rehabilitated, but its hermeticism, allusiveness and complexity have ensured that it will never be read by more than a few highly educated readers and scholars.

Guillermo Cabrera Infante (b. 1929) is, by general consent, with *Tres tristes tigres* (first version 1964, definitive 1967), author of the first Latin American comic classic with its hilarious vision of three hangers on and around in pre-revolutionary Havana. The novel has a similar theme to that of Edmundo Desnoes's *Memorias del subdesarrollo* (1967), which criticizes the posture of the petty-bourgeois intellectual, but when it transpired that Cabrera, like his characters, preferred unrepentantly to go on being a 'sad tiger' even after the Revolution, the Cuban authorities rapidly lost patience with this born iconoclast and in due course he went into exile. This was a pity, though perhaps an inevitable one, since at that time Cabrera was one of the most talented writers of the new wave.

His linguistic exuberance makes comparison with Lezama (as well as Carpentier and Sarduy) inevitable, but there is one major difference: where Lezama's work relies heavily on a Greek and Roman Catholic philosophical background, Cabrera Infante turns to popular – indeed, Pop – culture, and was the first to introduce the mass media into his fiction as a solid proposition and without parody or apology. On the contrary, it was educated or official culture which seemed to him to be risible. Cabrera's most ambitious work, *La Habana para un infante difunto* (1979), appropriately translated as *Infante's Inferno*, is also a major novel by any standards, not least in length, and an important biographical document. It is in effect an almost interminable sexual odyssey, with Cabrera, writing from London, recalling his early erotic experiences as an adolescent and as a young man in the tropical fleshpots of old Havana. Here too, as in *Tres tristes tigres*, nostalgia is a pervasive and ultimately perverse shaping emotion.

Fernando del Paso (b. 1935) is a Mexican writer who has tried harder than most to reconcile avant-garde literature with political writing, beginning with *José Trigo* (1965), which is based in part on the critical railway workers' strike in the late 1950s. In 1977 however he produced a huge novel, inspired directly by James Joyce's *Ulysses* and Rabelais's *Gargantua and Pantagruel,* as well as by chivalresque and picaresque fiction, entitled *Palinuro de México*. The echo of *Adán Buenosayres* is obvious in the title, as well as the fact that Palinuro, like Adán, is dead before the work starts. (The last chapter of *Paradiso* likewise relates the death of Cemí's alter ego, Oppiano Licario, and Cabrera's title, 'Havana for a Dead Infante' suggests an equally apocalyptic conception of the meaning of these colossal literary self-projections). Ironically enough, the weakness of Del Paso's work is the opposite of Lezama's, namely that the linguistic texture itself is perhaps insufficiently demanding to stretch the reader's consciousness to the dimensions required by Del Paso's 'Ulyssean' perspective. Thus although Del Paso is an entertaining and knowledgeable writer, and although the novel's fictionality fuses with Mexico's recent reality when Palinuro dies at the 1968 Tlatelolco massacre (in a section entitled 'Acta est Fabula: The Comedy is Over'), the narrative ultimately fails to achieve historical transcendence and is more of a Joycean improvization than a successful 'Ulyssean' novel. Del Paso's latest work is another monster production, *Noticias del imperio* (1987), about the episode involving the imposition of Emperor Maximilian and Queen Carlota of Mexico in the nineteenth century. It is considered by a number of critics to be one of Latin America's most accomplished historical novels.

The biggest of all Latin American novels thus far is Carlos Fuentes's *Terra Nostra* (1975), gargantuan both in length (almost 900 pages) and ambition. Its title makes plain an intention which we see, in retrospect, was also that of Marechal, Lezama, Cabrera and Del Paso, namely to lay claim to a territory and its history through a literary reconstruction which identifies that temporal space with the life of its author. Fuentes's ambition is the greatest of all, since his work is not only *not* confined to a capital city, or even a capital and its country, but lays claim to the whole of Latin America and Spain, that is to the whole Hispanic region over the whole of its history; indeed, it is really more ambitious even than this because it also whimsically modifies that vast history and invents its own variants. This is magical realism with a vengeance: the vengeance of Latin American culture against its Spanish paternity, the culmination of almost a century of literary parricide.

Fuentes, perhaps the most inherently talented writer of the past thirty years in Latin America, has consistently changed his literary style, and the title of his 1966 novel *Cambio de piel* is suggestive in this regard. Other novels include *Las buenas conciencias* (1959), the brief gothic classic *Aura* (1962), *Zona sagrada* (1967), *La cabeza de la hidra* (1978), *Gringo viejo* (1988) and *La campaña* (1992), the first of a trilogy of historical novels about the nineteenth century independence struggles. *Cristóbal Nonato* (1987) was one of a series of activities the endlessly self-circulating Fuentes undertook in honour of the forthcoming 1992 celebrations. Long before this, however, *Terra Nostra* was clearly intended as the Latin American novel to end all Latin American novels, a blockbusting total novel at the end of fiction, of the century, and, symbolically – given its apocalyptic overtones – of the world. In the process Fuentes playfully rearranges half a millennium in the history of Spanish and Latin American history, and begins by marrying Elizabeth Tudor of England to Philip II of Spain. Then Spain's historical figures, from Philip and Cortés to Franco, intermingle with such Spanish literary figures as Celestina, Don Quixote and Don Juan, plus a host of Latin Americans – not to mention other literary and historical characters drafted in as required from the whole of Western culture, including most of the writers of the 'Boom'. Sadly many critics have considered this work a failure, but it is certainly a grandiose one by a writer with more creative energy than most others could even dream of marshalling.

At this point our historical narrative runs into a problem. Despite its heading, 'Postmodernity', this third section has taken a quite orthodox course up to now. Granted, other writers would not necessarily agree in detail with either its preconceptions or its conclusions, but this has been a narrative with a central thematic and a developing plot, and one which incorporates a large number of authors and works which are, for the most part, 'canonical': that is to say, they would have been included by almost any other literary historian in the field. Thus although no other writer would have told the story in quite the same way, few traditional critics would strongly disagree with the fact that Mário de Andrade, Asturias, Borges and Carpentier were names to reckon with, if not the major precursors of the 1960s 'Boom', followed by Rulfo, Guimarães Rosa, Arguedas and Roa Bastos (this group is slightly less immovable); and probably no one in the entire critical world would disagree that the four great leaders of the 'Boom' itself were Julio Cortázar, Carlos Fuentes, Mario Vargas Llosa and Gabriel García Márquez.

But for the period 1975 to the present there would be no such agreement, and the problem is not only one of proximity and historical perspective. There is no consensus as to the important movements, authors or works. Now this may well be in part because no one has emerged to challenge the pre-eminence of the 'Boom' writers themselves. Indeed, Fuentes, Vargas Llosa and García Márquez remain overwhelmingly the most important and prestigious living writers (Cortázar having died in 1983). They have moved into middle age and – in literary terms – relative decline, though they have continued to write as energetically as before. But even as they continue to make grand literary gestures – Fuentes's *Terra Nostra* (1975) and *Cristóbal Nonato* (1987), Vargas Llosa's *La guerra del fin del mundo* (1981), García Márquez's *El amor en los tiempos del cólera* (1985), all major novels – the results are somehow slightly disappointing, essentially voluntarist works, there because the audience and the writers willed them, but perhaps not truly from the heart. The best of them is *El amor en los tiempos del cólera* – an international best-seller, moreover – but it is fair to point out that if that novel succeeds it is in part because it dramatizes our sense of a typically Latin American heroic failure. Its theme, after all – a man who waits more than half a century for the woman he loves – was one for the late 1980s: a brief, belated, totally private and largely symbolic triumph in the face of hopeless odds. But much more important, and a problem of a quite different conceptual order, is the fact that the whole concept of the canon, of an author, a work, a writing and acting subject, and even 'literature' itself have all been 'decentred', 'deconstructed' or 'placed under erasure', to use just a few of the critical terms which have emerged in the past twenty-five years. This means that the study of texts and discourses has been revolutionized in unprecedented ways and to an unprecedented degree, and it also means that the kinds of (literary) texts being produced has undergone an equally radical change, both in response to the same global transformations in cultural production which have altered critical writing and in response to changing critical expectations themselves. If one introduces back into this already complex problematic the long-standing problem of the extent to which Latin American cultural production is generated from within Latin American society itself and to what extent it is over-determined by 'external factors' (if these can be said any longer to exist) – that is to say, what we have earlier called the phenomenon of uneven development – then the theoretical problems confronting us are of a truly intimidating complexity.

This is not the place to examine this new problematic in any detail but its existence is worth noting. If we were to judge contemporary writers by the criteria used in mapping the narrative history thus far, few would seem to merit a whole page or even a paragraph rather than a line or two. However, history – even contemporary history – must be written, and what follows is a compromise – and in every way a provisional one – between the traditional history of authors and works and the new history of subject positions, discourses and texts. This is partly, on the positive side, an attempt to maintain a certain level of narrative coherence whilst responding to the changed cultural and critical situation; equally, and more negatively, its caution is explained by the uneasy feeling that this really is a less creative moment in Latin American narrative, that it will be recognized as such in some not too distant future, and that in that not too distant future we may again, despite everything, be back in a world, however much transformed, of more or less great authors and more or less canonical works. For the moment, at any rate, the Postmodern phenomenon has sharpened the distinction between the earlier narrative mode of literary history – more or less what the reader has experienced thus far – and what is often termed the 'encyclopedic' mode, which, for theoretical reasons, challenges the traditional division between elite and popular culture, eschews linearity and closure, and stresses particularity, contingency and randomness. In an age when 'grand' or 'master' narratives have fallen into disrepute, critics argue that it is contradictory to construct a literary history of the old kind.

Textuality, then, is the watchword, in an era where reality itself is deemed increasingly 'fictitious', because explicitly 'constructed' and therefore relativized. All previously existing certainties have been dissolved and the globalization of the mass media has annulled distance, divorcing the signifier from the signified, so that the problem of representation has come to dominate theoretical debate in the new era of detotalization and detemporalization. That is why nothing is clear in this present cultural panorama. There is little agreement about what Postmodernity is or when it began. Was it in the 1980s, when most critics and even the press began to talk about it? In the 1970s, when the oil crisis made it clear for the first time that neither the capitalist West nor the communist East was able to control the post-colonial 'Third World'? Or in the 1960s, the age of (illusory) revolution, both political and cultural? It may be a simplistic view, but perhaps Modernism reached its peak shortly after the First World War, completing not only the process initiated by the capitalist-imperialist scramble in the last quarter of the nineteenth century but also the era of European, and indeed Atlantic, hegemony. Postmodernity corresponds to the period after the Second World War (television, electronic music, computers, space exploration) and coincides with the completion of the rise to world dominance of the United States and the beginnings of the shift of the centre of gravity to the Pacific. Postmodernity and its cultural creature, Postmodernism, became dominant in the late 1950s and early 1960s, but their origins lay in the transformations of everyday life which began in the 1920s and which were reflected at that time in the international avant-garde movements and in the writing of Modernist authors like James Joyce and, indeed, Jorge Luis Borges. For this historian, then, as will have become clear above, the 'Boom' of the Latin American narrative completed the assimilation of Modernist procedures and also inaugurated the transition to what we now call Postmodernist modes of writing. Cortázar, Fuentes, García Márquez and Vargas Llosa are all writers who undertook that transition.

As we have seen, the 'Boom' was effectively bust by the time *Yo el Supremo* and *Terra Nostra* appeared in 1974 and 1975 respectively. It had been the culmination of fifty years of steady and coherent development in Latin American narrative, and in that sense was more of a climax than any kind of rupture with the past. In other words, it marked a particular stage in the process of modernity. It also signalled the moment when Latin American literature became integrated within the international 'mainstream' (to quote Luis Harss).[22] At the same time, however, the conjuncture which the 'Boom' represented saw the completion of one development – Latin American Modernism – and the beginnings of another – Latin American Postmodernism. Here the great precursors once again were Asturias, in whose early works much of Severo Sarduy and the Mexican new wave can be found in embryo, but above all Borges, who has revolutionized our understanding of the relations between texts, especially the relation between 'literature' and 'criticism'. The great instigator, however, was Julio Cortázar, whose *Rayuela,* like the 'Boom' itself, was trebly significant – in its own right, as a climax to Modernism, and as the point of departure for Postmodernism. It is surely no coincidence that Cortázar's works were produced from Paris in the late 1950s and early 1960s. This was not only the moment of the *nouveau roman* and the *nouvelle vague* but also of the *nouvelle critique.* As mentioned above, and each in their different ways, the great French theorists – Barthes, Derrida, Foucault and Lacan – were undermining the notions of the subject, the author and the work. The implications were revolutionary and their effects are still with us today, not only in literary criticism but in creative writing itself.

That said, it is difficult to find fixed patterns in the narrative fiction of Latin America over the past twenty years, and we shall have to settle for trends. Here the theoretical problems mentioned above and mere pragmatism come together in unholy alliance. For most of the period serious writers have been paralysed by the horrors and reverses of the continent's recent history. Ironically enough, the absence of a stable centre for Latin American culture – unless Paris is thought to play such a role – has had a decisive and possibly beneficial effect on the idea and the possibility of a 'Latin American Literature' and the particular 'Ulyssean' shape it has taken during its voyage into the mainstream. In a Postmodern era of pluralism, multi-culturalism and shifting identities, Latin America may even be considered a paradigm for future developments in the realm of cultural critique.

## Women's Rites

It is appropriate to begin with a brief survey of female writing and feminist writing, because its definitive irruption and apparent normaliza-

---

[22] Harss's book *Los nuestros* (1966), whose English version was entitled *Into the Mainstream* (New York, 1967), was a collection of conversations with Latin American authors which set many of the terms of critical debate about Latin American narrative from the late 1960s onward.

tion is without doubt the single most important phenomenon of the 'Post-Boom' era. The assumption by women of their own representation has inevitably put an end to the version of the great Latin American myths which reached their patriarchal apotheosis with the 'Boom' itself.

Progress in the twentieth century has been arduous for women writers. Even in poetry women have had to take a back seat, with only the Uruguayan writer, the significantly beautiful Juana de Ibarbourou, and the Chilean Gabriela Mistral (the first Latin American to win the Nobel Prize, in 1945) able to claim continental recognition until the very recent past. Nevertheless, in many countries, above all Argentina (Victoria and Silvina Ocampo, Beatriz Guido, Silvina Bullrich, Marta Traba, Luisa Valenzuela, and many others), Uruguay (Cristina Peri Rossi), Chile (Marta Brunet, María Luisa Bombal, Isabel Allende), Brazil (Raquel de Queirós, Ligia Fagundes Telles, Clarice Lispector, Nélida Piñón) and Mexico (Nellie Campobello, Elena Garro, Rosario Castellanos, Elena Poniatowska, Luisa Josefa Hernández), much excellent writing has appeared and opportunities for women are gradually increasing. In the 1980s and 1990s a few women became almost as well known as the best known men, though none has yet become the best known novelist or poet of their country. Similarly, in literary criticism women have begun to make their mark, and this is perhaps an especially significant phenomenon. They include Ana Pizarro, Beatriz Sarlo, Josefina Ludmer, Silvia Molloy, Sara Castro Klarén and Margo Glantz.

Elena Poniatowska (b. 1933) is one of Latin America's most remarkable narrators. Outside of Paz and Fuentes, she is probably the most important writer in Mexico today. Her father was a French-Polish émigré aristocrat, her mother the daughter of a Mexican landowning family which fled the country during the Revolution. In later years she strove conscientiously to integrate herself into Mexican national life, and today is possibly the country's best known journalist and arguably Latin America's most important producer of documentary narrative. *La noche de Tlatelolco* (1971) is the single most influential record of any kind of the 1968 massacre, in which her brother Jan died. And *Nada, nadie* (1988) is a truly moving testimony to the experience of the 1986 earthquake. Thus Poniatowska has produced the most lasting memorials to the two most significant events of Mexican history in the last two decades, the Tlatelolco affair and the great earthquake, as well as a series of other works such as *Querido Diego, te abraza Quiela* (1978), *Lilus Kilus* (1976) and *La flor de lis* (1988), something like a fictionalized autobiography. (Another child of émigré parents, Margo

Glantz (b. 1930), has made a similarly wide-ranging contribution to fiction and literary criticism: *Las genealogías,* 1981, is an outstanding contribution to women's autobiographical writing).

Poniatowska's documentary novel *Hasta no verte Jesús mío* (1969) is perhaps the most substantial example of Latin American documentary fiction and gives the fullest picture of its protagonist, Jesusa Palancares, a woman born in the interior, who took part in the Revolution and lived for more than forty years in Mexico City. Jesusa's view of the world excludes politics, and she has little sympathy for her fellow women (all 'soft touches'), but the political impact of the book is considerable. It is principally concerned with the endless work Jesusa has done throughout a long and lonely life, and her reflections on that and her other personal experiences. The combination of its artful construction and compelling story makes most social realist fiction seem artificial. In 1993 Poniatowska completed a favourite long-term project, *Tinísima,* a huge documentary novel about the photographer Tina Modotti, political activist in the 1920s and 1930s, sometime lover of Julio Antonio Mella, and feminist icon.

Brazil's most celebrated woman writer was Clarice Lispector (1925–77), author of *Laços de família* (1960), *A maçã no escuro* (1961), *Legião estrangeira* (1964), the stunning *A paixão segundo G.H.* (1964), and several other works of fiction and chronicles. Comparisons are often made with another Brazilian novelist with a penchant for intimate tales, Autran Dourado (b. 1926), author of extraordinary novels like *O risco do bordado* (1970), and the scintillating *Os sinos da agonia* (1974) about colonial Ouro Preto. One of a remarkable generation of Latin American women writers from East European backgrounds – including Elena Poniatowska, Margo Glantz, Alina Diaconú, Vlady Kociancich, Alejandra Pizarnik – Lispector was two months old when her Ukrainian parents arrived in Brazil. She was to become best known for her extraordinary explorations of feminine subjectivity, above all the way in which women are entrapped and isolated in a private world of helpless rage and frustration which they often conceal even from themselves. Lispector's best known novel was her last, the very brief *A hora da estrêla* (1977), which later became a successful film. It tells the story of the pathetic Macabéa, a half-literate typist from the country who comes to work in São Paulo, feeds spiritually on a diet of radio commercials and quiz shows, and ends up killed by a fast car just as she begins to dream of a Hollywood-style happy ending for herself. The French feminist theorist Hélène Cixous has suggested that Lispector's writing constitutes the most important body of fiction accumulated by any woman writer in the contemporary era, and not just in Latin America.

By far the most successful Latin American woman writer with the international reading public is the Chilean Isabel Allende (b. 1942), author of *La casa de los espíritus* (1982), *De amor y de sombras* (1984), *Eva Luna* (1987) and the very disappointing *El plan infinito* (1992), set in the United States. A work of world renown, *La casa de los espíritus* has also met with controversy: many critics have accused the writer of plagiarizing García Márquez or have asserted that the book is little more than an amateurish sentimental romance. Yet there is little doubt that it has brought the horrors of the Chilean coup to the attention of as many people as Costa-Gavras' film *Missing,* whose intentions were similar. There is a parallel recent endeavour from Brazil, *A República dos sonhos* (1984) by Clarice Lispector's best known successor, Nélida Piñón (b. 1935). Piñón, like Lispector, began by writing allusive, suggestive fiction, confirming the movement away from social realism after the 1940s; but she too, in the face of the military oppression of the 1960s and 1970s, has evolved towards a more historical mode. *A República dos sonhos* returns with a vengeance to the theme of Brazilian identity, in this case from the perspective of a woman whose grandparents migrated to Brazil from Galicia in Spain and made their fortune, despite the new land failing to turn out as the utopia of the deliberately ambiguous title. Piñón's very long book alternates between an insider and an outsider view of Brazil and again combines a personal and family saga with the history of the country.

It is not only men who are lured by the seductive force of fantasy in the River Plate region. As mentioned above, Silvina Ocampo (1906–93), sister of Victoria, was one of the pioneers of the genre, also worked by Onetti and Cortázar, in which the fantastic seeps uncannily out of everyday experience. More recently the Uruguayan writer Cristina Peri Rossi (b. 1941), in exile since 1971, has established a wide reputation for her ability to combine the fantastic, the erotic and the political in both short stories and novels, including *El libro de mis primos* (1969), the much admired *La nave de los locos* (1984), about the virtues of exile, *Una pasión prohibida* (1986), *Cosmoagonías* (stories, 1988) and *Solitario de amor* (1988).

The Argentine Luisa Valenzuela (b. 1938) is another exile who lives in the United States and has written one of the most vivid and original novels about the period following Perón's return in 1973. Its title, *Cola de lagartija* (1983), comes from one of the many instruments of torture recently invented in the Southern Cone. Valenzuela's previous works include *Cambio de armas* (1977; published 1982), which explores the more disturbing aspects of male-female relations against the background of the prevailing military repression, and *Aquí pasan cosas raras* (1979). *Cola de lagartija* however is a much more hypnotic novel, focused on the almost incredible figure of José López Rega, the self-styled minister of social welfare of President Isabel Perón (1974–6). He is portrayed as an insane Svengali committed to an atavistic crusade involving the most hideous impulses and blood rituals. Valenzuela's surrealistic language is reminiscent of the only extant prose work by the Argentine poet Alejandra Pizarnik (1936–72), *La condesa sangrienta* (1968).

Valenzuela has found a sisterly though even more disconcerting voice in the Chilean Diamela Eltit (b. 1949), author of *Lumpérica* (1983), *Por la patria* (1986), *Cuarto mundo* (1988) and *Vaca sagrada* (1992). Eltit remained in Chile after the Pinochet coup, and like a number of Argentine novelists contrived a line of fiction designed to be subversive yet illegible to the powers that be. Her perspective is provocative and aggressive, an intimidating example of an implicitly feminist work which aligns itself with every other form of marginalization. Eltit's work promises to develop in directions as radical as anything yet produced by a Latin American, whether male or female.

Other notable recent works by women writers are *Papeles de Pandora* (1976) and *Maldito amor* (1986) by Rosario Ferré (Puerto Rico, b. 1938); Postmodern pastiches of genre fiction by Ana Lydia Vega (Puerto Rico, b. 1946), like *Pasión de historia* (1987) or *Falsas crónicas del sur* (1991); the bolero-based *Arráncame la vida* (1985) by Angeles Mastretta (Mexico, b. 1949); *Como agua para chocolate* (1989) by Laura Esquivel (Mexico, b. 1950), a 'novel in monthly instalments, with recipes, love affairs and home remedies' which became a runaway international best-seller following the success of the movie adaptation; *Ultimos días de William Shakespeare* (1984) by Vlady Kociancich (Argentina, b. 1941); and *La mujer habitada* (1990), a work both political and magical realist by the well-known Nicaraguan poet Gioconda Belli (b. 1948). Among new writers emerging across the continent there seem to be as many women as men.

## Popular Culture and Pastiche

One of the aspects of Postmodernism agreed upon by most observers is that its cultural vehicles seek to reduce or abolish the gulf between 'high' and 'popular' culture. For many historical reasons, this is a trend well suited to Latin American cultural realities and popular culture has indeed been an increasingly influential source of material for Latin American writers since the transition from rural to urban fiction in the 1940s and 1950s. Cortázar's enthusiasm for jazz was an early antecedent of the shift. Mexico City became an influential cultural axis of the ensuing period and had its own mini-boom. In the swinging sixties that 'new wave' of hip young writers known as the 'Onda' emerged, centred on Mexico City's fashionable 'Pink Zone'. The movement involved a curious mixing-in of United States beat, pop and psychedelic culture with Latin American literary ingredients like the works of Borges, Cabrera Infante, Sarduy and above all Cortázar's quintessentially 1960s mode. Inevitably, the new wave struck a series of profoundly ambiguous postures both towards the idea of consumer capitalism in general and the Mexican state in particular. It has to be admitted that the 'Onda' appears to have produced no histori-cally transcendent works, but then it is a tenet of Postmodernism that words like 'transcendent' should be despatched to the critical dustbin. 'Onda' writers were young, cosmopolitan, anti-establishment and mainly male, purveyors of a narrative literature apparently grounded in the plea-sure principle though rarely far from political despair. Thus although few of them were overtly militant, they were often aggressively proletarian in their vocabulary and cultural tastes. Leading writers included José Agustín (b. 1944), writer of acid-rock novels like *La tumba* (1964), *De perfil* (1966), *Inventando que sueño* (1968) and *Se está haciendo tarde* (1973); Gustavo Sainz (b. 1940), author of *Gazapo* (1965), *Obsesivos días circulares* (1969) and *La Princesa del Palacio de Hierro* (1974), both mentioned above, and *Compadre Lobo* (1978); and Parménides García Saldaña (1944–82), author of another rock-and-roll novel *Pasto verde* (1968). At some distance from their wilder contemporaries were Juan García Ponce (b. 1932), mainly a short-story writer but later also author of a hugely ambitious socio-erotic novel, *Crónica de la intervención* (1982); and José Emilio Pacheco (b. 1939), an outstanding poet but also author of *Morirás lejos* (1967), *El principio del placer* (stories, 1972) and many other works.

Outstanding among the writers who fuse popular speech and popular culture into elusive avant-garde concoctions was the Cuban Severo Sarduy (1937–92), self-exiled from the revolutionary island after 1960. Sarduy joined the *Tel Quel* group in Paris and produced a series of dazzling linguistic exercises such as *Gestos,* (1963), *De dónde son los cantantes* (1967), *Cobra* (1975), *Maitreya* (1978), *Colibrí* (1982) and *Cocuyo* (1990). For some critics the colourful literary miscengenations of Sarduy make him one of the most important of recent Latin American writers, though a comparison with the apparently similarly intentioned novels of Argentina's Manuel Puig may lead to the conclusion that the Cuban's work, however alluring, remained external – literally – to the recent history of the continent. A younger writer, Eliseo Diego, (Cuba, b. 1951), has written *La eternidad por fin comienza un lunes* (1992), reminiscent of Sarduy in its neobaroque precision but more substantial in length and ambition.

Manuel Puig (1932–90) seems, by common consent, to be the most important writer to have emerged out of the confused and confusing process of Latin American fiction since the 'Boom'. His work fuses the sort of pop Postmodernism characteristic of Cortázar with the dialectical self-awareness of a Roa Bastos. Puig distances that which entraps and seduces him through irony and the techniques of the new journalism. His uniquely focused problematic includes mass and popular culture, Hollywood movies, TV soap operas and advertising, power relations and sexuality: in short, he surveys the tragic banality and alienation of life inside the capitalist cultural labyrinth with almost Brechtian ruthlessness. His major novels are *La traición de Rita Hayworth* (1968), *Boquitas pintadas* (1969), *The Buenos Aires Affair* (1973), *El beso de la mujer araña* (1976), *Pubis Angelical* (1979), *Maldición eterna a quien lea estas páginas* (1980), *Sangre de amor correspondido* (1982) and *Cae la noche tropical* (1988). These almost perfect pastiches bring us close to the real world which so many Latin Americans actually inhabit, a media labyrinth with no way out. As long ago as 1969, Carlos Fuentes remarked that melodrama was 'one of the bases of Latin American social life . . . When one lacks tragic consciousness, a sense of history or of oneself, melodrama supplies them: it is a substitute, an imitation, an illusion of being.'[23] No one has given a better insight into this phenomenon than Puig.

*El beso de la mujer araña,* made into a famous film, is perhaps Puig's most important novel. It brings together, in a prison cell, a homosexual and a revolutionary militant to create one of the most provoking and illuminating episodes in contemporary fiction. Half the novel, presented mainly through dialogue like a radio drama, is taken up with the stories told by Molina, the lower middle-class gay, to Valentín, the revolutionary activist from an upper-bourgeois background. These stories are not Molina's own, but are his immensely detailed recollections of second-rate

---

[23] Carlos Fuentes, *La nueva novela hispanoamericana* (Mexico, D.F., 1969), p. 47.

movies he has seen and loved. The other half of the novel is taken up with conversations between the two men outside of these personalized film narratives, the occasional interior monologue, and such documentary materials as prison reports and footnoted extracts from psychoanalytical and behaviourist theories of homosexuality. The overall effect is stunning in lucidity and dialectical impact. It seems safe to say that no one, anywhere, has written texts which are more radical, subversive or deconstructive than Puig, as he both registers and contributes to the extraordinary narrativization of existence in the postmodern era.

Puig's books often seem frivolous and even light-hearted, but they are deadly serious. Other popular, populist and popularizing novelists who have perhaps tried harder to be simply entertaining are Luis Rafael Sánchez (b. 1936), of Puerto Rico, author of the rumbustious *La guaracha del macho Camacho* (1980) and *La importancia de llamarse Daniel Santos* (1989), a fictional biography of the famous bolero singer; Mempo Giardinelli (Argentina, b. 1949), best-selling author of *¿Por qué prohibieron el circo?* (1976), *La revolución en bicicleta* (1980), *El cielo con las manos* (1982) and *Luna caliente* (1983); and Marco Tulio Aguilera Garramuño (Colombia, 1949), writer of provocative erotic fictions like *Breve historia de todas las cosas* (1975), *El juego de las seducciones* (1989) and *Los grandes y los pequeños amores* (stories, 1990). A quite different kind of postmodern phenomenon, reminiscent of Conrad and Greene but flatter and less melodramatic, is the remarkable Alvaro Mutis (Colombia, b. 1923), friend of García Márquez and author, in his sixties, of a stream of haunting novels about a wandering seaman, Maqroll the Lookout: they include *La nieve del almirante* (1986) *Ilona llega con la lluvia* (1988), *La última escala del tramp steamer* (1988), *Un bel morir* (1989), *Amirbar* (1990), *Abdul Bashur, soñador de navíos* (1991). Mutis has also written many stories and poems.

### Politics and Testimony

Overtly socialist committed writing of the kind going back to Icaza and beyond was already out of fashion by the time of the 'Boom'. The Peruvians Arguedas and Scorza had really marked its outer limits – and desperation – even before the Sendero Luminoso movement propelled their country into a hyper-reality beyond the reach of literary expression. Since the mid-1960s, however, the old social novels have been replaced by a more overtly political kind of writing.

In Mexico the experimental vogue of the alienated 'Onda' generation was brutally interrupted by the events of 1968 and the Tlatelolco massacre in the wake of the student movement. For the next decade and beyond many Mexican novels would be marked by these events: *Los días y los años* (1971) by Luis González de Alba, really more of a 'testimonio'; *El gran solitario de Palacio* (1971) by René Avilés Fabila; *La Plaza* (1971) by the best-selling Luis Spota, implicitly supportive of the government position in the dispute; *Juegos de invierno* (1974) by Rafael Solana; *El infierno de todos tan temido* (1975) by Luis Carrión; *Los símbolos transparentes* (1978) by Gonzalo Martré; *Si muero lejos de ti* (1979) by Jorge Aguilera Mora; *Al cielo por asalto* (1979) by Agustín Ramos; *Manifestación de silencios* (1979) by Arturo Azuela, grandson of Mariano; *Pretexta* (1979) by Federico Campbell; *Muertes de Aurora* (1980) by Gerardo de la Torre; *El león que se agazapa* (1981) by Norberto Trenzo; *Los octubres del otoño* (1982) by Martha Robles; *Héroes convocados* (1982) by Paco Ignacio Taibo; *Esta tierra del amor* (1983) by David Martín del Campo; and *Los testigos* (1985) by Emma Prieto, among many others. José Revueltas (1914–76), one of Mexico's most influential novelists of the last half century with works like *El luto humano* (1943) and *Los días terrenales* (1949), found himself incarcerated as an 'intellectual instigator' of the movement and wrote the brutal prison novel *El apando* (1969) by way of response. On a more recent episode, Carlos Montemayor (b.1947) has written *Guerra en el paraíso* (1991) about the guerrilla campaign led by Lucio Cabañas in the 1970s.

An upsurge of committed fiction from a socialist or communist perspective might have been expected in Cuba. The fact is, however, that while there have been as many novels and short stories as one might expect from a country of Cuba's size, and many of them interesting and accomplished, rather few of them have been about the post-revolutionary era as such, and none of those can be ranked unequivocally among the great Latin American classics. Indeed, the best known works have been non-revolutionary, such as *Tres tristes tigres* or *Paradiso*. Nevertheless, there have been many interesting novels: *Memorias del subdesarrollo* (1965) by Edmundo Desnoes (b. 1930), *Los niños se despiden* (1968) by Pablo Armando Fernández (b. 1930), *Canción de Rachel* (1969), an early testimonial novel by Miguel Barnet (b. 1940), *La última mujer y el próximo combate* (1971), a socialist equivalent of *Doña Bárbara* by Manuel Cofiño (b. 1936), *El pan dormido* (1975), a historical novel set in Santiago de Cuba by José Soler Puig (b. 1916), *El mar de las lentejas* (1979) by Antonio Benítez Rojo (b. 1931), and *De Peña Pobre* (1979) by Cintio Vitier (b. 1921), an ambitious panoramic work spanning the period from the 1890s to the 1970s and uniting the writer's Christian point of departure with his Marxist present. Perhaps Carpentier's *Consagración de la primavera* (1978) is the closest to an approved revolutionary text, integrating the past with the present, from 1920s Paris and Moscow to 1960s Havana and a window on the future. Like so many other novels, however, it ends at the moment of revolutionary triumph and the inauguration of a new socialist culture. As for the failure of works by younger writers to find success, political anxieties might seem the most obvious explanation (in his *Words to the Intellectuals* in 1961 Castro had declared 'Inside the Revolution, everything; outside the Revolution, nothing', and Article 38 of the 1976 constitution specifies that 'Artistic creation is free so long as its content is not contrary to the Revolution'), but an equally persuasive one is that writing fiction seems a solitary, unheroic and unassertive activity in comparison with film and television, poetry and song, art and dance.

The most important of the dissident Cuban novelists was Reinaldo Arenas (1943–92), whose early works, written from within the Revolution, were *Celestino antes del alba* (1967) and the celebrated *El mundo alucinante* (1969), a magical history of the life of Fray Servando Teresa de Mier in Mexico's pre-independence period. Had he been born outside Cuba, Arenas, who happened to be homosexual, would probably have become one of the most successful Latin American exponents of the magical realist manner, but fate decreed that he was to live in a country where the social realist – or, indeed, socialist realist – mode would dominate, and little by little he found this and other restrictions on his personal freedom not only unacceptable but quite literally intolerable, as the stories of *Con los ojos cerrados* (1972) began to show. In 1980 he took refuge in the United States and published *El palacio de las blanquísimas mofetas* and *La vieja Rosa,* and then, in 1982, launched his most substantial novel, *Otra vez el mar.* It tells the story of a disillusioned revolutionary poet and his wife, whose marriage falls to pieces at the same pace as their revolutionary commitment.

Jesús Díaz (b. 1941) is a quite different case. He fought as a high-school student against Batista, became leader of those same students after 1959, took part in the Bay of Pigs campaign, founded the magazine *El Caimán Barbudo* in 1966 and won the Casa de las Américas prize that same year with his short stories *Las años duros.* In 1969 to 1970 he participated physically in the ill-fated campaign to harvest 10 million tons of sugar and then prepared a first version of *Los iniciales de la tierra* at the height of the hard-line response to the Padilla affair in the early 1970s. The book was not well received and was not published. Díaz was by then working in the Cuban Film Institute (ICAIC) and became a successful director. He also produced a further short story collection, *Canto de amor y de guerra* (1978), and an important documentary work, *De la patria y el exilio* (1979), based around a film he made on the same subject. However *Los iniciales de la tierra* is in a sense the distillation of his life thus far, and is probably the most important novel written from within the Revolution by a writer who has lived through 'the hard years' (to quote his short story title). Yet Díaz, too, became detached from the Revolution in 1992, and published his latest novel *Las palabras iniciales* (1992) outside of Cuba.

It is in Central America in particular that the tradition of revolutionary literature has been maintained. Such classics as *Mamita Yunai* (1941) by the Costa Rican Carlos Luis Fallas (1911–66) and Asturias's *Trilogía bananera* have been followed by *Cenizas de Izalco* (1966) by the Salvadorean Claribel Alegría (b. 1924) and her North American husband Darwin T. Flakoll, on the 1932 uprising in El Salvador in which 30,000 peasants were massacred; *¿Te dio miedo la sangre?* (1977) and *Castigo divino* (1988) by the Nicaraguan Sergio Ramírez (b.1942), a leading Sandinista politician; the inspiring *La selva es algo más que una inmensa estepa verde* (1981) by another revolutionary novelist, Omar Cabezas (Nicaragua, b. 1950); an outstanding sequence of novels by Manlio Argueta (b.1935) of El Salvador, including *El valle de las hamacas* (1970), *Caperucita en la zona roja* (1977), *Un día en la vida* (1980) and *Cuzcatlán, donde bate la mar del sur* (1986), which provide brilliantly focused solutions to the problems of writing about peasant characters at a time of repression and revolution.

Writing political novels did not mean eschewing experimentation and complexity. In Peru Alfredo Bryce Echenique (b.1939), author of the long psychological novel *Un sueño para Julius* (1970), published *La vida exagerada de Martín Romaña* in 1981. It tells the story of a young Peruvian in 1960s Paris delegated by an extreme left group to write a socialist realist novel about the Peruvian fishing unions. Instead, the protagonist, who frequently curses the well-known novelist Bryce Echenique, writes an experimental work on an intranscendent subject in which its own author makes frequent appearances. Already in 1978 Manuel Scorza (1928–83), the last of the true indigenist novelists, had included himself and some of his own articles and documents in *La tumba del relámpago*, the culmination of his five-part series, *La guerra silenciosa*, about the Indian struggle for survival in the high sierras and their unsuccessful battle against the Cerro de Pasco Mining Company. In *La danza inmóvil* (1983), published in the year of his tragic death, Scorza went even further by writing a novel on Bryce's theme, but one which moved in exactly the opposite direction (it is also eerily reminiscent of Régis Debray's later *Masks,* whose format it also inverts): a writer in Paris, member of a Peruvian guerrilla movement, falls in love with a beautiful Parisian bohemian as he tries to write a story about a guerrilla in which he ransacks the styles and motifs of Cortázar, García Márquez and the rest. Scorza effectively dramatizes the forking paths open to Latin American writers today and emphasizes hilariously the seductions and temptations to which they are subject, thereby making a most incisive comment on self-referentiality and inter-textuality from the revolutionary Left. Finally in 1984, Peru's best-known writer, Mario Vargas Llosa himself, who had already played these games in *La tía Julia y el escribidor,* published *Historia de Mayta,* about a Trotskyist guerrilla of the 1950s. In this, a well-known novelist whose curriculum vitae appears to coincide precisely with that of Vargas Llosa, attempts, in an apocalyptic near future, to unravel the story of Mayta against a terrifying background of social dislocation. *El hablador* (1987) repeats the gesture.

Since the 1970s literature in Chile, Uruguay and Argentina has had to come to terms with a series of shattering political experiences. In Chile the accomplished metaphysical experiments of Donoso's *El obsceno pájaro de la noche* published in 1970, the year of Allende's election, were soon to seem frivolous. After Allende's overthrow in 1973 Antonio Skármeta (b. 1940), with *Soñé que la nieve ardía* (1975) and *Ardiente paciencia* (1985), and Ariel Dorfman (b. 1942), with *Viudas* (1981) and *La última canción de Manuel Sendero* (1982), among others, made the Chilean exile response to the coup. In Uruguay, which also fell into the hands of the military in 1973, Carlos Martínez Moreno's *El color que el infierno me escondiera* (1981) was a striking equivalent. In Argentina, where hysteria and philosophical pessimism have long been a staple ingredient of the national narrative mix (Arlt, Sábato), the decade 1973–82, and especially the period after the military coup of April 1976, was horrifying enough to make even the most optimistic despair. An army which represented the sacred values of the fatherland and its history attempted once again to impose unity on its own terms, this time by eliminating all those who saw things differently – writers among them. In 1976 Haroldo Conti (1925–76), author of the excellent *Mascaró, el cazador americano* (1975), who was awakened to his Latin American identity by a visit to Cuba, disappeared;

followed a year later by Rodolfo Walsh (1927–77), whose best known work was the documentary *Operación masacre* (1957), an early exposé of military repression. Walsh vanished shortly after sending an 'Open Letter' to the military denouncing the policy of disappearances. After that writers knew what to expect if they told the truth and published it inside Argentina.

Numbers of Argentine novelists, inside and outside the country, began to seek new ways of projecting what was going on inside its borders. Among the most interesting works were Puig's *El beso de la mujer araña* (1976); *El trino del diablo* (1974) by Daniel Moyano (b. 1928), another novel anticipating what was to come; *Cuerpo a cuerpo*, (1979) by David Viñas (b. 1929), on the military and their proletarian opponents over the past century, with the history of Argentina conceived as a war of conquest and extermination; *No habrá más penas ni olvido* (1980) by Osvaldo Soriano (b. 1943), on the absurd contradictions of Peronism; *Respiración artificial* (1980) by Ricardo Piglia, which works back through an authoritarian past to try to discover what had gone wrong in Argentina and indeed in his own family (the first words are: 'Is there a history?'); *A las 20.25 la señora entró en la inmortalidad* (1981) by Mario Schizman (b. 1945), on recent history viewed through the eyes of a bemused Jewish family; *La vida eterna* (1981) by Juan Carlos Martini, on symbolic struggles for power among prostitutes and pimps; *Conversación al sur* (1981) by Marta Traba (1930–85), a widely diffused dialogue of resistance among ordinary women; *Nada que perder* (1982) by Andrés Rivera (b. 1928), a reconstruction of the life of a union leader; *Hay cenizas en el viento* (1982) by Carlos Dámaso Martínez, on teachers turned undertakers burying murdered workers; *Cola de lagartija* (1983) by Luisa Valenzuela, discussed above; *Recuerdo de la muerte* (1984) by the ex-Montonero Miguel Bonasso, written in exile in Mexico, a more straightforward realist encapsulation of the 'dirty war', and in particular the efforts of the guerrillas and the counter-attack by the military, but a novel that also mixes dramatized fictional reenactments with documentary evidence, especially relating to repression and torture; and *La novela de Perón* (1985) by Tomás Eloy Martínez, who applied similar techniques – the interweaving of fact, documents and fiction – to an exploration of the central protagonist of the last half century in Argentina, General Juan Domingo Perón. All these novels are covertly or overtly political, most interweave the chronicle and journalism with narrative fiction. Many are obsessed, on the one hand, with documents of every kind (especially those that are falsified to distort reality and those that inadvertently falsify it in the first place), not least with legal sentences and death certificates, and on the other hand, with the almost ungraspable realm of memory or oral history. Above all, they are concerned with the nature of power, politics and reading and their interaction in Argentine history. It is worth noting that this is precisely the problematic carved out by Augusto Roa Bastos, who was still resident in Argentina when Perón made his fateful return in 1973. To that extent his *Yo el Supremo* is also an Argentine novel.

Perhaps the most important development in political writing, however, is a phenomenon centred on Latin American documentary narrative, a genre which in a sense has replaced the old journalistic 'chronicles' and the social realist novel (both of which still survive), though of course its roots go back to Sarmiento and Da Cunha – some would say to the first chronicles at the time of discovery (though others might counter that these were examples of 'magical realism' and that the Spanish picaresque novel is the true ancestor of the documentary). Its antecedents also include works by anthropologists and sociologists: Gilberto Freyre's *Casa grande e senzala* (1933), Ricardo Pozas's *Juan Pérez Jolote* (Mexico, 1956), the life of a Tzotzil Indian, and Oscar Lewis' enormously influential *Children of Sanchez* (1961) about the Mexico City slums and *La Vida* (1965) on prostitutes in Puerto Rico. From the late 1950s, as the social realist novel began to seem both patronizing and anachronistic, documentary works began to take a more overtly political and 'testimonial' turn, with Walsh's *Operación masacre* in 1957 perhaps the first of a series of committed, partly fictionalized – or merely narrativized – texts which have established an important and compelling tradition: Carolina Maria de Jesús, *Quarto de despejo* (1960), on a woman's life in the São Paulo slums; Miguel Barnet, *Biografía de un cimarrón* (Cuba, 1966), about an ex-slave; Domitila Chungara, *Si me permiten hablar* (1977), about oppression in the Bolivian mining camps; *Me llamo Rigoberta Menchú* (1985) by the Quiche Indian woman who won the Nobel Peace Prize in 1992; plus a whole series of harrowing prison memoirs by writers like Hernán Valdés, *Tejas Verdes: diario de un campo de concentración en Chile* (1974), Jacobo Timerman (b. 1923), *Preso sin nombre, celda sin número* (Argentina, 1981), and Alicia Partnoy's *La escuelita* (Argentina, 1986). Gabriel García Márquez himself returned to the documentary mode with *La aventura de Miguel Littín, clandestino en Chile* (1986).

## Towards 1992 and Beyond: The New Historicism

Consciously or unconsciously, Western writers and intellectuals have been thinking in terms of anniversaries, apocalyptic premonitions and concepts like the 'End of History' as the twentieth century has approached its end and a new millennium appeared on the horizon. The fashion for great commemorations probably began in the last quarter of our century with the United States bicentenary in 1976 and went on, somewhat incoherently, through Orwell's 1984 to Robespierre's 1989. Little did anyone imagine that in the year when the French Revolution was commemorated we would also witness the end of the Russian Soviet Revolution and with it, apparently, the end of the Cold War. That the Gulf War against Iraq should take place so soon afterwards, reviving the spectre, against a background of growing Islamic fundamentalism, of a return to the West's greatest battles at the dawn of the modern era seemed to be one of History's most sombre ironies. All of this tended to undermine mental and emotional preparations for what in the eyes of many was the greatest commemoration of all, namely the 500th anniversary of the so-called 'discovery' of the so-called 'New World' in 1492, although this celebration was already in trouble before its time arrived, in view of the objections of the American native peoples and their sympathizers, prompting Spain's euphemistic retitling of the year's events under that unconvincing slogan 'Encounter of Two Worlds'.

No one could have forseen the confused and radically altered global panorama confronting thoughtful observers in 1992. And yet it might be said that Latin American writers and historians were, deep down, already prepared for such confusion and anti-climax: prepared for it precisely by the 500 years of Latin America's previous history of hopes turned to illusions, triumphs turned to defeats. It seemed in retrospect that the continent was invented on a single day, by Columbus, five centuries ago, and that each republic, or fragment of the whole, was constantly making new beginnings only to find, 'many years later', that the route embarked on was yet another illusion. The difference now, of course, was that for the first time in its history, Latin America, always a 'land of the future', no longer had much faith in that future, was no longer, after the disillusionment of the 1970s and 1980s, producing new futures in which to believe. The fact that it shares this condition with the rest of the Western world is not much consolation for a continent built upon the concept of providential transformation.

This is no doubt why a region where the historical novel had never previously flourished has for the past twenty years begun to produce a succession of important and compelling historical narratives. The 'Boom' writers had used the apparently mythologizing structures and techniques of European Modernism against the grain, used them precisely to prevent their readers from mythologizing and to force them, somewhat arrogantly, to gaze on the new – perhaps pre-revolutionary – dawn. Now, older and wiser, those same writers were forced to recognize their own illusions and to gaze back upon a different, reinterpreted history. The disappointments, bitter ironies and regrets involved explain why parody and satire condition much of the writing which has appeared during this period. Here, as in so many other ways, the great precursor is undoubtedly Carlos Fuentes with *Terra Nostra* (1975) and he continued the trend with *Cristóbal Nonato* (1987), a novel which – taking its cue from Salman Rushdie's *Midnight's Children* – parodies both the idea of the discovery and of its celebration. *Terra Nostra* had appeared, significantly enough, at the same time as the three dictator novels always now linked together: Roa Bastos's *Yo el Supremo* (1974), Carpentier's *El recurso del método* (1975) and García Márquez's *El otoño del patriarca* (1975). Although each of those novels looked back at a distant past, it was obviously the desperately disappointing and disillusioning turn of events in the continent between the mid-1960s and mid-1970s which prompted their choice of theme and their meditation on Latin American history.

Of course the stereotypical representation of Latin America as a continent with an addictive taste for dictatorship is a travesty of its historical reality. Since the period of revolutions after 1810 it has been a region of liberal democratic constitutions on the European or North American models. It is precisely in the tension between this aspiration and reality, viewed both as a national and continental problem, as well as an individual one, that much of the force of the theme is concentrated, from *Facundo* (1845) and *Amalia* (1851) through *El señor Presidente* (1946) to the present. There have been innumerable novels about individual dictators, or about the problems of dictatorship, *caudillismo, caciquismo,* militarism and the like. Few of them have managed successfully to unite the specific instance – Francia, Rosas, Estrada Cabrera, Gómez, Pinochet – with the more universal concerns of tyranny, power and evil. The first important works were inspired by Argentina's Rosas. Sarmiento's *Facundo* examined the themes of civilization and barbarism, dictatorship and power, based on the case study of Facundo Quiroga and his relation to Rosas. José Mármol's *Amalia* conceived the problem, as Asturias's *El señor Presidente* later did, partly as a problem of the state, manifested through the will of some Monstrous Personage, violating the ordinary individual's privacy, both of home and of consciousness.

During the 1950s and 1960s, however, neither the dictator novel, nor its more general associate the novel of urban alienation, received much attention, because this again appeared to be a time of 'apertura', when the people were on the move and development seemed to provide the answers to the great problems of the continent and its future. In a directly sociological sense, the 'Boom' itself was associated with the transition to liberal democracy which had seemed to be evolving since the Second World War, along with industrialization, urbanization, and the growth of the middle sectors. Then came revolution in a small Caribbean republic, the rise and fall of liberal perceptions of Cuba between 1959 and the late 1960s (culminating abruptly in the events of 1971, the so-called 'Padilla Affair'), the growing gulf between Left and Right, with the gradual disappearance of the political centre, the struggle between guerrillas and military juntas, and the gradual reassertion of pessimism, disillusionment and despair associated in the end with the defeat of left and popular governments almost everywhere in the continent until the – in a way anomalous – triumph of the Sandinista guerrillas in Nicaragua in 1979.

In a sense, both García Márquez in *El otoño del patriarca* and Carpentier in *El recurso del método* aimed at easy targets – firing at the Right from the Left – whereas in *Yo el Supremo* Roa Bastos made a critique of the Left (for that is where he situated his protagonist Francia) from within the Left itself. Moreover, Roa's novel implicitly compared the past with the present, whilst there was little evidence at the time that the novels of Carpentier or García Márquez had much contemporary relevance – though with the passage of the years their parodic perspective is coming to seem more prescient. Perhaps the most immediately striking thing about them, however, was that their dictators were not even historical figures, but composite and essentially imaginary ones, and that they broke the tradition whereby the characterization of the dictator is oblique or in other ways problematical, without any obvious advantages accruing from such a risky venture. In short, they appeared to evade the challenges of the era – one of the bleakest periods in Latin American history – and they also ignored Lukács' recommendation that great men, even fictional ones, should be left off-stage when historical interpretation is involved (as Vargas Llosa had decided to do with Odría in *Conversación en la Catedral*), both entering the minds of their dictators at will.

*Yo el Supremo* seemed a work of a different order. Like Sarmiento's *Facundo*, it has a clear Latin American specificity. While it is unmistakably a novel about dictatorship both as a universal and as a Latin American problem, it takes its concrete force from, and continually returns to, the life and works of José Gaspar Rodríguez de Francia, the supreme and perpetual dictator of Paraguay from 1814 to 1840; and although it considers the function and meaning of writing in Western history as a whole, and the roles and duties of the Latin American writer since Independence, it cannot be separated from the predicament of one specific writer, Roa Bastos himself in the early 1970s, confronted with the dilemma of what to write, for whom to write, and whether in any case writing is anything other than an irrelevant or even cowardly thing to do in a continent where dictators are everywhere in power and where the great mass of the population is illiterate and condemned by uneven development to a consciousness anterior to that which has historically produced the novel as a literary form. Its central question, put starkly, is this: does the practice of writing fiction have anything at all to contribute to the process of national and continental liberation? Or is the writer condemned, perhaps fatally, to be on the other side? It is difficult to escape the conclusion that the novel was addressed above all to Roa's friends in Cuba, who were similarly trying to force the hand of history in the face of an imperialist blockade, while the relation of an austere individualist leader to a revolutionary collectivity was similarly being worked out.

It is impossible to understand the full dialogical significance of *Yo el Supremo* without first recognizing that it contains an implied critique of the Latin American 'New Novel', and second, and still more important, that it is structured around two great presences and two great absences. The presences are Francia, the all-powerful supreme dictator, the man who is everything, whose every thought and action is translated at once into objective reality, and whose audience is absolutely certain; and Roa Bastos himself, the 'compiler' of the book, alluded to within it as a fugitive and a traitor, a writer of fictions and fables, a man whose impact on his country is negligible after thirty years of exile, and whose audience, like that of all novelists, is wholly indeterminate. The two great absences are Stroessner, then (and until 1989) dictator of Paraguay and an example of one of the worst kinds of Latin American tyrant; and Fidel Castro, who may well have been the contemporary version of Francia in Roa Bastos's conception. The following, at any rate, is the nub of Roa Bastos's last judgement on his dictator: 'You turned yourself into a great obscurity for the people-mob; into the great Don-Amo, the Lord-and-Master who demands docility in return for a full belly and an empty head . . . No, little mummy; true Revolution does not devour its children. Only its bastards; those who are not capable of carrying it to its ultimate consequences. Beyond its limits if necessary.'[24] The Paraguayan writer's anxieties that Cuba's Revolution was heading for the same end as Francia's led him neither to renounce socialism nor to counsel despair, but to renew old questions and resuscitate earlier debates in preparation for the new historical period to come. In 1992 Roa published his long-awaited sequel *El fiscal,* which relates to Paraguay's long succession of dictators after Francia.

In Brazil, the military coup of 1964 interrupted the normal development of narrative fiction before the 'Boom' in Spanish America could really make its impact felt. Thus little overtly political or historical writing has been possible until quite recently. Significant exceptions were two valiant novels by Antônio Callado (b. 1917), linking country and city, *Quarup* (1967) and *Bar Don Juan* (1971), and *Gálvez, imperador do Acre* (1975) by Márcio Souza (b. 1946), a satire which cost him his job in the civil service. Other works like *Zero* (1974, though banned in Brazil) by Inácio de Loyola Brandão (b. 1936), *A festa* (1976) by Ivan Angelo (b. 1937), *Mês de cães danados* (1977) by Moacyr Scliar (b. 1937), *Em câmara lenta* (1977) by Renato Tapajos (b. 1943), *A grande arte* (1983) and *Buffo and Spalanzani* (1985) by Rubem Fonseca (b. 1925), were also novels which in a variety of ways – usually implicitly – attempted to explain Brazil's lurch into authoritarianism. (Also worthy of note is the remarkable novel *Maíra,* 1979, about the Amazon Indians by the well-known anthropologist and politician, Darcy Ribeiro). Nevertheless, since Mário de Andrade's formidable *Macunaíma,* no one had felt able to attempt a grand work uniting the whole of Brazilian history and culture in one big narrative work. In the mid-1980s, however, João Ubaldo Ribeiro (b. 1940), whose *Sargento Getúlio* (1971) was already widely admired, wrote perhaps the most ambitious novel in the history of Brazilian narrative, *Viva o povo brasileiro* (1984). This work of almost 700 pages covers the entire period from the Dutch occupation in the first half of the seventeenth

[24] A. Roa Bastos, *I the Supreme*, trans. Helen Lane (London, 1987), p. 423.

century to the late 1970s, and although centred on the fertile coastal strip around Bahia, it is clearly intended symbolically to embrace the whole of Brazil. The opening lines of the narrative proper return us tongue in cheek to the anthropophagous theme of the 1920s: 'The Capiroba enjoyed eating Dutchmen.' It ends with a storm blowing in from the ocean: 'No one looked up and so no one saw, in the midst of the storm, the Spirit of Man, lost but full of hope, wandering above the unilluminated waters of the great bay.' Ribeiro writes in an apocalyptic, sometimes overbearing tone, but it is refreshing to have a novel conceived for once on Brazil's own massive scale.

It was, of course, in Spanish America, and Spain itself, more than in Brazil, that novelists began to reflect on the beginnings and ends of both the colonial experience and the emancipation period of the early nineteenth century. Thus there have been several works about Columbus, including Alejo Carpentier's *El arpa y la sombra* (1980), the outrageous and disconcerting *Los perros del paraíso* (1983) by the Argentine Abel Posse (b. 1936), surely one of the most remarkable of all Latin American historical novels, and *Vigilia del almirante* (1993) by Augusto Roa Bastos. Abel Posse also turned to one of the most ambiguous and troubling figures of the colonial period, the rebel Lope de Aguirre, in *Daimón* (1978), as did the veteran Venezuelan Miguel Otero Silva (1908–85), campaigning author of *Fiebre* (1939), *Casas muertas* (1955), *Oficina no. 1* (1960) and *Cuando quiero llorar no lloro* (1970), in *Lope de Aguirre, príncipe de la libertad* (1979). *El entenado* (1983) by Juan José Saer (Argentina, b. 1937) is another novel set in the sixteenth century, whilst the same author's *La ocasión* (1988) recreates life on the Argentine pampa in the nineteenth century. Mario Vargas Llosa's *La guerra del fin del mundo* (1981) provided a brutally ironic commentary on the late nineteenth century confrontation between 'civilization' and 'barbarism' at Canudos in Brazil, so memorably registered in Da Cunha's *Os sertões* at the time. In 1987 Fernando del Paso published *Noticias del imperio,* his ambitious portrait of Maximilian and Carlota in Mexico following the French intervention. And in 1990 Carlos Fuentes, whose *Gringo viejo* (1985) had told the story of Ambrose Bierce in Mexico during the Revolution, turned back to the emancipation period with *La campaña* (1990), announced as the first of a trilogy of novels about the independence campaigns across the continent.

It is appropriate, however, to end with the image of one great Latin American icon, Simón Bolívar, as fashioned by another, Gabriel García Márquez. In 1989 García Márquez returned to his obsession with power and confronted the grandest political myth in the history of Latin America, that of Bolívar. *El general en su laberinto* is about the defeated hero's last journey towards his early death. It is, one might say, the 'Autumn of Another Patriarch' with a similarly incestuous relation between author and character. In his acknowledgments following the body of the text García Márquez confesses his own 'absolute lack of experience and method in historical research', but he shows little hesitation, in an age of parody and scepticism, in painting his late twentieth-century portrait in the boldest of colours, turning Bolívar, almost inevitably, into a character from the writer's own historical gallery. Like the protagonist of *El coronel no tiene quien le escriba,* endlessly waiting for his pension, Bolívar spends much of the novel waiting for a passport (though possibly hoping that it will never come). Like the Patriarchal Dictator wandering through the labyrinthine corridors of his autumnal palace, Bolívar wanders through the wintry labyrinth of his staggering decline and fall. And like all García Márquez's novels, the work is about defeat, not victory, about disillusionment, not the apotheosis of an idea. Bolívar is shown as a man who has succeeded in his great task as liberator of a continent but failed in the even greater endeavour of uniting it; and as a man who, mightily fallen, somehow retains his courage and greatness of spirit in even the most desperate and humiliating circumstances, at the end of his 'mad chase between his woes and his dreams'. Evidently García Márquez believes that this is an equally great aspect of the Liberator's character. Perhaps Bolívar's ultimate grandeur lay in his becoming an ordinary Latin American in his last months, the predecessor of all those other magnificent failures who struggle through the pages of Latin American fiction in the arduous kingdom of this world? Be that as it may, Columbus and Bolívar, as well known for their failures as for their successes, live once again in the pages of contemporary Latin American fiction.

Despite numerous efforts to characterize the 'Post-Boom' novel, it seems clear that we are not yet in a position to do so. For the moment at least, the 'Post-Boom' narrative is, quite simply, the novels which have appeared since the mid-1970s, and efforts to demonstrate radical new departures are usually just grist for the academic mill which rarely manage to propose entirely convincing formulations. One of the major phenomena, undoubtedly, is the accumulation of a body of determinedly self-referential fiction on a scale unseen in other parts of the world. This would seem to confirm the thesis that Latin America's historically dualist experience continues to magnify in intensity the intellectual's paradoxical self-awareness of his or her responsibility to the objects of their contemplation and representation. It has also facilitated the return of social realism under another guise, through an ideologically self-conscious mode of enunciation which mitigates some of the technical and philosophical inadequacies of earlier exponents of the genre. Nevertheless, despite such striking phenomena as the emergence of an important new generation of women writers, the narrowing of the gap between 'high' and 'popular' art, and a return in many cases to a simpler, more accessible mode of narrative discourse, the fact remains that the best known writers today are those who made the 'Boom' of the 1960s. Clearly we shall be well into the next century before the shape of Latin American fiction takes on some decisive new form.

# 3

## LATIN AMERICAN POETRY,
### c. 1920–1950*

### INTRODUCTION

Before the blossoming of narrative in the second half of the twentieth century poetry occupied a pre-eminent position and role in the world of Latin American literature. Before Borges, the short-story writer, interest and attention focused more on Borges as a poet; or on the Peruvian poet, César Vallejo, and the Chilean poet, Pablo Neruda, whose *Canto general* burst upon the scene in 1950, dividing the century into equal halves and becoming the prime testimony of Latin American consciousness. The Nobel Prize for Literature was awarded to the Chilean poet, Gabriela Mistral in 1945, more than two decades before the Central American novelist Miguel Angel Asturias, in 1967; it was awarded to Neruda himself, in 1971, more than a decade before the Colombian novelist, Gabriel García Márquez, in 1982. With the help of these four representative names, it is possible to observe a swing from poetry to narrative prose in the central forces that shape the literary process. The first half of the twentieth century is in fact characterized by the special relevance of poetry; without this antecedent and example, the emergence of narrative would be incomprehensible.[1]

Although from Vasconcelos to Paz and from Mariátegui to Salazar Bondy the essay also contributed to the development of Latin American cultural identity, it was poetry that first crossed national frontiers, formulating a global reality which reached the Spanish world as a whole. This

---

* Translated from the Spanish by Anthony Edkins.
[1] Borges conceived his stories as poetic pieces; time and again Cortázar reminded us that his narratives were built with structures of images; the relationship between Onetti – or, at least, the Onetti of *La vida breve* (1950) – and Neruda's *Residencias* is evident; and so on.

situation had existed since Rubén Darío (Nicaragua, 1867–1916), whose most mature poetry – the poems in *Cantos de vida y esperanza* (1905) – was in one way a search for a cultural definition of the Spanish-speaking peoples. Although in conceptual terms the result did not go beyond the idea of 'Latinity' (which appears in the ode 'To Roosevelt', for example, and in other poems of the same collection), his words were to find a very wide dissemination, due to a historic moment of Pan-American significance: the beginnings and the subsequent aggressive consolidation of U.S. domination over Latin America.

What Darío represented at the beginning of the century, with his wanderings in France, Spain and Majorca (as if to give active proof of his loyalty to the Latin and Mediterranean world), was repeated later by the Chilean Vicente Huidobro (1893–1948), whose work and personality followed the transatlantic course mapped out by the Nicaraguan poet. Between 1918 and 1924, during the years after the First World War Huidobro constantly crossed the Pyrenees to preach the good tidings of the Parisian avant-garde on the literary cafés of Madrid. He sowed the avant-garde and reaped ultraism. Indeed, his influence was to be far from negligible on the young iconoclasts who were then looking for ways and ideas to renovate poetic life in the old metropolis. Then, in the mid-thirties and on the brink of the Spanish Civil War, the presence of Neruda among the great poets of the so-called Generation of 1927 strengthened the links between both cultural hemispheres. This provides a key – a partial key, but no less crucial – to the historical leaning of this poetry. Faced with the consuming crisis of the conflict that was going to initiate the débâcle of the Second World War, leading Latin American poets, regardless of personal or national differences and subsequent divergences, presented a united front. Alongside the many intellectuals and writers who fought in the trenches or were alert to what was going on, the participation of Vallejo, Neruda, Nicolás Guillén, González Tuñón and even the young Octavio Paz emphasizes the cohesion that existed among them.

This group of poets was 'at one with its time' in its thinking and in its output. Such an encounter between poetry and history would not repeat itself – not, at least, to the same degree and with the same passion. 1936 and its adjacent years marked a high point in Latin American consciousness which, along the highways of Spain and the rest of Europe, began to comprehend the forces of chaos and negation. Latinity ceased to be sacrosanct. People saw that it was not immune to a barbarism that proceeded from its own tradition.[2]

In fifteen-year periods with regular intervals – 1905, *c.* 1920, *c.* 1935, 1950 – the poets' self-imposed cultural task coincided with a historical praxis of the first magnitude. The appearance of the *Canto general* in 1950 came at the beginning of the Cold War, which had brutally broken up the framework of alliances in force at the end of the Second World War, insinuating a repressive spirit into every corner of the subcontinent. It was not by chance that the *Canto general* was published simultaneously in Mexico and Chile, albeit clandestinely in the latter, the poet's own country. Poets were no longer fighting away from home; they had to fight to preserve their own habitat. In the scenario of bonfires and shadows which Neruda's great book unearths, we are able to notice an intensification of the poetic and critical perception of the continent. Between Darío's ode 'To Roosevelt' and the section of the *Canto general* devoted to Lincoln –'Que despierte el leñador' (Let the wood-cutter awaken) – the distance travelled is very great. Between the *Canto a la Argentina* (1910) – a breviary of progressive liberalism – and the dictatorial hell that is the focal point and nucleus of 'América, no invoco tu nombre en vano' (America, I do not invoke your name in vain), the distance is immeasurable. What had been a moment of U.S. expansion at the beginning of the century had now become an iron structure of domination. The *Canto general* had to respond to such a challenge by forging new weapons of consciousness.

The pages that follow aspire to describe this projection of Latin American poets and to determine the value of their contribution within the chronological framework which, broadly speaking, spans the century from its first decades until a little after 1950. To sketch a view of half a century of poetry is an almost impossible task. A complete list of poets should not, therefore, be expected. We are more interested in pointing out the strengths and general importance of this poetic development, and in combining an approach to its peaks with a description of the 'spirit of the valley' – a Taoist metaphor which, in these days, seems appropriate. On the other hand, bearing in mind that this is a contribution to a history of Latin America we shall also consider its historical dimension, that is, where it runs parallel with, or counter to, corresponding collective pro-

[2] Alejo Carpentier, who had already ironized the ideology of Latinity in *El recurso del método* (1974) composed a gigantic frieze of the period in one of his last novels, *La consagración de la primavera* (1978).

cesses, without losing sight of the specifically poetic properties of what is being studied (its aesthetic distance, as traditional jargon has it). Finally, because the cultural categorization of twentieth century Latin America is still in its infancy, it is preferable to dispense with a systematic formulation and to rely on a more modest approach, a purely heuristic outline. We shall talk, therefore, about decades, moments, phases, intervals of time, and so on. We shall seek to explain, after examining some aspects of literary *posmodernismo**, which will serve as a transition to the avant-garde: 1) the nationalist character common to the avant-garde of the twenties; 2) the moment of the intensification of American reality by means of the essential works published by Vallejo and Neruda during the thirties; and 3) a significant bifurcation in poetic tendencies from the end of the Second World War.

Prior to the 1920s, the poetry panorama is, essentially, characterized by the exhaustion of the *modernista* formula. *Modernismo* and Parnassianism-Symbolism, in spite of all their limitations, at least meant a certain dawning awareness of progress, hope and the future, among the enlightened elites of Spanish America and Brazil. The growing mimicry of the first of these movements and the academicism of the second are extinguished at precisely the same time as the Latin American nineteenth century, that is, at the end of the First World War. (Nevertheless, there are echoes of this dawning consciousness, which curiously bring together some important later essayists, including Vasconcelos and Mariátegui.)

Some time ago, the critic of Spanish origin, Federico de Onís, conceived a chronological ordering of poetry written before and after Darío which, although debatable as to detail, can serve as a point of departure.[3] Taking Darío's *modernista* work as a centre point, he distinguished a pre-*modernista* phase, placed approximately between 1882 and 1888, and then a *postmodernista* stage and one that was ultra-*modernista*. This last essentially coincides with what we call today the avant-garde or vanguardism. It is quite obvious that the first heading was too narrow to classify personalities with the range of a José Martí (1853–95) as forerunners. However, the most problematic stage of this chronology is the *posmodernista*.

---

* *Translator's note: Posmodernismo* and *modernismo* in this essay refer to Spanish literary movements. The terms have been left in Spanish to avoid confusion with Postmodernism of current critical usage.
[3] Federico de Onís, *Antología de la poesía española e hispanoamericana (1882–1932)* (Madrid, 1934), 'Introduction'. The author has the peak of Darío's modernism coincide with *Prosas profanas* (1886) and places the starting point of Postmodernism in 1905.

At present there is an undeniable tendency to reject the validity of that idea. The Mexican critic and poet, José Emilio Pacheco, a distinguished poetry scholar, flatly rejects it.[4] Pacheco is right to point out that *modernista* and *posmodernista* themes and styles are indiscernible in Darío's work until the point where it incorporates and subsumes them, making the abovementioned distinction irrelevant, when not entirely useless. What has come to be called *posmodernismo,* Pacheco argues, is one more aspect of the internal dynamism of *modernismo.* Therefore there is no need to make it a separate category.

There is a great deal of truth in this point of view. Nevertheless, it is possible to examine *posmodernismo* in two of its conditions: as a preliminary phase of individual poetic development; and as an orientation of *modernismo* towards the respective national realities from which the authors proceed – and especially towards their rural surroundings. Those national elements which then began to introduce themselves – *posmodernismo*'s rural approach within a predominantly cosmopolitan and at times exclusively urban *modernismo* – were what, in my opinion, justified the idea's raison d'être. National variable; region; rural landscape; also province – this series not only coherently counterpointed the emphasis on the great metropolis (Darío's cosmopolitan city), it also helped to fashion a tone of lasting resonance in subsequent poetry. In a certain sense, the subjectivity of Latin America's great poetry is closer to the *posmodernista* spirit than to the voice of Darío, even when his notable 'Nocturnos' are taken into account.[5] We have only to think of the question of tempo, so closely linked to tone and poetic subjectivity in general. This natural sympathy with the inwardness of the country created an oasis of the ordinary, a slow village rhythm, which was often at the opposite extreme to the *modernista* attitude – one much more aware of the actual moment and the seduction of the present. Sedimentation, then, not vibration, was the characteristic of this tempo. Archaism, anachronism, the traces and remains of a 'history' behind History were noticeable in that sensibility. This village tone sounded in the simple, luminous poems of Abraham Valdelomar (1888–1919), the Peruvian of the *Colónida* group, in which Mariátegui too participated around 1916; and it also found a strong, persistent echo in the Mexican, Ramón López Velarde (1888–1921), whose rural and provincial stamp – highly

[4] See, among his other publications, *Poesía modernista: una antología general* (Mexico, D.F., 1982), in particular, p. 12 et seq.
[5] This does not mean ignoring Darío's enormous influence. This influence was central in subsequent poetry, but it did not fundamentally affect tone or similar elements.

refined, of course – was duly noted by poets such as Neruda and Paz. In a brief, concentrated output (*La sangre devota*, 1916; *Zozobra*, 1919; and a poem of 1921, 'La suave patria') López Velarde called woman 'flor del terruño' (flower of the native soil), praised places and landscape in the province, and ended by unmasking 'la carreta alegórica de paja' (the allegorical wagon of straw) behind the official pomp of the nation and the state. Intimacy, then, peopled by echoes which began to be indigenous; the turning of the poet on himself to find himself inhabited by an earlier time that was colonial and passive.

It is a fact of incalculable consequences that, in the main, *modernismo* blocked observation of Latin America's agrarian hinterland. Country life which, in a poem like *Martín Fierro* (1872 and 1879), had displayed such strength, was sidestepped by the new aesthetic hierarchies that modernism imposed. At the most, it was converted into an alternative, but always subordinate, discourse, as happened in Argentina. When Darío inclined towards the countryside, when he looked out beyond the city (as he did on rare occasions), either he dealt with an offbeat mirage ('Del campo' in *Prosas profanas* anticipated the 'platonization' of which the gaucho would be the object in Ricardo Güiraldes, *Don Segundo Sombra*, 1926), or he restored the contours of a childhood Arcadia ('Nicaragua natal' in the ending of his *Cantos*). The enlightened groups who came together in *modernismo* (lawyers, artists, journalists) were unreservedly in the Sarmiento mould and did not understand the earthy agrarian or pastoral root that was fundamental to the richness of South America, about which they were so determined to sing. This began to change with the poets who were linked to *posmodernismo*, at first slightly, but in a direct, frontal manner as the century advanced.

Of course, the range was extremely wide and made room for infinite gradations. There was the grandeloquent attitude of the Peruvian José Santos Chocano (1874–1934), who turned the jungles of his *Alma América* (1906) into small plots of universal exoticism. It costs us an effort to read Chocano seriously today, but he had an enormous influence in many parts of Latin America. His trips to Puerto Rico aroused such enthusiasm in cultural and academic circles, no doubt due to his hispanophile, conservative position.[6] And not only there; his voice was imitated and his example followed in Mexico and Chile. Quite early on also, there was the rough

---

[6] See Arcadio Díaz Quiñones, *El almuerzo en la hierba. Lloréns Torres, Palés Matos, René Marqués* (Río Piedras, 1982), pp. 47 ff.

poetry of the Chilean Carlos Pezoa Véliz (1879–1908) who aggressively grafted *modernismo*'s sumptuary prospect on poverty's outlook. Bourgeois ostentation vanished in his plebeian poetry, giving way to the big city's poorer quarters, to the spaces frequented by life's defeated people. No longer the exotic jungle; instead, the appearance of dusty, grey parks in the bowels of the cosmopolitan city. Pezoa died too young to consolidate this poetic approach, but he did also leave a handful of peasant poems which went back to a folk tradition close to gaucho poetry. Furthermore, there was a whiff of spiritualistic agrarianism running through Spanish-American poetry around 1915, which was in closer harmony with *modernismo*'s aesthetic preferences. This was due to the influence of Rabindranath Tagore, who was translated from the English by Juan Ramón Jiménez and his wife, Zenobia Camprubí. This doubtless edifying agrarianism of the Bengali poet half-opened poetry's doors onto a space that was the background and backdrop of Latin American cities. Its concentration on the series of orchards, estates, vinyards and mountain ranges (i.e. latifundia), which were the real 'beyond' of the region's towns and capital cities, was *posmodernismo*'s salutary contribution.

As if miraculously, pictures of rural life began to bud – to abound, even. They were made aesthetic of course, but were responsive to work and activities that, until then, had not been considered worthy to enter the world of poetry. This was an extension of the repertoire, a stretching of the canon, which would necessarily set about making new expressive forms and – why not? – permitting a growing sensitivity towards 'the other', towards what *modernismo* had left outside. In this respect and without any hesitation, *posmodernismo* was clearly extra-modernista. As the countryside did not fit into a sonnet – and even less into the euphonies and preciousness of the prevailing fashion – it became necessary to devise small cycles (triptychs, pictures in series) which took account of the successive processes of farming and the complex reality that was being contemplated. Descriptions sketched the contours of a rural scene, allowing us to imagine what was lacking: the oligarchic context that made the experience possible. This is what we can see in Chilean *posmodernistas* such as Manuel Magallanes Moure (1878–1924) and Pedro Prado (1886–1952) – particularly in the latter's early work. The same motifs, but with greater depth and elaboration, are found in the Vallejo of *Los heraldos negros* (1918), his first book of poems; in the earliest work of Gabriela Mistral (1889–1957), a woman of peasant origin who lived the greater part of her life, before leaving Chile in

1922, in rural or provincial places; and in fragments of the Uruguayan Julio Herrera y Reissig (1875–1910), who in this way built a bridge for the invasion of the avant-garde (particularly in *Los éxtasis de la montaña*, 1904–7). Both fashions came together and merged in the Argentine Leopoldo Lugones (1874–1939) of *Lunario sentimental* (1909) and *El libro de los paisajes* (1917).

### THE 1920S: AVANT-GARDE AND NATIONALISM

If it were necessary to choose a distinctive characteristic of the avant-garde movements that occurred in Latin America in the period between the two world wars, perhaps the most definitive would be the close connection between nationalism and internationalism which they promoted and put into practice. There was a subtle combination of both dimensions, as if international influences were put to the service of national lyric poetry and, complementarily, as if the nationalist design could not be fulfilled without constant appeal to exogenous forces. A cultural parable through which the Latin American recognized himself *thanks to and in contrast with* the European world; and a central paradox of vanguardism, which was very probably expressing the real contradictions that often flower on the field of political battle. It was the exceptional atmosphere of the twenties, whose emotional mood fluctuated incessantly between exaltation and misery, between the poles of optimism and depression. In the internal logic of the subcontinent's literary processes, especially poetry, we have to see the nationalist consciousness the avant-gardes expressed as a potentiality, a greater degree of the *posmodernismo* national sensibility. However weak and partial this was, the radius of its vision was provincial – of the interior. The international ferment granted poetry at that time an incredible familiarity with the fate of its own country: in the case of Argentina, confidence; concern and enquiry in the case of Brazilian modernism. In the Caribbean, the area's regional peculiarity won through; while in Mexico some poets participated in elaborating an Iberian-American creed. There are, I would suggest, few places in the world where it would have been possible to title books of poetry as follows: *Argentina* (1927) by Ezequiel Martínez Estrada; *Raça* (Race) (1928) by Guilherme de Almeida; *Canto do Brasileiro* (Brazilian Song) (1928) by Augusto F. Schmidt; *A República dos Estados Unidos do Brasil* (To the Republic of the United States of Brazil) (1928) by Menotti del Picchia.

## Argentina

The poetry produced in Argentina during the Radical ascendency (1916–30) included work by Jorge Luis Borges (1899–1986), Oliverio Girondo (1891–1967) – possibly the poet with the most authentic avant-garde spirit – and many others (Martínez Estrada, Marechal, Molinari etc.). Later, all of them were to follow divergent paths and, around or after 1940, to complete outstanding works of great range. Nevertheless, if the diversity of their natures is left aside, what remains as a common denominator is a firm conviction about the nation's future, one in which – miraculously or deservedly – history has been tamed in the South Atlantic. They all had a blind belief in the Republic, with variations of course, but without real disagreement. There was an optimism that, in the light of subsequent events, is both ingenuous and frightening. It is impossible to understand the Argentine crisis of conscience, which increasingly grew from the military coup in 1930 until the dreadful dictatorship of 1976–83, without taking into account this complacent self-consciousness, which almost amounted to historical immortality. There was a meta-historical attitude setting the tone of this poetry, even in its most extreme avant-garde pirouettes.[7]

What, then, is the real basis of all this? An ideology accentuating the country's undoubtable achievements had been forming ever since the Independence centenary celebrations in 1910. It can most easily be seen at work in the essays of Ricardo Rojas. The 'tierra de promisión' (land of promise) – and doubtless it was for a huge mass of European outcasts (of whom Vincente Blasco Ibáñez, the Spanish novelist, spoke) had moulded the nation's collective ego. The enrichment caused by the war and the country's growing international role increased this aura of triumph, while butchery on a grand scale reigned in Europe and while, in the extreme north, Mexico gave the impression of being chaotic and lawless, Argentina was, *par excellence,* the most serious and responsible country, a model of well-being and civilization.

'Irigoyenism' did not shatter these convictions, rather, it extended and 'democratized' them. In spite of the Semana Trágica (Tragic Week) and a generally anti-worker policy, successive Radical regimes appealed to the middle classes, to their sense of progress and responsibility, provoking an

---

[7] Cf., for example, the *Odas para el hombre y la mujer* (1929) by Leopold Marechal, or the early poems of R. Molinari (*El imaginero*, 1927).

ideology of fusion and social amalgam. David Viñas has ironically recalled that the photographs of the period usually show Güiraldes and Arlt amicably together: the novelist of the ethos of the *pampa* and the novelist of the anguished city; Florida and Boedo;* a potential Right and Left which did not even conceive of the possibility of a future polarization.

That the crisis existed in embrionic form, can easily be verified by reading the numerous manifestations of critical thought, whether anarchist or socialist. José Ingenieros's work speaks for itself. And we have just mentioned Roberto Arlt, who comes closer to what we are expounding. In his narrative output, which began in the middle of the period we are discussing with *El juguete rabioso* (1926), the author perceived the underground currents of the crisis with unequalled lucidity.

However, this is not the case with poetry. To establish this rapidly, it is enough to turn to a book we have already mentioned, Martínez Estrada's *Argentina;* it gives us, though slightly exaggerated, a good example of what we are trying to describe. A short commentary will help us the better to understand, as a contrast, the singularity of *Fervor de Buenos Aires* (1923), Borges's undeniable masterpiece.

*Argentina (Poesías)* consists of two well-differentiated parts. The first includes a long poem with the same title, 'Argentina', which extends over several sections. This part closes with a Hymn dedicated to Argentina, in which the old political metaphor of the state as a ship is once again brought out from the dead and dusted: 'Argentina: tu nave reluciente' (your sparkling ship); 'tu nave triunfal' (your triumphant ship); 'velamen de oro' (golden sail); and so on. Malice and mockery aside, this book expresses the prevailing climate of those years with absolute ingenuousness; there is complete rapport between the poet and his society.

To do justice to Martínez Estrada, it should be added that his vision is weakly anti-Sarmiento, even in this part. There is a defence of the Indian which, however ambiguous Argentine indigenism seems after the pacification campaigns in the *pampa,* does not fail to stand out in a picture that is ideologically dominated by the alternative of civilization or barbarism.

But if the outward composition of this little book reveals the country's characteristic split, its second part abandons the hymn and begins to voice real concerns. It starts with 'La estancia' (the ranch) and ends with 'Buenos Aires', an extensive poem which gets watered down in 'Río de la Plata'.

*Translator's note:* Boedo is the name of a street in Buenos Aires where a group of left-wing writers used to meet; Florida is the name of another street where a group of more sophisticated writers met.

Everywhere, agrarian pictures in the *posmodernista* style – 'La oveja' (the sheep), 'Siembra' (sowing), etc. – keep filtering through; these, along with descriptions of indigenous realities (birds, trees, farm produce), lay the fragmentary foundations of a future national canticle. They were the materials and scaffolding of a building which soon would be seen to be cracked.

*Fervor de Buenos Aires,* the initial collection of Borges's poems, was one of Borges's best works, and a crucial contribution to this century's Spanish-American poetry. Its youthful awkwardness was patiently corrected throughout the author's life; he went on rubbing out, expurgating the old text, without spoiling his original intuitive creation in any way. The outcome – a reduced, always improved version – is the sum of some astonishingly rigorous aesthetic decisions; it perfectly captures the potentialities of the period.

The title is partly a subtle strategy, depending on a single letter. 'Fervor' (fervour) replaces 'hervor' (ferment), which brings too closely to mind the seething city and its crowds. While this is a naturalistic metaphor, extracted – *horresco referens!* – from transformations of matter, 'fervor' is associated with spiritual dispositions, coating and sublimating 'hervor'. From its title, then, this book transmutes a collective experience into a personal cult.

Inherent in the play with the language's articles, are some very simple stylistic expedients, which were skilfully described some time ago by Amado Alonso.[8] 'A' street in Borges – any old street – is soon shown as 'the' sought for and beloved street. And quite naturally, it ends up being 'street' without any article and with the purity and fullness of the unique. The absence of article in *Fervor* is precisely that, an indicator of fervour. This clever dematerialization renders the object weightless, prolonging it like an echo in the – fervent – intimacy of the subject.

There was a third poetic element determining Borges's vision of the city. It will have been noticed that his Buenos Aires was no longer the cosmopolitan city of yesteryear; it was an artifice of corners: districts, suburbs, fragments of remembered streets. A city imitating the province, viewed inwardly and crystallizing in a space equidistant from official centres and plebeian periphery. It was the 'platonization' of a Buenos Aires which had been and always would be. Borges accepted all this, writing in a prologue that he

---

[8] Cf. Amado Alonso, 'Estilística y gramática del artículo en español', in *Estudios lingüísticos (Temas españoles)* (Madrid, 1951), pp. 151–94.

withdrew from later editions: 'My fatherland – Buenos Aires – is not the expansive geographical myth these two words suggest; it is my house, the friendly *barrios*, those streets and hidden corners that are the well-loved devotion of my time . . . ' – 'A quien leyere' (To whoever reads).

A subjectivity *revises* the city. The verb is literal: the passer-by reads and deciphers this city with his eyes; his city and that of his forebears. He moves, he roams, he travels, he interprets. The city is a text: a spirit, in other words. Those who hold the key, those who know how to interpret it, how to read it, are trustees of tradition. The attitude is distant and can be calm, because this city is a long way off, more distant than history. Rosas is a bad memory, and he can be forgiven; the Independence epic (San Martín, our ancestors) is quite remote. Suddenly, however, we have these disturbing lines:

> Más vil que un lupanar
> la carnicería rubrica como una afrente la calle.
> Sobre el dintel
> la esculpidura de una cabeza de vaca
> de mirar ciego y cornamenta grandiosa
> preside el aquelarre
> de carne charra y mármoles finales. . .
> con la lejana majestad de un ídolo.

(Baser than a brothel/the butcher's shop marks the street like an affront./ Over the doorway/ the little sculpture of a cow's head/ with blind look and set of horns/ presides over the watercolour,/gaudy meat and bits of marble. . ./with the distant majesty of an idol.)

The brief poem – here in its more extensive version – was later reduced to five or six lines. In 'Carnicería' (Butcher's shop) everything is out of tune; ripples of bad taste shatter the friendly comfort of the streets: it is the reign of the 'charro' (ill-bred). No coincidence, then, that amid the spiritual fervour, such a place should be the centre of such sensations. A butcher's shop, a history of bloodshed, the Argentine economy, metaphysical hatred for the flesh as such – very Borgesian! From then on, *res* (head of cattle) was to be, for Borges, the reverse of *ser* (being).

## Mexico

In Mexico under Obregón and Calles the country was trying to reconstruct its civic life after the armed revolutionary conflict. When the conquests of the revolution appeared to have taken hold, the Cristero uprising reopened the war. We are dealing here with the exact opposite of Argentina. Opposed to the serious, patrician countenance of Southern worthies were heroes who had wagered on history with weapons in their hands. We get plebeian images of peasants, shepherds, miners, in disorderly collective mobilization. Chaos versus order; the barbarism of here and now versus the eternal civilization ruling down there. Consequently, the poetry of Mexico of that time is very different from that of Argentina.

From the initial example of José Juan Tablada (1871–1945) up until the forming of the *Contemporáneos* group, the Mexican avant-garde assimilated varied cultural movements, aesthetics and ideologies. First of all, orientalism, a current that was to have greater persistence in Mexico than in other countries, from Tablada to Paz (*Ladera Este,* mainly the fruit of the poet's stay in India as Mexico's Ambassador), by way of the influential *Estudios Indostánicos* (1920), which Vasconcelos wrote in San Diego, California, during his years of exile. Second, Castilian poetry: the resurgence of the lyric on the Peninsula, which was then in full flood, very soon reached the Mexican high plateau, greatly contributing to twentieth-century poetry. Seen from without it is the poetry of Mexico that shows most affinity with the Castilian tradition. (Perhaps for this reason Paz highlights his French connection.) European influence in general was to have considerable impact on the work of, for example, Villaurrutia. This amalgam produced some of the continent's richest avant-garde poetry.

Considered as an expressive unity, the most important work of this period was written by the *Contemporáneos* group. Nowhere else was there so varied and homogenous a flowering (homogenous at the level of technical competence; varied in the range of individual works) as that produced by Xavier Villaurrutia (1903–50), José Gorostiza (1901–73), Carlos Pellicer (1898–1977) and other members of the group. *Reflejos* (1926), Villaurrutia's terse initial work, and *Nostalgia de la muerte* (1930), the high point of his lyrical development, along with Gorostiza's substantial *Muerte sin fin* (1939), allow us to bring this judgement to bear. In what follows, we shall also highlight a minor work taken from early on in Carlos Pellicer's poetic development, because it seems to us representative of the spirit of a certain Mexican avant-garde.

The perceptive critic, José Joaquín Blanco, has discerned a double orientation within the *Contemporáneos* group. Only one of them interests us here, namely, what could be called the group's Vasconcelos wing, which was more allied to ideals that were detached from the revolution itself and which viewed events through Latin American eyes, following the example of the man who was guide to the young in the post-revolution reconstruction phase, the ideologue José Vasconcelos. Between 1921 and 1924 Vasconcelos held the posts of Rector of the University of Mexico and Secretary for Public Education. And it was precisely in 1924 that Carlos Pellicer published his second book of poems, *Piedra de sacrificios. Poema iberoamericano,* a work which very competently synthesized this tendency. With a prologue by 'The Master' and epigraphs from Darío, the book has a very explicit opening: 'América, América mía'; it appeals to the 'great international Ibero-American family', as Vasconcelos does not fail to point out in his introductory remarks. In effect, this extensive poem, which is conceived symphonically, names people and places in different parts of the continent, using a kind of travelling cinematic approach – a quality also noticeable in Vasconcelos's main essays. Bear in mind that Vasconcelos's *La raza cósmica* (1925), along with its historico-philosophical introduction about American *mestizaje* (miscegnation), was also a travel book in which the Revolution's intellectual delegate conveyed his impressions of Argentina, Brazil and other countries. The cinematic approach, in other words, characterized Pellicer's images and style from then on.

In his desire for knowledge of the immense reality he had chosen to celebrate, Pellicer multiplied perspectives in order to sense and embrace the American land. The phrase 'Desde el avión' (From the aircraft) opens two stanzas, shaping an aerial vision that, a quarter of a century later, the *Canto general* did not scorn. Above all, there was a perspective in depth, which showed the poet's immersion in the Americas:

> Y así desde México sigo
> creyendo que las aguas de América
> caen tan cerca de mi corazón,
> como la sangre en las liturgias aztecas.

(And so from Mexico I continue/believing that America's waters/fall as close to my heart/as blood in Aztec liturgies.)

This is decisive, it is a site for the *canto;* a lyrical path par excellence, in which the poetic subject becomes identified with experience of the past. The indigenous element reflects this tension, sometimes reaching beyond the optimism of Vasconcelos.

Thus, in spite of obvious technical immaturity, Pellicer created a poem filled with enormous possibilities. One example will suffice: in the fragment to Carabobo, using a language of unusual vigour, he was on the point of rising above the traditional liberal hymn extolling national glories. Although the poem fails to fulfil its promise, it leaves with us a magnificent line, which condenses all the grandeur of Bolívar's expedition: 'Un gran viento desmantelaba el cielo' (A great wind uncloaked the sky). Instead of superficial discussion, where the poem is a gloss on the political discourse, nature as the site and sphere of historical conflicts is granted a voice.

## Brazil

The character of the Brazilian avant-garde — the so-called *Modernismo* — is not an exception in the review we are conducting. On the contrary, the obsession with national identity would be bordering on caricature, were it not for the saving graces of humour and irony, so firmly etched into Brazilian literature. In Chapter 1 of this volume, Richard Morse has described the cultural significance of the work and actions of the two Andrades, Mário and Oswald, leaders of the Brazilian modernist movement from its origins at the beginning of the twenties until its extinction in the mid-forties. The connection between creative motivation and preoccupation with national and ethnic identity acquired an exemplary standing in their work. With Mário (1893–1945), the writer who led the movement with *Paulicéia desvairada* (1922), we can witness a model development, one that transformed him into a veritable strategist of contemporary Brazilian culture. His novel *Macunaíma* (1928), a masterpiece with a strange primitivism, his poetry texts published during the twenties, and his illuminating research into music and folklore, served as the basis for a systematic exploration into Brazilian reality. And Oswald (1890–1954), the author of a series of novels spanning three decades, for his part, entitled his most relevant poetry collection *Pau Brasil* (1925). In it he attempted a historical survey, aimed at retrieving national origins. Although chronology, tone and spirit are very different, there is a similarity between this attempt and the semi-historical poems, based on chronicles and accounts of voyages, with which the Nicaraguan, Ernesto Cardenal, began his poetic work at the end of the forties.

The events that mark the development of Modernism can be outlined as follows: a climate of cultural renewal began to form with the plastic arts (the Malfatti exhibition in 1917) and other incentives as a background;

and then, halfway through February, 1922, there was an explosion: São Paulo's Teatro Municipal put on three artistic festivals – one devoted to painting and sculpture, one to literature and poetry, and one to music. This rapidly spread from São Paulo to Rio, Belo Horizonte, and so on, but it encountered resistance in the north, where the intellectual views of Gilberto Freyre held sway. As we have said, 1922 was also the year in which *Paulicéia desvairada* appeared. Andrade wrote it after worriedly reading *Les Villes Tentaculaires* by the Belgian symbolist, E. Verhaeren. To compare Borges with Andrade at this point, and the Buenos Aires of the former with the São Paulo of the latter, is to go from the calm posture of the passer-by to the absolutely free, basically muscular attitude with which the Brazilian assaults his hallucinatory city. The book also had primitivist aspects which were to become more and more noticeable over the decade.

Within the framework we have suggested, the limit of this development is marked by the foundation of the *Revista de Antropofagia* (1928) and Oswald's 'Manifesto antropófago', which appeared in its first number. Primitivist postulates here reached a culminating point, coinciding and combining with the artistic-folkloric productions of the composer Heitor Villa-Lobos and Mário himself. A division in the modernist avant-garde between a socialist-leaning left and a Catholic, traditionalist right was beginning to take shape at the same time. It was as if the fascist sympathies of Italian Futurism and the Bolshevik orientation of a certain Soviet avant-garde had, by strange chance, coincided on Brazilian soil. In all events, the two tendencies shared a basic, common nationalism, which is emphasized by Wilson Martins in a study dedicated to this period: 'the nationalism, that in the guise of various avatars, would be one of the most imperious dogmas of Modernism and of Brazilian life then and to come'.[9] And he continues: 'Modernism preferred the nationalist course to cosmopolitanism, the course of primitivism to that of artifice, the sociological to the psychological, the folkloric to the literary, and . . . the political to the unpolitical'.

But, more important than the literary output generated during the years of the avant-garde – ephemeral in a world context – it must be remembered that during this time the contribution of two of the most important Brazilian poets of this century, Carlos Drummond de Andrade (1902–87) and Cecília Meireles (1901–64), was being prepared. From

[9] Wilson Martins, *The Modernist Idea* (New York, 1970), pp. 8, 94.

1925, the former was obviously part of the avant-garde climate, while the latter was influenced more by earlier symbolism and was as a general rule reserved when confronted by the appeals of the 'new'. These two, together with the significant figure of Manuel Bandeira (1896–1968), are possibly the most outstanding personalities in Brazilian poetry.[10]

Although Drummond's great poetic works were to come later (*Sentimento do mundo*, 1940; *A rosa do povo*, 1945), his first unique work – which falls within this chapter's chronological limits – signalled a clear distancing from the regional and nationalist concerns of the day. It did reproduce them, but with *detachment**, and with a quality of humour that was to be the the hallmark of his poetry from then on.

*Alguma poesia* (1930) – the title is every inch an euphemism, if the surrounding enthusiasm and elation are taken into account – collected poems written by Drummond between 1923 and 1930. It was dedicated to 'Meu amigo Mário de Andrade'. With an obviously autobiographical axis invested with an uninhibited mythology of ad hoc angels – 'o anjo terto' (the hurt angel) of his birth, 'o anjo batalhador' (the champion angel) of the denouement – the poet's infancy was recalled and cyclical sections about Brazilian life were introduced. After sketches of Rio, Belo Horizonte and other places, he rounds off:

> E preciso fazer um poema sobre a Bahia.
> Ma eu nunca fui lá.

(It's necessary to write a poem about Bahia/But I was never there.)

There was an epigrammatic wit, which was not incompatible with potential profundity, such as that exhibited in 'Quadrilha'. The fate of several frustrated lives – about which Mistral sang with unparalleled understanding in her ballad 'Todos ibamos a ser reinas' (All of us were going to be queens) – was here reduced to a miniature, as if the form itself were ironising the poor living parables described. Perhaps Antônio Cândido is the critic who has best caught the peculiarity of Drummond's poetry: 'In truth, with him. . .Brazilian Modernism attained the transcending of the verse, allowing the manipulation of the expression of space without barriers, where poetry's magic flow depends on the overall shape of the poem, freely arranged, which he glimpsed in his descent into the world of words.'[11]

---

* *Translator's note:* In English in the original text.

[10] Vinícius de Moraes (1913–80), another outstanding figure in the Brazilian poetry of this century, was to start his output in the following decade, at the beginning of the thirties.

[11] Antônio Cândido, *Vários Escritos* (São Paulo, 1970), p. 122.

Without any doubt, Cecília Meireles is one of the greatest women poets in the Portuguese language. Her main peer in Spanish America was the Chilean poet Gabriela Mistral, with whom she had strong ties of friendship. Although her earliest work – which began with _Espectros_ (1919) – was symbolist in style, she was later to find a voice of her own with her book _Viagem_ (1939), which she herself chose to head a collection of her complete works. The clarity of these verses and their extremely clear notation of nature's most subtle moments make this poetry a fascinating experience. It could only have emerged, as she recorded herself, from the 'silence and loneliness' of her childhood; and – we in turn add – from the enormous hurt that surrounded her existence. If, in accordance with Gide's dictum, to be classical a work must be permeated with a _profound clarity,_ then there is no poetry more classical than that of _Viagem_ and Meireles's subsequent works. A fragment of 'Música' suffices to give us an idea:

> Minha partida,
> minha chegada,
> a tudo vento. . .
> Ai da alvorada!
> Noite perdida,
> Noite encontrada

(My departure,/my arrival,/the wind at full blast. . ./Oh dawn!/Night lost,/night encountered.)

### The Andean republics

The avant-garde in Chile did not have any significant weight at this time. It can be reduced to Huidobro who published a slim volume, _El espejo de agua,_ in 1916, Neruda's transitional poetry, one or two works by Angel Cruchaga Santa María (_La selva prometida,_ 1920) and the emergent phase of two subsequently great poets, Humberto Díaz Casanueva (1908–92) and Rosamel del Valle (1900–63). In Ecuador, apart from Alfredo Gangotena (1904–44), who was a somewhat eccentric figure on the literary scene (the greater part of his books was written in French), the avant-garde as such could only claim the work – and the personality – of Jorge Carrera Andrade (1903–78). After publishing his first book, _El estanque inefable_ in 1922, and leaving the country in 1928, Carrera Andrade published his first avant-garde collection, _Boletines de mar y tierra_ (1930). He produced almost all his poetic work abroad, while working as an official connected with international organizations or Ecudaor's diplomatic corps. The avant-garde in Colombia came into being a little after the period with which we are now concerned, halfway through the thirties. The *Piedra y Cielo* (Stone and Sky) movement, around which it coalesced, included three leading poets: Jorge Rojas (b. 1911), who undeniably inspired it; Arturo Comacho (1910–82); and Eduardo Carranza (1913–85).[12]

## Cuba and Puerto Rico

In spite of differences in historical development, social structure and cultural traditions, Puerto Rico and Cuba are not too dissimilar, linked by the former's colonial situation and the neo-colonial domination suffered by the latter, which had begun to be consolidated under Gerardo Machado's dictatorship (1927–33). To begin with Cuba, there was an almost uninterrupted flow, embracing the work and activity of Rubén Martínez Villena, co-founder of Cuba's Communist party in 1925, the *Revista de Avance,* the research of Alejo Carpentier and the blossoming of Black themes in the poetry of Nicolás Guillén and Emilio Ballagas.

In effect, the first three books of Guillén (1902–89) registered an ascending curve of impressive significance, not only for the poetic possibilities that they offered, but more especially for their cultural implications for the Caribbean area and, therefore, for Latin America in general. In the field of poetry, it is probably Guillén who has contributed most to making Latin America aware that the African element is an essential ingredient of its ethnicity; that Africa, together with Europe and America, is the third continental angle in our historical triangle. To this end, the poet began to search through the Afro-Spanish cultural tradition so rich and abundant on the island; in particular, the traditional dance known as *son*. Underlying this were, doubtless, the interest in African cultures that had been starting to assert itself since the beginning of the century and, a little later, the impact of the North American Harlem Renaissance, and especially the work of Langston Hughes, the Black poet who visited Cuba in 1928. But, more than anything, it must have been the ethnographic, artistic and folkloric research, which was beginning to be carried out on

---

[12] See the excellent anthology *Poesía y poetas colombianos* (Bogotá, 1985) edited by the Colombian poet Fernando Charry Lara and Eduardo Comacho's magnificent studies, especially *Sobre literatura colombiana e hispanoamericana* (Bogotá, 1978).

the island, that contributed most to highlighting the Black cultural input: Fernando Ortiz's research, naturally, and the studies which later culminated in Alejo Carpentier's *La música en Cuba* (1946).

With *Motivos de son* (1930) Guillén achieved a powerful cultural synthesis; at heart, it rested on a very simple procedure: the translation of what already existed in the popular and musical area of the *son* to the level of poetry. The means were also simple, but extremely effective; they corresponded to the spirit of what he was attempting to combine. The Spanish octosyllable, as the basic metrical unit, was complemented with refrains, broken feet and repetitions, which exercised a polyrhythmic effect and ended up giving the poem an incantatory tone, one of magic trance. At the same time, ideological strategies were helping to overcome ethnic prejudice and to fight racism. In this way, the African theme, which, in colonial poetry (Caviedes, and others) was dealt with in terms of caste, acquired here a powerful form of cultural counter-effect.[13]

After a transitional work (*Sóngoro Cosongo. Poemas mulatos*, 1931) which immediately followed *Motivos de son,* but already displayed a greater social and political consciousness, *West Indies Ltd.* (1934) both strengthened this increasing scrutiny of the Caribbean arena and expressed an accusation against the foreign forces entrenched in the zone. The English title was a conspicuous indicator of linguistic alienation, economic exploitation and political colonialism. It portrayed not only the oppressor *establishment,** but – with a very characteristic Guillén twist – also the servility and submission it engendered in dominated peoples. These were Guillén's beginnings. His later *El son entero* (1947), *La paloma de vuelo popular* (1957) and the splendid poetry written after the Cuban Revolution make him a pivotal figure amongst the poets of Spanish America and the Caribbean.

In the sphere of poetry, Puerto Rican nationalist aspirations crystallized in the century's second decade with the work of Luis Lloréns Torres (1876–1944). Allied with the island's intellectual elite at a time when the plantation owners were beginning to feel the loss of their economic power and social ascendancy at the hands of the imperial metropolis, Lloréns started to shape a Utopian vision of the Antilles within the framework of the concept of *hispanidad.*[†] He elaborated a

* *Translator's note:* In English in the original text.
† *Translator's note:* Literally, 'Spanishness'; as a political concept, it implies an almost mystical relationship between Spain and her former possessions.
13 For this aspect in particular, see Jorge Ruffinelli, *Poesía y descolonización: viaje por la poesía de Nicolás Guillén* (Oaxaca, 1985), pp. 42 et seq.

programme of historical poetry centred on household gods and, using the
*decimas** of popular tradition, he extolled the peasant, the island countryman who, it seemed to him, was invested with all the positive virtues of
the race.

At the same time that Lloréns was producing the bulk of his poetic work,
Luis Palés Matos (1898–1959), a native of Guayama, published his first
book of lyrics, *Azaleas* (1915). From 1920, at least, he was trying to create
an Afro-Antillian poetry. This took shape in *Tuntún de pasa y grifería* (1937),
the fruit of a long gestation and also the subject of much subsequent
rearrangement (1950, etc.). The book's basic intention – a contrast to
Lloréns's White Hispanist assumptions – was to recover the Black half of
the island, as well as to affirm and assess his condition as a mulatto; also – in
response to the colonial situation – to fight against the attitude of stagnation and defeatism, which was widespread throughout the population.
Because of the fairness of its voice and tone (it neither stops short nor goes
beyond his country's historical potential); because of its taut structure – in
effect, the Martí tradition: 'Tronco' (Trunk), 'Rama' (Branch) and 'Flor'
(Flower), as if to create the fruit it were necessary to seek out the secret root;
and because of its generous relationship with Puerto Rican nationality,
*Tuntún de pasa y grifería* is a work without parallel in the Latin American
poetry of this century.[14]

## THE 1930S

The decade running from 1930 to 1940 was probably the most significant
in the development of Latin American poetry. During this time, poetry
reached its highest levels of revelation and expression. We have already
mentioned the early works of Guillén and the mature works of Villaurrutia
and Gorostiza in Mexico. In Chile the decade opened with *Altazor* (1931),
an exceptional poem by Vicente Huidobro, and it closed, we might argue,
with *Tala* (1938), the opus magnum of Gabriela Mistral up to that time.
In the same period Pablo Neruda's *Residencia en la tierra* (1935) and César
Vallejo's *Poemas humanos* (1939) appeared. Without doubt, these are two
key books in the history of Latin American lyrical poetry.

* *Translator's note:* A form of Spanish poetry employing a ten-line, octosyllabic stanza rhyming: a b b a a c c d d c.
[14] See Díaz Quiñones, *El almuerzo en la hierba,* whom I follow and abridge.

*Neruda*

Pablo Neruda (1904–73), who was born in provincial Chile at the beginning of the century, began his literary career with *Crepusculario* (1923), a still adolescent book pervaded by a melancholy that was very typical of the student generation of the twenties. The youthful tone took more coherent shape in *Veinte poemas de amor y una canción desesperada* (1924) which, in addition to being quite an editorial coup amid the meagre poetry offerings of that time, became a love breviary for many groups of young people throughout the continent. From province to capital; from Marisol to Marisombra* – as the poet was to say in his memories of *O Cruzeiro Internacional* (1962) – from student autumn to the summer tides of the south of Chile, these poems forged a sensitive, carnal experience whose power resided in their ambiguity and the endless fluctuation they set up between the intensity and vagueness of passion and desire.

With *Veinte poemas* the Nerudian subjectivity received its first objectivization in the world of amorous relationship. However, a different landscape asserted itself in the books which followed: the prose poems of *Anillos* (1926), the avant-garde narrative text *El habitante y su esperanza* (1926) and also that same year his ambitious and sombre poem, *Tentativa del hombre infinito*. This 'infinite man' who emerged into the Nerudian world was a new form of poetic subject, a nocturnal, wintry shape that went beyond the still aesthetic horizon of his earlier works. A strange, painful experience of reality, in which everything displayed a threatening face of adversity and resistance, had now become conspicuous. There was an ultimate feeling of devastation on every page. And, oddly, it was the rural note that predominated. Flooded countryside, uninhabited islands, torrential storms seemed to preside over the undermined confines of Neruda's new poetry. The poet was already on the road to his *Residencias*.

Four groups of poems can be established in *Residencia en la tierra*. This classification – entirely chronological – only takes account of the different phases of the book's structure. Their coinciding with the writer's geographical travels is by no means an exclusive criterion. More than anything, it emphasizes that the inclusion of new zones of experience represents a decisive element of poetic integration and an acceptable method of ordering. The four groups are: 1) poems written in Chile, before the poet

---

* *Translator's note:* An untranslateable pun: *sol* means 'sun', *sombra* means 'shade'; Marisol is a girl's name, Marisombra is a neologism invented by Neruda.

leaves his country (1925 or 1926–27) – in general, they present a violent, chaotic vision of nature and the world of men; 2) poems written in the East during his stay in different parts of Burma, Ceylon and Java (1927–32) – these poems, written in the middle of a colonial crisis affecting the Dutch and English domination in South East Asia, introduce us to the poet's daily oriental life, one of exile, poverty and despair; 3) poems written back in Chile on his return from Asia (1932–33) – they present pictures of bureaucratic labour, in other words, sterile exercises in a world of offices; poems such as 'Walking Around' and 'Desespediente' serve as good illustrations of this state of mind; finally, 4) poems written in Spain (1934–35), during the time of the Republic – these allow us a glimpse of a decidedly less pessimistic tone. The initial 'Galope muerte' opens up, at least partially, a quest for fertility, which seems to invade some pieces in *Cantos materiales*, chiefly 'Entrada a la madera' and 'Apogeo del apio'.

The poems in *Residencia en la tierra* are organized in an unusual way, far removed from the *postmodernista* composition of *Crepusculario* and the lyrical, sentimental tone of *Veinte poemas*. Divided into two *Residencias* – with the inclusion of five prose poems in the first – the book also offers another duality; a broad, solemn, almost ritual verse alongside poems in a minor key, concentrated miniatures. However, we are not given a dominant impression of variety, but rather one of homogeneity and intense, all-pervasive swell. Density, slowness, intensity are the values that preside over this Nerudian conception of form and language in *Residencia en la tierra*.

From a historical-spiritual angle, the *Residencias* signify the possibility of formulating new axiological hierarchies. Their obvious geological flavour gives clear warning of this. The 'tierra' (land/earth) of these *Residencias* are not only the planetary latitudes inhabited by the poet, but – also at a deep level – a kind of mineral coefficient. In the world of the *Residencias* and the polarizations of its imagination, the lower, the terrestrial, the nocturnal establish positive and supreme values, directly transmuting the axiological orientations implicit in all spiritualism.

At the same time, the subject that wanders through these poems turns out to be a strange mixture of contemporaneity and anachronism. Following very closely the historical avatars of a collective experience (with something of the explorer and a great deal of the colonial gentleman; and with partly the helpless citizen of the world, partly the impotent pioneer), the 'residential' personage is swathed in an enormous cosmic forbearance, as if resistance and passive warfare were the privileged resolutions of his soul. Signs are refreshingly inverted. As can be seen, we are not dealing with positive energy, capable of overcoming material obstacles, but with a current of contrary flow, in which a heroic 'patience' seems to be the only attitude possible in the face of such forms of devastation.[15]

From the foregoing it is apparent that the considerable influence of this poetry lies in the fact that Neruda seizes on the painful and traumatic collective experience of a society greatly scarred by historical impotence. If there is a poignancy in *Residencia en la tierra,* if we often reach the edge of desperation, it is because we are present at a history of destruction, of cataclysms, of blood spilt incessantly. With its restless images, with its stuttering syntax and language in general, it is a nightmare vision that we are taking by surprise. But this vision is only the transference of a very lucid consciousness of what characterizes the surrounding human world: oppression, poverty, the unshakeable shadow of immobility and death.

*Vallejo*

The case of César Vallejo (1892–1938) is slightly similar to that of Neruda, but fundamentally very different. Like Neruda, he began with a book of poems bearing a *posmodernista* stamp; like Neruda, he produced a significant avant-garde book at the beginning of the twenties. But these appearances are deceptive. In *Los heraldos negros* (1918) Vallejo was already making way – alongside many poems that are only echoes of *modernismo* – for a feeling of autochthony, expressed in Andean scenes and, above all, in an intense exploration of human suffering. The first poem, which gave its title to the book, was almost emblematic of pain the world over. Similarly, there was no avant-garde work – at least during the twenties – which could be compared with *Trilce* (1922) in terms of powerful effect. *Trilce* was a true *experimentum crucis* of the complex relationship between foreignness and a radical American consciousness. If the book is looked at from outside, the more obvious expedients of avant-garde poetry can clearly be seen, namely: orthographic violations, layout practices, broken syntax, and so on. But this is not the essential point. In a much stronger way than Neruda's *Tentativa, Trilce* contains a substantial local appeal, making it the first formulation of an endogenous avant-garde. The Peruvian landscape, the highlands, the suffering face of the entire country are resoundingly

[15] On the subject of Nerudian 'patience', see the penetrating pages Alain Sicard dedicates to it in *La pensée poétique de Pablo Neruda* (Lille, 1977).

assimilated in a tone of expression and a complex manner of feeling. 'Aventura y el orden' (Adventure and order) are here placed at the disposal of a deepfelt cause, which is nothing more than knowledge of self. *Trilce*'s vanguardism is definitely 'ours'; Mariátegui wisely saw that the essential 'indigenous voice' was flowering in Peruvian poetry.

Vallejo left the country in 1923, the year following the publication of *Trilce*. He left behind him the valuable work experiences of his youth (the mine and the sugar plantation), where he had been able to see at first hand the exploitation of many of his fellow countrymen. He had also left behind — a bleak memory — his brief but wrongful encarceration. He was never to return to Peru, spending the greater part of his life in Paris and Spain. His interest in the achievements of contemporary Marxism led him to travel on three occasions around 1930 to the Soviet Union, then in its full socialist construction stage. His social and political faith was strengthened by this experience; it fortified his militancy as a member of the Communist Party (in both France and Spain). The endless discussions among students of his work about whether Vallejo was 'Christian' or 'Marxist', a 'dialectician' or an 'existentialist', are ultimately senseless, however many examples are put forward. His Marxism was at once orthodox and original; and in his prose works he has left us pages which are both obscure and illuminating, but they are always governed by his poetic sensibility and imagination. There is a definite experience of suffering in Vallejo. It was originally moulded by religious forms and symbols, and later elucidated by means of social, political and historical categories. This tension, far from harming the coherence of his work, was extremely productive. It caused him to maintain a poetic discourse that was always faithful to the undergone experience — his and others. What Jean Franco has called 'his devastating attack on the individualized subject' is an integral part of the paradoxical design of possibly one of the most complex Latin American imaginations.

Soon after his return from the Soviet Union, Vallejo wrote a handful of poems which amounted to one of the first layers of his future *Poemas humanos* (1939) and which almost forms a separate group within this collection.[16] They are 'Salutación angélica', 'Los mineros', 'Gleba' and 'Telúrica y magnética'. According to Franco, the influence of the first of these can be underlined in this way: 'it proposes in an inequivocal fashion

---

[16] For the involved publication problems of *Poemas humanos*, see Americo Ferrari's concise note ('C. V. entre la angustia y la esperanza'), in César Vallejo, *Obra poética completa* (Madrid, 1982).

what will become a central issue in the 'Spain poems' – a poet-prophet who is not avant-garde or vanguard but, as it were, bringing up the rear. It is not the poet who produces a new consciousness but the militant'.[17]

In effect, 'Salutación angélica' (Angelic Salutation) uses a title with a Christian flavour in order to celebrate the birth of the 'Bolshevik' as the embodiment of the new man in the march of history. This, unlike the representatives of nations and specific states, overcomes and goes beyond 'el beso del límite en los hombros' (the limited kiss on the shoulders). The image of this man of the present who looks towards the future is devised in terms that are at once political slogans of the period and religious allusions:

> y aquesos tuyos pasos metalúrgicos,
> aquesos tuyos pasos de otra vida.

(and those metallurgical steps of yours,/those steps of yours of another life.)

Furthermore, at the poem's outcome, the Bolshevik triumph does not eliminate the situation of the poet and other peoples in other parts of the earth:

> me dan tus simultáneas estaturas mucha pena,
> pues tú no ignoras en quién se me hace tarde diariamente,
> en quién estoy callado y medio tuerto.

(your simultaneous heights greatly grieve me,/for you do know in whom I'm daily made late,/in whom I'm silent and half blind.)

This feeling of limits and of mutilation, centred in the domain of corporeal human nature, was to reach an impressive development in Vallejo's posthumous poems, particularly the fifteen pieces that made up *España, aparta de mí este cáliz.* The Spanish conflict, which sharpened the poet's already wounded sensibility to the point of an eminently lucid delirium, transported him to an intense meditation upon the body as the vehicle of human solidarity. For example, in 'Himno a los voluntarios de la República' (Hymn to the Republic's Volunteers), he wrote:

> ¡Constructores
> agrícolas, civiles y guerreros,
> de la activa, hormigueante eternidad: estaba escrito
> que vosotros haríais la luz, entornando
> con la muerte vuestros ojos;

---

[17] Jean Franco, *César Vallejo: The Dialectics of Poetry and Silence* (Cambridge, Eng., 1976), p. 168.

que, a la caída cruel de vuestras bocas,
vendrá en siete bandejas la abundancia, todo
en el mundo será de oro subito
y el oro,
fabulosos mendigos de vuestra propia secreción de sangre,
y el oro mismo será entonces de oro!

(Builders, farmworkers, civilians and soldiers,/of busy, ant-like eternity: it was written/that you would be light,/half-closing your eyes with death;/ that, at the cruel fall of your mouths,/abundance will arrive on seven trays, everything/in the world will suddenly be made of gold/and the gold/ fabulous beggars of your own blood's secretion,/the gold itself will then be made of gold!)

Eternity is here constructed anew with the active energy of the many; but what is stressed above all is a solidarity leaning towards the beyond, a posthumous solidarity which is rooted in the sacrifice of the combatants. A dialectical vision of death, in the end convergent (although not identical) with what Neruda expresses in 'Alturas de Macchu Picchu' (1946). In Vallejo, however, it is articulated within the paradigm of a Spanish Lazarus (see poem XII, 'Masa'): the corpse immortalized through collective achievement. The book's provocatively evangelical title attains an air of parable, in which human history is visualized through eyes of a miracle – the miracle of blood and death – unifying *España*'s dominant voices, namely the public oration and the religious sermon.

The *Poemas humanos*, then, suggest a powerful inversion of values, something that also happens in *Residencia en la tierra*. The body is no longer seen as the modern and classical *locus* of the individual and individualism; it is inhabited by elements of the community and society. Vallejo had already begun a tenacious deconstruction of the human organism in *Trilce*. The points of spiritualist privilege (eyes, brow) were substituted in *Trilce* by an overbearing invasion of the shoulder, the lower members, or the extremities. This tendency continued and grew even greater in his poetry of the thirties. Grey hairs and nails – those expendable remains of the flesh – become fossils of the family circle ('canas tías' (aunts with white hair), and so on); and the clothes that human beings dress in become the skin of other beings: each re-enacts his own life with the work and suffering of the great many as background. Thus, by means of this double avatar, images of the corporeal are extended and prolonged beyond the limits of the singular individual, integrating and *incorporating* signs of the collective, that is, the productive groups and society in general.

LATIN AMERICAN POETRY AT MID-CENTURY

As we come to the mid-century after the end of the Second World War, we see Latin American poetry consolidating its cultural importance on the continent. At the same time, it begins to reach an increasingly international audience. The decade's most memorable events were undoubtedly the Nobel Prize for Literature awarded to the Chilean poet, Gabriela Mistral (1945), and the publication of the *Canto general* in 1950. With its award, the Swedish Academy were honouring a body of work that, from its very beginnings, had been marked by pacifism and deep compassion for the suffering of the weak, ever the victims of this century's panorama of war. The prize was given for a work that was in full flow and which, to a high degree, summed up the trajectory we have been outlining so far. A poetry with an archaic slant that was both bitter and intense had followed the still provincial and rural verse of *Desolación* (1922). *Tala* (1938) was Mistral's characteristic contribution to the endogenous avant-garde and the Americanism of the thirties. At the time she received the Nobel Prize, Mistral was working on part of her last collection of poems (*Lagar*, 1954), which was to appear three years before her death in 1957.

With the *Canto general*, Neruda completed a poetic project that had absorbed him for nearly ten years, from 1938 until early 1949, when he had to leave Chile following persecution of the Communist party in his country. Begun in years of freedom and hope during the victory of the Popular Front, the book was finished under oppression, in clandestine circumstances within the shadow of exile. Neruda's stay in Mexico around 1940 and his journey to Machu Picchu in 1943 were decisive in expanding his project from the 'Canto general de Chile' (a part that remains as section VII of the whole) into, simply, the *Canto general*, American in source and scope. With fifteen vast sections, the book opens with an almost Utopian vision of the pre-Columbian world. It unfolds the collective American experience from the Spanish conquest up to the wars of the twentieth century, and it culminates with the complementary halves of a grandiose objective cosmography – 'El Gran Océano' (The Big Ocean) and an autobiographical elaboration 'Yo soy' (I am) – in which the poet's body and spirit are conceived as the product of his country's natural environment and the struggles of its people. It can surely be claimed that, by virtue of its epic dimensions and the structural variety of the poetic forms it embraces, this great Nerudian book is one of this century's fundamental works. [18]

In Argentina Borges – whose work, we have seen, was initiated within the framework of the avant-garde at the beginning of the twenties – undertook an appraisal of his own poetry by means of an anthology that he prepared and published in 1943 (*Poemas, 1922–1943*). It marked a significant point in Borges's trajectory, in that he re-orientated his work in a classical direction, almost purging it of avant-garde tendencies, while at the same time he injected it with a metaphysical air, which had not existed before as such and which could be accounted for as the result of the author's own stories influencing his poetry from within. From that time on, it became hard to distinguish the poet from the storyteller. Both poems and short stories were chosen by Borges for his underlying purpose of systematically excluding the novel, with all the dangers of 'realism' and the prosaic that, according to him, this genre carried with it. In Borges the poet a further facet of the author of *El Aleph* (1949) and his other stories will always be seen, confirming the immense distance that there is between his work and Latin American history. A distance that, whether or not a sign of persistent Buenos Aires cosmopolitanism, is also – paradoxically – a characteristic reaction to turning points in Argentina's history, and particularly to a specific view of universal history. In fact, deconstructing history, which appears to be the most obvious indicator of Borges's literary apparatus, is also the cover for one of the most refined philosophies of history ever undertaken by one of our men of letters. On the map of universal history, with commendable tolerance, Latin American culture co-exists with other civilizations forged by humanity throughout the planet over the centuries; but the common denominator of this history has always been violence (invasions, the incursion of nomadic tribes, and so on). Latin America also participates in this consubstantial violence. Tolerance is pluri-cultural and avoids every attempt at ethnocentrism; violence is ubiquitous and, in the interests of this same tolerance, it passes from culture to culture, it is culture itself *at work*, * carrying and contributing to the fertile synthesis, transfer and movement of tradition, and so on. It can be noted that the butcher's shop, which appeared

---

* *Translator's note:* In English in the original text.

[18] A significant detail for the relationship between literature and politics: when he died in Bolivia, Ernesto 'Che' Guevara was carrying a treatise on Calculus and a copy of the *Canto general* in his military rucksack.

modestly in a corner of Borges's first book (see above), now becomes the symbol of a civilization built on barbarism. (His own experience of his country and the contemporary period, perhaps?)

In Mexico, Octavio Paz (b. 1914) first anthologized himself in *Libertad bajo palabra* (1949). Almost all his earlier poetry – *Luna silvestre* (1933), for example, and subsequent books, especially his poetry written in Spain – were excluded from his selection by Paz. He gave special emphasis to his surrealist phase in the forties. This had led him in 1943 to start editing the influential review, *El hijo pródigo*. His poetry – likeable when it has a symbolist slant – basically inherited the tradition created by the *Contemporáneos* group and it was to obtain its best results later with *Piedra del sol* (1957), *Salamandra* (1958–1961) (1962) and *Ladera Este* (1962–1968) (1969). However important Paz may be in Mexican literature – and his importance tends at times to overshadow the existence and value of other poets, such as Efraín Huerta, José Emilio Pacheco and the group belonging to *La espiga amotinada* – it seems fair to claim that his work is not that of an 'originator' in the proper sense nor does his poetry break new ground. His poetry is an echo – albeit a harmonious, refined echo almost always controlled by a painstaking competence – of his great predecessors in the first half of the century, particularly Villaurrutia and Gorostiza.

More names can be singled out in other parts of Latin America. Some poets reaffirmed or renewed their creative impulse. In Chile, for example, Humberto Díaz Casanueva, halfway through the decade, published one of his most mature poems (*Requiem,* 1945). Pablo de Rokha (1894–1968), a poet born on Chile's central coast, who brought a rural note and new forms of social poetry to the Chilean repertory, definitively affirmed his already prolific output in the same period. In Cuba, at the same moment that Guillén was giving a retrospective look at the whole of his output (the already mentioned *El son entero* of 1947), the entirely different work of José Lezama Lima (1910–76) was growing and developing. Following *Muerte de Narciso* (1937), he published several books of poetry in the forties, from *Enemigo rumor* (1941) to *La fijeza* (1949). It was a basically hermetic poetry, whose codes still need deciphering (and this is said in spite of Cintio Vitier's important critical contribution). Finally, special mention must be made of Eunice Odio (1922–74), the great Costa Rican poet who was to live most of her life outside her own country, mainly in Mexico, and who began her dazzling output with *Los elementos terrestres* (1947), but her work was practically unknown or ignored until it was posthumously rescued from oblivion and she was given the place she rightfully deserved.

As regards the national variations that are crystallized by mid-century, how can we give even a summary account of tendencies and the richness of poetic temperaments, so heterogeneous by any reckoning? The lack of symmetry with which the phenomenon expresses itself in the continent's different regions further complicates matters. A simple contrast between Peru and Ecuador is sufficient example. In the former, the tradition established by Vallejo was maintained in the work of Martín Adán (1908–85), Carlos Germán Belli (b. 1927) and many more. In Ecuador, the best literary talent seems to have been absorbed by narrative prose, under the influence of the great indigenist novel of the thirties no doubt.

The case of Colombia is particularly interesting. Between the main poets of earlier periods and the few important voices that can be found around 1950, there was considerable continuity; this gives the Colombian poetry of the present century a very clear profile. If there is anything that characterizes the work of José Asunción Silva (1865–96) – often limitingly considered to be a pre-*modernista* poet – it is his overwhelming · musicality. The country's best critics have noted a similar musical gift in the varied and multifaceted work of León de Greiff (1895–1976) and in the frugal output of Aurelio Arturo (1909–74), which is more or less concentrated in one book (*Morada al sur,* 1963) and in a handful of poems. Rooted in Colombian regionalism, an Arcadian breath of fresh air impregnates the work of Arturo who, together with Eduardo Cote Lamus (1928–64) and Fernando Charry Lara (b. 1920), exemplify the best of Colombian poetry.

In spite of the existence of talented poets such as Líber Falco (1906–55), Roberto Ibáñez (b. 1907) and Juan Cunha (1910–85), it is evident that the most telling characteristic of the poetry of Uruguay is the strong feminine presence at its inception. No other Latin American country has ever had such an amount of splendid poetry written by women. Following in Delmira Agustini's wake are the numerous publications of Esther de Cáceres (1903–71), Clara Silva (1903–76), Idea Vilariño (b. 1920) and, a little later, Ida Vitale (b. 1938) and Circe Maia (b. 1932), two estimable present-day poets. The main star of this Pleiad was, of course, Sara Iglesias de Ibáñez (1904–71) who, from her *Canto* of 1940 to her posthumous poems of 1973, elevated and dignified the Uruguayan poetic imagination.

Along with the better known names of Antonio Arraiz (1903–62) and Vicente Gerbasi (1913–93), the figure of Juan Liscano (b. 1915) is dominant in Venezuela. He published two of his first books – *Contienda* (1942) and *Humano destino* (1949) – in the decade that here concerns us. The unhappy tone of the first and the eager exaltation of the second foreshadowed the powerful work he has since produced. Liscano is, without doubt, Venezuela's principal poet.[19]

The excitement provoked by the Argentine poetry of those years is curious. In contrast with the more powerful note of some nations' poetry – that of Peru and Nicaragua, for example – and perhaps because of the very dispersal of poetic energy encouraged by a somewhat external avant-garde, the Argentine lyric seems to lack a distinctive stamp. By virtue of its very variety, which includes a highly diversified regional poetry (in Rosario, Córdoba, Mendoza and Bahía Blanca), a cohesive force is apparently lacking. The individual poet and the group maintain a somewhat erratic relationship and fail to establish a harmonious tradition. This view is deceptive, however. There is no poetry more subtle, more intense or more complex than the work of Enrique Molina, Alberto Girri and Olga Orozco, whose output commenced precisely in the forties. This trio of writers – less publicized than their continental peers – is definitely of world standing.

Enrique Molina (b. 1910) revealed a deep-felt reverence for the planet's beauty in a striking series of volumes, including *Las cosas y el delirio* (1941), *Pasiones terrestres* (1946) and *Costumbres errantes o La redondez de la tierra* (1951). At the end of his first book the Earth was 'this adorable planet' and in a later work he spoke of the 'nomadic brilliance of the world', placing on record his travels over the world's surface. At a much later date, *Monzón Napalm* (1968) was not only to carry this planetary geography to extremes, but also to give evidence of an intensification of Molina's historical consciousness, without substantially altering the aesthetic line he has faithfully followed since he commenced his work. Predominant in his poetry is a dignified, polished verse, with more pathos than Girri and, arguably, with less intensity than Orozco – a compact, well-ordered world which makes Molina's voice one of the most authentic in the Latin American poetry of today.

Alberto Girri (1919–91) and Olga Orozco (b. 1922) began their work in the same year, 1946, the first with *Playa sola* and the second with *Desde lejos*. Girri's poetic imagination, which was forged with *Playa sola* and *La coronación de la espera* (1947) is possibly one of the purest that exists in the Spanish-American world today. His autobiographical 'I' – with its past

[19] Consult the anthology prepared by René L. F. Durand, *Algunos poetas venezolanos contemporáneos* (Caracas, n.d.). J. Sánchez Paláez (b. 1922) and Guillermo Sucre (b. 1933), who began to publish at the beginning of the 1970s, should be added.

history, its psychological labyrinths, its intellectual tics – becomes lighter
and more compact, until it turns into a completely lyrical 'I', inhabited
only by the reverberations of time and the shifting mirage of material
things. It is a poetry at once temporal and essential, which is situated in
exact equilibrium between perception and image. Girri's poetry also establishes equidistance between anguish and desire on the one hand, and the
subject's calmness and ultimate serenity on the other. In the slow swing of
his verse, which is both sensitive and meditative, we can glimpse the
secret yearning and transparent choreography of dreams.

Olga Orozco's *Desde lejos,* signalled this poet's mature entry into South
American letters. *Desde lejos* was, above all, an evocation of woman's
immediate concern: the family home, the grandmother's protective
shadow, the southern landscape. But the forceful dimensions of the *pampa*
wipe out all comforting trace and sow a wind of idolatry, an untameable
climate of great devastation peopling the intimacy with nature's violent
powers. Orozco's poetry, made out of pain and wisdom, with grand ritual
and tiny gestures, lying between the soul's composure and the ever imminent verge of catastrophe, propagates the voice of one of the major spirits
of the time.

The position of Nicaragua in the picture of Latin America poetry is
truly exceptional. During the long night of the Somozas, which lasted half
a century from the assassination of Sandino until the victory of the Sandinista Revolution, a group of poets was able to provide a bastion for
resistance from both inside and outside the country, and to maintain it in
spite of repression and torture. While Alfonso Cortés declined into madness in 1927, José Coronel Urtecho (1906–94) managed to survive long
years of real internal exile, and Ernesto Cardenal (b. 1925) was able to
create the revolutionary and evangelical experiment of Solentiname.
Grouped together between Master and disciples were poets of the stature
of Manolo Cuadra (1907–87), Pablo Antonio Cuadra (b. 1912), Joaquín
Pasos (1914–47) and Ernesto Mejía Sánchez (1923–89). Directly or indirectly, sooner or later, they all participated in a poetic development with
the following characteristics: early contact with the most renovative North
American poetry (with Salomón de la Selva (1893–1958) as a forerunner
in his *El soldado desconocido,* 1922); the crucial role played by José Coronel
Urtecho in absorbing foreign influence, taking certain elements from
Pound who, it should not be forgotten, was a stinging critic of 'usury' in
the capitalist system, even if he did espouse Italian fascism; and the
individual exposition of the works of the above mentioned poets. Both

priest and poet, Ernesto Cardenal who became Minister of Culture after the Sandinista revolution in 1979 embodied the living movement from dictatorship to freedom, from his first historic poems, written during his stay in Mexico at the end of the forties, up to his decisive *Canto nacional* (1973).

From this overall picture it is easy to get the impression of a growing ideological polarization in the poetic tendencies of those years. More recent experience has come to confirm that, if not a polarization in the strictest sense, we are dealing with a bifurcation that expresses clearly defined options on a continental level which are, essentially, of a political and historical nature. These poets could not ignore the global conflict between capitalism and socialism and it strongly affected their poetry and the thinking that moulded their lives. On the one hand, a *Canto general* (1950) in the manner of Neruda and a *Canto nacional* (1973) in the manner of Cardenal, postulating resistance to political oppression and the creation of new ways of collective living; and on the other, 'orientalism' in the vein of Paz and historical-universal metaphysics *à la* Borges, advocating the status quo. A divergence and antithesis that does not exclude space for the expression of dreams, which surface in the poetry of Girri or Orozco. The obscure splendour these poets seek – sometimes blindly – is not opposed to that other, committed poetry, whose conscience and clarity make it see itself as companion of the social forces in ascendancy on the continent. The chiaroscuro of dreams dwells there as well. How could it be otherwise? The forms that give Latin American poetry of the first half century and subsequent years its exceptional vibrancy and recognizable authority in contemporary literature as a whole are the forms of history, nature and Utopia.

# 4

---

# LATIN AMERICAN POETRY SINCE 1950

## INTRODUCTION

By the 1950s Latin American poets were writing within the context of their own continental traditions. From Rubén Darío's break with the post-colonial Hispanic tradition in the 1890s, to the following generational break embodied in Vicente Huidobro's avant-garde poems in the 1920s and César Vallejo's experimental *Trilce* (1922), the desire to be as modern as possible by absorbing the latest modes from Europe continued to dominate Latin American poetry. A typical avant-garde poem from the 1920s refused to conform to metre as a definition of what was poetic (i.e. free verse), and sought a new kind of subjective sensibility through playing with syntax, punctuation, common sense, and obvious metaphorical associations, in order to express the novelty and originality of the 'romance' of technology ushered in by the cosmopolitan twentieth century. This typical avant-garde poem serves, at a formal level, as a mould that includes the Brazilian *modernistas* as much as the Mexican *estridentistas*. One of the most representative collections of this period was Carlos Oquendo de Amat's *5 metros de poemas* (1927).[1] A third wave of Latin American poets who wanted to 'make it new' were less Europeanized. Here the emblematic collection was Pablo Neruda's *Residencia en la tierra I y II* (1935), whose title was a proclamation of an earthy or materialistic position. Neruda idiosyncratically created a new generational style exploring telluric, or sensual, relations with the empirical world that did not apparently feed off culture. In 1930 Carlos Drummond de Andrade claimed that stupidity made poets sigh for Europe where in fact only making money counted. What emerged from these Latin

---

[1] On Brazilian modernism, see John Nist, *The Modernist Movement in Brazil* (Austin, Tex., 1967); on the *estridentistas*, Luis Mario Schneider, *El estridentismo: una literatura de la estrategia* (Mexico, D. F., 1970). On Oquendo de Amat, Mirko Lauer and Abelardo Oquendo, *Vuelta a la otra margen* (Lima, 1970).

American avant-garde traditions was that individual poets writing in the 1950s not only had a general Western tradition available through a proliferation of translations, but also fluid, emergent native Latin American traditions.

The Romantic seeking of originality over several generations, where poetry is an individual's coming to terms with an inner, subjective status, exploring multi-layered consciousness through language, must be counterbalanced by an equally crucial Latin American tradition that sees the poet's role as subservient to a social revolution, or to a more public persona. The starting point for this tradition would be Rubén Darío's public and denunciatory poems like 'Salutación del optimista' from *Cantos de vida y esperanza* (1905), or the nationalistic Brazilians like Manuel Bandeira, and passes through all the poets like Pablo Neruda or Nicolás Guillén, who reacted to the rising evil in Europe by changing their poetry to make it communicate immediately, to be understood by those who might not read, or buy, books of poems. This politicized tradition centres on César Vallejo's posthumous poems, on Neruda's post 1950s populist stance, and includes the Brazilianization at work in post 1920s Brazilian poetry.

As crucial as the traditions for poets beginning to publish in the 1950s was the social status of the poet. Here a poet's charisma, close to that of a shaman, in cultures in the process of defining themselves against Europe, and in relation to their neighbours, and shared histories, still seduced younger poets into wanting to become poets. At an anecdotal level, Manual Bandeira had a sign outside his workplace saying that a parking space was reserved 'for the Poet'. Pablo Neruda was usually referred to simply as the 'Poet'. As living from poetry was impossible poets like Pablo Neruda, Vinícius de Moraes, João Cabral de Melo Neto, Octavio Paz, Jorge Carrera Andrade, Jaime García Terrés, Raúl Zurita, Juan Gustavo Cobo Borda, and Homero Aridjis, to mention a few, were given glamorous diplomatic posts. Others like José Lezama Lima, or Carlos Drummond de Andrade (thirty years in the Brazilian Ministry of Education), or César Fernández Moreno (at UNESCO), or Ernesto Cardenal (Minister of Culture in the Sandinista government in Nicaragua), have worked in bureaucracies. Poets in Latin America were and are rewarded for being poets in a continent with high levels of illiteracy, and little access to 'high culture'. Poets are asked to take part in debates, give opinions, be a conspicuous role mode. Pablo Neruda's post-1950s poetry cannot be separated from his role in the Chilean Communist party, ending up as ambassador under Salvador Allende in Paris. Octavio Paz's public utterances, from his condemnation of the U.S. invasion of Santo Domingo in 1965 and the massacre of over 300 students in Tlatelolco in 1968, to his contested views on Cuba and Nicaragua, come from his respected status of 'poet'.[2]

As the publication of poetry lies outside the economics of the marketplace for the vast majority, most poets begin by paying for their own editions. This presents enormous freedom for poets, and problems for a critic. A poetry press like Ediciones Ultimo Reino in Buenos Aires has a huge list of poets in print. Contemporary poetry presses proliferate. There is a history of Latin American poetry to be written around the status of these small presses and little magazines. Typical examples would be Victoria Ocampo's magazine *Sur* and its press, running from the 1930s to the 1970s, or Peruvian poet Javier Sologuren's one-man effort at publishing poets in his La Rama Florida press from the 1960s, or Octavio Paz's more prestigious Vuelta press.

Within this living dialogue between generations and traditions that can never be fossilized into a fixed tradition, the genre of poetry itself remains viable in Latin America. In advanced Western countries the poem has been forced into small presses, university presses, and creative writing departments. That poetry is not economically rewarding has affected the social status of a poet. Poets have become marginalized voices in a mass culture doped on TV and videos, with fewer and fewer readers of poetry outside Academe. Latin American poets are equally aware of this demise of poetry within society's values. They may ridicule the Romantic status of poet as special or visionary or social critic, but as they never submitted to the pressures of the commercial market continue to want to call themselves poets.

Finally, in Latin America, as in the late Eastern block countries, poets found a new role in hostile political situations, and became 'witness' writers, even guerrillas. They took a step beyond Neruda's position in 'Alturas de Macchu Picchu' (1946), that he would let the voiceless working class speak through him;[3] they actually took up arms for them.

In what follows I have chosen four loosely defined poetic traditions into which I group representative Latin American poets. These are the surreal-

[2] See Paz's poem 'Intermitencias del oeste (3)' in *Ladera este* (Mexico, D. F., 1969), his essay *Posdata* (Mexico, D. F., 1970), and 'En Santo Domingo mueren nuestros hermanos' from 'Viento entero' (1969).
[3] Neruda's 'Alturas de Macchu-Picchu': 'Yo vengo a hablar por vuestra boca muerta. . . . Acudid a mis venas y a mi boca / Hablad por mis palabras y mi sangre.'

ist and post-surrealistic tradition, the guerrilla and political poetry tradition, the concrete and neo-baroque tradition, and lastly the anti-poetry tradition.

Parisian surrealism condensed all the theories about liberation and writing in the air in the 1920s, and turned them into manifestos with codes, invoking anarchic and revolutionary theories from Charles Fourier to Trotsky, whom André Breton visited in Mexico in 1938. As an exploration of latent and repressed mind levels, offering a *technique* of self-liberation, a praxis, surrealism was by far the most influential artistic movement of the mid-twentieth century. From an early stage Spanish and Latin American painters were involved (Dalí, Buñuel, Picasso, Lam, Matta, Tamayo, and so on), even some poets who changed language and wrote in French like the Peruvian César Moro. But it was in the 1940s and 1950s that surrealism had a real effect on poets and painters, offering at worst facile metaphorical outpourings.

Embryonic surrealist groups grew up in Argentina around Aldo Pellegrini in 1928, and later in Chile around Braulio Arenas in 1938, but it was in Mexico and Argentina in the 1950s that surrealism threw up noteworthy poets. In the Mexico of the 1950s Octavio Paz (b. 1914), after eleven years abroad, and befriending the surrealist leader André Breton in Paris, challenged the official revolutionary orthodoxy in both polemical essays like *El laberinto de la soledad* (1950) and in poetry like *¿Aguila o sol?* (1951). Paz's surrealism incorporated a utopian belief in the transforming powers of art in a sterile political context of betrayal of revolutionary beliefs, and moral corruption. Paz opposed his finely evaluated surrealist beliefs against the PRI of the 1950s and 1960s. He reinterpreted Aztec myths, redefined the liberating action of poetry in changing consciousness, and offered an alternative revolutionary tradition that was immensely influential on writers like Carlos Fuentes and Juan Rulfo. Paz's presence in Mexican culture increased with his surrealist study of inspiration, and the role of a poet in society and history, in *El arco y la lira* (1956), and with long dense poems re-evaluating history and myth like *Piedra de sol,* (1957). His later less programmatic (and less surreal) works from India where he was Mexican ambassador like *Ladera este* (1969), or his poems about returning to Mexico after a nomadic life abroad in *Vuelta* (1976) and his many acute essays, have created a persona against whom it has been hard to fight for younger Mexicans. Paz almost single-handedly recast the Mexican poetic tradition along avant-garde lines with his anthology *Poesía en movimiento* (1966). Winner of the Nobel Prize for Literature in 1990, he remains today an excellent poet, running a powerful literary magazine *Vuelta,* and dominating Mexican cultural politics. The younger poet José Emilio Pacheco (see below) spoke for many when he said in 1966: 'His poetry and prose have ensured that my discovery of what I wanted to say could begin; they have illuminated me.'[4]

In Argentina, a surrealist nucleus resurfaced around a fine literary magazine *A partir de cero,* with three numbers appearing between 1952–56, and edited by poet Enrique Molina (b. 1910).[5] This group opposed both the Peronist philistine neo-fascist cultural policies, as well as the cosmopolitan *Sur* magazine group around Victoria Ocampo, and Borges. Like Paz in Mexico, with whom they had contacts, Enrique Molina and Francisco Madariaga envisaged surrealism as an inner transformation, and a defence of the values of the imagination. They did not turn to political action. Enrique Molina's crucial book *Amantes antípodas* (1961) asserts surrealism as a rush of sensuous images suggesting Molina's erotic paradise as an island, or port, or childhood town (Bella Vista on the Paraná river) with degradation, and tropical decay, liberating the mind from utilitarian concerns (and language). Molina has constructed a theory of sensation (as opposed to intellect) as the only path towards understanding reality. He said to Danubio Torres Fierro: 'sensations alone can touch, smell, taste and affirm the diversity, the irreductible, infinite diversity of matter and beings.'[6] Poetry is a recreation of this sensational understanding through words evoking mental sensations. The opening poem of this collection defines poetry as 'sudor de instintos' [sweat of instincts] that changes the poet into a 'bestia inocente' [innocent beast]. Further poems describe journeys (Molina once worked as a merchant seaman) to white-hot, passionate places far away from overcrowded Buenos Aires. 'Etapa' [Stage] proposes a surrealist anti-family, anti-home ethic: 'Corrompidos por un esplendor de ríos y de grandes sorpresas hemos perdido para siempre la paciencia de las familias./ Fuimos demasiado lejos. Libres y sin esperanza

[4] Pacheco in *Confrontaciones: los narradores ante el público* (Mexico, D. F., 1966), p. 246. On Paz's surrealism, see Jason Wilson, *Octavio Paz* (Boston, 1986). On surrealism in Mexico, see Luis Mario Schneider, *México y el surrealismo (1925–1950)* (Mexico, D. F., 1978).
[5] On Argentine surrealism, see Graciela de Sola, *Proyecciones del surrealismo en la literatura argentina* (Buenos Aires, 1967).
[6] Danubio Torres Fierro interviews Molina in *Memoria plural* (Montevideo, 1986), p. 188. (My translation).

como después del veneno y del amor / nuestra fuerza es ahora una garra de
sol / los labios más infieles/ y apenas nos reconocemos por esas extrañas
costumbres de tatuarnos el alma con la corriente' (Corrupted by a
splendour of rivers and great surprises we have lost for ever the patience of
families. We went too far. Free and without hope like after poison and love
our force is now a claw of sun, the most faithless lips, and we hardly
recognize ourselves in this strange custom of tatooing the soul with the
current).[7] Molina's poetry does not develop much from the 1960s, despite
an attempt at an anti US-in-Vietnam collection *Monzón napalm* (1968). He
himself derived his tropically metaphorical style from Pablo Neruda's
earthy 1930s poetry: 'I think that the greatest resonance in my poetry has
to be secretly identified with those poems by Neruda, who is to me a
colossal poet to whom I owe the atmosphere, the climate of my poetry'.[8]
Molina is also a painter, and exhibited in the surrealist show in Buenos
Aires in 1967. His surrealism is ethical, a 'compromiso total de vivir la
poesía'.[9]

Francisco Madariaga (b. 1927) is also a fine surrealist without ever
being orthodox to the Parisian school, following the mould of Paz and
Molina by attempting to apply his poetics to his own life. His first
collection *El pequeño patíbulo* appeared in 1954, followed by his two best
collections *Las jaulas del sol* (1960) and *El delito natal* (1963). His complete
work was collected as *El tren casi fluvial* in 1987. His compressed, tele-
grammatic poems are set in Corrientes, with dunes, lagoons and wild
nature, suggesting a landscape of passion, and total commitment to intense life. Both Molina and Madariaga link mental life with marginalized,
tropical places, writing what could be called a 'criollo' surrealism where
metaphor is seen as the linguistic tool that unlocks the mind's potential,
and direct experience as more intense than culture.

The most extremist Argentine 'surrealist' poet is Alejandra Pizarnik
(1936–72) for whom poetry is an exploration of inner being cut off from
any references to some empiric outside. In her short poems, often in prose,
only the subjective counts. At the same time, these inner depths resist
words, so that Pizarnik's poetics are on the edge of silence. A short poem
from her fourth book, *Arbol de Diana* (1962, with a prologue by Octavio
Paz) outlines her endeavour: 'Por un minuto de vida breve/ única de ojos

[7] Molina, *Amantes antípodas* (Buenos Aires, 1961), p. 31.
[8] Horacio Salas interviews Molina in 'Vivir su poesía', *Análisis*, 477 (1970), p. 50. (My translation.)
[9] Molina's complete works appeared as *Obra poética* (Caracas, 1978) and *Obra completa* (Buenos Aires,
1989). His sole novel is *Una sombra donde sueña Camila O'Gorman* (Buenos Aires, 1973).

abiertos / por un minuto de ver / en el cerebro flores pequeñas / danzando como palabras en la boca de un mudo' (For a minute of brief life, unique with open eyes, for a minute of seeing small flowers in the brain dancing with words in the mouth of a mute). Pizarnik enjoyed a reputation as a *poète maudite*, whose final suicide seemed to confirm the agony of her verse. At the heart of her work is an attempt to turn herself into a work of art. But there is a lack of music, a yearning for death and self-destruction that throws up images of mirrors, an intense narcissism, walls, rooms and loneliness. Her work has attracted cult readers to its risky plight, and pity for the poet's sense of being 'gagged' ('este canto me desmiente, me amordaza' (this song refutes me, gags me)), and exiled into a dull adult's world, like an Alice expelled from Wonderland, facing death: 'La muerte siempre al lado. /Escucho su decir. / Sólo me oigo' (Death always by my side I listen to its saying. I only hear myself).[10]

Marco Antonio Montes de Oca (b. 1932) is a Mexican poet whose surrealistic inspired poems try to trap the sensuality of an ever-changing reality through strings of metaphors. Championed by Octavio Paz, the prolific Montes de Oca collected his poems in 1987. His poetics are a search for 'tiempo vivo' (living time), for 'el vértigo maravilloso' (marvellous vertigo). An early collection *Fundación del entusiasmo* (1963) defines his work, for his poems enthusiastically celebrate life as in 'Atrás de la memoria' (Beyond memory) where the poet is born into 'la profunda felicidad /Que uno siente cuando conoce el aire' (the deep happiness that one feels when one knows air). His poetry explores inspiration, his own creativity. He wants to fly: 'Pido volar / En vez de ser ayudado por los vientos' (I demand to fly instead of being aided by the winds), where flying is believing that words have the magic to lift you out of mundane reality. Words are the 'llaves maestras de los pechos' (the master keys of our chests). His later work has passed through a 'concrete phase' (see below the section on concrete poetry), and then become more colloquial and disenchanted, but without abandoning his 'geiser' of rich metaphors so that Eduardo Milán could say about his complete poems: 'It is almost impossible to find in Latin American literature a body of work of such proteic intensity.'[11]

[10] Pizarnik, 'Los trabajos y la noche' (1965), in *Antología consultada* (Buenos Aires, 1968), p. 73. See Cristina Piña, *Alejandra Pizarnik* (Buenos Aires, 1991). Pizarnik's complete works appeared as *Obras completas* (Buenos Aires, 1990).

[11] *Fundación del entusiasmo* (Mexico, D. F., 1963), pp. 73 and 101. Montes de Oca's complete poems appeared as *Poesía reunida* (Mexico, D. F., 1971), and as *Pedir el fuego* (Mexico, D. F., 1987). Milán, *Una cierta mirada* (Mexico, D. F., 1989), p. 101. (My translation.)

Another Mexican poet, Homero Aridjis (b. 1940), also participated in the surrealistic adventure. There is a torrential quality to Aridjis's early poetry that suggests a litany, almost a lyrical narrative. *Mirándola dormir* (Watching her sleep) (1964) is the poet's meditation on a sleeping woman, borrowing magical insights from Octavio Paz's view of woman in *Piedra de sol* (Sun stone) (1957). The long poem incorporates dialogues, monologues and mind-flow sequences in long lines with repeated words and leitmotifs. Woman becomes all women, Eve and Bérenice, man's opposite without whom there is no revelation, no poetry. Aridjis's lyrical expansion reaches its climax in *Perséfone* (1967). In this erotic lyrical novel, without a plot or well-defined characters, Aridjis recreates the Goddess of the Dead and the Underworld, an insatiable amorous woman turned into a whore in a brothel. Aridjis privileges the gaze, and names erotic parts in a hypnotic litany. Several passages embody his theory of regenerative love pulling people back to their 'confused beginning' and origins, charting a descent into a more meaningful self. The men who arrive at the brothel 'had left their brains, hearts and teeth in a closet, had put on their sense at random and in haste, putting memory on their knees and souls in their genitals'. All the time Persephone, slightly absent and mysterious, controls this erotic ritual of self-knowledge.

Aridjis has also mastered the short lyric. In *Los espacios azules* (The Blue spaces) (1968), and especially in *Quemar las naves* (To Burn the Boats) (1975) and *Vivir para ver* (1977) we see how vision predominates in poetry celebrating light, this world, and the here and now. In 'Quemar las naves' Aridjis moves from Cortés's daring act of burning his boats, to impersonating several Mexican figures from Aztec deities to Emiliano Zapata. The poem 'Carta de México' (Letter from Mexico) captures Aridjis' sense of the haunting Mexican past: 'Por estas callejuelas/ ancestros invisibles/ caminan con nosotros' (Along these backstreets invisible ancestors walk with us), that ends with the sun shining on the poet's face, who will also become transparent. Ardijis is genuinely lyrical, not letting his intellect interfere with the poem's music. He tends to expand endlessly and rely on a piling up of images and repetitions to create sense.[12]

The surrealistic tradition privileges the word as capable of recreating reality through the imagination. It relies on opening the mind's verbal

---

[12] Aridjis's complete poems *Obra poética, 1960–1986* (Mexico, D. F., 1988). See Emir Rodríguez Monegal's interview in *El arte de narrar* (Caracas, 1969). Aridjis's novels include *1492. Vida y tiempo de Juan Cabezón de Castilla* (Mexico, D. F., 1985) and *Memorias del nuevo mundo* (Mexico, D. F., 1988).

sluice-gates to allow words to emerge beyond the self's control. Another surrealistic strand situates reality completely within language itself. A suspicious critical attitude to the inner thought processes is the theme of Venezuelan poet Rafael Cadenas (b. 1930). He writes a poetry of divided selves, of the mind's 'trampas'. 'Combate' from *Falsas maniobras* (1966) sets the poem solely in the arena of the poet's inner selves: 'Estoy frente a mi adversario. /Lo miro . . . lo derribo . . . Veo su traje en el suelo, las manchas de sangre . . . él no está por ninguna parte y yo me desespero' (I'm opposite my adversary. I look at him . . . knock him over . . . I see his suit on the ground, blood stains . . . he is nowhere and I get desperate). Cadenas's poems border on aphorisms and prose, there is no outer reality, yet the inner self barely exists; 'Tú no existes' (You don't exist) he writes about himself in 'Fracaso' (Failure).[13]

Argentine poet Roberto Juarroz (1925–95) began publishing in 1958, collecting his 13 books under the same title *Poesía vertical* (Vertical poetry). He also deals with inner verbal paradoxes, relating the slippery self to devious words, rather than to understanding current history, writing a poetry of 'ser' (being), of 'pensamientos' (thoughts). The consistent, solid self is dismantled in sudden inversions and enigmas. Breaking down automatic verbal associations, allows liberating insights to enter the mind, as he claims in his essay 'Poesía y realidad' (1987). In poem 2 of *Tercera poesía vertical* (Third Vertical Poetry) (1965), he plays with his false identity: 'El otro que lleva mi nombre / ha comenzado a desconocerme' [the other who carries my name has began to unknow me], to end 'Imitando su ejemplo, / ahora empiezo yo a desconocerme. / Tal vez no exista otra manera / de comenzar a conocernos.' [Imitating his example I now begin to unknow myself. Perhaps there is no other way to begin to know yourself] Inside the self is a 'vacío' [emptiness], that is also the emptiness of the apparently solid outside world. Juarroz's nihilistic, quasi-Buddhist stance, depends on defying words. In Juarroz's work (as in Cadenas's) the process of writing (and reading) a poem is clearing the mind of its rubble so that reality appears as it really is: 'Bautizar el mundo/ sacrificar el nombre de las cosas/ para ganar su presencia' (To baptize the world, to sacrifice the name of things to win their presence). His creed is completely mentalist: 'La imaginación es la verdadera historia del mundo'

---

[13] Cadenas, *Falsas maniobras* (Caracas, 1966), p. 15. Cadenas's first three books were collected in 1979. *Memorial* (Caracas, 1977) contains work from 1970–75. See José Balza, *Lectura transitoria sobre la poesía de Rafael Cadenas* (Caracas, 1973).

(Imagination is the real history of the world). There is no local colour, no reference to South-American-ness.[14]

Many further names could be added to the Latin American surrealistic tradition, but all share an apolitical stance, a belief in the liberating power of the imagination, a trust in words as carrying hidden enriching meanings, and a belief that the world and history are distorted by the traps of language itself. In the 1950s and 1960s important literary magazines like Raúl Gustavo Aguirre's *Poesía Buenos Aires* (Argentina), Sergio Mondragón's *El corno emplumado* (Mexico), *El techo de la ballena* (Venezuela),[15] Gonzalo Arango and Jaime Jaramillo Escobar's *Nadaísmo* (Colombia), Miguel Grinberg's *Eco contemporáneo* (Argentina), amongst many others, develop surrealistic rebellion by incorporating the U.S. beat poets, jazz, and later the hippy movement, slowly to become politicized in the late 1960s.[16]

POLITICAL POETRY

The Cuban revolution offered a way forward for many Latin American poets concerned with the scandalous injustices of their continent; it was possible to combine impatience for change with a revolutionary poetics. The icon of the 1960s and 1970s, Che Guevara, who died in Bolivia with a copy of Neruda's *Canto general* in his backpack, was seen as a poet who renounced writing to act, a kind of Rimbaud. The Romantic purifying act that changes a political stalemate allowed a generation of Latin American poets to combine praxis with art, writing a literal poetry, often directly against the obscure, mentalist metaphors of the surrealists, whose writing changed nothing.

Salvadorean poet Roque Dalton (1935–75), one of Latin America's most charismatic guerrilla poets, was executed by a dissident wing of his own revolutionary party. In an interview with Mario Benedetti in 1969, Dalton labelled himself a 'nieto de Vallejo' (Vallejo's grandson).[17] Dalton,

---

[14] The first volume of Juarroz's complete poems appeared in Buenos Aires in 1993. See his 'Poesía y realidad', *Academia argentina de letras* (1987), 371–405.

[15] See Edmundo Aray: 'Se quiere encender petardos dentro de la literatura' and 'La búsqueda de investigación de las basuras' in 'La actual literatura de Venezuela', in *Panorama actual de la literatura latinoamericana* (Madrid, 1971), p. 124.

[16] An orthodox view of Latin American surrealist poetry is Stefan Baciu, *Antología de la poesía surrealista latinoamericana* (Mexico, D. F., 1974). Baciu uses 'parasurrealista' for surrealistic poets. See his 'Algunos poetas parasurrealistas latinoamericanos', *Eco*, (Octobre 1980), 591–601, which includes Juarroz.

[17] Mario Benedetti, *Los poetas comunicantes* (Montevideo, 1972), p. 33.

like many of his generation, had turned to César Vallejo's colloquial, posthumous poetry that did not shun personal emotions, contradictions, humour, irony, sarcasm or satire. Vallejo's 'human' poems broke with metre, and reached out to its audience by employing slang, and stressing the vitality of voice. Vallejo showed how a poetry of plain truth need not flinch from being circumstantial, and being immediately understood by a sympathetic reader. By adapting Vallejo's kind of poetry guerrilla poets could become witnesses to their age.

Another crucial factor in Vallejo's influence was that he showed that a political poet did not need to prove his political stance by promoting party doctrine. For Vallejo a socialist poet evidenced 'an organic and tacitly socialist sensibility'. Vallejo's revolutionary intellectual was someone who 'fought writing and combating simultaneously'.[18] The most liberating consequence of Vallejo's lead was that subjectivity spread outwards into public life so that 'love' and 'politics' were freed from alienation. The key term here is *sincerity*, and the sincerity of a poem was tested by the poet's actions.

As a poet Dalton came into prominence when he won the Casa de las Américas poetry prize in 1969 for *Taberna y otros lugares* (Tavern and other places). In the poem titled 'América Latina' we have the intercontinental Cuban view, and why art cannot achieve the necessary revolution, for the poet may face the moon, employ foreign words, scratch his little violin, but that does not stop him smashing his face against the 'harsh wall of the barracks'. In 1973 he had joined the guerrilla group Ejército Revolucionario del Pueblo (ERP) without relinquishing writing poems. In fact he also tape-recorded a long interview with a militant survivor of the 1932 Izalco massacre, published as *Miguel Mármol* (1974). But his sarcastic poems written in Cuba began with *El turno del ofendido* (1963). It includes a short poem titled 'General Martínez': 'Dicen que fue un buen Presidente / porque repartió casas baratas / a los salvadoreños que quedaron . . . ' (They say you were a good president because you handed out cheap houses to the salvadoreans who remained) which illustrates Dalton's rhetoric of direct names, and the gruesome irony of free houses for the few peasants not killed by the army. Dalton returned to name Martínez when the ex-president was assassinated, in a long poem 'La segura mano de Dios' (The sure hand of God), written from Ahuachapán prison. This 1963 collection ends with a poem 'Lo terrible' confessing how Dalton had changed: 'Ahora la ternura no

---

[18] César Vallejo quotations from Angel Flores (ed.), *Aproximaciones a César Vallejo* (New York, 1971).

basta/ He probado el sabor de la pólvora' (Now tenderness will not do. I have tasted gunpowder). Again this symbol is literal, for only gunpowder will change all that Dalton records as evil and corrupt in his society. His *ars poetica* (1974) yokes real poetry with revolutionary action for poetry 'is not made of words alone'. The poem 'Historia de una poética' from *Poemas clandestinos* (1975) ends justifying his art for telling 'the plain truth'. Reading Dalton's words is to read the impressionistic, ironic diary of a combatant in the on-going Central American disasters.

The Argentine poet Juan Gelman (b. 1930) hit the headlines in his own country when he was sentenced to death by a faction of the Montonero guerrilla group to which he belonged. Later Gelman was not allowed to return to Alfonsín's democratic Argentina because of a pending arrest, despite the disappearances of Gelman's son and pregnant daughter-in-law. Following Menem's amnesty of the military, Gelman went into exile in Mexico in protest. Much of Argentina's turbulent history of the last thirty years can be read into Gelman's life and poems. He remains one of Argentina's more admired poets.

Gelman does not hide behind literary artifice. In his linked poems 'Carta abierta' (Open letter) he names his disappeared son, along with all the grim details. More importantly, Gelman's poetry both denounces existing social limitations, and offers a violent change. Gelman told Benedetti in 1971 that the Cuban revolution changed his feeling of impotence towards the Argentine communist party, fossilized in bureaucracy and Stalinism. He said: 'When we take power I think that the world will feel in a different way'; Revolution will usher in a new sensibility. Like Dalton, Gelman turned back to César Vallejo who 'profoundly influenced me both personally and in my poetry'. Like Vallejo Gelman does not separate politics from his deepest personal emotions. Real poetry is the consequence of ethical choices; 'el resultado de una manera de vivir' (the result of a way of living). [19]

All Gelman's emotive poetry is literalist. He stands against the surrealists − 'Te juro que no estoy haciendo surrealismo' (I swear I am not making surrealism). In 'Belleza' (Beauty) he mocks Octavio Paz, Lezama Lima and Alberto Girri as over-cultured symbolists, as idealist liberals. Poems do not end with poetic emotions, but lead to action: 'este poema / no se termina en estas páginas' (this poem does not end with these pages). The poet has no doubts about capitalism's egoism, about class society, about foreign intellectuals who do not understand Latin America, who do not know how a 'picana eléctrica' actually feels. He's working for the 'entierro del capitalismo' (burial of capitalism). Poet and revolutionary become synonymous.

From *Velorio del solo* (Funeral wake for the solitary man) (1961) Gelman establishes his guerrilla identity. The short poem 'Nacimiento de la poesía' links gun shots with words. In *Gotán* (1962, 'tango' respelt) Gelman evokes the erotic thrill of clandestine guerrilla activity in the Montoneros as 'como un hombre que entra temblando en el amor' (as a man who enters into love trembling). This book ends with Gelman's rebirth as the Guevarist New Man. *Cólera buey* (1967) links the guerrilla's 'bellas aventuras' (beautiful adventures), with 'tiros en la noche' (shots in the night). The poem 'Masacres de guerrilleros' (Massacres of guerrillas) ends with a boast 'por fin hay muertos por la patria' (at last people have died for their country). His next collection *Fábulas* (1971), eulogizes guerrilla groups. The topic of *Hechos* (poems written between 1974–78) is the clandestine life 'probando pistolas acomodando cargadores / los compañeros // parecen brillar inmortales o lejos de la muerte/ vivos/ en el esfuerzo de probar/ sin// pensar en la suerte adversa favorable' (trying out fitting charges the compañeros seem to shine immortal far from death alive struggling to prove settle without worrying about good or bad luck). Gelman has dispensed with punctuation, with metaphor. From exile in 1976 Gelman recalled 'la alegría de combatir', and guerrilla friends killed and 'disappeared' as he fights political apathy.

A name of a dead 'combatiente' that occurs often in Gelman's poetry is his poet friend Francisco 'Paco' Urondo, a Montonero leader killed in a shoot out in 1976. Urondo had written an essay *Veinte años de poesía argentina, 1940–1960* (1968), criticizing the poets before him for vague anti-Peronist stances, and a total lack of real political commitment. Urondo was one of the intellectual leaders of the 1960s and 1970s, becoming rector of Buenos Aires university after being released from prison under Argentina's caretaker president Cámpora in 1973. Urondo's choice of death rather than surrender became heroic for Gelman, and many others.[20] In a conversation with Roberto Mero, Gelman evokes this exemplary status: 'despite clandestinity, Urondo did not stop writing and fin-

[20] On Urondo, see Jason Wilson, 'The poet as hero', *London Magazine* (February, 1987), 51–60; (trans. in *Culturas. Suplemento de Diario 16*, 128, 1987, iii–v and in *Hojas universitarias*, Bogotá, 4/32, 113–24).

ished a book of poems before he died. I repeat, this example is very important'.[21]

However, Gelman's poems are more than sincere reflections of a revolutionary out to change consciousness for they are crafted with suppressed punctuation, no capitals, lines ending with dashes, neologisms, gender changes, and slogans in a melancholic, colloquial and angry tone. Many of the poems are one long question. He ensured that poetry has been rescued from academic analysis, and literary history, to be read as a *testimonio* to a fanatic mind-frame that both fascinates and repels.[22]

Many poets took up arms to change their societies as quickly as possible, and to recover a sense of personal authenticity. The best known are Otto René Castillo, a Guatemalan poet, who joined Fuerzas Armadas Rebeldes (FAR) in 1966, was ambushed and tortured to death in 1967, the Nicaraguan Leonel Rugama (1950–70) who died under Somoza, and the Peruvian Javier Heraud (1942–63).[23] There are even more poets whose poems invoke a similar ideology but who did not become guerrillas, who just resisted under dictatorships. The Honduran poet Roberto Sosa (b. 1930) summed up the options: 'For Central American writers there is no road left but to be in favor of the oligarchies or against them.'[24]

When Ernesto Cardenal (b. 1925), the charismatic, ex-Sandinista minister of culture, and priest, began publishing his poems in the 1940s it was under two critical influences, one literary, the other political. As we had argued, literary surrealism had an enormous liberating impact in Latin American poetry for it seemed to combine personal freedom of expression within a revolutionary context. Cardenal first published poems in 1946 in free verse. However the ferocious political situation under the successive dictatorships of the Somozas made Cardenal reconsider the point of merely personal liberation in a written text. From this questioning emerged one of the constants of Cardenal's developing poetics: namely, the position of the poet's 'ego' is made secondary to the need to write a poem that urges action. By taking the *effect* of the poem on the reader as central to the poem's area of action, the more Romantic notion of the poem as the sincere expression of the poet's own inner world is relegated to the past. Cardenal discovered the means to carry out his new perception of the

[21] Roberto Mero, *Conversaciones con Juan Gelman. Contraderrota, Montoneros y la revolución perdida* (Buenos Aires, 1989), p. 120.
[22] Gelman's poetry was collected in 2 vols. as *Interrupciones* (Buenos Aires, 1988).
[23] See Mario Benedetti's anthology of assassinated guerrilla poets, *Poesía trunca. Poesía latinoamericana revolucionaria* (Madrid, 1980).
[24] Sosa interview in Sosa, *The Difficult Days* (Princeton, N.J., 1983), p. xi.

role of the poem in an illiterate country like Nicaragua through his reading, while studying at Columbia University in New York (1947–9), of Ezra Pound. Cardenal began translating Pound, aware that most of the Latin American poets of his generation were still looking towards French culture, especially surrealism. To Cardenal, Pound's *Cantos* with their incorporation of quotations, with the collage technique of confronting documentary texts with Chinese poems, and with their ambitious attempt to go beyond the limitations of an individual's private world, suggested a new technique Cardenal called 'exteriorismo', paying more attention to the outer than to the inner world.

The political context to Cardenal's poetry further drives the ego-obsessed Romantic out of the poems. In 1961 in Mexico Cardenal published his *Epigramas,* based, through Pound, on reading Latin and Greek poets. Cardenal developed a counterpointing technique of opposing the classical past (Caesar, etc.) with the Central American present (Somoza). By pretending to write love poems, he avoided direct political denunciation. His little poem 'Imitación de Propercio' (Imitation of Propertius) ends 'Y ella me prefiere, aunque soy pobre, a todos los millones de Somoza' (And she prefers me, poor, to all Somoza's millions). Through Pound, Cardenal also learnt that a poem must be clear, and immediately understood, as Cardenal said to his muse Claudia: 'Los he escrito sencillos para que tú los entiendas' ('I wrote them simply so that you will understand them).

For protest poetry to work on its audience it must be direct, immediately understandable, and in Latin America, readable aloud. Pablo Neruda had lead the way in the late 1930s with his realization that a poem must be read aloud to spread beyond the confines of the printed word, and the few who can afford to buy books. All Cardenal's post-1950s poetry is narrative. It avoids the condensation of meaning in metaphors, and uses the syntax of prose.

In some ways Cardenal, by expanding what can be included in a lyrical poem, becomes the unofficial historian of Nicaragua, then Central America, and finally for the whole Latin American continent. In *Hora 0* (1960) there are poems with specific references to local revolutionaries like Adolfo Báez Bone or Sandino; he names places, dictators, characters from the past and the present that have no universal poetic appeal as such but represent his version of evil. This moral vision allows Cardenal to blend his Christian messianism (he was ordained in 1965 in Colombia) with his reading of Marx. *Salmos* (1964), combines he re-writing of the Biblical psalms with his critique of Somoza. This political-religious vein continues through the poems of *Oración por Marylin Monroe y otros poemas* (1965) where in the title poem Cardenal mentions Monroe's last unanswered phone call and ends 'Contesta Tú el teléfono' (You (Lord) answer the phone). The title of that poem shows how Cardenal has moved beyond Pound to the pop-culture of the United States of the 1960s giving Marylin Monroe, an Andy Warhol icon, a moral value. His criticism of US consumer culture flows from this stance.

In the collections *El estrecho dudoso* (1969) and *Homenaje a los indios americanos* (1969) Cardenal expands his poems into the history of the conquest of Central America, and catalogues the pre-Columbian Indian heritage, based on archival studies, incorporating voices and documents into the poems so that a reader actually learns about the forgotten past. A good example is 'Economía de Tahuantinsuyu' (Economy of Tahuantinsuyu) where Cardenal contrasts capitalist North American with Pre-Columbian uses of money where political truth and religious truth 'eran para el pueblo una misma verdad' (were but the one truth for the people). The poem that best draws together Cardenal's radical moral vision is his lament on the death of his Trappist poet mentor Thomas Merton (whose poems he translated into Spanish in 1963) which ends 'Sólo amamos o somos al morir./ El gran acto final de dar todo el ser. / o.k.' (We only love and we only are on dying [when we die]. The final act of giving all one's being. o.k.). Read in conjunction with the notes he was allowed to write during his stay at the Trappist monastery – see *Gethsemani Ky* (1960) – and few would doubt Cardenal's deserved position as a poet.[25]

Engaged poetry is defined by its political circumstances; it forces literal references on to the reader to remove doubt; it challenges a surrealist leaning on deep associations; it relies on voice and colloquialisms, and above all, its imperative is to communicate emotionally. A prime intention was to make poetry matter again in the struggle for social justice, and this still concerns younger poets.

## CONCRETE AND NEO-BAROQUE POETRY

Poetry has always had a formal side despised by the post-Romantic poets to the extent that the Parisian surrealists, in their first surrealist manifesto of 1924, claimed that anybody could be a poet and write poetry because

---

[25] See Cardenal's *Antología* (Buenos Aires, 1971).

poetry was the unconscious manifesting itself in surprising images. Throughout the twentieth century, metre has been slowly abandoned for a free verse that promised to mirror a free imagination. Against this belief many poets have argued that form and craft define the poem. There is an alternative tradition enshrining the poem as a game with words that goes back to the Golden Age master Luis de Góngora, and up to the Spanish poets clustered around Federico García Lorca who celebrated Góngora's tricentenary in 1925 with public acts in his homage.

This verbalist tradition mocks the literalist engaged poets, as well as those surrealists who believed in the magic qualities of words. Instead it asserts that poetry is purely verbal, and written, a game with a complete dictionary. Within the Hispanic tradition Góngora's *Soledades* (1612–17) defined poetic genius as making a reader creatively guess at metaphors. In the twentieth century this destructive playfulness was characterized by Vicente Huidobro in his polemical long poem *Altazor,* (1931) as provoking a 'cataclismo en la gramática' (cataclysm in grammar), and the 'simple sport de los vocablos' (the simple sport of words). Huidobro's seventh canto is nonsensical, neologisms perhaps imitating the new song that Huidobro's superman-poet hoped to write, beyond conventional Spanish.[26] César Vallejo's *Trilce* (1922), the title itself a neologism, also played with words so that a poem tended towards a visual object, with unexpected use of capitals, and no punctuation. Following Apollinaire's *calligrammes,* Huidobro had a poem called 'Moulin' (written in French) that was shaped like a windmill. During the same experimental period Juan José Tablada (1871–1945) also played with typography imitating a woman's eyes in the line 'rOstrOs de una mujer' where the capitalized O's look like 'her' eyes.

The most notorious group of poets who broke down the barriers between a poem and a picture were the pioneer Brazilian concrete poets grouped around the magazine *Noigandres* (a Provençal word derived from Ezra Pound), founded in 1952 by Augusto de Campos (b. 1931), and aided by his brother Haroldo de Campos (b. 1929) and Décio Pignatari (b. 1927). Concrete poetry was unofficially launched at an exhibition in São Paulo in 1956. Later a meeting with the Swiss-Bolivian Eugen Gomringer in Ulm, Germany, set up the international movement (which spread to Britain with Ian Hamilton Finlay). The Brazilian concretists are internationalists, and appear to begin from scratch in attempting to come to grips

[26] Vicente Huidobro, *Obras completas*, Vol. 1, (Santiago, 1963), p. 393.

with modernity, but they also look back to Mallarmé, Ezra Pound, e.e. cummings, and rediscover Oswald de Andrade.

The term 'concrete' is opposed to 'abstract', that is, these poets isolate the sign itself, the materiality of the word, its semantics not its phonetics. An early Haroldo de Campos poem (1956) is word play 'O āmago do ōmega' (Core of omega) where the pun leads to the heart of linguistic matter. His 1979 poem 'Esboço para uma nékuia' (Sketches for a Nekuia) has the word 'branco' (white) capitalized in a corner of an entirely white page. The whole poem has isolated words drifting across the page's empty white spaces so that the poem is understood pictorially first, without metre, or much syntax. Haroldo de Campos accompanies the poem with a learned note; he is professor of literary theory, a specialist on Poundian ideogrammes, a translator of James Joyce's *Finnegans Wake*.[27]

Augusto de Campos's verbal-visual experiments are hard to reproduce as he plays with typefaces, collages, and puns. 'Olho por ôlho' (eye for an eye) is made of clippings of eyes in the shape of a pyramid or skyscraper. 'A rosa doente' (O sick rose), based on a short William Blake poem, curls into the shape of a rose, using italic typeface. Décio Pignatari, a graphic artist and professor of information theory, has an engaged concrete poem from 1958 subverting a Coca-Cola advert, and moves in capitalized puns from 'beba coca cola' (drink coca-cola) to 'babe' (to slobber), 'caco' (pieces), 'cola' (glue), and ends 'cloaca' (sewer). Another Pignatari concrete poem has a US dollar bill with a face of Christ rather than Washington, with the title 'Cr$isto é a solução' (Chri$t is the solution). Another is a cine-poem with large single letters spelling 'ILFE', each one on a page, forcing the reader to re-organize them into 'LIFE'.[28]

Despite their debt to technology, and their roots in a Brazil that had just created Brasília out of nowhere in the style of Le Corbusier, the concrete poets were seen as critical poets, especially of manipulation through advertising. A later group round a magazine *Praxis* and led by Mário Chamie (b. 1933) developed this critical visualized text. Chamie's poem 'TV' is a good example of combining verbal games with a political message. One positive aspect of these verbal experiments was to undermine automatic verbal opulence by objectifying single words. All the

<hr>

[27] See Haroldo de Campos interview with Julio Ortega in *Syntaxis* 8–9 (1985), 15–32. Most of his poetry was collected in *Xadrez de Estrelas. Percurso textual, 1949–1974* (São Paulo, 1976).

[28] Augusto de Campos collected his poetry in *Viva vaia* (São Paulo, 1979), and again in 1986. Décio Pignatari's collected poems can be found in *Poesia pois é poesia (1950–1975)* and *Poetc (1976–1988)*.

major concrete poets moved on into further formal experiments playing with meta-texts, with neologisms, to Haroldo de Campos's 'Galactic' project finally published in 1985.

If there is an avant-garde still today in Latin America it follows from the kind of work the concretists were doing in Brazil, one of the few movements to cross out of Brazilian literature and attract poets like Octavio Paz, Severo Sarduy and Néstor Perlongher. It also pushed Hispanic poets to rediscover poets like Argentine Oliveiro Girondo (1891–1967) whose last book *En la masmédula* (1954), is one long attack on the word and syntax, creating a kind of ur-talk, stripping language of its expressiveness to make it just a material object, as Tamara Kamenszain has noted.[29] Equally crucial to this neo-baroque avant-garde is the role of Cuban José Lezama Lima (1912–76), whose complete works were published in 1970, and who wrote an opaque poetry based on obscure metaphors, that highlighted the sound of the word at the expense of sense, but densely allusive to literary history, whose point was that it mysteriously defied literal meanings.

Paris-based Cuban Severo Sarduy (1937–94) has broken the boundaries between prose and poetry, and in collections like *Big Bang* (1974) playfully mixes allusions to science and sex typographically, following the concrete poets. In his essay *Barroco* (1974), he quotes Lezama Lima to define Góngora's baroque strategies as the elimination of part of a term, ellipsis, in order to make the other part stand out. To suppress half the metaphor was to eliminate ugliness, and evil, by never naming it, saying something for something else. This is the peculiar feeling that reading Lezama Lima gives of half understanding the meaning. In this sense neo-baroque poetry is anti-realist, anti-literalist, and teasingly playful.

In Argentina the collection *Oro* (1975) by Arturo Carrera (b. 1948) can only read as a typographically inventive litany where the words and short phrases are not much more than the pure sound of an *escriba* (scribe) just writing, and the reader just using his eyes, displacing meaning continuously. In his later *Arturo y yo* (1980), mockingly re-creating childhood perceptions of the 'campo', one line can be converted into a poetics, 'el sonido puro que rapta el deseo' (pure sound that abducts desire). The sound of language wakes up secret desires, that cannot be defined except as 'gozo' (pleasure), anticipation of a meaning that never quite happens.

---

[29] Oliveiro Girondo, *Obras completas* (Buenos Aires, 1968). Tamara Kamenszain, *El texto silencioso: tradición y vanguardia en la poesía sudamericana* (Mexico, D. F., 1985), p. 19.

Argentine Néstor Perlongher (1949–93) takes this neo-baroque into politics with his *Alambres* (1987) that ends on the litany poem 'Cadáveres' (corpses) where, as Perlongher said in an interview, the references are omitted. The title of his latest book *Parque Lezama* (1990) is a pun on an actual plaza in Buenos Aires, and a tradition harking back to the poet Lezama Lima. The poem 'Danzig' opens in baroque Spanish with 'La rutilancia de las lentejuelas / en un rimmel de tan marmóreo transparente / el rebote de los ojares . . . ' Perlongher explained his subversions of meaning when he evoked his love of the word 'jade' in Spanish, which forced him to complete it by saying 'jadeo' (panting), where the first word jade contains a secret erotic charge.[30]

There are formalist poets writing against surrealist facilities, and political faiths, who turn to the craft of metres, and the defamiliarizing of pure pleasure in sounds. One of the best known is the Peruvian Carlos Germán Belli (b. 1927) who uses baroque Spanish syntax, allusions, and anachronisms in an expressionist attempt to capture contemporary anguish and 'carencia' (lack). His neo-baroque stance is not similar to Lezama Lima, but by colliding old forms with modern misery manages to capture the present in Peru. In his first collection *Poemas* (1958) the poem 'Segregación N. 1' defines the area of his poetic explorations as an insignificant Peruvian faced with authorities: 'Yo, mamá, mis dos hermanos / y muchos peruanitos / abrimos un hueco hondo, hondo / donde nos guarecemos,/ porque arriba todo tiene dueño' (I, mother, my two brothers and many little Peruvians open a deep deep hole where we can hide because above everything has an owner), to end with a wonderful diminutive: 'y nosotros rojos de vergüenza, / tan sólo deseamos desaparecer / en pedacititos' (and we red with shame only want to disappear into tiny little bits). The downtrodden bureaucrat-poet emerges questioning his body, his love-life, being a Peruvian, as in later collections Belli contorts his syntax, relies on deliberate archaisms, and hyperbaton. By *¿Oh hada cibernética* (O cybernetic fairy) (1962), he counterpoints the classic language of the Spanish Golden Age, with a black-humoured nihilism, as in 'Una desconocida voz . . . ': 'una desconocida voz me dijo:/ 'no folgarás con Filis, no, en el prado,/ si con hierros te sacan/ del luminoso claustro, feto mío;'/y ahora que en este albergue arisco / encuentro me ya desde varios lustros,/ pregunto por qué no fui despeñado, / desde el más alto risco, / por tartamudo o cojo o manco o bizco' (an unknown voice said to me You will

[30] Luis Chitarroni interviews Perlongher in *La papirola*, 3 April 1988, 10–14.

not couple with Filis in the field, no, not even if they take you out with irons from the luminous cloister, o my fetus).[31] In Belli's case the deliberate archaisms heighten the drama of coping with actuality. Belli collected his poetry under the significant title *El pie sobre el cuello* (1967) that perfectly describes his ironic view of the downtrodden poet today. When he presented this book in Lima Belli recalled his development: 'Like other Latin American poets I was dazzled by surrealism' so much so that he preferred the sound of words to their sense. Then he turned to baroque extravagance: ' . . . I try to dominate an atemporal syntax that is not of our time, based on hyperbaton and elipsis. I deliberately affect my language with archaisms.'[32] In 1970 he published *Sextinas y otros poemas* where the verse form gives the title, a homage to formalism.

## ANTIPOETRY

Several critics have seen in anti-poetry the style that matches the post-1950s period, for anti-poetry is a questionning of the value of poetry and of the inflated egos of poets from within the poems. Anti-poems correspond to what the critic Michael Hamburger called the 'new austerity' and arose out of 'an acute distrust of all the devices by which lyrical poetry had maintained its autonomy'. Anti-poetry as defined empirically by Hamburger is based on the urge to communicate as directly as prose; it seeks to reveal socio-political concerns without metaphors, and it uses humour and irony to deflate, to demythify.[33]

In Latin America anti-poetry is a reaction to the kind of self-restricted aestheticism embodied in Juan Ramón Jiménez's 'poesía pura' against which Pablo Neruda argued vehemently for a poetry that was 'impura', that desublimated art, that reeked of sweat and work and the street. But it was another Chilean, Nicanor Parra (b. 1914) who coined the term anti-poetry in his *Poemas y antipoemas* (Poems and antipoems) (1954). It is apt that 'poems' appears in this title as well, for a limited definition of anti-poetry in Parra's case was his reaction against his first lyrical, but never re-edited, collection *Cancionero sin nombre* (Song Book without a name) (1937). Anti-poetry is first of all, anti-lyrical poetry, because lyrical poetry does not capture the alienation and anguish of the age in its 'sweet music'.

[31] Belli, *El pie sobre el cuello* (Montevideo, 1967), pp. 16–17 and 45–6.
[32] Javier Sologuren, *Tres poetas. tres obras. Belli. Delgado. Salazar Bondy* (Lima, 1969), pp. 35–6.
[33] Michael Hamburger, *The Truth of Poetry. Tensions in Modern Poetry from Baudelaire to the 1960s* (London, 1969), p. 220.

Critic Fernando Alegría defined three elements in anti-poetry in an essay published in 1970. It narrates; it has humour; it uses colloquial language. He discovered a tradition that begins with the Mexican Ramón López Velarde, passes through César Vallejo, into Nicanor Parra, Gonzalo Rojas, and Ernesto Cardenal. Alegría summarised: 'anti-poetry which has been anarchic, an anti-rhetorical shawl, found a direct, violent language that restored a lost reality to man'.[34] Anti-poetry has been accused of not being political enough (by Roberto Fernández Retamar),[35] but its basic strategy was to make poetry more important through making it demotic.

Anti-poetry in Brazil also reflects a growing scepticism towards subjective lyrical poetry defined early on by Manuel Bandeira's urge to say 'as coisas mais simples e menos intencionais' (the simplest and least intended things), to the later works of Carlos Drummond de Andrade (1902–87) epitomized in his title *Lição de coisas* (Lesson of things) (1962). Drummond's return to simplicity appeals to his roots, in his family poems, and like César Vallejo, asking his mother 'e o desejo muito simples' (the very simple desire) to mend his soul. Direct, anti-metaphorical poems about tables ('A mesa', 1951), stones, apples. Earlier in 'Nosso tiempo' (1945) Drummond had defined this new aggressive poet as somebody who 'declina de toda responsabilidade/ na marcha do mundo capitalista / e com sus palavras, intuicões, símbolos e outras armas / promete ajudar / a destruí-lo / como uma pedreira, uma floresta, / um verme' (declines any responsibility in the march of capitalist society and with his words, intuitions, symbols and other weapons promise to help destroy it like a stone, a flower, a worm). Drummond's 'No meio do caminho' (1930) ('In the middle of the journey', echoing Dante) selects the stone as brute evidence of existence.[36]

João Cabral de Melo Neto (b. 1920) takes up this 'stone' in his poem 'A educacão pela pedra' (1966) where the bare stone symbolises the sertão's dry hardness, and becomes a poetics 'para aprender da pedra/ a de poética, sua carnadura concreta' (to learn from the stone a poetics, its concrete flesh), and thus 'e no idioma pedra se fala doloroso' (in a language of stone one speaks painfully). Cabral de Melo Neto's *Duas aguas* (1956), can be seen as a watershed of this paring down of lyrical poetry in Brazil where his long poem 'Uma faca só lâmina' (1955) (Only the blade of a knife) ends

[34] Fernando Alegría, 'La antipoesía', *Literatura y revolucíon* (Mexico, D. F., 1971), pp. 204 and 240.
[35] Roberto Fernández Retamar, 'Anti poesía y poesía conversacional en América Latina', in *Panorama actual de la literatura latinoamericana* (Madrid, 1971), p. 342.
[36] See Carlos Drummond de Andrade's *Nova reunião*, 2 vols. (Rio de Janeiro, 1983).

with his poetics of 'the presence of reality' as more pressingly real than an 'image' of it. Like the Hispanic anti-poets, Cabral de Melo Neto had moved on to this distrust with lyrical aesthetics from surrealism's rebellion against organized social life.[37]

As early as 1948 Nicanor Parra sought 'a poetry based on facts and not combinations or literary figures. In this sense I feel closer to a scientist. I am against the affected form of traditional poetic language . . . '; and all this because he wants to trap 'modern life' in a poetry that coldly, scientifically, looked at contemporary man.[38] As a theoretical physicist (he became a professor, even wrote a textbook on relativity) Parra began writing anti-Neruda poems in England in 1948. Over his career as a poet he has progressively eliminated lyrical elements until he gave up writing poems, and in 'Artefactos' (1972) just copied down graffiti, or cut out bits from newspapers. Poetry to Parra, like to Drummond, was always outside the poet's subjectivity, in 'cosas' [things]. He refuses effusive and emotional reactions; he denies the ego its omnipotent place at the centre of personality. Many of his 1954 poems are about degradation, exhaustion, failure, hysteria. The poet 'es un hombre como todos' (a man like anybody else); there is nothing special about being a poet. The new anti-poetry is not humanistically uplifting; it does not teach people how they should be. Anti-poetry for Parra simply mirrors the absurdity of life ('la vida no tiene sentido' – life has no sense), that culture and thinking get you nowhere. Parra, like Drummond, takes a stone to invert aesthetics. To Manuel Durán he said in 1972: 'My personal experience is that the ugliest stone is superior to the most beautiful statue.'[39]

His self-portrait as a teacher summarises his world view in its sarcasms, and shifts of tone: '¿Qué me sucede? -¡Nada! / me los he arruinado haciendo clases: / La mala luz, el sol, / La venenosa luna miserable. / Y todo ¡para qué! / Para ganar un pan imperdonable / Duro como la cara del burgués / Y con olor y con sabor a sangre./ ¡Para qué hemos nacido como hombres / Si nos dan una muerte de animales!' (I have ruined my life teaching. The bad light, the sun, the miserable, poisenous moon. What is happening to me? Nothing. And all this, for what? To earn unforgiving bread as hard as a bourgeois's face and with the smell and taste of blood. Why were we born as men if they kill us like animals?). From a working-class background, brother to Chile's great folk singer Violeta Parra (1917–

[37] See João Cabral de Melo Neto, *Poesia completa, 1940–1980* (Lisbon, 1986).
[38] Parra in Huga Zambelli, *13 poetas chilenos* (Santiago, Chile, 1948), p. 79. (My translation.)
[39] Durán interviewed Parra in *Plural*, 6 (1972), pp. 10–13. (My translation.)

67), Nicanor Parra kept his distance from political parties, saw himself as a 'francotirador' (sharpshooter), was denounced by Cuba as the result of having had a cup of tea with Mrs Nixon in 1970, stayed independent in Chile under Pinochet, and whose black humour has not endeared him to any faction. As he said in 'Telegramas' (1970): 'Yo simplemente rompo los moldes' (I simply break moulds). His unpredictable amalgam of vulgarity, nostalgia, contradictions, humour and exaggerations is based on the persona of buffoon to society's serious intellectuals. Anti-poetry is a violent critique of existing society: 'mi postulado fundamental proclama que la verdadera seriedad es cómica' (My fundamental postulate is that true seriousness is comic). In his long poem 'Los vicios del mundo moderno' (The vices of the modern world) he stated: 'El mundo moderno es una gran cloaca' (the modern world is a sewer). His recent work impersonates a nineteenth-century religious crank called the 'Cristo de Elqui'.[40]

Within the Chilean national tradition Parra served as an antidote to the sensual dominance of Pablo Neruda's partisan poetry. Many excellent younger poets followed in Parra's wake of mocking and demythifying, especially Enrique Lihn (1929–88) who had edited a selection of Parra's poetry in 1952 and Gonzalo Rojas (b. 1917), who had emerged from the Chilean surrealist group. But anti-poetry travelled beyond Chilean frontiers. A good example comes with the Mexican poet Jaime Sabines (b. 1925) whose down-to-earth prosey poems stand out against the serious poetics of Octavio Paz. Sabines, like Parra, writes an urban, anguished poetry, where the poet is not protected by culture and education, what he calls the 'tufo de literato' (the stink of a literary man). In his poetry there are few cultural references, and the language is direct, communicative, vulgar, emotional and colloquial. Like Parra again he uses antithesis, paradox and opposites to provoke emotions, rather than metaphor and images. He too believes in reality: 'la realidad es superior a los sueños' (reality is superior to dreams). Nothing is especially poetic; he exploits bad taste, discards discretion. For Sabines the only answer to disease and death is sex: 'No hay más/ Sólo mujer' (there is nothing else. Only woman). He defines life: 'Uno nació desnudo, sucio / en la humedad directa,/ y no bebió metáforas de leche' (one was born naked, dirty, in direct humidity and did not drink metaphors of milk).

Sabines began publishing with *Horal* (1950). His main collection

---

[40] Parra collected his poems in *Obra gruesa* (Santiago, Chile, 1969). Later work includes *Sermones y prédicas del cristo de Elqui,* (Valparaíso, 1979), *Hojas de parra* (1985), and *Chistes para desorientar a la poesía* (Madrid, 1989).

*Tarumba,* appeared in 1956, and his collected poems *Recuento de poemas* in 1962, followed by *Nuevo recuento de poemas* in 1977. His street-wise poetics emerge in 'A estas horas, aquí' (At these hours, here): 'Habría que bailar ese danzón que tocan en el cabaret de abajo,/ dejar mi cuarto encerrado / y bajar a bailar entre borrachos./ Uno es un tonto en una cama acostado,/ sin mujer, aburrido, pensando, / sólo pensando' (I would have to dance this dance they're playing in the cabaret below, leave my stuffy room and go down and dance with drunks. One is a fool lying in bed, without a woman, bored, thinking, only thinking) where the colloquial voice speaks directly about experience.

A younger Mexican poet (and excellent fiction writer),[41] José Emilio Pacheco (b. 1939) began his writer's career working on the literary magazine *Estaciones* attacking Paz in 1957 for being 'contaminated' by Parisian surrealism. A few years later in 1961 Pacheco publicly declared that Paz's version of surrealism had led to his best poetry. Over those years Pacheco had been seduced into admiring Paz's version of what it meant to be a poet in post-revolutionary Mexico. However, as Pacheco has said, his generation grew up with cinema as the cultural model, and with the 1959 Cuban revolution as their version of 1960s liberation (more politicised than their European counterparts).[42] This has allowed Pacheco to move into an area of writing that is completely his own, distancing himself politically, and owing little to Paz.

The book of poems that heralded this change in tone was *No me preguntes cómo pasa el tiempo* (1969), where the title proclaims Pacheco's particular vision of life and art as grounded in inexorable passing time. Passing time is one of the great lyrical and emotional themes of poetry, and Pacheco explores this in fascinating ways. One strand that typifies his work is the stress on dismissing the traditional poet's ego. Pacheco has consistently refused to glorify himself, dislikes giving interviews, and places the poem above its creator the poet. He often impersonates a historical character, puts on a mask, and employs ironic set-phrases, leading critics to talk of his 'collage' technique.

Following this avoidance of his own ego Pacheco is a great respector of the lyric tradition while at the same time affirming that nobody reads poetry any more, and that it has lost its cultural importance, thus affirming an ambivalent belief in the 'survival of the genre'. His poem 'Crítica

---

[41] Pacheco's fiction includes *El viento distante* (Mexico, D. F., 1963); *Morirás lejos* (Mexico, D. F., 1967); *Las batallas en el desierto* (Mexico, D. F., 1981).
[42] Pacheco in *Confrontaciones. Los narradores ante el público* (Mexico, D. F., 1966), pp. 246–8.

de la poesía' (Critique of Poetry) reveals this in brackets: '(La perra infecta, la sarnosa poesía, / risible variedad de la neurosis, / precio que algunos hombres pagan/ por ño saber vivir. / La dulce, eterna, luminosa poesía)' (The infected bitch, flea-bitten poetry, / a laughable variety of neurosis, / the price which some men pay / for not knowing how to live. / Oh sweet, eternal, luminous poetry.) In a confessedly post-Borgesian way Pacheco is aware that poetry only happens in a written poem, that he is a poet only when he writes a poem. This anti-Romantic stance remains subversive today, and links Pacheco with the anti-poetry tendency.

Another consequence of Pacheco's exploring passing time is his sense of relativity. The poet is a chronicler who comments on events from the limitations of his period. Fashions change, and history accelerates (a title of a short poem) so that passing time undermines any certainties, any 'truths'. Pacheco's poetry is littered with ironic references from the 1960s youth culture (for example, in a wonderful poem called 'Kodak'), from 1960s political positions. As a chronicler he has commented on the Vietnam war, on the massacre of students in Tlatelolco in 1968, on the ecological disaster that is Mexico City, and most recently on the 1985 earthquake in that city. Just the titles of his collections confirm this complex investigation into time and art from *Desde entonces* (1980), to *Tarde o temprano* (1980), which collects his poetry from 1958 to 1978. In 1986 he published *Miro la tierra,* hinting at the way he cooly observes life, followed in 1989 by *Ciudad de la memoria.* His distinctive voice is at odds with the more literal and obvious politicized poets, as well as those who still affirm the prestige and magic of art.

Another anti-poet who became a *cause célèbre* in 1971 was the Cuban Heberto Padilla (b. 1930). In his second collection of poems *El justo tiempo humano* (1962), written between 1953 and 1961 when he lived abroad in the United States and in London, there is a sequence dedicated to William Blake that contrasts his age with Blake's, but both share a fear of persecution by 'un inspector de herejías' (inspector of heresies), as if poets were natural dissidents to any regime. This outsider pose ended for Padilla in this book with his acceptance of a new role in revolutionary Cuba. In the title poem he accuses himself: 'Tú soñador de dura pupila, / rompe ya esa guarida de astucias / y terrores./ Por el amor de tu pueblo, ¡despierta!' (You dreamer with the hard pupil, break your cunning shelter of terros. For love of your people, wake up!). Publication of poems in Cuba was a problem due to the U.S. blockade and paper shortages but Padilla won the UNEAC (Union of

Cuban Writers and Artists) prize for *Fuera del juego* (off-side; out of play) (1969). When the book came out his irreverent attitude got him in deep trouble. We find a few poems in praise of Castro's revolution, and others mocking revolutionary seriousness, especially concerning Russia. Padilla adopted a Parra-like irony, even iconoclasm, which jarred with revolutionary earnestness. Padilla was aware that art does not always conform, that it is immoral, and warns himself in a short poem: 'No lo olvides, poeta. En cualquier sitio y época / en que hagas o en que sufras la Historia,/ siempre estará acechándote algún poema peligroso' (Don't forget it poet. In whatever place or period in which you make or suffer history some dangerous poem will always be lying in wait for you). His anti-poetry poetics push him to speak the truth ('Di la verdad'). He defends the apathetic Lezama Lima, accused of being an 'observer', an apt description of all anti-poets. In the title poem Padilla mocks the poet's role in the new society by saying no poets fit. The poem ends: '¡A ese tipo, despídanlo! / Ese no tiene aquí nada que hacer' (that chap, sack him. He's got nothing to do here). In the ironic 'Instrucciones para ingresar en una nueva sociedad' (Instructions to enter the new society) Padilla looks at the good Russian communist as optimistic, obedient, sporty and always applauding.[43]

When *Fuera del juego* was published UNEAC slipped in a note declaring it disagreed with Padilla's counter-revolutionary ideology. Following this Padilla was detained, and finally in court repented ('I have committed so many mistakes') in an extraordinary speech that puts the sincerity of his poetry in doubt. In this speech he despises his poet's pose: 'Yo, bajo el disfraz de un escritor rebelde, lo único que hacía era ocultar mi desafecto a la revolución' (I, under disguise of a rebel poet, have only hidden my hostility for the revolution). He criticized his *Fuera del juego* as packed with 'bitterness' and 'pessimism'; he lamented complaining about Cuba to foreign friends (like Enzensberger), lamented being a friend to Lezama Lima, and praised the revolution for getting him work. The Padilla case polarized the intellectual world with luminaries like Sartre, de Beauvoir, Calvino as well as Europeanized Latin Americans like Cortázar, Paz and Vargas Llosa signing a letter condemning Cuba, published in several newspapers.[44]

[43] Quotations from Padilla, *El justo tiempo humano* (Barcelona, 1970), pp. 71 and 88; *Fuera del juego* (Buenos Aires, 1969), pp. 17, 41 and 56. Padilla's novel is *En mi jardín pastan los héroes* (Barcelona, 1981); his memoirs, *Autoretrato del otro: la mala memoria* (Madrid, 1989).

[44] See 'Documentos. El caso Padilla' in *Libre*, 1 (1971), 95–145. (My translations.)

When the Peruvian poet Antonio Cisneros (b. 1942) won the Casa de las Américas poetry prize in 1968 for *Canto ceremonial contra un oso hormiguero* (Ceremonial song against an ant-eater) he confirmed that a new kind of poetry spoke to readers excited by Che, Mao and liberation movements. Cisneros did not adapt surrealism, or modify Neruda or Vallejo; he sounded different, wrote a narrative, mocking poetry with sudden shifts, juxtapositions, collage quotations, and colloquialisms, reminiscent of Ezra Pound, and U.S. beat poets like Allen Ginsburg.

At the heart of Cisneros's poetic lies a peculiar sense of being a stranger in his own country, at odds with the official histories, and uncomfortable with the rich Inca past (like the Mexican José Emilio Pacheco with his Aztec past). His uneasy distancing from the conquistadores, and from contemporary Lima society, allowed the poet to range through Europe and European cultures with a similar sense of it not quite meaning anything, illustrating Ezra Pound's 'botched civilization' from a Peruvian point of view.

His best poems present him as a politicized hippy who mocks his own bourgeois background and first marriage. He contrasts sordid power, and a rotten past with ecstatic moments lying on his back in the sun, or making love in the open. The old Inca sun becomes his point of reference, whether in St James's Park or in Budapest where the poet – 'el gran haragán' (the great layabout) – equates his years of exile, teaching in European universities, with cold rain and silence. But although Cisneros quotes from Leonard Cohen, and scatters his poems with 'piss' and 'shit', he is not just a sun-loving hippy seeking new sensations and refusing to work or think. His rebelliousness is more politicized (Cuba, guerrilla sympathies), and toughens his poetry. He is not seduced by European glamour. In a poem written from Southampton University he mocks those who believe in the reality of their cars, and that where they are 'is the world', where people are alienated by comfort, homes and a convenient forgetfulness. Life in rainy England leaves Cisneros shut 'entre mi caja de Corn Flakes / a escribir por las puras / sin corona de yerbas ni pata de conejo que me salven' (inside my box of Corn flakes / writing for the heck of it/ without a crown of herbs nor a rabbit's foot to save me)'. When Cisneros returned to live in Peru he continued his misfit's role of critic, turning to a religious and radical ecological view of Peru's poor stranded in 'an ocean of seaweed and jelly fish and a sandbank of shit'. Cisneros is honest, his irony deflates many of his culture's myths. He said: 'My country has a fabulous past but that culture does not belong to me anymore, and I can only appreciate its remains like any stranger',[45] where he speaks not only for Peruvians, but for all Latin Americans faced with their severed past, and the realities of underdevelopment.

The same shift towards a literalist anti-poetry can also be discerned in Brazilian poetry. Ferreira Gullar (b. 1930, real name José Ribamar Ferreira) is a good example. His second collection *A luta corporal* (The bodily struggle) where he sought an honest, precise poetry about things, sometimes close to the avant-garde appeared in 1951 (in 1958 he joined the Concretists in *Noigandres*). From 1964 he opposed the military until he went into exile in 1971. On his return he published *Poema sujo* (Dirty poem) (1977) that sums up his intention at looking at the seamy side of urban life. His anti-poetry poetics are summed up in the opening of 'A vida bate' (Life strikes): 'Não se trata do poemas sim do homem / e sua vida' (This does not deal with poems but with men and their life). In 'A casa' the poet asks who speaks, and locates simple things like a coin, or a mouse: 'Fala / talvez o rato morto fedendo até secar' (Perhaps the dead mouse speaks, stinking until it dries up). Gullar's poetry of things is subversive, politicized. In 'Coisas da Terra' (Things of the earth) he writes: 'São coisas, todas elas, / cotidianas, como bocas/ e mãos, sonhos, greves, / denúncias/ acidentes do trabalho e do amor. Coisas, / de que falam os jornais / as vezes tão rudes / as vezes tão escuras / que mesmo a poesia a ilumina com dificuldade' (They are things, all of them, daily, like mouths and hands, dreams, strikes, denunciations, work or love accidents. Things that newspapers talk about at times so crude, at times so obscure that even poetry illuminates them with difficulty). In another poem 'Agosto 1964' the poet is 'fatigado de mentiras' (tired of lies) as he returns from work in his bus he says 'Adeus Rimbaud,/ relógio de lilazes, concretismo,/ neoconcretismo, ficcões da juventude, adeus,/ que a vida / eu a compro à vista aos donos do mundo. / Ao peso dos impostos, o verso sufoca, / a poesia agora responde a inquérito policial-militar' (Farewell Rimbaud. Clock of lilac, concretism, neo-concretism, fictions of youth, farewell, for life, I will buy on sight from the owners of the world. Under the weight of taxes, verse suffocates, and poetry now responds to a secret police inquiry).[46] This farewell to the grand lyric tradition has been assumed by

[45] Cisneros in L. Cevallos Mesones, *Los nuevos* (Lima, 1967), p. 14. (My translation.) Cisneros's other main books: *Commentarios reaies*, (Lima, 1964); *Agua que no has de beber* (Barcelona, 1971); *Como higuera en un campo de golf* (Lima, 1972); *El libro de Dios y de los húngaros* (Lima, 1977); *Crónica del Niño Jesús de Chilca* (Lima, 1982).

[46] Gullar's complete poems in *Toda Poesia (1950–1980)* (São Paulo, 1989).

countless Latin American poets worried by what is actually happening in their societies.

## CONCLUSION

Whether a poet retreats into his own privacy, and subjectivity, or whether he or she sacrifices the word for a cause, poets and poetry continue to matter in a continent where most poets pay for their own editions, and where poets still represent a symbolic position in society. Poetry continues to be the voice of exacerbated individuality. As historic tendencies and tastes change so too will forgotten poets, marginalized into irrelevancy for a time, emerge.

When it comes to poets writing after 1950 a critic has to choose between selecting poets on subjective criteria, and finding representative voices. However, only an eclectic position allows space for the differing responses to life and tradition that charge the best poems with value. To select names from the mass of poets writing in the 1970s and 1980s is a more dubious critical task. In an essay in 1989 I put forward Horacio Castillo, Ricardo Herrera, Juan Gustavo Cobo Borda, and Reynaldo Pérez Só as poets who speak for the chaotic present some call Postmodernism.[47] In a recent essay Juan Gustavo Cobo Borda chose Antonio Cisneros, Raúl Zurita, Eduardo Mitre, Darío Jaramillo and David Huerta as most likely to survive their period.[48] Eduardo Milán selected poets who question language itself like Haroldo de Campos, Roberto Echavarren, Néstor Perlongher, Arturo Carrera, or Emeterio Cerro as those experimenting beyond the poetics of the 1960s and 1970s.[49] Perhaps the most judicious way to evaluate contemporary poets is through the excellent anthologies by Julio Ortega (1987) and Juan Gustavo Cobo Borda (1985) that break down the barriers between Latin American countries.[50] The freedom that Latin American poets have attained today in relation to their own rich, and diversified, poetic traditions, yet often faced with distressing social and personal circumstances, is epitomized by Colombian poet Juan Gustavo Cobo Borda's dictum: 'Escribir como se nos dé la gana' (To write as we want to).

---

[47] See Jason Wilson, 'Después de la poesía surrealista', *Insula,* 47 (1989), 47–9.
[48] Juan Gustavo Cobo Borda, 'Latinoamérica en su poesía: 1930–1980', *Boletín cultural y bibliográfico,* XXVIII (1991), 34–53.
[49] Eduardo Milán, *Una cierta mirada* (Mexico, D. F., 1989).
[50] See Julio Ortega, *Antología de la poesía hispanoamericana actual* (Madrid, 1987); Juan Gustavo Cobo Borda, *Antología de la poesía hispanoamericana* (Mexico, D. F., 1985) See also José Antonio Escalona-Escalona, *Muestra de poesía hispanoamericana del siglo XX* (Caracas, 1985); Jorge Boccanera, *La novísima poesía latinoamericana* (Mexico, D. F., 1982).

# 5

# INDIGENOUS LITERATURES AND CULTURES IN TWENTIETH-CENTURY LATIN AMERICA

## SOURCES AND INTERPRETATION

During the last half-century accounts of indigenous America have pointed to a deeper and wider coherence, and a greater resilience, than was formerly recognized in academic and official discourse, notably in mainstream Anglo-American social anthropology. As early as the 1950s, Claude Lévi-Strauss celebrated not just the coherence of American culture but its prime role in the 'cumulative history' of the planet, pointing to its distinctive achievement in such endeavours as plant genetics, medicine (anaesthetics, poisons) and mathematics. Since then scholarship has abundantly vindicated this view while drawing in further areas of common reference, like cosmogony and visual language.

In the matter of script, analysis has revealed characteristics common to the recording systems used in the two principal urban societies of the continent, Tahuantinsuyu or the Inca empire of the Andes, and Mesoamerica. Both the quipu of Tahuantinsuyu, whose logic and codes have been adequately described only in the last few decades, and the books of Mesoamerica are notable for their numeracy and their reliance on such principles as place-value notation. Mesoamerican script conventions have generally become more comprehensible thanks in part to high-quality reproductions of inscribed texts and superb facsimiles of the screenfold books and codices. The hieroglyphic script peculiar to the lowland Maya is now being successfully read according to phonetic principles (advocated by the Soviet scholar Yuri Knorosoz), which effectively link living Maya speech with signs shaped 1700 years ago.

The 'Mixtec-Aztec' or iconic script used elsewhere in Mesoamerica has also been elucidated through study of the principal literary genres associated with it, the ritual books discussed in K.A. Nowotny's grossly under-read *Tlacuilolli* (1961), and the histories or annals (*xiuhtlapoualli*). The patterning of space characteristic of the ritual texts has been fruitfully compared with current practices among the Huichol in Mexico, and the Pueblo, Navajo and other heirs of the Anasazi in the southwestern United States. In the deciphering of the annals, a breakthrough was made by Alfonso Caso when he assigned Christian dates to the life of the Mixtec hero Eight Deer (1001–63 AD) and several preceding generations; and re-examinations of texts from Metlatoyuca and Itzcuintepec now confirm the seventh-century AD Chichimec base date given or suggested in other texts from Cuauhtitlan, Chalco, Nepopoalco, Cuauhtinchan and Coixtlahuaca. Moreover, as they are increasingly deciphered, these inscribed and other early documents are being accorded a long-denied place in Mesoamerican literary history. At the same time, beyond Mesoamerica, the Taino of the Caribbean and the Moche of Peru, among others, have inspired analogous attempts to incorporate ancient inscription and design into the literary corpus.

In the case of recording systems which use verbal language itself, rather than a visual or tactile correlative, a major insight was gained by Marc de Civrieux in his work on the Makiritare Carib cosmogony *Watunna*.[1] In his introduction to the Spanish edition of this work (1970), Civrieux shows how memory of its considerable length is preserved in highly encoded chants, which are not readily intelligible in ordinary language. This model has important implications for the concept of 'orality', as this has been so liberally applied to native American literature since the days of Montaigne, especially by those structuralists working along lines set out by Claude Lévi-Strauss.

Closely akin to Civrieux in their approach, other anthropologists have in the last two decades developed decidedly literary techniques for dealing with native texts from all parts of the continent. Within the framework of discourse theory and ethnopoetics, Dell Hymes, Jerome Rothenberg, Dennis Tedlock, Joel Sherzer and others have come to place greater emphasis on visual presentation on the page, highlighting through typography such concepts as stress or pace in performance, and indeed text itself, paying attention above all to the notion of line, as in verse. Their efforts have brought startling new life to older texts that had been buried in amor-

---

[1] For translations into Spanish, English and other major languages of the native texts discussed in this chapter, see bibliographical essay 5.

phous prose, for example by the Bureau of American Ethnology, and are enhancing the reproduction of currently recorded texts.

Bringing this scholarly effort home, native Americans themselves have become increasingly articulate about their culture and their texts. They have recovered an authoritative voice of their own, especially when speaking from common ground. The shift is now being actively registered in the programmes and policies of the United Nations, the International Labour Organization and other major international bodies. It has resulted in radical changes in the approach of the Instituto Indigenista Interamericano in Mexico, as is made evident in the fiftieth issue of its publication *América Indígena* (1990). Only in this revised framework may we sensibly approach the literary production of native America, its world view and its resilience.

## WORLD VIEW AND COSMOGONY

The literal bedrock of native thought, American cosmogony has in recent years acquired dramatic relevance for those interested in ecology and the possible survival of the human species. It is best approached from within, via certain native-language 'classics', which directly convey native world views and whose published alphabetic versions date from the sixteenth century to the present. The earliest of them emerged from the Spanish invasion of the urban cultures of Mesoamerica and Tahuantinsuyu, and include the *Popol vuh* and the Book of Chumayel of the highland and lowland Maya, the Nahuatl *Inomaca tonatiuh* or Legend of the Suns, and *Runa yndio*, the Quechua manuscript of Huarochiri. Today these narratives are supplemented by others from surrounding and intervening areas, like the Navajo *Dine bahane* from Anasazi, now the southwest of the United States, the *Tatkan ikala* from the Cuna islands off Panama's Caribbean coast, and the Huinkulche narrative of the Mapuche homeland that straddles the Andes between Argentina and Chile. From the rain forest, that last great bastion now under genocidal assault, come the Guarani *Ayvu rapyta*, the Carib *Watunna,* and extensive narratives by the Huitoto, Desana, Shuar and many others, all of them published for the first time in our century.

Common to these American versions of genesis is the scheme of world-ages, of plural creations which end in flood, eclipse and other catastrophes. The emergence of our human species is posited as a late though climactic event in the story of life forms and is threaded particularly through the long and hazardous line proper to vertebrates (fish, saurian, bird, monkey). Humankind's distinctive genius, Cain's, is to have learned how to feed itself, to have developed genetically the most nourishing and beneficent plants, first gourds and tubers like manioc and then beans and cereals. In the Anasazi and Maya texts the cereal maize is even held to be the substance of humankind, according to the doctrine that you are what you eat. In the moral terms of this scheme, the encounter with Europe and the West is most often diagnosed as regress to a less cultured age.

Deriving directly from the still vigorous practice of shamanism, the epic part of this cosmogony deserves special attention, also because it is the one that mediates in principle between the grand metamorphoses of creation, on the one hand, and specifically human history, on the other. The epic hero who braves the underworld and walks like the 'travellers' or planets into the sky is the prototype of the initiate shaman, the curer, the midwife and the psychopomp, bearer of the soul on its journey after death, as Mircea Eliade has shown in *Shamanism: Archaic Techniques of Ecstasy* (1964) and his other fundamental studies of shamanism. A kind of appendix to the Carib *Watunna*, 'Medatia' published in David Guss (ed.), *The Language of the Birds* (1985), is a version of such journeys and practices; the work of a apostate, it is without doubt one of the most powerful pieces of literature to have emerged from America this century.

Dealing in alterations of consciousness and sense perception, these epics also operate shifts between the dimensions of time: the four days of mourning on earth are four years for the spirit travelling beyond, just as a night may stand for a moon, in the midwives' count of nine, or for a year of migration history. Far exceeding Western linearity, just this understanding or articulation of time was enshrined in the great calendar systems of the continent, especially Mesoamerica, where indeed elements of it continue to inform lives among the Maya in highland Guatemala, for example, or the Mixe in Oaxaca.

Through these same recurrent shamanic ciphers, the whole world age scheme is also translated into territory, justifying native occupation of it on the cosmic scale. Hence, ritual Mesoamerican texts like the Féjérváry screenfold and the Aubin Ms. 20 establish the paradigm maps of the four quarters, usually orientated to east or west, and the geological quincunx, usually orientated to north or south. In Tahuantinsuyu, according to Guaman Poma, the same logic underlies the placing of the four huaca mountains – Pariacaca, Sauriciray, Vilcabamba, Coropuna – that guard

Cuzco's huaca Pacaritambo, the place of emergence. Today these ritual maps continue to be made and used. Closely following the designs found in the Mesoamerican books, the Navajo make therapeutic sand and dry paintings which also affirm territory, specifically the concept of the homeland Dinetai on the continental divide. Further, in identifying the four mountains or landmarks that guard their place of emergence and Dinetai, to northeast, northwest, southwest and southeast and to either side of the continental divide, the Navajo quincunx finds perfect analogues among the Cuicatec and the Mixe in highland Oaxaca, and even among the Mapuche who until only a century ago held the southern Andean passes between what are now Argentina and Chile. Thus placing and representing territory, ritually and in actual map designs, in itself not only remembers the homeland but inspires the reason and energy for its defence, and even its recovery.

Particularly strong ritual geography of this kind has been shown to characterize the Andes. Vast as it is, this area is held together in Quechua terms by certain key concepts, like the legend of Inkarri whose head and body – capital and four limb-provinces – wait to re-unite, or the female anatomical landscape which places the head in Quito, the navel in Cuzco (which is what cuzco means) and the uterus in Tiahuanaco, Copacabana and the 'mother' lake Titicaca. Moreover, emerging from cosmogony the very strata of geology are similarly construed along the whole length of the cordillera, as reptilian monsters who had to be laid to rest yet who may embody and prepare the way for cataclysmic change and political earthquake or revolution: Amaru in Quechua, Catari in Aymara and Kai-kai in Mapuche. Indeed, as is well known, with the prefix Tupac, Amaru and Catari named the leaders of the great native uprising in the Andes in 1780, the former being an Inca name also used by a guerrilla group in Peru today.

While telling a story and naming their space in this way, these cosmogonies construct the world as they construct themselves. In other words they are complex literary artifacts, which reflect on their own beginnings, argument and even ontology. And contrary to the Positivist assumptions of older anthropologists, this order of sophistication tends to be the greater the more 'primitive' its origin. Such is the case for example with the remarkable Huitoto creation published by Konrad Preuss in *Die Religion und Mythologie der Uitoto* (1921).

Since these texts are so consciously and finely articulated, it is important to note the process whereby they have ended up in alphabetic script

on the printed page. The optimum example here is the *Watunna* narrative
of the Makiritare or Soto Carib, first because it originates in that part of
America which effectively has remained least known and understood from
the outside. It was brought before Western eyes as a result of the Franco-
Venezuelan expedition that went in search of the true sources of the
Orinoco as late as 1950, in the area that proved to coincide largely with
Makiritare territory. Indeed, this geography is integral to the argument of
the text, as it recounts the world ages centering itself on the western end
of Pacaraima, the ridge that stretches from Roraima (the 'botannical el
dorado' of South America as it has been called) towards Marahuaka, and
the improbable Casiquiare canal that links the Orinoco and Amazon drain-
age systems. Then, once encountered, *Watunna* proved extremely difficult
to transcribe and in fact parts and episodes are put together differently in
the versions in Spanish (1970) and English (1980). The difference resulted
from continuing discussion between the editor, Marc de Civrieux, and the
Soto authors, about how to resolve the problem of reducing to a single
linear sequence a text whose structure depends originally on dense poetic
language and on cycles of performance. Similar issues have also surfaced in
editions of Desana cosmogony, the main point of reference in Reichel-
Dolmatoff's *Amazonian Cosmos* (1971), as well as studies by other Colombian anthropologists. Working with Berta Ribeiro, Umusin Panlon and
other Desana shamans prepared their Brazilian version (1980) with the
explicit purpose of correcting previous mistakes and misreadings. The first
outsider to publish the Tupi-Guarani version of rainforest cosmogony on
any scale, the German anthropologist Kurt Onkel, lived so long and
intensely among the authors and bearers of these texts that he himself
became Guarani and changed his name to Nimuendaju. The life of his
successor, León Cadogan, took a quite similar course, a fact reflected in his
handling of the core doctrine of '*ayvu rapyta*' or 'origin of human speech'.

In these and several other cases what is being defended is the integrity
of the text itself, a concept for which little room has been traditionally left
in mainstream anthropology, notably in structuralist approaches to American 'myth'. This approach was best exemplified in the four volumes of
Lévi-Strauss's *Mythologiques* (1967–74) which, remarkable as they are in
revealing intellectual coherence over wide geographical areas, deal only in
synthesized units of myth, never allowing the concept of text or its integrity to function at all.

Taking such care in reproducing and editing native cosmogonies is by
no means an idly literary matter: the whole system of shamanic apprentice-

ship, for one thing, depends on the prior existence of an authorized text. Cuna society, in this sense, acknowledges a hierarchy of sub-genres or 'ways' (ikala) – childbirth epics, funereal epics and so on – that derive from the major cosmogony *Tatkan ikala,* consigning all to notebooks in a special form of pictographic script. In other words, expressing things properly is essential in the whole process of native education that stems from such world views. Unequivocal statements on this point have recently been made by the Piaroa, neighbours of the Soto, and the Shuar, once better known as the dread head-shrinking Jivaro. In the last decade the Shuar have produced a whole series of textbooks in their language for use by children in schools, topics and moral lessons being drawn directly from the story of the world ages. In a similar vein, the Tzotzil and other highland Maya continue to read the eclipse as the warning against human exploitiveness issued previously in the *Popol vuh,* in a passage which prompted the Cuban novelist Alejo Carpentier correctly to identify American cosmogony as the only one in the world to have warned against the perils of machine technology.

At all events, as a live body of knowledge, cosmogony in this sense underpins nothing less than a philosophy of life, one which formulates in its own way such questions as the human spot in the environment, individual ambition within the collective, and substantive gendering (appealing to a dualism far more subtle than those Western binaries that oppose female earth to male fecundator, and so on). The cogency with which it does so exposes a certain absurdity in Leopoldo Zea's reaffirmation, at the XII Interamerican Congress of Philosophers in Buenos Aires in August 1992, of the idea that philosophy was born in America on 12 October 1492. This New World doctrine was openly endorsed as native American by no fewer than 120 American nations when they met at a conference in Quito in July 1990, in order to work out their common policy towards the Columbus quincentenary. Overriding local and other differences, they drew up a manifesto that made precisely this ecological reading of the world into a first political principle.

## RESILIENCE AND MEDIUM

Recognizing formulations like these we can better hope to understand the tenacity of native literatures and cultures, against odds which elsewhere in the world have usually proved terminal. Rather than some pure 'primitive' superstition that necessarily fades before the 'civilized' advance, it is a

question of beliefs and practices that can also absorb and adapt. At the
brute economic level, ways of turning the intrusive economy to advantage
have effectively been found, as in the world-famous and much-studied
cases of the Navajo silversmiths and the Otavalo weavers, and the Cuna
who market appliqué designs taken from the molas featured in their
shamanic texts. In Mexico, the Huichol have similarly adapted dream
maps and designs (*neirike*) traditionally incised on gourds, working them
into vivid yarn-paintings sold in thousands to tourists; appealing ultimately to the same iconographic tradition and Mesoamerican visual language, the Otomi papermakers of Pahuatlan and the Nahuatl painters of
Xalitla, Guerrero, have worked together to produce screenfold books and
pages of *amate* or bark paper that they sell locally and internationally. The
Cuna, Otomi and Nahuatl products are especially significant since they
incorporate elements from the heart of cosmogony – the Cuna tree of life
whence the ocean flood (*mu*) issues, the twelve lords of the underworld
below Pahuatlan, or the communal harvests of Xalitla – and indeed for
the outsider may serve as a first guide to that cosmogony, prompting
enquiry into the anterior meaning of these texts, their proper message. At
the same time, commercial reproduction has been set up so as not to
vitiate native belief and education.

In all this, what anthropologists have termed 'acculturation' (since
apparently they recognize only one culture, theirs) may sooner be evidence of inner resilience, the ability to choose from the foreign source and
mould it for one's own purposes. In literature, a finely calibrated measure
of this process is available in the study of translations that have been made
into native languages since Columbus and which in recent decades have
come to form part of conscious programmes of cultural renovation. Robert Laughlin, Neville Stiles, Carlos Montemayor and other field workers
report the intense desire of native peoples to translate into and thereby
strengthen their own languages, not just in the legal and political discourse but in poetry and fiction. The Zapotec version of Brecht's ode to
study, published along with comparable pieces in the Tehuantepec literary
review *Guchachireza,* is exemplary here. In tune with the Instituto
Indigenista Interamericano's revised notion of literacy and education,
native translators have also brought Western literary works into their
languages through the educational and pedagogical programmes of such
bodies as Proyecto Experimental de Educación Bilingue (PEEB) in Peru
and Centro de Investigaciones y Estudios de Sociología y Antropología
Social (CIESAS) in Mexico, while in Ecuador bilingual illustrated books

in Quechua and Spanish, that re-tell traditional tales, are being produced for use in schools.

Bound up in all this is the question of medium and technology. While the classic industrial revolution indeed generally had a devastating impact on native society, today the more refined technology of the transistor and the microchip has proved less culturally predetermined and has been more readily turned to native advantage. The corpus of Quechua songs which has had so long a life in the Andes is now finding modes of survival and dissemination via transistor recordings, like those by the Rumi llajta group who also perform a version of the drama Apu Ollantay. The same is true in the case of the Embera-Chami and Chocó songs of Colombia, where ethnomusicology is being redefined for similarly immediate social, political and pedagogical ends. The Navajo in the United States, the Paez in Colombia and the Kayapo in Brazil are also known for the video-tape versions they have made of their experience, not least their ceremonies and songs. The Paez work with the Consejo Regional Indígena del Cauca (CRIC), a body that has suffered intense persecution in the last decade, and have focused on the annual encounter instituted in Toribio in 1987; the Kayapo are recognized as part of a 'grassroots' media movement that also includes the Nambikwara and the Xavante. Classic texts have also become the subject of film, in such cases as the Mendoza Codex (Tlacuilo), *Popol vuh* and *Watunna*. As for the computer, a recent essay by the Mexican Otomi (Ñähñu) writer Jesús Salinas Pedraza reveals how it has been a main aid to the redesigning of the Ñähñu alphabet and the production of the native-language texts hungrily demanded by villages throughout Otomi territory. In its novelty, this project has refined relationships and roles, notably that of the 'informant'. Traditionally the anonymous Indian who supplied data to the Western writer, from Bernardino de Sahagún in the sixteenth century to Robert Redfield in the twentieth, the informant here becomes the computer programmer who helps the native writer. Jesús Salinas also notes how the success of the Ñähñu project has led to collaboration with Indian groups elsewhere in Mexico, and beyond. Most recently (1991–), it has served as a model for the Quechua in Ecuador, and the Aymara in Bolivia (Aymara having been previously identified by some as the form of human speech closest to computer language).

Finally, a feature of recent decades generally has been the emergence of scholarship about native America published by native Americans, among them Luis Reyes (Nahuatl), Ramón Arzápalo (Maya), Petu' Krus (Tzotzil

Maya), Salvador Palomino of the Consejo Indio de Sud America and Abdón Yaranga (Quechua) and Juan de Dios Yapita (Aymara). Nahua-speakers in Tepoztlan, Morelos, have carefully edited the text of 'Ecaliztli Tepoztecatl' (The Challenge of Tepozteco), the play performed annually in that town. Tzotzil scholars and writers associated with the Sna Itz'ibajom in San Cristobal de Las Casas since 1982 have explicitly confirmed their need to go beyond the old role of 'informant' and to become researchers in their own right.

## MODERN AUTHORS

Collective authorship has undoubtedly been the norm in native literary production. Although the signatures of individual scribes (*u tzib*) are legible in certain hieroglyphic inscriptions of the Maya Classic period (300–900 AD), the post-Classic books are clearly the work of several hands, as are the post-Cortesian alphabetic transcriptions and adaptations known by the name Chilam Balam. The authors of the Cuauhtitlan Annals, one of the major histories in Nahuatl, discussed and agreed in committee the text we have today, while the native scribes who wrote in Latin out of courtesy to the friars typically used the first person plural ( . . . *quod vocamus* . . . ) in introducing their work. The same is the case with the first major collection of Quechua poems to be published in the original language, 'por unas parias': *Tarmap pacha huaray*, Tarma, Peru, 1905. This is just as much because of a social and political preference as it is because of the sheer nature of the texts themselves. What single individual could ever have dreamt of laying claim to a text so ingenious and all-encompassing as the *Popol vuh?*

In recent years, individually named native authors have nevertheless become more visible, partly because of Western cataloguing and marketing preferences, and partly for reasons internal to their culture. For these authors have chosen to occupy that hazardous space that lies between traditional community and the hail of insult from beyond the community. In other words, to work as a writer in this sense in a native American language of itself implies a major literary and political choice. In each case, forgoing a more likely market the writer gains a range of expression not necessarily available in imported languages like Spanish, Portuguese, English, French and Dutch. Even at the grammatical level, American languages cast gender and person differently, as we noted above. Nor is it easy to find equivalents for certain of those key concepts that have been defined over many centuries of experience in, say, agriculture, the field garden where many of the world's finest plants were first cultivated, lovingly invoked as chacra (Quechua), conuco (Carib), kol (Maya) and milpa (Nahuatl); or the philosophy that never fully divorces place from time, in the 'earth-moment' called pacha (Quechua), mapu (Mapuche) or neka (Cuna). Such notions of time and space derive from that American cosmogony of world ages, whereby previous creations inhere in our present and are constantly alluded to in everyday situations.

Again, choosing to write in the native language allows the author an attitude towards the official imported language of his or her country, either by exulting in autonomy and refusing to admit even a word of it, or by incorporating it dialectically for sarcastic or other ends.

Guarani playwrights, among whom Julio Correa (*Sandía Yvyvy*) and Tadeo Zarretea (*Mitá Reko Mará*) are well-known names, have long been a feature of the theatre in Paraguay, where moreover works in Spanish are commonly translated into that language. In Chile, a special position is occupied by *Nepey ñi güñün piuke* (*Se ha despertado el ave de mi corazón*) (1989) by the Mapuche poet Leonel Lienlaf. From the Mapuche heartland of Temuco, Lienlaf was only nineteen when he wrote the thirty-five poems in this collection, which belongs to the recent Mapuche literary renaissance (Sebastián Queupul, Martín Alonqueo, Elicura Chihuailaf; plus Victorio Pranao and others who have appeared in the 'Küme dungu' series of texts published in collaboration with the University of Temuco). Lienlaf is exemplary in drawing on the deeper Mapuche and native tradition while giving his lines an edge that is very much here and now. The mountain that saved people from the flood, Threng-threng, still serves as a promise of refuge when seen from a boat out at sea ('Boat Song'); and in Temuco, another mountain Nielol remembers the quite recent times when all the houses there were Mapuche. Yet in 'They tore the skin off his back' the wounds inflicted by the savage invasions of the late nineteenth-century, on both sides of the Andes, threaten even the idea of native coherence. Previous Mapuche versions of this violence are found in accounts of the life of Calfucura, hero of the pampa, and in the notable autobiography of Pascual Coña (1930). In what is perhaps the most intense and difficult poem of the collection 'Footsteps' (Rupanum), the experience of walking through Mapuche time, up to the intrusion of the 'cross' and the 'sword', coincides with feeling the growth of the tree. As such the analogy drawn between plant growth and human movement belongs to the wider native

American tradition. In the epic section of the *Popol vuh* the fortune of the Twins as they pass through the underworld is paralleled by that of the maize plant left at home: the plant thrives as the traveller fares. The particular analogy with the tree recalls the tree cults of the Chilean Mapuche, evident in a host of place names (including Temuco itself), and in the east-facing tree-post or *rehue* which once centred every community. In cosmogony, each leaf of each tree tells its story.

The great power to the north in the old Mapuche world view, Tahuantinsuyu or the 'four districts' of the Inca empire lives on in the language of ten million or more speakers of *runasimi* or Quechua, in the Andean countries of Bolivia, Peru and Ecuador. Quechua even extends its literary presence into Andean Argentina while far to the north, in the Sibundoy valley of southern Colombia, the very dialect of the old capital Cuzco still records the 'Sayings of the ancestors' and the events of every day. Always pressing hard beneath the surface of the Hispanic culture imposed on these countries, Quechua runs unbroken through the Colonial and Independence periods and issues into the twentieth century in the Tarma anthology of 1905. Its particular strengths have been the drama and song that were so highly developed at the court in Cuzco, in cycles of kingship plays, and a repertoire of poetic modes that include the *wayno* and the *yaravi*. Even within the last few decades the tragedy concerning the death of the Inca emperor Atahuallpa at the hands of Francisco Pizarro was still being performed in the Bolivian Andes, evidence of a living dramatic tradition into which are now being fed works by such modern Quechua theatre groups as Yuyachkani. In the 1960s, Kilku Waraka (Andrés Alencastre) published poetry in Quechua which astounded José María Arguedas with its classical force.

Contemporary Quechua poets, enduring a civil war brought on by centuries of racist outrage against them, have turned especially to the *wayno,* the poetry of its words being matched in performance by that of its Andean music. A leader in the movement in question, Lino Quintanilla chose the *wayno* to celebrate the taking back of stolen peasant lands in Andahuaylas in 1972; urging resistance in his hometown Huamanga (Ayacucho) in another *wayno,* Eusebio Huamani decries the *sinchi* police, whose mottled green uniforms identify them as arrogant parrots that infest home and fields. A *wayno* of quite devastating power is 'Viva la patria' by Carlos Falconi, which like Lienlaf's 'Rupamum' uses the technique of incorporating Spanish words in order to deconstruct and ultimately revile them, to the extent that the 'patria' in question is exposed as vicious hypocrisy, an imposition both incoherent and insulting on all those who are not Latin or white.

The question of racial conflict and of identity within the nation state recurs in Mexico and the other countries that emerged from Mesoamerica, that other great urban focus of pre-Columbian times. And again, modern authors give their edge to the poetics and rhetoric of the old language, in this case the Nahuatl once spoken at the courts of Tenochtitlan and Texcoco. This recuperation may involve no more than re-stating the aesthetics and philosophy of 'flower-song' (xochi-cuicatl) or Nahuatl poetry itself, as this has been preserved for example in the sixteenth-century manuscript known as the Cantares mexicanos. Hence, Natalio Hernández Hernández's poem 'Our ancestral singers' (Nocolhua cuicate, 1987) delicately revives Nahuatl binary phrasing in invoking the old capacity to 'say and know', 'say and sing'. Or, as in a poem by Fausto Hernández Hernández, a traditional mode like the 'orphan song' (*icno-cuicatl*) may be employed to express the current predicament of children and families in Nahuatl-speaking Veracruz who have been abandoned by parents obliged to migrate to alien cities: the title 'Tototl' ([migrant] bird) can refer to either gender, women having in fact borne much of this burden, earning money as they can in the hope of eventually helping those they left behind. Other verse recalls the cadences of Nahuatl rhetoric and oratory. This aspect of Nahuatl has a long history of its own and in 1524 was superbly exemplified in the speech addressed by the Aztec priests to the Franciscan missionaries who wished to convert them to Christianity. In Luis Reyes's poem (1988) 'How many Nahua are we?' ('Keski nauamaseualme tiitstoke?'), there is the same flexibility of persona, from humble to self-assertive, the same dry irony and open sarcasm. Representing the non-Indians of Mexico is the coyote, the trickster, opportunist and scavenger whose pre-social instincts belong to a pre-human age, according to North American cosmogony in general: 'Four hundred years have taught us/ what coyote wants.'

Within Mesoamerica, the Nahuatl tradition is matched by that of the Maya, lowland and highland, among whose classics are numbered the Books of Chilam Balam and the *Popol vuh*. Indeed in the case of the lowland Maya it is possible to trace a continuous line from the hieroglyphic texts of pre-Cortesian times through the Books of Chilam Balam up to such modern authors as Dzul Poot, whose stories immerse us in the geography of the Chilam Balam towns, indicating its hidden but live significance for Maya speakers today. This view is borne out by the

authors of Maya texts included in Allan F. Burns's *An Epoch of Miracles*
(1983), which includes a salutary re-writing by Paulino Yama of the US
archaeologist Sylvanus Morley's account of his dealings with the Maya at
Chichen Itza in 1934–5. Among highland Maya authors, the Quiché
Victor Montejo has, like Rigoberta Menchú, documented the genocidal
campaigns of the Guatemalan government of the 1980s, linking the
resistance of the Maya to their cosmological beliefs (*The Bird who Cleans
the World*, 1992). Writing in Tzotzil, Petu' Krus is the first native
woman to have received the Chiapas prize for literature.

Then, in addition to Nahuatl and Maya, other Mesoamerican languages
are now making their first true literary appearance, notably those which
like Zapotec and Otomi (Ñähñu) belong to the most ancient Otomanguan
family, scarcely known hitherto through alphabetic texts. In this respect,
Carlos Montemayor's *Los escritores indígenas actuales* (1992), which gathers
these new beginnings together, is a definite landmark. Distinguished yet
unrecorded as a source language and a 'wild' style in the Nahuatl court
poetry, Otomi is said to have been used by Nezahualcoyotl the poet-king
of Texcoco (1402–72), when he composed his laments: now thanks in part
to the computer, it is the vehicle of poems like Thaayrohyadi Bermúdez's
'Tsi Mahkitaa Lerma', a heartfelt ode to the 'father-river' Lerma, which
passes on its ecological message by honouring of the old water gods. A
counterpart to 'How many Nahua are we?', Victor de la Cruz's Zapotec
poem 'Tu laanu, tu lanu' uses half-rhyme to ask 'Who are we? What is our
name?'.

## IMPACT ON LATIN AMERICAN LITERATURE

With regard to native precedent, the story of Latin American literature in
this century has largely been one of recuperation and what Angel Rama
called 'transculturation'. After decades of Indianism and indigenism, in
which Indian characters tended to be little more than the hypothetical
constructs of Romantics or social realists, native culture began to make a
profound impact on Latin American literature, as classic texts at last
became accessible thanks to scholarly translations and editions. The result
has been a major case of intertextuality, a concept which however has most
often been reserved in Latin American criticism just for the impact of
Western and Old World literature.

The *Popol vuh* is a good example of this interaction. Alluded to in the
*mundonovista* work of the Modernistas, like Rubén Darío's poems

'Tutecotzimi' and 'Momotombo' with their references to the creator 'Hurakan' and the proud military strength of the Quichés and Cakchiquels, this highland Maya text provided the only geographically recognizable episode in Salarrue's Atlantis fantasy *O-Yarkandal* (Cuzcatlán [San Salvador], 1929). It then became the decisive element in the work of Miguel Angel Asturias, who translated it (from Georges Raynaud's French) when in Paris and included whole passages in his *Leyendas de Guatemala* (1930). In 'Gaspar Ilóm' (1945), later the opening chapter of *Hombres de maíz* (1949), engagement with the Quiché text can be shown to have transformed completely Asturias's view of his compatriot Maya, curing him of the racism evident in his early thesis *El problema social del indio* (1923), and revealing to him the reasons for the military resistance to white invasion offered by Ilóm's prototype, who actually existed, in Cuchumatanes at the turn of the century. This literary conversion has in practice continued through the life of his son who adopted the name Gaspar Ilóm as the member of the URNG guerrilla forces. In tacit homage, Alejo Carpentier drew on and quoted Asturias's translation of the *Popol vuh* in *Visión de América* (1948) and in the novel which grew out of those essays, *Los pasos perdidos* (1953), which develops most fully his notions of a deeply rooted and autonomous American culture, 'lo maravilloso americano'. Carpentier's readings of the flood and world-ages have scholarly value, as has his remarkable intuition of the links between this Mesoamerican scheme and that of the South American rainforest. Even Jorge Luis Borges, hardly an *indigenista* by calling, turned to the *Popol vuh*, quoting it in the climactic moments of the Jaguar Priest's vision in 'La escritura del dios' (1949). In Amparo Dávila's short story 'El patio cuadrado' (*Arboles petrificados* 1977), an anthropologist tries to 'cross over' (in the terms of Borges or Cortázar) to the native American world represented here by the actual text of the Quiché play *Rabinal Achí*. In the 1960s Ernesto Cardenal began incorporating Quiché-Maya originals into his *Homenaje a los indios americanos* (1969) a work of continental range in which the *Popol vuh* cosmogony and its marvellous evocation of the beginnings of earthly life are directly linked to the creation dates of hundreds of millions of years recorded in the hieroglyphic inscriptions of the Maya ('Mayapan').

Of these examples, Asturias's 'Gaspar Ilóm' and Cardenal's *Homenaje* in particular alert us to a political reading of the *Popol vuh* which is also found in narratives like Virgilio Rodríguez Beteta's *Los dos brujitos mayas* (Guatemala City, 1956), with its highlighting of Xibalba's 'Halcones de la muerte' and 'Mansión tenebrosa de la Desaparición', and Rosario Castellanos's *Balún Canan* (Mexico, 1957). The catastrophic deaths accorded to the exploiters of this world and the epic struggle of the Twins against the power-mad cigar-smoking Lords of Xibalba have found especial resonance in popular literature in Mexico and Central America: these motifs inform consciousness-raising plays performed by La Fragua theatre group in Honduras in the 1970s and the Lo'il Maxil group in Chiapas in the 1990s, as well as the paintings of Juan Gallo in Chiapas, and of Juan Sisay, recently assassinated in Quiché, Guatemala; and they underpin the tenacity revealed in the autobiography of Rigoberta Menchú (1983). In Nicaragua, Pablo Antonio Cuadra read in the story of the Twins' mother Ixquic (Blood Woman), daughter of the Lords of Xibalba, a sign of the end of Somoza's bloody tyranny ('El jícaro', 1978). More recently, the Salvadorean author Manlio Argueta, currently in exile in Costa Rica, has updated Asturias's account of peasant resistance in El Salvador in *Cuzcatlán donde bate la mar del sur* (1986), where again the philosophy and world view inscribed in the *Popol vuh* are shown to be an irreplaceable sustaining force.

Likewise incorporated into Asturias's *Leyendas de Guatemala* and Cardenal's *Homenaje,* the Chilam Balam books of the lowland Maya have passed into Latin American literature having themselves been the focus of the centuries-old 'caste war' of Yucatan that ended effectively only with Lázaro Cárdenas's wise concessions of the 1930s. Just this role is made explicit in the revivalist novel *La tierra del faisán y del venado* (1934) by Antonio Médiz Bolio, translator of the Chilam Balam book of Chumayel; and in what has proved to be one of the best-selling Mexican novels ever, Ermilo Abreu Gómez's *Canek* (1942), named after the leader of the 1761 Maya uprising who looked forward to the nineteenth-century Caste War (1848) and back to the last leader of the independent Maya (1697), also Canek. The question of Maya historical consciousness and its articulation in hieroglyphic and later in alphabetic texts is developed in several of the poems in Cardenal's *Homenaje* ('Oráculos de Tikal', 'Katun 11 Ahau', '8 Ahau', 'Ardilla de los tunes de un katun').

Within Mesoamerica, the matching Nahuatl tradition of cosmogony exemplified in the Sunstone of Tenochtitlan, the Legend of the Suns and the Cuauhtitlan Annals has been generally a pervasive force in the work of Octavio Paz and Carlos Fuentes, while the epic story of Quetzalcoatl's descent to the underworld Mictlan, in its current rural versions, gave shape to Juan Rulfo's *Pedro Páramo* (1955). By far the most directly influential text in the Nahuatl corpus has, however, been the

*Cantares mexicanos,* a collection of poetry initially from the court of Tenochtitlan which a recent translation by John Bierhorst (1985) suggests has similarities with the nineteenth-century Ghost Dance songs of the Sioux and other Plains Indians (a view hotly contested by the Mexican Nahuatl expert Miguel León-Portilla). Already in the sixteenth century, Ixtlilxochitl popularized the 'laments' of his ancestor Nezahualcoyotl (1402–72), the poet-king of Texcoco who belonged to the *Cantares* tradition and who was made even more famous by W. H. Prescott's *Conquest of Mexico* (London, 1843), as well as such Christianizing nineteenth-century Mexican poets as Juan José Pesado, Augusto Roa Barcena, Villalón, José Tercero. This century, the *Cantares* began to be read as testimony to the cultural wealth of the Middle America, the place that stretched from Rubén Darío's birthplace Nicaragua in the east to Mexico in the west and whose ancient coherence underlies modern political divisions. In the wake of the Mexican Revolution and the new translations by Angel María Garibay prompted by that event, the Cantares acquired greater resonance in the poetry of Octavio Paz, Marco Antonio Montes de Oca, José Emilio Pacheco, Rubén Bonifaz Nuño and Homero Aridjis, as well as that of the Nicaraguans Pablo Antonio Cuadra and Ernesto Cardenal.

In recreating the brilliant verbal images of the *Cantares*, both Cuadra and Cardenal go further in relating them back to their visual precedent in the screenfold books of Mesoamerica, like the Borgia Codex. These same ancient books are vividly reproduced in words in *Los perros del paraíso* (1987), by the Argentine Abel Posse, part of a 'trilogía americana' that in fact touches repeatedly on native American literature. And in modern Mexico they have become a notable resource for political satirists, for example the illustrated pages of *Quetzalcoatl no era del PRI* by Eduardo del Rios (RIUS), and the brilliant series of cartoons and narratives featured in *El Ahuizote* (a supplement of *La Jornada*), that provided a keenly irreverent response to the 1992 celebrations.

As for the other great urban focus of ancient America, Tahuantinsuyu, literary historians have amply reported the enduring vogue of the *yaraví,* a verse form that had its roots in the *haravek* of the Inca court in Cuzco and which was widely cultivated by the Spanish American Romantics and their successors, including the Nobel-prize winner Gabriela Mistral. Another court genre, the kingship drama, finds its way into the Bolivian novel *El valle* by Mario Unzueta (1962), which indeed preserves the Quechua perspective on Pizarro's murder of the emperor Atahuallpa. Published only within the last half-century, the Quechua narrative from Huarochiri *Runa yndio* gave title and shape to *El zorro de arriba y el zorro de abajo* (1971), the posthumous novel of José María Arguedas (who also translated this text as *Dioses y hombres de Huarochirí;* 1966), and to Manuel Scorza's *Garabombo el invisible* (1972), part of the quintet devoted to the account of the Pasco uprising of 1962. Also published and transcribed only in recent decades, Guaman Poma's account of the European destruction of Tahuantinsuyu, based as it was on *quipu* archives, has similarly come to strengthen the cry for political change in the Andes, especially the vivid page-drawings that have now become universal currency.

That part of America which has resisted invasion still in this century, the rainforest of South America has also preserved a literary wealth that led Italo Calvino, for one, to characterize it as 'the universal source of narrative material, the primordial magma . . .'[2] Reflected in the poems and novels of José de Alencar, Gonçalves Dias and the nineteenth-century Brazilian Americanistas, the Tupi-Guarani cosmogony transcribed in *Ayvu rapyta* has subsequently entered a dialectic with western philosophy and religion in Cardenal's *Homenaje* ('Los hijos del bosque de las palabras-almas') and in novels by the Brazilian anthropologist Darcy Ribeiro (*Maíra*, 1976) and the Paraguayan Augusto Roa Bastos (*Hijo de hombre*, 1961; *Yo el supremo*, 1974): *Maíra* and *Yo el supremo* both feature for example the hallucinatory blue jaguar of solar eclipse. In an uncharacteristic gesture – given his general demeaning of Indians in his novels of Peru and in his Brazilian *La guerra del fin del mundo* – Mario Vargas Llosa borrowed the cosmogony of the Machiguenga making it the centrepiece of *El hablador* (1987), and showing how the very survival of these Arawak-speaking people on the uppermost Amazon depends on their remembering their history and place in the universe.

A last and special chapter in this record is that of the Carib texts from the Pacaraima area defined in the great Makiritare Carib charter *Watunna*. Working alone and mostly in ignorance of each other, many South American writers have drawn on the corpus epitomized by *Watunna* and contributed to previously by such visitors as Humboldt, Schomburgk, Koch-Grünberg and Armellada, a story told in part in Carpentier's 'Visión de América' (1948).[3] In English-speaking Guyana W. H. Hudson's *Green Mansions* (1904) and Wilson Harris's *Palace of the Peacock* (1960) draw in

---

[2] Italo Calvino, *If on a Winter's Night a Traveller*, p. 94, quoted by Gerald Martin, *Journeys through the Labyrinth* (London, 1989), p. 356.
[3] See *Ensayos*, vol. 13 of *Obras completas* (Mexico, D.F., 1990).

their different ways on Carib accounts of mystic ascent to Roraima up east-flowing rivers possessed of their own will and life. The Brazilian Mário de Andrade turned to the Taupilang-Arekuna epic of Makunaima when writing his novel of the same title (*Macunaíma*, 1928), which sends this hero on a journey south from Uaricoera to São Paulo and back again. In Venezuela, the third country to share Roraima as a landmark, Rómulo Gallegos anticipated Wilson Harris's story 'Kanaima' in diagnosing Canaima, the title of his story of the north-flowing Caroni river (1935), as the particular homicidal madness which *Watunna* tells us was induced among the Carib by the White invasion. Other versions of Canaima appear in Eduardo Galeano's American trilogy *Memoria del fuego* which, moreover, opens with a creation passage from *Watunna*. It is just this continual resonance of Pacaraima cosmogony which prompted Carpentier's notable intuitions on the subject and his cross-references to the *Popol vuh* in *Visión de América* and *Los pasos perdidos*.

Another study could record a similar story of impact on Western literature more widely, that includes such figures as D. H. Lawrence, André Breton, Antonin Artaud, Alfred Döblin and many others. The intertextual phenomenon as such is decidedly twentieth-century, and definitive. Recovering native classics and sensing their continuing vigour in native societies today has been a turning point for many modern Latin American writers.

# 6

# LATIN AMERICAN MUSIC,
## c. 1920 – c. 1980

## INTRODUCTION

In general terms, the history of Latin American art-music composition in the twentieth century begins with a period of nationalist assertion, with neo-Romantic and neo-classical countercurrents, followed by a period of openly experimental tendencies. These trends occurred at times concurrently in the various Latin American republics, but musical nationalism appeared above all from the 1920s to the 1950s, neo-classicism and other neo-tonal aesthetic orientations at various times from the 1930s, while experimentalism and the avant-garde in music prevailed from the early 1960s. The output of Latin American composers was considerable, revealing a wide compositional diversity, according to historical period, geographical location and special socio-cultural conditions and circumstances. There was at the same time a significant development of music professionalism, supported by professional associations and by institutions of learning, including the national conservatories inherited from the nineteenth century and, from the 1930s, some state and private universities. A number of opera houses were erected or reconstructed from the beginning of the century, and national symphony orchestras emerged in the major countries of the continent in the 1920s and 1930s.

Historically the art music of twentieth-century Latin America had its antecedents in the colonial period and, above all, in the nineteenth century when numerous elements of the great European classical tradition were implanted in the continent. Following the wars of independence, several of the emerging nations established national music institutions. They were, however, dominated by foreign professionals and visiting virtuosi, especially in the latter part of the century. Italian opera and

307

lighter musical theatre genres, art-songs and piano music (mostly of the salon type) dominated the cultivated musical life, although symphonic and chamber music made their appearance in some of the larger cities during the second half of the century.

The earliest attempts to write music in a definable national style were generally undertaken after the mid-century. Opera proved to be particularly conducive to dramatic and musical expression of national themes and values. In Mexico, for example, the opera *Guatimotzin* by Aniceto Ortega (1823–75), premiered in 1871, relies on a libretto based on a romanticized Aztec theme and incorporates some native elements. In Peru, an Italian, Carlo Enrique Pasta, wrote the first opera on a Peruvian theme, *Atahualpa,* premiered in Lima in 1877 and José María Valle Riestra (1858–1925) attempted in *Ollanta* (1901) to create a national opera, but only the libretto had reference to national culture. The Argentine composer Francisco A. Hargreaves (1849–1900) drew on folk-music sources or simply folkloric associations in his operas, which include *La Gatta bianca* (1885) and *El Vampiro* (1876). The operas *Pampa* (1897) and *Yupanki* (1899) by Arturo Berutti (1862–1938) borrow actual folk melodies from the *gaucho* and Andean Indian traditions. In Brazil, Antônio Carlos Gomes (1836–96) followed the Romantic Indianist movement in some of his operas, particularly *Il Guarany* (1870) whose libretto is based on a celebrated novel by José de Alencar and whose overture in its final version became virtually a second national anthem. Verdi who heard and saw *Il Guarany* in Ferrara in 1872 called it the work of a 'truly musical genius'. The native contents of Gomes's operatic style, however, are rather limited: his libretti treat Brazilian subjects (Indianism, abolition of slavery), but largely in a symbolic manner.

The late nineteenth century and early part of the twentieth century saw the emergence of musical nationalism, particularly in Mexico, Cuba, Colombia, Argentina and Brazil, under the influence of similar trends in Europe. Romantic nationalism at that time could be described essentially as the 'creolization' of European salon dances (polkas, mazurkas, waltzes, schottisches) together with a new attention to vernacular music genres, and the incorporation in a stylized fashion of certain characteristic elements of 'native' music into a prevailing European Romantic music vocabulary. It should be borne in mind that the aesthetic ideas of composers of such national music represented the typical middle class and upper class values of the time. That such values reflected the cultural-artistic dependence on Europe should surprise no one, since the art-music tradition in Latin America was part and an extension of Western civilization.

Among the numerous Mexican pianist-composers of the latter part of the nineteenth century who contributed substantially to the characterization of Mexican national music were Juventino Rosas (1864–94), an Otomí Indian whose set of waltzes *Sobre las olas* (1891) won him international fame, Tomás León (1826–93), Julio Ituarte (1845–1905), Ernesto Elorduy (1853–1912), and Felipe Villanueva (1862–93). Through a stylized arrangement of popular airs and dance rhythms, these salon-music, popular composers made vernacular music presentable to concert audiences. Elorduy and Villanueva, particularly, devoted themselves to the *danza mexicana,* influenced by the Cuban *contradanza,* the source of numerous Caribbean dance forms, such as the *habanera* and the *danzón,* all emphasizing typical syncopated rhythmic figures that became characteristic of numerous Caribbean and Latin American popular music genres.

In Cuba, Manuel Saumell (1817–70) and Ignacio Cervantes (1847–1905) cultivated the *contradanza* and through it took the first decisive steps toward musical nationalism. Saumell excelled in the small, intimate salon piano piece of a frankly popular style in which an extraordinary variety of rhythmic combinations prevails. Cervantes, a concert pianist, wrote twenty-one *Danzas cubanas,* for piano (1875–95), which incorporate elements of both Afro-Cuban and Guajiro folk music traditions into a Romantic piano style. Particularly conspicuous in these pieces is the use of one of the most typical rhythmic figures of Afro-Caribbean traditional music, the syncopated rhythm known as *cinquillo* in Cuba.

In Colombia, the first attempts to write music of a national character dated from the 1840s, when Henry Price (1819–63), born and educated in London, settled in Bogotá and wrote the piano piece *Vals al estilo del país* (1843), a stylized *pasillo,* one of Colombia's most popular dances. But it was at the end of the nineteenth century that nationalist composition within a Romantic style began to emerge more generally. José María Ponce de León (1846–82), composer of opera and sacred music, took an early interest in national music; works such as *La Hermosa Sabana* (1881) and *Sinfonía sobre temas colombianos* (1881) were partly based on typical folk dances like the *bambuco, pasillo* and *torbellino.*

The early phase of Argentine musical nationalism developed from the mid-nineteenth century, and centered on the cowboy (the *gaucho*) of the pampas who came to symbolize the national folk and to epitomize the country at large in the early part of the twentieth century. The various dances and songs of the pampas were the major sources to which the first nationalist composers turned. Francisco Hargreaves, for example, in his *Aires nacionales* (1880), for piano, stylized such typical folk songs and dances as the *gato, estilo, vidalita, décima* and *cielito*. The father of Argentine musical nationalism, however, is generally considered to be Alberto Williams (1862–1952) who first found his inspiration in gaucho folk music in the 1890s. The various albums of the *Aires de la Pampa* (begun in 1893), totalling over fifty pieces for the piano, include *vidalitas, gatos, zambas,* and a large number of *milongas,* one of the forerunners of the tango. In his *Primera Sonata Argentina,* Op. 74 (1917), Williams relied on the athletic gaucho dance known as *malambo* for the scherzo movement, thereby opening the way to similar treatment of the dance by later nationalist composers. A true understanding of the expressiveness of Argentine native music is found more readily in the works of Julián Aguirre (1868–1924) whose piano pieces (*Aires Nacionales Argentinos*) and songs (*Canciones Argentinas, Cueca, Vidalita*) reveal a strong empathy for native music and a sophisticated *criolla* inspiration.

In Brazil, the piano piece, *A Sertaneja,* written by the amateur composer Brasílio Itiberê da Cunha (1846–1913) and published in Rio de Janeiro in 1869, opened the path to Romantic music nationalism in its reliance on melodic and rhythmic traits of the urban popular music of the time, particularly the *modinha* (a sentimental song type), the Brazilian tango (especially as cultivated by Ernesto Nazareth, 1863–1934) and the *maxixe* (a popular dance deriving from the European polka). A closer adherence to national musical sources appeared in some of the works of Alexandre Levy (1864–92) whose *Suite brésilienne* (1890), for orchestra, ends with a *Samba* movement based on two traditional tunes and a multitude of rhythmic patterns closely related to contemporary urban popular music. Among the various works of nativistic persuasion written by Alberto Nepomuceno (1864–1920) were the piano piece *Galhofeira,* the String Quartet No. 3 (subtitled 'Brasileiro'), and the *Série brasileira,* for orchestra. *Galhofeira*'s syncopated accompaniment pattern is derived from similar rhythms found in urban popular forms, such as the *maxixe* and the *chôro.* The last movement, *Batuque,* of the *Série brasileira,* is based on the composer's early piano piece, *Dança de negros,* imitating symphonically Afro-Brazilian dance music, by stressing rhythmic elements and simulating through orchestral texture density the responsorial from Afro-Brazilian singing.

## MUSIC NATIONALISM, 1920S TO 1950S

As an aspect of culture, music did not escape during the first half of the twentieth century the influence of the rapid development of nationalism in the socio-political life of the Latin American republics. Although musical nationalism lost its importance in Europe after about 1930, it remained a viable current in Latin America well into the 1950s. Latin American musical nationalism, however, cannot be defined in general terms; its expression, meaning and function varied with the individual composer and the specific socio-musical conditions in a particular region, country or even city.

### Mexico

Although the composer Manuel M. Ponce (1882–1948), considered the pioneer of Romantic nationalism in Mexican music, advocated a native musical development during the years of the Mexican Revolution (1910–20), it was not until the late 1920s and the 1930s that the Indianist movement responded to the search for a national cultural identity and reached its full development in Mexican art-music. The central figure in this development was Carlos Chávez (1899–1978) who, in a 1928 lecture at the Universidad Nacional in Mexico City, praised the pre-Conquest virtues of Indian music as expressing 'what is deepest in the Mexican soul', and the musical life of pre-Columbian Indians as 'the most important stage in the history of Mexican music'.

Chávez exerted a profound influence in Mexican musical life from the 1920s to the 1950s, not only as a composer, conductor and a teacher but also as a writer on music and a government official. His own adherence to nationalist composition was followed by many of his students, although he was not an exclusively nationalist composer. His own direction toward Indianist, primitivistic style began with the ballet *El Fuego Nuevo* (1921) and culminated with the *Sinfonía India* (1935–6) and *Xochipilli-Macuilxochitl* (1940). Although the subjective evocation of Indian music (whether that of contemporary tribes or remote pre-Columbian high cultures) remained a fundamental concern, Chávez also paid attention to the mestizo folk tradition and to urban popular music. His music has been characterized as 'profoundly non-European' perhaps as the result of the obvious exoticism of his Indianist works but, more importantly, as the consequence of the unique, austere style of such works that combine modernistic and primitivistic elements. The indigenous musical features of his works identified by the composer himself are also found in several of his non-Indianist works and include modal melodies (both pentatonic and diatonic), frequent use of rhythmic ostinatos and consistent underlying rhythmic units, irregular metres, cross-rhythms and syncopation, and frequently changing tempos. In addition, the predominant linear (polyphonic) texture of many of Chávez's works can be related to his statements about polyphony in Indian music of Mexico and the primary value assigned to melody and rhythm rather than harmony in primitive music. The use of copies of ancient instruments, particularly the two-keyed slit drum, *teponaztli,* and the *huehuetl* (a cylindrical, one-headed Aztec drum), and of numerous other percussion instruments or the percussive treatment of other instruments, are also related to primitivistic Indianism. The harmonic vocabulary of Chávez is decidedly modern and akin to contemporary European practices. This vocabulary includes parallelisms, harsh dissonances, sevenths, ninths and octaves, and non-triadic three-note chords (quartal and quintal harmonies), that is, non-Romantic harmonies.

The *Sinfonía India,* one of the best-known Mexican orchestral works of the twentieth century, relies on authentic Indian melodies and native instruments, such as Indian drum (Yaqui drum), clay rattle, water gourd, *teponaztlis* and a large *huehuetl.* The melodic material of the various sections presents a Cora Indian melody used as the first theme of the first allegro, a Yaqui Indian melody used as the second theme, and a Sonora Indian melody as the main theme of the slow middle section. The grandiose finale of this work relies on a Seri Indian melody and epitomizes Chávez's Indianist style in its repetitious structure, brilliant orchestral and cross-rhythmic effects, and its exuberant, driving force.

During his twenty-one years as music director and conductor of the Orquesta Sinfónica de México (OSM, founded in 1928), Chávez favoured the contemporary repertory and championed the works of Mexican composers. His active participation in the International Composers' Guild and the Pan American Association of Composers also contributed to the development of Mexico City as an important musical centre of the hemisphere. As director of the National Conservatory (1928–34), he provided true academic leadership in music education by initiating basic reforms of the curriculum, organizing concerts of all kinds, and by establishing three research units for the study of folk and popular music, of music history and bibliography, and of new musical possibilities. His interest in electric sound reproduction while he was in the United States in 1932, resulted in his book *Toward a New Music: Music and Electricity* (New York, 1937).

Besides his incursion into Indian and mestizo folk music, Chávez also expressed on occasions his sympathies with the post-revolutionary ideology in such populist work as the 'proletarian symphony' *Llamadas,* the 'Mexican ballad' *El Sol,* and the *Obertura Republicana* (retitled later *Chapultepec*), involving an arrangement of the provincial military march, *Zacatecas,* the nineteenth-century salon waltz, *Club Verde* and the revolutionary 'canción mexicana', *La Adelita.*

Among Carlos Chávez's students who were directly influenced by their teacher in their early compositions were Blas Galindo (1910–93) and José Pablo Moncayo (1912–58). Together with Daniel Ayala (1906–75) and Salvador Contreras (1912–82) they formed the 'Grupo de los Cuatro' to promote their activities in nationalist music. Both Galindo's *Sones de Mariachi* and Moncayo's *Huapango,* presented at the Museum of Modern Art in New York in a series of concerts in conjunction with the exhibition Twenty Centuries of Mexican Art (1940), are overtly nationalist pieces with direct borrowing of mestizo folk tunes (particularly *sones*) and the imitation of specific folk dance rhythms and of regional folk music ensembles. In his later works, however, Galindo cultivated a neo-classic style and eventually adhered to the twelve-tone method of composition.

Next to Chávez, the nationalist composer who won the wide international reputation was Silvestre Revueltas (1899–1940). Most of his compositions date from the last ten years of his short life. His first orchestral piece, *Cuauhnahuac* (1930) ('Cuernavaca'), exhibits a highly chromatic, at times violently dissonant harmony, together with a colourful orchestration and a vigorous rhythmic drive. The latter is better expressed in another orchestral piece, *Sensemayá* (1938), considered Revueltas's best work. Inspired by the poem of the Afro-Cuban poet Nicolás Guillén, *Sensemayá* is a sort of onomatopoeic imitation of the sounds and rhythms of Afro-Cuban traditional religious music. The rhythmic ostinatos combined with highly dissonant harmonies and short, repetitive melodic motifs, remind one of Stravinsky's *The Rite of Spring*. Revueltas's good humour and spontaneity is clearly reflected in *8 x Radio (Ocho por Radio)* (1933), for an octet chamber group, and in the tone poem *Janitzio* (1933). (Janitzio is the resort island of Lake Pátzcuaro; Revueltas referred to this piece as his contribution to national tourism.) Indeed, such works derive their basic contents from characteristic mestizo folk music models. In other works, such as his

*Homenaje a García Lorca* (1936), Revueltas combined his nationalistic tendency with neo-classicisim.

Other Mexican nationalist composers of the same generation were Luis Sandi (b. 1905) and, to a lesser extent, Miguel Bernal Jiménez (1910–56). Sandi, particularly interested in choral music and conducting, followed the Indianist trend in such works as *Yaqui Music* (1940) and *Bonampak* (premiered 1951), while Bernal Jiménez, a native of Morelia, explored Michoacán's folk musical traits in his *Suite Michoacana* (1940) and *Noche en Morelia* (1941). His opera *Tata Vasco* (1941) written for the celebration of the fourth centenary of the arrival of the first bishop of Michoacán, Vasco de Quiroga, incorporates some national elements such as popular religious songs and traditional Indian instruments.

After about 1950, musical nationalism in Mexico declined rapidly when new aesthetics and their corresponding styles emerged. By this time Mexico had been able to establish a truly professional musical life, with the official backing of some government agencies, such as the Instituto Nacional de Bellas Artes (founded in 1946 by President Miguel Alemán), and even the possibility of music publishing with the appearance also in 1946 of the Ediciones Mexicanas de Música.

## Cuba

Just as Mexican artists found in the Aztec Renaissance of the 1920s and 1930s one of the major sources for their artistic expression, Cuban artists of the same period rediscovered Afro-Cuban culture (known as *afrocubanismo*) as the essential source of national characterization. Despite the advocation of an Indianist approach to musical nationalism by Eduardo Sánchez de Fuentes (1874–1944) who, as an opera composer cultivated Italian *verismo* based on pseudo-Caribbean Indian music, all of the members of the 'Grupo Minorista' (established in Havana in 1923) explored the African elements of Cuban folk and popular culture. For the two most outstanding representatives of music nationalism in Cuba, Amadeo Roldán and Alejandro García Caturla, *afrocubanismo* remained the most appropriate source of national expression.

Amadeo Roldán (1900–39) wrote the first major symphonic work, *Obertura sobre temas cubanos* (1925), indicating the new trend. Besides the utilization of authentic Afro-Cuban musical instruments, this and other works by Roldán explore the prevailingly rhythmic character of Afro-

Cuban music. Roldán's most celebrated work, the ballet *La Rebambaramba* (1927–8), based on a story by the well-known poet, novelist and musicologist Alejo Carpentier, relies on numerous folk elements, such as Afro-Cuban mythology, Cuban *contradanzas* of the nineteenth century, and popular *comparsas* (processional groups of Afro-Cuban cultmen). His second ballet, *El milagro de Anaquillé* (1928–9), also based on a story by Carpentier, relies on both Guajiro (Cuban-Hispanic folk song and dance) and Afro-Cuban (Abakuá initiation ceremonial music) folk traditions. Roldán treated the folk music sources in a modern, dissonant style. In his six chamber music pieces, *Rítmicas* (1930), he tended to recreate subjectively the spirit of Afro-Cuban music, stressing at the same time the refinement of his harmonic and tone-colouring language. *Motivos de Son* (1934), eight songs for soprano and an ensemble of seven instruments, a set of Nicolás Guillén's poems, reveals the composer's skills as a lyrical melodist, a highly effective orchestrator, and an accomplished technician in his treatment of rhythmic intricacies associated with Afro-Cuban dances.

Alejandro García Caturla (1906–40), a student of Nadia Boulanger in Paris in the late 1920s, was exposed to the avant-garde music of the period and came under its direct influence, particularly in reference to polytonality and poly-rhythms. His profound empathy for Afro-Cuban culture and people is felt in all of his creative output. His approach to Cuban folk music (both Afro-Cuban and Guajiro) was unorthodox, in that he attempted to create his own unique style with some important elements derived from many folk music genres. His *Tres danzas cubanas* (1927), for orchestra, the Afro-Cuban suite *Bembé* (1928), and the symphonic movement *Yamba-O* (1928–31) on the poem *Liturgia* by Alejo Carpentier, all show a very advanced, exuberant style, with highly imaginative harmonies and instrumental and rhythmic effects. Pentatonic melodies related to Afro-Cuban folk music contribute frequently to the primitivistic nature of his music. The composer-musicologist Adolfo Salazar compared Caturla's style with that of the Cuban popular *son* itself. The main traits of that style consist of a 'generally pentatonic melody, presented by an instrument of a distinct timbre, in a tonally indefinable sonorous atmosphere, sustained by the multiplicity of simultaneous rhythms played by typical instruments'.[1] Both Roldán and García Caturla held a significant place in

---

[1] Adolfo Salazar, 'La obra musical de Alejandro García Caturla', *Revista Cubana*, XI, 31 (January 1938).

twentieth-century Cuban music not only because of the high quality of their works, rooted on national sources but transcending these in unique, modern styles, but also because they contributed, each in his own way, to raising the level of music professionalism in their country.

In the 1940s and 1950s, the Spanish-born composer José Ardévol (1911–1981) dominated the Cuban music scene as an influential teacher and composer. He settled in Havana in 1930 and, although he shared at first the aesthetic ideals of the 'Grupo Minorista', he eventually adhered to neo-classicism which, in his view, carried a greater international meaning. He explored Cuban folk music elements on a few occasions, as in his *Suite Cubana No. 1* (1947) and *No. 2* (1949). Two of his students, Argeliers León (1918–91) and Hilario González (b. 1920), followed the nationalist trend up to the 1950s. Both as a composer and an ethnomusicologist, León maintained his interest in Afro-Cuban music, as revealed in his works *Escenas de ballet* (1944), *Danzón No. 2* (1945), *Yambú, Bolero y Guaguancó* (1956), and *Akorín* (1956), among others. González's most typical nationalist works include *Tres preludios en conga* (1938), *Danzas cubanas* (1938), and two cycles of *Canciones cubanas* (1940, 1945), in which the composer handles rhythmic patterns of folk and popular music in a very personal manner, within a strikingly dissonant style.

## The Andean Republics

From around 1920 Vicente Emilio Sojo (1887–1974) and Juan Bautista Plaza (1898–1965) exerted strong leadership towards the renovation of music composition in Venezuela. Sojo helped found the Orquesta Sinfónica Venezuela (1930) and the choral association Orfeón Lamas. He taught at and directed (from 1936) the National School of Music of Caracas, and in those capacities, he influenced a large number of student-composers. In his compositions, he developed a rather overt national style combined with Impressionistic techniques. Plaza who occupied the post of chapelmaster at the Caracas Cathedral for twenty-five years wrote religious music and a series of works for various media in which he cultivated 'música criolla', that is, songs and dances of partially European origin, such as the *joropo*, Venezuela's national folk dance, related to the Spanish *fandango*. His *Siete canciones venezolanas* (1932) may have been inspired by the example of Manuel de Falla in his own *Siete canciones españolas*, each drawing on a different popular genre. Plaza set poems by Luis Barrios

Cruz, himself a nationalist and a 'poeta llanero' (of the plains or 'llanos' and hence of the popular tradition of that area). The settings borrow certain characteristics of popular songs and dances but there is no strict imitation. *Joropo* rhythmic patterns are cleverly combined in Plaza's *Fuga criolla* (1932), for string orchestra, with the essential polyphonic nature of the fugue.

Among the following generation of Venezuelan composers Evencio Castellanos (b. 1915), his brother Gonzalo Castellanos (b. 1926), Inocente Carreño (b. 1919) and Antonio Estévez (b. 1916), could be counted as nationalist composers, although not exclusively so.

The most influential Colombian composer of the first half of the twentieth century, Guillermo Uribe-Holguín (1880–1971), combined a good technical command of the great tradition of European music with an excellent assimilation of national elements. The latter are particularly evident in the 300 piano pieces known as *Trozos en el sentimiento popular* (1927–39). The melodic, rhythmic and formal characteristics of such folk-popular dances as the *pasillo* and the *bambuco* provide the basis for some of these pieces. Other nationalist works, such as the *Second Symphony*, Op. 15 (1924), subtitled 'del terruño', and the *Suite típica* Op. 43 (1932), for orchestra, are programmatic and their musical descriptions or associations favour the vernacular elements.

Other Colombian composers representative of the nationalist trend were Daniel Zamudio (1885–1952), author of the study *El Folklore musical de Colombia* (1944), José Rozo Contreras (1894–1976) who relied in part on the Afro-Colombian folk music tradition of the Chocó area, and Antonio María Valencia (1902–52) who, as a student of d'Indy in Paris, received a solid training in composition. Valencia's *Chirimía y bambuco sotareño* (1930) originally for piano and orchestrated in 1942, and *Emociones caucanas* (1938) for violin, piano and cello, represent some of the best examples of his nationalist style, made up of evocations of national life and nature through the stylization of popular dance music. His early training in Europe is reflected in his frequent reliance on Impressionist techniques of composition.

Among those of the following generation of composers who maintained an interest in national music, albeit in an indirect and non-exclusive manner, were Luis Antonio Escobar (b. 1925) and Blas Emilio Atehortúa (b. 1933).

Musical nationalism in Ecuador found its first proponent in the Italian Domenico Brescia, director of the Quito Conservatory of Music from 1903 to 1911, and composer of such works as *Sinfonía ecuatoriana* and *Ocho variaciones* on an Indian song, both written in the 1920s. Indianist styles were developed subsequently in the works of Segundo Luis Moreno (1882–1972), a well-known folklorist and musicologist, Luis Humberto Salgado (1903–1977) and Pedro Pablo Traversari (1874–1956). These styles generally reveal an overt reliance of Indian music and dance, either through direct borrowing of themes and scales or through programmatic allusions to native legends and national history.

The search for national identity among Peruvian composers found a logical direction in the 'indigenismo' (Indianist) movement. A number of folklorist-composers active from the 1920s wrote piano pieces, art songs and fewer orchestral pieces, all reminiscent in varying degrees of highland Indian and mestizo traditional musical expressions. Traits related to such folk genres as the *huayno, triste* or *yaraví*, particularly descending pentatonic melodies and characteristic cadential and rhythmic practices, are found in the music of composers such as Daniel Alomía Robles (1871–1942), José Castro (1872–1945) and Manuel Aguirre (1863–1951). The most prolific and influential composer of nationalist persuasion was Teodoro Valcárcel (1902–42) whose 30 *Cantos de alma vernacular* and *Cuatro canciones incaicas* reveal an imaginative stylization and genuine understanding of traditional Indian music material.

Inadequate academic training in music in Peru was somewhat remedied with the settling in Lima in the 1920s and 1930s of several European-born musicians. Among these the most influential were Andrés Sas (1900–67) and Rodolfo Holzmann (1910–92). Sas not only taught a large number of Peruvian composers but stimulated through his own research a better penetration of pre-Columbian music. His own compositions exhibit a general folkloristic nationalist style, with clearly French Impressionist harmonic practices as can be seen especially in *Rapsodia peruana* (1928) and *Poema indio* (1941). As a professor of composition at the National Conservatory of Music, Holzmann exposed his students to the newest European trends, particularly atonality and serialism. Over the years, he collected and studied Peruvian folk and primitive music, but despite this interest he never did advocate for himself the Indianist style. Some of his works of the 1940s are related to a few aspects of Peruvian folk music, such as the *Suite sobre motivos peruanos* and the *Suite arequipeña,* but such incursions appear more circumstantial. His later works relied on other contemporary trends.

Bolivian nationalist composers during the first half of the twentieth century utilized a Romantic stylization of folk music elements rather than relying directly on traditional Indian music. Among others, these composers include Simeón Roncal (1870–1953), Eduardo Caba (1890–1953), Teófilo Vargas Candia (1886–1961), Humberto Viscarra Monje (1898–1971) and José María Velasco Maidana (1900–70). Roncal was particularly effective, as a composer, in the stylization of Bolivia's national dance, the *cueca*. His twenty *cuecas* for the piano are highly virtuosic pieces, written in the character and the spirit of nineteenth-century Romantic salon music. Velasco Maidana, considered by many the leading nationalist composer of his country, wrote ballets and tone poems describing or evoking Aymara–Quechua myths and music.

In Chile, Indianism and nationalism in general had few adherents; the cultivated tradition in Chilean music was strongly Europeanized. There were, however, a number of exceptions. Pedro Humberto Allende (1885–1959) was the first to cultivate a national style in a context of French Impressionist techniques. Musical Indianism was followed especially by Carlos Lavín (1883–1962) and Carlos Isamitt (1885–1974), both composers and folk music researchers. Lavín carried out field research among the Araucanian Indians and incorporated his knowledge and impressions in his own works, such as the *Mitos araucanos* (1926), for piano, and *Fiesta araucana* (1926), for orchestra. The same occurred with Isamitt whose works of most obvious Indianist persuasion include *Friso araucano* (1931), for voices and orchestra, and the piano *Sonata 'Evocación araucana'* (1932).

## Argentina and Uruguay

A number of Argentine composers in the twentieth century kept alive the nationalist current initiated in the latter part of the nineteenth century in opera, ballet, symphonic and chamber music. In the 1930s, Juan José Castro (1895–1968) appeared as the leading figure of the movement, especially with his *Sinfonía argentina* (1934) in three movements ('Arrabal', 'Llanuras', 'Ritmos y Danzas'), and his *Sinfonía de los Campos* (1939), a 'pastoral' work evocative of the pampa folk traditions. His approach to musical nationalism, however, is not overt but rather based on a few references to folk or popular music genres (as in *Tangos*, for piano, 1941, or *Corales criollos nos. 1 and 2*, for piano, 1947), or a sublimation of these (as in the *Corales criollos No. 3*, for orchestra, 1953). His operas *La Zapatera prodigiosa* (1943) and *Bodas de sangre* (1953) on texts by García Lorca, attest to his strong affinity with Spanish music. Castro's contemporary, Luis

Gianneo (1897–1968), contributed to Argentine national music, over a period of thirty years, in a consistent and comprehensive manner. His nationalist style relied on Indian music elements of northern and north-western Argentina, the *música criolla, gauchesca* tradition, and urban popular music represented by the *tango*. The latter is given prominence in his *Variaciones sobre tema de tango* (1953), for orchestra.

Alberto Ginastera (1916–83), recognized as one of the leading creative personalities in twentieth-century Latin American music, came of age during the high tide of Argentine musical nationalism. The first period of his activity as a composer reveals an objective, deliberate treatment of vernacular elements, but his reputation as the most notable national composer of his generation was established in the late 1930s and 1940s, with such works as the *Danzas argentinas,* for piano (1937), the ballets *Panambi* (1937) and *Estancia* (1941), *Obertura para el 'Fausto' Criollo* (1943), *Suite de danzas criollas* (1946) for piano, and several solo songs. This period that Ginastera himself has qualified as one of 'objective nationalism' (1937–47) is characterized by a strong reliance on the *gauchesco* tradition, both literary and musical, a clearly tonal musical idiom, including however, extremely dissonant passages. *Estancia* includes sung and recited excerpts from the epic poem *Martin Fierro* (1872) by José Hernández, which connects the work at once with the gaucho. Furthermore, the last section of *Estancia,* titled 'Malambo', establishes a direct link with the *malambo* dance, a vigorous, now extinct competitive dance of the gauchos. Here Ginastera makes the most of the intricate rhythmic organization of the dance. At the same time and as early as 1937 in the third of the *Danzas argentinas,* Ginastera tried his hand at polytonality, both melodically and harmonically, anticipating later stylistic developments.

From about 1947 to 1954, Ginastera moved into a phase of 'subjective nationalism', beginning with the first *Pampeana* (1947) and the First String Quartet (1948) and ending with the *Pampeana No. 3* (1954), for orchestra. Here the national musical elements are sublimated and stated in a subdued manner. Referring to his Piano Sonata (1952), for example, Ginastera maintained that 'the composer does not employ any folkloric material, but instead introduces in the thematic texture rhythmic and melodic motives whose expressive tension has a pronounced Argentine accent'. One particular trait reappearing until 1953–4 is the conspicuous use of the natural chord of the guitar, with the open strings (E-A-D-G-B-E) often presented in chromatically altered form. This 'symbolic' chord retained a close association with Argentine folk and popular music traditions. *Pampeana No. 3*, called a 'symphonic pastoral', still related indirectly to Argentine folk music, but the techniques of composition are based, for the most part, on non-national elements such as tone rows, although the feeling of tonality is still evident. Beginning with his String Quartet No. 2 (1958), Ginastera turned to neo-expressionist aesthetics and ceased to be associated with musical nationalism as such.

Uruguay's first nationalist compositions appeared in the 1910s and 1920s. The works of Alfonso Broqua (1876–1946), Eduardo Fabini (1882–1950), Luis Cluzeau Mortet (1889–1957) and Vicente Ascone (1897–79) are the most representative. Fabini, in particular, was the champion of nationalism in his country. His tone poem *Campo*, premiered in 1922, is generally considered the Uruguayan 'national' work par excellence. In this and other works, such as *La Isla de los Ceibos* (1924–6) and the series of *Tristes*, for various media (1925–30), he re-creates rather than imitates directly elements of Uruguayan folk music.

## Brazil

The most prolific and creative composer of his generation in Brazil, indeed in Latin America, Heitor Villa-Lobos (1887–1959), approached the art of composition with spontaneity, sophistication and individuality. His non-conformity, in his life as well as in his music, often resulted in originality and success. He always felt a deep empathy and affinity with Brazilian popular culture and, although he was not an exclusively nationalist composer, his works of nationalist inspiration represent his most original contribution to Brazilian twentieth-century music.

Born and raised in Rio de Janeiro, Villa-Lobos's first musical experience as a guitar player originated among the *chorões*, or popular strolling, serenading musicians. This provided him with a first-hand, practical knowledge of urban popular music of the turn of the twentieth century. That music exerted a profound influence on him throughout his life. From about 1905 to 1913, he travelled extensively all over the country and discovered the richness of the various regional folk musical traditions, albeit his approach to such materials was not scientifically orientated.

In February 1922, Villa-Lobos participated in the 'Week of Modern Art' in São Paulo, that celebrated *modernismo* in modern Brazilian culture, a trend based on the principle of the adoption of avant-garde European techniques in the arts combined with a renewed promotion of national subject matters. (In fact, Villa-Lobos had already anticipated much of this, particularly in his ballets and tone poems, such as *Uirapurú, Saci-Pererê* and *Amazonas,* all composed in 1917.) Before leaving for Europe in 1923, he wrote the *Nonetto* (subtitled 'Impressão rápida de todo o Brasil'), one of his most typically nationalistic compositions. Besides the reliance of Brazilian popular percussion instruments (*chocalhos, cuíca, reco-reco,* among others), the work draws on the dance rhythmic character and colour blendings of popular music and stylizes somewhat the improvisatory nature of the music of the *chorões*.

During the 1920s, Villa-Lobos wrote some of his most celebrated piano pieces (*A Prole do Bebê No. 2,* 1921; *Cirandas,* 1926; *Rudepoema,* 1921–6), the series of *Choros,* and the songs of *Serestas.* The sixteen *Choros* were written from 1921 to 1929, a period of experimentation corresponding to his exposure to new European styles combined with his subjective re-creation of the musical manifestations of the various popular and primitive cultural traditions of Brazil. *Choros No. 5,* subtitled 'Alma brasileira' (Brazilian soul), for solo piano, characterizes the serenading music of the popular *chôro,* with its lyrical quality emanating from the *modinha,* a sentimental song genre of eighteenth- and nineteenth-century Luso-Brazilian tradition. The middle section of this piece, in contrast to the first, typifies the dance-like repertory of the *chorões,* with characteristic popular rhythmic patterns. *Choros No. 10* (1926), 'Rasga o coração' ('Rend my heart'), for large orchestra and mixed chorus, represents the composer's most successful attempt to integrate local musical elements with some of the European contemporary techniques of the time. The latter include above all a richly dissonant harmony with polytonal effects and multiple syncopations with poly-rhythmic passages. The national elements are the subjective re-creation of primitivistic musical practices, particularly through the imitation of Indian melodic material and the use of onomatopoeic vocal effects, echoing the phonetic character of Indian languages.

The 1930s and 1940s were dominated by the composition of the nine *Bachianas Brasileiras.* The composer referred to this set as a 'genre of musical composition in homage to the great genius of Johann Sebastian Bach'. Conceived as suites, that is, a sequence of dance movements with preludes and arias, these works were intended essentially as a very free adaptation to Brazilian folk and popular music of certain Baroque procedures. Villa-Lobos felt, not without some justification, that there existed some clear affinity between certain of Bach's contrapuntal and rhythmic procedures and those of Brazilian folk and popular music. In effect, the

*Bachianas* won international acclaim not only for the curiosity aroused by their evocation of Bach but also for their captivating melodic and harmonic contents and their exciting rhythmic qualities. With a few exceptions, each movement of the *Bachianas* bears a double denomination, one formalistic relating to the Baroque suite, the other clearly nationalistic. Their melodic contents tend to be quite lyrical and the harmonies Classical and strongly tonal. Examples of Romantic, lyrical melodies abound in the *Bachianas,* but none as expressive as the soprano line of the 'Aria-Cantilena' in *Bachianas Brasileiras* No. 5 (1938–45), the best-known work of Villa-Lobos. The improvisatory character of that long vocal phrase and the ingenious accompaniment (by a cello ensemble) suggesting an amplified version of a picked style of guitar playing add to its powerfully expressive qualities.

Brazilian musical nationalism also had strong adherents in Camargo Guarnieri (1907–93) and Francisco Mignone (1897–1986). Guarnieri's large production covers several decades of intense activity. His first works of clearly nationalistic character were the *Canção Sertaneja* (1928) and the *Dansa brasileira* (1928). Mário de Andrade, the influential Modernist writer and the spokesman for musical nationalism, acknowledged Guarnieri's *Sonatina,* for piano (1928), as the work of an extraordinarily imaginative composer. Among the chamber music works of the 1930s, Guarnieri began a series inspired by the popular *chôro* and his association with Andrade resulted in 1932 in a one-act opera, *Pedro Malazarte,* for which Andrade wrote the libretto. His numerous solo songs, from *Impossível Carinho* (1930) to *Vai, Azulão* (1939), are considered the composer's best contribution to this medium. His total song output reveals the effective use of Afro-Brazilian and Amerindian folksong characteristics. In the 1940s and 1950s he wrote his best orchestral pieces: three symphonies, an *Abertura Concertante* (1942) and several orchestral suites (*Brasiliana,* 1950; *Suite IV Centenário,* 1954; *Suite Vila Rica,* 1958). These works typify his unique style, based on the nationalist aesthetic, but with a substantial stylization of national elements, and a special attention to the technical craftsmanship of composition. Among the numerous piano pieces written by Guarnieri the fifty pieces in five albums entitled *Ponteios* (1931–59) are fine examples of this neo-classical linear writing and harmonies combined with rich lyricism.

Francisco Mignone was also prolific. His extensive production covers almost all musical genres of the Western tradition. He first cultivated a neo-Romantic style and, from around 1929 to about 1960, he combined a strong native orientation with post-Romantic and neo-classic styles. Representatives of this orientation are the ballets *Maracatu de Chico Rei* (1933), *Batucajé* (1936), *Babaloxá* (1936), and the four *Fantasias Brasileiras,* for piano and orchestra (1929–36). In them he uses Afro-Brazilian subjects and actual themes or stylized folk and popular dances. Urban popular music forms and contents influence overtly many piano pieces by Mignone, particularly the two sets of waltzes, *Valsas de Esquina* (1938–43) and *Valsas Choros* (1946–55), which are reminiscent, in their Romantic inspiration, of the piano music of the popular composer Ernesto Nazareth (1863–1934). From the late 1950s, Mignone followed a more eclectic approach to composition. He was less directly concerned with nationalist expression and gradually developed an interest in experimenting with new-music techniques, as in the *Variações em busca de um tema* ('Variations in search of a theme') (1972).

Among the numerous Brazilian nationalist composers of subsequent generations, José Siqueira (1907–85), Radamés Gnatalli (1906–88), Luiz Cosme (1908–65), Cláudio Santoro (1919–89), César Guerra Peixe (1914–93) and Oswaldo Lacerda (b. 1927) have been the most successful, albeit not exclusively nationalist.

COUNTERCURRENTS, 1920S TO 1940S

Although musical nationalism prevailed in Latin America well into the 1950s, other currents, some opposed to nationalism and others indifferent to it, emerged from the beginning of the twentieth century. A number of composers in the various republics attracted to the most advanced techniques and aesthetic of their period were frankly opposed to nationalism; they felt that musical nationalism and particularly national music styles demeaned Latin American music in general by resorting to an easy exotic regionalist expression. They also sought to gain recognition through the intrinsic quality of their works rather than through what could be construed as external means. In general, however, the majority of composers up to the 1960s followed an eclectic path, cultivating varying styles which combined national and non-national stylistic elements. Specific countercurrents were not adhered to systematically, although the main trends were, besides post-Romantic and neo-Romantic, Impressionist, neoclassical expressionist and, after mid-century as we shall see, serialist and variously experimental.

*Mexico*

As we have seen, the post-Revolutionary period in Mexico strongly favoured the development of musical nationalism. Yet one important figure who came to prominence in the 1910s and 1920s gave no attention to national music. Julián Carrillo (1875–1965) who studied in Germany and Belgium for almost five years came under the influence of late German Romantic music but also favoured in some of his early works a complex harmonic vocabulary, including at times extreme chromaticism and an intricate contrapuntal technique. He is, however, remembered essentially as one of the pioneers in the cultivation of microtonality. His theories of microtones, which he called *Sonido 13* ('Thirteenth Sound'), won him an international reputation. *Sonido 13* stood for him as the symbolic representation of the division of the octave beyond the twelve semitones, that is, microtones of various sizes down to sixteenths of a whole tone. In one of his first microtonal works, *Preludio a Colón* (1922) for soprano, flute, guitar, violin, octavina (a string instrument designed by the composer) and harp, Carrillo uses quarter, eighth and sixteenth tones. The microtonal effects enhanced by specific performance traits such as glissandi, harmonics, vocal portamentos and mutes, create a wailing, incantatory, eerie atmosphere which appeared quite futuristic for its time. For later works, he had instruments constructed to microtonal specifications, particularly microtonal pianos, which attracted the attention of the Czech Alois Hába and the Russian Ivan Vischnegradsky, both early proponents of microtonal music. In 1926, Carrillo's microtonal *Sonata Casi Fantasía* was performed in a concert of the League of Composers at New York's Town Hall, with resounding success. Leopold Stokowski himself took an immediate interest in Carrillo's theories and helped develop his reputation, by commissioning him to write a work for the Philadelphia Orchestra, resulting in the *Concertino* (1927) for violin, guitar, cello, octavina and harp (all in microtones) and orchestra (in traditional semitones). With this work, the composer applied for the first time his theories of 'musical metamorphosis', a forward-looking method of treatment of musical structures involving new possibilities of transformations and permutations of melodic, harmonic and rhythmic materials. Carrillo further explored microtonality in later works such as *Horizontes* (1951), various concertos, *Balbuceos* (1959) and the Mass for Pope John XXIII (1962). In retrospect, Carrillo appears as the precursor of ultrachromaticism and one of the most important pioneers in the field of sound experiments in the early part of the century.

While the ideas of Julián Carrillo were unique in Mexican music of the time, a number of Mexican composers were concerned with keeping up to date with European contemporary idioms, concurrently with their nationalist profession of faith. The case of Carlos Chávez himself is quite revealing. As a composer and the main conductor of the Orquesta Sinfónica de México, Chávez always strove to promote the 'new music' of a particular period. His *Seven Pieces for Piano* (1923–30), published in the United States in Henry Cowell's New Music Series in 1936, are written in the complex, international avant-garde style of the 1920s. In the period 1930–50, he wrote several non-nationalist works, relying wholly or partially on contemporary European techniques. Significant examples are the *Sinfonía de Antígona* (1933), the *Diez preludios para piano* (1937), the *Toccata* for percussion instruments (1942), and the Violin Concerto (1948–50). The *Sinfonía de Antígona,* one of Chávez's orchestral masterpieces, is certainly akin to the neo-classical style of Stravinsky, in its archaic modal flavour, sobriety, austere character, thematic polyphony and its wind-dominated orchestration. Likewise, the systematic diatonicism and linearity of the Ten Preludes, as well as their predominant two-voice polyphony and their diatonic, parallel static harmonies, identify them as excellent examples of the neo-classical movement of the 1930s. The Violin Concerto exemplifies the composer's mature compositional process. As a grand virtuoso work, this concerto reveals further the attachment of the composer to classical techniques, such as melodic inversions, variations, retrograde formal organization and highly demanding and effective virtuosic writing, all of them treated in a very personal, imaginative matter.

Silvestre Revueltas, the other major Mexican national composer of the time, also paid attention to neo-classical stylistic idioms. His *Homenaje a García Lorca* (1936), while maintaining a uniquely Mexican character, is one of the most successful examples of the assimilation by a Mexican composer of the neo-classical style. The second movement – 'Mourning for García Lorca' – particularly is neo-classical in its aesthetic, characterized by a static, contemplative character and a general economy of musical means.

The Spanish-born Rodolfo Halffter (1900–87) settled in Mexico in 1939 and exerted a profound influence on Mexican art-music developments in the subsequent decades, particularly as a professor of composition at the National Conservatory, as the editor of the journal *Nuestra*

*Música* (from 1946) and the manager of Ediciones Mexicanas de Música. As a composer, Halffter had a close affinity with Manuel de Falla's neo-classicism of the 1920s. He developed a personal language whose austere character and highly expressive restraint are conveyed through tonal and polytonal feelings, complex rhythmic patterns related to Spanish folk music, predominant linearity and contrapuntal elaboration, and refined diatonic and dissonant harmony. His most significant works written in Mexico in the 1940s are the Violin Concerto Op. 11 (1939–40), the ballet *La Madrugada del Panadero* (1940), *Homenaje a Antonio Machado* (1944), for piano, and the *Epitafios* (1947–53), for a cappella chorus.

Although Blas Galindo did not abandon altogether the nationalist expression of his early works, he cultivated in the 1940s and early 1950s a style reminiscent of neo-classicism. His harmonic practices especially became more cosmopolitan at that time, as seen in such works as the Violin Sonata (1945) and the *Siete Piezas para Piano* (1952).

## Cuba

In Cuba, both Amadeo Roldán and Alejandro García Caturla had instilled their nationalist style with very modernistic practices, particularly harmonic and rhythmic complexities, that lend a contemporary expression. Beginning in the 1940s, however, José Ardévol became the leader of modern Cuban composition. In 1942, together with some of his students, he founded the Grupo de Renovación Musical whose aim was the creation of a Cuban school of composers 'which could reach the same degree of universality obtained by other countries'. The most important members of the group included Harold Gramatges, Edgardo Martín, Julián Orbón, Hilario González, Argeliers León, Serafín Pro and Gisela Hernández. Ardévol stood as the spokesman and leader of the group. While the credo of the group stressed the independence of its members from any pre-established trend, the neo-classical movement appeared at first as one of the most adequate currents for their purposes. Craftsmanship and competence in the knowledge and treatment of musical composition were emphasized. In the early 1930s, Ardévol himself wrote in an atonal style or followed the twelve-tone method. But gradually he adhered to neo-classicism in the late 1930s and the 1940s. His most revealing works of this period include six *Sonatas a tres* (1937–46), two Concerti Grossi (1937), the ballet *Forma* (1942), and the Concerto for Piano, Winds, and

Percussion (1944). The *Sonata a tres No. 1*, for oboe, clarinet and cello is conceived as a Baroque trio sonata as to instrumentation and form. Systematic imitations and contrapuntal elaboration occur throughout the work. In the ballet *Forma* for four-, five- and six-part choruses and orchestra, the voices are treated in the manner of ancient Greek drama, commenting upon the action in a non-participatory way. Once more, the harmonic staticity of the choral numbers is typical of neo-classical techniques of the period.

Almost all of Ardévol's students associated with the Grupo de Renovación Musical cultivated a neo-classical style, often combined with a neo-nationalism early in their career (the 1940s), but they followed quite different paths during the subsequent decades. The youngest and most independent member of the group, Julián Orbón (b. 1925), developed (together with Aurelio de la Vega) into the most outstanding Cuban composer of his generation. His earlier works, dating from the mid-1940s, exhibit a direct influence from the Spanish neo-classical style of Falla and Cristóbal Halffter. After 1950, he found a more personal style, harmonically more tense and less committed to tonality (as, for example, in his *Tres versiones sinfónicas*, 1953).

### The Andean Republics

In Colombia Guillermo Uribe-Holguín came increasingly under the influence of French Impressionism, particularly in the harmonies and orchestration of his works of the 1920s. His compatriot Carlos Posada-Amador (1906–48) had the same experience in the 1930s, while Santiago Velasco Llanos (b. 1915) showed a preference for neo-classicism. And in Peru, Rodolfo Holzmann exposed his many students to various contemporary European styles and advocated openly an alternative to nationalism. He was himself influenced by Paul Hindemith's new tonal system and emphasis on craftsmanship in the composition training. In some of Holzmann's most characteristic works of the 1940s, including *Divertimento Concertante* (1941) for piano and ten woodwinds, the *Cantigas de la Edad de Oro* (1944), for small orchestra, the *Tres Madrigales* (1944) for voice and piano, and the *Concierto para la Ciudad Blanca* (1949) for piano and orchestra, his attachment to tradition can be seen in the formal designs, compositional processes and general reliance on the tonal system—treated, however, in a modern vein.

Among the Andean nations it was Chile, however, that took the lead position during the 1930s and 1940s in the production of significant non-nationalist compositions. Chilean musical life underwent a profound transformation in the 1920s, as the result of the activities of the Sociedad Bach under the leadership of Domingo Santa Cruz (1899–1987) and especially of the creation of the Facultad de Bellas Artes (1929) within the University of Chile. Santa Cruz exerted a considerable influence from the 1920s to the 1950s as teacher, administrator and composer. As Dean of the Faculty of Fine Arts at the National Conservatory, reorganized later as the Faculty of Musical Arts and Sciences, he helped establish a successful system of musical instruction in the country under the control of the university. As a composer, he wrote a number of important works. His first orientation went towards both Impressionist neo-classicism, and atonal stylistic elements. The *Five Pieces for String Orchestra,* Op. 14 (1937), for example, exhibit a rich, contrapuntal style with technical and formal elements akin to Baroque and Classic practices. At the same time the essentially horizontal writing generates at times a polytonal harmony. Later works, such as the *Sinfonía Concertante* Op. 22 (1945) and the *Preludios Dramáticos* Op. 23 (1946), illustrate further his attachment to the Western art-music heritage. He did not eschew, however, the 'Latinidad' of his own heritage: many of his themes reveal a strongly Hispanic character, particularly the type of melodic ornamentation associated with Andalusian folk singing or typical rhythmic motives associated with Spanish folk dances. Santa Cruz was also active and successful as a choral composer in the 1940s. His compositions include *Cinco Canciones* Op. 16, for mixed chorus or soloists, *Tres Madrigales,* Op. 17, for mixed chorus, *Cantata de los Ríos de Chile,* Op. 19, and *Egloga,* Op. 26. These represent a special expression of his aesthetics. The *Tres Madrigales,* for example, are highly dramatic settings (with texts by the composer), combining an expressively harmonic counterpoint with monodic, recitative-like designs.

Santa Cruz's contemporaries such as Enrique Soro (1884–1954), Alfonso Leng (1894–1974) and Jorge Urrutia Blondel (1903–1981) cultivated above all post-Romantic and Impressionist styles. Acario Cotapos (1889–1969), who lived in New York from 1917 to 1927, was associated with the avant-garde of the time and, like Edgard Varèse, refuted all academicism and established trends. His early works (for example, *Le Détachement vivant,* 1918, or the *Tres Piezas Sinfónicas,* 1923) reveal a vivid imagination and independence, which found further expression in his later works, such as *Balmaceda* (1958), considered revolutionary.

Of the next generation, Alfonso Letelier (b. 1912) and Juan A. Orrego-Salas (b. 1919) were quite active in the 1940s. Both belong to the generation of Chilean composers sometimes classified as 'formalists' because of their adherence to the stylistic aims of neo-classicism. Among Letelier's numerous works of this period, the *Sonetos de la Muerte* (1942–8), for soprano and orchestra (on sonnets by Gabriela Mistral), and the piano *Variaciones en Fa* (1948), exemplify his stylistic preference. In the *Sonetos* he succeeds in depicting the dramatic substance of the poems, by treating the vocal line as a free recitative, in the character of 'endless melody', by utilizing dissonant and dense harmonies and contrasting dynamics. Several of the variations in the piano *Variaciones* are stylized Baroque dance forms (gigue, allemande, minuet, gavotte), in which homophonic and polyphonic textures are combined.

Orrego-Salas enjoyed the widest international reputation among Chilean composers. He was influenced by the aesthetic orientation of Domingo Santa Cruz, his teacher of composition at the Santiago National Conservatory. Thus his early works of the 1940s follows an imaginative and effective neo-classic style. The *Canciones Castellanas* Op. 20 (1948), for soprano and a chamber ensemble are settings of early Luso-Spanish Renaissance poetry, in which modal and linear writing prevails. A rhythmic intensity and a skilful treatment of timbres quite characteristic of the composer's musical language pervade these songs. Occasional Spanish traits also appear in this work, such as arabesque-like figurations and rhythmic patterns. Orrego-Salas turned to the orchestra more readily in later works, but his First Symphony (1949) and his *Obertura Festiva* Op. 21 (1948) denote already a very colourful, virtuoso orchestral writing.

## Argentina and Uruguay

In the 1920s a few Argentine composers began to move away from folkloric nationalism. Such figures as Juan José Castro, his brother José María Castro (1892–1964), Floro M. Ugarte (1884–1975), and Jacobo Ficher (1896–1978) attempted in varying degrees to assimilate European contemporary techniques. Juan José Castro's quest for a more international style is evident in his *Allegro-Lento e Vivace* (1930), for orchestra, in which Impressionist and Stravinskian influences abound. Although Ugarte's primary interest lay in music nationalism, some of his works of the 1920s are conceived within a post-Romantic style and aesthetic. Of Russian origin,

Ficher remained attached in the 1920s to the post-Romantic Russian composers, particularly Scriabin, but his subsequent works (symphonies, piano and violin sonatas) have greater affinity with neo-classicism.

Dodecaphony, considered in the 1930s the most radical trend in musical composition, had its first Latin American champion in the Argentine composer Juan Carlos Paz (1901–72). With the Castro brothers, Ficher, and others, Paz founded the Grupo Renovación in 1929, with the aims of advocating a deeper involvement of Argentine composers with European modern trends, leading to the renovation and updating of art music in their country. Paz, however, withdrew from the Group because of irreconcilable differences as to the methods to achieve such goals, and founded the Conciertos de Nueva Música (1937), eventually creating his own group, the Agrupación Nueva Música (1944). This latter organization went further in the promotion of the avant-garde, particularly the music of the serial composers Schoenberg and Webern, and the experimentalists such as Varèse, Cowell, Cage and Messiaen. Largely self-taught, Paz's attitudes and enthusiasm for new musical ideas had a beneficial influence on a number of later composers.

Juan Carlos Paz was the only composer of the period who sustained a consistent campaign against musical nationalism. Up to about 1934, he cultivated an essentially neo-classical style, characterized by a linear writing, polytonal and at times atonal harmony (*Three Pieces for Orchestra, 1930, Octet for Wind Instruments, 1930*). With the *Primera Composición en los 12 Tonos* (1934), Paz turned to dodecaphony, but always used the twelve-tone methods in a free, personal way, radically different from Schoenberg's manipulations. A good illustration of Paz's treatment can be seen in the *Tercera Composición en los 12 Tonos* (1937), for clarinet and piano. All four sections of the work – 'Toccata', 'Tema con variaciones', 'Canción', and 'Tempo de giga' – utilize the same row, in its prime and retrograde forms without inversions or transpositions of it. As opposed to Schoenberg, Paz does not avoid chordal or tonal implications in the arrangement of the basic row material. Here he utilizes octaves and chords such as triads, sevenths, and ninths quite deliberately, and he repeats several notes of the row or presents them out of order. Another aspect of Paz's musical style was revealed with the work *Rítmica Ostinata* Op. 41 (1942), for orchestra. This composition abounds in virtuoso contrapuntal and rhythmic writing. The title itself indicates the repetitive nature of the work, which has the character of a large toccata, due to the prevailingly fast tempo, constant quaver and semi-quaver figurations, numerous ostinatos, and to the brilliant orchestration. The harmonic idiom is wholly chromatic and dissonant.

Among other Argentine composers representative of the 'international' trend, Roberto García Morillo (b. 1911), the Spanish-born Julián Bautista (1901–61), and the Austrian-born Guillermo Graetzer (1914–92) stand out. García Morillo began writing in the 1930s in a modernistic style and appeared until the 1950s as an eclectic composer, thereafter showing a clearer orientation towards neo-classicism. In works such as *Las pinturas negras de Goya* (1939), *Tres pinturas de Paul Klee* (1944), and the cantata *Marín* (1948–50), he developed an increasingly complex language which includes an intensified, dissonant and often atonal harmony and an original treatment of rhythm. Bautista belongs to the Spanish neo-classic school of the 1920s to the 1940s. His style is primarily contrapuntal, harmonically advanced and formally traditional. Graetzer's training in Austria and Germany orientated him towards the new tonal style developed by Hindemith. As a teacher he became influential in the field of music education.

Among the few Uruguayan non-nationalist composers active in the early part of the twentieth century were César Cortinas (1890–1918) and Carmen Barradas (1888–1963). Cortinas wrote in a style combining Romantic elements of the late nineteenth century (especially in his piano works) with a Puccini-like lyric intensity (in his songs and his opera, *La última gavota,* 1915), while Barradas who wrote primarily for the piano was exceptional for her interest in experimenting with revolutionary notation. Beginning in the 1940s, Uruguayan music matured enough to be able to achieve an international reputation. The composers most in evidence during the 1940s were Carlos Estrada (1909–70), Héctor Tosar E. (b. 1923), and, to a lesser extent, Guido Santórsola (b. 1904). Estrada, who studied at the Paris Conservatoire, cultivated a sober neo-classical style. His incidental music for Paul Claudel's *L'Annonce faite à Marie* (1943) and Paul Verlaine's *Les uns et les autres* (1950) as well as his numerous settings of French poems reveal his strong empathy for French culture. Tosar's most important works were written after 1950, but his talent as a composer is already evident in the 1940s. In his *Sinfonía No. 2* (1950), for strings, for example, he reveals a decisively modernistic style of enormous rhythmic vitality, rich harmonic resources and original timbral and dynamic effects. The Italian-born Santórsola was particularly influential as a conductor and string player, having founded the orchestra of the Uruguayan Cultural Association. In his works he drew at first on Uruguayan folk music, but later turned to serial techniques.

A particularly important figure active in Montevideo from the 1930s was the musicologist Francisco Curt Lange (b. 1903), who had emigrated to Uruguay from Germany in the late 1920s. Besides his invaluable services as a researcher of Latin American music, he systematically promoted the music and musicians of Latin America the world over. He founded both the Inter-American Institute of Musicology and the unique Editorial Cooperativa Interamericana de Compositores which published numerous piano, choral and chamber music works by composers of the Western Hemisphere. In 1985, he received, together with the U.S. musicologist Robert Stevenson, the 'Gabriela Mistral' Prize awarded by the Organization of American States' Department of Cultural Affairs.

## Brazil

During the first quarter of the twentieth century Brazil had a Europeanized school of composition represented mainly by composers such as Francisco Braga (1868–1945), a post-Romantic, Glauco Velasquez (1884–1914), an Impressionist, and Henrique Oswald (1852–1931), a post-Romantic eclectic. Alberto Nepomuceno himself wrote many works in a non-nationalist vein, such as *Sinfonía* in G minor (1894), *Valsas humorísticas* (1903), for piano and orchestra, numerous choral works, all of post-Romantic inspiration and technique. There is no doubt, however, that Villa-Lobos's works of the period 1915–30 represent the boldest achievement in Brazil in the assimilation of contemporary techniques of composition. Despite its nationalistic intention and substance, Villa-Lobos's music relied on such techniques as polytonality, polyrhythm, dissonant polyphonic textures and experimental tone colouring.

The major innovating movement in Brazilian composition came from the Música Viva group, founded in 1937 under the leadership of the German composer Hans-Joachim Koellreutter (b. 1915). The group's manifesto of 1946 declared its frank opposition to folkloristic nationalism and was viewed by many as an anti-national campaign. The current that became associated with this campaign was dodecaphony because Koellreutter himself favoured it in his own works of the 1940s. At first his treatment of atonality and twelve-tone techniques was rather dogmatic, as in *Música* (1941) and *Noturnos* (1945), but he used them more freely and personally in subsequent works. His influence as a teacher of composition was felt especially in Rio de Janeiro, São Paulo, and Salvador (Bahia), the three major centres in the country for the future development of new music. Among his many students were Cláudio Santoro and César Guerra Peixe (see above).

Santoro orientated himself between 1939 and about 1947 towards atonality and a pragmatic twelve-tone technique. His early works are abstract, with the exception of the semi-programmatic *Impressões de uma fundição de aço* ('Impressions of a steel foundry') for orchestra (1942). The Sonata for solo violin (1940) is written in an atonal style but retains the structure of the Baroque sonata. Moreover, this atonal style does not rely on the twelve-tone technique. In the First Sonata for Violin and Piano (1940), however, Santoro follows serial techniques in a free manner. In a few of his vocal works of the period he also follows Schoenberg's vocal technique known as *Sprechstimme*, as in *Asa Ferida* (1944) which includes a passage with the indication that the recitation of the text should be interpreted as 'spoken song'. Other works of the 1940s (Second and Third Symphonies, First String Quartet, *Música para cordas*) reveal Santoro's eclecticism with definite preference for classic structure, Baroque polyphony, atonal and polytonal harmonies and rhythmic drive. Guerra Peixe appeared in the 1940s as a decided apologist of atonality and twelve-tone music in Brazil. He wrote several works based on serial techniques, such as *Sonatina 1944*, for flute and clarinet. Soon, however, he turned to what he called a 'curious sort of music' that could combine two apparently irreconcilable trends – twelve-tone and nationalist music. The necessary compromise, which required some alteration of both serial technique and typically national musical elements, proved untenable. But Guerra Peixe produced original, well-conceived works (such as the *Trio*, for flute, clarinet and bassoon, in 1948) which need no theoretical affiliation.

Another composer associated with the Música Viva group was Luiz Cosme (1908–65), who turned to non-national sources in his later works. From 1946 to about 1950, he increasingly avoided the tonal system and made free use of the twelve-tone method. His last work, *Novena à Senhora da Graça* (1950), for string quartet, piano, narrator and female dancer, relies to a certain extent on some dodecaphonic techniques and is free of national implications.

From the 1930s to the end of his life, Villa-Lobos tended to write in a more abstract manner, that is, without the obvious programmatic intention of his earlier works. Although he remained close to Brazilian national sources as in his *Bachianas*, he concurrently displayed an interest in neo-tonal and post-Romantic styles with little or no nationalist references. The *Missa de São Sebastião* (1937), for example, and many other choral works, are good indications of this tendency. Among his later works, the *String Quartet No. 17* (1957) shows a new aesthetic direction towards an austere simplicity, expressed through a rather terse and abstract style.

In general, the countercurrents witnessed in Latin American music from the 1920s to about 1950 indicate the definite awareness of a number of composers of a need to innovate and rejuvenate Latin American composition by liberating it from the subjection of musical nationalism. The consequent individualism and eclecticism developed in full during the next three decades.

## CONTEMPORARY MUSIC, 1950s TO 1970s

Since the middle of the twentieth century the profound transformations that have affected art-music in Latin America have resulted in a variety of styles and in a diversity of aesthetics. Before the Second World War social and intellectual conditions in Latin America had reflected a strong dependence on Europe and, to a lesser extent, North America; consequently musical nationalism appeared to many as a logical orientation since it responded to the need for national identity and assertion. But, although political and economic subordination, particularly in relation to the United States, continued after 1950, cultural dependence diminished considerably. A new tendency, at least in the larger cities, towards a greater cosmopolitanism gradually emerged. Foreign elements still prevailed but were deliberately assimilated within a new frame of mind. Many progressive Latin American composers speculated that in the process of assimilating the 'new music' of Europe and North America a natural qualitative selection would occur, followed by an imitation, recreation and transformation of foreign models according to the local artistic environment and individual needs and preferences. The progressive and avant-garde composers of the period realized that they had a great deal to contribute as Latin Americans to these new cosmopolitan musical trends.

In the 1960s new, experimental musical currents emerged in most countries of the continent. Those adhering to such currents, however, soon discovered that official support for the performance of their music by national orchestras or for its publication and commercial recording was not readily forthcoming. Several prominent Latin American composers were forced to settle in Europe, the United States and Canada. Conditions for new music composers did gradually improve, however, in the 1960s and 1970s, especially in Argentina, Chile, Brazil, Venezuela and Mexico. In co-operation with the International Society for Contemporary Music (ISCM), several national organizations were formed; a few electronic music studios were developed; some professional schools or universities updated their music curricula; state broadcasting systems gave some attention to contemporary music; and several private and state institutions began to subsidize festivals of new music. Beginning in 1958, the Organization of American States organized and sponsored the Inter-American Music Festivals in Washington, D.C., always premiering new works of Latin American composers. From the early 1960s, the OAS also promoted the publication of a series of scores, including some works by young composers. In the 1970s contemporary music festivals, summer workshops and courses, such as the Latin American Course on Contemporary Music held in various countries, occurred more frequently and brought together not only prominent figures from Europe but also young composers from the entire continent. Thus, the isolation of the majority of composers and the lack of interaction among them in previous decades tended to disappear. With it, a sense of new identity within the contemporary music scene became stronger among Latin American composers.

### *Mexico*

Although Mexican musical life no longer revolved around him after about 1955, Carlos Chávez remained active as composer, conductor and teacher. He delivered the Charles Eliot Norton lectures at Harvard University in 1958–9, out of which came his book *Musical Thought;* and he opened a workshop in composition in 1960 at the Mexico City Conservatory, which he directed until 1964 and in which several young Mexican composers got their training and experience. Chávez's compositions of the period include four symphonies, the opera *The Visitors* (1953–6), the cantata *Prometheus Bound* (1956), *Resonancias* (1964), for orchestra, *Clio* (1969), a symphonic ode, the ballet *Pirámide* (1968), *Initium* (1971), for orchestra, *Concerto for Trombone and Orchestra* (1976), and several piano and chamber music pieces. In contrast to earlier works, *Sinfonía No. 4* (1953), subtitled *Román-*

*tica,* is lyrical and emotional in character and rather classical in formal designs. *Sinfonía No. 5* (1953), for string orchestra, clearly indicates Chávez's penchant for neo-classicism. Among his most significant works of this period are *Soli II, III* and *IV* (of 1961, 1965, 1966, respectively). *Soli II* is for wind quintet, *Soli III* for bassoon, trumpet, timpani, viola and orchestra, and *Soli IV* for French horn, trumpet and trombone. The appearance of each instrument (or group of solo instruments) as soloist in each movement justifies the titles. The directing principle in these pieces, according to the composer, is that of non-repetition, the avoidance of standard sequence, symmetry and recapitulation and of the 'repetitive procedures implicit in the Viennese serial technique'. Instead, Chávez resorts to the element of renewal of musical materials. This principle affects the melodic writing which is made up of wide-ranging, disjunct and chromatic motifs that establish an improvisatory character, as seen in *Soli II.* In addition, the composer's concern for clarity, terseness and novelty of instrumental blendings finds its best expression in these works.

Twelve-tone and other serial techniques gained the attention of several Mexican composers during the 1950s and 1960s, at first under the guidance of Rodolfo Halffter who himself turned to twelve-tone methods in the early 1950s (for example, *Tres Hojas de Album,* for piano, 1953, and *Tres Piezas* for string orchestra, 1954). In these and subsequent works, however, he applies the techniques very freely, and the Spanish rhythmic traits noted in his earlier works reappear occasionally. Among Halffter's students who followed serial techniques was Jorge González Avila (b. 1926), primarily a composer of piano music. Atonality and serialism, that is, the serialization of more than one parameter, found more acceptance among younger Mexican composers. Joaquin Gutiérrez-Heras (b. 1927), for example, cultivated a free atonal style, in works such as the *Woodwind Trio* (1965). In the case of Mario Kuri-Aldana (b. 1931), another student of Halffter, we find the development of a highly individual style based on traditional procedures but expressed in a contemporary language mixed with neo-classical and neo-nationalist elements. His research on Mexican folk and Indian music influenced his compositions somewhat, as in works such as *Peregrina agraciada* (1963) or *Concierto Tarahumara* (1981). A modern style rooted in national sources also appears in some of the works of Leonardo Velásquez (b. 1935).

Foremost among the Mexican followers of avant-garde techniques and aesthetics from the 1960s were Manuel Enríquez, Héctor Quintanar, Eduardo Mata, Manuel de Elías and Mario Lavista. Enríquez (1926–94) was a student of Peter Mennin at the Juilliard School in the mid-1950s and at that same time came under the influence of Stefan Wolpe who orientated him to serial techniques. He then kept up with all avant-garde music developments and, as the director of CENIDIM (Centro Nacional de Investigación, Documentación e Información Musical 'Carlos Chávez') and the founder of the Mexican Society for Contemporary Music, was influential in the promotion and dissemination of such developments in his country. In 1971 he worked at the Columbia-Princeton Center for Electronic Music, but the electronic medium did not figure prominently in his works. Rather Enríquez favoured neo-expressionist atonality, serialism and aleatory music. His first serial work was *Preámbulo* (1961), for orchestra. He himself qualified his *Tres Invenciones* (1964), for flute and viola, the culmination of his admiration for Webern. After that date, chance operations appeared more frequently in his works, such as the Sonata for violin and piano (1964), *Ambivalencia* (1967) and *A Lápiz* (1965). From around 1967, he adhered more fully to indeterminacy, a principle first espoused by John Cage in the 1950s, whereby chance operations or random procedures create compositions with a certain degree of unpredictability and a variability of the sequence of sections in a work, often referred to as 'open form'. One of the first works by Enríquez relying systematically on open form was his *Second String Quartet* (1967), in which he applied graphic notation, a type of non-specific notation in which different symbols, drawings of different sizes and shapes, give general directions to the performer who can combine at will any of the numerous possibilities. In later compositions, such as *Él y Ellos* (1975), he wrote in a highly virtuosic, free style.

Héctor Quintanar (b. 1936) worked with Chávez in the Composition Workshop in the early 1960s and took over its directorship from 1965 to 1972. In 1970 he became the founding director of the electronic music studio at the Mexico City Conservatory. As a composer, Quintanar developed from a style akin to Webernian serialism and Penderecki-like experiments with new sonorities (in such works as *Galaxias,* for orchestra, 1968) to electronic music, aleatory techniques and mixed media. He pioneered the study and composition of electronic music in Mexico. Eduardo Mata (1942–94) combined freely in his works from the mid-1960s aspects of serial and aleatory techniques. In the 1970s and 1980s he dedicated himself primarily to his orchestra conducting career. Manuel Jorge de Elías (b. 1939) studied first at the School of Music of the National University of Mexico and at the National Conservatory, and later in Europe with

Stockhausen and Jean-Etienne Marie. In the 1960s he cultivated a serial style mixed with aleatory procedures and also paid attention to the electronic medium. His *Vitral No. 3* (1969), for orchestra, sets forth some of the typical performance practices of new music, such as rhythmic patterns produced by tapping the mouthpieces of brass instruments with the palm of the hand, and it combines counterpoints of discontinuous, unrelated lines with various series of clusters.

Mario Lavista (b. 1943) represented in the late 1960s and 1970s the extreme left wing of the Mexican avant-garde. While a student in Europe he became acquainted with the Hungarian composer György Ligeti who exerted some influence on his aesthetic development. In the early 1970s he studied electronic music in Tokyo. More than his colleagues, he appears as a bonafide experimentalist. Improvisation and chance operations were utilized in the most unconfined manner. He explored new sonorous possibilities, combined electro-acoustic and visual elements, and attempted to expand the concepts of musical time and space. In works such as *Pieza para un(a) pianista y un piano* ('Piece for a pianist and a piano') (1970) he applied John Cage's principles of indeterminacy and non-self-expression.

### The Caribbean and Central America

In Cuba the leader of the Grupo de Renovación Musical, José Ardévol, began to pay attention to atonality and serialism from around 1957. During the early years of the Cuban Revolution, he played a major role as National Director of Music in the reorganization of the country's musical life. Thanks to him, Cuba has enjoyed since then a remarkable freedom of musical expression, conveyed not only through his own stylistic development but through that of other members of the Grupo, like Harold Gramatges, Edgardo Martín, and Argeliers León, and of a number younger composers discussed below. From around 1965, Ardévol combined a post-Webernian serialist style with a few aleatory techniques, as in the cantatas *La Victoria de Playa Girón* (1966) and *Che Comandante* (1968). The same orientation is found in Gramatges's works, especially *La muerte del guerrillero* (1968), on a text by Nicolás Guillén, and *Cantata para Abel* (1974), for narrator, mixed chorus and ten percussionists. Martín ceased to compose during the period 1953–9 when he joined Fidel Castro's movement against the Batista regime. Several of his works of the 1960s reflect his political conviction. *Cuatro Cantos de la Revolución* (1962), *Así*

*Guevara* (1967), the cantata *Canto de héroes* (1967) and *Cinco Cantos de Ho* (1969), on texts by Ho Chi Minh, all reveal an eclectic language, with some serialist techniques permeating his abstract works of the period.

The younger, progressive composers most in evidence in the 1950s and 1960s included Juan Blanco, Aurelio de la Vega, Carlos Fariñas and Leo Brouwer. Blanco (b. 1920) learned on his own the techniques of *musique concrète* and electronic music which he was among the first Cubans to explore beginning in the early 1960s (*Música para danza,* 1961, *Estudios I–II,* 1962–3). Chance operations first appeared in *Texturas* (1963–4), for orchestra and tape, and with *Contrapunto espacial I* ('Spatial Counterpoint I') (1965–6) began a series of five major works belonging to so-called spatial music, that is, music in which the actual location of the sound sources, live or recorded but generally transmitted through loudspeakers, becomes integral to the structure of the work. In the last two of the 'Spatial Counterpoint' pieces, Blanco combined the spatial concept with that of theatre music, calling for actors and acting musicians.

Together with Julián Orbón, Aurelio de la Vega (b. 1925) is the best known Cuban composer of his generation. In the early 1950s, he developed a highly chromatic language combined with a strong rhythmic drive, and a virtuoso style of writing for traditional instruments which remained one of his constant concerns. He also cultivated free atonality, in such works as *Elegy* (1954) and *Divertimento* (1956), and unorthodox twelve-tone techniques, as in the String Quartet 'In Memoriam Alban Berg' (1957). From 1953 to 1959, he directed the music department at the Universidad de Oriente in Santiago de Cuba. Around the mid-1960s, by which time he was professor of composition at the California State University in Northridge, he abandoned gradually serialism for electronic means, open forms and aleatory procedures, while continuing to explore new sonorities. The effective expression of his colour blendings and structural organization is best expressed in two works of 1973: *Tangents,* for violin and pre-recorded sounds, and *Para-Tangents,* for trumpet and same pre-recorded sounds. The timbres and the expressive aspects of the solo instruments are explored in a dialogue fashion with the electronic sounds. Indeterminacy appeared in later works such as *Olep ed Arudamot* (1974) (the retrograde form of 'Tomadura de pelo', or 'Pulling one's leg') for non-specific instrumentation, the *Infinite Square* (1974), and *Undici Colori* (1981), with graphic projections by the composer.

Carlos Fariña (b. 1934) turned to serialist aesthetics in the 1960s, after an early interest in national music sources, and Leo Brouwer (b. 1939) after a similar nationalist concern became one of the most talented and recognized composers of the Cuban avant-garde. After the Cuban Revolution, Brouwer's contacts with the contemporary Polish avant-garde (Penderecki, Lutoslawski) and with Luigi Nono prompted him to adopt more readily new-music techniques. From around 1962, he wrote in a post-serialist and aleatory manner. His *Sonograma I* (1963), for prepared piano (following the ideas of Cage) is generally considered the first piece of aleatory music in Cuba. In the late 1960s and 1970s, he cultivated mixed media, first with *Cantigas del tiempo nuevo* (1969), and wrote major works for the classical guitar.

In Puerto Rico, new music has had several followers. Héctor Campos-Parsi (b. 1922) who had cultivated a rather overt nationalistic style in his early works and neo-classicism in the 1950s turned to atonality and serialism in the 1960s. He was active and influential in the promotion of music education in his country and of music research at the Institute of Puerto Rican Culture founded in 1955. Rafael Aponte-Ledée (b. 1938), a student of Ginastera and Gandini at the Buenos Aires Torcuato Di Tella Institute, followed such trends as serialism, electronics and indeterminacy.

Although he considers himself a nationalist composer, and his early works rely on aspects of Panamanian folk song and dance, the most significant works (since the late 1940s) of the Panamanian composer, conductor and teacher Roque Cordero (b. 1917) have been written in an almost exclusively serialist idiom. His *Second Symphony* (1956) exemplifies his treatment of the dodecaphonic technique. The symphony is based on three related tone rows used freely, that is, with melodic and harmonic repetitions and octave doublings. One typical trait quite common in Cordero's music is the use of frequent *ostinatos* which create a rather complex rhythmic organization. An increased concern for timbral effects, virtuoso writing and rhythmic intricacies appeared in his works of the 1960s, such as the *Violin Concerto* (1962) and the *Third Symphony* (1965). The *Violin Concerto* is a truly virtuoso work, with a technically very demanding solo part, and a virtuosic treatment of the orchestra. The basic twelve-tone set involves various forms and transpositions that make up the thematic and developmental materials. Further works (Concertino for viola and string orchestra, 1968 and Variations and Theme for Five, 1975) evidence Cordero's strong individuality in handling serialism while maintaining a Latin flavour without being nationalist.

Central American composers who have paid attention to non-nationalist currents include the Guatemalans Ricardo Castillo (1894–1967), José

Castañeda (1898–1978), who was one of the first to experiment with polytonality, microtonality and serialism, Salvador Ley (b. 1907), Enrique Solares (b. 1910) and Joaquín Orellana (b. 1937); the Nicaraguan Luis A. Delgadillo (1887–1964); the Costa Rican Bernal Flores (b. 1937), professor of composition at the University of Costa Rica and director of the department of music of the Ministry of Culture, who wrote in an atonal and serial style; and Gilberto Orellana (b. 1942), from El Salvador, who also adhered to serial techniques.

### The Andean Republics

In Venezuela the development of contemporary composition from the 1960s was encouraged by the establishment of the Instituto Nacional de Cultura y Bellas Artes (INCIBA), which promoted national prizes for composition, the Caracas Music Festivals, and the creation of laboratories of electronic music. The composers most in evidence during the late 1960s and 1970s were Antonio Estévez (b. 1916), who turned to electronic music after 1970, José Luis Muñoz (b. 1928), who used aleatory techniques, and Alexis Rago (b. 1920), who wrote in a neo-tonal style. Alfredo del Mónaco (b. 1938) worked at the Columbia-Princeton Electronic Music Center and studied at Columbia University. He wrote in the electronic medium (*Cromofonías I*, 1967, *Metagrama*, 1970), in a combination of traditional instruments and electronic sounds (*Alternancias*, 1976), and in computer music (*Synus-17/251271*, 1972). With the settling in Caracas of the Greek composer Yannis Ioannidis (b. 1930), younger Venezuelan composers who studied with him were readily exposed to contemporary music. Among his students were Alfredo Rugeles (b. 1949) who shows an impressive command of contemporary techniques whether he writes for traditional instruments (*Mutaciones*, 1974, for string orchestra, *El Ocaso del Héroe*, 1982, for narrator, mixed chorus and chamber orchestra) or realizes his compositions on tape (*Things-phonia*, 1978).

   In Colombia, the most active representative of contemporary music have been Fabio González-Zuleta (b. 1920), Luis Antonio Escobar (b. 1925), Blas Emilio Atehortúa (1933), and the Belgian born Jacqueline Nova (b. 1938). In his Violin Concerto (1958) and Third Symphony (1961), González-Zuleta pursued a polytonal and atonal style; later works explored serial techniques. Atehortúa became in the 1960s and 1970s one of Colombia's foremost contemporary composers. His music incorporates a rich rhythmic construction with effective colour blendings. Occasionally he used serialist techniques rather freely (e.g. *Cinco Piezas Breves,* 1969, *Partita 72,* 1972), but remained essentially attached to neo-classical compositional ideals (e.g. *Brachot para Golda Meir,* for orchestra, (1980), *Suite for String Orchestra,* 1982).

The only Ecuadorian composer since the 1950s to have espoused readily experimental aesthetics is Mesías Maiguashca (b. 1938) who, after an early training at the Quito National Conservatory, studied at the Eastman School of Music in the United States, and at the Torcuato Di Tella Institute in Buenos Aires. He worked in close contact with Stockhausen during 1968–72 as a collaborator at the Electronic Music Studio in Cologne and then remained in Germany as a freelance composer. His discovery of electro-acoustic techniques led to such major works as *Hör Zu* (1969) on tape, *A Mouth Piece* (1970) for amplified voices, and *Ayayayayay* (1971) on tape. After his *Übungen für Synthesizer* (1972) he turned to mixed media, as in *Oeldorf 8* (1973).

In Peru, while Rodolfo Holzmann continued to develop the neo-classical style of his earlier works—as in *Introitus et Contrapunctus* (1974) and *Sinfonía del Tercer Mundo* (1979), for example—beginning in the 1960s some of his students gave Peruvian music a truly contemporary character. Composers such as Enrique Iturriaga (b. 1918), Celso Garrido Lecca (b. 1926), Enrique Pinilla (1927–89), Francisco Pulgar Vidal (b. 1929), Leopoldo La Rosa (b. 1931), José Malsio (b. 1924), and especially César Bolaños (b. 1931) and Edgar Valcárcel (b. 1932) advocated a clear anti-nationalist attitude but were also conscious of the need to assert a Latin American personality in their new music. Admittedly subjective and vague, such an attitude has nevertheless motivated these composers to a cultivation of contemporary styles treated in a unique manner. Iturriaga, for example, attempted to integrate some native and European elements. Garrido Lecca developed a style in which contemporary European practices (atonality, quartal and quintal harmonies) are juxtaposed with locally derived musical traits (use of pentatonic scales), as in his Suite for Woodwind Quintet (1956). Enrique Pinilla put into practice his conviction that the modern composer should try his hand at all techniques available to him. He therefore cultivated a polytonal and atonal language and, in the 1960s, serialist and electronic music procedures. Pulgar Vidal and La Rosa have written primarily in a modernistic neo-nationalist vein but also have cultivated freely twelve-tone and aleatoric techniques, while Malsio, a student of Hindemith at Yale University and of Schoenberg in Los An-

Los Angeles, favoured polytonality in his works of the 1950s and atonality in the 1960s.

César Bolaños and Edgar Valcárcel represented in the 1960s and 1970s the progressive avant-garde of Peruvian music. From the very beginning of his career Bolaños orientated his activity as a composer towards experimental music in the electronic medium and towards indeterminacy. He studied at the New York RCA Institute of Electronic Technology and at the Di Tella Institute in Buenos Aires in the 1960s. From about 1970 he carried out experiments, at Honeywell Bull Argentina, in the application of computer science to music composition. Works created by this process have been referred to generically as ESEPCO (Estructuras Sonoro-Expresivas por Computación) and have included *Sialoecibi* (ESEPCO I), for piano and a narrator-mime actor, and *Canción sin Palabras* (ESEPCO II), subtitled 'Homage to non-pronounced words', for piano with two players and tape. As theatre music, the stage action becomes an integral part of the instrumental performance. His use of mixed media involved a range of activities from performance-theatrical actions to abstract audio-visual environmental movements. Valcárcel cultivated various contemporary techniques, from dodecaphony to electronic and aleatory procedures. As one of the most creative personalities of the Peruvian avant-garde, his development as a composer has been symptomatic of the Latin American composer of new music in general, in its assertion of the composer's intellectual freedom and its attempts to contribute unique features to new music expressions.

Most Bolivian composers who developed an interest in contemporary music studied abroad and often felt alienated upon returning to their country. Jaime Mendoza Nava (b. 1925) cultivated a neo-classical style in which appear some elements of native music of the Bolivian plateau (pentatonicism and characteristic rhythms). Gustavo Navarre (b. 1932), a student at the Paris Ecole Normale de Musique, created a neo-Romantic language combined, on occasions, with traits of Bolivian folk music. Atiliano Auza-León (b. 1928) wrote in a neo-classical vein at first and turned to twelve-tone technique in the 1960s. The most in evidence of the Bolivian composers in the 1960s and 1970s was Alberto Villalpando (b. 1940). He began using serialism in his First String Quartet (1964) and *Variaciones Tímbricas* (1966), for soprano and chamber ensemble, but turned to electronic and aleatory techniques in later works.

In Chile, where the University of Chile continued to be the main pillar supporting the country's extraordinarily dynamic musical life, the foundation of the Philharmonic Orchestra of Chile (later renamed the Municipal Philharmonic), the establishment of several chamber ensembles at the Catholic University, and the issuance of commercial recordings of Chilean music and a series of score publications by the Instituto de Extensión Musical (1959), all strongly stimulated musical composition. Domingo Santa Cruz remained attached to his neo-classical style, characterized by contrapuntal textures and linear chromaticism, though he was not as prolific as in previous decades. His Opus 28 (*Seis Canciones de Primavera*) dates from 1950, Opus 32 (*Endechas*) from 1960 and Opus 37 (*Oratio Jeremiae Prophetae*) from 1970. He wrote in an increasingly dissonant harmony and textural complexity and his dramatic and highly expressionist sense was reinforced during this period. In the case of Juan Orrego-Salas, from 1961 director of the Latin American Music Center at Indiana University, the neo-classical elements of his earlier works remained the underlying basis of his style, but with the adoption of twelve-tone procedures (restricted, however, to pitch selection) atonality prevailed in his works of the 1960s and 1970s. His *Sonata A Quattro*, Op. 55 (1964) reveals the concern for formal clarity and balance, irregular rhythmic aggregates, and an artful handling of timbres with original instrumental effects. The monumental *Missa* 'In Tempore Discordiae', Op. 64 (1968–9) and the oratorio *The Days of God*, Op. 73 (1975) illustrate the composer's skilful writing for voices, his dramatically refined character, and his remarkable talent for combining traditional and contemporary compositional techniques and ideas.

Among the Chilean composers of the 1920s generation Gustavo Becerra-Schmidt (b. 1925) has been one of the most successful. His works cover a considerable range of styles and genres. He began in the early 1950s as a neo-classicist (e.g. in the Violin Concerto, 1950 and the First String Quartet, 1950), then adopted the serialist method of composition around 1955, but maintained classical formal concepts. Webernian influences are felt in such works as the Third String Quartet (1955) and the First Symphony (1955–8) in which pointillistic procedures (associated with Webern) appear frequently. In the early 1960s he combined the serial method with what has been called a 'complementary polychordal system', involving also the twelve tones of the chromatic scale but divided into groups or 'polychords', of various pitches. Becerra felt that such a system was less restrictive than dodecaphony. During the 1960s, he introduced aleatory techniques in his works, as in the Concertos Nos. 1 and 2 for guitar (1964, 1968), the String Quartet No. 7 (1961), and the oratorio *Macchu Picchu* (1966), on a poem by Pablo Neruda. Becerra's aesthetic thought has been moulded by his socio-political views, as his choice of texts indicates. Influenced by Marxist philosophy he set to music poems or texts by Chilean poets or writers such as Neruda, Gabriela Mistral and Nicanor Parra, or simply texts on such subjects as Lenin's death, the Guatemalan revolutionary struggle, the Vietnam war and Allende's death (in the work *Chile 1973*, for voice and chamber orchestra).

Other Chilean composers representative of the musical avant-garde have been León Schidlowsky (b. 1931), Fernando García (b. 1930), and Miguel Aguilar-Ahumada (b. 1931). In 1955 Schidlowsky became a member of the Agrupación Tonus, a private musical association for new music, which he directed in 1957. He has been influential as a composer conscious of his social function and deeply devoted to questions of a socio-political and religious nature. He has shown a particular concern for the misfortune of the Jewish people throughout the world, which accounts for the pronounced mysticism of many of his works. His large output reveals a phase of expressionist and dodecaphonic style (1952–6) followed by one of adherence to total serialism (1959 to c.1963), then since about 1964, one of utilization of aleatory procedures. García also reveals a deep preoccupation with the socio-political conditions of the Third World (*América Insurrecta, 1962, La Tierra Combatiente*, 1965, both on texts by Neruda). His serial works of the 1960s' reflected special care in the treatment of tone colour. Aguilar-Ahumada has been a rather eclectic composer. He developed from an early influence of Hindemith, Bartók and Stravinsky and the early expressionism of Schoenberg and Berg to a post-Webernian serialist style and in the mid-1960s to aleatory procedures combined with electronic sounds (e.g., *Texturas*, 1965).

The first experiments in electronic music were initiated by Juan Amenábar (b. 1922) and José Vicente Asuar (b. 1933), who created in 1955 the Taller Experimental del Sonido (Experimental Sound Workshop) at the Catholic University in Santiago. Amenábar's *Los Peces* (1957) is generally considered the first tape composition in Latin America. Asuar, a trained acoustic engineer who was influential in the establishment of electronic music studios in several cities throughout Latin America, experimented with electronic music pieces (the first, *Variaciones Espectrales*, in 1959), and computer scores programmed for traditional instrumental ensembles (such as *Formas I–II*, 1970–72, for orchestra), and for complete electronic sound synthesis.

*Argentina and Uruguay*

After 1950, Argentina (and especially the capital Buenos Aires) developed the most flourishing musical life in Latin America. This was due to the renewed vitality of older institutions, the upsurge of new-music activities in national and private universities, and the generally improved level of music instruction in both public and private institutions. Among the latter, the Latin American Center for Advanced Musical Studies at the Di Tella Institute in Buenos Aires was unique. Established in 1962 and directed by Alberto Ginastera, the centre offered two-year fellowships biannually to twelve composers from Latin America, contracted with world-renowned composers to conduct composition seminars, established an electronic music studio (directed by Francisco Kröpfl), and sponsored concerts and festivals of the faculty members' and fellows' works. Several groups for the dissemination of new music were created in Buenos Aires, including the Asociación de Jóvenes Compositores de la Argentina (1957) with such members as Mario Davidovsky and Alcides Lanza, the Agrupación Euphonia (1959) (later renamed Agrupación Música Viva) established by Gerardo Gandini and Armando Krieger, and the professional Unión de Compositores de la Argentina (1964).

Among the composers born prior to 1920, Ginastera and, to a lesser extent, Juan Carlos Paz continued to be productive during the 1950s and 1960s. Ginastera's phase of neo-expressionism began with the Second String Quartet (1958) which relied extensively on twelve-tone techniques but retained the strong rhythmic drive of earlier works. In this and later works (e.g. *Cantata para América Mágica*, 1960, for soprano and a large percussion ensemble), twelve-tone techniques are often combined with other procedures, microtonal, polytonal, non-serialist, or atonal. In his orchestral and instrumental works of the 1960s and 1970s Ginastera explored very effectively new-music techniques and continued to search for new sonorities in the established vocal and instrumental media. Works such as the Violin Concerto (1963), the *Estudios Sinfónicos* (1967–8), the Piano Concerto No. 2 (1972), the *Serenata* (1973), for cello, baritone and chamber ensemble (on text by Neruda), or the Sonata for Cello and Piano (1979) combine the colourful exploration of clusters, microtonal and aleatory structures, are highly virtuosic and retain a clear affinity with Classical formal designs. Ginastera's aesthetic ideals during the last twenty years of his life have been equated with Romantic surrealism, because of a noted predilection for the supernatural, the fantastic and the ritualistic. This predilection finds no better expression than in his drama works of the 1960s, namely the operas *Don Rodrigo* (1963–4), *Bomarzo* (1966–7) and *Beatrix Cenci* (1971). In both aesthetic philosophy and musical technique, these are typically expressionistic works, involving tragic situations emerging from the neurotic states of morbid and pathological characters. The resounding success of these operas resulted not only from their timely libretti (making them relevant to contemporary western society) but also from the large spectrum of musical means put into action to express their intense dramas. During the 1960s Paz wrote two orchestral works and a few chamber and instrumental works that revealed a free atonal, intuitive style open to all sorts of rhythmic and timbral experiments. His language retained a post-Webernian quality, especially in the pointillistic treatment of timbre and the high concentration of thought, as can be seen in the five *Núcleos* (1962–4) for piano.

Among the numerous Argentine composers active from the 1950s, Roberto Caamaño (1923–93), Hilda Dianda (b. 1925), Francisco Kröpfl (b. 1928), Alcides Lanza (b. 1929), Mario Davidovsky (b. 1934), Gerardo Gandini (b. 1936), and Armando Krieger (b. 1940) deserve mention here. Together with García Morillo, Caamaño was the most significant neoclassical composer. He wrote some orchestral works, but his major contributions was in sacred and secular choral music. From around 1960, Dianda developed an earnest interest in new-music techniques. Her search for new sonorities was evident in such works as *Núcleos* (1963), *Ludus I* and *II* (1968, 1969), in which a virtuoso writing prevailed. The Hungarian-born Kröpfl was one of the most successful composers of electronic music in Argentina. His original treatment of the medium is evident in the series of works that addresses some specific electronic technical problems: *Exercise in textures, Exercise with impulses, Exercise in motions,* and *Exercise with coloured noise,* all from the early 1960s. From his association with the Columbia-Princeton Center (1965–71), Lanza also developed a major interest in electronic music, but electronic sounds tended to be incorporated with those of traditional instruments (e.g. *Plectros II, Interferencias I* and *II*), or were associated with mixed media. In the 1970s, when he made his career in Montreal, he relied increasingly on indeterminacy, those works calling for traditional instruments disclosed at times electronically conceived aleatory, as in *Eidesis III* (1971). From 1960 Davidovsky was resident in New York, also working at the Columbia-Princeton Electronic Music Center. His early works exhibited an atonal, abstract lyric style.

His first work exclusively in the electronic medium was *Study No. 1* (1961). Since then he has given more attention to the combination of electronic materials and traditional instruments, as shown in the series of several pieces entitled *Synchronisms* (from 1963 on), for various instruments and tape. Gandini, a pianist-composer, developed a coherent style based on a free utilization of serial techniques and a keen treatment of timbres. His *Música Nocturna* (1964) is an outstanding example of the composer's expressive power which includes numerous instrumental effects, contrasts between static parts and fast, elusive and delicate figures, and an acute pointillistic treatment of the minute material at work. In the late 1960s and 1970s aleatory procedures became an integral part of his compositions. Krieger first wrote in a largely post-Webernian vein but soon turned to aleatory procedures in his search for new sonorities with classical instruments. He has written considerably for the piano, his own instrument as a performer. Particularly striking and novel in his piano works are his experiments with registers, dynamics and timbre, including harmonics and sonorities extracted from clusters.

In Uruguay, the composers who followed some of the most advanced styles were León Biriotti (b. 1929), Antonio Mastrogiovanni (b. 1936), José Serebrier (b. 1938) and Sergio Cervetti (b. 1941). The music of Biriotti developed from a language imbued with considerations of craftsmanship (e.g., *Sinfonía Ana Frank,* 1964) to a total serialist style and the use of electronics. He has been particularly concerned with questions of set theory, which he refers to as a system of structures through permutations ('Sistema de Estructuras por Permutaciones') of ordered sets. This combinatorial-like method was applied in his *Espectros* (1969) for three orchestras, *Permutaciones* (1970), for chamber orchestra, and *Laberintos* (1970), for five instruments. Mastrogiovanni created a free serial style and from the early 1970s produced a few electronic music pieces and orchestral and chamber music works with special attention to new treatment of textures and timbres. Serebrier, on the other hand, attempted to instill a characteristic Latin American flavour in some of his works, especially through an intricate and clever treatment of rhythm (as in *Partita,* 1956–8, for orchestra). A resident of the United States for many years, he was very active as a conductor and helped disseminate Latin American contemporary music. In his works of the 1970s (e.g. *Colores Mágicos,* 1971) he explored simultaneously mixed media techniques, serialism and the concept of spatial music. Cervetti, who also settled in the United States, represents the left wing of the Uruguayan avant-garde. After an early interest in serialism he became attracted to electronic music (*Studies in Silence*, 1968; *Raga III*, 1971), chance operations, and mixed media in the form of theatre music in such works as *Peripetia* (1970) and *Cocktail Party* (1970), resorting to visually intricate and provocative graphic notation.

## Brazil

Only after 1960 do we witness radical changes in Brazilian twentieth-century music. Important musical activities developed after that date in several major Brazilian cities, such as Rio de Janeiro, São Paulo, Santos, Recife, Salvador, and, to a lesser extent, Belo Horizonte, Brasília and Curitiba. Several groups were established to promote new music ideologies, such as the Grupo Música Nova in Santos and São Paulo, the short-lived Grupo Musical Renovador in Rio de Janeiro, and the very active Grupo de Compositores da Bahia in Salvador. Several festivals of avant-garde music took place in Rio (1962, 1966, 1969, 1970), a total of eighteen festivals Música Nova de Santos (1964–82), and several events since the late 1970s entitled Bienal de Música Brasileira Contemporânea, organized by the Sala Cecília Meireles of Rio de Janeiro. The Brazilian Society of Contemporary Music was formed in 1971 and became affiliated with the ISCM. With few exceptions, institutions of higher learning, however, paid little attention to new music.

The music of Cláudio Santoro underwent profound stylistic transformations, with a return to serialism (Symphony No. 8, 1963), the reliance on micro-tuning combined with static sound-blocks, and random choice of scraping instruments (e.g. in *Interações Assintóticas*, 1969). Aleatory procedures also entered into his compositions in the late 1960s (*Cantata Elegíaca*, 1970) and a combination of electronic music with traditional instruments often involving chance operations appeared in the works of the 1970s (e.g. the six *Mutationen*, 1968–72, *Aus dem Brecht-Zyklus*, 1974, for soprano and synthesizer, *Cantata 'Aus den Sonetten an Orpheus'*, 1979).

Edino Krieger (b. 1928), a student of Hans J. Koellreutter in Salvador (Bahia), then Copland and Mennin in the United States, turned to twelve-tone methods during the late 1940s but a few years later developed a slightly nationalist neo-classic language (as in *Chôro*, 1952; *Abertura Sinfônica*, 1955; and especially *Brasiliana*, 1960). From about the mid-1960s, he utilized freely some serialist organization and other advanced techniques, as in *Fanfarras e Sequências* (1970). As the Director of the Music Institute of FUNARTE (Fundação Nacional de Arte) since 1980 he has been influential in promoting further contemporary music in Brazil but has been less productive as a composer.

The members of the São Paulo/Santos Música Nova Group most in evidence during the 1960s and 1970s were Gilberto Mendes (b. 1922), Rogério Duprat (b. 1932) and Willy Corrêa de Oliveira (b. 1938). Mendes came to composition rather late and has been essentially an experimentalist. His earliest and most original works are settings of concrete poems by Brazilian avant-garde poets such as Décio Pignatari, Haroldo de Campos and José Lino Grünewald. The choral piece *Beba Coca-Cola* (1966), subtitled 'Motet in D minor', on a poem by Pignatari, explores the sonic structure of individual syllables, with microtonal vocal effects mixed with talk, chanting, howling and shouting. The ending of the piece calls for a theatrical display of a strip bearing the word *Cloaca* which appears as an altered form of 'Coca-Cola', in an obviously critical, anti-advertising and anti-imperialist gesture. Mendes has also been interested in exploring the visual aspects of the music world. Many works since the mid-1960s (e.g. *Blirium c-9, Vai e Vem, Son et Lumière, Santos Futebol Club, Pausa e Menopausa*) exhibit a clear affinity for Cage's concept of indeterminacy and music theatre. Duprat was, together with Mendes and Corrêa de Oliveira, the major spokesman for the Música Nova group. Beginning as an atonalist and serial composer, he later cultivated electronic music and mixed media. He also explored the application of a computer to electronic music (*Experimental Music*, 1963). From about 1965 he worked mainly as an arranger of urban popular music. Mass communication and its implications for new-music creation was one of the major interests of Corrêa de Oliveira. In the early 1960s he turned to serial techniques (e.g., *Música para Marta*, 1961) and wrote numerous scores for plays utilizing the electronic medium. But from about 1965 he was stimulated by aleatory techniques applied to sound collage of borrowed materials from Western music and combined with controlled passages (*Divertimento*, 1967). A number of original works also resulted from his association with Brazilian concrete poets. *Cicatrizteza* (1973) for female voice is a true tour de force of imagination in the various vocal effects and its treatment of theatrical elements.

Among the numerous composition students of Camargo Guarnieri in the São Paulo area, José Antonio de Almeida Prado (b. 1943) and Raul do Valle (b. 1936) deserve special attention. Almeida Prado succeeded in freeing himself from Guarnieri's influence around the mid-1960s, when he began to develop a style in which a post-Webernian serialist character (rather than strict techniques) often prevailed, together with highly individualized harmonic and timbral effects and rigorous formal structures. Later works (*Pequenos Funerais Cantantes*, 1969, *Livro Sonoro*, 1973, for example) reveal the mystic temperament of the composer. The oratorio *Thérèse, L'Amour de Dieu* (1975) shows some technical affinity for his former teacher Olivier Messiaen's *La Transfiguration de Notre Seigneur Jésus Christ*. Raul de Valle also developed a highly original language based on atonality and exploration of new sonorities. His most successful works include the Mass *Da Nova e Eterna Aliança* (1974) and *Cambiantes* (1974), for percussion.

Among the composers active in Rio de Janeiro during the 1960s and 1970s, Marlos Nobre (b. 1939) came to occupy a prominent position within the Brazilian avant-garde. Stylistically he moved from an early nationalistic concern mixed with the dissonant style of Milhaud to twelve-tone techniques, free serialism and aleatory procedures with nativistic overtones. Many of his works have the natural exuberance found in that of Villa-Lobos, particularly in their dramatic intensity, projected through special timbral effects, rhythmic drive and highly contrasting dynamics (e.g. *Ukrinmakrinkrin*, 1964; *Rhythmetron*, 1968; *Concêrto Breve*, 1969; *Mosaico, In Memoriam*, 1970). Also in Rio (in alternation with New York City) Jocy de Oliveira (b. 1936) has been successful since the 1970s in multimedia works.

The composer most in evidence in the new capital of Brasilia after 1960 was Jorge Antunes (b. 1942). As a trained physicist, Antunes developed a special interest in electronic music which he studied at the Di Tella Institute, then at the University of Utrecht and with the Groupe de Recherches Musicales in Paris. He pioneered in electronic-music composition in Brazil (*Valsa Sideral*, 1962, *Auto-Retrato sobre Paisaje Porteño*, 1969, *Historia de un Pueblo*, 1970) and cultivated from about 1965 what he called 'integral art' or mixed media including not only sounds and colours but odours and flavours (e.g. *Ambiente I*, 1965). In his orchestral, chamber music and choral works (e.g. *Isomerism*, 1970, *Music for Eight Persons Playing Things*, 1970–71; *Catástrofe Ultra Violeta*, 1974; *Congadasein*, 1976; and *Proudhonia*, 1973), he relied a great deal on aleatory procedures.

The Salvador (Bahia) Seminários Livres de Música were founded in 1954, under the leadership and direction of Hans J. Koellreutter, and became during the 1960s and 1970s a dynamic centre for new music. The person largely responsible for this development was the Brazilian composer of Swiss birth, Ernst Widmer (1927–90) who settled in Bahia in 1956, and was very influential as the teacher of a whole generation of local composers. Widmer's own output shows him to be an eclectic. He developed from a moderately modernist style in the early 1950s to an intermittent involvement in avant-garde music in the 1960s. His profound dislike of dogmatic attitudes in composition resulted in a wide variety of compositional resources, from tonal, modal, polytonal and serial idioms (as in *Sinopse*, 1970), to an alternation of aleatory procedures and totally controlled elements (as in *Pulsars*, 1969; *Quasars*, 1970; *Rumos*, 1972), to aleatory and spatial-music effects (as in *ENTROncamentos SONoros*, 1972).

The most creative younger members of the Bahian Group of Composers have been Rufo Herrera (b. 1935), Lindembergue Cardoso (1939–89) and Jamary Oliveira (b. 1944). The Argentine-born Herrera settled in Brazil in 1963 and lived in Salvador in the 1970s as a freelance composer. Besides exploring new timbres in works for traditional instruments and electronically generated sounds, he has also experimented with aleatory procedures and collages. He was one of the first in Bahia to organize mixed-media events. Cardoso created a typical avant-garde local style in the late 1960s, made up of a combination of aleatory processes with fixed elements (*Via Sacra*, 1968, *Pleorama*, 1971, *Toccata* for piano, 1972). Oliveira, who also experimented with aleatory processes and was prepared to try any technique, tonal or atonal, that he believed might help to express a given idea, cultivated in the late 1960s an unorthodox twelve-tone technique. Among his most significant works were *Conjunto II* (1968), *Interações* (1970), *Congruencias* (1972) and *Ludus* (1973). In the late 1970s, he became interested in the application of computer techniques to music composition.

The younger generation of Latin American composers, born in the 1950s and early 1960s, have thus a vital tradition of art-music to draw upon. Some composers in the period from the 1950s to the 1970s no doubt suffered from what is called the 'terrorism of the avant-garde.' But in following international models the Latin American composer has automatically transformed them in order to authenticate them. Gustavo Becerra has referred to the Brazilian *sotaque* (regional accent) in contemporary music. This can be extended to the music of all Latin American countries. While it is difficult to point out precisely where and how the *sotaque* manifests itself in the considerable music production since 1950, its existence can hardly be questioned.

## A NOTE ON POPULAR MUSIC

The term 'música popular' in both Spanish and Portuguese has denoted traditionally the generic sense of music of the people, encompassing what folklorists and ethnomusicologists call folk and traditional music as well as urban popular music. Since the 1950s, however, 'música popular' has gradually assumed the contemporary sense of urban, commercial and mass-mediated music. It is to this sense of popular music that the note addresses itself. Urban popular music represents musical repertories, genres and behaviours specific to urban areas. It is generally disseminated through commercial outlets such as the publication of sheet music, radio and television broadcasts and, above all, the recording industry. It reflects the social stratification of a particular area, whether social strata are conceived in socio-economic, generational, or ethnic terms. In addition, certain Latin American popular music movements, genres and styles have frequently resulted from socio-political participation and criticism.

As an urban phenomenon Latin American popular music first developed in the early nineteenth century, primarily as an upper-class activity involving semi-popular theatrical genres and salon music and as a parallel to art-music traditions. It is impossible, however, to attempt to trace a homogeneous, unbroken tradition of urban music because of insufficient documentary sources. In many cities and towns the interpenetration of folk and urban cultures remained dynamic well into the twentieth century. Since the 1920s, and particularly after the Second World War, however, urban growth in most Latin American countries resulted in a massive development of urban cultures. In some of the largest cities, this growth and the consequent cultural diversity have been quite extraordinary. Urban popular music has expressly reflected that diversity, often in ethnic and socio-economic terms.

Fashionable European and other foreign species of popular music have always been present in the major cities. Thus, the main nineteenth-century ballroom dances such as the waltz, mazurka, polka, schottische, contredanse, and others were readily adopted in all cities and with time suffered the process of 'creolization' or 'mestisaje', that is the transformation into local, national genres. The waltz, for example, served as a forerunner to a large number of popular dances in the whole continent, with different names such as *pasillo* or *vals del país* in Colombia, *vals criollo* in Peru, *vals melopeya* in Venezuela and *valsa-choro* in Brazil. The great European salon music tradition also left a strong imprint on Latin American urban music and provided an important source for numerous popular genres of the twentieth century. In addition, the prevailing romantic character of many popular song types originated in that tradition whose gentility came to be combined with the *criollo* tradition of Latin American cities. The influence of North American Tin Pan Alley and other popular genres had its obvious repercussions in the hybrid forms that developed in the 1920s and 1930s (for example, the *rumba-fox,* the *Inca-fox* and the *samba-fox*). The big jazz band era of the 1930s and 1940s also left its imprint on the performing media of many Latin American urban popular forms. In the 1950s, several attempts were made, particularly in Cuba, Puerto Rico and Brazil, to develop Latin expressions of jazz, and the 1960s and 1970s witnessed assimilations of rock 'n' roll and rock music some-times fused with local folk-urban traditions, which gave rise to substantial innovations. Concurrently *música folklórica* in urban contexts became part of the *peña* fashion established in the 1960s and was the point of departure of a new style associated with political movements, a style that in a short period of time took on a pan-Hispanic American character.

## Mexico and the Spanish Caribbean

Much Mexican popular music of the nineteenth century was influenced by European salon music. One of the best examples of that influence comes from the set of waltzes *Sobre las Olas* (1891) by Juventino Rosas (1868–94), one of the first Mexican popular composers to win international fame. The most national popular genres of nineteenth-century Mexico were the *jarabe* and the *danza mexicana*. Since then the *jarabe* has been practised by most popular musicians in popular bands or ensembles, including *mariachis*. Those *jarabes* in triple metre were often easily transformed into fast-tempo waltzes, as was the case of the famous 'Cielito lindo', believed to have been written by a Quirino F. Mendoza during the Mexican Revolution. The *danza mexicana* stemmed from the Cuban *contradanza,* itself transformed by the Andalusian tango and the Cuban *habanera,* which stressed the duple metre structure and the basic dotted rhythm and the feeling of disjunction between duple and triple divisions of the beat that came to epitomize many Latin American and Caribbean popular dances. In Mexico, the *danza* was cultivated by composers such as Ernesto Elorduy (1853–1912), Felipe Villanueva (1862–93) in the salon music tradition, and later by Miguel Lerdo de Tejada (1869–1941) who was the first major popular composer popular composer who transformed the *danza* into a vocal genre. Many popular pieces originally written as simple songs were performed as *danzas* or *habaneras,* such as 'La Paloma' and the well-known 'La Cucaracha', popularized during the Mexican Revolution.

Despite the variety of dance music genres since the beginning of the twentieth century, the *canción mexicana,* and especially the *canción romántica mexicana* came to epitomize the whole domain of Mexican popular music. The modern history of the romantic *canción* begins with the publication in 1901 of Lerdo de Tejada's 'Perjura'. It is a history of catchy melodies that have remained in the collective memory of the Mexican people. Besides its obvious kinship with Italian opera, the *canción* has been influenced by other popular song genres, especially the Cuban *bolero.* The special type of *canción* known as *ranchera* is more distinctively Mexican in that it originated from folk-song tradition and retained specific performance characteristics of that tradition. As an urban genre, it appeared in the 1920s, at first primarily to accompany sound films, and was popularized in the 1930s. *Canciones* and *boleros* have been written by the hundreds since the 1920s. By far the most popular composer of his generation was Agustín Lara (1897–1970), whose song 'Granada' was an international hit. Other famous composers of *canciones* and other genres were Tata Nacho (Ignacio Fernández Esperón, 1894–1968), author of some two hundred songs, and Guty Cárdenas (1905–32), immortalized among his countrymen by his songs 'Rayito de sol', 'Nunca', and 'Caminante del Mayab'. The 1930s also saw the further development of urban popular music with the establishment of the first regular recording companies, the Victor Talking Machine Company, which opened its Mexican factory in 1935, and several years later Columbia Records. The first radio station to pay attention to popular music was XEW Radio in Mexico City ('La Voz de la América Latina') which began broadcasting in 1930 and maintained its leadership role until about the mid-1950s, when television took over.

In the 1940s, urban composers began to pay attention to the *corrido,* the folk ballad of Mexico. In the process of urbanization, the *corrido* underwent a few changes, that is, predominantly duple metre, *copla* (quatrain) literary form, vocal duet and trio performance in harmonized fashion, and *mariachi* and *norteño* ensemble accompaniment. The best illustration of the phenomenal popularity of a modern *corrido* is 'Juan Charrasqueado', written in the 1950s by Victor Cordero (b. 1914). José Alfredo Jiménez (1926–73) was very successful with his *corridos* evoking historical events or the beauty of the Mexican provinces performed in a *ranchera* style.

Cuba has exerted enormous influence on the development of numerous Latin American popular musical forms throughout this continent. From the *habanera*, the *son cubano*, the *danza cubana*, and the *bolero* to the *mambo*, *rumba*, *conga*, and *chachachá*, Cuban music has either shaped the *criollo* music genres in other countries of the continent or been adopted in toto at various periods as fashionable dance music. Of the many popular forms, the *habanera* and the *son* first characterized Spanish Caribbean music. A typical example of a composed *habanera* was Eduardo Sánchez de Fuentes's piece entitled 'Tú,' published in 1894. The *son*, which became urbanized during the 1910s, has a strong syncopated rhythmic accompaniment, resulting in the folk version in a typically Afro-Cuban polyrhythmic texture, and is generally considered the basis of modern *salsa* music. As a dance the Cuban *bolero* stresses a duple metre and the same rhythmic pattern of the early *habanera*. Since the 1920s, the *bolero* has been essentially a vocal genre of highly romantic and sentimental character whose lyrics stress love themes of the most varied types. One of the most popular composers of *boleros* was Ernesto Lecuona (1896–1963), immortalized by songs like 'Malagueña', 'Maria la O', and 'Siboney', and many others.

The traditional *rumba* has three recognized sub-types, the *guaguancó*, the *columbia*, and the *yambú*. Musically and choreographically, the first of these was the forerunner or the urban *rumba* that developed around the 1920s. As a dance, the *rumba* deals with courtship and the male domination over the female and involves extensive hip and shoulder motions and a pelvic thrust known as *vacunao*. The urbanization of the dance retained the hip and shoulder movement, but the *vacunao* was made less obvious or disappeared altogether. This urbanization was also due to numerous dance bands that developed in the 1930s, the first to gain popularity being the Havana Casino Orchestra of Don Azpiazu. The most commercialized of all in the United States was that of Xavier Cugat.

The specific new Cuban song known as *nueva trova* reflects the ideals, the history and the struggles of the Cuban Revolution. This musical movement, which gave rise to protest music in several South American countries in the 1960s, was not one of protest as such but rather of expression and promotion of the revolution's ideology. The movement started and grew spontaneously among young people who wanted to express through song their experience and feeling within the revolution.

Among the numerous Caribbean dances, the *merengue* which originated in the Dominican Republic, has enjoyed popularity throughout the Caribbean and South America, particularly in the Central American countries,

Puerto Rico, Venezuela and Colombia. The Haitian *méringue* developed its own *créole* character but is related to the Dominican counterpart. Venezuelan popular music shares common musical characteristics with both the Caribbean and the Andean area. The most popular genres, however, the *joropo*, the *valse*, and the *merengue*, are typical native (*criollo*) expressions. As a music and literary genre, the *joropo* has been cultivated by popular composers since the latter part of the nineteenth century and has remained the most characteristic national dance of Venezuelan popular music. In the 1910s, it was associated with light theatrical pieces, the most successful of which was the *joropo* of the *zarzuela* or comic opera *Alma Llanera*, written in 1914 by Pedro Elias Gutiérrez.

## The Andean Countries

Since the beginning of the twentieth century, Andean urban popular music of clear national derivation has frequently consisted of urbanized renditions and therefore transformations of folk songs and dances. In Colombia the most popular forms have been the *bambuco*, the *porro*, the *cumbia*, and the *pasillo*. The vocal part of the urban *bambuco* involves a duet of male voices singing in parallel thirds, although originally it was a serenading song for solo voice. No dance form has had the lasting popularity in Latin America of the *cumbia*, originally an Afro-Panamanian and Colombian (Atlantic coastal area) folk dance. In its urbanization the *cumbia* lost some of its choreographic figures, such as the typical hip movement and the zig-zag motion of the male dancer, but the musical characteristics are generally similar. The *pasillo*, another widespread popular dance-song, also known in the nineteenth century as the *vals del país*, is a moderately slow waltz-like dance whose rhythm does not stress the downbeat as in its European counterpart. Sung by either solo voice or duet in parallel motion, it is accompanied by either piano (in the salon context), the *tiple* (a treble guitar) and guitar supported by tambourines and 'spoons', or an *estudiantina* (a string ensemble).

Ecuadorian popular music includes the *sanjuanito*, the *pasillo*, and the *cachullapi*, among other genres. Much like the Peruvian *huayno*, the *sanjuanito* is a dance in duple metre, strictly instrumental with syncopated melodies frequently in the minor mode, with a regularly and strongly accented accompaniment. The *pasillo* from Ecuador enjoys popularity both in the highland mestizo communities and in the coastal area, particularly the city of Guayaquil.

Popular music in the various Peruvian cities and towns reflects to a large extent local musical traditions. Thus, cities like Cuzco, Ayacucho and Arequipa exhibit a popular musical style akin to the mestizo folk music tradition of the highland region. The popular *huayno*, similar to its folk counterpart but performed by urban ensembles with an instrumentation foreign to the folk tradition, has maintained its strong status among highland urban communities. Coastal cities such as Trujillo, Chiclayo, or Piura in the north and Pisco and Ica in the south have popular music expressions related to the *criollo* tradition, for example, the *marinera* and the *vals criollo*. The Lima population at large favours the *criollo* music genres, especially the *vals criollo*. Originated in Lima between 1900 and 1910, the *vals* became the main musical expression of the urban working class throughout the 1920s and 1930s. Cultivated by composers such as Felipe Pinglo Alva, Laureano Martinez, Carlos Saco, Filomeno Ormeño and Alicia Maguiña, the *vals* contains lyrics that reflect in general the psychology of the Peruvian people at different times, their cultural personality, and their conflicts, attitudes, and value systems resulting from their reaction to social conditions. A specific type of urban popular music, identified particularly with the youth of the 1970s and 1980s, is *chicha* music, combining Caribbean-like and Afro-Peruvian dance rhythms with melodies of a predominantly Andean related style.

Bolivian popular composers have cultivated the *huayño popular*, the *cueca*, the *yaravi*, and the *taquirari*. The stylized *cuecas* for piano written by Simeón Roncal (1870–1953) continue to enjoy popularity among Bolivian pianists. As in the other highland Andean areas, the Bolivian *yaravi* is a melancholy love song. The *taquirari*, a sung dance, originated in the eastern provinces of Beni and Santa Cruz; the singing almost invariably calls for parallel thirds or sixths. In the cities and towns of the Bolivian plateau, the *bailecito*, similar to the *cueca*, has been extensively cultivated. The *carnavalito*, spread throughout the country, is a characteristic popular dance in which the rhythmic hemiola (a simultaneous duple and triple beat, thereby creating a rhythmic ambiguity) prevails. Since the 1960s, festivals of 'música folklórica' in urban settings have given rise to the development of a new style and sound of popular music recreating and stylizing aspects of indigenous and mestizo music. As a strictly urban phenomenon this trend toward folk music revival and 'música criolla' rested primarily in the hands of members of the middle and upper classes. These musicians became highly proficient performers on indigenous musical instruments and adopted truly traditional and folk music genres, albeit in a more or less free style. In 1965, the La Paz 'Peña Naira' opened as an urban cultural centre. This is where the group 'Los Jairas' began, at first under the direction of the famous *charango* (small ten-string guitar) player, Ernesto Cavour. In the 1970s, the most popular and influential group was 'Savia Andina', made up of four highly professional musicians consisting of a guitar player/singer, a percussionist, a *charango* virtuoso, and a player of *quena* (Indian end-notched vertical flute), *zampoña* (panpipe), and occasionally *tarka* (another Indian whistle, vertical flute) or *mohoceño* (large flute). Subsequently, the group 'Los Kjarkas' enjoyed wide popularity throughout the Andean nations.

In addition to the adaptations of international forms of popular music, Chilean urban music consists of such popular forms as the *cueca* and urban versions of *tonadas, tristes, carnaval,* and *tiranas.* The Chilean *cueca*, a dance with song, alternates rhythmic figures in 6/8 and 3/4 metres. The singing is done by one or two voices, accompanied by guitar, *charango*, flute and *bombo* (double-headed drum). The 'Nueva Canción' movement, which spread to the whole of Latin America in the 1960s, originated in Chile. Following the example of the Cuban model, this movement was associated with social protest, labour movements and reform, and the strongly revolutionary sentiment of the period. The New Song movement centred around a group of talented musicians-poets of whom the main figures were Violeta Parra (Sandoval); her children, Angel and Isabel Parra; Patricio Manns; and Victor Jara.

### Argentina and Uruguay

Among the various popular music genres of Argentina and Uruguay since the beginning of the twentieth century none epitomizes as deeply the social and cultural history of those countries as the tango. For this reason alone, the tango has remained by far the most important popular form that originated in both countries. In the Rio de la Plata area, the tango came to symbolize the hopes, successes and failures of the millions of European immigrants who hoped to work in the farms but settled in the *arrabal* or ghettos of Buenos Aires and Montevideo. The *milonga*, a dance of Afro-Argentine and Uruguayan folk tradition in duple metre and syncopated rhythm, probably contributed to the development of the tango in the area. Choreographically, the tango is in part a local adaptation of the Andalusian tango, the Cuban *danzón* and *habanera*, and, to a lesser extent, of the European polka and schottische. Essentially three types of tango developed: the strongly rhythmic instrumental *tango-milonga* for popular orchestras, the instrumental or vocal *tango-romanza* with a more melodic and romantic character, and the accompanied *tango-canción*, which is strongly lyrical and sentimental. It is in the *tango-canción* that the major themes characteristically associated with the tango as popular culture appear. Carlos Gardel (1887–1935), a popular idol who continued to fascinate most Argentines well into the 1970s and 1980s, was particularly important in making the tango fashionable throughout the Western Hemisphere and in Europe. His major contribution was to transform it into a song genre of social and cultural significance. Perhaps the most successful tango ever composed was 'La Cumparsita' (1917), written by Gerardo Matos Rodriguez in Montevideo. Other representative popular pieces of the 1920s were Julio César Sanders's 'Adiós Muchachos', Enrique Santos Discépolo's 'Yira, yira', Angel Villoldo's 'El Choclo', Juan Carlos Cobián's 'Nostalgias', Francisco Canaro's 'Adiós, pampa mia' and Edgardo Donato's 'A media luz'. The tango revival of the 1960s and 1970s brought about stylistic innovations. The so-called new tango movement, whose leading exponent was Astor Piazzolla (1921–92), included the appearance of tango suites transformed into ballets.

## Brazil

The popular music of Brazil began to acquire stylistic originality during the latter part of the nineteenth century. The sentimental love song, *modinha*, and the song-dance *lundu*, cultivated in the salons since the period of Independence, began to be popularized among urban musicians in the 1870s. Local adaptations of European urban dances, particularly the polka, gave rise to new genres such as the *maxixe*, the *tango brasileiro*, and the *choro*, whose most successful composers were Joaquim Antonio da Silva Callado (1848–80), Francisco Gonzaga (1847–1935), and Ernesto Nazareth (1863–1934). The *choro* of the 1920s to the 1940s stressed virtuoso improvisation of instrumental variations and the consequent counterpoint of remarkable imagination as in the pieces of the Velha Guarda band of Pixinguinha (Alfredo da Rocha Viana, 1899–1973).

Carnival, first organized on a regular basis in the late 1890s in Rio de

Janeiro, stimulated the development of urban popular music. At first simple marches, polkas and waltzes were used, but the most typical carnival genre, the urban samba, emerged during the second decade of the twentieth century. The first recognized samba to be recorded was 'Pelo telefone' by Ernesto dos Santos, nicknamed Donga, in 1917. From that date, the samba became standardized as an urban genre. Several species of the form appeared from the 1920s, including the folk-like dance known as *partido-alto* and the *samba de morro* (sometimes referred to as *batucada*, i.e., with percussion emphasis) cultivated by people of the *favelas* (hillside slums) and the first samba 'schools' of Rio de Janeiro. Around 1928 two significant new developments affected the samba: the creation of the first samba schools and the advent of the genre *samba-canção*. Both epitomized the dichotomy that separated the music of the lower classes and that of the middle and upper classes. The *samba-canção* was meant for middle- and upper-class consumption. Melodically and textually it was strongly reminiscent of the older *modinhas*, while harmonically and rhythmically it was influenced in the 1940s and 1950s by the Cuban *bolero* and the 'fox-blues'. Together with other hybrid forms such as *samba-choro* and *samba-fox*, the *samba-canção* dealt with love and unhappiness often in superficial or melodramatic terms. One of Brazil's popular idols, Francisco Alves (1898–1952), was a singer of *samba-canções*. Among the most recognized composers of urban sambas were José Luiz de Morais (alias Caninha) (1883–1961); Ary Barroso (1907–64), who won international acclaim with his samba 'Aquarela do Brasil'; Noel Rosa (1910–37); and Carlos Ferreira Braga (alias João de Barro) (b. 1907).

In the 1950s, the urban samba in its ballroom context suffered the influence of the big band with stereotyped arrangements seeking to emulate the American big jazz band sound of about ten years earlier. The reaction to such arrangements led to the development in the mid-1950s of the samba jazz phenomenon (influenced by the cool sound and aesthetics of Miles Davis) and, in turn, to the *bossa nova* movement of the late 1950s, which provided Brazilian popular music with new currents and a dynamic vitalization that brought about in the 1960s and 1970s highly sophisticated musicians, notably Antônio Carlos (Tom) Jobim (1927–94). The group of musician-poet-performers known as 'Tropicália' emerged in the mid-1960s and included such different personalities as Caetano Veloso, Gilberto Gil, Gal Costa, José Carlos Capinam, Torquato Neto, Tom Zé, Nara Leão and the composer-arranger Rogério Duprat. Sociopolitically, this group meant to awaken the consciousness of the middle class to the Brazilian tragedy of poverty, exploitation and oppression and to point out the true nature of the modern Brazilian reality. Musically, the 'Tropicália' movement brought about substantial innovations by widening the Brazilian musical horizon through adherence to and adaptation of the most relevant musical trends of the 1960s and 1970s, for example, the rock-Beatles phenomenon and the experimental new musics of the electronic age.

The history of recorded music represents an essential aspect of the development of popular music throughout Latin America and the Caribbean but can hardly be sketched at present with any degree of completeness and accuracy, except for the recording careers of some of the famous musicians.

CONCLUSION

This chapter has provided ample evidence of the great musical achievements of Latin America during the period under consideration. Especially since the 1950s the music of Latin America has been recognized in the major centres of the western world and many of its eclectic voices have been heard worldwide. As the century unfolds, we witness an acute new awareness of cultural identity in Latin American art and popular music that reflects the diversity of the Latin American nations and the Latin American people. Popular music genres especially have become key identity markers and have contributed to the considerable growth of pluralistic artistic expression. Art-music composers frequently complain about the diminishing possibilities of expansion of their artistic activities. Thus, we find numerous examples of music composition, especially in Mexico, Cuba, Brazil and Argentina, that unconsciously or intentionally blur the established boundaries of the popular and art-music traditions, thereby questioning the old aesthetics as the value system of the elite artist-composers. We might speculate that more attempts at integrating urban musics will occur. Although the Latin American art-music tradition of the twentieth century has been considered essentially an extension of that of Western Europe, new aesthetic processes may well change that perception within the next generations.

# 7

## LATIN AMERICAN ARCHITECTURE,
### *c*. 1920 – *c*. 1980*

### INTRODUCTION

By the 1870s the majority of the newly independent Latin American countries appeared – to greater or less degree – to be on the road to social and political stability. Relative economic prosperity resulting from Latin America's accelerated integration into world economy and the arrival of thousands of immigrants from all over the world, but above all from Europe (especially the Mediterranean basin), had at least two important consequences for Latin American architecture. First, it brought skilled labour that was quite different from the local workmanship that had sufficed until then; secondly, a new acculturation on a global scale meant exposure to styles and sensibilities distinct from those which had prevailed until then. Between the 1870s and the 1920s governments and the new rising bourgeoisie used architecture as one of the most visible means of giving themselves an aura of respectability, and they did so by imitating European and North American models.

During this period neo-classicism – refined or popular, as it was handled by masons steeped in the millennarian formulas of the Old World – began to disappear, giving way to eclectic designs typical of the nineteenth century: neo-romanesque or neo-gothic, Italian Renaissance, *Beaux-Arts,* or simply the picturesque styles of the European countryside: Andalusian, Basque, Norman, Swiss or English, appropriated for suburban residences or homes built in the mountains or at the beach. An ingenious mechanism then came into play: *obligatory* styles for various types of buildings. Thus, for example, the 'Roman' (with the addition of a cupola) lends itself to

---

*A preliminary draft of this chapter was translated from the Spanish by Elizabeth Ladd. The chapter was substantially revised by the Editor.

legislative palaces, and the 'Italian' or the 'French' (complete with mansard roof in tropical climates) is required for most public structures or for private buildings that lay claim to a certain degree of nobility. This leaves neo-romanesque or neo-gothic for churches or religious establishments in general. We can find, too, totally exotic examples like certain Arabian houses, or even more arbitrary and maladapted Chineses-style buildings. Who was responsible for these exploits? Mostly it was French or Italian architects who had come to Latin America looking for work, or else had simply been recruited to teach.

In general, architecture at the end of nineteenth century met a common fate in nearly all the Latin American republics: there was a reaction against everything Spanish or Portuguese that might even remotely conjure up memories of colonial dependence. Instead, the ideal was anything that evoked the rest of the highly civilized Europe: France, Italy, England, Germany. Progressive governments turned to foreign architects and engineers or to those natives who had European (or North American) technical and artistic training. Architects built structures with eclectic façades, although they were constructed with traditional techniques; engineers undertook the execution – during the same period – of roads, bridges, railroads, factories or packing plants using a modern technology that already included industrial prefabrication in wood and metal structures.

If in architecture the general trend was the imitation of the European, it is worth remembering that in some countries with strong indigenous tradition – such as Mexico or Peru – there were some attempts at 'Neo-Mayan' or 'Neo-Incan' pavilions, especially to represent these nations at several international exhibitions. This well-intentioned nationalist display was doomed to failure, since pre-Columbian architectonic forms – solid and practically without interior spaces – had nothing to do with the functions of Western style 'indoor living' which the civilized European world had been practising at least since the time of the Romans.

The 'neo-colonial', on the other hand, sprang up all over the continent, and was not entirely absurd, since its plans, functions, building materials and methods were perfectly rooted in Latin American tradition. Mexico was the first country to build in the neo-colonial style – as we shall see in more detail below – and this display of cultural nationalism appeared there at least twenty years before it did in any of her sister countries.

It might be said that all the great stylistic movements of the nineteenth century had repercussions on Latin American architecture: neo-classicism; romanticism, which produced, for example, the neo-gothic and all the fantasies of the 'picturesque' styles and a sort of folkloric *costumbrismo* based on completely foreign characteristics; eclecticism, the most important vein practised above all by French and Italians, although there were also a few local architects who had studied with foreign teachers in their own country or in Europe; and finally positivism which partly explains, for example in Mexico during the Porfiriato, the popularity of structures that strove to be 'modern' and 'progressive'. This last movement towards modernity was so important that in assessing the period 1870–1920 as a whole there is no doubt that the structures built by engineers – perhaps because they attract more attention – always appear more interesting and important than the works of architects. Railroad stations, markets, ports, hospitals, prisons, schools, factories, warehouses, the first department stores, were principally buildings with metal skeletons that were often exposed to view in an honest manner, although on other occasions they were disguised following the conventional prejudices of the epoch.

There was an obsessive preoccupation with 'style' desired by both those who commissioned the work as well as the architects who carried out their design.

In the first years of the twentieth century, the abovementioned 'historical' recipes were followed by new architectural and design formulas, different from everything that came before. French and Belgian *Art Nouveau,* Viennese *Sezession,* Italian *Liberty* or *Floreale* and Catalan *Modernismo.* Compared to the routine attempts to re-use the traditional styles of the past, all these ventures into a new aesthetic – while not always very well balanced – at least seem to suggest original solutions consonant with the daily functions of contemporary life. These architects did not hesitate to use a variety of techniques simultaneously or to mix materials. On the contrary, they did everything possible to use metal structures combined with stone, brick walls, large windows and skylights of clear or multicoloured glass. All this was an attempt to 'integrate' – rightly or wrongly – the 'box of walls' that contained the building proper, with its decoration in paint or in mosaic, ceramic, marble, wood or bronze. These solutions might appear as simply decoration or, better still, incorporated into such utilitarian features as roofs, floors, wall coverings, light fixtures, and so on. All these were capable of rendering the various buildings in which they were used more impressive and unified.

Among the mature professionals of the fifty years before the 1920s the following deserve mention: in Mexico, Refugio Reyes and Antonio Rivas Mercado; in Cuba, Joaquín Ruiz y Ruiz and Bernardo de la Granda; in Venezuela, Luciano Urdaneta and Juan Hurtado Manrique; in Colombia,

Mariano Santamaría and Julián Lombana; in Chile, Manuel Aldunate and Fermín Vivaceta: in Argentina, Jonás Larguía and Ernesto Bunge (who studied in Germany); in Uruguay, Ignacio Pedralbes and Juan A. Capurro; in Brazil, two urban engineers Paulo de Frontin and Saturnino Brito and, among others, the architect Bernardo José de Melo.

It must be recognized, however, that for the most important public works it was usual to hold international competitions, which produced a great flow of foreign professionals, always dominated by the French and Italians. In Mexico, the Palacio de Bellas Artes (1904–34) and the Central Post Office (1904), both in Mexico City, were the work of the Italian architect Adamo Boari. In Colombia the outstanding buildings in Bogotá were those that formed the National Capitol (1846–1926), by the Englishman Thomas Reed and an infinity of successors, among whom was the Italian sculptor Pietro Cantini, although the architect who changed the tastes of the epoch was the Frenchman Gaston Lelarge. Chile was dominated by two architects who came from France to teach and, at the same time, managed to get the best commissions: C. F. Brunet de Baines, who built the first Municipal Theatre which burned down and was rebuilt by his countryman Lucien A. Henault, who also designed the University of Chile and the National Congress, both in Santiago. In Argentina the great event of the end of the nineteenth century was the founding *ex nihilo* of the city of La Plata. The plans were drawn by an Argentine architect, Pedro Benoit Jr. and the different public buildings were awarded – through competition – to a constellation of architects that included Germans, Swedes and a Belgian, Julio Dormal, who later settled in the country. In Montevideo, the great builder of that epoch was the Italian civil engineer Luigi Andreoni, who was responsible for the Uruguay Club and the new Italian Hospital, and who also finished the Central Railroad Station.

In Brazil the great architects at the turn of the century were, in São Paulo, Francisco de Paula Ramos de Azevedo (1851–1928), who was responsible for the Caetano de Campos School and the Government Palace; and in Rio de Janeiro a Spaniard, Adolfo Morales de los Ríos, who designed the School of Fine Arts. Later in São Paulo the Swedish architect Carlos Eckmann distinguished himself as designer of the School of Commerce, but above all of the lovely Villa Penteado. In Rio the Frenchman Victor Dubugras – who worked primarily in Argentina – designed the most elegant residences in the city.

From the 1920s there developed throughout Latin America a consciousness of national identity. The fundamental differences that separate every thing Latin American – at whatever latitude – from the tradition of the West, taken in this case as an all-encompassing general term, became more apparent. Of course, there would still continue to be a considerable number of architects and plastic artists who were content to remain more or less repeating the academic ways. A few younger, more talented and, above all, more audacious architects would embark on an exploratory vanguard, influenced in particular by Le Corbusier. Finally, a third category which thought of itself as original, although it did not admit cosmopolitan novelties, would try desperately to find its own formula. In painting and sculpture this would be called 'indigenism', 'return to earth', with the consequent justification and exaltation of the artists' own cultures, autocthonous and colonial. In architecture, an equivalent movement would also seek motifs of inspiration in earlier forms, some in the pre-Columbian, but especially in an intense revival of the colonial.

## MEXICO

Several buildings were erected in Mexico City in the neo-colonial style during the early years of the twentieth-century: the enlargement of the University by Samuel Chávez; the rebuilding of the City Hall by Manuel Gorozpe; the Cervantes Library; the Escuela Normal and the Benito Juárez School by Carlos Obregón Santacila. Some years later, Augusto Petricioli would, in turn, contribute a new plan for the National Palace (1927), uncovering the *tezontle* – a dark red volcanic stone – that was part of the original construction which had been plastered over in the nineteenth century. The Mexican neo-colonial phenomenon is interesting because it occurred at least twenty years before the style appeared in the rest of Latin America, a situation doubtless due to the prestige of the omnipresent colonial buildings that served as models and inspiration. It is easy, therefore, to understand why the style passed rapidly to the domain of private building, for the most part badly interpreted.

The aesthetically contrary posture is the one which the vanguard quickly assumed. Along the most serious line of the strictly functional we find José Villagrán García (b. 1901), whose design for the Granja Experimental at Popotla (1925) influenced many of his own students, including Juan O'Gorman (1905–83) – also a distinguished painter, Alberto Aburto and Juan Legarreta. The style these architects used was simple and, because of that, economical, and this fact contributed to the state's commissioning several public works from them. The Hospital de Huipilco was built by Villagrán;

the Centro Escolar Revolución and the Coyocán School were entrusted to O'Gorman, who between 1927 and 1938 took the opportunity to design about thirty school buildings, in addition to a dozen private houses, among them the home-studio of Diego Rivera.

The most orthodox functional works of the period – other than those already mentioned – were created by Enrique del Moral, Enrique Yáñez, Mario Pani and Salvador Ortega. These men built in the public interest some of the gigantic multi-family housing complexes. There were also innovations in religious architecture, like the church of the Purísima (1946) in Monterrey, by Enrique del Moral, who, in collaboration with Fernando López Carmona, also produced the church of San Antonio de las Huertas. The Spanish architect Félix Candela, in collaboration with López Carmona, created the Santa Monica Church (1966) and, working alone, built a little masterpiece – the church of the Medalla Milagrosa, both located in the Federal District.

The culmination of the 'international' style (as it was also called) can be seen best, however, in the Ciudad Universitaria (1950–54) which, under the direction of the architect Carlos Lazo, includes buildings by Villagrán García, the partnership of Cacho, Sánchez and Peschard, Enrique del Moral and Mario Pani, and O'Gorman with Martínez Velasco y Saavedra. The University buildings are important because of their scale and their deliberate monumental effect. The relative failure of some of the pavilions consists, perhaps, in the unnecessary and forced integration of mosaics, polychrome reliefs and sculpture – a 'plastic support' that this powerful architecture did not need.

At more or less the same time, but in the private sphere, Luis Barragán (1902–89), one of the greatest of modern Mexican architects, created the development of Pedregal de San Angel in what had been a field of lava considered worthless by the real estate developers. Among the luxurious modern homes first built there are houses by Barragán himself, Pedro Ramírez Vázquez (b. 1919), and many others. In 1957, Barragán – collaborating with the then young German-born sculptor Mathias Goeritz (b. 1915) – designed and built the so-called Satellite City Towers, genuine 'monumentos a la nada', since they consisted of simple shafts of concrete, painted in different colours. They are fanciful towers whose mission is to provide a true 'centre of gravity' around which a confused suburban landscape is organized – for better or worse. The rest of Barragán's scarce but exquisite work lies exclusively in gardens, convents and private homes.

It appears that around the 1960s, the buildings commissioned by the state had to be obligatorily meaningful and even symbolic of the tacit message they embodied. They excelled in the modern style which, at that point, was already considered the 'official' expression of government. Rising above the merely nationalist, it sought to create – in its own eyes and those of foreigners passing through – an image of Mexico as a country in the vanguard, in which the naive 'local colour' lent by well or badly imitated historical styles was kept in check. In this sense, the surpassing Mexican work of the century is, without doubt, the Museum of Anthropology (1963–5), by Pedro Ramírez Vázquez, in collaboration with Rafael Mijares. In this building unfolds a true transposition of pre-Columbian and colonial elements in terms of an architecture that is contemporary, bold and perfectly functional. These same architects designed the Museum of Modern Art (1964) and the Aztec Stadium (1965).

Other names worthy of mention in Mexican official architecture are: Enrique Yáñez, a specialist in hospital complexes; Alejandro Zohón, who built the Mercado Libertad in Guadalajara; A. Pérez Rayón, designer of the Instituto Politécnico Nacional (1965); and, finally, Pedro Moctezuma, author of the austere Pemex (Mexican Petroleum) buildings. Among public works, it would be unfair to leave out the excellent example of the Olympic Pools (1968) by the architects Recamier, Valverde and Gutiérrez Bringas and the Olympic Stadium (1968), produced by Félix Candela in collaboration with Castañada Tamborell. A colossal work of almost 'symbolist' proportions is the Military College (1977), designed by the architect Augustín Hernández, which tries to recapture something of the pre-Columbian grandeur, at the risk of losing everyday practicality.

Also in the 1970s the team directed by the architect Orso Núñez deserves mention; it was responsible for the Nezahualcóyotl concert halls and the imposing National Library (1974–9) on the periphery of University City and at the edge of the so-called Espacio Escultórico (see Chapter 8). However, dominating public and private commissions during these years were the team of Abraham Zabludovsky and Teodoro González de León. Their work includes the ultramodern buildings of Infonavit, the Colegio de México (1977) and the new Museo Tamayo (1980). In collaboration with F. Serrano they also designed the austere Mexican Embassy in Brasília, which is a fine example of the best contemporary Mexican architecture.

CENTRAL AMERICA

At the end of the nineteenth century there were few notable buildings in Guatemala, whose capital was built and rebuilt after the various earthquakes that dot its troubled history. And few were built in the early decades of the twentieth century, with the exception of the National Palace (1919), designed by Rafael Pérez de León. Architectural modernity arrived only slowly in this country, and when it did it seems to have followed its more simplistic patterns in which 'modern' was the equivalent of cubical, stripped, smooth and white. Those responsible for it lacked a true understanding of the principles of the best functionalism, which relate above all to floor plans and sections, not merely to volumes and façades. This seems clear, for example, in the Municipal Palace (1954–8), designed by Roberto Aycinema, whose exterior boasts the great mosaic *Canto a la raza* by the Guatemalan painter Carlos Mérida (who lived in Mexico). Something similar might be said of another voluminous structure, the Guatemalan Institute of Social Security (1957–9), also designed by Aycinema, this time with Jorge Montes Córdova. These semi-functionalist plans are also reflected in the Civic Center of Guatemala, which consists of several public buildings including the Dirección General de Bellas Artes, the National Radio Station, the National Theater and the Museum of Modern Art. Interesting works of the 1960s and 1970s are the Rectory of the University City, and, also in the capital, the National Mortgage Credit Building, the Bank of Guatemala and the National Library and Archives.

Panama, an independent state from the beginning of the twentieth century, has become – thanks to the Canal – a more or less free zone for international trade through which, necessarily, a great deal of money circulates. Thus it is not surprising that its modern buildings exhibit a marked 'tropical North American' style, which assumes all the advantages of ultra-modern technology. Nevertheless, the progress of architecture was very slow. The Faculty of Engineering, which also trains architects, was not founded until 1941, and a real Faculty of Architecture was not established until 1962, in accordance with the models brought by two Panamanian architects, Guillermo de Roux and Ricardo Bermúdez, both educated in the United States. These two architects designed various buildings of relative importance, such as the annex to the Faculty of Sciences, the Savings Bank and the Bank of Urbanization and Rehabilitation. Collaborating with Octavio Méndez Guardia, they also designed the University, made up of the different faculties, with the library strategically located on the highest piece of land available.

In Cuba and Puerto Rico until the end of the nineteenth century the architectural models still came from Spain, but after the Spanish-American War the influence of North American architecture was dominant. During the first three decades of the twentieth century the great buildings of Havana were for the most part designed by U.S. architects and built by U.S. companies. This was the case, for example, with the Hotel Nacional (now the Havana Libre), by McKim, Mead and White. The styles which still dominate in these buildings are either French classicism (revised by the Academie des Beaux-Arts) or 'Californian' on a gigantic scale, correctly designed but with no serious attempt at architectonic innovation. In the Havana of the twenties, other enormous buildings were erected like La Metropolitana, designed by Purdy and Henderson. The Parliament building (1929) was built in neo-classical style, with the indispensable cupola, designed by Raul Otero in collaboration with J. M. Bens and others.

In Puerto Rico, after a Hispanizing trend which produced the Puerto Rico Casino (1918), the Capitol (1925) was built in official classical style. However, in Río Piedras, the University Tower (1936–7) by Rafael Carnoega Morales and Bill Shimmelpfenning boasts a deep-rooted Spanish affinity. The same occurs, around the same time, with the Puerto Rican Atheneum and the School of Medicine, both in San Juan. Within the presumed 'colonial' stylistic norms also rose the 'skyscraper' of the Cuban Telephone Company in Havana (1927), the first of its kind in the city, designed by the architect Leonardo Morales.

Within the current opposed to historicism, two movements began to reach the Caribbean, movements which moved in parallel in nearly all of Latin America in the 1930s. These were functionalism and, to abbreviate, the style we will call art deco. The latter, for example, was brought to Havana by the architect E. Rodríguez Castells, designer of a famous building for the Bacardi Company (1929), the noted rum distiller. Also on the Cuban scene various Spanish immigrants made their appearance, including the architects Martín Domínguez and R. Fábregas, many of them members of a group called GATEPAC which was affiliated to the Congrés International d'Architecture Moderne in Barcelona. People like Domínguez and Fábregas transmitted the message of functionalism, which would soon produce interesting designs like those by two local architects, Alberto Camacho and the future colonial art historian Joaquín Weiss (1894–1968), who diffused, above all, designs belonging to the Germanic version of rationalism. In Puerto Rico several excellent foreign professionals appeared: the first was a Czech, Antonin Nechodoma (who died prematurely in 1928), an imitator of Frank Lloyd Wright, whose Prairie Houses he made known with great sensitivity and talent; the second was a German, Henry Klumb (b. 1905), a direct disciple of Wright, from whom the new buildings on the university campus were commissioned.

By the 1940s, Cuba was already more in step with the derogatorily labelled 'international style'. The architect Emilio de Soto built apartment buildings in Havana along these lines, and even the Maternidad Obrera clinic (1939) in Marianao. However, the real point of departure for the best modern tendencies took place through people like Max Borges and Mario Romañach, who specialized more than anything else in private homes. Large projects, meanwhile, were awarded to Emilio del Junco, Miguel Gastón and Martín Domínguez, who designed, for instance, the Radio Center (1947). The Library of the Sociedad Económica de Amigos del País (1946) is the work of the architects Govantes and Cabarrocas; the Miramar Clinic (1947) was designed by Rafael Cárdenas.

In the Caribbean it has frequently been the luxury hotels that have served to introduce and diffuse modern architectural trends. First there were those of the Vedado neighbourhood in Havana, later those of San Juan in Puerto Rico, like the Caribe Hilton, by Toro, Ferrer and Torregrosa, the Sheraton in Kingston, Jamaica, by Shearer and Morrison, and the Hotel Jaragua in Santo Domingo, designed by G. González.

In the fifties there was a great stirring of architectural activity throughout the Caribbean. Thus, for example, in Havana Arquitectos Unidos enlarged the Edison Institute (1954), while Ernesto Gómez Sempere completed the great residential complex of Focsa (1956). In Puerto Rico, Klumb on some occasions reminds one of Frank Lloyd Wright, as in the Fullana house, and on others of Le Corbusier in Ronchamp, as in the case of the Church of Carmen in Cataño. In Santo Domingo, still under the dictatorship of Trujillo, the following buildings were erected: the Model Prison, the Archivo General de la Nación, the Reserve Bank of the Republic and, finally, the Government Palace (1947), designed by the architect Guido D. Alessandro. During the same period the French architect

Dunoyer de Segonzac built the Basilica of Higüey, using daring parabolic concrete arches.

In Cuba after the Revolution the buildings best representing the new architectural experimentation were the East Havana Neighborhood Unit (1959–3), by Roberto Carrazana, Reynaldo Estevez, Hugo Dacosta and others; and the famous National School of Plastic Arts and the National School of Dance, in Cubanacán (1960–3), by Ricardo Porro, Vittorio Garatti and Roberti Gottardi, which were an attempt at an original synthesis of African and colonial elements, the substrata of Cuban culture. Perhaps the most transcendental was, however, the Ciudad Universitaria José Antonio Echeverría (1961–70), on the outskirts of Havana, the work of a panel of architects which included H. Alonso, M. Rubio, F. Salinas, J. Montalván and J. Fernández. All the required conditions are present in this excellent design: consideration of the climate, transparency of walls, the provision of abundant areas of shade.

In the seventies, 500 schools were built for no less than 300,000 children. Three important projects should be mentioned: the V. I. Lenin Vocational School (1972–4), by Andrés Garrudo; the Máximo Gómez school (1976), in Camagüey, by Reynaldo Togorcs; and the Ernesto Guevara Palace of the Pioneers (1979), by Néstor Garmendia. Finally, built along very pure aesthetic lines, we must mention the new Cuban Embassy in Mexico City (1977) and the José Martí Monument (1978) in Cancún, both created by the talented architect Fernando Salinas.

During this same period in Puerto Rico there were several very important buildings erected: the conventional Ponce Museum, by the U.S. architect Edward Stone; the María Libertad Gómez Elementary School in Cataño, the work of Lorenzo Rodríguez de Arellano; and the Library of the Interamerican University of San Germán, which shows the influence of Rudolph and Saarinen. In the building for the legislators, the annex to the Capitol in San Juan, Toro and Ferrer achieved a tropical lightness of great purity, while Ramírez de Arellano, in the religious centre and chapel of the Interamerican University, leaned decidedly towards an aesthetic 'climate' that recalls the old neo-colonial assumptions.

Finally, in the Dominican Republic, the post-Trujillo democratic governments undertook an intense building campaign, which avoided the past dictatorial 'monumentality'. Notable buildings include the Juan Pablo Duarte Cultural Center, which comprises the National Library by Danilo A. Caro, the Museum of the Dominican Man by José A. Caro, the

National Theater by Teofilo Carbonell, and the Gallery of Modern Art by J. A. Miniño, and the main branch of the Central Bank, which opens onto a plaza, from designs by the architects R. Calventi and P. Piña.

## COLOMBIA

Colombia represents, in architecture, another special case, since it is one of the few South American countries that has at least three large cities of the first order: Bogotá, the capital, Medellín and Cali. With the general prosperity of the beginning of the century the need for public works multiplied and a few privileged architects dominate the principal projects. The most important were the French architect Gastón Lelarge and two Colombians, Julián Lombana (who died in the 1920s) and Mariano Santamaría (1857–1915). During the first quarter of the century the interior of the country was provided with a number of important buildings, such as the Government House of Antioquia, built by the Belgian architect Al Goovaerts, the one at Manizales, by the North American J. Vawter, and the Edificio National in Cali, built by another Belgian J. Maertens. During the same period the cathedral of Villanueva, originally designed by the French architect Charles Carré, was built (1875–1929) in Medellín. The cathedral in Manizales (built 1927–37) was designed by another French architect, Auguste Polty. In the latter case the structure was of concrete and since it was left unfinished (it was projected as a 'gothic' building) it gives the false impression of having been an advanced work for its time.

Two local architects, Guillermo and Alberto Herrera Carrizosa, produced a true revolution in taste when they created the La Merced neighbourhood in Bogotá between 1937 and 1942, with the houses in 'Tudor' style. At the end of the thirties, the campus of a new National University – very deteriorated now – was planned by another foreigner, Leopoldo Rother, who was inspired by Le Corbusier's first period. The outstanding elements of this campus were the Faculty of Architecture building, the Hydraulics Laboratory and the Faculty of Law building. However, the more mature contribution was made by another architect from abroad, the Italian Bruno Violi, who between 1939 and 1943 built the Faculty of Engineering with obvious Italo-German references. The great national commissions continued: for example the Radium Institute (1937–9) in Bogotá designed by A. Wills, and his plan for the National Library (1937–9) which reflects a complex of evocations that run the gamut from contemporary fascist architecture to North American influences.

The most transcendant architectural turning point occurred, however, between 1946 and 1958. It began with the 'messianic' visit of Le Corbusier to Bogotá, for which a development plan was rapidly sketched. Two works greatly inspired by Le Corbusier were also built at this time: the '11 de Noviembre' Baseball Stadium (1947–9) in Cartagena, by Ortega, Solano, Gaitán and Burbano, with the help of the engineer González Zuleta; and the David Restrepo Maternity Clinic, built in the fifties by the firm of Cuellar, Serrano and Gómez. Then the second Corbusian generation began to return – including some who had worked directly with the master in Paris. The first great impact among young Colombian architects was made by Germán Samper, who participated in the group that designed and built the Central Mortgage Bank where he showed evidence of extraordinary adaptation and imagination. Perhaps the most outstanding of these collaborations was, however, that formed by Rogelio Salmona and Hernán Vieco in their design for a group of multi-family dwellings in bare brick, called San Cristóbal (1964–5 and 1967–8), whose form set themselves apart from the 'cubical' canons of architecture and approached the free integration of Alvar Aalto.

Meanwhile, at the end of the 1950s, unrelated to these fashions, Gabriel Serrano and Gabriel Larga had created the El Dorado Airport, one of the best planned airports in the world. The rest is nearly all contemporary history as the great Colombian projects of the time were divided up among the powerful and more efficient partnerships. One of them, Esguerra, Saenz and Urdaneta (later joined by Samper), was responsible, in Bogotá, for the Luis A. Arango Library and the Avianco skyscraper. In Medellín they built the strange tower for the Coltejer Company. Their rivals – in those years – were, most importantly, Cuellar, Serrano and Gómez, who also had a busy construction schedule. Finally, a little later another group appeared, Rueda, Gutiérrez and Morales, designers of many complexes of definite interest like the residential developments of El Bosque (1972) and Santa Teresa (1977–8), both in the Bogotá environs.

But the work that is undoubtedly the mark of the decade of the seventies is the Park Towers (1968–72) designed by Rogelio Salmona, three skyscrapers of exposed brick with elegant curved stories that ascend in steps forming terrace gardens. This nearly obsessive reevaluation and return to brick – first carried out by Gabriel Serrano – has been brilliantly continued, not only by Salmona but also by Fernando Martínez. It is perpetuated in single buildings, like Los Cerros (1982), by Salmona himself, and in small residential developments like the ones already mentioned as well as others: La Calleja and La Candelaria, by Campuzano, Herrera and Londoño; Sorelia (1974–5) and Brapolis (1976–7) by Billy Goebertus and Juan G. Botero; and finally, along the same lines, the El Polo del Country (1979–80) built by the firm of Brando, Rueda and Sánchez. The dissident is the architect Jorge Piñol, whose best known works are not in exposed but in plastered brick, through which he tries to revive the white architecture of the architectonic cubism of the twenties.

## VENEZUELA

It was not until 1937 that we first see symptoms of architectural and urban innovation in the Venezuelan context when the government of the day appointed a group of French urban planners to take charge of the modernization of Caracas. This group included Maurice E. H. Rotival, who presided over the preparation of a Master Plan approved in 1939. At the same time, the Venezuelan Cipriano Domínguez was put in charge of designing the Centro Simón Bolívar (1950–60), in accordance with the 'modernized' norms of the Beaux-Arts style: a great central avenue with identical buildings and two symmetrical coloured towers that were designed by the great architect Carlos Raúl Villanueva (1900–78).

Villanueva, a key figure in the history of Venezuelan culture, had earned his architecture degree in Paris in 1928, and scarcely a year later opened his own office in Caracas, a city in whose transformation he would later play a major part. As early as 1935 the authorities commissioned him to design the Museum of Fine Arts in the Los Caobos neighbourhood. Villanueva dared to conceive an edifice of a single story with an attractive sculpture patio in the shape of a quarter-circle. In 1939 he created the Gran Colombia School and, during the 1940s, he also developed the El Silencio neighbourhood, where he tried to preserve something of the colonial ambiance, designing a plaza with fountains and statues surrounded with porticos in the vernacular tradition. Villanueva's *magnum opus*, however, was the monumental University City in Caracas, completed in several stages over twenty years, from the middle of the 1940s to the middle of the 1960s. Here we find ourselves at the opposite pole from the contemporary Cuidad Universitaria in Mexico City. Indeed, the fact that the Caracas project is an individual undertaking and the Mexican one eminently collective is what separates them from the outset. Villanueva continued to contribute other projects: the Olympic Stadium (1952), with a capacity of 30,000 spectators; the Baseball Stadium, somewhat later and capable of holding the same number of fans; and finally, the Olympic Pool, whose galleries support a daring concrete roof.

In the private sector in Caracas, beginning in the fifties, there appeared an urgent demand for really modern structures adapted to the climate and the local style of life. In 1950, the architects Guinand and Benacerraf erected the important Edificio Montserrat. Among the first tall buildings – of which there would be so many later – was the Edificio Polar (1952–4) in the Plaza Venezuela, the work of the architects Martín Vegas Pacheco and the Uruguayan José Miguel Galia, who had settled in Caracas.

The system of multi-family dwellings – in spite of having been severely criticized – continued to be practised as the only answer to the enormous uncontrolled growth of Caracas. Thus, the Caricuao complex, designed by the architects Alcides Cordero, Carlos Becerra and other collaborators, was extended. Meanwhile, Guido Bermúdez was building the Unidad Habitacional Carro Grande (1951–4) in the Valley of Caracas. The Cerro Piloto (1954), on the other hand, although supervised by Bermúdez himself, also involved other participants – J. Centellas, C. A. Brando, J. Hoffman, J. A. Mijares, J. A. Ruiz Madrid, J. Noriega and, as consultant once again, the omnipresent Villanueva.

Among the urban projects on a grand scale Ciudad Guayana deserves mention above all – an artificial creation, the product of a governmental decision, situated at the confluence of the Orinoco and the Caroni Rivers, where building began around 1960. During the 1960s other official commissions were made: for example, the School of Medicine of the Vargas Hospital (1961), designed by the architect Nelson Donaihi; the Maturín Industrial School, by Ignacio M. Zubizarreta; and, lastly, also by the same architect, the Escuela Artesanal El Llanito (1962) in Petare. We must also point out several later works by José Miguel Galia: the Bank of Caracas, the Banco Metropolitano and the interesting exposed brick tower of Orinoco Insurance. An Argentine who works successfully in Venezuela is Julio César Volante; he offered his own style in the Andrés Bello University with its severe façade. Finally, worthy of note are the Venezuelan Tomás José Sanabria, to whom we owe the Ince building, and the powerful Hispano-Venezuelan firm of Siso, Shaw and associates, who were responsible for the Parque Central – begun in the seventies – which contains three colossal 'cliffs' thirty-five stories high with a 400 meter façade, finished off with two towers of mirrors which – for better or worse – have definitively changed the urban skyline.

ECUADOR

After a glorious colonial past, Ecuadorian architecture entered a lethargic phase that lasted for at least 150 years. Modernity appeared very late, and that it did so at all is, in part, thanks to the strong personality of the Austrian architect Oscar Edwanick and to the fact that the Quito authorities in 1946 asked two competent professionals – the architects Guillermo Jones, an Uruguayan, and Gilberto Gatto Sobral, an Ecuadorian – to organize a Faculty of Architecture. One of the first interesting vanguardist works, without doubt, is the San Francisco de Sales School (1955) in Quito, created by the Swiss architect Max Erensperger. Also outstanding are several private homes designed by Jaime Dávalos together with Gatto Sobral. Dávalos, like Durán Ballen and Wilson Garcés, had studied in the United States and they brought the latest architectural ideas to Ecuador. Other distinguished professionals who should be mentioned are Milton Barragán, Juan Espinosa, Ruben Moreira and Mario Solís A worthy building from the 1970s – before oil wealth produced a rash of new buildings in Quito – is the Municipal Palace (1975), built near the Cathedral and the Government Palace on one side of the central plaza. Moderate in scale and neutral in design, it is the work of the architects Diego and Fausto Banderas Vela, who received their training and degrees in Montevideo.

PERU

Peru, like all Latin American countries, including Brazil, seems to have gone through a real architectural identity crisis between 1920 and 1940. On the one hand, there was a return to the pre-Columbian (the equivalent of 'indigenismo' in painting), although hardly a trace remains of the indigenous influence in the National Museum of Anthropology and Archaeology in Pueblo Libre, a suburb of Lima, and there is only the vaguest of hints in the Peruvian pavilion at the Paris International Exhibition (1937). On the other hand, by contrast revival of appreciation for the colonial assumed considerable proportions in Peru, doubtless because it is the country – in this part of the continent – where the greatest number of colonial buildings of value are still standing. The architect Rafael Marquina seems to have started the trend with his Desamparados railway station in Lima. Marquina, together with Manuel Piqueras Cotolí, developed (beginning in 1925) the Plaza San Martín in 'neo-colonial' style, in spite of the fact that in the surrounding area vaguely French style buildings were appearing as, for example, the Hotel Bolívar (1938). Similarly, neo-colonial was the Plaza de Armas (1945), designed by the great historian of colonial architecture, Emilio Harth-terré (1899–1983) and José Alvarez Calderón. It is hard to believe that these four architects, plus other specialists like Carlos Morales Macchiavello and Héctor Velarde, could have succumbed to the same error: they allowed excellent buildings to disappear – they even demolished them – in order to reconstruct a historic city like Lima in 'pseudo-colonial' style, invented from head to toe. Velarde himself, in one of his books, defends this 'revival' which, at bottom, represents nothing more than a naive affirmation of nationalism.

Nevertheless, the Master Plan of Lima (1946), which literally gutted the old city, at the same time accepted the advent of the contemporary style that had already had an opportunity to manifest itself in several works by Alfredo Dammert, Juvenal Monge and Santiago Agurto Calvo. In this new spirit the National Stadium (1952) was constructed in Lima, with a capacity for 60,000 spectators – the work of the architects A. Jimenos and J. Caycho and the engineer H. Pisatti. During this period the neo-colonialist Alvarez Calderón 'converted' to modernism, and collaborated with Walter Weberhofer on the Atlas Building (1956), which exhibits obvious Corbusierian influence. E. Rodriguez Larraín and T. Cron distinguished themselves in the same vein. Finally, the Colonia Huampani project (1956), by the architects S. Agurto, L. Vásquez, C. Cárdenas and J. Ramos, was an important step towards vanguard planning.

During the 1950s and 1960s the Peruvian government commissioned several modern buildings in Lima, including the Ministry of Finance by G. Payet, and the Ministry of Education by E. Seoane, both of mediocre quality. At the same time there were some excellent intransigently functionalist projects like the Jorge Chávez Airport in Lima, the Cuzco Airport, and a residence designed for the Peruvian Air Force. Other notable buildings in Lima were the Faculty of Architecture, part of the National University of Engineers; several neighbourhood developments such as San Felipe, Santa Cruz and Palomino; and, later, the Civic Centre (1971), designed by the architects A. Córdova, J. Crousse, J. García Bryce, M. A. Llona, G. Málaga, O. Núñez, S. Ortiz, J. Páez and R. Pérez León y Williams. This impressive, and controversial, agglomeration of spaces, terraces and little plazas in the 'brutalist' style has literally changed the old face of the city, since it rises between the colonial neighbourhoods, now very run-down, and the new residential sections which as yet have little character.

Among other distinguished Peruvian architects Miguel Rodrigo in particular deserves mention. Rodrigo designed, among other things, the Central Mortgage Bank of Peru in El Callao, the port of Lima. On occasion, he collaborated with Miguel Cruchaga and Emilio Soyer – for example, in designing the Ministry of Fishing, a very high quality structure, within an aesthetic of sharply contrasted masses made, deliberately, of exposed concrete. Also important are Walter Weberhofer, whom we have already mentioned, and Daniel Arana, creators of the Petroperu building, which for some time was the tallest building in Lima. The firm of Ibérico, Tanaka and Lozano completed another great public work that cannot be visited for security reasons: the Ministry of Defence. Finally, other talented architects who worked in partnership are Federico Cooper Llosa, Antonio Graña and Eugenio Nicolini. They built several new pavilions for Lima's Catholic University, the San Miguel Trade Center and a multitude of private buildings, always displaying designs of the highest quality.

BOLIVIA

In Bolivia, the link between European-inspired architecture, the neocolonial and modernity was the architect Emilio Villanueva (1884–1970), who was born in La Paz and received his degree in Engineering and Architecture in Santiago de Chile. Villanueva is important for his dual role as urban planner and architect, and for thirty years he exerted a powerful influence over the shape of his native city. As a young man he designed the Military College (1914, now demolished) and the General Hospital (1916), but his really important work is the City Hall (1925), which recalls the one in Brussels. It is built in an unexpected Flemish Renaissance style not often seen in South America. A brief neo-colonial period did not contribute much to his career, until after passing two years with his family in Paris, he returned to build two more interesting buildings: the Hernando Siles Stadium (1930, demolished in 1975) and, more important, the thirteen-storey tower in one solid block of the Universidad Mayor de San Andrés (1941–8) in La Paz. This functional construction – symmetrical in floor plan and façade – has only a few decorative elements at the entrance, inspired by motifs from the ancient Tiahuanaco culture.

From the 1960s modern architecture made forward strides, little by little, in the principal Bolivian cities, although many of the buildings erected suffer from more or less conventional design. A notable exception is the University of Oruro (1971), by the architects Gustavo Medeiros (a Bolivian who studied in Córdoba, Argentina) and his countryman and partner Franklin Anaya. It consists of a series of powerful blocks made of rough concrete. Another interesting figure on the contemporary scene is the architect Alcides Torres, principally the author of the German Club in La Paz (1965) and the building for Yacimientos Petrolíferos Bolivianos in Santa Cruz de la Sierra.

## CHILE

After the inevitable eclecticism, historicism and a few excursions into *art nouveau*, such as that practised by the Catalan architect A. Forteza at the beginning of the century, Chile moved more and more in the direction of modern architecture. In this vein we find two important figures, both native architects: Sergio Larraín and Jorge Arteaga, who designed the precocious 'rationalist' Oberpaur Building (1928–9) in Santiago. Arteaga also designed the Bulnes Gate (1923–32) in the Plaza de Armas in Santiago. During this period José Smith Miller and Josué Smith Solar built the monumental Hotel Carrera, also in the capital. In the centre of Santiago the Barrio Cívico represents, in turn, the most substantial urban planning effort of this era in Chile: it includes a series of solid public buildings – severe and smooth – surrounding the elegant Palacio de la Moneda, the neo-classical masterpiece of Joaquín Toesca completed at the end of the eighteenth century. Sergio Larraín was not only the teacher of several generations of architects, but also – with other collaborators – the designer of the impressive Naval School in Valparaíso, which remained unfinished for many years. In association with Diego Balmaceda and others, he later created the Presidente Frei barrio in Santiago (1965).

Another important figure in contemporary Chilean architecture is Emilio Duhart. A disciple of Gropius, Duhart later worked in Le Corbusier's studio in Paris during the period when he was drawing up the plans for the city of Chandigarh in Northern India. He is best known for the magnificent headquarters of the United Nations Economic Commission for Latin America, (1960–6), which he built in Vitacura, a suburb of Santiago. The building, a dominant horizontal, recalls Corbusierian solutions, both in its relationship to the mountainous terrain – with which it does not want to merge – and the visual play of its masses and the bold use of rough-finished concrete. Duhart later designed the dignified and refined Chilean Embassy in the Barrio Parque of Buenos Aires.

Generally, the youngest Chilean architects worked in teams. The group composed of C. Bresciani, H. Valdés, F. Castillo and C. G. Huidobro were the creators of several now classic multi-family dwellings such as the Portales Neighbourhood Unit (1961–3) in the so-called Quinta Normal in Santiago. They worked also with the architects Larraín, Bolton and Prieto on another series of collective apartments, called Torres de Tajamar. Finally, without collaborators this time, they also designed buildings for the Universidad Técnica del Estado in Santiago.

The Corporación de la Vivienda (CORVI) directs and organizes the construction of multi-family housing for the entire republic. One of the most interesting is that built in 1966 in Santiago by the architects V. Bruna Camus, V. Calvo Barros, J. Perelman and O. Sepúlveda Mellado. In the provinces at least two very successful CORVI projects deserve mention: one in Salar del Carmen in Antofagasta, in which the architects M. Pérez de Arce and J. Besa performed the difficult feat of harmoniously adapting ultramodern cubic forms to a desolate landscape; the other in Población Astorga in Valparaíso, the product of a collaboration between O. Zacarelli and J. Vender.

Finally, we must mention a building of some purity, beyond the merely utilitarian: the Benedictine Chapel and Monastery in Las Condes (1964), near Santiago, designed by two architects who are themselves members of the Benedictine order: brothers Gabriel Guarda (also a noted historian) and Martín. They achieved, with a minimum of means, one of the most attractive and restrained works in South American vanguardist architecture of the pre-war years.

## ARGENTINA

The first young Argentine architects to follow modern ideas – then revolutionary – were Alberto Prebisch and Ernesto Vautier, who conceived a project (never realized) for Ciudad Azucarera in Tucumán (1924), inspired by two great French architects, Garnier and Perret. When at the end of the 1920s Le Corbusier gave a series of lectures in Buenos Aires, his ideas were well received, not only among students and young professionals, but also among intellectuals and some of the ruling class. Thus Antonio U. Vilar and his brother Carlos, two architects who had begun their careers building 'historicist' buildings, soon converted to functionalism, becoming widely known among the public at large for a series of white service stations built for the Argentine Automobile Club.

Around this same time we encounter the original creations of two free spirits, the Italian Mario Palanti and the Argentine Alejandro Virasoro. From Palanti we have the Pasaje Barolo (1922) in Buenos Aires, a strange tower that has been classified as 'expressionist', consisting of bulbous forms that distract from its main lines. At the opposite pole, Virasoro is known as the 'champion of the right-angle': his signature work is the Casa del Teatro (1928), another structure of about twenty stories also located on a major central avenue in Buenos Aires. Virasoro's style is derived from art deco, a mannered style that does not, however, lack character and elegance.

Those who accepted neither functional vanguardism nor art deco practised eclectic international styles, including the 'neo-colonial', which we have already discussed in the context of Mexico and Peru. The best theoreticians and specialists in colonial art were Martín S. Noel, Juan Kronfuss, Angel Guido and Mario J. Buschiazzo, who fell into the temptation of practising the controversial 'revival' style. Noel built the Argentine Pavilion at the Iberoamerican Exhibition in Seville (1929), the Argentine Embassy in Lima, and a two-family residence for himself and his brother, today converted into the Fernández Blanco Museum of Colonial Art.

As if to neutralize this backward-looking effect, the first skyscrapers had already begun to appear in Buenos Aires – office and apartment buildings – which would radically transform the urban profile. The purest of them are the Comega Building (1933), by Joselevitch and Douillet and, above all, the true masterpiece which is the Kavanagh Building (1934–6), by Sánchez, Lagos and de la Torre, thirty-five stories high and for many years the tallest building in the entire world made of reinforced concrete. Alberto Prebisch, mentioned above, was a very gifted professional architect who, nevertheless, built relatively few buildings. His two principal works, however, continue to be highly visible in the heart of the Argentine capital, as it was he who designed the controversial Obelisco (1939) and the Gran Rex cinema (1936–7), a model of functional reserve and elegance, on Avenida Corrientes.

Among the architects of the next generation, Jorge Ferrari Hardoy and Juan Kurchan, who worked with Le Corbusier in Paris, stand out; their eight-storey house on Calle Virrey del Pino (1943) in the Belgrano district of Buenos Aires remains a classic in Argentine architecture. Other significant creations of the decade of the forties, several of them in the provinces, include the well-known 'Casa-puente' (1945) by the architect Amancio Williams in Mar del Plata, the Atlantic beach resort, and in Tucumán the new University built on a wooded hillside and the Hospital Antiluético (1948), both to the credit of the architects Eduardo Sacriste and Jorge Vivanco.

In the 1950s two large architectural practices in Buenos Aires appear to have vied for the majority of public and private commissions. One of them was formed by Sánchez Elía, Peralta Ramos and Agostini (known by the acronym SEPRA), which in addition to innumerable 'towers' of rental apartments, designed the great ENTEL Building (1951) in Buenos Aires and the more conventional Córdoba City Hall (1953). The other still powerful firm was directed by the brilliant architect Mario Roberto Alvarez who worked alternately alone or with different associates. He built, for example, with Oscar Ruiz, the impeccable San Martín Municipal Theater (1954–60) in Buenos Aires, which has not become dated.

Another figure, a little younger and more revolutionary, is the architect-painter Clorindo Testa (b. 1923), who often collaborated with other professionals without ever forming a stable partnership. With SEPRA Testa designed the most controversial building in Argentina of the last thirty years: the Bank of London and South America (1960–64) in Buenos Aires. At the opposite pole we find two architects, Claudio Caveri Jr. and Eduardo Ellis, who produced very little but were the fortunate designers of one of the most popular and influential buildings in Argentina – the little Church of Our Lady of Fátima (1956–7), in Martínez near Buenos Aires. In fact, although its design is modern, this church in its proportions and the way its materials are treated, recalls solutions within local tradition; one might even say it is a valid variation on the neo-colonial, similar to what Luis Barragán achieved in Mexico. Of this same generation also worthy of note are Horacio Baliero and Carmen C. de Baliero, authors of the Panteón Israelí in Mar del Plata (1965) and the Argentine Pavilion in Madrid's Cuidad Universitaria; and Juan Manuel Borthagaray, architect of the Ollé Pérez house (1966) in Punta del Este.

In the 1970s three practices captured much of the important work: Solsona, Manteola, Sánchez Gómez, Santos, Petchersky and Viñoly, designers of an important television station and numerous apartment buildings; Baudizzone, Díaz, Erbin, Lestard and Varas, which became known when it won the competition for the Municipal Auditorium of Buenos Aires (1972, never built); and Kocourek, Katzenstein, Castillo and Laborda, who – among other works – built the Conurbán Tower (1973) in Buenos Aires, In the interior of the country the leading figure was Miguel Angel Roca in Córdoba, his native province, where he won important commissions such as the Paseo Azul Commercial Center, the Conjunto Habitacional Consorcio Sur (1972–7) and the Consorcio Habitat (1972–8). Some Buenos Aires architects also designed for the provinces. E. Kocourek, mentioned above, is the author of the International Hotel (1978) in Iguazú, facing the Cataracts; Antonini, Schon and Zemboráin built the Stadium and Sports Center at Mar del Plata (1975–7); finally, Llauró and Urgel were responsible for the Hospital de Orán in the province of Salta.

URUGUAY

In Uruguay the *magnum opus* of the first third of the twentieth century was the large and complicated construction of the Legislative Palace in Montevideo. This monumental edifice was first entrusted to the Italian architect Victor Meano. On his premature death in 1904 the job was temporarily assigned to J. Vazquez Varela and A. Banchini, and in 1913 it was awarded to another Italian, Gaetano Moretti, who only finished it 20 years later. In another category, the Palacio Salvo skyscraper (1923–8), for many years the tallest in South America, is, like the Pasaje Barolo in Buenos Aires, the work of Mario Palanti, although in the latter case the Italian architect collaborated with the engineer L. A. Gori Selvv. In a style more sober than that of these concrete skyscrapers, other important works were built in this era, including the Edificio Central (1931), a true tribute to art deco, and several 'modern' private residences, like the Perotti house (1931), designed by the architects De los Campos, Puente and Tournier. Other well-known names are Carlos Gómez Bavazzo and Guillermo Jones – mentioned in connection with Ecuador – the latter having been one of the most prolific builders in Punta del Este.

From the same period several designs and executions by the influential architect and teacher Mauricio Cravotto are worthy of mention. He was responsible for the design of the Palacio Municipal (1929, which in its realization was lower than in Cravotto's original plans), the Master Plan of Montevideo (1930) and later the Rambla Hotel (1940). Around the same time the architect Carlos Surraco built the Hospital de Clínicas (1930), important for its size and the quality of its design. The most significant event in the history of Uruguayan architecture in the first half of the century was, however, the appearance of the exceptional figure Julio Vilamajó (1894–1948) whose designs, from his private house on the Boulevard Artigas (1930) to his masterpiece the Faculty of Engineering

(1938), demonstrate a constant striving for excellence. M. Muccinelli and R. Fresnedo Siri designed the Faculty of Architecture, much more conventional than that of Engineering, although not without its own brand of elegance. Also built in Montevideo in this period was the ANCAP Corporation building, the product of a collaboration between the architects B. Arbeleche and R. Lorente, and the Panamerican Building, designed by Raúl Sichero.

The Spaniard Antonio Bonet, who practised in Argentina, realized his most transcendental work in Punta Ballena, Uruguay: the Berlingieri house (1946) and the Solana del Mar (1947), which were to have a marked influence on both banks of the Río de la Plata. The Uruguayan engineer Eladio Dieste, by contrast, was an 'outsider' who made himself the champion of the most traditional 'poor' material in South America: bricks. In his hands, however, bricks, together with iron reinforcements, join the most modern techniques to achieve structures of true vanguardist boldness without any folkloric or romantic concessions. In the fifties, the other outstanding figure in Uruguay was the architect Mario Payssé Reyes, who was impressive for his refinement in the use of materials, his elegance and innate sense of beautiful proportion. Later he built the new Embassy of Uruguay in Buenos Aires, a work which is, however, not one of his best. Finally, among recent Uruguayan architects of note, we must mention Nelson Bayardo, author of the admirable Urnario (1961) in the North Cemetery in Montevideo, and Mariano Arana, who in addition to being an architect and professor much admired by his disciples has, as head of the well-known Urban Studies group, done much to save the old parts of Colonia and Montevideo.

## PARAGUAY

In Paraguay several outstanding architects deserve mention, including Genaro Espínola, who like the Bolivian Medeiros and the Argentine Testa was both an architect and painter; Carlos Colombino, who created the dwellings adapted to the climate, traditions and typically Paraguayan materials, without succumbing to folklorisms of dubious merit; and Pablo Ruggero, author of the interesting Xerox building, in which he tried to preserve the technique and aesthetic of brick, which is closely linked to the history of Paraguayan construction. Finally, in Asunción there are a number of interesting works by José Puentes, an Argentine architect who has become a naturalized Paraguayan citizen; these include numerous modern adaptations of the great mansions of the nineteenth century and, above all, a radio transmitting station on the outskirts of the capital.

## BRAZIL

The only modern school of Latin American architecture that has merited a worldwide reputation in this century has been the Brazilian, although today it must be said that, unfortunately, its hour of glory is already past.

Modernism had its origins in São Paulo. It was a movement stimulated at first by a group of intellectuals and artists, both older people and enthusiastic young people, all of whom organized the famous week of Modern Art in 1922. In architecture the movement was launched by the writings of Mário de Andrade and the practice of a Russian architect, Gregori Warchavchik (1896–1972), who had studied in Odessa with Tatlin and Lissitsky, and with Piacentini in Rome. Warchavchik came to São Paulo in 1923 and, barely two months later, published a pair of manifestos in defence of 'rationalism'. He built his first revolutionary house in 1927, followed by the Casa Modernista (1930) in Pacaembú, which was decorated with paintings by the artists Tarsila do Amaral and Lasar Segall.

During the revolution of 1930, which brought Getúlio Vargas to power, two tendencies which had appeared to be antagonistic – neo-colonialism and modernism – became united under the leadership of a highly prestigious architect, Lúcio Costa (b. 1902). There emerged, little by little, the elements which were to constitute the strength of modern Brazilian architecture: a functionalism *sui generis,* with local traits – like the use of tiles – and, above all, the exaltation of the climate and tropical vegetation. The two visits made by Le Corbusier to Brazil, one in 1928 and another in 1936, proved fundamental for the diffusion and triumph of rationalist principles. There is no doubt that the *pilotis* and the *brise-soleil,* so indispensable there for climatic reasons, are his influence, but in the hands of Brazilian architects they surpassed their merely functional roles and came to constitute a proud symbol of tropical affirmation. In chronological order the principal realizations of the movement are: the Ministry of Education and Culture (1937–43) in Rio de Janeiro, by the team directed by Lúcio Costa with the participation of Le Corbusier himself; the district of Pampulha, Belo Horizonte (1943–44) built by Oscar Niemeyer (b. 1907) – who would become the best-known Latin American architect of the century – and two 'classics' of modern Brazilian architecture, the residential complex Pedregulho (1950–2) and the Museum of Modern Art (1954–8), both in Rio de Janeiro, constructed by another great architect, Affonso Eduardo Reidy (1909–64).

In São Paulo, simultaneously, a parallel movement was developing which, while modern, nevertheless tried to distinguish itself from the Rio de Janeiro current. The two principal local figures there were Rino Levi and João Vilanova Artigas. The latter not only founded the Faculty of Architecture and Urban Planning in São Paulo (1961–8), but also built its main buildings; they are different—less theatrical and spectacular—from those by Niemeyer for the new capital Brasília.

The main event of this period was indeed the 1956 competition for the design of Brasília for which Rino Levi presented a very daring but practically unrealizable plan. The prize was won by Lúcio Costa, with Oscar Niemeyer as architect of the principal public buildings. From the moment of its conception, Brasília consecrated urban planning ideas – based on Le Corbusier's *Ville Radieuse* – that were already at least thirty years old. Now, with the benefit of historical perspective, its design, as well as the individual buildings, has been harshly criticized. Among the buildings designed by Niemeyer – who displayed in them the true imagination of a sculptor – we find the Cathedral, the Theater and the Civic Center, composed of two tall rectangular prisms and two segments of a sphere, each of which houses one branch of the legislature.

In São Paulo – in opposition to the school that gave rise to Brasília – the first disciples of Vilanova Artigas began to appear in the sixties. They were principally Paulo Mendes da Rocha, Pedro Paulo de Mello Saraiva, Carlos Millan, Décio Tosi, João W. Toscano, Abrahão Sanovicz, Ubirajara Giglioli and Fábio Penteado. The architect Joaquim Guedes designed innumerable public and private buildings in São Paulo. Rui Ohtake continues to astonish us with imaginative solutions of strange volumetric forms.

Brazil after the early sixties, however, seemed to be living on its architectural reputation. Rio Janeiro, São Paulo and even Brasília were transformed by the intervention of great engineering companies, whose only interest was commercial. See, for example, the enormous Avenida Central Tower, by Henrique E. Mindlin, in Rio Janeiro, which has no character: it is just one more North American style skyscraper. Nevertheless, there were a few who resisted this trend, notably the great architect Sérgio Bernardes (b. 1919), who seems less 'formalist' than Niemeyer in

Brasília. Bernardes' contributions include the Mercado das Flores in Rio de Janeiro, the Palácio do Governo (1966) in Fortaleza, and the Hotel Tambaú (1971) in João Pessoa, a low circular structure, closed on the exterior except for the side facing the sea.

CONCLUSION

The architecture of Latin America during the second half of the nineteenth century was not always of the highest quality. New governments emerging from the morass of civil wars are not the best qualified or most cultivated vehicles capable of commissioning works of supreme aesthetic significance. Everything was improvised. Young local architects, just out of school, found themselves entrusted with major structures for which they were indubitably not ready. As for the foreign architects who came from a Europe already contaminated by eclectic historicism across the whole repertory of styles, they offered Latin America the same warmed-over dishes with which they had earned their livings – poorly or well – in their native countries. Some of the best, such as, for example, the excellent French architect René Sergent – famous on the European level – did not even bother to cross the Atlantic in order to supervise the three or four palatial homes he built in Buenos Aires for as many Argentine millionaires.

Nevertheless, some of the designs from the turn of the century are perfectly respectable: for instance the one of the National Theatre in Mexico (now the Palace of Fine Arts), by the Italian architect Adamo Boari, which was an original attempt to integrate, within a modern European scheme, certain autochtonous elements. These are most visible in the sculptural decoration of the façades. Likewise the National Congress of Buenos Aires, by another Italian, Victor Meano, seems a noble and successful work with an original cupola of elliptical profile whose slender proportions confer an individual stamp on the building. Even today some of these buildings, with their excellent design, quality materials and skillful execution, remain as outstanding points of reference that stand out in the rather insipid grid of the majority of Latin American cities.

From the 1920s a choice had to be made between two options: the conservative, typical of the 'Southern Cone', which was in love with French and Italian architecture; and the modernist as, for example, in the case of the Mexicans who came immediately after the Revolution, or, thirty years later, the still more famous 'Brazilian school', which flourished from the 1940s to the mid-1960s.

Some twentieth-century Latin American architects can be placed at the highest international level: for example, the best of the Mexicans, Luis Barragán and Pedro Ramírez Vázquez (whose works include the Museum of Anthropology in Mexico City); the Cuban Fernando Salinas; the Colombians Rogelio Salmona and Germán Samper; the Venezuelan Carlos Raúl Villanueva (whose works include the University City in Carracas); the Argentines Jorge Ferrari Hardoy, Juan Kurchan, Clorindo Testa; the Uruguayans Julio Vilamajó and Mario Payssé Reyes; to say nothing of the veritable legion of great Brazilians architects (and urban planners) of the 'golden age': Lúcio Costa, Oscar Niemeyer, Affonso Reidy and Sérgio Bernardes (all from Rio de Janeiro) and João Vilanova Artigas (from São Paulo). Many of the above are distinguished enough to confer on Latin America a good place in the history of modern world architecture. It is true that some others, the most famous being the Cuban Ricardo Porro, the Chilean Emilio Duhart, the Uruguayan Carlos Ott, the Argentines César Pelli and Emilio Ambasz, have lived and practiced abroad, which is a way of reminding us that chronic political and economic crises do not favour budding architectural talents and that they, like delicate plants, can only flower fully when they can benefit from the opportunities to be found in the highly developed countries.

# 8

## LATIN AMERICAN ART SINCE $c.$ 1920*

### INTRODUCTION

Beginning in the 1870s Latin American art was gradually transformed by a dual phenomenon. On the one hand, increasing numbers of European (especially French, Italian and Spanish) teachers of drawing, painting and sculpture – some recruited, others simply on a 'cultural adventure' – arrived in the New World. At the same time increasing numbers of young Latin American artists, with scholarships or prizes if they did not have private resources, departed for Europe to pursue their studies in Paris, Florence, Rome, Madrid or some other centre of Western European art. Most Latin Americans returned to their own countries, either to teach or, commissioned by the government, to depict images of national heroes in bronze or on canvas, immortalizing the principal events of independence in large-scale works of art. Simultaneously, however, monumental change – in part a struggle against the inertia of the academies – was taking place in the art world in a number of different European cities: principally in Paris, but also in Vienna, Amsterdam, Berlin and Moscow. It was not for the avant-garde artists of Europe at first simply a question of subject matter, but something more immediate: the treatment of sunlight, the use of colour, as well as the validity of everyday themes which were considered pedestrian by the academies. In other cases, the driving force behind the new painting was the reinterpretation of the artists' own landscape or the assimilation of non-Occidental forms of art. In a word, the flight from the classical canons, a flight to which photography partly contributed, opened a door to other ways of perceiving and interpreting reality. And what happened was not confined to the limits of a few cities within national or

*A preliminary draft of this chapter was translated from the Spanish by Elizabeth Ladd. The chapter was substantially revised by the Editor.

continental boundaries. The most 'advanced' European art movements crossed the Atlantic and reached first the United States and then LatinAmerica, albeit after a delay produced by the physical and psychological distance separating the two continents. Thus, Latin American artists were gradually exposed to naturalism, impressionism, post-impressionism and symbolism. But if the first exhibition of Impressionism dates from 1874, the Argentine and Mexican Impressionists – to cite only two examples – do not begin to express themselves in this style until twenty-five or thirty years later. Eventually, the delays in Latin America's reception of, and response to, the vanguard in art became shorter. In the case of Cubism and Fauvism, for example, there was a lag of only ten or fifteen years. And after the Second World War, thanks to modern media of diffusion, art, including Latin American art, became universal.

We do not find any extraordinary figures among Latin American painters and sculptors of the late nineteenth century as we do in literature (for example, the Nicaraguan poet Rubén Darío), but a considerable number of artists of the period deserve to be remembered. Thus, for instance, in the heroic genre of historic evocation, the Venezuelans Martín Tovar y Tovar and Arturo Michelena and, above all, the Uruguayan Juan Manuel Blanes were outstanding, as were the Colombians Epifanio Garay and Ricardo Acevedo Bernal, the Argentine Eduardo Sívori and the Catalan artist who practised in Mexico, Pelegrín Clavé, in the field of portraiture. At this time Latin American art was practically unaware of the continent's indigenous people; only the Mexican painter Juan Cordero dared to represent a few of his classmates with their own characteristic racial features. Other compatriots of his, such as José Jara, took advantage of historical themes to present a realistic version of the Indians, while the Peruvian Francisco Laso and the Brazilian Rodolfo Amoêdo idealized indigenous types in a semi-academic compromise.

Among notable artists painting in the style which might be called native *costumbrismo*, Teófilo Castillo, who was inspired by Ricardo Palma's *Tradiciones peruanas,* and the Brazilian José Ferraz de Almeida Junior, who was more faithful to the social reality that surrounded him, which he did not attempt to improve, are worth of attention. In landscape painting a variety of painters fom all latitudes distinguished themselves: the Argentine Prilidano Pueyrredón depicted like no one else the vast transparent dome of sky that dominates the *pampa;* the Romantic Ecuadorian Joaquín Pinto did lyrical interpretations of the mountains of his land; and, in an opposing style, we have the Mexican José María Velasco, the 'scientific' observer who transcribed the landscape of his country, with its climate and its unmistakable geology and flora.

The female nude was practically a prohibited genre in respectable houses at that time, but nevertheless several artists dared to treat it, including the Brazilian Eliseu Visconti and – in a still more realistic manner – the Chilean Alfredo Valenzuela Puelma. On the other hand, *intimistas* were well received by a bourgeois society that liked to see its own world and faces reflected in realistic paintings. Good practioners of this style were Cristóbal Rojas, a very sensitive Venezuelan who died young; the Argentine Severo Rodríguez Etchart, little known even in its own country; and the talented Chilean Juan Francisco González, a refined colourist. In social painting, which the Argentines later seemed to ignore, we nevertheless find two notable Argentine examples: Pío Collivadino and the ecclectic and less literal Ernesto de la Cárcova, the author of *Sin pan y sin trabajo* ('No bread and no work'), a genuine political painting. Another Argentine Martín Malharro was an impressionist, although a latecomer, who interpreted the local landscape in somewhat romantic terms. We should mention, too, a contradictory Puerto Rican painter, Francisco Oller, who was alternatively a naturalist with little imagination and the best impressionist ever born in Latin America. In Paris he made friends with Pissarro and Cézanne and, under their influence, returned to his island to evoke the crude but beautiful light in the tropics as no one else has done.

In Latin America – as in the rest of the world – it has always been more difficult to find good sculptors that good painters, especially if we mention only the names of those who reached a truly high level of artistry. At the end of the nineteenth century, within the tradition of the heroic nude – especially the male nude – we have the Mexican Manuel Vilar, and if we look for a more modern expression we find his compatriot Miguel Noreña, who created the classic *Cuauhtémoc* on the Paseo de la Reforma in Mexico City. The Chilean Virginio Arias astonishes us even today with the pathos of his group *El Descendimiento* ('The Descent'). More along the lines of Carpeaux, Rodolfo Bernardelli, a Brazilian born in Mexico of European parents, became in his country the representative of a 'pictorial' type of sculpture which was dynamic and sensitive. Finally, the Argentine Francisco Cafferata, who would have become the greatest naturalist sculptor in his native land if he had not died so young, deserves mention.

We now turn to Latin American art in the twentieth century and especially in the period from the crucial decade of the 1920s to the 1970s and 1980s. The subject will be treated chronologically, country by country.

MEXICO

At the beginning of the twentieth century, there was only a handful of important painters in Mexico. One, Joaquín Clausell (1866–1935), who was a lawyer by profession, decided to paint in the impressionist style after a brief sojourn in Europe and became its best representative in Mexico throughout his long career as a painter. Clausell was above all a great landscape artist who travelled tirelessly throughout his country and was appointed director of the Ixtacalco School of Outdoor Painting.

In contrast to this objective painter, a faithful interpreter of nature, Julio Ruelas (1870–1907), who was a subjective artist, lived a short but intense life and 'burned himself out' with his iconoclastic and mysogynist violence. He studied first in Mexico and later in Karlsruhe, Germany with the master painter Mayerbeer. Ruelas distinguished himself more as an illustrator for the *Revista Moderna,* founded in 1898 by a group of intellectuals who considered themselves to be in the vanguard, than as a painter. He is remembered above all for a splendid print, *La Crítica,* done using the technique of etching which he had learned in Paris a few years before his premature death.

Saturnino Herrán (1887–1918), who was twenty years younger than Clausell and lived an even shorter life than Ruelas, was perhaps exaggeratedly glorified by the critics of his time but must be considered an indispensable element within the Mexican national conscience. What Clausell did with landscape, Herrán tried to do with ethnic types and their respective regional costumes. His *Tehuana* (1914) is a classic of Latin American painting and, in spirit corresponds to what some artists like Zuloaga had achieved in Spain, although Herrán always realized his work in a lighter and more optimistic vein. Born in the same year as Herrán, Roberto Montenegro (1887–1968), by contrast, enjoyed a very long life. He studied in Paris from 1906 to 1919, but when he returned to his native country he kept in mind the 'naive' artists, especially those who had painted ex-votos. In this sense a meeting took place within him between a cultivated and a popular orientation that contributed to the Mexican artistic maturity. He painted at the easel; he did frescoes; he was a printmaker; and he even wrote an important book on the art of Mexico in the nineteenth century: *Pintura mexicana, 1800–1860* (1933).

One figure who cannot be linked to any other because he played the role of a true precursor of mural painting was Gerardo Murillo (1875–1964), who called himself Dr Atl, the name by which he is best known. Atl was a man of action; in his youth he went to Italy and France, becoming involved with the Anarchist and Marxist movements, at the same time associating with the artistic avant-garde in Paris. A restless innovative painter he invented several 'dry' colours (the 'atl-colours'). With these he painted his views of volcanoes – the principal theme of his art, which he developed throughout his life. This did not prevent him from being, at the same time, an excellent portrait painter. His extreme nationalist attitude counted more than anything else in facilitating the advent of the muralist movement. By 1910, supported by a group of young people – which included José Clemente Orozco – he organized a successful dissident and revolutionary exhibition.

While Dr Atl was one of the cultivated forerunners, we also find popular antecedents of muralism. It should be remembered, first of all, that in nineteenth-century Mexico there had always been a tradition of naive mural painting, on the walls of, for example, the *pulquerías* – usually executed by anonymous artists. Secondly, there was also a line of popular graphic artists, like Gabriel Gahona (1828–99) or, much more important, José Guadalupe Posada (1851–1913). The case of Posada is extraordinary because working for newspapers, without any formal training, he became the 'natural illustrator' of the reality of his era. Most of his prints – generally woodcuts but sometimes metal engravings –reveal a formidable intuitiveness. A picturesque character, he worked in view of the public in his tiny studio in the centre of Mexico City. For artists like Rivera and Orozco, for example, his style represented an example of how to reach the public without being vulgar or condescending.

The topic of Mexican muralism must be approached as what it unquestionably is: the Latin American art movement that had the greatest repercussions on the continent as a whole and on the rest of the world in the course of the twentieth century. It will be discussed below by examining the work of its most famous figures, the artists traditionally labelled the 'big three': José Clemente Orozco, Diego Rivera and David Alfaro Siqueiros.

Today it seems relatively easy to discern the various causes that would explain the success of this true 'school', so different in its means and objectives from all the other great modern art movements of this century. From the outset we must realize that in the historical process – in any place or time – if a group of artists appears and behaves as a true 'generation', the effect on public opinion is much greater than if each of those same artists had tried individually to follow his own path. Furthermore, if the idea that motivates this group is simple and easy to grasp, better still: one can then say that the 'message' will be transmitted, and through it the contact between artist, work of art, and at least a portion of the public will be established to some extent. Finally, one indispensable element must be added: the work of art must possess positive values without which the message would not be captured – and these must be not only artistic values but also social and even ideological.

Mural art, when it reached its full expression, exhibited all those characteristics we have just listed as necessary for success and recognition, although it must be admitted that this recognition was somewhat relative. It certainly existed at the international level, but not in Mexico itself. The mass of the Mexican people were unable to decipher these painted murals, although the utopian aim of their creators was to 'reach the people' in order to contribute to their civic education. Today, of course, the situation looks totally different: mural art is accepted as 'historic' with as noble a pedigree as pre-Columbian or colonial art.

Leaving aside questions of quality and quantity, it is interesting to compare the Mexican with the Cuban case. After their Revolution the Cubans literally 'papered over' the island with posters, both normal-sized and monumental. Perhaps they had learned a lesson of Mexico: when they saw that 'the public did not go to the images', they turned things inside out and decided that 'the images would come to the people'. Between the two revolutions, that is between 1930 and 1960, what Mexican mural art represented from the aesthetic, social and political point of view – and it was certainly much better than the social realism of the Soviet Union – was quickly grasped and often badly imitated by a number of Latin American painters who, confronted similar problems of expression, wished to convey a message which, if not revolutionary, was at least rebellious.

In describing the unique phenomenon of Mexican mural art in detail, it must be made clear from the outset that we are talking about the idea of a single intellectual and not an initial impulse by one or more painters. This intellectual was José Vasconcelos, who, on being appointed Secretary of Education in 1921, invited a series of young artists to execute huge mural compositions for several public buildings. And the truth is that Vasconcelos himself did not have very clear ideas about how to reach the objectives he had outlined. We might add that two of the future 'greats' – Rivera and Orozco – erred in their first efforts when they were unable to liberate themselves from the nineteenth-century notion of 'allegory' that was linked to monumental-scale painting. It was, instead, painters who were later considered less important, like the Frenchman Jean Charlot (1898–1979) and the Mexican Ramón Alva de la Canal (1898–1981), who best understood the importance of the themes that should be addressed: popular themes, with concrete references to familiar events, portrayed without falling into the misty symbolism with which Rivera and Orozco began their work on the walls of the Escuela Preparatorio in Mexico City.

Good mural art would be, by definition, revolutionary and Marxist, nationalist and indigenous. In this art, in rather Manichean fashion, the forces of good (those just mentioned) confront the forces of evil, represented by Spain, Catholicism, the *conquistadores* and, in modern times, capitalism. This is the ideological line followed by Rivera and Siqueiros; we will see that Orozco seems to have been more relaxed, treating these themes in a more general manner and with a greater power of synthesis that augmented the impact of his work.

Diego Rivera (1886–1957) was born in Guanajuato into a middle-class family and went to Mexico City as a young boy to study at the Academy of San Carlos. The precocious career he had undertaken later took him to Spain – on a scholarship – in 1907, where he studied with the painter Chicharro, a *costumbrista* of colourful brilliance. Beginning in 1908–9 Rivera tried his luck in Paris, where he associated with vanguard artists like Picasso and Braque, who were in the full swing of Cubism, a style Rivera imitated successfully. When he returned to Mexico in 1921, he accepted Vasconcelos' offer and, after a few tentative first efforts, began to decorate the Ministry of Education building (1923–8). From this moment he discovered his own language, which he would develop, if unevenly, for the rest of his life. Among Rivera's most famous murals are the ones located at the National School of Agriculture in Chapingo (1923–7) and at the National Palace in Mexico City (1929–35 and 1944–51). He also painted, with the various degrees of success, murals in Detroit, New York and San Francisco. At the same time, Rivera always led a double career as a muralist and an easel painter (specializing in portraits).

José Clemente Orozco (1883–1949) was born in the state of Jalisco, but went to the capital as a child. As a young man he began to study at the School of Agriculture, where he unfortunately suffered an accident that left him with a maimed left arm for the rest of his life. Then he studied at San Carlos with Dr Atl, following the vanguardist movements in his teacher's footsteps. When his father died, Orozco had to earn a living as an architectural delineator and as a caricaturist, so that when he came to paint his first murals at the Preparatory School he sometimes approached the work with a markedly ironic intent, although he would soon realize that this was not appropriate. From 1927 to 1934 he had to live in exile in the United States, where he left several murals: for example Pomona College in California; the New School for Social Research, New York; and especially Dartmouth College, New Hampshire. When he returned to Mexico he did some of his best work, such as the murals that decorate the stairway of the Government Palace (1937) and the vault and cupola of the Hospicio Cabañas (1939), both in Guadalajara.

David Alfaro Siqueiros (1896–1974) might have become a great artist had he led a different life, but spent a third of his agitated life in jail, travelled extensively, took part in the Spanish Civil War, and was militant all his life on behalf of the extreme leftist ideas he always held. Nevertheless, his style was daring, such as, for example, the use of very exaggerated perspective and foreshortening that add drama to the themes presented. He was also innovative in technique, spraying industrial colours and using a new paint (pyroxiline) spread directly onto stone panels. Perhaps Siqueiros's best work, apart from some spectacular easel paintings, are the murals painted with a spraygun – *La Libertad, Cuauhtémoc* – which today occupy a place of honour in the Palace of Fine Arts in Mexico City. He painted large compositions in the Social Security Hospital and the Historical Museum in Chapultepec. He taught in the United States where he left at least one disciple who would become famous: Jackson Pollock, the inventor of drip painting.

Of course the 'big three' had numerous followers, to the point where it might be said that mural art held back the normal progress of painting in Mexico for many years. Among the most illustrious of these was Rufino Tamayo, scarcely younger than Siqueiros, whose career we will view in detail below. Others who should be mentioned are Juan O'Gorman, Alfredo Zalce, Pablo O'Higgins, Leopoldo Méndez, Jorge González Camarena, José Chaves Morado and Federico Cantú. Of these, perhaps Juan O'Gorman (1905–83) is the most interesting: an architect-muralist-painter of note, in association with other artists he not only planned the building for the Library of the National University in Mexico City, but also covered its cubical mass with a gigantic mosaic of coloured stones representing images inspired by pre-Columbian art.

This long and complex period of mural art – which by the middle of the century had become a real obstacle to the development of Mexican art – had major repercussions in the rest of Latin America. Cubans like Victor Manuel, Colombians like Pedro Nel Gómez, Ecuadoreans like Camilo Egas, Peruvians like José Sabogal, tried to imitate the formula and some even travelled to Mexico to learn it. In Argentina – through Siqueiros – there was a mural art movement whose best representative was Lino E. Spilimbergo. However, the Argentine who painted with a content that most paralleled Mexican mural art was Antonio Berni (1905–81), first through his large rectangular oil paintings and later through collages on a colossal scale, in which he used the cast-offs of the undiscriminating consumer society. Finally, from the point of view of absolute transcendence, the Brazilian Cândido Portinari (see below) was the one artist who could be compared in greatness to his Mexican predecessors; his strong celebratory compositions neither belittled historic themes nor themes of daily life. Thus, although some of the names mentioned here will appear again below, it should be made clear that when mural art is discussed in Latin America – praised or criticized, as is always the case with important movements – the reference is not to one country only nor one specific historical moment, but in a much more general way to a school that would forever transform the notion of Latin American art. In other words, it became one of the principal vehicles for that obsessive concern with *identity* – a concept that seems to make Latin Americans so anxious.

Leaving the world of mural art, the two most important creators who were contemporary with the movement were without doubt the Guatemalan Carlos Mérida, to whom we will refer later, and Francisco Goitia (1882–1960). Originally from Zacatecas, Goitia studied in Europe for eight years, first in Spain and then in Italy. When he returned to his own country it was to occupy himself first and foremost with archaeological and ethnographic questions. Thus a great artist was lost, and an original one within the context in which he lived and worked. As a painter, Goitia represents a violent expressionism, more direct but less 'committed' politically and socially than that of the muralists. His *Tata Jesucristo* (1927), for example, is a small masterpiece.

Four other interesting names from this period of Mexican art history are Castellanos, Agustín Lazo, Meza and Michel. Julio Castellanos (1905–47) was always under the influence of post-muralism, even when he did easel painting. His figures seem deformed, whether in pain or violent joy, reacting in the style of the humble folk who inspired them. Agustín Lazo (b.1910) belongs to another breed of artists. A cultivated man whose friends were writers, Lazo translated Goldoni and Pirandello and even designed the sets for their plays when they were staged. Guillermo Meza (b.1917), on the other hand, was a master of the nude who continued, to some extent, the line of the muralists, but he was more of a naturalist and less grandiloquent than they. Finally, Alfonso Michel (1898–1957) was a very fine 'chamber painter' who lived in Europe from 1923 to 1930, and only dedicated himself exclusively to painting during the last ten or eleven years of his life.

The impression has been given – perhaps exaggerated – that between 1920 and 1950 everything that happened in Mexican art came under the rubric of muralism. But there also existed dissident or simply naive artists who continued to express themselves as they could and as they wished. One of them – who has been newly appreciated in recent years – was Antonio Ruiz 'El Corzo' (1897–1964), author of the unforgettable *Sueño de Malinche* (1939) in which he realizes an ingenious syncretism between woman and landscape, united with deliberate symbolic meaning. An equally important figure is Maria Izquierdo (1906–55), who is not simply one more 'naive painter', but someone who tried to practice an art that was not academic in any way, a kind of painting which, precisely because of its total freedom, seems surprisingly modern today.

Along similar lines, but expressed with much more violence, is the art of Frida Kahlo (1907–54), who in spite of having been Diego Rivera's wife for many years, did not adopt a single aspect of the master's style. A brilliant, intuitive painter, she shows herself under two very distinct and perhaps complementary aspects. In some small 'autobiographical' canvases about her unhappy life – which she spent either in bed or in a wheelchair because of an accident – she does not surpass the mediocre quality of the ex-votos; by contrast, her portraits are admirable, especially the self-portraits, like the so-called *Las Dos Fridas* (1939), clearly her masterpiece.

The next escape from the dictatorship of muralism was achieved by a series of immigrant foreign artists. As a result of the Second World War, several surrealists came to Mexico, a place they saw as – in their own words – a providential country. We will begin with the most important, the Austrian-born Wolfgang Paalen (1905–59), whose international career was already quite advanced before he came to Mexico in 1939. Years later he founded the magazine *Dyn* (1942–4), of which only six numbers were issued. Paalen's mind-set was like that of the early Dalí or, even better, Yves Tanguy. In his best pictures he demonstrates a great power of evocation inspired by nature. A Spaniard, Remedios Varo (1900–63), and an Englishwoman, Leonora Carrington (b.1917), are painters of literary 'obedience'. Varo departs from an invented story which she 'dresses' in a concrete manner: elongated characters disporting themselves in a world of transparent objects. Carrington lets her uncontrollable imagination soar, painting beings who perform hard-to-comprehend actions. Both have a good sense of mystery and display a delicate and intriguing colour scheme.

Although because of his age and importance Rufino Tamayo (1899–1991) might have appeared earlier in this history, this is the best place to discuss him. On the one hand, he was a contemporary of the muralists – whom he survived by many years – and on the other he was already a modern painter who possessed all the boldness of the best universal painting of his time, integrating it into a decidedly Mexican figurative and chromatic scheme, without ever falling into the merely folkloric. It is true that Tamayo, in the beginning, also practised murals and painted in the traditional manner, at a time when as a young artist he could not refuse to do so. These paintings are, however, excellent, and bear his already unmistakable personal stamp. Above all, Tamayo was, more than anything else, an easel painter, as he himself realized early in his career. When he agreed to execute enormous mural paintings, he knew that he would do them with the same technique he always used, that is, by painting on canvas which was later attached to the wall in question. Tamayo's strange world consists of a very personal distortion in which the synthesized figures move across backgrounds of very strong or very pale colours – depending on the situation. The 'skin' of his painting is never totally smooth; it was rather granular and opaque.

It seems appropriate here to turn to Pedro Coronel (1923–85) who, without imitating Tamayo, was unable to avoid belonging to his tradition. Coronel was one of the few 'lyrical' abstract painters in Mexico who preferred pure form to figurative painting, always producing forms with well-defined contours, using ample quantities of paint and generally very 'thick', intense colours. Another 'outsider' who deserves mention is Juan Soriano (b.1920) of Guadalajara, who, like Pedro Coronel, belongs to the strange family of improvisers. Unbelievably precocious, this intelligent and lucid man is simultaneously a supreme craftsman. If he paints in an unpredictable manner it is not to surprise, but because he has so many resources to draw on that he himself does not know what he is going to conjure up on every occasion. Soriano's dominant characteristic is, after all, a certain way of seeing the world in which elements of reality mix with a strong dose of popular Mexican art, including its macabre connotations. He has often approached – successfully – abstraction, only to return immediately to his beloved figurative art.

As an introduction to geometric abstract art, we have waited until now to present a precursor like Carlos Mérida (1891–1984), who was born in Guatemala but from the thirties lived and worked in Mexico during the full flowering of mural art, in a way setting himself against this trend. Mérida's style has two roots: on the one hand his work may be read in a surrealistic key, but his main enthusiasm has been to 'geometrize' a coloured reality: characters, costumes, dances of his Guatemalan homeland. He returned there several times to carry out commissions for large semi-figurative mosaics, although he considered himself basically an easel painter.

If present-day Mexican painting is divided by generations, that of Tamayo and Mérida is followed by that of Coronel, Soriano and Gerzso. We have already discussed the first two. Gunther Gerzso (b. 1915), for a long time a set designer for stage and screen, also dedicated himself actively to painting after the surrealists came to Mexico. He himself seems to have begun with this style, although his later work would scarcely lead one to suspect it. Fortunately, he stopped being an orthodox surrealist – with all its literary connotations –to become a pioneer in a kind of geometric painting in which several other very talented painters, whom we will analyse later, were to follow. Gerzso's painting always shows the obvious presence of different planes that are superimposed on one another, creating real depth. Each of these 'walls' – as they might be called – displays its own colour and its own material, and this gives his paintings, which take a long time to complete, a nobility of style which is not common in this period.

One of the most original and well-rounded Mexican artists is Manuel Felguérez (b. 1928). He was born in Zacatecas and, after studying in Mexico City, spent some time in Paris working under the sculptor Ossip Zadkine. Felguérez was – with Lilia Carrillo – one of the few Mexicans who successfully practised 'informalism', a style of abstract art that exalted the materials his works were made of, whether in painting or sculpture – that is, its texture. Later he developed towards more purely geometric bases, two-dimensional or three-dimensional, where colour and surface still retain their importance. In the 1980s his work became more rigid and systematic – even to the point of working with computers – although he then returned to the search for effects of colour and materials, avoiding the smooth, homogeneous, brilliant surfaces that fascinated him for a time.

Although there are other examples of abstract artists in Mexico, Vincente Rojo (b. 1932), one of the painters who had the most influence on the favourable reception of this type of art, especially in the field of graphic design, merit special attention. Born in Spain, he came to Mexico at the age of sixteen, where he has worked for nearly his whole career. This secretive man seems to feel comfortable when he organizes his work as the development of a series dictated by intuition. Each of these series confronts an artistic problem to which he tries to find a compound solution. Thus we have seen *Señales, Negaciones, Recuerdos* and, finally, in the 1980s a series entitled *Mexico bajo la lluvia*.

Figurative art did not lose its validity in Mexico during the 1960s, but, as in the rest of Latin America, in order to survive it had to focus on what we have elsewhere called 'critical figuration.' That is, the figure is treated in a negative, cruel manner – a desecration. This manner of returning to the world of objects and, primarily, to the world of people with their bodies and their faces, might be expressed through satire or inoffensive irony. Among the satirists, we must first mention Alberto Gironella (b. 1929), who seemed to be leaning towards the study of literature when, beginning in 1958–60 with his 'variations' on the Niño de Vallecas and Queen Mariana of Austria – glorified by Velázquez – he began to express himself through painting. He was successful with this, and on trips to Europe he was received enthusiastically by the surrealist group, one of whom, Edouard Jaguer, became his sponsor. Gironella – a great craftsman and painter – was not content with these forms of expression. He also made huge collages, which are really 'assemblages', collections of heterogeneous objects which he seasons with acid pictorial commentaries, a sort of derisive, mocking monument.

Along similar lines, though less aggressive, we find two foreign artists who nevertheless made their careers in Mexico: Roger Von Gunten (b. 1933), a Swiss, and Brian Nissen (b. 1939), an Englishman. The first, more attached to visible reality, transforms it through what we might call a 'joyful expressionism' that uses a beautiful palette dominated by the blues and greens of the countryside in which he lives, far from the large cities. Nissen's trajectory, on the other hand, is obviously related to English pop art of the sixties. Nevertheless, once in contact with the complex Mexican world, he evolved toward a delicate art, halfway between pure painting and three-dimensional creation.

The best known native Mexican of this generation is undoubtedly Francisco Toledo (b. 1940), born in Juchitán, Oaxaca, to which he always returns, after prolonged stays in New York or Paris. This polymorphic artist is a talented painter, printmaker, ceramist and weaver. His expression seems to consist in a "return to the source' and his works are based on recapturing prehistoric caves where ancestral signs combine – the supreme irony – with the day-to-day instruments of our machine-age culture. The drawing is tense and precise in the prints, but in the paintings the sandy material with which he works obviates any possible rigidity. The opaque colours are always orientated towards a dominant hue (blue, ochre, red) which confers unity on each work. Another figure who deserves special mention is José Luis Cuevas (b. 1933). A great draughtsman and graphic artist, he must today be placed beside the best contemporary painters of his country; he is unique and indispensable to current Mexican art.

In the 1970s a curious phenomenon occurred in Mexican art – equivalent to what we might call a 'lost generation'. There seems to have been few original artists born between 1940 and 1950, who would have been expected to reach maturity twenty-five or thirty years later. This vacuum was filled – precariously – by a few outbreaks of what was then considered the 'vanguard'. However, compared with the enthusiasm with which these manifestations (which we will summarize under the generic name of 'conceptual art') were practised in Argentina, Brazil and later Colombia, Mexican developments were relatively poor. Perhaps more interesting were the manifestations of 'street art', which deliberately mixed musical and literary elements with the plastic arts. All these phenomena had a political-social protest character, developing in a climate similar to that of the old 'happenings' of the fifties.

On the other hand, with the advent of the eighties, Mexico witnessed extraordinary renewal in the field of the visual arts. Painters, sculptors, draughtsmen and printmakers proliferated. New, fairly independent artists appeared, some of whom had begun to work during the 'conceptual' era. One of the most brilliant is the painter-sculptor Gabriel Macotela, whose ideas are interesting because although they reflect earlier experiences of other artists (Tamayo, Toledo) they appear interpreted in an original way and in a context other than abstraction. Also worthy of attention are painters such as the four Castro Ieñero brothers – each one with his specific individuality – Santiago Rebolledo and a few others. It is no longer possible to divide them into abstract and figurative categories, as we might have done twenty years ago. They already belong to a world which is eclectic by definition: novelty resides in the formula which each one finds to express himself.

Since colonial times, sculpture has been traditionally less important in Mexico than painting. Nevertheless, at the end of the nineteenth century a few competent, if not great, artists appeared; for example, Miguel Noreña (1843–94), who was trained in Europe and who, on his return, received several important commissions: the Monument to Hidalgo in Dolores; the Monument to Father Llanos in Orizaba; and the work that made him famous, the noble figure of Cuauhtémoc which stands in a plaza on the Paseo de la Reforma in Mexico City. At the beginning of the twentieth century the architect Antonio Rivas Mercado, collaborating with the Italian sculptor Enrique Alciati, raised the column of the Monument to Independence (1902–16) on the same broad avenue that leads to the Chapultepec woods.

True modernity made its appearance with a sculptor such as Guillermo Ruiz (1896–1964), who in 1934 raised a colossal statue of Morelos on the island of Janitzio in the middle of Lake Pátzcuaro. The work, forty metres high, is basically made of reinforced concrete covered with stone blocks which were cut to size after they were put in place. The enormous stylized figure lifts its right arm to the sky while the left grasps the hilt of the sword of justice. Two contemporaries of Ruiz were Ignacio Asúnsolo (1890–1965) and Oliverio Martínez (1901–38). They helped to fill the need apparently felt by every new country to cover itself with congratulatory monuments. Asúnsolo created the Monument to the Fatherland (1924) and Martinez, who died young, designed the powerful figures that decorate the outside of the dome of the Monument to the Revolution (1933). Luis Ortiz Monasterio (b. 1906) chose also the stylized tendency of large masses and scarce details in the Monument to Motherhood in the Federal District, which can be compared to the statue of the same theme by Asúnsolo erected in Monterrey. Seldom do we find busts or heads among so much more or less allegorical monumental production. But those of the composer Silvestre Revueltas by Carlos Bracho and of the painter Francisco Goitia by his friend Asúnsolo deserve mention.

The fact that between 1900 and 1930 not many quality sculptors were born in Mexico may explain in part the influence of foreign artists who were ready to fill the need for three-dimensional expression, whether figurative or abstract. Several of these became famous. Preeminent was Francisco Zúñiga (b.1914), who was born in Costa Rica but spent practically his whole life in Mexico. Zúñiga was, without a doubt, the most popular figurative sculptor in spite of the sameness of his theme: the Indian woman, fullbodied and either nude or clothed only in her *huipil,* a kind of sleeveless blouse. At the opposite pole from Zúñga we find another foreigner: Mathias Goeritz (b.1915), a German refugee with a degree in philosophy who, after fleeing the Nazi regime, came to Mexico in 1949. Goeritz alone would change the face of sculpture in his adopted country, by trying to recapture –through his intransigent abstract sculptures – the greatness and solemnity of ancient pre-Columbian art. Needless to say the architects saw him as an indispensable collaborator. Luis Barragán planned with the then young Goeritz the Towers of Satellite City (1957), one of the fundamental features of modern Mexico City. In spite of the fact that he had been internationally known for many years, Goeritz still produced new work, above all in the collective enterprise called Espacio Escultórico ('Sculpture Space') in Mexico City.

Another influential non-Mexican sculptor was Rodrigo Arenas Betancur (b.1921); born in Colombia, he went to Mexico to study in 1944, and has remained there ever since. Although in is native country he had the opportunity to execute a gigantic equestrian statue of Bolívar – whom he represented nude – perhaps his most popular creation is his vertical image of Prometheus (1951) in Mexico's University City. Finally, the Frenchman Olivier Séguin worked with success for several years in Mexico before returning permanently to his own country. To him is owed several large abstract sculptures in public places, especially in Guadalajara, which have certainly contributed to the diffusion of this form of non-figurative art.

Again in the abstract tradition two Mexican women sculptors of comparable talent, although their formal characteristics are opposed, are outstanding: Angela Gurría and Helen Escobedo. Gurría's work always seems like a memory of things seen, that is, her works are of 'biomorphic' inspiration; Escobedo, on the other hand, is a stubborn practitioner of the hard geometric line, with which she often achieves great artistic purity. Of the same generation there is another notable painter-sculptor worthy of mention: Federico Silva (b.1923), who worked first in Siqueiros' team, and later became completely independent. Today he is one of the best abstract sculptors on the continent, whose works, although reaching sometimes considerable size, show a subtle and balanced 'skeleton', as for example with a piece suspended above the central hall of the National Library. Fernando González Gortázar (b.1942) is an architect-sculptor who was born in Mexico City, but at the age of four moved to Guadalajara, where he still resides. In his double role as architect and sculptor he follows the tradition set in motion by the great landscape architect Luis Barragán. Gortázar is also fond of pure geometric form, which he plays with on every scale and with different materials, combining them frequently with water in motion to create fountains of great originality.

Goeritz, Escobedo and Silva all took part in the design and execution of the abovementioned Sculpture Space in Mexico City. On the campus of the Autonomous National University of Mexico (UNAM), a vast field of black lava, untouched by human hands since the creation of the world, was set aside. The intent was to erect several sculptural works there. After serious reflection, the artists concerned decided to leave the land intact, barely accenting it with a circle 120 metres in diameter formed of natural elements. The sculptures themselves were installed outside the lava field and represent some of the best examples of abstract sculpture on the continent.

## CUBA

In Cuba which declared itself an independent country only in 1902 art – like culture in general – had been strongly marked by Spanish colonial rule. Even after the change in Cuba's political status the academies continued to dispense the same antiquated, conventional teachings. The most distinguished artists of the beginning of the twentieth century were Armando Menocal (1861–1942) and Leopoldo Romañach (1862–1951). Menocal, who had been a classmate of the great Spanish painter Sorolla, decorated the Presidential Palace in Havana, although his *forte* lay in the field of portrait painting. He stands out for having used a more brilliant palette that that of his immediate Cuban predecessors. Romañach, on balance, much the better painter, was also trained in the Spanish and Italian painting tradition, although he had occasion to visit Paris. In spite of this, he did not have any contact with impressionist or post-impressionist innovations, but only with the academic art of his time.

When Romañach returned from Europe, he was appointed professor of 'colouring' at the Academy of San Alejandro and around 1920 his pupils included, among others, Victor Manuel, Eduardo Abela, Fidelio Ponce de León and Amelia Peláez, which is to say, those who would be the best representatives of vanguard Cuban painting in the next thirty years. Little by little, these students lost interest in the obsessive 'chiaroscuro' that seemed to be Romañach's principal preoccupation as a teacher. The magazines and the reproductions of the great painting of the end of the nineteenth and the beginning of the twentieth centuries were now coming freely into Cuba and naturally the younger painters wanted to follow these new paths.

In 1924 Victor Manuel (1897–1969) rebelled against official teaching and took as a model Mexican muralism. In the same year Amelia Peláez (1897–1968), who had studied at the Art Students' League, had an exhibit in New York, where she had gone for training after spending several years at the Grande Chaumière, a private academy in Paris which was very popular among Latin Americans. In 1926 the Hispano-Cuban Institute of Culture was created to organize the more advanced exhibitions. A year later the poet Jorge Mañach began to publish the *Revista de Avance*. In 1929 the Lyceum was organized and, almost simultaneously, the Plastic Arts Foundation. It should be mentioned that the Communist Party and the José Martí Popular University were also founded in Cuba during the 1920s. Artists who considered themselves avant-garde identified with these popular struggles and their artistic creed followed the same path. This situation was demonstrated when Eduardo Abela (?–1966) exhibited his painting *Guajiros* (1928), which revealed the direct influence of Diego Rivera. In its violent colour, its search for a certain naivete, the use of national themes and figures, it introduces the deliberate line that avant-garde Cuban art was to take in this period. Later, the Estudio Libre de Pintura y Escultura, directed by Abela himself, would employ two young teachers about whom we will say more later: René Portocarrero and Mariano Rodríguez (who signed his name simply Mariano).

The Cuban painter Wifredo Lam (1902–82) is customarily regarded – along with Rufino Tamayo, the Mexican, and Roberto Matta, the Chilean – as one of a triumvirate of great Latin Americans all born around the turn of the century. Lam, who was of mixed Chinese and African background, after the obligatory presence at San Alejandro, went to Madrid where he pursued more or less conventional studies, and by the time he was twenty-six he had already exhibited in the Spanish capital. His fate, however, was determined on a trip he made to Paris where he had the opportunity to meet Picasso, with whom he formed a friendship that would last the rest of his life.

It seems odd today that Picasso, in Paris, would be the one to introduce Lam to black African art, a revelation that would definitively change the young Cuban's art. It was also providential that he met André Breton and the French painter André Masson in 1940 when the three of them sailed on the same ship from Marseilles to the Caribbean. The great 'popes' of surrealism accepted him on this historic crossing and from the moment Lam disembarked in Cuba one can say that his painting followed a sure path. The proof of this is his admirable painting entitled *La Jungla* (1941), which is perhaps his masterpiece and today hangs in the Museum of Modern Art in New York. However, while Lam may have found his racial and spiritual roots in his African forbears, this did not exhaust the possibilities of Cuban artistic expression. His contemporary Amelia Peláez, inspired by the coloured glass in tropical doors and windows, filled her canvases with a profusion of flowers, fruit, fish and everday objects. She offered an optimistic, objective art, while Lam always followed the subjective, anguished path.

Fidelio Ponce de León (1896–1957), mentioned earlier, was an independent personality who having abandoned his art studies reappeared in the thirties. He is a kind of 'intuitive expressionist' who barely pays attention to drawing in order to concentrate on strong colours and thick paint. When he died the National Museum in Havana organized an exhibition (1958) of 115 of his paintings. Felipe Orlando (b. 1911), who through his irregular career went from figurative art to abstraction with a surrealist connotation which is very particular to him, emigrated permanently to Mexico in 1949. Mariano Rodríguez (1910–90) also had connections, although sporadic, with Mexico, since it was there that he was a disciple of the painter Manuel Rodríguez Lozano, who introduced him to the secrets of his trade. But while the master used neutral, somber colours, the disciple – when he began to find his own way – would be a man of a bright palette. His series of cocks and cockfights, figurative at first, became gradually almost abstract. This was his best period. A few years after, he regressed to a diluted figurative style loaded with confused political content, without achieving the direct effect of good 'propaganda' as represented, for example, by the best Mexican mural art. Another important Cuban painter was René Portocarrero (1912–85), who studied at the Academia Villate and later at San Alejandro. By 1945 he had exhibited in New York, and fifteen years later the National Library in Havana organized a retrospective of his drawings and water colours. In 1966 he had a special gallery at the Venice biennial and there he introduced a kind of *horror vacui,* the result of which is that his canvasses are literally filled with signs presented frontally, all worked in thick paint: a heavy 'static baroque'.

Cundo Bermudez (b. 1914), who later emigrated to Puerto Rico, has always been an inventor of strange themes linked to a kind of 'naive surrealism'. Another voluntary exile is Mario Carreño (b. 1913), who visited Mexico, France, and Italy, lived in Spain for a few years and then in New York for a time before settling permanently in Chile. His art has 'travelled' with him: starting as a figurative form of folkloric fantasy, it became rigorously abstract and then returned to a cold and measured representation. Another wanderer is Luis Martínez Pedro (b. 1910), who in 1932 moved to New Orleans. He participated, however, in the Exhibition of Cuban Contemporary Painting organized by the Casa de las Americas in 1960.

We must finally mention a few artists who have made their reputations in revolutionary Cuba. Some are exclusively painters, such as Fayad Jamis (b. 1930), a strange case of a poet-painter who studied at San Alejandro and has exhibited in Europe at the Salon Réalités Nouvelles (1956), the Paris Biennial (1959) and, above all, the Exhibition of Cuban Painting in London (1967). Originally an abstract painter who tended to use blots of dark colours, his work later derived – for better or for worse – from what some writers call 'magic realism'. Other talented artists only practised easel painting sporadically, launched as they were on a fundamental public mission, forming the official popular graphics teams, in, for example, the Organization of External Support, the Committee for Revolutionary Action, the Casa de las Americas, the Union of Writers and Artists, and the Cinematographic Institute. In spite of the fact that the works – posters or what they called 'vallas' (enormous signs that might cover a whole building) – had to be anonymous, a few names always leaked out. Among the most distinguished artists we must mention Raul Martínez (b. 1927), who practised 'nationalist neo-primitivism', and Alfredo Rostgaard (b. 1943), who created some unforgettable poetic images.

In the same period, several fine Cuban painters for reasons of political dissidence lived in exile, where they continued to produce art. Some of the most famous include Emilio Sánchez, who lives in New York but who tirelessly paints architectonic canvasses in which brightly coloured tropical houses are represented. Another talented Cuban, Agustín Fernández, works between New York and Puerto Rico. A painter whose art has nothing to do with the superficial image of a tropical country like Cuba. Fernández is a hyper-realist whose canvases are accumulations of metallic objects with reflections, all represented in solemn greys and blacks. Of the painters who live in Paris, two can be mentioned: Joaquín Ferrer and Jorge Camacho. Ferrer is one of the finest and most mysterious Latin American painters of all those who work in Europe. With perfect technique, he draws angles and curves with ruler and compass, delimiting monochromatic areas, creating non-figurative paintings which nevertheless are fascinating to even the most demanding viewer. Camacho, a much younger man, shows the influence of the Chilean Roberto Matta and the Mexican Francisco Toledo, although his work is entirely original. Over neutral backgrounds – usually ochres – move strange half-human, half-animal forms, painted in iridescent and phosphorescent colours that make them even more dynamic.

As in the rest of Latin America, sculpture in Cuba is of lesser importance than painting. Juan José Sicre (1898–1974) is the most famous Cuban sculptor of his time. He began his studies in 1916 at the Academia Villate, and continued two years later at San Alejandro. Beginning with a scholarship in 1920, Sicre went to Madrid, Paris and Florence, remaining in Europe until 1927, when he returned to Cuba and was appointed to a teaching position at San Alejandro. His best known works are a statue of Victor Hugo (1936) in the El Vedado neighbourhood of Havana, a colossal head of heroic proportions representing José Martí (1939), and a series of portraits and contributions of a religious nature. Norberto Estopiñán (b.1920), born in Havana, where he later became Sicre's disciple at the Academy of San Alejandro, is also worthy of mention. He works in wrought iron or bronze, in a non-figurative style, inspired by primitive cultures. The best Cuban sculpture of this century, however, can be found in the work of one great figure: Agustín Cárdenas (b.1927), who was born in the Cuban providence of Matanzas, but who has lived and worked in Paris since 1955, achieving international fame. Cárdenas works directly on the most noble of materials: wood, stone and marble. He is also the type of artist usually characterized as having a 'biomorphic' inspiration. In his work masses always are defined by large twisting curves, melting into one another due to the great care with which he polishes the surfaces to make them gleam in the light.

## DOMINICAN REPUBLIC AND HAITI

In the Dominican Republic it can be said that modern painting begins with Abelardo Rodríguez Urdaneta (1870–1932), an academic painter who did historical paintings and scenes of local colour. A breath of fresh air arrived later with the Spanish painter José Vela Zanetti (b. 1913), who subsequently emigrated to Puerto Rico. Among local talents we should mention Jaime Colson (b. 1904) and Darío Suro (b. 1918), who studied first in his own country and later with Diego Rivera and Agustín Lazo in Mexico. Suro is probably the best known artist from the Dominican Republic, although he usually lives in the United States.

In the city of Santo Domingo in 1965 – motivated by the U.S. intervention – the combative and bold Frente Cultural was created. He brought together artists from different generations and artistic approaches, as is evident in an Exhibition-Competition held in November 1965 in the Palace of Fine Arts. Artists as different from one another as Silvano Lora and Ada Balcácer joined together to pose the question of art and the social function of the artist. Both still create art today in accordance with their traditional media: for example, Lora insists on political testimony; Balcácer uses myth and dreams to convey her message. A younger artist, Danilo de los Santos (Danicel) creates an obsessive female figure, Marola, who must be interpreted for her symbolic meaning. Another outstanding contemporary figure is Orlando Menicucci (b. 1949), a self-taught painter who is always halfway between abstraction and representation.

Haiti achieved international recognition in the field of art with the founding of the Art Center in Port-au-Prince in 1944. The person responsible for this institution was the North American painter DeWitt Peters, who fought harder than anyone else to establish a meeting place for Haitian artists that did not depend on any government subsidy and that would provide them with a place to exhibit and publicize their work. Of those who participated at the outset, only three could be categorized as 'popular' artists: Philomé Obin (1892–1984), Rigaud Benoit (1911–86) and the sculptor Valentin. DeWitt Peters, however, was convinced that the most interesting aspect of Haitian art was primitive or naive art, especially the work of the exceptional Hector Hyppolite (1894–1948), who in addition to being a painter and decorator was a Voodoo priest. (He had long been a practitioner of *vévé*, a ritual design made with flour on the ground before the beginning of a ceremony.)

Unlike Obin or Benoit, Hyppolite, because of his role as an 'intermediary', had to paint in a hurry. Many other artists – too many, obviously – have tried to continue this naive tradition (genuinely or otherwise), to the point where Haiti has been turned into a marketplace for this type of painting – a marketplace in which there are many false primitives who nevertheless represent one of the country's richest sources of income.

## CENTRAL AMERICA

The Central American countries do not have a strong modern art tradition. It might be said that they passed directly from a mediocre colonial art – with the notable exception of Guatemalan imagery – to the contemporary period without any major transition. After the Second World War, however, many talents were revealed, some of whom, like Carlos Mérida (Guatemalan) or Francisco Zúñiga (Costa Rican), have already been mentioned in our discussion of Mexico. Many artists from the Mexican provinces and from neighbouring Central American countries always been attracted to Mexico City.

Guatemala seems to have produced the most distinguished artists. Besides Mérida, González Goyri, Mishaán and Abularach deserve mention. Roberto González Goyri (b. 1924), a sculptor who was born in the capital, although he studied in the United States, executed between 1964 and 1966 a number of important reliefs in his native city. Rodolfo Mishaán (b. 1924), also from Guatemala City, fell under the influence of the famous Mérida, considered a national hero. Finally, Rodolfo Abularach (b. 1933) has become known in Latin America for a theme which seems to have become an obsession with him: the representation of a great open eye. Mishaán and Abularach have lived for many years in the United States. However, all in all – if we make an exception of Francisco Zúñiga – of the present generation the most important Central American artist is Armando Morales (b. 1927). Born in Granada, Nicaragua, he went to the capital, Managua, where he learned drawing and painting. In 1957 he travelled extensively in South America, and three years later – on a Guggenheim grant – he went to live in New York, where he stayed for twenty years and pursued his aptitude for graphic art. Morales, who was an admirable abstract painter, returned some years ago to representational art of the metaphysical type, which he achieves through very pure drawing and a strange iridescent palette.

COLOMBIA

At the beginning of the twentieth century Colombia had only one outstanding artist: Andres de Santamaría (1860–1945), who was born in Bogotá,
but was taken to Europe as an infant. There, he studied in England and
France, finally taking up permanent residence in Brussels, where he later
died. However, the seven years that he spent intermittently in his native
country were enough to classify him as an indispensable link in the Colombian artistic chain of awareness. It has to be said, however, that most of the
painting that was produced in Colombia during the first thirty years of the
century was somewhat unimaginative. Among the few who contributed to
different and revolutionary movements in the 1940s and 1950s was
Guillermo Wiedemann (b. 1905), who was born in Munich, Germany, and
studied art in his native city. Fleeing from the Nazi terror, he took refuge in
Colombia in 1939, and was at first overwhelmed – like so many
foreigners – by the 'tropicalism' that he tried to express on his canvases. In
the 1950s, however, with the same seriousness he had put into his figurative art, he began to cultivate 'lyrical' abstraction and was the major
precursor of this style in Colombia.

Besides Edgar Negret – strictly speaking a sculptor – whom we shall
consider later, two artists are considered to be undisputable abstract masters
in Colombia: Obregón and Ramírez Villamizar. Alejandro Obregón (1920–
92), born in Barcelona, lived from childhood on the shores of the Caribbean,
which has always been his great source of inspiration. In 1958, he began an
active career that fascinated the Colombian critics of the time, since they
found him to be semi-figurative, semi-abstract, and able to pose the problem of Latin American expression in his paintings. Eduardo Ramírez
Villamizar (b. 1923) was an inspired painter-sculptor. He presents the opposite case to that of Obregón: he is one of the few Colombians – the other is
Omar Rayo – who was tempted by the purity of geometry. Omar Rayo
himself (b. 1928), born in Roldanillo, is an artist who engraves obsessive,
labyrinthine reliefs of black lines on a white ground, when he is not
pursuing – as well – the revelatory relief on paper of a real object. Skipping
a generation, there are two Colombian women painters who are interested in
this same avenue, although they approach it in a less insistent manner:
Fanny Sanin, who lives in New York and paints symmetrical pictures in
muted colours; and Ana Mercedes Hoyos, of Bogotá, who at first created
ambiguous canvasses in a style that lay between the figurative and the
abstract, and more recently has made incursions into conceptual art.

In figurative art, the most famous figure is Fernando Botero (b. 1932), who was born in Medellín and by 1951 was exhibiting in the capital. Later he studied in Madrid, at the Academy of San Fernando, where he doubtless learned his excellent technique. Is Botero a modern or a reactionary in art? Fifty years ago his paintings would have been rejected as conformist. Botero is a creator of *sui generis* images whose principal characteristic is that he 'inflates' everything he paints – people, animals, objects. Going against the tide of automatic avant-gardism, thanks to the quality of his work and his humour, Botero has commanded higher prices than any other Latin American artist. What remains uncertain is whether his painting will endure or whether it will become simply another momentary curiosity.

If in Botero we discern an element of social criticism, through the mocking treatment of reality, in his compatriot Beatriz Gonzalez this criticism becomes satirical and merciless. She attacks religious and patriotic myths and even the themes of daily life, and instead of applying her paintings on canvas, she affixes them – like permanent lacquers – on furniture or vulgar objects: an original use of Pop Art, Colombian style. Figurative artists to the core are the brothers Santiago and Juan Cárdenas Arroyo, but they are very different from each other in spite of their attachment to the visible 'document'. Santiago is the best hyper-realist in his country, using amusing *trompe-l'oeil* effects in which we see a tacit irony. Juan, perhaps less imaginative in his provocations, concentrates on representing people in enclosed or open spaces. An able portrait artist, perhaps his work as a printmaker is more interesting than his paintings.

The 1970s saw the appearance of the new art of Colombia, especially as it concerns a handful of draughtsman-painters. One of the most brilliant is, without doubt, Luis Caballero (b. 1943), who studied in Bogotá and Paris – the city where he lives and where he began as a great figurative artist of distortions. Older now, he has become an inspired interpreter of the young male body in attitudes of maximum tension. Another of these excellent draughtsmen-painters is Gregorio Cuartas, from Medellín. Influenced by the Italian *Quattrocento,* which he studied first-hand, Cuartas draws with a hard line which also, recently, is enriched with strange sombre colours on small canvases of intense magic.

In Colombian sculpture as in Colombian painting at the beginning of the twentieth century there is only one name of any real interest, that of Romulo

Rozo (1899–1964). Born in Chiquinquirá, Rozo studied in Bogotá, Madrid and Paris. As soon as he returned, his government sent him on a diplomatic mission to Mexico, which was a crucial episode, since he established his career in that country, building monumental sculpture and teaching. Rozo and Rodrigo Arenas Betancur (see above) have several things in common: not only did both emigrate to Mexico, but they also both aspired to the stylization of form, simplifying masses through the use of large planes without detail.

Later came a radical revitalization. Two great sculptors of the same generation as Arenas Betancur – Negret and Ramírez Villamizar, whom we have already mentioned as painters – entered the scene with new ideas that were diametrically opposed to what preceded them. Edgar Negret (b.1920) was born in Popayán and studied in Cali, where he would later settle. In 1948 he travelled to the United States and stayed there for about ten years, with intermittent trips to Europe. He sculpts in welded metal which he cuts, folds, perforates and embosses, as if he were trying to create fantastic 'useless machines'. These solemn and elegant creations are invariably painted monochromatically: in black, white, red or, most recently, yellow. They always have a matt finish with not a hint of reflection. Eduardo Ramírez Villamizar was born in Pamplona – in the north of Colombia – but he studied architecture and fine arts in Bogotá. As a painter, he revitalized the genre with his strictly geometric constructivism and his smooth technique. In 1955 he began to work in sculpture, first in small reliefs or large mural compositions. He also lived for several years in New York, concentrating there on three-dimensional sculpture which he sometimes painted in bright colours. His conception of form is basically monumental and accordingly he creates huge works which, in spite of their severity, are integrated with the landscape of his native country.

At the opposite pole we have Feliza Bursztyn, a sculptress who died young. She was the first and most gifted of the 'junk sculptors' in Colombia. At first she created static pieces by accumulating heterogeneous metallic materials; later she launched 'crazy machines', which both intrigued and irritated the Colombian public during the 1960s. The breach, however, remained open. Also worthy of mention is Bernardo Salcedo (b.1942), an architect and sculptor born in Bogotá. His temperament shows in his fabrication of invented objects, in which he arbitrarily combines certain elements taken from reality: old dolls, photographs, knives and saws which he modifies and combines in strange and elegant assemblages. His work adds an ironic note to contemporary Colombian sculpture.

## VENEZUELA

In spite of the fact that Venezuelan painting had some outstanding artists at the turn of the century, it must be recognized that except for Emilio Boggio – an impressionist who lived in Europe – the rest were content with a more or less academic approach.

Something more meaningful took place, however, with the arrival on the scene of Manuel Cabré (1890–1983). Although he had studied with Herrera y Toro – one of the important precursors – Cabré had a new vision of painting, or to put it better, of the light of the Caracas Valley. The attempt to represent it on canvas was a task that occupied his entire long life. For him art was not a matter of portraits or heroic themes of Independence or even of the intimate details of daily life. What Cabré wanted was nothing less than to pay supreme attention to the nature of his region, which he interpreted on a monumental scale.

The fact that this approach became generalized into what we call the Caracas School does not mean that more advanced Venezuelan painters did not also experiment – at the same time – in other, frequently totally divergent, directions. We refer to the style of the greatest twentieth-century painter to have been born in Venezuela – Armando Reverón (1889–1954). This genial *clochard*-to-be of tropical painting began a sensible career first studying in Caracas (1904), then going to Europe ten years later (1914–21), with long stays in Madrid, Barcelona and Paris. It was only when he returned from Europe that Reverón began to explore the light of the Caribbean coast, first painting 'blue' with fuzzy technique and Goyesque themes, and later turning to a 'white' period, renouncing the city and taking refuge in the wild beach at Macuto. He then entered his 'brown' period, in which the brushstrokes are almost lost in the neutral colour of the burlap he used to paint on.

The First World War brought home Rafael Monasterios (1889–1961) and Federico Brandt (1879–1932) from Europe, bringing with them a fresh view of the new conception of painting. Brandt is a painter of people and things in the home; his palette is refined and cheerful. In contrast, with Monasterios we return to nature captured in a pale palette, without the subtle visual transposition of Reverón. A similar case is that of Antonio E. Monsanto (1890–1948), a good *plein-air* painter who had learned the lessons of Impressionism. In the following period the most interesting artists are Francisco Narvaez, Marcos Castillo and Juan V. Fabbiani. We will discuss in particular Francisco Narvaez when we turn to the topic of Venezuelan sculpture. Castillo and Fabbiani were above all painters of the nude – a genre not practised in Venezuela until then: the first treats them in flat colours, and the second in large masses. Since both taught at the School of Plastic Arts in Caracas, they naturally had a great deal of influence over the young artists of the day.

Hector Poleo (b.1918) is the painter who provides the link with the generations to follow. He went through several periods: he was strongly influenced by Mexican painting – both in subject matter and technique – and he then pursued a kind of highly constructed surrealism. Later he turned to mistier, almost abstract evocations.

From then it might be said that the history of modern Venezuelan art was written both in Caracas and in Paris, that is with the creation of the group that baptized itself 'The Dissidents'. It included Guevara Moreno, Debourg, Regulo Pérez, Barrios, Vigas, Arroyo and Peran Erminy. At first all of them were in favour of a violent abstraction that later would take the form of kinetic art or neo-plastic geometricism. However, there still remain vestiges of figurative art in some of them, which were given concrete expression by Oswaldo Vigas, Omar Carreño, Humberto Jaime Sánchez, Jacobo Borges and Alirio Oramas.

During the late 1950s several groups were formed in Caracas – for example, Sardio, El Techo de la Ballena, La Tabla Redonda and those around the publication *Crítica contemporanea* – and in Maracaibo two main movements arose: Apocalipsis, and another around the magazine *40° a la sombra*. From 1960 figurative painting became diversified. Younger artists began to express themselves: Virgilio Trómpiz with the stylized human figure; Hugo Baptista, who painted doors in dazzling colours, but developed towards more diluted, non-representational canvases. Marisol Escobar devoted herself completely to sculpture and went to New York where she pursued her career in pop art.

Venezuelan kinetic art in Paris had a complex internal history of its own. We will begin with Alejando Otero (b.1921), who was in Paris from 1945 to 1952. A talented figurative artist, he learned a great deal from Picasso and began to use that influence successfully. Nevertheless, on his return to Venezuela he broke with that facile approach and invented what he called 'colour-rhythms': white panels painted in impasto, striped with black and containing geometric areas of intense colour. Later we will follow Otero's development that led him to three-dimensional expressions. Jesús Rafael Soto (b. 1923), who had studied in Caracas and rapidly rose to be director of an art school in Maracaibo, was in Paris in 1950. During his first five years in Europe he did scientific research on certain phenomena known in optics but generally not used until that time in art. He discovered that if a freely moving element passes in front of a background with vertical black and white stripes, the human eye imagines it perceives a vibration. After thirty years of recognition, Soto created other intriguing optic illusions like his 'fields of bars' or, even better, his 'penetrables' –virtual forests of nylon threads which viewers traversed in amusement or alarm.

Carlos Cruz-Díez (b. 1923) reached Paris in 1959, after a brilliant career in his own country as a prominent industrial designer. If Otero and Soto were above all intuitive, Cruz-Díez showed, in contrast, a systematic sensibility and mentality. He gave the name *fisiocromías* to his most widely known experiments, which consist of systems of vertical bars set on end and painted different colours. As the spectator moves in front of it, the panel is transformed into a series of successive geometric compositions, each one different from the others. As in the case of Soto, there is a virtual movement in the background – not only a real one – that justifies the label of kinetic art which is applied to this trend initiated first of all by Alexander Calder.

Venezuelan art in the 1980s, after the perhaps exaggerated 'boom' of kineticism, protected by the state, the foundations and the rich collectors, was beginning to concede the preeminent position to other manifestations. Jacobo Borges (b. 1931), for example, always an interesting artist, became in his mature years probably the best neo-figurative artist in Latin America. His broad recent canvases possess a purely pictorial dynamism, that is, they are never simply drawings coloured in *a posteriori*. As in the work of the great colourists of earlier times, the form is born from the colour that the brush – as sensitive as a seismograph – applies on the canvas. Other talents continue to flourish and it is practically impossible to take account of all of them. Particularly worthy of mention is Edgar Sánchez (b. 1940), first for his drawings, and then also as a painter. His art is mainly expressed through the amplification of details – on a colossal scale – of nude or clothed bodies which he represents with minute, icy precision. In other cases, his works consist of isolated features, like several mouths that appear to have separate lives of their own, without a face to support them, emerging painfully from a fragment of spread out skin.

In sculpture, the only great name from the beginning of the century is that of the already mentioned Francisco Narvaez (b. 1908), who belonged to the generation of artists who produced stylized figures, and who were the vanguard of the era of his youth. His Fountain of Las Toninas in the El Silencio neighbourhood of Caracas belongs to this period. However, after 1950 Narvaez became an abstract biomorphic artist, with a more architectonic tendency in his latest works. He is a man who has worked in all techniques and with all materials, listening to what each medium has to offer and taking it as his inspiration.

  We discussed the kineticism of Soto and Cruz-Díez under painting, because many of their works were murals. We cannot do the same with the recent work of Alejandro Otero: his 'pyramids' or 'rotors' are three-dimensional, that is, true 'spatial sculptures'. Ingenious, monumental, constructed of stainless metals, reflective of light from all angles, they are proliferating throughout the world as 'signs' of the Venezuelan spirit, that is to say, of a country orientated towards the future. As far as spatial sculpture is concerned, we must also mention the name of Gego (Gertrudis Goldmichdt, b. 1939), a German architect established in Venezuela who displays an aerial conception of sculpture, using spiderwebs made of wire or knotted cords, which paradoxically reveal to the viewer the indeterminacy of open space. And finally, another architect, Domingo Alvarez (b. 1935), deserves attention. He won a competition for the Monument to Venezuelan Aviation, which was, unfortunately, never built. It consisted of a Solar Plaza with mirrors that reflected the whole sky on the earth. Alvarez also constructed labyrinths of mirrors which, in their way, play with the ambiguity of space.

## ECUADOR

The first new principle in Ecuadorean art in this century was stamped by indigenism, discussed above. Its most illustrious promoter was Camilo Egas (1899–1962). After 1912, a group of young men including Egas and his friend José A. Moscoso (who died in the prime of life) benefited from the presence in Quito of two men who had been 'imported' from Europe.

One was the Frenchman Alfred Paul Bar, summoned to teach drawing and painting; the other was an Italian, Luigi Cassadio, who acted as instructor of sculpture. In Egas's case, Bar's presence was crucial, since he made him see the Ecuadorean landscape in Impressionist terms. Egas would go to Rome and the Academy of San Fernando in Madrid to continue his studies, travelling extensively in Europe until he decided to settle in the United States, where he achieved a certain recognition by exploiting the lode of pre-Columbian America with its typical characters, attire and customs.

Victor Mideros (b. 1888) also studied in Quito with Bar. Mideros followed the indigenist current – with more realism than Egas – before becoming interested in a mystical painting rendered in classical terms. He is an indispensable figure because he represents the nexus with the next generation, as he was, for example, the teacher of Eduardo Kingman (b. 1911), another indigenist painter who shared with Egas the honour of creating the pictorial decoration in Ecuador's pavilion at the New York World's Fair (1939). The artist who attracted most attention, however, was a controversial figure: Oswaldo Guayasamín (b. 1919), who was born in Quito and studied at the National School of Fine Arts there. In his work the traces of Mexican muralism are obvious, as well as the influence of Portinari in Brazil (see below) and even Picasso of a certain period. With these elements and his own statements, which he certainly does not lack, he has been able to elaborate a declamatory image of suffering humanity.

In the middle of the fifties the first signs of abstract art appeared in Ecuador. Two very different personalities initiated it: Manuel Rendon (b. 1894), who was born in Paris, although his family was Ecuadorean, and was twenty-six years old when he moved to Guayaquil, where he has remained ever since; and Araceli Gilbert (b. 1914), a native of Guayaquil, which is where she began her studies with Hans Michaelson before moving to New York to continue her training with Amedée Ozenfant, the French purist. Ecuadorean painting evolved a style we must characterize as concrete, that is, a severe non-figurative expression based on geometry.

Among the direct or indirect disciples of these two artists we may count younger men like Enrique Tábara (b. 1930), who is also from Guayaquil. He began his career painting landscapes and regional themes, and when later he approached informalism it was under the influence of Michaelson and Rendon, although it was the years he passed in Barcelona that brought him to monochrome painting with emphasis on the material. When he returned to his own country, he attempted a pre-Columbian symbolism, pasting natural elements on his canvases, a collage worked with constructivist methods.

Luis Molinari Flores (b.1929), like those mentioned above, was born in Guayaquil, but his training was more international since he studied in Buenos Aires and spent many years in Paris and New York. His works exhibit a rigorous geometry, inspired by Vasarely. Oswaldo Viteri (b.1931), his contemporary, was born in Ambato; in contrast to the intellectual Molinari Flores, he aspired to a popular art, using burlap in his work, with which he fashioned little dolls that were supposed to represent the South American expression.

Later there was a return to figurative art, represented above all by artists like Felix Arauz, who through the use of oil paint and sand tried to approach that *art brut* practised by Dubuffet. Finally, even conceptual art seems to have reached Ecuador, in the person of Maurice Bueno, who was trained in the United States. His materials are taken from nature, such as water, earth and fire; his techniques are, by contrast, ultramodern and include neon light and laser beams.

In sculpture, the only interesting figure is the sculptress Germania de Breilh, who studied at the Faculty of Fine Arts in Ecuador and also, later, in the United States. The cast iron pieces by this artist are reminiscent of the solutions of the Spanish artist Chillida, while when she works full forms in andesite, one can not help thinking of the great French sculptor Arp.

PERU

The glorious colonial past of Peru, rather than being an advantage for the development of modern art in the country, has represented a burden, a true millstone around the art community's neck.

By way of introduction, we will begin our discussion with Daniel Hernández (1856–1932), who in spite of being still a traditional artist, served as a transition, especially in his work as a teacher. Born in a rural area, Hernández moved to Lima at the age of four, and after studying there was sent to Europe in 1875 by the government to finish his education. He spent ten years in Rome, and in Paris he made friends with the Spanish painters Pradilla and Fortuny, from whom he must have learned the cursive manner of handling his brushes. He was a fast and accurate painter, although his great historical paintings often seem grandiloquent. He portrayed many female nudes, and several portraits of much better workmanship and penetration than the large official pictures. From 1918 he was the director for many years of the National School of Fine Arts from where he exercised undeniable influence. Another important artist was Carlos Baca-Flor (1867–1941), a strange case of internationalism, whose situation was similar to what happened with Santamaría in Colombia and Boggio in Venezuela. In fact, one must ask whether Baca-Flor's cosmopolitan career had any influence at all on the painting of his native country. He lived in Paris and was a mundane portraitist of real universal fame.

Hernández had problems with several rebellious students at the School of Fine Arts. The one who stood out immediately as the leader of the future indigenist movement was José Sabogal (1888–1956), who by 1909 had already made a trip to Europe. Five years later we find him studying in Buenos Aires, and between 1922 and 1925 he lived in Mexico, linking himself closely to Rivera and Orozco. The indigenists pursued a regional and racial ideal that had to represent the human figure in accordance with local archetypes, although they also extended their quest to the portrayal of landscape, customs and dress. Among those converted by Sabogal were: Julia Codesido, Jorge Vinatea Reinoso, Alejandro González, Enrique Camino Brent and Camilo Blas. Their respective works are diminished by the extreme simplification of the drawing, the careless composition, the aggressive colours, all of which seem more fitting to tourist posters than to serious art. Perhaps the only Peruvian painter who reflects the life of the people spontaneously – and not through an intellectual process – is Mario Urteaga (1875–1959), a sort of *naif* artist born in Cajamarca, who had the grace (in both senses of the word) to be able to paint simply what he felt. His humble little rural or urban scenes, in muted tones like those of the real earth, tell us more about an authentic reality than any pompous declamation.

A wave of internationalism swept across Peru with two other painters: Grau and Gutiérrez. Ricardo Grau (1907–70) was born in Burdeos and studied in Brussels. Returning to the country of his parents, his catalytic role seems today even more important than his artistic career proper. In fact, Grau would launch three decisive battles in Peru: for colour (as the principal organizing element of the picture and not simply the subject), for the freedom to experiment (with emphasis on the individual in the face of nationalism), and finally, for the search for *plastic* thinking, instead of the 'literary' impositions from which indigenism had not been able to escape. Quite different, but important in his own way, was Sérvulo Gutiérrez (1914–61), who began as a self-taught artist until he was able to study for eight years in Buenos Aires with the great Argentine painter Emilio Pettoruti. Gutiérrez' masterpiece is without a doubt his canvas *The Andes* (1943), in which a crude, strong female nude represents – better than in the case of Guayasamin – the unavoidable South American reality. Perhaps the most noticeable difference between Sabogal and Grau, as compared to Gutiérrez, was that the latter was never an intellectual, and perhaps because of this his pictures offer a direct, living testimony.

Abstraction would also reach Peru thanks to a foreigner: A. C. Winternitz (b. 1906), who was born in Vienna but as a young man moved to Italy where he specialized in mosaic and stained glass work. In 1939, when he moved to Lima, he taught the techniques of mosaic and founded the School of Plastic Arts at the Catholic University where he had as his disciple – among others – Fernando de Szyszlo, the most important present-day Peruvian painter. Winternitz, with his knowledge and sensitivity, was, then, an indispensable link in the evolution of art in Peru.

Fernando de Szyszlo (b. 1925) studied first at the Catholic University, and then spent several years in Europe, where he went to complete his studies. When he returned to his own country, he himself taught at the same school where he had been educated. Szyszlo's art demonstrates that there is no hard and fast line between the figurative and the abstract. In his paintings what appears at first to be totally invented, in the end seems to evoke – voluntarily or involuntarily – the memory of something already seen, and that comes from the rich repertory of pre-Columbian art, to the point where his painting could be classified as 'indigenist abstraction', or, better yet, 'abstract indigenism'.

We must not neglect three painters from the intermediate generation who, in addition to practising their art, were also teachers. Ugarte Elespuru (b. 1911) shows the influence of Mexican muralism, at least in the vast panel he painted for the assembly hall of the old Saint Thomas School in Lima. Ugarte Elespuru wrote, furthermore, the most useful of the manuals on modern Peruvian painting. Alberto Dávila (b. 1912), although faithful to the regionalist theme, knew better than the indigenists how to construct his pictures, organizing them around geometric schemes, perhaps invisible to the uninitiated. Sabino Springuett (b. 1914) is someone in whom there is also a struggle – as in Dávila – concerning the old conflict between localism and universalism.

Within Szyszlo's generation we find other painters whose style ranges from informalism to the most minute cult of detail. Among those who painted 'tactile mists', we have, for instance, Milner Cajahuaringa, Venancio Shinki and Arturo Kubotta, who today lives in Brazil. In the opposite camp are those who use reality as a starting point – seen or imagined – and then devote themselves to transcribing it implacably. The most important figure of this group is probably Herman Braun (b. 1933), who was born in Lima and began his career as an architectural designer. In recent years he has become one of the best Latin American hyper-realists, although in his canvases some deliberate incongruity always appears, which links him almost in an obligatory way with surrealism. Braun has lived in Paris for many years. The surrealist *par excellence* is Tilsa Tsuchiya (1932–84), of Japanese lineage, but born in Lima, who also lived in Paris for a long time. Tilsa – as she is often called – was a patient and imaginative miniaturist who created her works in small dimensions, populating them with imaginary beings and illuminating them in pure, brilliant colours.

The isolated figure who embodies 'intellectualism' in Peruvian art today is the poet-painter Eduardo Eielson (b. 1923), who has lived in Rome for years. He has been creating modern *quipus* (knotted woollens used by the Indians to register dates and facts), perhaps of little interest artistically, but they are precursors of conceptual art. In a younger generation we find Gerardo Chávez, who after graduating from an art school in Lima, travelled to Europe in 1960, living first in Rome for two years and since then in Paris, where he exhibits frequently. Chávez, at the beginning of his career, was influenced by both Matta and Lam, although at present he is totally confident in his own art. He reveals himself as a 'fantastic' figurative artist of great imagination.

Modern sculpture in Peru really begins with Joaquín Roca Rey (b. 1923), who was born in Lima and trained at the National School of Fine Arts, but perhaps received his real education beside the great Spanish sculptor Victorio Macho, who worked in Lima and left many sculptures there. Roca Rey has tried everything in sculpture: sometimes figurative work with a declamatory emphasis (for example, his *Monument to Garcilaso,* in Rome);

sometimes experimenting with complicated abstractions in iron, as he did in the 1950s and 1960s. However, his role as a teacher is important, not least for having helped to train the most distinguished contemporary Peruvian sculptor today, Alberto Guzmán, and another outstanding artist, Armando Valera Neyra.

Alberto Guzmán (b. 1927) was born in Talara and studied in Roca Rey's classes in Lima. Later, in 1960, he won a scholarship to go to France, where he has remained ever since. Guzmán is the first Peruvian who seems to have really embraced modern art, not treating it superficially. Another well-known sculptor from Peru is Fabián Sánchez (b. 1935), who was born in Ayacucho, studied in Lima and went to live in Paris in 1965. Sánchez is a very curious artist, in the sense that he neither carves nor models. Using old sewing machines, he makes them look like large 'insects' that move by means of a perfect and silent technique, which makes them even more alarming. The surrealist reference is clear, and in part it has validated his current reputation.

## CHILE

The twentieth century in Chile begins with the figure of Pablo Burchard (1875–1964). Born in Santiago, Burchard studied successively at the German School, the National Institute and the University of Chile, graduating with a degree in architecture. Later he enrolled in the School of Fine Arts to study with Pedro Lira, one of the best Chilean artists of the previous generation. Comparing Burchard's mature style with that of his antecedents – Valenzuela Llanos, the landscape artist, or J. F. González, the brilliant *plein air* painter – we can see that Burchard is less aerial than they, since he 'constructs his paintings through colour,' colour that is thereby transformed into the dominant element of his painting.

From 1912 the School of Fine Arts was directed by the Spanish painter F. Alvarez de Sotomayor, a decided partisan of *costumbrismo*. This teacher was responsible for training excellent technicians in the use of painting materials (he initiated them in the tricks of the trade), but at the same time he held back all attempts at lyricism and that exploration of unknown paths that seems to be the supreme goal of youth. Some of these disciples belonged to the Group of 1913, in which several good painters were active: Pedro Luna (1894–1956), intimate and refined, whose canvases are characterized by their blurry contours; and his opposite, Arturo Gordon (1883–1945), who was slightly vulgar but, representing popular scenes as in *The Cockfight* or *La Cueca* (a great dance), became a great favourite. Finally, we must mention Julio Ortiz de Zárate (1885–1946), a solid constructor of still lifes, who after belonging to the Group of 1913 reappears in the Montparnasse movement (see below).

As art instruction had been deteriorating in Chile, an enterprising Minister of Public Instruction, Pablo Ramírez, decided in 1929 to close the School of Fine Arts. He sent about thirty promising young artists to Paris. Among those Chilean artists who returned (some, like Manuel Ortiz de Zárate, stayed) were the sculptors José Perotti, Tótila Albert, Laura Rodig and Julio A. Vásquez, and the painters Vargas Rozas, Camilo Mori and Julio Ortiz de Zárate. They joined to form the Montparnasse circle, led by Pablo Burchard, who only visited Europe during the last years of his life. The most famous figure from this group was Camilo Mori (1896–1976), who was born in Valparaíso, studied at the School of Fine Arts in Santiago, and later travelled extensively in Spain, Italy and France, where he lived for many years. Mori was a painter of extreme facility and elegance, with such versatile talent that perhaps this very virtue has damaged the judgement that his work deserves today. Landscapes, still lifes, figures, all were topics for Mori's avid brush; he painted in so many different styles that at times it is difficult to recognize him from one picture to another.

Of the so-called 'revolutionaries' in the decades from 1940 to 1960, the best known is Roberto Matta (b. 1911), who was born in Santiago and studied architecture, receiving his degree in 1931. Three years later he was in Paris working in the studio of the famous architect, Le Corbusier. In 1937 he joined the surrealist movement and, at the same time, began to exhibit his strange drawings and then incipient painting. Before he was thirty, Matta had all his expressive means at his disposal: his drawings show an 'automatic' freedom (as prescribed in surrealist theory); his colours flow strangely and inventively, forming vast expansions that serve as the background for a multitude of machines and 'humanoids', engaged in actions that we cannot decipher. Another architect-painter, Nemesio Antúnez (b. 1918), began to paint in the United States, where he had gone to do postgraduate work. Is Antúnez a surrealist too? We would say that what he does is, at least, 'fantastic' painting in which he deliberately presents a confusion between reality and pure imagination, to the extent that all of his paintings, instead of trying to solve enigmas, on the contrary seem to propose them. Enrique Zañartu (b. 1921) is a painter and sculptor of reliefs, although his name more often is associated with printmaking, a medium in which he is a notable practitioner. After his abstract, dark-toned graphic work, Zañartu later surprised us with an antithetical attitude: the creation of small white reliefs of extraordinary refinement. Rodolfo Opazo (b.1925) presents yet another version of the 'latent surrealism' of many of the best contemporary Chilean painters. Instead of working with that elemental magma to which Matta is accustomed, Opazo practised a kind of free association of scales and diverse objects; whether real or invented, they intrigue us through their quality of 'ectoplasm', fixed on the canvas with extraordinary lucidity. Ricardo Yrarrázaval (b.1931), born in Santiago, is a painter-ceramist who carries on both careers in parallel. At first it seemed as if ceramics would be the dominant voice, since his paintings consisted of horizontal stripes of earthy colours superimposed in strata, but later he changed completely to caricatured figures in lively, sharp colours. On a very individual track, always bordering the fantastic, we find Ernesto Barreda (b.1927), also an architect, a fact soon revealed to anyone who sees his posessive paintings. In them, he represents exclusively doors, windows and walls, dislocated in relation to each other, alarming in their very frontal presentation. This whole world appears decrepit and in ruins. Barreda, conscientiously imitating the texture of stone, the grain of wood, tries to transmit his vision using only white, black, grey and ochre.

The political situation in Chile from the early 1970s resulted in some unfortunate exiles, like for example José Balmes (b.1917) and Gracia Barrios (b.1926), two abstract artists of high quality who later turned to figurative art with an expressionist accent, and Guillermo Núñez (1930), a painter and set designer, who worked along conceptual lines. Balmes, Gracia Barrios and Núñez have all been living in Paris for several years.

Another artist integrated in the contemporary Chilean artistic scene is the Cuban Mario Carreño (b.1913). The style with which Carreño made his name was geometric, although inspired by forms from nature, a little like the case of Carlos Mérida. Beginning in 1958, when he moved to Chile, the architects immediately solicited his collaboration, which they thought would harmonize with the severity of modern buildings. Later in his complex career – perhaps in compensation for his earlier position – Carreño returned to figurative art encompassed in a kind of classical revival. Roser Bru (b.1924) was born in Barcelona, Spain, but is totally at home in her adopted country. In good Mediterranean style, one senses in this painter a kind of aplomb, a sense of proportion; the forms she uses, with their harmonious colours, produce works of great serenity.

Finally, we turn to several Chileans who live outside their country. They could not be more different from each other. Claudio Bravo (b. 1936), of Valparaíso, after studying in Chile went to Madrid in 1961, before moving to Tangier, where he continues to paint successfully. Bravo is a hyperrealist, as the style has been called in recent years, with a disconcerting visual acuity equalled only by the dexterity of his hand. However, the spectacular duplication he achieves in his painstaking oils astonishes or disquiets without moving us. This has not prevented him from enjoying fame and commanding high prices. There are at least three significant expatriates living in New York: Mario Toral, Enrique Castrocid and Juan Downey. Toral (b. 1934) is a figurative artist who lets himself be carried along by his galloping imagination, conjuring up strange indeterminate objects before our eyes which almost always refer to the female nude. He is a skilled draughtsman, and perhaps drawing is the medium which best lends itself to the representation of his personal fantasies. Castrocid (b. 1937) is by contrast deliberately iconoclastic, without knowing too well what target to aim at. In 1966 he exhibited sculptures and a series of robots which clearly attempted to announce the future. Later – by several years – he turned to some curious 'anamorphoses', distorted representations which only appear recognizable from a single point of view. Downey (b. 1940), a disciple of Nemesio Antúnez, after winning several prizes with semi-figurative painting, moved on to compose 'fake' maps and graphics, which at first sight seem scientific but in reality arise from his playful and delirious imagination.

Modern sculpture in Chile begins with the already mentioned José Perotti (1898–1956), who belonged to the Montparnasse movement. In 1920 he went to Madrid at the Chilean government's expense and his teachers there were Sorolla, Romero de Torres and the sculptor Miguel Blay. In addition he later worked in Paris with Bourdelle, and this strange combination of influences explains his eclecticism, a tendency which was also characteristic of his time. A more significant figure is Lorenzo Domínguez (1901–63). He was born in Santiago and studied medicine in Madrid, but in 1926 he abandoned this career to devote himself to sculpture under the tutelage of the Spanish sculptor Juan Cristóbal. When he returned to South America in 1931 he exerted great influence, not only through his own works, which were solid and well defined, but also through his dedication to teaching. Domínguez, who worked directly in marble and even harder stones, expressed himself through compact forms and hieratic, monumental content.

Chilean sculpture has been dominated by women. Juana Muller (1911–52), of Santiago, studied in Paris with Zadkine, although she was above all a follower of the great Brancusi. Her premature and accidental death deprived the art world in her country of a key figure. Lily Garafulic (b. 1914) was born in Antofagasta and studied in Santiago. She was a pupil of the figurative Lorenzo Domínguez, but her own art was abstract. Marta Colvin (b. 1917) was born in Chillan but educated at the Academy of Fine Arts in Santiago. In 1948, on a scholarship, she also worked with Zadkine in Paris. In 1957 she made an educational trip that took her to the highlands of Peru and Bolivia where – according to her own report – her interest in pre-Columbian sources was awakened. She later tried to evoke this character in her abstract sculpture, carved in stone or wood, without literally copying any earlier monument, although always inspired by the pre-Columbian. She lives today in Paris.

We conclude with Raul Valdivieso (b. 1931), who belongs to a generation that cannot be described in terms of the essentially false abstract-figurative dichotomy. He began by manipulating non-representational forms and today is increasingly reverting to the transposition, in sculptural terms, of an image he extracts from human, animal, or vegetable forms. His masses, compressed like seeds or shells, follow the traditional path of compact sculpture, caressed by the hand or the chisel. Valdivieso alternates the materials, textures, finishes and even the colours of the stones with which he works.

## BOLIVIA

The study of art in twentieth-century Bolivia must begin with Cecilio Guzmán de Rojas (1900–50). From a young age he exhibited his work in his own country, but then, thanks to a scholarship, he was able to continue his studies at the Academy of San Fernando in Madrid, where his teacher was Julio Romero de Torres. When he returned to his country in 1930, he was appointed director of the School of Fine Arts, and he used this position to exert his influence. Guzmán de Rojas is an indigenist in his own style, but he lacks the social concern that was the most important aspect of this movement. He concentrates solely on picturesque themes, which he stylizes in a decorative manner. It must be recognized, however, that his painting is of higher quality than that of most Peruvian painters of this school, and his colours are deep and intense. One of his contemporaries was Jorge de la Reza (1900–58), who studied at Yale and possessed, like his countryman, a great aptitude for mural decoration, which he hardly ever used. His colour range seems deliberately restricted.

Everything in the Bolivian art world changed with the revelation of its finest artist: Maria Luisa Pacheco (1919–74), originally from La Paz, who studied first in her native city and later in Madrid (in 1951–2) with Daniel Vázquez Díaz, an excellent Spanish figurative artist. From 1956 until her death she lived in New York, where she created most of her work. Since she gave considerable importance to the material she worked with, it is not unreasonable to assume that she was tempted by informalism, which was so much in vogue among South American artists of the 1950s. She did, however, resist this facile solution, partly because she aspired to achieve the 'plastic equivalent' of the rugged landscape of her own country, which must have been engraved on her retina.

Alfredo La Placa (b. 1929) is another outstanding Bolivian painter who avoided figurative art, although his pictures always evoke a kind of 'ghost' of concrete things. Today he is one of the best known artists in Bolivia. Alfredo da Silva (b. 1936) twenty years ago seemed to be a typical abstract lyricist, with emphasis on materials, as if the viewer had to re-translate the forms and colours of the painter into the terms of authentic nature. Enrique Arnal (b. 1932), like the rest of his generation, returned to figurative painting, although his style is neither distorted nor critical. His object was, until a few years ago, to conjure up an anonymous figure from the highlands, a silhouette without features profiled against a backlit scene, which is set off in many of his paintings by the simple frame of a door that leads to nowhere.

Moving to geometric and kinetic art in Bolivia, we mention here Rodolfo Ayoroa (b. 1927), who was born in Bolivia and studied in Buenos Aires. For many years he has lived and worked in the United States, but without dissociating himself from his native country. Ayoroa is a precision creator of silent optical machines that cast a genuine spell on the viewer; recently he has also been painting canvases on a small scale in which he displays great geometric imagination and an exultant gamut of colour.

The only relevant figure in modern Bolivian sculpture is Marina Núñez del Prado (b. 1910), who was born in La Paz, where she began her studies and soon became well known. During her career she passed from a fairly literal naturalism to a comprehension of form that cannot be interpreted as merely abstract, since in her work everything departs from the seen object, which she reduces to forces and tensions in an always elegant resolution. She works in *quayacan* wood and in the hardest Andean stones. She has lived in Quito for many years.

The seeds of modern art were planted in Paraguay by Ofelia Echagüe Vera (b. 1904), a painter who studied in Asunción until the government gave her a scholarship to work in Montevideo with the Uruguayan D. Bazzurro and later in Buenos Aires with A. Guido and E. Centurion. Apart from her work itself, Echagüe Vera is interesting because she also devoted herself to teaching. Her disciples include Pedro di Lascio, Aldo del Pino and especially Olga Blinder. These artists form the traditional nexus from which the vanguard would afterwords become established. Olga Blinder (b. 1921), originally from Asunción, began her studies at the Paraguay Atheneum. Later she worked with Livio Abramo, a Brazilian artist who has lived in Paraguay since 1956, with whom she further developed the technique of woodcut prints, a medium in which she excelled. Important as a well-rounded artist (she is also a painter) Olga Blinder is thus one of the fundamental promoters of change who was active in Paraguayan art circles in the 1950s. Of course, she was not alone. Josefina Pla (b. 1909), who was born in the Canary Islands, was active alongside her. Pla is the widow of an important Paraguayan ceramist and painter who signed his name Julian de la Herreria. Herself a ceramist and critic, she took part in the arduous struggle to connect Paraguay with the rest of Latin America and the world. At this time – 1950 – the Center for Plastic Artists was created to oppose the traditionalists. However, when one of the members of this group went to the second Biennial in São Paulo, Brazil in 1953, the dynamic Pla founded the New Art Group, which included Olga Blinder, Lili del Monico and the sculptor José Laterza Parodi.

The best contemporary Paraguayan artists include Carlos Colombino and Enrique Careaga. Colombino (b. 1937) was born in Concepción and is a painter-architect of great merit. At the beginning of his career he invented what he called 'xylopaintings' (wood panels carved and painted). Later, he also experimented with some large screens in the form of hands or figures of cutout profiles. Thereafter, still pursuing his xylopaintings, his images were not abstract but figurative – 'faceless portraits', as he calls them. Careaga (b. 1944) was born in Asunción and is, by contrast, a pure geometric artist. He studied in Paraguay and later went to live in Paris for a few years, where he discovered the world of Vasarely: that is to say, a *trompe l'oeil* art of hard edges and bright colours.

Modern Paraguayan sculpture is represented by two figures: José Laterza Parodi and Hermann Guggiari. Laterza Parodi began his career as a ceramics disciple of Josefina Pla. His initial sculptures were figurative and 'Americanist', although later they were derived from a not entirely gratuitous abstraction, since they are always related to the character of the wood from which they are carved. When he expresses himself as a ceramist, however, he resorts to another repertory – such as the human body – of highly stylized forms. Guggiari, although he took some lessons from the sculptor Pollarolo, can be called a truly self-taught artist. In 1943 he received a scholarship to go to Buenos Aires, where he associated with good teachers and fellow students. Three years later, he returned to his own country as a trained sculptor with mastery of all his expressive techniques. Of these the most important aspect is his skill in working metal until he produces certain lacerations which, although figurative, clearly signify the explosion of a frank violence and are not merely a pretext for decorative formalism.

ARGENTINA

Argentine art – like that of Mexico and Brazil – is more complex than the art of the rest of the continent, and there was important activity there at the end of the nineteenth and the beginning of the twentieth centuries. Perhaps we should begin with Miguel Carlos Victorica (1884–1955). Born in Buenos Aires he was so precocious that his family hired a private teacher for him until he was old enough to enroll in the Estimulo Association for Fine Arts, a private school where he studied with some of the most brilliant painters of the preceding generation: De la Carcova, Sivori, Della Valle and Giudici. Victorica went to Europe in 1911 and stayed there for seven years, which were crucial to his career. In modern Argentine painting, Victorica embodies expression through colour, since the weak structure of his paintings is organized – and saved – in exclusively chromatic terms. The forms take shape against neutral backgrounds by means of large isolated spots of iridescent colour which together form an extremely aerial and tactile kind of 'archipelago'.

The opposite pole – in terms of personality and artistic attitude – is represented by another great Argentine painter: Emilio Pettoruti (1892–

1971). Born in what was then the new city of La Plata (located fifty kilometres from Buenos Aires), Pettoruti was awarded a scholarship by the provincial government in 1913 to study in Italy, the country where his parents were born. Just as the First World War was about to begin, he left for Europe, to stay in Florence for several years; he also travelled all over Italy in order to study the Renaissance masterworks from which he learned his own impressive craft. The content of his paintings, however, arises from various sources. As the youngest of the futurists, he adopted from them the *parti-pris* of simplification, although to their dynamism he preferred a well-tempered staticism like that of synthetic cubism. Finally, there is also in his pictures a kind of magic that brings them close to Italian metaphysical painting. Pettoruti returned to Argentina in 1924 and it was there that he would realize his best work. By the time he moved to Paris for the last twenty years of his life, his career was already essentially completed.

Argentine painting tended to be cosmopolitan, especially after 1920. That is, in contrast to what was happening in other cultural centres, the Argentines had difficulty in finding an easy identity to assume, as had been the case, for example, with indigenism in the Andean countries. The vanguard was restricted, thus, to pursuing the European currents which, after a certain lag, reached the Argentine schools. The most impatient artists finished their own education in the Old World, in one of the great Italian cities of art or, better still, in Paris, studying for the most part not in the official but in private schools.

Among the best of those who went to Paris were Hector Basaldúa (1895–1978) and Horacio Butler (1897–1983), who caught the delightful fever of the Paris school. Basaldúa expressed it in pictures and theatre set designs, and Butler painted in grey and olive-green tones using short brush-strokes in pursuit of Cezanne. Only Raquel Forner (1902–87) liberated herself from this elegant contagion. Unlike the others, once she had learned her trade well, as they all had, she produced a much more fantastic and dramatic kind of painting, especially in her portrayal of the Spanish Civil War on bold monumental canvases. Another Paris-educated Argentine who did not follow the tacit assignments of the 'school' was the provincial Ramón Gómez Cornet (1898–1964), who reduced the violence of Mexican indigenism – the Andean version was so artificial it hardly mattered – to a note of melancholy village life. His characters are Indians or Mestizos, but since the reassertion of their proud heritage is absent or merely implied, they seem to consider themselves simply second-class citizens.

Argentina differs from the rest of Latin America in the sense that it has a generation of modern artists who might be said to fall into the category of what the French call *petits-maîtres,* offering an irreplaceable kind of 'chamber-painting'. These include Eugenio Daneri (1881–1970), an earthy painter of humble scenes of Buenos Aires and its neighbourhoods and Miguel Diomede (1902–74), who painted still lifes 'in a whisper'. More assertive were another pair of painters: Spilimbergo and Berni. Lino E. Spilimbergo (1896–1964) was a great draughtsman and painter in the Italian style – that is, a classical painter – who bathed his figures in intense, bright colours. His pictures showed, at first, exaggerated 'fugitive' views, which he gradually abandoned in favour of anonymous portraits in which one can see solemn, monumental figures with large, staring eyes. Antonio Berni (1905–81) began painting surrealistic pictures, which eventually made political and social statements. The colours Berni used at the time were intense and crude, and the drawing showed an expressive, hard line. (Much later, another 'reincarnation' awaited him, when he was able to take advantage of the 'pop' experience to create large collages of popular celebration that had their moment of glory.)

In Argentina, unlike Chile, there is no stable tradition of surrealism. Nevertheless, one strange, indefinable personage is intriguing: Alejando Xul Solar (1888–1963), a sort of follower of Klee but with esoteric facets, who is the exception that proves the rule, and perhaps because of this his work has gained favour today in critical opinion. Official surrealism, however, did not appear in Argentina until the arrival of the Spanish artist Juan Batlle Planas (1911–65), creator of grey deserts across which prophets stride carrying shepherd's crooks, and veiled women are draped in soft colours of blue and lavender.

Between 1930 and the end of the Second World War Argentina saw a healthy reaffirmation of local values, exemplified by figures like the Uruguayan Figari and the Argentine Victorica, who showed in their work that one could be 'national' without painting in a folkloric style, and that 'intimate-ism' is more natural to the Argentine character than the effects of sentimental pathos. On the other hand, the youngest and most restless artists were inspired – almost without knowing it – by the constructivism of another Uruguayan, the great Torres-García (without feeling themselves obliged to follow his tiresome symbolism), and also by that formal exactness and perfection that was always an essential feature of Pettoruti's work. We refer here to 'concrete' art, a hard abstraction which was undoubtedly inspired by everything that was *not* French in European art. Tomás

Maldonado (b. 1922), who would later have a brilliant career as a theoretician and designer in Europe, and Alfredo Hlito (b. 1923), the most important painter of the movement, were the heroes of this new path which, in 1945, baptized itself 'Agrupación Arte Concreto-Invención.' However, under the impulse of the founders – Carmelo Arden Quin (b. 1913) and Gyula Kósice (b. 1924) – another revolutionary movement was to emerge: Madí, which postulated total freedom and allowed every kind of creation, without distinguishing between painting and sculpture. Colleagues in the first group were: José Antonio Fernández Muro (b. 1920), Sarah Grilo (b. 1920), Miguel Ocampo (b. 1922) and, later on, Clorindo Testa (b. 1923), better known as an architect. All of them had brilliant careers, and their work is in general less rigorous and more sensitive than what they had proposed in their youth.

Other artists born a few years later went to Paris in 1958 in search, above all, for the sponsorship of the Hungarian-Parisian Victor Vasarely. The principal figure among these *émigrés* is Julio Le Parc (b. 1928), who won one of the grand prizes in the Venice Biennial of 1966. Also worthy of mention are Francisco Sobrino (b. 1932), Hugo Demarco (b. 1932) and Horacio García Rossi (b. 1929). They were the great inventors and practitioners of kineticism, an art based on the effects of optics and movement, whether the real movement of the object or the virtual movement of the spectator. Independent, but still in the same framework, are three other Argentines in Paris: Luis Tomasello (b. 1915), creator of what he calls 'chromoplastic atmospheres', and those two inspired optical machine 'engineers', Marta Boto (b. 1925) and Gregorio Vardánega (b. 1923).

The sixties was the great period of the Instituto Di Tella, whose art section was directed by the well known and controversial critic, Jorge Romero Brest. It was the heyday of everything rash and the triumph of extreme youth, from which some elements of value, especially in the field of theatre, would emerge. In 1961 under the name Otra Figuración four new painters began to exhibit their work: Rómulo Maccić (b. 1931), Ernesto Deira (1928–86), Luis Felipe Noé (b. 1933) and Jorge de la Vega (1930–71). The painting of these outsiders consisted of a kind of figurative expressionism. They represented a genuinely 'angry generation' of Argentine artists.

What happened to the other movements that were never entirely extinguished? Lyrical abstract art ended up as 'informalism', as exemplified by several notable black and grey canvases by Clorindo Testa, although in most cases it became mixed with a kind of non-figurative surrealism, if one can use such an expression. Strict surrealists had already appeared between 1930 and 1940 in the group called Orion, which included, among others, Orlando Pierri (b.1913), Leopoldo Presas (b.1915), and Ideal Sánchez (b.1916), although the last two later abandoned the style. The best-known Argentine orthodox surrealist is Roberto Aizenberg (b.1928), who exquisitely interprets his rich interior world of desolate landscapes and mysterious architecture.

In conclusion, we must not omit the other independents, who include several of the best artists, some of whom stayed home in Argentina, and some of whom sought their fortune elsewhere, but especially in Paris and New York. Among the former is Rogelio Polesello (b.1939), a painter of canvases and a 'constructor' in transparent acrylics, who applies to all his works such geometric rigour and sensitive colour treatment that they become all exceedingly appealing. Of those who left home, the most outstanding Argentine in New York would seem to be Marcelo Bonevardi (b.1929), also halfway between painting and abstract sculpture, as he creates panels of wood covered with painted canvas, panels that are true architectonic 'constructions' and have niches and objects incorporated into them. Antonio Segui (b.1934), born in Córdoba, is the best known Argentine living in Paris. He is a combination of painter-engraver-draughtsman who, through the use of black humour, pokes fun at the stereotypes of his native country, defects and transgressions that stand out more sharply because of the distance created by the fact that he has lived and worked in Paris for the last twenty years.

If Argentine sculpture was perhaps less conventional than its painting in the first thirty years of this century, this is due to the presence of an exceptional artist – Rogelio Yrurtia (1879–1950). This sculptor was sent to Europe at an early age on a scholarship awarded by his own government. His case was unusual at the time, because instead of going to Florence or Rome, he went directly to Paris, where he breathed in the inspiring genius of Rodin. Both in Paris and on his return to Buenos Aires, Yrurtia contributed to the creation of some of the most impressive monuments in the Argentine capital: *Dorrego* (1907, erected in 1926), the *Hymn to Work* (1922), and the *Mausoleum of Rivadavia* (1932), in which, although the oppressive architecture is of questionable merit, the splendid figures of Action and Justice certainly are not. Pedro Zonza Briano

(1886–1941), a man of very humble origins, began his studies in Buenos Aires, but in 1908 he won the Rome Prize, which allowed him to go to Italy for the first time, although later he would establish residence in Paris. The nature of Zonza Briano's sculpture is different from that of Yrurtia: the younger man is frankly more in Rodin's orbit, as is very noticeable in the melting of one mass into another producing pictorial chiaroscuro effects.

There are too many good Argentine sculptors to permit us to speak at length about all of them. The only alternative is to group them according to style, putting those who model by pure sensibility on one side and those we will call the architectonic sculptors on the other. Among the first we have Alberto Lagos (1893–1960) and, above all, Luis Falcini (1889–1970), an admirable romantic. Among the second, we must mention with praise Troiano Troiani (1885–1963), grandiose in the best way, a little in the Italian manner, and on the highest level, José Fioravanti (1896–1982), more solemn than Troiani and more successful with his public works, several important monuments in Buenos Aires. Alfredo Bigatti (1898–1960) is more declamatory, but his figures perhaps gain in dynamism what Fioravanti's lose because of their static nature. Bigatti, who worked in 1923 in Bourdelle's studio, learned from the French sculptor a care for the treatment of form that we also find – even more exaggerated – in Pablo Curatella Manes, another of Bourdelle's Argentine disciples. Curatella Manes (1891–1962) was the first Argentine sculptor to pursue a notable double career as both figurative and abstract artist, having been a member of the Cubist movement since 1920. Although he simplified his figures into large straight or curved planes, when he approached abstraction his exceptional talents as a plastic artist asserted themselves still more.

Two other notable Argentine sculptors were trained in Paris, where they lived until their deaths. Sesostris Vitullo (1899–1953), who had studied in Buenos Aires, appeared in Paris in 1925 to join Bourdelle's studio. As in the other cases we have noted, Vitullo failed to catch the 'heroic' style of the master. He did learn from him, however, how to schematize form using a semi-abstract, semi-figurative approach, which he translated by carving directly on stone and wood. Alicia Penalba (1913–82) is an interesting case because of the about-face she executed during her career. At the advanced School of Fine Arts in Buenos Aires she had studied drawing and painting, but as soon as she reached Paris in 1948 she signed up for a course in printmaking at the Academy. Only later did she discover her

her true vocation, which was sculpture. She spent three years in Zadkine's studio, becoming his most brilliant disciple of that period. Penalba always practised that form of abstraction which we have already characterized as 'biomorphic'. Her works contain a reminder of the vegetal world which she interpreted on different scales, in different metals and finishes, from the monumental to the tiny jewel.

Among the best known sculptors who remained predominately in Argentina is Líbero Badii (b. 1916). After studying in Buenos Aires he travelled to Europe following the Second World War, where he consolidated his style, which is always figurative in the last analysis, although it also exhibits a stylization that is one of his characteristics. Enio Iommi (b. 1926) is a self-taught artist who grew up in a family of Italian sculptors. Before he reached his twentieth birthday he was already a concrete artist, following the movement we alluded to earlier in our discussion of painting. In this period Iommi was only interested in working with hard materials — like stone and stainless steel — to build geometric forms that expressed a 'gesture' almost without occupying a place in space. Much later, after 1977, he became interested in other problems, whose resolution involved the association of the most heterogeneous materials in the construction of 'ironic monuments', a tradition that appears in Latin America mainly among Colombians and Argentines.

## URUGUAY

Like the incomparable Juan Manuel Blanes (1830–1901) in the nineteenth century an Uruguayan painter Joaquín Torres-García (1874–1949) brought fame not only to his country but to the whole continent in the twentieth century. It is difficult to summarize such a full life. The son of a Catalan family, he moved with his parents to Catalonia at the age of seventeen. Educated from youth at the Barcelona Academy, the young Uruguayan seems to have appropriated, during his career, the whole history of art for his personal use. Thus, beginning with a 'classical' period within the Mediterranean tradition, he spent some time in Italy and then passed two difficult years in New York (1919–21), where perhaps his response to the skyscrapers, with their vertical and horizontal masses, provided the seeds of his future constructivism. He returned to Paris in 1922, where he joined other artists who shared his tendency. There he painted 1,500 pictures in which he put his theories into practice. Finally, returning to Montevideo in 1934, he founded the Torres-García Workshop where he had some brilliant disciples, among them his own sons Augusto and Horacio. What is the nature of a Torres-García painting? It depends on the period examined. First, he moves from normal figurative art to a synthesis of flat mass and colour, without any chiaroscuro or volume. Later, at the culmination of the style, the painting is reduced to the division of its surface, according to the 'golden section', and the presentation of virtual 'logos' that represent the sun, man, a clock, and so forth. All is painted in white, black and grey, with an extreme severity that is never unintentional.

Although Pedro Figari (1861–1938) was born before Torres-García, he did not become a full-time painter until 1920, when he was nearly sixty years old. Figari studied drawing and painting as a child, but later concentrated on his career as a lawyer, which he practised all his life alongside his distinguished role as a politician. In 1921 he left all his duties in these fields and moved, first to Buenos Aires and later, in 1925, to Paris, where he painted for nine years. He is the antithesis of Torres-García. For Figari, what matters is a fleeting impression of the whole that also implies movement, translated into brilliant spots of colour. His South American themes portray city and countryside as they might have appeared in the nineteenth century. This featuring of local themes was important because it inspired other South Americans to try to recapture their own history without succumbing to facile folkloricism.

Another excellent painter who, like Torres-García, lived for relatively short periods in his own country, was Rafael Barradas (1890–1929), who left Uruguay at the age of twenty-two and returned later only to die young. Barradas settled in Spain, where he pursued his entire career. Spain thus claims him as its own artist. His painting consists of an interpretation of everyday life in terms of simplified lines and masses which are presented in a deliberately greyish, neutral colour scheme. Other painters like José Cúneo (1887–1970), on the other hand, in spite of making numerous trips to Europe, felt closely linked to their own country. It is revealing that his series have titles like 'Ranches', 'Moons', or 'Uruguayan Watercolours', and are treated in the expressionist manner – dark, dense, thickly painted interpretations of the tellurian South America. Later on, when he had switched to informalism, he signed his canvases Perinetti, which was his mother's maiden name. Unlike Torres-García, this excellent painter apparently left no artistic heirs.

José P. Costigliolo (b.1902) boasted of being an outsider, as was Cúneo in his way, *vis-à-vis* the tacit dictatorship of the Torres-García Workshop. Costigliolo began to paint abstractly in 1929, although until 1946 he had to earn a living working in advertising. His figurative painting is reminiscent of the work of the Guatemalan Mérida – the solutions are not infinite – but, on the other hand, his pure abstractions are completely original and quite unique in the Río de la Plata region.

Julio Alpuy (b. 1919) seems to us – with the exception of the sculptor Gonzalo Fonseca – the most original of Torres-García's disciples. Without abandoning the master's method, he never renounced figurative art, which he projected onto his canvases or his carved, polychrome wooden reliefs. We must also mention Washington Barcala (b. 1920), who joined the Torres-García Workshop in 1942, where he learned an austere discipline, but one that never lacked grace and sensitivity. In his later work Barcala did geometric painting of counterposed solid-colour planes with smooth surfaces, to which he added relief elements that enrich the texture of the whole.

To end this list – from which, naturally, many names are missing – we should mention two contemporary artists who are very different from each other. Nelson Ramos (b. 1932) studied two different painters, the Uruguayan Vicente Martin, a figurative painter, and the Brazilian Iberé Camargo, a semi-abstract one. His most characteristic works are panels on which he builds up in a neutral pigment, with an occasional isolated element of bright colour, as if he were working in relief. He is not only looking for the 'material nature' of the work, but also trying to find a relation between verticals and horizontals, between surface and depth. The lesson of Torres-García has still not been completely forgotten in Uruguay. José Gamarra (b. 1934) studied in Montevideo and Rio de Janeiro, thanks to a scholarship. He has lived in Paris for more than twenty years, where he launched a brilliant career creating a sort of 'pictograph', like the symbols in cave paintings, in which he alludes to America before the 'Discovery'. Now, for several years he has adopted the apparent stance of a *naif* wise man, whereby he denounces the political situation in most of the countries of Latin America. This style of admirably painted 'comic strip' allows him to recreate a continent that seems more like something dreamed of than something real.

Modern Uruguayan sculpture begins with several very talented artists who cannot, however, be called avant-garde. For example, José I. Belloni (1882–1965), the son of Swiss parents, who studied in Lugano, Switzerland and spent many years after in Europe, is a 'popular' sculptor in the best sense of the word. His best known work, *La Carreta*

(The Wagon) (1929), conferred a degree of fame on him that is difficult to match in the Río de la Plata. José Luis Zorrilla de San Martín (1891–1965), the son of the celebrated national poet Juan Zorrilla de San Martín, studied in Montevideo and won scholarships in 1914 to Florence and in 1922 to Paris, where he stayed for many years. A naturalist like Belloni, Zorrilla's style exhibits other characteristics. He is almost always grandiosely declamatory, but he nevertheless masters all the resources of his own theatricality. He created several heroic monuments both for his own country and for Argentina. His most serene work is without doubt the marble tomb of Monsignor Mariano Soler in the Cathedral of Montevideo.

Turning to the contemporary scene, we should first mention Germán Cabrera (b. 1903), who was born in Las Piedras and began his studies with the Argentine Luis Falcini in Montevideo. He spent many years in Venezuela and later, in 1946, abandoned his figurative style to devote himself to welding metals in accordance with the informalist canon of the 1950s. Later, he made large roughcut wooden boxes, which contain in their centre a kind of explosion of abstract forms made of metal. Leopoldo Novoa (b. 1919) was born in Montevideo, but spent his adolescent years in Spain, returning to Uruguay in 1938. Self-taught, he was indirectly influenced by Torres-García. Since 1961 he has lived and worked in Paris where, after a period of gigantism exemplified by the mural of the Cerro Stadium in Montevideo, he has turned to more sensitive creations on a normal scale.

One of the best contemporary Latin American sculptors is the Gonzalo Fonseca (1922), who was born in Montevideo and who at the age of twenty had become one of Torres-García's first disciples. Later Fonseca, who worked as an archaeologist in the Middle East, tended towards solid sculpture. His works, which are usually on a small scale, are carved directly in stone. Rather than merely abstract, they tend to be architectonic, since they are reminiscent of tombs excavated on the slopes of mountains, processional staircases, sacrificial terraces – that is, any kind of monumental form with a solemn, severe appearance. We conclude with Enrique Broglia (b. 1942), who was born in Montevideo, and had the good fortune to be able to study with the great Spanish abstract sculptor, Pablo Serrano. Broglia spent his early years in Madrid, later set up a studio in Paris, and finally settled in Palma de Mallorca. In his solid sculpture, his creations often play with the surprising effects of torn metal. In his later work, Broglia contrasts exterior surfaces of dark, opaque bronze with interior ones that are polished, bright and capable of reflecting the world around them.

Three isolated events set the stage for the advent of modern art in Brazil. The first was an exhibition by the Lithuanian painter Lasar Segall (1891–1957) in São Paulo in 1913; the second a show of works by Anita Malfatti in 1917; and finally, in 1920, the 'discovery' by a group of artists and intellectuals of the work of the sculptor Victor Brecheret. Then came the famous Semana de Arte Moderna, also in São Paulo, in February 1922. An avant-garde group of intellectuals, sponsored by wealthy and influential patrons of the arts, organized a festival at the Municipal Theatre that lasted for three nights, with poetry readings, music recitals, lectures and visual arts exhibitions. The group, made up of musicians, poets, writers, architects and plastic artists, was trying to achieve something whose goal was, in the words of Mário de Andrade, 'to fight for the permanent right to pursue the aesthetic quest, the actualization of Brazilian artistic intelligence, and the establishment of a national creative consciousness'.

Among those present who were to have important careers were two women, Anita Malfatti and Tarsila do Amaral. Anita Malfatti (1896–1964), who studied in Germany with Lovis Corinth and at the Art Students' League in New York, brought back a strident violence from her travels, unknown in Brazil until then. Unlike the more contained and sadder violence of Lasar Segall, Malfatti's projected itself through a heightened sense of colour that the painter would later lose forever. Tarsila do Amaral (1890–1973) only began to practise art at the age of thirty. In 1922 she went to Paris to study in the studios of Leger, Lhote and Gleizes, and she continued to experiment when she returned to São Paulo for a few months in time to attend the Week of Modern Art festival. Tarsila's first paintings collided with the taste of the aesthetes. They contained microcephalic figures with enormous feet and hands. It was really the first stage of the future movement of Anthropophagia, which Oswald de Andrade – Tarsila's husband – would develop later in the form of a Brazilian cultural theory. However, this 'ideological' period – which pleased her critical compatriots – lasted, in fact, only a short time. The artist turned afterwards to a highly constructed geometrical figuration in pastel tones. Another version of this 'Brazilianism' – carried to extremes – can be found in the work of Emiliano Di Cavalcanti (1897–1976). He was born in Rio de Janeiro but had his first exhibit in São Paulo in 1917. Di Cavalcanti is, above all, a painter of women, especially mulattas, and the night life of Rio de Janeiro, where he spent his whole life. In a way he seems to be a precursor of Cândido Portinari, who never had Di Cavalcanti's charm, although on the other hand, he surpassed him in depth of meaning.

Cândido Portinari (1903–62) was born in Brodosqui, in the state of São Paulo, and was the second of twelve children. His parents, Italian immigrants, were humble farm workers. As a child he was sent to Rio de Janeiro where he completed his elementary education and then enrolled in the Escola de Bellas Artes. He soon won a scholarship, which enabled him to spend two years in Paris, from where he made frequent trips to Spain and Italy, to be inspired by the great fresco painters of the Renaissance. His work was rewarded when in 1935 he won a prize from the Carnegie Institute in Pittsburgh. Suddenly his own country now 'discovered' him and showered him with commissions, many of which he carried out in collaboration with the architect Oscar Niemeyer. An example of this partnership is the chapel of Saint Francis in Pampulha, on the outskirts of Belo Horizonte. Portinari's passion was the monumental form, to which he then applied subdued colours which were nothing like the loud hues that might have been expected from a tropical painter. In spite of having been a man of leftist political attachments, Portinari also painted many Christian religious themes, and not only with respect, but with love.

Here it is necessary to compare the relative weight of the cultural movements in Rio de Janeiro and in São Paulo, cities which are traditionally rivals. In the thirties, a group of artists from São Paulo founded the Familia Artistica Paulista, which held exhibitions in the country's two major cities. Around the same time the Salon Paulista de Bellas Artes began, followed by the salon of the Artists' Union and the May salons (1937–9). These were really an anticipation of the São Paulo Bienal, which began in 1951. In Rio de Janeiro, exhibitions began to be held on a more and more regular schedule, partly thanks to the efforts of the Association of Brazilian Artists. These shows took place at the Palace Hotel and were held from 1929 to 1938. The decade of the 1940s – with the resistance to the dictatorship of Getúlio Vargas and the euphoria over the end of the Second World War – reflects a liberation that can be seen in a certain trend of expressionism. Other names began to appear in both the major centres, like Volpi and Bonadei in São Paulo; and Guignard, Cícero

Dias and Pancetti in Rio de Janeiro. At the same time in the state of Rio Grande do Sul Vasco Prado, Danubio and Scliar are worthy of note, and in the Northeast, Rego Monteiro and Brennand.

Alfredo Volpi (1896–1988) was a figurative painter who began by painting female nudes but soon turned to the theme that made him popular: houses, flags, banners, anything that could be subjected to a geometric plan in bright, straightforward colours. Aldo Bonadei (1906–74) studied in Florence and exhibited characteristics of the Italian school of the 1930s. Using nature as a starting point, he abstracted it in harmonious, pale colours, although his figures always had a Mediterranean solidity.

Alberto de Veiga Guignard (1896–1962) studied in Florence and Munich but, reacting against tradition when he returned to Rio de Janeiro in 1929, decided to 'become' a *naif,* and painted several beautiful works that are pleasing precisely because of their anti-cultural aspect. Cícero Dias (b. 1907) was born in Recife and worked in Rio de Janeiro after 1925. In his pictures, or more precisely in his watercolours, he reveals himself as a naive surrealist, and perhaps this is why he is important in the anemic Brazilian art scene of the period. After returning from a stay in Paris, Dias became interested in abstract art and in 1948 he executed a non-figurative mural in Recife that may have been the first one in the country.

Guignard, the 'cultivated *naif*', and Dias, the 'spontaneous *naif*', bring us to José Pancetti (1902–58), whose attitude was naive although his painting was not. A sailor whose wandering life oscillated between Italy and Brazil, he painted like a self-taught artist, sometimes giving away his paintings to his shipmates, until in 1932 he began to study art, and soon became one of the best landscape painters in the country. Carlos Scliar (b. 1920) recorded scenes of the riograndense countryside in his linoleum prints. At the same time he pursued a praiseworthy pictorial career which consists of a kind of post-Cubism in warm but muffled colours. Vicente do Rego Monteiro (1899–1970) was a painter who divided his life between Brazil and Paris. His formal characteristic was to reduce the human figure to geometric forms, endowing it with a strong impression of actual relief; he generally used ochres and browns.

Until the 1940s Brazilian artistic activity was restricted. There were hardly any galleries and artists often had to earn a living with a second job, in the best of cases by teaching. Furthermore, art criticism remained almost exclusively in the hands of journalists, literati and poets, although professionals now began to appear on the scene. These include Brazilians like Lourival Gomes Machado and Mario Pedrosa, and foreigners like Jorge Romero Brest, the Argentine specialist who was invited to give a series of lectures in São Paulo in 1948.

Although the essayist Mário de Andrade had been insisting for ten years on the need to create museums in Brazil, only in 1947 did the wealthy newspaper proprietor Assis Chateaubriand found the Museu de Arte de São Paulo (MASP). In 1948 the São Paulo industrialist Francisco Matarazzo Sobrinho created the Museum of Modern Art (today called the Museum of Contemporary Art). In 1951 Matarazzo also founded the São Paulo Bienal, the most important show of its kind in Latin America which has been held every two years ever since. 1948 also saw the foundation of the Museu de Arte Moderna (MAM) in Rio de Janeiro, although the present building by Affonso Reidy belongs to the 1950s.

Perhaps unjustly, we must omit from our discussion certain fine artists of this period, including some, Heitor dos Prazeres (1898–1966) and the well-known Djanira da Motta e Silva (1914–79), who are categorized by Brazilian critics as 'primitives', and who seem to us, in general, overvalued. Some local painters, like Antonio Bandeira and Cícero Dias, still went to live in Paris. In exchange, some foreigners decided to live in Brazil; for example, Samson Flexor, who did geometric abstract art, Almir Mavignier, Ivan Serpa and Abraham Palatnik. New Brazilian talents, who were able to establish a 'bridge' between figurative and abstract art included Milton Dacosta, Maria Leontina and Rubem Valentin.

In 1956 the São Paulo Museum of Contemporary Art organized its first exhibition of concrete art, bringing together, as in 1922, poets and plastic artists. After the second exhibition, two groups began to take shape. One, formed around Waldemar Cordeiro, Geraldo de Barros and Luis Sacilotto, aspired to 'pure form' with no symbolism at all. The other, with Lygia Clark (1920–88) and Hélio Oiticica (1937–80), sought a more organic vision. As their differences grew, the movement baptized 'neo-concrete' emerged in 1959 at an inaugural show in Rio de Janeiro, only to dissolve two years later. This was the moment when figurative art infiltrated, in the new form of North American-influenced pop art.

We now turn to the 'traditional' abstract or semi-abstract artists, such as the painter-draughtsman Iberé Camargo (1914–94). He draws his native countryside with affection, and in contrast also builds up dark paint on paintings which are – for him – figurative, but with extreme distortion. Another first class artist is Tomie Ohtake (b. 1913), of Japanese origin, who composes impeccable canvases which are divided into 'free' geometric zones that she covers with strange colours and that harmonize very well with each other. To continue with the Japanese Brazilians we may mention Manabû Mabe (b. 1924), whose colour work is astonishing, although his paintings gradually became less and less structured. A step further towards informalism is represented by Flávio Shiró (b. 1928), who lives in Paris and paints in greys or dull colours that take shape in thick, opaque applications of paint. Different from all these artists is Arcángelo Ianelli (b. 1922), who belongs to the hard edge school of abstraction. His style consists of the superimposition of translucent planes in only two or three colours, which nevertheless suggest the impression of depth.

In the early sixties art became politicized. There were groups of students who arrived at aesthetic questions only by starting with social reality. This process was, however, interrupted by the overthrow of democracy by the military in 1964. Now, with political art prohibited as subversive, a return to figurative art occurred, including manifestations such as 'happenings'. This did not prevent the period from 1967–72 from being in terms of art one of the most active the country had seen. Here is a list of the major manifestations: the Opinião exhibition (1965 and 1966), at the Museum of Modern Art in Rio de Janeiro; Brazilian Vanguard (1966), in Belo Horizonte; the Brazilian New Objectivity Show (1967), also at the Museum of Modern Art, which included artists like Vergara, Gerchman, Magalhães, Leirner and Nitsche. It was a figurative exhibition, but it was not organized in the traditional manner but with a critical eye, analysing the trend towards technology and utilization. It included the *object*, the *environment*, and even the spectator as *creator* of the work on display. At the same time it stressed the step from the 'object' to the 'idea', which the critic Roberto Pontual calls 'the leap from the retina to the mind'. That is to say, we find ourselves face to face with what is called conceptual art.

This does not mean that painting – as painting – had disappeared from Brazil. Here are two examples that demonstrate the contrary. Antonio Henrique Amaral (b. 1935) is a São Paulo native who began as a printmaker and became one of the best painters in the country. Using a hyperrealist approach in the North American style, he nevertheless managed to imbue his paintings with explosive political content. At the beginning, Amaral discovered the theme of bananas: pierced, sliced, in bunches, he represents them in enormous, detailed images. Of course these paintings demand to be read differently from what they seem to represent. Later this painter found other 'tropicalist' motifs which, however, he did not carry off as well. João Cámara Filho (b. 1944), of Recife, became the figurative *engagé* favourite of Brazilian criticism. His painting, more than simply aggressive, is truculent, with long series of paintings on political or sexual themes. They aim to do more than break a taboo, which is surprising in such a liberated country. The explicit message is overstated. On the other hand, not everyone appreciates the intrinsic pictorial quality of these works, which come dangerously close to pamphlet art.

At the beginning of this section we mentioned the sculptor Victor Brecheret (1894–1955) as a precursor of modern art. A native of São Paulo, he studied first in his own city, then from 1913 to 1916 in Rome, and the next three years in Paris where he fell under the combined influence of Rodin, Bourdelle and Mestrovic. He even adopted certain art deco mannerisms, which he later transformed into monumental sculpture. In 1920 he exhibited the maquette of his *Monument to the Bandeirantes,* but he did not begin work on the colossal sculpture until 1936; it was finally unveiled in São Paulo in 1953. Brecheret was a sculptor of compact, stylized figures with unmistakable round, glossy volumes. He was one of those rare artists who was equally at home on a small scale as on the monumental, and who moved with natural ease from bronze to smooth or rough-textured stone.

One of the pioneers in the field of women's sculpture, which has recently become so important in all of Latin America, was María Martins (1903–73). After starting out as a painter, she turned to sculpture and studied in Paris and then, during the Second World War, with Lipchitz in New York where she moved from surrealism to the strictest abstraction. She has important works in Brasília, both in the Alvorada Palace and the Ministry of Foreign Relations. The hero of Brasília, however, is Bruno Giorgi (1908–92), who was born in the state of São Paulo but lived in Italy, his parents' homeland, for many years. He began his studies in Paris with Maillol, whose influence is evident in his solid forms with vague details in stone. At other times, however, he worked with a linear silhouette which is very legible from a distance, as in the case of *Os Guerreiros,* which has become a kind of logo for Brasília. Franz J. Weissmann (b.1914) was born in Vienna, Austria, but moved to Rio de Janeiro at the age of ten, where he later studied sculpture with the Polish artist Zamoyski. In 1946 he moved to Belo Horizonte, where, together with the painter Guignard, he founded the first modern art school in that city. Weissmann is an intransigent purist in contemporary Brazilian sculpture.

His work is abstract, geometric and metallic, and these qualities are expressed through solemn structures on a large scale.

With Lygia Clark we completely depart from the framework of traditional sculpture, and find ourselves on the edge of certain experiments which at first could be assimilated into a sculptural approach, but later became pure 'actions' in which the artist encouraged the participation of the spectator through movement. A diametrically opposite approach – not intellectual but almost ecological – is found in the work of Franz Krajcberg (b. 1921), who was born in Poland and came to Brazil in 1948. After going through an abstract phase, in the sixties he began to use elements taken directly from nature in his work, such as stones, leaves and roots. He presented these either without modification or painted overall in opaque colours. Yet another view is the one of Ione Saldanha (b. 1921), who began as a figurative painter and then was overtaken by abstraction. In her most recent work she creates spatial sets in which she presents forests of bamboo shoots coloured horizontally in bright, lively hues. An outsider in his manner is Mario Cravo Júnior (b. 1923), from the state of Bahia. He is a draughtsman, printmaker, sculptor and man of action. He was one of the founders of the first modern art show in Salvador in 1944. In his sculptural work he uses every kind of material, including very modern ones like polyester. He built a large geometric fountain in the port area of the city of Salvador.

Certain 'marginal' artists whose production can be assimilated – with good will – into the category of sculpture include Wesley Duke Lee (b. 1931), who in 1967 began to show large constructions which he calls 'spatial ambientations', and his friend Nelson Leirner (b. 1932), who is interested in activating the participation of the spectator. Leirner works with objects from real life, linked together in an arbitrary manner with the use of new techniques such as neon light. There are other artists who are just as avant-garde as these, except that they do not seek to provoke, nor are they committed to the latest fashions in art. Abraham Palatnik (b. 1928) was born in Rio Grande do Norte and emigrated with his family to Israel, where he was educated. When he returned in 1948 he became the pioneer of kinetic art in Brazil, and was one of the first artists in the country to perceive the importance of technology as applied to the aesthetic experience. Sérgio de Camargo (1930–90), on the other hand, was purely a sculptor. He was born in Rio de Janeiro but studied in Buenos Aires with Pettoruti and Lucio Fontana. He lived in Paris until 1974, and then returned permanently to Rio. Camargo is a sculptor of truncated solids, which he 'accumulates' or presents in the form of totem poles or 'vibrating walls' all in one colour. At first he worked with white-painted wood, but then he used marble from Carrara which is undoubtedly a higher quality material. Camargo is considered one of the most important artists of his kind on the continent. Finally, Yutaka Toyota (b. 1931) deserves mention. He was born in Japan and went to school there. After travelling through Europe he returned to São Paulo (which he had previously visited only briefly) in 1962. He is an abstract sculptor who uses shiny metal, to which he adds the effects of colour. Many of his voluminous public works are endowed with movement, which makes them even more fascinating.

## CONCLUSION

After a rather dull period from around the 1870s to the First World War, where we find some academic artists following the European ecclecticism of the time, at the beginning of the 1920s a kind of artistic 'explosion' took place throughout Latin America. It was one of the most fertile, inventive and innovative moments in the development of its plastic arts. Latin American artists, like North American, and for that matter Australian or Japanese, were fascinated by the European vanguard of the early twentieth century. The fact of their having been inspired by or having imitated the advanced western models and norms, in their transition from a more or less dead academic art, not only does not constitute an original sin, but was a most spontaneous and healthy response. Without anyone planning it in advance, around this time things began to change and become revitalized, in Mexico thanks to muralism, in Brazil with the Semana de Arte Moderna, and in the Southern Cone with the widespread success of the so called 'School of Paris'. Twenty-five years later, immediately after the Second World War the foreign model was what for convenience – without naming its subspecies – we call the 'New York School'. The best Latin American art of this century, however, is independent and distinct from its presumed models: only the mediocre and second-rate artists have naively or intentionally imitated what came to them from outside.

Here are some concrete examples. The three best known Mexican mural painters alone revived the mural, an art form that had fallen into disuse; their contemporaries, – with exceptions like Puvis de Chavannes – had been praticising the genre in a routine and lifeless manner. Each of those Mexican artists approached the mural in his own way. Rivera 're-read' the Italian *Quattrocento* and infused it with modern political content. Orozco worked on a monumental scale and relied on gray, black and touches of yellow and red to evoke apocalyptic flames and banners. Siqueiros introduced new sorts of pigments, exaggerated foreshortening and perspective. This had never been done before, and Europe and the United States at the time paid more than benign attention to this Mexican painting. The works of these three painters are still preserved on the walls of several important North American institutions.

When Torres-García, who was educated in Barcelona, Paris and New York, returned to Montevideo to found his Workshop, he was not influenced by Mondrian, as has falsely been said. Colleagues in the *Cercle et Carré* movement (which the Uruguayan had begun with the Belgian Michel Seuphor), Torres-García and Mondrian are, strictly speaking, two painters who are independent from one another. It is easy to see that constructivism, in the case of the Dutch artist, was carried to its theoretical extremes: white striped with black and the frugal use of primary colours. Torres-García, on the other hand, of Mediterranean origins, practised his art through that inherent quivering hand – 'with feeling', as they say in the art studios – investing his works with a strange symbolism. Nothing like that had ever been seen in the world.

Was Matta, the Chilean who was discovered by the 'official' surrealists, merely one more surrealist? Hardly. His formula, invented by him alone – and not pursued intellectually – is a fantastic visceral image vision, a premonitory biological-cosmic science fiction. And it is certainly not the case that he imitated the Armenian-North-American Arshile Gorky; rather the reverse is true, and this can be corroborated by comparing their respective chronologies.

And what can be said of the Argentine kinetic artists: Le Parc, Demarco, García Rossi, Tomasello and their Venezuelan counterparts: Soto, Cruz-Diez and Otero? They all went to Paris in the fifties and declared themselves followers of the Hungarian Vasarely (who came from the Bauhaus) and the North American Calder. All those stubborn South Americans produced innovations which for years were not appreciated in the very city where they wanted to be recognized, until the Germans, Italians and English began to imitate them. Then there are the North Americans themselves, who, when they talk about 'op art', only mean a brief cultural fad in New York – until it was snuffed out by advertising and design – a visual expedient which in reality they had copied from the art produced for years by the Latin American kinetic group in Paris.

Besides the great figures of the 1920s and 1930s we can perhaps find ten to twenty careers in Latin American painting and sculpture in the second half of the twentieth century, sharing originality and substance and making a distinctive contribution to the art of the world. The time has come to discover them, just as the best Latin American literary figures were discovered twenty to thirty years ago by a surprised and delighted international public.

# 9

---

## LATIN AMERICAN CINEMA

### INTRODUCTION: THE SILENT ERA

With the advent of the centenary of cinema, each country has a story to tell about the arrival of moving pictures in the last decade of the nineteenth century. On 6 August 1896, in Mexico, C. F. Bon Bernard and Gabriel Veyre, agents of the Lumière brothers, showed the President of Mexico, General Porfirio Díaz and his family the new moving images. Three weeks later they gave public screenings. And they began to film the sights of Mexico, in particular those in power in the land: Díaz on his horse in Chapultepec Park, Díaz with his family, scenes from the Military College. At the end of the year Veyre left Mexico and arrived in Cuba on 15 January 1897. He set up in Havana, at 126 Prado Street, and a few days later the local press announced screenings in the Parque Central alongside the Tacón theatre. Particular favourites were the 'Arrival of the Train', 'The Puerta del Sol Square in Madrid' and 'The Arrival of the Czar in Paris'. Veyre went down to the fire-station in Havana to film the activities there. He took along with him María Tubau, a Spanish actress who was the star of the theatre season. It is said that she wanted to see the fireman at work. What is more likely is her early fascination with a medium, still in its infancy – the shots of the firemen last one minute – which would incorporate theatre and its forms into a new language. It would not be long before the public would prefer actresses like María Tubau on screen to endless shots of their ruling families in public or at leisure, or of worthy demonstrations of civic duties, for the cinema released dreams of modernity, opening up new horizons of desire.

In 1896 moving images had also arrived in Argentina and Brazil. The first establishment in Rio de Janeiro to projet the new medium on a regular basis was the aptly named Salão de Novidades set up by two

455

Italian immigrants, the Segreto brothers, in 1897. They soon changed the name of their hall to Paris no Rio, in deference to the pioneering work of the Lumières and as an assertion that the cultural modernity of the European metropolitan centers had found a home in the South.

Cinema took root in the developing cities of Latin America during the next twenty years. 'Along the way', wrote Clayton Sedgwick Cooper in Rio de Janeiro in 1917, 'sandwiched in between business, art, press, politics, are the omnipresent and irrepressible moving picture theatres, which here in Rio de Janeiro, as in every South American city and town from the top of the Andes to Patagonian Punta Arenas, give evidence by their number and popularity of the picture age in which we live . . . The people of the country . . . are getting expert with the moving picture camera, and more and more purely national subjects, having to do with the plainsmen's life or description or romances set in the interior of the big Republic, are finding their popular following.'[1] Speed, motorized transport (trams and trains), artificial light, electricity cables, radio aerials were signs of the changing perceptions of modernity and the growth of a culture industry in which cinema would become central. But it was also a 'peripheral modernity', in Beatriz Sarlo's apt phrase, in societies of uneven development.[2] In the case of cinema, progress required advanced technologies which increasingly only the metropolitan centres could provide.[3]

Cinemas, rudimentary or sophisticated, mushroomed in the urban centres and from these centres, the itinerant film-maker/projectionists could follow the tracks of the railways which, in the interests of the export economies, linked the urban metropolis to the interior, projecting in cafés and village halls or setting up their own tents (*carpas*). As early as 1902, there were some 300 cinemas in Mexico. A heterogeneous public learned to dream modern dreams. 'In the cinema', Carlos Monsiváis has written, 'they learned some of the keys to modern life. The modernization presented in films was superficial but what was seen helped the audiences to understand the change that affected them: the destruction or abandonment of agricultural life, the decline of customs once considered eternal, the oppressions that come with industrialisation . . . Each melodrama was an encounter with identity, each comedy the proof that we do not live

---

[1] Clayton Sedgwick Cooper, *The Brazilians and their Country* (New York, 1917).
[2] Beatriz Sarlo, *Una modernidad periférica: Buenos Aires, 1920 y 1930* (Buenos Aires, 1988).
[3] On 'peripheral' modernity in Brazil, see Roberto Schwarz, 'The cart, the tram and the modernist poet', in *Misplaced Ideas: Essays on Brazilian Culture* (London, 1992), p. 112.

our lives in vain.'[4] It was an audience whose horizons of desire were already being expanded by mass circulation popular literature, the sentimental serial novels, and new magazines in the style of the Argentine *Caras y Caretas,* which began publishing at the end of the nineteenth century, together with the radio and the record industry which made great advances in the 1920s.[5]

The values and themes embedded in the early filmic melodramas, as in the serial novels, hark back to 'pre-modern' moments, to the values and stabilities of the neighborhood, the *barrio,* as opposed to the dangers of the new. Critics have argued that the Mexican sentimental naturalist novel *Santa,* published by Federico Gamboa in 1903, contains many of the keys of later Mexican melodramas: the eternal values of the provinces (the book opens in the idyllic village of Chimalistac) as opposed to the vice of the cities (the heroine ends up in a brothel in the centre of the city). The provinces are populated by hard-working, respectful, honourable families, organized by beatific mothers, in the setting of harmonious nature. The city is the site of immorality, sensuality, disease and death. A women is pure and good as a virgin, but can become perverted when seduced.[6] The first of many versions of *Santa* was filmed by Luis G. Peredo in 1918. The lyrics of tango, in the 1910s and 1920s in Argentina, work with similar simple oppositions: a protagonist is often stranded in the world of modernity ('Anclado en Paris' – anchored in Paris), dreaming and singing nostalgically of his mother, friends, the lovers' nest (*bulín*), the *barrio.* In contrast, an *ingenu(e),* is propelled into the world of modernity, prostitutes have hearts of gold, the *barrio* offers the site for homespun wisdom. The trauma of the new is both desire and threat. If Peter Brook is correct to argue that melodrama is 'a fictional system for making sense of experience as a semantic field of force [that] . . . comes into being in a world where the traditional imperatives of truth and ethics have been violently thrown into question',[7] then it can be seen as a way of structuring the values of a post-revolutionary Mexico, or of the inhabitants of São Paulo or Buenos Aires caught in the maelstrom of the new.

Melodrama was also the dominant mode of the French and particularly

---

[4] Carlos Monsiváis, 'Mexican cinema: of myths and demystification', in John King, Ana M. López and Manuel Alvarado (eds.), *Mediating Two Worlds: Cinematic Encounters in the Americas* (London, 1993), p. 143.

[5] Beatriz Sarlo, *Jorge Luis Borges: A Writer on the Edge* (London, 1993), ch. 1.

[6] Gustavo García, 'Le mélodrame: la mécanique de la passion', in P.A. Paranagua (ed.), *Le Cinéma Mexican* (Paris, 1992), p. 177.

[7] Peter Brook, *The Melodramatic Imagination* (New Haven, Conn., 1976), pp. 14–15.

Italian films that dominated the world market up to the 1910s, and millions of first and second generation Italian immigrants throughout Latin America as well as *criollos,* could enjoy the stylized gestures of the great divas, Francesca Bertini, Pina Menichelli, Hesperia and Maria Jacobini. Yet it would be to the Hollywood star system that audiences in Latin America would be drawn once the U.S. film industry resolved the disputes of the Patents War and began to invade the world market from the mid-1910s, initially with the successful superproductions of D. W. Griffith. Lillian Gish and Mae Marsh worked with Griffith and soon they and a number of other emblematic idols could be found in photojournals throughout Latin America: Theda Bara, John Barrymore, Rudolph Valentino, Mary Pickford, Gloria Swanson and in particular Greta Garbo and Marlene Dietrich. All over Latin America, dozens of such journals appeared: *Cinearte* in Brazil, *Hogar y Cine, Cinema Chat* and *Héroes del Cine* in Argentina, *La Gaceta Teatral y Cinematográfica* in Cuba. All disseminated modern dreams, marketing the desire for the new. And the emblems of the new were the stars of Hollywood. From about 1915, the pre-eminence of Hollywood cinema was established. By December 1916 the trade newspaper the *Moving Picture World* could remark, 'The Yankee invasion of the Latin American film-market shows unmistakable signs of growing serious. It may before long develop into a rush as to a New Eldorado.'[8] North American films could achieve such dominance because in general they were amortized in the home market (which contained about half of the world's movie theatres) and could thus be rented cheaply abroad. U.S. distributors, taking advantage of the semi-paralysis of European production in the First World War, gained control of foreign markets almost without competition and successfully combated renewed opposition after the war.[9] The modern dreams of Hollywood were more complex and more entertaining than rudimentary national cinemas as Jorge Luis Borges noted. He talks of going to the cinema in Lavalle Street which, even today, contains the highest proportion of cinemas in Buenos Aires. 'To enter a cinema in Lavalle Street and find myself (not without surprise), in the Gulf of Bengal or Wabash Avenue seems preferable to entering the same cinema and finding myself (not without surprise) in Lavalle Street.' Why support the national product, thought Borges, if it was badly made: 'To idolise a ridiculous scarecrow because it is autochthonous, to fall asleep

[8] Quoted in Kristin Thompson, *Exporting Entertainment* (London, 1985), p. 79.
[9] Thomas H. Guback, 'Hollywood's international market' in T. Balio (ed.), *The American Film Industry,* revised ed. (Wisconsin and London, 1985), p. 465.

for the fatherland, to take pleasure in tedium because it is a national product – all seem absurd to me.'[10]

If Hollywood provided the images of modernity and the technological sophistication of the new medium, Latin America, in particular Mexico, could offer the United States a series of exotic images of bandits, 'greasers', noble savages and beautiful señoritas. It is not the purpose of this chapter to explore U.S. or European images of Latin America, to chart the shifting positions of Hollywood as cultural ethnographer, creating rather than reflecting images of 'otherness'. This analysis can be found elsewhere.[11] It is interesting to note, however, that Mexico, in both U.S. documentaries and in fictional films (especially the Western), appears as both desire and threat. It has been well remarked that 'Mexico is the Western's id. South of the border is to the body politic of the Western what below the belt is in popular physiology – a place where dark desires run riot, a land not just of wine, women and song, but of rape, treachery and death.'[12] U.S. newsreel cameramen followed closely the vicissitudes of the Mexican Revolution. For a time, before he had the audacity to lead a raid across the border, Pancho Villa was the 'star' of the Revolution, a presence which beguiled journalists and film-makers from John Reed to Raoul Walsh. Villa even signed a film contract with Mutual Film Corporation and, in return for $25,000, gave them exclusive rights to film 'his' war. Publicity material on billboards and hoardings throughout the United States boasted Mutual's new signing: 'Mexican War, Made by Exclusive Contract with General Villa of the REBEL Army. First reels just in and being rushed to our branch offices. These are the first moving pictures ever made at the front under special contract with the commanding general of the fighting forces.'[13] Carlos Fuentes, the Mexican novelist, imagines Pancho Villa's relationship with his cameraman, Raoul Walsh. 'He promised Walsh, the gringo with the camera "Don't worry Don Raúl. If you say the light at four in the morning is not right for your little machine, well, no problem. The executions will take place at six. But no later. Afterward we march and fight. Understand?" '[14]

The overwhelming majority of films made in Latin America in the silent

[10] Jorge Luis Borges, quoted in E. Cozarinsky (ed.), *Borges y el cine* (Buenos Aires, 1974), p. 54 (both quotations).
[11] See George Hadley-García, *Hispanic Hollywood: The Latins in Motion Pictures* (New York, 1990).
[12] Ed Buscombe, 'The Magnificent Seven'; in John King et al. (eds.), *Mediating Two Worlds*, p. 16.
[13] Quoted in Margarita de Orellana, *La mirada circular: el cine norteamericano de la revolución mexicana* (Mexico, D.F., 1991), p. 74.
[14] Carlos Fuentes, *The Old Gringo* (New York, 1985), pp. 170–71

era were documentaries. As Jean-Claude Bernadet, the Brazil critic, has argued from his exhaustive style of the press in São Paulo, documentary film-makers could carve out a niche that international competitors were not concerned with: regional topics, football competitions, civic ceremonies, military parades. These documentaries reflected society's self-image, especially that of the aristocracy: its fashions, its power, its ease and comfort in modern cities and in a spectacular rural landscape. The scenes of virgin landscape could be incorporated into the discourse of modernity, by showing the raw strength of these young developing nations.[15]

Fictional films, from the few remaining examples that are still available for viewing – the film heritage of Latin America from this period has been largely lost through neglect, indifference, lack of money and resources, or catastrophic fires or floods in archives – reveal a melange of styles: an imitation of Hollywood, a strong influence of theatre melodrama and the presence of acts and artists from the vaudeville shows, burlesque reviews and circuses which were the main components of popular culture in the 1910s and 1920s. One temporarily successful attempt to harness the popularity of music to the silent screen in Brazil was the 'singing films', where duos or even whole companies sang behind the cinema screen, attempting a rudimentary synchronization. In Argentina, the film-maker José 'El Negro' Ferreyra drew explicitly on the world of the *barrio* conjured up in the lyrics of tango. He could sometimes count on Argentine band leaders such as Roberto Firpo to give his films live backing. Remarkably, the first animated feature film in the world was produced in Argentina – *El Apóstol* (The Apostle, 1917), animated by Quirino Cristiani and produced by Federico Valle. Most films, however, did not reveal such technical virtuosity.

Ferreyra, the most prolific director in Argentina, was an auto-didact, as were most of the pioneers of the medium throughout the region. All sought to work in the interstices of the dominant Hollywood model and found a certain support in local audiences who were not yet so used to the sophisticated language and techniques of Hollywood that they would turn their back on more rudimentary national products. Different countries could point to at least one director who could consolidate a body of work: Enrique Díaz Quesada and Ramón Peon in Cuba, Enrique Rosas, Miguel Contreras Torres and Mimi Derba in Mexico, or Humberto Mauro in

[15] Jean-Claude Bernadet, 'Le documentaire', in P.A. Paranagua (ed.), *Le Cinéma Brésilien* (Paris,

Brazil. A brief focus on Mauro reveals the limits of the possible for film-makers in Latin America.

Born in Minas Gerais, Humberto Mauro (1897–1983) was brought up in the region of Cataguases. His early work shows the artisanal dynamism of a pioneer. He began by dabbling in the new technologies, working with electricity, building loudspeakers for radios, learning the techniques of photography from the Italian immigrant Pedro Comello.[16] Mauro and Comello together studied the techniques for making movies. In 1925, Mauro set up Phebo Films and made a film *Na primavera da vida* (In the Spring of Life) using family and friends as actors: his brother is the hero who rescues Eva Nil (Comello's daughter) from a band of bootleggers. This film brought Mauro to the attention of the Rio-based critic and cultural maecenas Adhemar Gonzaga who founded the film journal *Cinearte* in the mid-1920s and later his own production company Cinédia. Mauro's next feature, *Thesouro perdido* (Lost Treasure 1926), which starred himself together with his brother and his wife Lola Lys, won the *Cinearte* prize for the best film of the year. After this success, Rio producers tried to attract him to the city. Come here, they argued, 'cinema is the art of the tarmac.'[17]

Mauro stood wavering between these two influences – urban Brazil and the *sertão* (the backlands) – a tension that structures his following film *Braza dormida* (Burned Out Embers 1928). A landowner from Minas lives in Rio, but returns to his country estate with a new overseer. The overseer falls in love with the landowner's daughter and she is sent to Rio to avoid his amorous advances. The film comments on Cataguases and Rio as opposite poles of desire. Rio would eventually draw Mauro in, when he was invited by Adhemar Gonzaga to film the stylish *Lábios sem beijos* (Lips Without Kisses, 1930). His last feature in Cataguases was only financially viable thanks to the investment of the actress Carmen Santos, who also starred in the movie *Sangue mineiro* (Minas Blood, 1930) which once again places sophisticated characters in a love triangle set in the interior of Minas. By this time Mauro, accompanied in his last two films by the inventive cinematographer Edgar Brasil, was recognized as the most accomplished director of the day in Brazil, a reputation enhanced by his stylish talkie *Ganga bruta* (1933).

There was little avant-garde exploration of the medium itself in the

---

[16] On the fascination of new technologies in the 1920s, see Beatriz Sarlo, *La imaginación técnica* (Buenos Aires, 1992).
[17] Bernadet, 'Le documentaire', p. 231.

1920s. If certain theorists of modernism, such as Walter Benjamin, talked of the inherently radical and experimental nature of cinema, these arguments found few echoes among the practitioners. Nor did the modernists in Latin America itself spend much time discussing cinema – the favoured forms were poetry, the novel and in particular the plastic arts. When the visionary Minister of Education in post-Revolutionary Mexico, José Vasconcelos, sought to define a cultural project for Mexico and looked for emblems of post-revolutionary optimism, he turned to the plastic artists and not to film-makers. Vasconcelos was bitterly opposed to cinema: he saw it as the work of the devil of the North, the United States, and, furthermore, there were no great cineastes, on a par with Orozco, Siqueiros or Rivera.[18] Genuinely radical, avant-garde, movies were a rarity. One notable example, *Limite* (The Boundary, 1929), was filmed in Brazil by the precocious Mario Peixoto who at, the age of eighteen, revealed a vision and a technical mastery uncommon in Latin America at the time. In 1988, almost sixty years after it was made, a panel of critics voted *Limite* the best Brazilian film of all time.

The state of Latin American cinema at the advent of the talkies was thus parlous. Directors worked within a medium and a marketplace dominated by Hollywood, though some had the raw energy to draw on strong national traditions of popular culture – melodrama, theatrical spectacle, or vaudeville and tent shows – to make movies which could attract a local audience. In Billy Wilder's classic analysis of an ageing silent movie star, *Sunset Boulevard* (1950), the 'heroine' Norma Desmond (Gloria Swanson) looks with delight at one of her famous silent roles and remarks to her 'captive' young scriptwriter: 'We had faces then!'[19] What would happen when these faces would be required to speak? No one in Latin America quite knew. A columnist in the Mexican paper *Ilustrado* remarked on 3 October 1929 that the installation of the vitaphone would raise entrance prices and would flood the market with English speaking films, comprehensible only to the minority: 'the vitapahone is the most modern calamity. Syncronized films are capable of harming the ears through their never-ending, dreadful sound-tracks . . . And it is not just a question of music, for these films will impose the English language on us. And frankly, the only people who have the right to impose a language on ourselves are

[18] See Gabriel Ramírez, *Crónica del cine mudo mexicano* (Mexico, D.F., 1989), pp. 203–4.
[19] I am grateful to Carlos Monsiváis for reminding me of this scene. See Monsiváis's beautifully illustrated *Rostros del cine mexicano* (Mexico, D.F., 1993).

Mexicans. Or not?'[20] In Brazil, on the other hand, Adhemar Gonzaga greeted the arrival of sound with optimism: these developments, he felt, would deal a death-blow to foreign films, drowned out by the songs and vernacular of contemporary Brazil. He ought surely to have been right; but he was wrong.

### THE 1930S: THE COMING OF SOUND

The availability of synchronized sound in the late 1920s created a new, complex, situation in Latin America. Many shared the optimism of Adhemar Gonzaga: if the image could be understood everywhere, surely language and music were particular to specific cultures? Yet the expense and complexity of the new systems were too much for poorer countries; they would wait for many years to have access to these technologies. At the beginning, in Europe, only the Elstree Studios in Britain and U.F.A. in Berlin had the equipment in place, and Italian, French and Spanish producers and directors flocked to their doors. The universal language of cinema now gave way to the Tower of Babel and the confusion of tongues. How would this affect the dominance of Hollywood in the world?

The conversion to sound coincided with the 1929 Depression, which slowed down, albeit briefly, new technological options. Dubbing films, for example, was impossible in the first years since there was no means of mixing sound. Hollywood was thus in some confusion. The first, rather desperate attempts to preserve their market share abroad was to make foreign-language versions of Hollywood films. N. D. Golden, the head of the Film Division at the U.S. Department of Commerce stated the policy: 'Hollywood must make films spoken in five languages – English, Spanish, French, German and Italian – if it wants to keep for its films its great foreign markets.'[21] Hundreds of actors and aspirant script-writers from Spain and Latin America – Carlos Gardel, Xavier Cugat, Lupita Tovar, Mona Maris, Juan de Landa, Imperio Argentina, Tito Guizar were among the most distinguished – flocked to Hollywood and to other studios that opened in New York, London and Paris, to take part in 'Hollywood Spanish-Language Films'. In 1930, Paramount set up a huge studio at Joinville, in the outskirts of Paris, which could initially make films in five languages. By working a twenty-four hour schedule, it at one stage

---

[20] Quoted in Angel Miguel Rendón, *Los exaltados* (Guadalajara, 1992), p. 212.
[21] Quoted in Juan B. Heinink and Robert G. Dickson, *Cita en Hollywood* (Bilbao, 1990), p. 22.

reached a delirious twelve languages. This experiment lasted until the mid-1930s, with peak production in 1930 and 1931. Historians have made a recent inventory of these films and show that sixty-three films were made in 1930 and forty-eight in 1931.[22] After that numbers declined. There are many reasons for the relative failure of this scheme. Films were expensive to make and did not return a profit. Local audiences wanted to see the Hollywood stars and were not happy to tolerate their Hispanic substitutes. Accent, dialect and even physiognomy varied wildly with each line-up of Latin American and Hispanic actors, something that producers could not detect – to them one Hispanic looked and sounded very much like another – but a detail that did not escape the 'Hispanic' public, who were irritated when an Argentine had a Mexican brother and a Catalan sister. By the early 1930s, dubbing and subtitling had improved and Hollywood, coming out of the Depression, regained or even increased its market share. The Motion Picture Producers and Distributors of America (MPPDA), was an effective pressure group for U.S. films, seeking to maintain an 'open door' policy in the face of possible tariff, quota or exchange restrictions.

If the substitution of actors in mainstream Hollywood productions did not work, Hollywood could boast of a few successes in the field of Hispanic language films. Paramount had the wit to sign up tango singer, Carlos Gardel who, by the late 1920s, was a superstar throughout Latin America thanks to the growth of the record industry and the spread of radio. The simple plots of his films were structured around his extraordinary voice – Gardel needed to sing at least five tangos per movie and the audience often interrupted screenings to make the projectionist rewind the film and play the songs again. The main successes were *Melodía de arrabal* (Arrabal Melody, 1932), *Cuesta abajo* (Downward Slope, 1934) and *El día que me quieras* (The Day you Love Me, 1935). One Buenos Aires cinema cabled Paramount with the enthusiastic news that: '*Cuesta abajo* huge success. Delirious public applause obliged interrupt showing three times to rerun scenes where Gardel sings. Such enthusiasm has only rarely been seen here'.[23] The songs in *Cuesta abajo* are indeed worth hearing again, especially 'Cuesta Abajo', 'Mi Buenos Aires querido' (My Beloved Buenos Aires) and 'Olvido' (Forgetting), composed and orchestrated by the Argentine band-leader and composer Alfredo Le Pera in collaboration with

[22] For a complete filmography, see Heinink and Dickson, *Cita en Hollywood*.
[23] Simon Collier, 'Carlos Gardel and the Cinema', in J. King and N. Torrents (eds.), *The Garden of Forking Paths: Argentine Cinema* (London, 1987), p. 28.

Gardel. Song, dance, melodrama: these were the ingredients of Gardel's success with Paramount and these were also the ingredients of early sound cinema in Latin America: Gardel was being groomed to become a crooner in English-language Hollywood films (a slow process since he did not have a great ear for languages, as his few words of spoken French in *Cuesta Abajo* reveal), but his career came to a tragically early end when he was killed in a plane crash in Colombia in 1935.

Local entrepreneurs in Latin America soon realized the possibilities opened by sound and, in countries with a large domestic market – that is to say, Argentina, Brazil and Mexico – investment was made in machinery and in installations. Some rudimentary studios such as the Chapultepec Studios had been built in Mexico in the silent era. This complex was bought and expanded in 1931 by Nacional Productora to make 'talkies', beginning with *Santa*. Mexico Films followed suit – eleven of the twenty-one films made in 1933 were filmed in their studios. CLASA studios were set up in 1934. In Argentina two major studios were opened – Lumitón in 1932 and Argentina Sono Films in 1937 – to exploit the commercial potential of tango-led national cinema. In Brazil, Adhemar Gonzaga established the Cinédia Studios in 1930 and the versatile Carmen Santos, a pioneer woman in a male dominant industry, founded Brasil Vita Filmes in 1933, both in Rio de Janeiro, which was to become the almost exclusive centre of Brazilian film production in the 1930s and the 1940s. Other small Latin American economies found it difficult to respond to the new conditions. It would take until 1937, for example, for Cuba to produce its first feature length sound film *La serpiente roja* (The Red Snake), directed by Ernesto Caparrós, drawn from a popular radio serial.

Most of the first actors, directors, cinematographers and technicians, especially in Mexico, had received some rudimentary training in Hollywood or in New York, in bit parts or in small jobs, and early films showed both vitality and technical proficiency. *Santa,* for example, shot in 1931, was directed by Antonio Moreno, a Spanish actor who had worked in Hollywood; the cinematographer was a Canadian Alex Phillips and the two principle actors Lupita Topar and Donald Reed had played Hispanic parts in Hollywood. By 1933, Mexico was producing films of lasting quality: among the twenty or so movies that come out in that year we find Fernando de Fuentes's *El prisionero trece* (Prisoner Number 13) and *El compadre Mendoza* (Godfather Mendoza) and Arcady Boytler's *La mujer del puerto* (The Woman of the Port). Russian emigré Boytler stylishly directed this film which, after *Santa,* firmly established the prostitute melodrama in Mexico. The heroine is betrayed by her fiancé who causes the death of her father. Bereft, she drifts into prostitution and, in a genuinely tragic ending, unwittingly sleeps with her long-lost brother. Andrea Palma — Dietrich in Vera Cruz — is a splendid Mexican vamp with her deep voice, hanging cigarette and haughty disdain. She had worked as a wardrobe assistant to Dietrich and manages to create one of the first lasting images of enigma and sadness in a rudimentary film milieu.

The films of Fernando de Fuentes of the mid-1930s establish the genre of the melodrama of the Revolution, reflecting and perhaps making sense of the huge social and cultural upheavals of the post-revolutionary period. De Fuentes early vision, like that of the novelists of the Revolution, is sombre. In *El compadre Mendoza* an opportunistic landowner is faced with the dilemma of remaining loyal to a kinsman, a general in Zapata's army, and a character clearly modelled on Zapata, and thus court economic ruin, or to betray the kinsman and save his own skin. Mendoza, under the mute, accusing gaze of his housekeeper, chooses to preserve his hacienda, but will be haunted forever by the sight of his compadre, hanged by Carranza's forces at the entrance to the estate. In the later *Vámonos con Pancho Villa* (Let's Go with Pancho Villa, 1935), Fuentes portrayal of the revolutionary forces is equally bleak as a band of friends, the Lions of San Pablo, decide to join up with the forces of Pancho Villa, but find their noble sentiments caught in a world of anarchy, stagnation and corruption. The final speech of a revolutionary in this film: 'Is this an army of men or a troop of dogs?' reverberates with tragic power.

De Fuentes captures a period and a nation in transition. 'The nation' is reflected in·the faces of the principle actors, but also in the extras, as Carlos Monsiváis explains. 'Underlying philosophy: if the revolution taught us to look at ourselves, it is now necessary to specify who we are, that's to say, how the mirror of cinema accepts, essentialises or distorts us.' Soon, through persistent repetition, the 'people' of the cinema screen become 'the people': 'It is no exaggeration to state that when a Mexican of those years wants to conjure up an image of "the people", he or she can only refer to film images.'[24] These popular images are the backdrop to the main scenes of the Revolution, but they are also the faces of the family, the neighbourhood, people 'like us'. Director Juan Orol used Sara García as everyone's mother in *Madre querida* (Beloved Mother, 1935), the story of a boy sent to a reform institution, an action which causes his mother to die

[24] See Monsiváis, *Rostros del cine mexicana*, p. 10.

of a broken heart on Mother's Day. García later starred in a string of maternal melodramas such as *No basta ser madre* (It's Not Enough to Be a Mother 1937) or *Mi madrecita* (My Little Mother, 1940) and most famously, *Cuando los hijos se van* (When the Children Leave, 1941), directed by Juan Bustillo Oro.[25]

If Fernando de Fuentes made his most complex films about the Revolution, his most successful film – and one of the most successful films of all time in Latin America – was *Allá en el Rancho Grande* (Out On the Big Ranch, 1936). The image of the singing charro, the emblem of Mexican virility, was at one level clearly a reworking of Roy Rogers and Gene Autry films, but it added a particular Mexican pastoral fantasy to the model and also drew on Mexican popular cultural forms – the *canción ranchera* from Guadalajara and the Bajío. Song from the countryside was to become an essential part of national cinema, the sentimental underpinning linking scenes together and giving greater weight to specific situations. Singing stars – in this film Tito Guízar and in later *comedias rancheras* Jorge Negrete – become popular all over the continent. So popular that the film industry changed direction and concentrated its energies on rural dramas, set in rural bars, or in the world of Mexican *fiesta,* with *charros,* beautiful señoritas in folk costumes, mariachis and folk trios.[26] These rural melodramas are structured by paternalist feudalism, with casts of honest landowners and noble workers, harking back to a time before the Revolution when God was in heaven and benevolent, firm fathers such as Porfirio Díaz were in control and everyone knew their place. Ironically these films appeared during the radical administration of Lázaro Cárdenas (1934–40) who put agrarian reform as one of his firm priorities. Cárdenas, however, did not seek to interfere with a form that was becoming an important export item throughout Latin America. The image of the singing charro was Jorge Negrete who was arrogant, *criollo* and severe, an aristocrat, conquering the world and all its women. From his earliest film *La madrina del diablo* (The Devil's Stepmother, 1937), his image changes little: it offered the rural Mexican way of being a man.[27]

The urban equivalent to singing cowboys were the night-club crooners, Agustín Lara and, later, Pedro Infante. The scene moves from the rural cantina to the night-club or brothel, the cabaret. Lara sings the songs that

---

[25] Charles Ramirez Berg has an interesting analysis of this film as a 'classically transparent text' in his *Cinema of Solitude: A Critical Study of Mexican Film, 1967–1983* (Austin, Tex., 1992), pp. 16–28.
[26] See Monsiváis, in P.A. Paranagua (ed.), *Le Cinéma Mexicain* (Paris, 1992), pp. 143–53.
[27] See Monsiváis, *Rostros del cine mexicana*, p. 12.

become the stuff of *caberetera* melodrama articulating for the first time the desires and threats of a new morality, or amorality, when tradition had been turned upside down by the Revolution and by a developing, urban-centred, modernity. In Lara's idealized night life, the forbidden seemed almost within reach, the brothel was the space of exalted passions and sensibilities (*Santa* again). Pedro Infante, as we will see later, moves from night-club crooner, to the voice of the urban dispossessed in a number of key melodramas of the late 1940s. If Mexican cinema by the end of the 1930s could be said to have a toe-hold in the domestic market – figures for the decade show that Mexican film account for 6.5 per cent of the home market (Hollywood accounting for 78.9 per cent) – it was largely as a result of musical features.

It took Mexican producers a number of years almost to stumble over a successful box-office formula. Argentine producers knew from the outset that tango would be at the heart of their endeavours. Paramount in the United States had seen the profitability of Gardel: if Argentine cinema could not now afford Gardel, it could at least use his friends, the singers, band leaders and musicians of the cabaret circuit in Buenos Aires and abroad (for tango had swept Europe and the United States in the 1910s and 1920s). As in Mexico, the six hundred or so movie houses in Argentina in the early thirties were showing almost exclusively North American films, but exhibitors would not turn down a tango film. Manuel Romero, who had worked with Gardel as a librettist, was to become one of the most successful directors of the 1930s with films such as *Mujeres que trabajan* (Working Women, 1938) and the extremely popular *Los muchachos de antes no usaban gomina* (Back Then, Boys Didn't Use Hair-Cream, 1937), which starred Mireya, the woman oblivious to the advances of rich men around town. He followed these with a series of musical melodramas which often took well-known tangos as their titles, such as *Tres Anclados en Paris* (Three People Anchored in Paris, 1938). 'El negro' Ferreyra, the pioneer of silent cinema, made a successful transition to 'talkies' with a series of evocative portrayals of the *arrabales* (outskirts) and *barrios* of Buenos Aires, such as *Calles de Buenos Aires* (Streets of Buenos Aires, 1934) and *Puente Alsina* (Alsina Bridge, 1935).

In 1936, Ferreyra teamed up with Libertad Lamarque and helped to make her a star the rival of Gardel. Lamarque's life story, like that later of Eva Perón, seemed to come out of the plot of a tango melodrama. Born of humble origins in the provinces, she moved to the city and worked her way up through cabaret and vaudeville, ekeing out a meagre existence in a world of duplicitous men and false glamour. She wrote the script of, and starred in, the 1936 film *Ayúdame a vivir* (Help Me Live) directed by Ferreyra. This film set a style for the musical in Argentina in which the song lyrics, as in operetta or its Spanish cousin, the *zarzuela*, are built into the scripts as moments of dramatic punctuation. Gardel films, by contrast, stop when the star sings a song. These plots – the naive in the world of modernity, the tart with a heart, the *barrio* as pre-modern site of stability – and the songs could be repeated with small variations. The new immigrants to the city flocked to these movies and could empathize with the heroine who was pure and moral, struggling against the odds.

In Brazil, the musical vehicle was the *chanchada*, drawn from the vaudeville sketches of Brazilian comic theatre, as well as music and dance forms revolving around carnival. One of the first, Wallace Downeys' *Coisas nossas* (Our Things, 1931), a 'Brazilian Melody', broke all box-office records in São Paulo on its release. Such films would incorporate singers already popular on the radio and in popular theatre: Paraguaçu and Noel Rosa and the orchestras of Gaó and Napoleão Tavares and Alzirinha Camargo. The amalgamation of different aspects of the developing culture industry was quite clear. Wallace Downey, for example, was a high-ranking executive in Columbia records. Cinédia Studios led the way, with successes such as Gonzaga's *Alô, Alô Brasil* (1935) and *Alô, Alô Carnaval* (1936), featuring the talented Miranda sisters. Carmen Miranda, as a singer and as a hoofer, became a major star in Brazil, with more than 300 records, five films, and nine Latin American tours, before she erupted onto the New York stage 1939 and was immediately bought up by Fox. There, 'her explicit Brazilianness (samba song-and-dance repertoire, Carnival-type costumes) was transformed into the epitome of *latinidad*.[28] Even the most stylish Brazilian director, Humberto Mauro, was drawn to *samba* in *Favela de meus amores,* (Favela of My Loves 1935), a film which broke taboos by seeing samba not in its folklorist, tourist variation, but as a product of the vibrant popular culture of the shanty towns of Rio.

An essential aspect of *chanchada* was the stand-up comedian and the resulting plethora of verbal and visual gags. Two stars that were to emerge in the 1940s out of this tradition were Grande Otelo and Oscarito. But the first, internationally successful, comic of Latin American cinema was Mari-

---

[28] Ana López, 'Are all Latins from Manhattan?', in Lester D. Friedman (ed.), *Unspeakable Images: Ethnicity and the American Cinema* (Urbana, Ill., 1991).

ano Moreno, Cantinflas. He began as a tumbler, a dancer and a comedian in the popular *carpas* (tents). With his greasy shirt, crumpled, sagging trousers and large, scuffed shoes, he epitomized the *pelado,* the scruffy, street-wise neighbourhood wide-boy (the *arrabal* occupied a similar real and symbolic space in Mexico to the one we have already mapped out in Argentina), who deflates the pomposity of legal and political rhetoric. *Cantinflismo,* acting like Cantinflas, becomes a mode of speech where, delivered at breakneck speed, words go in desperate search of meanings. In his third film *Ahí está el detalle* (That's the Crux of the Matter, 1940), in the final court scene, he so disrupts the proceedings that the judge and the officials end up using the same nonsense language. In this movie he teamed up with Joaquín Pardavé, another comedian, whose trickster persona had the distinction of a resonant voice, a top-hatted elegance and a well-turned moustache. Manuel Medel was another perfect comic foil to Cantinflas in *Aguila o sol* (Eagle or Sun, 1937) and in *El signo de la muerte* (The Sign of Death, 1939). But it is the face and the acrobatics of Cantinflas that are memorable: his extraordinary arching eyebrows, leers, and his elastic limbs which contort into impossible positions. Cantinflas's films later became repetitive and hollow, but in the late 1930s and early 1940s he was at the peak of his inventiveness. It was not merely empty political rhetoric that caused Diego Rivera to include Cantinflas in his magnificent mural in the Insurgentes Theatre as a defender of the poor. Not a defender to lead them out of misery, but a man who could alleviate that misery with a few good or terrible gags.

Argentina, Brazil and Mexico, therefore, could maintain some presence in the home market and Argentina and Mexico even became successful exporters to the rest of Latin America by the late 1930s. The initiatives were based on private capital. The state, in Mexico under Cárdenas and even under Vargas's Estado Novo in Brazil, did little to protect or to sponsor local production. But several local producers exploited the market quite successfully. Apart from a number of 'quality' films that can be found in the canon of each country, the main concern is the box office, 'where', Monsiváis has written, 'success is assured by issuing films like orders, weep, repent, enjoy the beautiful unity of the family, swear never to break the rules, depart this vale of tears with an indulgent smile, get drunk . . ., serenade the whole town, kiss the hand of the little old mother, go directly to the nearest happy ending'.[29]

[29] Monsiváis, 'Mexican cinema', in John King et al. (eds.), *Mediating Two Worlds,* p. 145.

## THE 1940S: A 'GOLDEN AGE' OF CINEMA?

### *Mexico*

In 1940, Mexico and Argentina vied for Spanish-language dominance of the Spanish American film market. By 1945, the argument was settled in favour of Mexico, with more than a little help from north of the border. The U.S. Good Neighbor Policy of the 1930s had worked to improve the negative stereotyping of Latin America and, at the outbreak of war, a government agency, the Office of the Co-ordinator of Inter American Affairs (CIAA), was set up under Nelson Rockefeller to orchestrate economic and cultural programmes in Latin America. Nelson Rockefeller, for example, sent Orson Welles as a goodwill ambassador to Brazil in the early 1940s and supported Walt Disney in his two cartoon films *Saludos Amigos* (1943) and *The Three Caballeros* (1945), where Donald Duck teams up with new friends, the parrot José Carioca, symbol of Brazil, and the pistol-clad *charro* rooster Panchito. One bird absent from the jaunts was Martin the gaucho, since Argentina incurred the wrath – and, in the case of Secretary of State Cordell Hull, the obsessive hatred – of the State department by refusing to enter the war. The United States, as part of a package of restrictions, denied Argentina access to raw film stock, while simultaneously building up the Mexican film industry. While Argentina went into a partial decline in production, Mexico entered a fleeting 'Golden Age'. The success of Mexican cinema in the 1940s was thus given a boost by U.S. policies, but it was also guaranteed by the emergence of directors and cinematographers and the consolidation of a star system. Financial support was offered, from 1942, by the Banco Cinematográfico which was based on private capital, but with guarantees from state bodies such as the Banco de México. The closed shop union structures which were later to strangle the industry were evolved in these years.

Of the genres established in the 1930s, the revolutionary melodramas of Fernando de Fuentes found a worthy successor in the work of Emilio 'el Indio' Fernández, together with his 'team', the cinematographer Gabriel Figueroa, script writer Mauricio Magdaleno and the stars Dolores de Río and Pedro Armendáriz. In films such as *Flor Silvestre* (Wild Flower, 1943) and *María Candelaria,* 1943, Figueroa's expressive cinematography captures, in allegorical fashion, the moment of Adam and Eve in the garden of Mexico, the expressive physiognomies of the main characters, which harmonize with the expressive nature of the landscape: its lowering clouds, the emblematic plants, the play of light and dark, the shadows cast by the heat of the sun. Of course there are traces of Eisenstein's influence in this imagery (Eisenstein had spent nine months in Mexico in 1931 working on a film project that eventually he could not edit), and of photographers such as Paul Strand, but it is wrong to see the work of 'El Indio' and Figueroa as merely copying, or pandering to, European and North American images of the 'noble savage'. Both were original talents. Mexico, in these films, is elemental, atavistic, the site of primal passions, a violence from which can be forged a new progressive nation.[30]

The founding family on which this nation could be forged was made up of screen idols, Dolores Del Río and Pedro Armendáriz. Del Río had been a star in Hollywood from 1925 to 1942. There she appeared in twenty-eight films as the instinctual savage who could be tamed by love and western culture, or as a more distant, exotic, beauty. Her star appeal was beginning to fade in Hollywood by the early forties and her relationship with Orson Welles was running out of steam. She was ready for a change and 'El Indio' Fernández persuaded her to play a humble peasant girl in *Flor Silvestre* who falls in love with Juan, a landowner's son, and marries him secretly against the wishes of his severe parents. When the Revolution begins, the son's father is killed and he takes vengeance on the bandits masquerading as revolutionaries. They in turn take his wife and child as hostages and Juan, to save them, delivers himself to a firing squad, where Dolores faints over his dead body. Such were the cataclysmic moments of heroism and struggle, Dolores explains many years later to her son – a conversation which frames the main narrative – out of which modern Mexico could develop and prosper. This bald plot outline suggests conventional melodrama, but 'El Indio' carries it off with great gusto, while his 'perfect' couple, Dolores del Río and Pedro Armendáriz, convey tragedy in their stoic faces in a dialogue of elegant glances. Del Río was required to radiate a quite, hieretic beauty. Her partner, Armendáriz by contrast was a mixture of passion, tenderness, rage and joy. Del Río went on to work again with 'El Indio' in *Bugambilia* in 1944, with Roberto Gavaldón en *La otra* (The Other Woman, 1946) and with Alejandro Galindo in *Doña Perfecta* (1950). These directors allowed her to escape from 'El Mexican aesthetics of 'El Indio' into other, more nuanced roles.

[30] Monsiváis, 'Gabriel Figueroa', in *Artes de México*, 2 (Winter 1988), p. 63.

The other major star in Mexico in the 1940s was María Félix. Octavio Paz has recently paid homage to her own distinct, beauty and appeal. He begins by analysing the myths of womanhood in Mexico, from the Virgin of Guadalupe and La Malinche to the revolutionary Adelita and adds: 'The myth of María Félix is different. In the first place, it is modern; secondly, it is not entirely imaginary, like all the myths of the past, but rather the projection of a real woman . . . she was, and is, defiant of many traditional conventions and prejudices . . . María Félix is very much a woman who has been bold enough not to conform to the idea of womanhood held by the machos of Mexico. Her magnetism is concentrated in her eyes, at once serene and tempestuous – one moment ice, the next fire. Ice that the sun melts into rivers, fire that becomes clarity.'[31] She came to play in a number of films whose titles reveal the on-screen persona outlined by Paz: *Doña Bárbara, Maclovia, La mujer de todos* (Everyone's Woman), *La devoradora* (The Devourer), *La generala* (The General). She had an impressive debut in *El peñon de las ánimas* (The Crag of the Spirits, 1942), playing alongside the already famous Jorge Negrete. Her third film, *Doña Bárbara* based on the famous twenties regional novel by the Venezuelan Rómulo Gallegos, gave Felix the image that would be repeated, with variations, over the next decade: the haughty, self-contained woman, the devourer of men. In marked contrast to the family melodramas of the 1940s, with Sara García as the self-abnegating mother, which rigidly upheld a patriarchal code, María Félix seemed to offer a revolt within this system. This revolt was, in the main, contained in the filmic narratives, which remain male centered. If Doña Bárbara humiliated other people around her, having been brutally raped, the film (and the book) is mainly concerned how an enlightened man Santos Luzardo, can tame and defeat this woman, rather than exploring the woman's point of view.[32]

That self-declared most macho of film directors El Indio Fernández sought finally to depict the taming of the shrew in his *Enamorada* (In Love, 1946), which paired Félix with Pedro Armendáriz. The plot, based loosely on Shakespeare, is straightforward. During the Revolution, general Reyes (Armendáriz) takes Cholula and falls in love with the beautiful Beatriz (Félix), daughter of the rich Don Carlos. She is going to marry a North American, Roberts, and treats the revolutionary badly. However, after a number of twists, Beatriz leaves Roberts on the eve of her wedding and

31 Octavio Paz, introduction to *María Félix* (Mexico, D.F., 1992), p. 13.
32 See Ana López, 'Tears and Desire', in *Iris,* 13 (Summer 1991).

follows Reyes as his *soldadera*.[33] This is the film where the style of the
cinematographer Gabriel Figueroa can be seen to excellent effect. Figueroa
himself singles it out as one of his favourite films: 'Among the scenes I
remember most enjoying as a cameraman is the end of *Enamorada*. I mention
this scene because it has everything, and particularly an extraordinary visual
emotion, as in the scene where the long shadows of the soldiers are projected
into the heroine's house, and she begins to run among the shadows. That's a
very striking scene, in which it is not technique but imagination that
counts.'[34] Figueroa and other distinguished cinematographers – Agustín
Jiménez, Jack Draper, Alex Phillips, Rosalío Solano – helped to define the
dominant images of Mexican cinema throughout the forties and early fifties.

Not all Mexican stars were involved in revolutionary melodramas or in
bucolic rural idealizations of hacienda life such as Jorge Negrete's *Ay
Jalisco, no te rajes* (Oh Jalisco Don't Give Up, 1941). The modern city
increasingly became both the backcloth but also one of the major themes
of cinema. Director Ismael Rodríguez who had made successful *ranchera*
films such as *los tres García* (The Three Garcías, 1946) turned to films
which examined the culture of poverty of *barrios* of Mexico City: *Nosotros
los pobres* (We the Poor, 1948) *Vds los ricos* (You the Rich, 1948), *La oveja
negra,* (The Black Sheep, 1949). And in Pedro Infante he found an actor to
personify the best aspects of the common man: tender, honest, handsome,
long suffering, one of the boys. His saintly *novia* was often played by
Blanca Estela Pavón and together they had a number of memorable scenes
and song duets. These films are impossible to summarize since they contain myriad characters – structured loosely around a main character, the
carpenter Pepe el Toro played by Pedro Infante, and his financial, amorous
and family problems – who appear in different sketches. Among these are
the lumpen women comedians, 'La Guayaba' and 'La Tostada' (Amelia
Wilhelmy and Delia Magaña). *Nosotros los pobres* moves at a very fast pace,
full of songs, gags, jokes and aching sentiments, and became for many
years the biggest box-office success in Mexico.

While earlier images of the city are more earnest and attempt a gritty
realism the films of Rodríguez had made no pretence to be realist. *Distinto
amanecer* (A Different Dawn, 1943), directed by Julio Bracho, set mainly
in the nightworld of Mexico City, successfully incorporates the structures
of *film noir* into a political thriller. Alejandro Galindo's *Campeón sin corona*

[33] For an analysis of the film, see Jean Franco, *Plotting Women: Gender and Representation in Mexico*
(London, 1989), pp. 148–52.
[34] Gabriel Figueroa, 'Un pueblo despojado de color', *Artes de México,* 10 (Winter 1990), p. 47.

(Champion Without a Title, 1945), examines the world of the urban poor and the attempts of a working-class boy, played by David Silva, to escape his background through his boxing talents. Interestingly, the theme of the underprivileged fighter trying to achieve advancement through his fists, became a favoured form in Hollywood narratives about Mexican Americans such as *Right Cross* (1950), *The Ring* (1952) and *Requiem for a Heavyweight* (1962). In Mexico, however, it was not boxers but rather masked wrestlers who would seize the popular imagination from the 1950s.

Awareness of the problems of Mexican Americans north of the border, but also of the fascination with border crossings help to account for the success of the comedian Germán Valdés, Tin-Tan. He plays a Mexican-American *pachuco*, the zoot-suited, upwardly mobile con man who can talk and dance his way out of any situation in a mixture of Spanglish idioms and border-music rhythms. By the late 1940s, the origins of Tin-Tan – the border towns such as Cuidad Juárez, the mass migrations (legal and illegal) across the border, the Americanization of Mexican culture – were all to become an irreversible part of the modern, urban Mexican experience. And Tin-Tan energetically expounds a frenetic, hybrid modernity in some of his best films, *El rey del barrio* (The King of the Barrio, 1949), and *El revoltoso* (The Rebel, 1951).

One of Tin-Tan's most regular co-stars was the exotic dancer Yolanda Montes, 'Tongolele'. Different rhythms were invading the nightclubs of Mexico City, from the North, but more particularly from the Caribbean and the south. Boleros were increasingly used in films to intensify particular heightened moments of melodrama, but there was also a considerable growth in more exotic rhythms, in particular the rumba, danced by the memorable María Antonieta Pons, Rosa Carmina and Amalia Aguilar, Meche Barba and, in particular, the Cuban Ninón Sevilla. Ninón Sevilla raised the heart-beat of audiences and critics throughout the world. The young critic turned director Francois Truffaut wrote in admiration in *Cahiers du Cinema* in 1954 under the pseudonym Robert Lacheney: 'From now on we must take note of Ninón Sevilla, no matter how little we may be concerned with femine gestures on the screen or elsewhere. From her inflamed look to her fiery mouth, everything is heightened in Ninón (her forehead, her lashes, her nose, her upper lip, her throat, her voice) . . . Like so many missed arrows [she is an] oblique challenge to bourgeois, Catholic and all other moralities.'[35]

[35] Quoted in Jorge Ayala Blanco, *La aventura del cine mexicana* (Mexico, D.F., 1968), pp. 144–5.

To a certain extent, the films of Ninón Sevilla, directed in the main by Alberto Gout, continued the successful formula of *caberetera* films of the 1930s and 1940s, but the conditions of the late 1940s are depicted with a vulgar dynamism which is quite new. The post-war cosmopolitanism and early developmentalism which marked the Presidency of Miguel Alemán (1946–52) find a complex reflection in these extravagantly sexual and deliberately provocative movies. *Aventurera* (Adventuress, 1949) is the most accomplished film of Gout and Sevilla. Agustín Lara, the famous balladeer and crooner of the genre, once again supplies the appropriate lyrics, sung by Pedro Vargas, which serve as a leitmotif throughout the film: 'Sell your love dearly adventuress / Put the price of grief on your past / and he who wants the honey from your mouth / must pay with diamonds for your sin / Since the infamy of your ruined destiny / Withered your admirable spring, / Make your road less harsh / Sell your love dearly, adventuress.' Sevilla indeed exacts a price: by the end of the film, many of the protagonists have met grisly ends and genteel Guadalajra society is in ruins.[36]

Despite the excesses of these movies, the woman is still the site of 'spectacular' pleasure, the object not the subject of the narrative. Men occupied positions of power in the industry. The only woman film-maker of this period was Matilde Landeta, just as the actress and director Mimi Derba in the 1920s and the actress, producer and director Adela, 'Perlita' Sequeyro in the 1930s had been exceptional women film-makers in Mexico in earlier decades. Landeta had served a long apprenticeship as a script girl on almost one hundred features (from 1933) and later as an assistant to the major directors of the period. She made three features: *Lola Casanova* (1948), *La Negra Angustias* ('Black' Angustias, 1949) and *Trotacalles* (Street Walker, 1951). These films are interesting not merely as the work of a woman previously 'hidden from history' but also because they test the possibilities of an articulate pro-feminism in a male industry and society. Landeta would have to wait until the late 1980s, however, to be joined by a significant number of Mexican women working behind the camera.

The above analyses have pointed to the main trends in Mexico's most dynamic decade of film-making. The volume of output was considerable. Whereas in 1941, Mexican cinema had only 6.2 per cent of the domestic market, by 1945 this had risen to 18.4 per cent and by 1949, to 24.2 per cent. Over the decade, the average was 15.1 per cent. In 1949, Mexico

---

[36] See Eduardo de la Vega Alfaro, *Alberto Gout (1907–1966)* (Mexico, D.F., 1988).

produced a remarkable 107 films.[37] Figures are not available for the market share of Mexico in the rest of Latin America, but the impact was considerable: the stars of Mexican cinema, Cantinflas, Jorge Negrete, Tin-Tan, Pedro Infante, Dolores Del Río, María Félix, Pedro Armendáriz and Ninón Sevilla became firm favourites throughout the continent. Mexico acted as a mini-Hollywood, making the battle for survival of national cinemas even more difficult.

### Argentina

Argentine cinema showed some of the dynamism, and indeed the quality, of Mexican cinema in the 1940s, but was forced to struggle in the early period against U.S. embargoes. This decade has received little critical attention and indeed the films of the period have only in a few cases been well preserved, so any analysis is necessarily provisional. In broad terms, however, the most successful genre of the 1930s, the musical comedy, continued until the mid-1940s, with Libertad Lamarque an ever-popular star. In 1946, however, Lamarque quarrelled with the Perons and left for Mexico where she established another successful career in films that often aped directly the well-proven Argentine formulae. In *Soledad* (Solitude) directed by Tito Davison in 1948, for example, she plays a young Argentine orphaned maid who is tricked into marriage, seduced and abandoned by a self-serving man. In Mexico, she is portrayed as both mother and entertainer and she holds her own with the greats. In 1946 Luis Buñuel paired Lamarque with Jorge Negrete in *Gran Casino* (1946), though Buñuel is not prepared to give her, or the portly Jorge Negrete, any special treatment. As Michael Wood has pointed out, 'There are . . . nice gags in this film: a love scene played straight by the principals while the camera lingers resolutely on a sickening-looking patch of oily mud; an insistence on showing Lamarque in extravagant close-ups and soft focus, so that she looks like a movie-star in a museum, a rehearsal for *Sunset Boulevard*.'[38]

As urbanization increased and Argentine cinema became more secure, more complex urban dramas took the place of the *barrio* melodramas. The most interesting of the pre-1950 period was Luis César Amadori's *Dios se lo pague* (God Bless You, 1948), which was nominated for an Oscar. The

---

[37] María Luisa Amador and Jorge Ayala Blanco, *Cartelera cinematográfica, 1940–1949* (Mexico, D.F., 1982), pp. 373–8.
[38] Michael Wood, 'Buñuel in Mexico', in *Mediating Two Worlds*, p. 42.

location is the central streets of Buenos Aires, where an extremely intelligent beggar plies his trade outside a church and outside an aristocratic club. As the narrative develops, the spectator gradually discovers that the tramp is a mysterious millionaire who takes time out on the streets to obtain a clear perspective of the hyprocrisy of life. The melodrama uses its urban locations to great effect: the main streets of Buenos Aires, where dandies and tramps rub shoulders; the *arrabal,* the Colón opera house (and an operatic conceit which requires a working knowledge of *Lohengrin,* the knight of the Grail to be fully understood); the aristocratic salons, the sight of conspicuous consumption and of the snares and delights of the modern; the town-house where the female protagonist is stifled and the Church, which resolves the tensions and blesses the new union. Other sophisticated and assured works, which mark a clear 'coming of age' include the urban comedy of manners directed by Francisco Mujíca, *Los martes, orquídeas* (Orchids on Tuesday, 1941), in which a father invents a romance for his melancholic daughter Mirtha Legrand (who suffers, like Catherine Morland, from reading an excess of romantic literature), an invention that gradually becomes a reality.

For historical-national melodramas Argentina lacked the symbols (a strong pre-Columbian past, a recent 'revolution' and a discourse of revolutionary nationalism) available to Mexico. The gaucho was only infrequently used as a symbol of a frontier society and there was little attempt to create a 'Southern' to vie with the symbolic strength and resonance of Hollywood's Westerns. Attempts at creating a national epic were made in the early 1940s by a group of writers, directors and actors who formed the group Artistas Argentinos Asociados (Associated Argentine Artists) and made two melodramas on nineteenth-century topics, *La guerra gaucha* (Gaucho War, 1942) and *Pampa bárbara* (Barbarous Pampa, 1945). *La guerra gaucha* in particular, based on the famous account by writer Leopoldo Lugones, that traces the Independence struggles of Güemes and his gaucho bands in Alto Peru in the 1810s, is full of achingly noble, Manichean, nationalist, sentiments and makes a rather rudimentary attempt to capture the grandeur of the landscape. It was a success at the box-office but came at a time when the mirror of liberal nationalism was being cracked, offering up new, unexpected and sometimes murky reflections.

In the artistic/intellectual community, most viewed the period of the first Peronist regimes (1946–55) as one of cultural obscurantism. Cinema was under the control of a Subsecretariat for Information and the Press, which acted as a form of propaganda ministry, monitoring newspapers and radio broadcasts as well as the cinema. Perón deliberately cultivated his matinée idol looks and his clear resemblance to Carlos Gardel, while Evita had come up through radio soaps and had had minor roles in the film industry as Eva Duarte. Both were, therefore, extremely conscious of the power of the image. A number of directors and actors found the regime claustrophobic and limiting and went to live abroad or else imposed strict self-censorship: Luis Saslavsky, who had directed a number of films, including the stylish comedy thriller *La fuga* (The Flight, 1937), Hugo Cristensen and the ineffable Libertad Lamarque. In these conditions, the quality of Argentine cinema fell and there was a marked decline in box-office receipts.

Perón did, however, offer the first state support for Argentine cinema. Up until his regime, producers were mainly weak and divided and at the mercy of distributors and exhibitors who had a strong investment in promoting North American films. Perón sponsored various measures to protect the Argentine film industry which included the establishment of screen quotas and distribution on a percentage basis for Argentine films, state bank loans for financing film productions, a film production subsidy programme and restrictions on the withdrawal of earnings from Argentina by foreign-controlled companies.[39] These measures were to have little effect, however, since the United States would not accept restrictions on repatriating profits, exhibitors ignored screen quotas and production money tended to be made available to safe, non-innovative, directors who could turn out formulaic, profitable B-movies. Money therefore chased, and generated, mediocrity. There are, of course, a number of clear exceptions to this state of affairs with distinguished films by Leopoldo Torres Ríos, *Pelota de trapo* (Rag Ball, 1948), his son Torre Nilsson (see below), Hugo Fregonese, in *Apenas un delincuente* (Just a Delinquent, 1950), and Hugo del Carril's evocative *Las aguas bajan turbias* (Muddied Waters, 1952) which returns to the genre of gritty realism. In the main, however, protectionism and autarchic nationalism did not generate any film renaissance.

## *Brazil*

Given the linguistic 'limitation' of Portuguese, Brazilian cinema could never hope to reach the markets available to Mexican cinema. The battle,

[39] See Ana López, 'Argentina 1955–1976', in King and Torrents (eds.), *The Garden of Forking Paths*, p. 50.

therefore, was over the home market. It had managed to consolidate a domestic public through music, dance, song and comedy and these successful ingredients continued into the 1940s. A new production company Atlântida, the brainchild of cineastes José Carlos Burle, Alinor Azevedo and Moacyr Fenelon, had initially intended to support political, realist cinema and made a first feature *Moleque Tião* (Boy Tião, 1943) based on the life of Sebastião Prato, 'Grande Otelo', who was already a well-known actor. They soon discovered, however, that socially committed films could not guarantee economic stability as the title of a later film ironically pointed out: *Tristezas não pagam dívidas* (Sadness Doesn't Pay Off Debts, 1944). Their commerical breakthrough came when they teamed Oscarito, Brazil's most brilliant comic, with Grande Otelo. This duo made a number of successful comedies throughout the forties, which attracted the attention of Luiz Severiano Ribeiro, who ran the country's major distribution and exhibition circuits. He bought Atlântida in 1947 and for the first time in Latin America, a country could boast a vertically integrated industry – one which, like Hollywood, had control over production, distribution and exhibition – however small this might be. Money could be made in *chanchadas* which featured Oscarito, Grande Otelo and other popular performers such as Zé Trinidade, Wilson Grey and Zezé Macedo. Ribeiro's buy-out occurred in the year in which the Vargas regime decreed that each movie house should show at least three Brazilian films a year. These movies were unashamedly 'popular' appealing to a large working-class audience. As such, they would be despised by middle-class critics, who aspired to a more modern, technically proficient and internationally acceptable cinema. The wish to provide an alternative to 'low brow' *chanchadas* would be one of the reasons for the development of the Vera Cruz Company in November 1949.

Production rose from ten features in 1946 to twenty in 1950 (one-fifth of Mexico's film output), as Atlântida helped to regenerate the industry. Cinédia, which had ceased production started up again and had a major success with *O ebrio* (The Drunk, 1947), directed by the multi-talented Gilda de Abreu who was already a singer, actress, writer and theatre director before she embarked on a film career. The most sophisticated comedy of the time was by an independent producer and director Silveira Sampaio, *Uma aventura aos 40* (An Adventure in the 1940s, 1947). Another woman cineaste, Carmen Santos produced, directed and starred in *Inconfidência Mineira*, 1948, a project that she had developed for over a decade, and which she could partly film in her own small studios. This artesanal approach would be derided in the overwhelming ambitions of Vera Cruz.

The Vera Cruz film company emerged from the optimistic conditions of post-war São Paulo, following the break-up of the Estado Novo, a return to conservative democratic practices and a brief economic boom. São Paulo lived through a time of intense cultural activity. In the short space of six years, the city witnessed the birth of two art museums, a prestigious theatre company, several schools, a film library, a biennial exhibition of plastic arts and a large number of concerts, lectures and exhibitions. Many of these cultural initiatives were financed by a group led by the industrialist Francisco Matarazzo Sobrinho. Vera Cruz was linked to the complex of institutions based on his prestige and fortune, notably the Museum of Modern Art and the Brazilian Comedy Theatre.[40]

The reasoning of the group was based on economic principles. Hollywood's hegemony, it was argued, relied on its access to the technologies which allowed it to 'universalize' its comparative advantages. The way forward, therefore, was to invest massively in the industry. The company built large, costly studios, imported all the most up-to-date equipment and brought over skilled European technicians. Approaches were also made to have Brazil's most internationally famous cinematographer, Alberto Calvacânti, who lived in Europe, as head of the organization. He eventually took on the job but stayed for only one year. The project was posited on penetrating international markets, which proved impossible, and it was too expensive to be maintained by the domestic market alone: its productions cost about ten times the average Atlântida film. Up until 1954, it made eighteen films, the best-known being Lima Barreto's *O cangaceiro*, 1953, which was to have a great impact on the directors of the subsequent generation. In the end, however, the whole project was too overblown for the home market conditions of Brazil. Was there, then, an alternative to the *chanchadas?*

By the early 1950's it appeared that the creative energies of the forties were beginning to wane and that the market would increasingly dictate the type of movie available. In Mexico, it was found that quick formulaic films, *churros* (known after the doughy pastry) – singing cowboys, maternal melodramas, Cantinflas and Tin-Tan making up to six films a year, sex

---

[40] See Maria Rita Galvão, 'Vera Cruz: a Brazilian Hollywood', in R. Johnson and R. Stam (eds.), *Brazilian Cinema* (London, 1982), p. 273.

comedies – could provide acceptable profits. The structure of film financing, through the Banco Cinematográfico, favoured monopolization of a few producers, exhibitors and directors such as Emilio Azcárraga and William Jenkins. The major powers could set up an 'insider' financial operation, while the two main unions, the Sindicato de Trabajadores de la Industria Cinematográfica (STIC) and the elite breakaway union, the Sindicato de Trabajadores de la Producción Cinematográfica (STPC) ran a closed-shop policy which effectively closed the door on young film-makers for some twenty years.[41] A similar move to monopoly control by a few 'safe' producers has been observed in Perón's Argentina, where state credits chased mediocrity, which bred on these conditions of plenty. In Brazil, with the collapse of the Vera Cruz experiment, cinema was in a state of flux, though the popularity of *chanchada* showed no signs of diminishing as the spectacular parody *Nem Sansão, nem Dalila* (Neither Samson nor Delilah, 1954) reveals.

No other country in Latin America was experiencing a crisis since only a handful of films were made anywhere else and these tended to be timid imitations of Argentine and Mexican genres.[42] Film historians can find isolated titles in each of the Latin American republics, but no developed industry. In Chile an attempt was made in the 1940s to stimulate cinema through state investment. The state agency, CORFO, set up to deepen Chile's import-substitution industrialization and economic modernization, saw cinema as an important growth industry and in 1942 gave 50 per cent finance to set up Chile Films. Costly studios were erected but, as in the case of Vera Cruz in Brazil, the project was over-ambitious and Argentine film-makers ended up by using most of the facilities. Manuel Alonso's *Siete muertes a plazo fijo* (Seven Deaths at an Appointed Time, 1950) and *Casta de roble* (Caste of Oak, 1954) point to a certain vigour in film-making in Cuba before the Revolution. Isolated directors such as Rafael Rivero in Venezuela (*Juan de la Calle*, 1941) or the Colombian Máximo Calvo (*Flores del Valle*, 1941) and small production companies like Amauta films in Peru, which in the late 1930 and early 1940s produced some fourteen musicals and melodramas, show that all over the continent attempts were made to develop the new art form. Yet these are traces of

---

[41] On the emergence of a 'new' Mexican cinema from the 1940s, see Berg, *Cinema of Solitude: A Critical Study of Mexican Film,* introductory chapter.

[42] For the early days of cinema in other countries, see, for example, Hernando Salcedo Silva, *Crónica del cine colombiano, 1897–1950* (Bogotá, 1981); Ambretta Marrosu, *Exploraciones en la historiografía del cine en Venezuela* (Caracas, 1985); Alfonso Gumucio Dagrón, *Historia del cine bolivano* (Mexico, D.F., 1983).

individual works, rather than developed 'national' cinemas, in home markets dominated by Hollywood and, to a lesser extent, movies from Mexico and Argentina.

## THE 1950S: TOWARDS A NEW CINEMA

The early 1950s witnessed a slow but appreciable shift in the appreciation of cinema among intellectuals and middle-class sectors more generally. Cine Clubs and discussion groups were set up, which explored the theory and practice of film aesthetics. It was from this moment that the gap between what Pierre Bourdieu has called the 'autonomous' principle in art (appreciation by peers, legitimation on the basis of aesthetic values) and the 'heteronomous' principle (value as constructed by the marketplace), began to widen.[43] While students debated the value of cinema, and talked about the new vogue of neo-realism, popular audiences still flocked to (and even now regularly support) the formula films. The great attraction in Mexico in the 1950s and beyond was the 'cine de lunchadores', the masked wrestlers, in particular the legendary 'El Santo' (Rodolfo Guzmán Huerta) who had 15,000 bouts in the ring and starred in twenty-one films. In Argentina, audiences were much more interested in the increasing revelations of Isabel Sarli's body (in the sex comedies with Armando Bo) rather than in neo-realism. It is necessary to make these remarks since critical histories, especially those of the recent period of 'new cinema', tend to ignore what does not fit neatly into a progressive or socially concerned canon.[44]

In Cuba, the journalist and critic José Manuel Valdés Rodriguez founded a Department of Cinematography in the University of Havana in 1949 together with a cinémathèque which preserved copies of old prints. The cultural society Nuestro Tiempo was made up of figures who would later attract world attention such as Néstor Almendros, Guillermo Cabrera Infante and Tomás Gutiérrez Alea. In Brazil film journals like *Fundamentos* openly questioned the excessive spending of Vera Cruz and suggested that low-cost cinema should become the norm in Brazil. Film congresses met in São Paulo and in Rio in the early fifties to debate the different options. Cinema Clubs and filmothèques were set up in the

---

[43] See Randal Johnson's edition of Pierre Bourdieu's essays in *The Field of Cultural Production: Essays on Art and Literature* (London, 1993).
[44] The only book-length study of 'popular' cinema in Latin America is Jorge Ayala Blanco, *La disolvencia del cine mexicano: entre lo popular y lo exquisito* (Mexico, D.F., 1991).

major cities and influential critics, such as Alex Viany and in particular Paulo Emílio Salles Gomes, presented alternative critical strategies. In Chile a film club was established at the Universidad de Chile, which edited a journal, produced a radio programme and gave weekly screening of foreign films, and in 1959 a Centre for Experiemental Cinema was formed under the direction of a young documentary film-maker Sergio Bravo. In Argentina, especially after 1955, film clubs mushroomed and universities opened film departments. By 1955 in Mexico, there was already in existence a federation of Mexican Cine Clubs. The winds of change were beginning to blow across the continent.

Cine clubs and journals created a climate of increasing awareness of cinema as an art form. They also provided a forum for debates about the future of Latin American cinema. In the early 1950s, the major influence, the most possible and appropriate model, seemed to be neo-realism. Robert Kolker explains why: 'The neo-realists wanted the image to deal so closely with the social realities of postwar Italy that it would throw off all the encumbrances of stylistic and contextual preconception and face the world as if without mediation. An impossible desire, but in it lay the potential for yet other assaults on cinema history . . . [with] location shooting, poor working-class subjects played by non-professionals, use of the environment to define those subjects, an attitude of unmediated observation of events'.[45]

Alongside the fascination with neo-realism, young French critics around the journal *Cahiers du Cinéma* could offer interesting ideas to young Latin American theoreticians/film-makers. The 'politique des auteurs' spoke against the domination of bland and anonymous commercial studio productions and rediscovered individual voices rebelling within the system. *Cahiers* critics would discover the mavericks within Hollywood, and reassess the Western, or Minnelli or Hitchcock. Latin American critics in the main dismissed Hollywood altogether and all of the 'old' Latin American cinema, seeking instead the 'new' in terms of social and political relevance.

Practical as well as theoretical models were thus on offer and a number of aspirant film-makers made the pilgrimage to Italy, to learn at the feet of the neo-realist theorist Zavattini and others. Gabriel García Márquez talked in the mid-1980s of the strong influence of Italian cinema in that period: 'Between 1952 and 1955, four of us studied at the Centro

[45] Robert Kolker, *The Altering Eye: Contemporary International Cinema* (Oxford, 1983), p. 44.

Sperimentale in Rome: Julio García Espinosa, Vice Minister of Culture for Cinema in Cuba, Fernando Birri, the great pope of the New Latin American cinema, Tomás Gutiérrez Alea, one of its most notable craftsmen and I, who wanted nothing more in life than to become the film-maker I never became.'[46]

With hindsight we can perceive the contours of a new movement, but as yet film practitioners in Latin America were working in isolation, unaware of each others interests. We are still at least a decade away from being able to talk of a Pan Latin American movement. Certain precursor figures are important. In Brazil, Nelson Pereira dos Santos has recognized his debt to neo-realism: 'The influence of neo-realism was not that of a school or ideology but rather as a production system. Neo-realism taught us, in sum, that it was possible to make films in the streets; that we do not need studios, that we could film using average people rather than known actors; that the technique could be imperfect, as long as the film was truly linked to its national culture and expressed that culture.'[47] In 1955 Pereira dos Santos filmed the documentary *Rio 40 Graus* (Rio 40°, 1955) which focused on the slum dwellers of Rio, following the movement of five peanut-sellers throughout the city. Two years later he made *Rio Zona Norte* (Rio, Northern Zone, 1957), on the life of the Samba composer Espirito da Luz Soares. The composer is played by Grande Otelo who is given a different narrative function to that of black comic in numerous *chanchadas:* here he represents a man exploited by class and race, but who still inspires a strong popular culture. The young critic Glauber Rocha, saw Pereira dos Santos as an exemplary *auteur,* one who could give dignity to Brazilian cinema, showing that cinema could be made 'with a camera and an idea', a phrase that would later become one of the foundational definitions of Cinema Novo in Brazil.

In Argentina, Leopoldo Torre Nilsson and Fernando Birri offered two very different models. Torre Nilsson was the poet of aristocratic decadence. His *La casa del ángel* (The House of the Angel, 1957) was greeted with praise by 'new-wave' critics and film-makers such as Eric Rohmer who hyperbolically called it 'the best film to have arrived from South America since the beginnings of cinema.'[48] Torre Nilsson was a 'modern' *auteur.* Informed by Bergman, French New Wave and its British contempo-

[46] Gabriel García Márquez, quoted in *Anuario 88,* Escuela Internacional de Cine y TV (Havana, 1988), p. 1.

[47] Quoted in Johnson and Stam (eds.), *Brazilian Cinema,* p. 122.

[48] Quoted in Jorge Abel Martin, *Los filmes de Leopoldo Torre Nilsson* (Buenos Aires, 1980), p. 30.

raries Karel Reisz and Lindsay Anderson and in close collaboration with
his wife, the writer Beatriz Guido, he explored the contradictions and
decline of Argentine upper-class and genteel bourgeois society in such
films as *Graciela* (1955), *Angel* (1957) and *La caída* (The Fall, 1959). Torre
Nilsson gave prestige to Argentine cinema and helped to encourage a
younger generation of cineastes, formed in the cine clubs and in film-
making societies, who would create a temporary 'new wave' in the early
1960s.

While Torre Nilsson in Buenos Aires was exploring urban decadence, in
the city of Santa Fé in the north Fernando Birri, on his return from the
Centro Sperimentale in 1956, sought to use neo-realist principles to explore the hidden realities of Argentina. He set up a film school at the
Universidad Nacional de Litoral and made an important early documentary *Tire Dié* (Throw us a Dime, 1958) helped by a large group of his
students. They observed and recorded young shanty-town children who
daily risked their lives running along a main railway line begging for
coins. Before the final cut, he showed the film to the inhabitants of the
shanty towns and incorporated their suggestions. He also took the film on
tour, with a projector loaded onto an old truck, stopping at different
remote communities who were outside main exhibition circuits. Birri in
this and later documentaries and in his fictional feature *Los inundados*
(Flooded Out, 1963) anticipated, and in fact theorized in a number of
important essays, filmic practices which were to become important in the
1960s when, with the advent of portable, flexible 16mm cameras, the
dream of 'a camera in hand and an idea in the head' could become a reality.
Birri talked of national popular cinema, of the need to adopt and transform neo-realism in the context of Latin America and to break with the
distribution and exhibition circuits of commercial cinema, incorporating
working-class and peasant audiences into more democratic cultural practices. This final aim was to become one of the elusive chimeras of political
film-making in the 1960s.

The Spanish exile director Luis Buñuel made some twenty films in
Mexico between 1946 and 1965 including the memorable *Los olvidados*
(1950), *El* (1952) *Nazarín* (1958), *El angel exterminador* (1962) and *Simón
del desierto* (1965). He disagreed with the orthodoxies of neo-realism,
seeking not to present things as they are, but rather how the desires and
the state of mind of the observer charge these things with new meanings
and new ways of seeing. His unique blending of documentary, psychological, religious and surrealist motifs were not fully appreciated in a 1950s

Mexican context dominated by formulaic films, but he became an example and an inspiration for Mexican critics and cineastes in the 1960s.

## THE 'NEW CINEMAS' OF THE 1960S

The 'new' cinemas in Latin America grew up in the optimistic conditions of the late 1950s and early 1960s in Latin America. Two fundamentally different political projects were modernizing and radicalizing the social and cultural climate: the Cuban Revolution and the myths and realities of developmentalism in, for example, Kubitschek's Brazil and Frondizi's Argentina. We should not, as revolutionary Cuba lies in tatters in the mid-1990s, underestimate the radical impact of that revolution in Latin America throughout the 1960s. It seemed to most an exemplary nationalist, anti-imperalist movement which demonstrated a clear need for commitment and political clarity and held out the utopian possibility of uniting artistic and political vanguards. Cuba as a model influenced Latin American film-makers long before Cuban cinema came of age in the mid to late 1960s. This revolutionary impulse combined with a clear sense of cultural moderniza-tion in decade in which the intellectual community felt that it could be 'contemporary with all men' in Octavio Paz's evocatively optimistic phrase. This optimism was, at least in part, grounded in economic and political realities, but realities that could be subject to acute variations. As an historian of cultural modernity puts is: 'All the modernism and anti-modernisms of the 1960s, then, were seriously flawed. But their sheer plenitude, along with their intensity and liveliness of expression generated a common language, a vibrant ambience, a shared horizon of experience and desire . . . The initiatives all failed, but they sprang from a largeness of spirit and imagination and from an ardent desire to seize the day."[49]

In every country, new agendas were being set, new problems debated: how Cuba would develop a state, 'socialist', cinema; the relationship between film-makers and the state in a dependent capitalist context; the problems of production in conditions of scarcity (what Glauber Rocha called 'the aesthetics' of hunger) or outside the main commercial networks (evolving what the Argentines Getino and Solanas would call a 'Third Cinema'); the problem of how and where to distribute and exhibit work, in a context controlled by strong local capital, or, more usually, by mo-nopoly capital; the question of the appropriate film language for particular

---

[49] Marshall Berman, *All That is Solid Melts into Air: The Experience of Modernity* (London, 1983), p. 33.

situations (which would be very different in the altiplanos of Peru and Bolivia to that in the urban centres of Argentina or Uruguay); the whole vexed question of what constituted a 'national' reality in the context of an increasing globalization of culture; the uneasy relationship between film-makers (largely middle-class intellectuals) and the people they purported to represent; and the very nature of popular culture itself.

## Brazil

Brazil led the way, in both theory and practice, in a movement that became known as Cinema Novo. 'Cinema Novo is not one film, but an evolving complex of films that will ultimately make the people aware of its own misery.'[50] Here Glauber Rocha articulates one of the paradoxes of the process: that of creating 'popular' cinema for a public not used to political cinema inside the industrial complex, a popular cinema, there-fore, that was not for popular consumption. The young, largely Río de Janeiro based, film makers of the early sixties, Glauber Rocha, Nelson Pereira dos Santos, Ruy Guerra, Carlos Diegues, Joaquim Pedro de Andrade adopted a variety of styles but shared the view that they were expressing a radical national, and Latin American, identity in opposition to a neo-colonial cultural system. Here the influential think-tank, the Instituto Superior de Estudos Brasileiros, offered a model of developmen-tal nationalism, and the idea that an intellectual elite should be the critical conscience of underdevelopment. The key films of the period up to the military coup of 1964 were set in the main in the countryside, and in particular the desolate Northeast of Brazil, the deserted backland, the *sertão*, with its poverty, its mythical social bandits, the *cangaceiros*, and messianic leaders. Three films in 1963, Pereira dos Santos's *Vidas secas* (Barren Lives), Ruy Guerra's *Os fuzis* (The Guns) and Glauber Rocha's *Deus e o diabo na terra do sol* (Black God, White Devil) were all filmed in the northeast and explored the nature of unequal development and different forms of oppression. Glauber adopted some of the forms and structures of northeastern popular culture: the ballads and the mythical stories of *cordel* (broadsheet) literature. In these and other important fictional films, such as Carlos Diegues's *Ganga Zumba*, 1963, a film based on the seventeenth-century maroon community of Palmares, and Paulo Cesar Saraceni's *Porto*

[50] Glauber Rocha, 'An Aesthetic of Hunger', quoted in Johnson and Stam (eds.), *Brazilian Cinema*, p. 71.

*das caixas* (1962) there was a similar attention to the plight of the urban and rural poor and a shared utopian belief that the film-maker could lead the process of social change.

The military coup of 1964 effectively put an end to these left-wing and populist dreams, but for a time, until a more radical coup in 1968, left-wing culture still continued to flourish[51] albeit within state-defined limits. The state also began to invest in culture and set up a National Film Institute in 1966 to offer subsidies and to impose the compulsory exhibition of national films. Radical film-makers were thus wooed by 'the philanthropic ogre', Octavio Paz's telling phrase for the state, a complex situation which Glauber Rocha allegorized in his next film *Terra em Transe* (Land in Anguish, 1967). For critic Ismail Xavier, *Terra* analyses, 'The contradictions of a socially engaged artist who, misinterpreting himself as a decisive agent in the struggle for power in society, is obliged to confront his own illusions concerning the "courtly life" in an underdeveloped milieu and discovers his peripheral condition within the small circle of the mighty. Defeated, the artist enacts the agony of his illusory status, the death of his anachronistic view.'[52] Other films focusing on the ambiguous response of intellectuals to power were Paulo Saraceni's, *O desafio* (The Challenge, 1967) and *O bravo guerreiro* (The Brave Warrior, 1968) by Gustavo Dahl.

The coup within the coup of December 1968 further radicalized the situation, heralding what critics have called the third phase of Cinema Novo, 'cannibalist-tropicalist' phase, where the nature of power and oppression was explored by allegory. Certain film-makers such as Glauber Rocha and Ruy Guerra were forced into exile for short periods, while others resorted to indirect forms of criticism, often through more popular forms such as comedy. Joaquim Pedro de Andrade's adaption of the 1920s novel by Mario de Andrade, *Macunaíma,* has cannibalism as a central metaphor and follows the racial and social transformations of the trickster Macunaíma (played by Grande Otelo) as he travels from the Amazon to the modern city of São Paulo. Pereira dos Santos's *Como era gostoso o meu francês* (How Tasty Was My Little Frenchman, 1971) has the sixteenth-century Tupinambá Indians ingesting, and taking on the powers of, the French colonists. Cinema Novo directors, despite the severity of dictatorship, still had hegemonic power and state subsidies. Their dominance was ridiculed

---

[51] See Roberto Schwarz, *Misplaced Ideas*, pp. 126–59.
[52] Ismael Xavier, 'Allegories of underdevelopment': From the 'aesthetics of hunger' to the 'aesthetics of garbage', unpublished Ph.D. dissertation, New York University, 1982, p. 116.

by a brief by vigorous underground (Udigrudi) movement of the late
1960s which, in Xavier's phrase, proclaimed an 'aesthetic of garbage', an
aesthetic of futility, in the place of Glauber's rebellious, active 'aesthetic of
hunger'. Rogerio Sganzerla's *O bandido da luz vermelha* (Red Light Bandit,
1968) and Julio Bresanne's *Matou a famila e foi ao cinema* (Killed the Family
and Went to the Cinema, 1969) expressed this new, caustic sarcasm,
which hurled its disgust, like garbage, in the face of Cinema Novo and the
state. The compromises reached in the 1970s, however, would give the
state an increasingly upper hand.

*Argentina*

In Argentina, the young film-makers initially followed the example of
Torre Nilsson, rather than the more radical-populist proposals of Birri.
With some help from the newly founded Film Institute, INC, Argentine
'new wave' followed its Parisian counterparts in exploring middle-class
anomie and alienation or the sexual rites of passage of the young, set in the
cafés and streets of Buenos Aires. Or, like their Brazilian counterparts,
they drew inspiration from literature, in particular the work of Jorge Luis
Borges and Julio Cortázar. Films like Manuel Antin's *La cifra impar* (The
Odd Number 1962), and David Kohon's *Tres veces Ana* (Three Times Ana,
1961) were enjoyed by a sophisticated urban elite. Lautaro Murúa showed
the sordid side of the 'City of Dreams' Buenos Aires in his *Alias Gardelito*
(1960), while Leonardo Favio took Truffaut's *Les quatre cent coups* several
brutal stages further in his analysis of orphanage life: *Crónica de un niño solo*
(Chronicle of a Boy Alone, 1964).

The brief period of non-Peronist political regimes between 1955 and
1966 saw an ever increasing radicalization of politics and, by extension, of
culture. Perón was in exile, but he in many ways controlled the political
agenda. When the military under Onganía decided to take control in
1966, many artists and intellectuals reacted to these conditions by fighting the government in all areas of intellectual activity. The discourse, by
now, was nationalist, populist and, in many cases Third Worldist.[53] Concepts such as 'the people', 'the nation' and 'The Third World' were given a
new positive value and the word *extranjerizante* (foreign loving) was used as
a term of abuse to describe the 'false' cosmopolitanism of the liberal
tradition. The most representative film of this populist radicalism, in the

[53] For an analysis of the period, see Oscar Terán, *Nuestros años sesenta* (Buenos Aires, 1991).

tradition of Fernando Birri (whom it quotes), was Fernando Solanas and Octavio Getino's, *La hora de los hornos* The Hour of the Furnaces, 1966–8).

*La hora* is a colossal four-hour work, in three parts, which explores neo-colonalism and violence as the legacy of Argentina's economic and cultural dependency on Europe and talks of the present and future in terms of radical Peronism. It is a formally complex and ideologically Manichean work, but it became a rallying-point of resistance to Onganía and was seen clandestinely on the shop floor, in village halls or in private houses. Solanas and Getino theorized the work of their group Cine Liberación in a seminal essay 'Towards a Third Cinema', a term that has passed into the critical canon as a way of describing cinema from three continents, Asia, Africa and Latin America. The roots of Third Cinema for the film-makers, however, lie in Peronism. Third Cinema, posed an alternative both to first cinema, Hollywood, and to second cinema, a-political *auteurism*. Cinema in these terms had to produce works that the system cannot assimilate and which explicitly fought the system. Viewing *la hora* with hindsight, its faith in Perón seems pathetically misplaced. This is not to deny, however, the radical impact of the film, and the film-makers declarations, at the time. By 1970, Argentine politics and culture had entered a radical phase. All sectors looked to Perón to save a situation that was spiralling violently out of control. His return in 1973, however, was to create more problems than it solved.

*Mexico*

The strength and stability of state power in Mexico had always managed to defuse radicalism by coercion or cooptation. Equally the film industry was the most solid in Latin America, with jealously guarded vested interests. Change in this context was, of necessity, less spectacular than in other parts. Buñuel, as we have seen, spent the fifties making films in Mexico, but like Simon of the Desert (*Simón del desierto,* Mexico, 1965), one of his film titles, he was very much a voice crying in the wilderness; he could not rewrite alone the dull chapter of 1950s cinema. He would be an example, however, to a group of critics and cineastes – José de la Colina, Rafael Corkidi, Salvador Elizondo, Jomi M. García Ascot, Carlos Monsiváis, Alberto Isaac, Paul Leduc and Fernando Macotela – who in the 1960s formed a group *Nuevo Cine* (New Cinema) and edited a journal (which ran an excellent double issue on Buñuel). In 1962, Elizondo –

later to become one of Mexico's best vanguard writers – bluntly attacked the reigning orthodoxy of protectionism and a fading genre and star system. 'The system minimizes risks and establishes a certain security for investors. The system, in short, approves the following theorem: *A bout du souffle* would have been a much better film if instead of being directed by Godard with Belmondo and Jean Seyberg, it had been directed by Cecil B. De Mille and Vivien Leigh and Marcello Mastroianni.'[54] One film came from the group in the early 1960s, Jomi García Ascot's depiction of Spanish exile life *En el balcón vacío* (On the Empty Balcony, 1961), but they would all become leading film-makers, writers or critics in the decade of the 1960s.

An incentive to renovate cinema came from the film union STPC, which organized an experimental film competition in 1964/5. The prize was won by Rubén Gámez's *La fórmula secreta* (The Secret Formula) with Alberto Isaac's *En este pueblo no hay ladrones* (In this Town there are no Thieves), the first major film adaptation of a García Márquez short story, as runner up. These films were part of a sixties movement in which, as Carlos Monsiváis acutely observes, the Mexican public was also looking for different self-images: 'Socially and culturally what happens in that this (new) cinema is a clear product of the demands of the middle classes to find reflected their problems and their desire for access to universality, to cosmopolitanism in the face of the excesses of a cultural nationalism that had lost its force and dynamism and had become a series of grotesque formulae.'[55] Cultural nationalism was opposed by a movement known as 'la onda' a rag bag of different modernisms, in fashion, music and avant-garde literature. The 'hip' director of the 'onda' was the Chilean Alejandro Jodorowsky with *Fando y Lis* (1967) and *El topo* (The Mole, 1970).

Modernization and internationalization were accompanied in the late 1960s by a major political crisis when the Partido Revolucionario Institu-tional (PRI) found itself opposed by a strong student movement. This crisis was resolved in a horrifyingly brutal fashion on 2 October 1968, when troops opened fire on a demonstration of mainly students assembled in the Plaza of the Three Cultures in Tlatelolco, Mexico City. Many hundreds died in this massacre, which marked a watershed in the develop-ment of modern Mexico. In the widespread revulsion following the massa-cre, all intellectual groups condemned the government. The next presi-

---

[54] Quoted in *Hojas de cine: Testimonions y documentos del Nuevo Cine Latinoamericano*, Vol. II (Mexico, D.F., 1988), p. 42.
[55] *Hablemos de Cine*, 69 (1977–8), p. 26.

dent, Luis Echeverría, who took power in 1970, needed to restore the prestige of the presidency through conciliation. A major platform of his campaign would be to garner the support of artists and intellectuals.

## Cuba

It would take until the late 1960s for Cuban cinema to have much impact outside its national frontiers. One reason for this was the fact that the new revolutionary government was forced to begin almost with nothing. Conscious of the importance of cinema and radio in a revolutionary context it set up in March 1959, three months after the triumph of the revolution, the Cuban Institute of Cinematographic Art and Industry (ICAIC), which gradually, with the nationalization measures of the early 1960s, took over not only production but also distribution and exhibition throughout the country. The aims were lofty: to create a new cinema for the spectator, but also to create a new spectator for cinema.

Cuba had a small nucleus of film-makers with slight experience. A short documentary *El mégano* (The Charcoal Workers) had been made in 1954 as part of the Cine Club movement and the production staff on this short would become Cuba's earliest film makers: Julio García Espinosa, Tomás Gutiérrez Alea, Alfredo Guevara, Jorge Haydú and Jorge Fraga. Alfredo Guevara was put in charge of ICAIC and, in conditions of scarcity, gave over most of the limited resources to newsreel production and to documentary film-making, under Santiago Alvarez. It would be Alvarez who set the standards – supported by visiting European documentary film-makers such as Chris Marker and the veteran Joris Ivens – for radical, innovative documentary film-making during the years 1959–66, which can be seen as a period of apprenticeship.

How could the regime seek to create a new spectator for cinema when its own new cinema was evolving so slowly? A number of measures were adopted. A Cinemathèque was set up which showed film cycles from existing archive material. Television also included courses on film criticism. A film journal *Cine Cubano* began publication. In the countryside, mobile cinema units – projection equipment loaded on to Soviet trucks – toured the countryside, giving some outlying communities their first experience of the movie image. A ten-minute short by Octavio Cortázar, *Por primera vez* (For the First Time, 1967) recorded one such event in Oriente province.

Such educational advances, like that of the literacy campaign, were quantifiably successful. More complex, however, was the definition of the role of culture itself in the Revolution. Critic and film-maker Julio García Espinosa talked in *Cine Cubano* in 1964 of the existing splits: 'On the one side chauvinism, on the other cosmopolitanism; on the one side tradition, on the other fashion; on the one side sectarianism, on the other pseudo-philosophical speculation; on the one side the intransigent revolutionary, on the other the utopic liberal-spiritual confusion creates its own myths.'[56] A major dispute grew up over the temporary banning of a short documentary *P.M.*, made by Saba Cabrera Infante and Orlando Jiménez in a free cinema style in 1961. It caused Castro to intervene in 1961 and give his famous verdict in 'Words to the Intellectuals' which talked of the need for fellow travellers to commit themselves in the long term to the current process: 'within the Revolution, everything, against the Revolution, nothing'. A number of film-workers left Cuba in the early years: Néstor Almendros, Fernando Villaverde, Fausto Canel, Alberto Roldán, Roberto Fadiño and Eduardo Manet as well as the well-known critic and writer Guillermo Cabrera Infante. In general it can be said that ICAIC was in the liberal camp, trying whenever possible to defend artistic plurality against the more intransigent parts of the cultural political elite and providing an umbrella organization for artists in other disciplines whose experimentation was frowned upon: Saul Yelin's poster art, Silvio Rodriguez and Pable Milanés in music who joined Leo Brouwer's Grupo Sonoro Experimental and the multi-talented writer Jesús Díaz. It was to take until the 1980s for a clear Cuban exile cinema to express itself in the United States.

By 1966, film-makers could point to concrete advances. Santiago Alvarez had established a new style of newsreel and began working in documentary, turning scarcity into a signifier, remodelling second-hand sources such as news photos and television clips and developing a poetic and politically effective film collage in such documentaties as *Now* (1965); *Hanoi Martes 13* (Hanoi, 13 Tuesday 1967) and *Hasta la victoria siempre* (Until Victory, Always, 1967). It was to such work that Coppola would refer in a much quoted statement on a visit to Cuba: 'We do not have the advantages of their disadvantages.' 1966–7 saw two major fictional films: Tomás Gutiérrez Alea's comedy on bureaucracies *La muerte de un burócrata* (Death of a Bureaucrat, 1966) and Julio García Espinosa's picaresque parody *Las aventuras de Juan Quin Quin* (The adventures of Juan Quin

[56] Julio García Espinosa, *Cine Cubano*, 23–5 (1964), p. 20.

Quin, 1967). *Juan Quin Quin* is to date the largest grossing Cuban film, with over three million spectators. At last ICAIC could begin to make popular fictional films which helped to fill the gap left by the North American blockades and the rather stolid Hollywood substitutes that could be found in Eastern Europe. 1968 and 1969 saw several important works, Octavio Gómez's *La primera carga al machete* (The First Machete Charge, 1969), Humberto Solás' three-part *Lucía* (1968) and Gutiérrez Alea's *Memorias del subdesarrollo* (Memories of Underdevelopment, 1968), based on a novel by Edmundo Desnoes.

Towards the end of *Memorias,* a documentary insert shows Castro issuing a defiant speech to the world during the Missile Crisis in October 1962. 'No one is going to come and inspect our country because we grant no one the right. We will never renounce the sovereign prerogative that within our frontiers we will make all the decisions and we are the only ones who will inspect anything.' There was no space for individual questioning in such a polarized world, in 1962, or more acutely between 1968 and 1971, where a siege economy, the failure of the ten-million-ton sugar harvest, counter-revolutionary violence and political isolation helped to form an embattled mentality which claimed its casualties. The most notorious of these was the poet Heberto Padilla who was briefly imprisoned and gave an abject public recantation in 1971, much to the dismay of leading North American, European and Latin American intellectuals who wrote two open letters to Castro, complaining of the regime's actions. The decade of hope, therefore closed in crisis, heralding a period of what the Cuban critic Ambrosio Fornet has called the 'grey years' of Cuban cultural life.

*Chile*

In the south of the continent the decade ended with the optimistic hope that the Chilean democratic road to socialism could become a reality. Throughout the 1960s, film-makers in Chile had been actively involved in the political process. Sergio Bravo's university based Centre for Experimental Cinema helped to form young cineastes such as Domingo Sierra and Pedro Chaskel. Bravo himself made a documentary film of Salvador Allende's 1963/4 election campaign *Banderas del pueblo* (Banners of the People, 1964) which was banned by government censors. The defeat of the left alliance under Allende in 1964 caused a widespread internal debate not just over electoral politics but also about the need to work in the cultural field to wrest 'common sense' values away from the control of the right or Christian Democracy. Under the Frei administration (1964–70) there was to be a flowering of activity in theatre, music and cinema, and the years 1968–9 saw the maturity of Chilean cinema. Five features came out: Raúl Ruiz's *Tres tristes tigres* (Three Sad Tigers); Helvio Soto's *Caliche sangriento* (Bloody Nitrate); Aldo Francia's *Valparaiso mi amor* (Valpaaraiso My Love); Miguel Littín's *El chacal de Nahueltoro* (The Jackal of Nahueltoro) and Carlos Elsesser's *Los testigos* (The Witnesses). These film-makers came from different ideological and aesthetic tendencies, from the inventive maverick Raúl Ruiz to the sombre neo-realism of Francia, but they can be seen as a group, working with very scarce resources: the films by Ruiz, Elsesser, Francia and Littín were made consecutively, with the same camera. Aldo Francia, a doctor by profession, also organized a famous 'Meeting of Latin American Film makers' at the Viña del Mar film festival in 1967. This would be one the key events in growing awareness of cineastes across the continent that they were working with similar ideas and methods. Raúl Ruiz makes the point: 'Suddenly we found ourselves with a cinema which in a very obvious and natural way, without any cultural inferiority complex, was being made with very few resources, with the resources that we could acquire and with a freedom that earlier Latin American and European cinema did not have. Suddenly we found ourselves with all the advantages.'[57] These film-makers would support the Popular Unity campaign in 1970.

### Bolivia, Peru, Colombia and Venezuela

A film-maker who attracted attention at Viña del Mar was the Bolivian Jorge Sanjinés, who came from a country with scant tradition in film. In the aftermath of the National Revolution of 1952, the government established the Bolivian Film Institute, the ICB, which produced government newsreels, but lacked the resources or the trained personnel to exploit to the full symbolic and propaganda aspects of the revolution. One film-maker stood out in the 1950s: Jorge Ruiz who made two important ethnological films *Vuelve Sebastiana* (Sebastinana, Come Home, 1953) and *La vertiente* (The Watershed, 1958). Social cinema was extended by Sanjinés and the group he formed around him, the grupo Ukamau (named after their first major feature *Ukamau* (That's How it is, 1966)). Sanjinés

---

[57] Raúl Ruiz, interview in *Araucaria de Chile*, 11 (1980), pp. 101–18.

had studied in Chile at Sergio Bravo's newly opened film school and on his return to Bolivia formed a friendship and working partnership with Oscar Soria, Bolivia's foremost script-writer, who had collaborated with Ruiz in the 1950s. Sanjinés's work in the 1960s, and beyond, looked to highlight the problems of Bolivia's workers, peasants and indigenous peoples, but not in any patronizing way: instead the group tried to find a language appropriate to the rhythms and practices of popular culture. Their most successful film was *Yawar Mallku* (Blood of the Condor, 1968), which helped bring an end to the activities of the U.S. Peace Corps in Bolivia. But the film did not satisfy the group at the level of form: 'It was not that they [the Indian peoples] could not understand what was being said', Sanjinés wrote, 'it was rather a formal conflict at the level of the medium itself, which did not correspond to the internal rhythms of our people or their profound conception of reality. The substantial difference lay in the way in which the Quechua-Aymara people conceive of themselves collectively, in the non-individualistic form of their culture.'[58] Film-making in future would deal with the history of the collective, seeking to reactivate the popular memory denied by the hegemonic powers: the memory, for example, of the massacre of miners in June 1967, in the Siglo XX mines, which the group reconstructed in *El coraje del pueblo* (Courage of the People, 1971). The Banzer coup of 1971 ushered in a new hard-line regime in Bolivia and caused the group to rethink their working practices.

In Peru, theoretical debates about cinema in the 1960s were more sophisticated than filmic practices. The journal *Hablemos de Cine* founded in 1965, took up debates about 'new' cinema in Latin America. There had been a tradition of ethnographic film-making in Peru, especially based in Cuzco around the work of Manuel Chambi (the brother of the famous photographer Martin Chambi) and Luis Figueroa. This Cuzco school remained strong throughout the 1960s. Peru could perhaps boast of one *auteur*, Armondo Robles Godoy, but the main impetus towards film-making would come in the 1970s, as a result of state measures following the 1968 military coup of Géneral Velazco.

The same opportunities could be found for film-makers in Colombia and in Venezuela in the 1970s, when state support was consolidated. Before then, in the 1960s, film-makers worked infrequently and, in the main, in isolation. In Colombia, the documentary film-makers, Carlos Alvarez and in particular, Marta Rodriguez and Jorge Silva – with

---

[58] Jorge Sanjinés, quoted in *Framework*, 10 (1979), p. 3.

*Chircales* (Brick-Makers 1968–72) – followed the 'new cinema's' interest in social documentary. In Venezuela Margot Benacerraf made a remarkable documentary *Araya* in 1958, while Román Chalbaud's fiction *Caín adolescente* (Adolescent Cain, 1958) showed an early talent which would develop in more favourable conditions a decade later.

The decade of the 1960s, therefore, saw the emergence, out of different national contexts, of a group of radical film-makers and critics who would define their work as 'new Latin American cinema'. They sought to join their diverse projects into a broader ideological and cultural agenda capable of encompassing the continent.[59] The idea was, of course, utopian, but in the late 1960s it seemed as if the dream might become a reality. Film-makers met in different congresses in Viña del Mar (1967 and 1968) and in Mérida, Venezuela (1968), and proclaimed the birth of a new movement of Latin American cooperation and solidarity. It was a moment when theoretical statements about 'cinema of hunger', 'imperfect cinema' or 'third cinema' seemed linked to a dynamic practice. Perhaps this indeed was the 'hour of the furnaces' which would light up and guide liberation struggles throughout the continent.

## THE 1970S: STATE REPRESSION, STATE-LED DEVELOPMENT

The decade of the 1970s witnessed several interlocking trends that profoundly affected the development of cinema: the brief revolutionary optimism of the early seventies, in particular in Chile, Argentina and Uruguay; the spread of dictatorship throughout the southern cone with military coups in Uruguay (June 1973), Chile (September 1973), and Argentina (March 1976) which dislocated the intellectual community and sent many into exile; and the growth of state-led cinema in Brazil (under somewhat less repressive military rule since April 1964), in Mexico and in hitherto 'minor' film cultures, Venezuela, Colombia and Peru.

The narrow victory of the Popular Unity parties in the election of 1970 showed that the Chilean road to socialism would be full of hazards. The film-makers greeted the election victory with an enthusiastic manifesto penned by Migual Littín, and Littín himself was put in charge of the state institution Chile Films. He lasted for only ten months, tiring of bureaucratic opposition (many officials had guaranteed jobs in Chile Films and

[59] Zuzana M. Pick, *The New Latin American Cinema: A Continental Project* (Austin, Tex., 1993).

could not be replaced) and inter-party feuding as the different members of Popular Unity demanded a share of very limited resources. Few films were made between 1970 and 1973 and the state bodies could do little to affect distribution and exhibition. The United States imposed pressure in a number of ways. The Motion Pictures Export Association ordered the suspension of exports of U.S. films from June 1971 and Chile Films was forced into bilateral exchanges with Bulgaria, Cuba, Hungary and Czechoslovakia to fill to vacuum.

Raúl Ruiz was the most productive film-maker of the period, with a number of films in different styles such as *La colonia penal* (The Penal Colony, 1971), *Nadie dijo nada* (No One Said Anything, 1971), *La expropriación*, 1973 and *El realismo socialista* (1973). Littín was working on an ambitious feature *La tierra prometida* (The Promised Land) when the 1973 coup occurred and post-production took place in Paris. The most exemplary film which traced the radicalization of Chile in 1972 and 1973 was Patricio Guzmán's *La batalla de Chile* (The Battle of Chile), a documentary in three parts which was edited in exile in Cuba. The first parts, 'The Insurrection of the Bourgeoisie' deals with the middle-class revolt against the Allende government in the media and in the streets. 'The Coup d'état' continues this narrative, adding in the bitter quarrels among the left over strategy, while the third part 'Popular Power' looks at the work of mass organizations in 1973. In the first years of exile, this film became Chile's most evocative testimony abroad and received worldwide distribution in campaigns of solidarity. Paradoxically, Chilean cinema, which had little time to grow under Popular Unity, strengthened and became a coherent movement in exile.

The military coup in Uruguay in 1973, put an end to what had been for a time a lively film culture. The main protagonists of the 1960s had been the documentary film-makers Ugo Ulive and Mario Handler, and they were supported by a local independent producer and exhibitor Walter Achugar who pioneered the distribution of Latin American new cinema in Uruguay as a way of stimulating local production. In conjunction with the Argentine producer Edgardo Pallero, they were responsible for setting up the Cinemateca del Tercer Mundo in Montevideo in November 1969, which worked in production, distribution and exhibition. In the political radicalization of the early 1970s, the Cinemateca was a very visible target. In May 1972, two of its directors, Eduardo Terra and Walter Achugar were arrested, tortured and detained. As the long night descended in 1973, the artistic community spread into exile.

Both Chilean and Uruguayan artists initially found refuge in Argentina, for Perón had returned in June 1973, ushering in a brief period of civilian rule. The situation was tense and violent, as all sectors, from the far right and the military to the guerrilla groups and the left, thought that Perón would offer them support but there was a brief period of nationalist, populist, anti-imperialist euphoria in the film industry. Between 1973 and 1974, fifty-four films were made and cinema audiences rose by some 40 per cent. Cineastes focused on the heroes of Argentine history and adapted literary texts by José Hernández, Roberto Arlt and Manuel Puig. The most successful films were the anti-imperialist epics: Héctor Olivera's *La Patagonia rebelde*, Richardo Wullicher's *Quebracho,* and Leonardo Favio's *Juan Moreira.* Some more gentle, intimate, themes were portrayed such as Sergio Renán's *La tregua* (The Truce), but in the main artists and intellectuals were caught up in a political voluntarism.

Perón's death in 1974 and the assumption to power of his minor actress wife, Isabel, caused a spiralling violence. Factionalism grew within Peronism, the guerrilla groups continued a campaign of violence and right-wing death squads acted with impunity. Film-makers were just one of the sectors affected by the growing terror and repression. Many received death threats and escaped into exile even before the coup of March 1976.

From the mid-1970s and for the rest of that decade and beyond, the countries of the Southern Cone of Latin America lived through the bleakest period of their history. While repression was at its height, cultural expression was severely limited. In film, production dropped and a diet of inoffensive comedies or musicals became the norm. In the main it was foreign producers and distributions that benefitted: the North American Motion Picture Export Association recorded greatly increased profits in Argentina in the late 1970s. Yet no one could benefit from the blatant censorship which banned certain foreign films, or mutilated others, rendering them incomprehensible. Military men intervened in the state cultural institutions, military minds 'defended' the morality of the nation and of the family. A small 'catacomb' culture built up in the different countries in an attempt to keep intellectual debate alive, but high-visibility industries such as cinema had few opportunities to express difference.

The exiles suffered different problems, of displacement from community and isolation within their host communities. Most have described the process in positive terms, as Zuzana Pick reminds us: 'Forced to communicate with and engage in new cultural (and sometimes linguistic) contexts, these film-makers broadened the thematic concerns of their work and extended their practices beyond the affiliation with national communities',[60] into new expressive territories. The best example of a director adapting to new circumstances is the case of Raúl Ruiz. He went penniless to Paris, with his wife, the editor and film-maker Valeria Sarmento. His first film, which dealt with the exile community there, was entitled *Diálogo de exilados* (Dialogue of Exiles, 1974). It was greeted with hostility by the Chileans, who thought that his ironic, playful tone was inappropriate to the seriousness of the situation. Ruiz, now in almost a double exile, moved towards the world of French film-making. He was fortunate that the specialist institution, INA (Institut National de l'Audiovisuel) had been set up to commission experimental work. With the support of INA and other institutions, Ruiz gained the reputation of being one of the most innovative directors in Europe, the subject of a special issue of the film journal *Cahiers du Cinéma* in 1983. He has remarked that working in the stable conditions of Europe has given him 'an experience of production and a sense of craft that does not exist in Latin America, the idea of professional development and advancement, and the possibility of various technical skills converging into one.'[61] His films constantly navigate, like the sailors in *Les Trois couronnes du matelot* (Three Crowns of a Sailor, 1982), between Europe and America, in a hybrid style which is neither narrowly nationalist nor cosmopolitan. Eduardo Cozarinsky, the Argentine film-maker who went into voluntary exile in Paris with the return of Perón in 1973 has remarked that Ruiz and other film-makers (like Cozarinksy himself and the Argentines Eduardo de Gregorio and Hugo Santiago) 'can illuminate France, and consequently its cinema with a lateral light that emphasize volume and texture, rather than the harsh front-lighting which flattens everything out.'[62]

Valeria Sarmiento, Ruiz's wife, is one of several Chilean women cineastes to have developed their careers successfully in exile. It is from about the mid-1970s, throughout the continent, that the work of women film-makers became increasingly prominent, in different contexts, putting forward gender issues which had been largely ignored by the first wave of new cinema in the 1960s.[63] Sarmento's best-known film, *Un hombre, cuando es un hombre* (A Man When He is a Man) 1982, was shot in

[60] Pick, *New Latin American Cinema*, p. 156.
[61] Interview with Raúl Ruiz, in Pick, *New Latin American Cinema*, p. 177.
[62] Eduardo Cozarinsky, 'Les realisateurs étrangers en France: hier y aujourd'hui', *Positif*, 325 (March 1988), p. 42.
[63] On the development of women film-makers, see Pick, *New Latin American Cinema*, pp. 66–96, Luis Trelles Plazaola, *Cine y mujer en América Latina* (Río Piedras, P.R., 1991), and the special issue of the *Journal of Film and Video*, 44/3–4 (Fall 1992 and Winter 1993).

Costa Rica with a crew of Chilean exiles from Europe and was edited in Paris. It explores the world of machismo through *ranchera* music and *boleros*. This success was followed by *Notre Mariage* (Our Marriage, 1984) and the feature *Amelia López O'Neill* shot in Chile in 1990. Marilú Mallet made a number of important documentaries in Canada, while Angelina Vásquez found great support in Scandinavia, working and filming on Chile. Miguel Littín, Chile's best-known director from the Popular Unity period, was exiled in Mexico, receiving the support of president Echeverría. He became an explicit spokesman of Latin American cinema in exile, making a large budget Third World epic *Actas de Marusia* (Letter from Marusia, 1975) before funding dried up in Mexico in the late 1970s. These directors and others like Gaston Ancelovici in Paris and Pedro Chaskel in Cuba, showed the great energy and adaptability of Chilean film-making in the diaspora.

This was not the case for every director in exile. Fernando Solanas, for example, completed post-production work on his Peronist *Los hijos de Fierro* (The Sons of Fierro) in 1978 in Paris, but felt himself to be marginal, as an Argentine, but also as a Peronist. He never became a critical success like Raúl Ruiz and worked for a number of years to finance his film on exiles *Tangos: el exilio de Gardel* (Tangos: the Exile of Gardel) which he began filming in 1981, but could not complete until the mid-1980s, when Argentina had returned to democracy and co-funding became available.

In Bolivia, the Banzer coup of 1971 caused the Ukamau group to split. One part, under Antonio Eguino, opted to stay in Bolivia, and make films which were commercial but also socially responsible: *Pueblo Chico* (Small Town, 1974) and *Chuquiago,* 1977 (the Aymara name for La Paz). Sanjinés pursued a more radical option in exile and managed to make *El enemigo principal* (The Principal Enemy, 1973) in Peru and *Fuera de Aquí* (Get out of Here, 1976) in Ecuador until the fall of Banzer allowed him to return temporarily to Bolivia in 1979.

The experience of exile was thus ambivalent. It allowed some directors the freedom of distance, while it closed possibilities to others. It could be seen as an extension of the premises and aesthetics of the New Latin American cinema, but also as a moment of closure, or shifting of interests. In a period of transnational globalization the nation itself became a prime target. In terms of film, Hollywood by the mid-1970s had staged a remarkable comeback and, writes Thomas Elaesser, 'it was American movies, the package deal and big-business production methods which became more than ever the dominant model on both European and world markets'.

The new independent cinemas, whether national, politically interna-
tionlist or author – based, gradually found themselves forced into coexistence on the Americans' own terms or all but vanish altogether. In so far as
spectators returned to the cinema, it was to watch Hollywood blockbusters'.[64] There was a danger, in these circumstances, that the only audience
for radical, exile, Latin American cinema was on the international festival
circuit, where they became part of European radical chic.

Some countries sought to minimize this risk of deterritorialization by
offering major state funding, and other support, for national cinemas. In
this period, Brazil and Mexico led the way. By the time directors such as
Glauber Rocha and Ruy Guerra had returned to Brazil from brief periods
of exile in the early seventies, Cinema Novo had largely disappeared as an
integrated *movement* for social change. It was the Cinema Novo directors,
however, who would dominate film-making in the next two decades,
under the aegis of the state. Embrafilme, the state body, had been set up
in 1969 as an international distribution agency, but its activities extended
and in 1975, it began to work in production and exhibition as well as
distribution, taking virtually a monopolistic control over cinema in the
country. The screen quota for Brazilian films increased dramatically from
forty-two days in 1959 to 140 days in 1981. Under the direction of
Roberto Farias (1974–79) Embrafilme's budget rose from $US 600,000
to $US 8 million. Embrafilme distributed over 30 per cent of Brazilian
films in the 1970s and controlled between 25 and 50 per cent of annual
film production. The market share of Brazilian cinema increased from 15
per cent in 1974 to more than 30 per cent in 1980 and the number of
spectators for Brazilian films doubled.[65]

Such figures of growth seem to offer an irrefutable case for working with
the state. Yet the dilemma remained that Embrafilme was supported by a
repressive military government. Most film-makers decided to make a pact
with the state and produce socially responsible films from inside the system,
across the range of themes. Literary works were adapted, from light sex
comedies, Bruno Barreto's *Dona Flor e seus dois maridos* (Dona Flor and Her
Two Husbands, 1976) based on Jorge Amado's novel which became the
most successful film in Brazilian history, to the sombre realism of
Graciliano Ramos's fictional world, evoked in Leon Hirszman's *São Bernardo*
(1972). History was reexamined in Joaquim Pedro de Andrade's *Os*

[64] Thomas Elaesser, 'Hyper-Retro-or Counter Cinema', in *Mediating Two Worlds*, p. 121.
[65] Randal Johnson, *The Film Industry in Brazil: Culture and the State* (Pittsburgh, 1987), pp. 171–2.

*inconfidentes* (The Conspirators, 1972) and Carlos Diegues' *Xica da Silva* (1977), while Nelson Pereira dos Santos revised the early Cinema Novo's view that 'the people' were alienated masses that had to be educated out of false consciousness, by positing instead that they are repositories of popular wisdom, that intellectuals should tap in to. His *O amuleto de Ogum* (The Amulet of Ogum, 1974) and *Na estrada da vida* (Road of Life, 1980) deal, in this respectful way, with both popular religion and popular song. Ruy Guerra brought up to date his *Os fuzis* in *A queda* (The Fall, 1976), which finds the main military protagonist of the earlier film now as a construction worker in São Paulo. Women film-makers such as Ana Carolina and Tizuka Yamasaki also begin to emerge in this period, perhaps the most successful in Brazilian history. Ana Carolina made the first of a trilogy of surrealist, anarchist films, *Mar de Rosas* in 1977. Yamasaki made shorts in the 1970s, before releasing her first feature, a study of Japanese immigration into Brazil, *Gaijin: Caminhos da Liberdade* (Roads to Freedom) in 1980.

In Mexico the Echeverría administration (1970–76) sought to alleviate the loss of confidence caused by the massacre of students at Tlatelolco in 1968, by deliberately wooing intellectuals. Many prominent figures gave the new president their support. Leading novelist Carlos Fuentes accepted the Ambassadorship of Mexico in Paris and argued that 'above all, Echeverría lifted the veil of fear that Díaz Ordaz had flung over the body of Mexico. Many Mexicans felt free to criticize, to express themselves, to organize without fear of repression.'[66] Echeverría was particularly active in the area of cinema. He put his brother Rodolfo in charge of the Banco Cinematográfico, which was immediately reformed. He founded the Mexican Cinemathèque, established a film school, the CCC (Centro de Capacitación Cinematográfica) and gradually increased the role of the state in production and exhibition. In 1971, the state funded five films and private producers seventy-seven films; in 1976 private producers funded only fifteen features, while the state's share had gone up dramatically to thirty-five features. The major studios, Churubusco and América were turned over to state cinema, and the first-run cinemas were required to screen Mexican films.

This modernization of the film industry was accompanied by the development of a new generation of film-makers who had trained in the 1960s and now found that they had financial backing for their projects. Arturo Ripstein's *El castillo de la pureza* (The Castle of Purity, 1972), Jaime

[66] Carlos Fuentes, *Tiempo mexicano* (Mexico, D.F., 1971), p. 166.

Hermosillo's *La pasión según Berenice* (The Passion According to Berenice, 1976) and *Matineé*, 1976, Felipe Cazal's *Canoa*, 1975, Paul Leduc's *Reed: México insurgente*, (Reed, Insurgent Mexico, 1970) and his documentary *Etnocidio: notas sobre el Mezquital* (Ethnocide: Notes on the Mezquital, 1976) and Marcela Fernández Violante's *De todos modos Juan te llamas* (Whatever You Do, It's No Good, 1975) were all successful feature films in Mexico and abroad. The set-back to this success was the lack of continuity in presidential policies from one *sexenio* to the next. President López Portillo (1976–82) put his sister Margarita in charge of the film industry and she effectively dismantled the Echeverría system. The state withdrew funding, or else supported unsuccessful and very costly international co-productions and the old producers returned offering a diet for the late seventies of sex comedies, mild pornography, strong language and violent gun-runners.

The Cuban state in the early seventies, in the aftermath of the Padilla affair, clamped down on intellectual and artistic diversity. It is sometimes argued that the film industry escaped these restrictions[67] but such an analysis fails to convince. This phase ended in 1975 when a Ministry of Culture was set up. The ICAIC became part of that Ministry, but although output increased the range of topics under discussion did not. Just as the Brazilian military had supported films on slavery and independence movements, so the black Cuban director Sergio Giral found official approval for a trilogy on slavery and slave rebellions: *El otro Francisco* (The Other Francisco, 1973), *Rancheador* (Slave Hunder, 1975) and *Maluala* (1979). At one level it can be argued that these films celebrate black insurrection, but they also demonstrate a sense of nationhood forged by black struggle, posit an unproblematic transculturation, and create a pantheon of heroic guerrillas, a useful iconography for a black population about to engage in a bloody war in Angola. Rather than talk about contemporary problems of race, ICAIC perferred to 'imagine' a community based on harmony. In general ICAIC worked predominantly in historical themes, leaving the present to be explored only fleetingly.

A film more sensitive to contemporary problems, *De cierta manera* (One Way or Another, 1974), was made by Cuba's only woman feature director to date, Sara Gómez who died of asthma before the final cut. The work was completed by Alea and García Espinosa. It deals quietly and sensitively with worker's responsibilities, with *machismo*, with the black popula-

[67] See in particular Michael Chanan's analysis in *The Cuban Image* (London, 1985).

tion and with the alienating effects of popular religion. The campaign for women's rights was taken up in Pastor Vega's *Retrato de Teresa* (Portrait of Teresa, 1970) which portrays the break-up of marriage as the wife is involved in the home, in factory work and in cultural activities which incur the wrath of her two-timing husband. Gender is more interestingly examined than race in the films of the 1970s and in this the films reflect the political and social imperatives of the time.

Experimentation in narrative was largely abandoned as there was a deliberate shift to capture a more 'popular' audience, using a more transparent style. Fornet has called this the 'nationalization of traditional genres, by giving them new progressive contents'.[68] Several Manichean, conventional films were made in this way: Manuel Pérez's *El hombre de Maisinicú* (The Man from Maisinicú, 1973) and *Río Negro* (1977), and Octavio Cortazar's, *El brigadista* (The Literacy Teacher, 1977). All these are macho adventure stories, where the good guys are revolutionary and the bad guys are counter-revolutionary. No other nuances are needed or offered. Gutiérrez Alea made a complex film, also about slavery, *La última cena* (The Last Supper 1976) and Humberto Solás and Octavio Goméz made experimental films in this period, but there was a great deal of mediocre, conventional, work and few signs of new blood in either directors or actors. The Revolution was growing older and more bureaucratic and tensions – both internal and external – were hampering creativity. Solás's *Cecilia,* made in 1981 and released a year later, seemed to bring together a number of different worries. An established director had spent an inordinate amount of ICAIC's yearly production budget on a hackneyed costume melodrama and an ageing superstar cast. The part of Cecilia Valdés demanded a betwitching actress in her teens or early twenties. Instead the part was given to Daisy Granados, a splendid actress, but a woman looking her forty-plus years. Changes were clearly in order.

In Colombia, Venezuela and Peru, the state led significant developments in film-making in the mid-1970s. In 1971 a 'ley de sobreprecios' or 'surcharge law' was passed to support Colombian film-making, it stipulated that a Colombian short film should accompany any new release in the country. These would be subsidized by offering producers a share of raised box office prices. Results in terms of quantity were spectacular. In 1974 two feature films were made through private investment, but ninety-four shorts appeared through the surcharge system. A number of these were of

---

[68] See Fornet's essay in P.A. Paranagua (ed.), *Le Cinéma Cubain* (Paris, 1990), pp. 92–6.

poor quality, but in general it can be said that the scheme created new independent film companies and gave directors and technicians valuable training. Some directors – Marta Rodríguez, Jorge Silva, Carlos Mayolo, Luis Ospina and Carlos Alvarez – had already made documentaries in the 1960s, but others such as Lisandro Duque, Jorge Ali Triana and Ciró Durán also benefited from these new conditions.

Government measures also looked to encourage feature films. Screen quotas were imposed for national films (twenty days in 1977 and thirty days in 1978). Colombia had the third largest cinema audience in Latin America after Brazil and Mexico (80 million spectators in 1984) and it was felt that a percentage of that market could help to make Colombian films economically viable. A film governing entity FOCINE (Compañía de Fomento Cinematográfico) was set up in 1978 to promote national cinema, financed by an 8.5 per cent levy on cinema tickets. At the outset it offered advance credits to film projects up to 70 per cent of total costs and also credits to buy film equipment and stock. But when loan payments were not made, FOCINE decided in 1983 to move into full-time production. The limitations and benefits of the system would be seen in the next decade.

During the sixties a lively film culture had grown up in Venezuela, with the work of Román Chalbaud and Clemente de la Cerda among others. In September 1968 the University of Mérida had sponsored a festival of Latin American documentary cinema in September 1968 which brought together work by Solanas, Sanjinés, Santiago Alvarez, Glauber Rocha and Tomás Gutiérrez Alea, and six months later, as a direct result of the festival, the Universidad de los Andes (ULA) had founded a documentary film centre, which became absorbed into a department of cinema. This department became an important training ground and also production centre throughout the 1970s, with established directors such as Carlos Rebolledo and Michael New. In 1975, perhaps prompted by the critical and commercial success of the Mexican Mauricio Wallerstein's *Cuando quiero llorar, no lloro* (When I Want to Cry, I Don't Cry, 1974) and Román Chalbaud's, *La quema de Judas* (Burning the Judas, 1974), the state began to support feature films and between 1975 and 1980, with oil revenues booming, the state financed twenty-nine features. It was also stipulated, through this period, that at least twelve Venezuelan films should be exhibited a year. For once exhibitors needed little encouragement since most film-makers adopted the strategy of making deliberately commercial, popular, films which would also contain elements of social protest.

Ramón Chalbaud's *El pez que fuma* (The Smoking Fish, 1977), Carlos Robeolledo and Thaelman Urgelles's *Alias: el rey del joropo* (The King of the Joropo Dance, 1978) and Clemente de la Cerda's *Soy un delincuente* (I'm a Criminal, 1976) are exemplary in this respect. In 1981, the Fondo de Fomento Cinematográfico (FOCINE) was established to consolidate this work.

In Peru the military government that came to power in 1968 decreed that Peruvian films should receive 'obligatory exhibition' in the country and since there were very few feature films, the documentary short became the favoured form. Over 150 production companies were set up to make films for this new exhibition space. As in Colombia quality varied, but a number of important film-makers all made significant documentaries in this period: Luis Figueroa, Federico García, Arturo Sinclair, Francisco Lombardi and Nora de Izcué. The investment in equipment and the growth of film making experience also inevitably led to the production of feature-length films. Indigenous themes were explored in Luis Figueroa's adaptations of the novel *Los perros hambrientos* (The Hungry Dogs, 1976) and *Yawar Fiesta* (Bloody Fiesta, 1980) and Federico García's *Kuntur Wachana* (Where the Condors are Born, 1977). 1977 also saw the first feature-length film by Francisco Lombardi, *Muerte al amanecer* (Death at Dawn) which was a great box-office success. At the end of the decade, therefore, Peruvian cinema was in a relatively healthy state.

## 1980S AND EARLY 1990S: FROM REDEMOCRATISATION TO NEO-LIBERALISM

The decade of the eighties began with cinema showing optimistic signs of growth. At the outset of the nineties there were fewer grounds for optimism, as most countries, in the cold neo-liberal wind, found investment in film a dispensable luxury. Throughout the decade, the economic problems were immense. All over the world cinema had to maintain a market share against the other attractions of the entertainment industry, in particular television and the new world of cable and satellite. In order to survive, Hollywood companies diversified and became part of conglomerate networks. This diversification was a hedge against losses which was a luxury that no Latin American film-maker could entertain, unless the state, in a few cases, was willing to pick up the tab. Cinema was maintained precariously, against a background of declining audience and the attractions of the new electronic media.

Television would prove to be a rival, rather than ally of cinema. The big media conglomerates, Globo in Brazil and Televisa in Mexico have successfully exported *telenovelas* throughout the world, but there is no tradition of commissioning feature films for television. In Brazil in 1981, 1792 films were shown on television; of these 88 were Brazilian (4.91 per cent of the total); of the 88, very few were quality Cinema Novo titles: they were in the main, *pornochanchadas*. Television would also increasingly become a place of work for film-makers unable to finance features or documentaries.

The strongest industries in the 1970s had been state-driven: Brazil, Mexico, Peru, Venezuela, Colombia and, in a different context, Cuba. For a time production remained strong in Brazil despite the economic crises and the dramatic fall in cinema audiences as the TV giant Globo increased its market share with successful game shows and, in particular, soap operas. Several Cinema Novo directors had untimely deaths – Glauber Rocha, Joaquim Pedro de Andrade and Leon Hirszman – but others such as Nelson Pereira dos Santos (*Memórias do cárcere,* 1984) and Ruy Guerra (*Erendira,* 1982, *Opera do malandro,* 1986) produced important work. Several women, Ana Carolina, Suzana Amaral and the Japanese-Brazilian Tizuka Yamasaki directed major features which were successful in the home market. Ana Carolina completed her trilogy of films begun in the 1970s with *Das Tripas Coração* (1982) and *Sonho de Valsa* (1987). Yamaski followed the success of *Gaijin* with *Parahyba, Mulher-Macho* (1983) and *Patriamada* (1985). Amaral successfully adapted Clarice Lispector's final novel *A Hora da Estrela* in 1985. Yet this model of state-funding was entering into crisis. Randal Johnson summed up the situation as follows: 'Embrafilme became the major source of production financing, creating a situation of dependence between the state and so-called 'independent' film-makers and in itself became a marketplace where film-makers competed against each other for the right to make films. This, in turn exacerbated tensions within the industry and created a situation in which the play of influences was often more important than the talent of the film-maker or the quality of the final product. As a consequence, public sector investments in the cinema lost social legitimacy. Brazilian President Fernando Collor de Mello's dismantling of Embrafilme in 1990, represented the *coup de grâce* to a poorly conceived and misguided policy of state support.'[69] However misguided the state support, it had at least sustained

---

[69] Randal Johnson, 'In the belly of the ogre', in *Mediating Two Worlds*, pp. 211–12.

film-makers for twenty years. Without this support, there was in the early 1990s a dramatic fall in production.

The same problems of clientelism and bureaucratic wranglings dogged the development of Colombia's film industry. Some directors of FOCINE were popular singers or boxing promoters. Even though FOCINE could boast in 1988, its tenth anniversary, of some 200 feature, medium length and short films including Mayolo's *La mansión de Araucaima* (The Mansion of Arucaima, 1986), Ospina's *Pura sangre* (Pure Blood, 1982), and Jorge Ali Triana's *Tiempo de morir* (A Time to Die, 1985), from 1986 it scarcely managed to offer any support in production or exhibition. Few directors were able to make more than one feature, especially after FOCINE withdrew from production in 1990. The state, it seemed, had no strategy for the 1990s. In its place, film-maker Sergio Cabrera proposed *La estrategia del caracol* ('The Strategy of the Snail', 1993), which, in January 1994, was on its way to becoming the biggest grossing box-office Colombian film of all time. In the first month of its release in Colombia it attracted an extraordinary 750,000 spectators, a figure that rivalled the year's audience for *Jurassic Park* in Colombia. The film tells of a group of tenants who share a large old house in the centre of Bogotá and are subject to imminent eviction. Their resistance, stage-managed by an old exiled Spanish anarchist, with the help of a lawyer outwits the yuppie tenament owner, his corrupt legal advisers and brutal henchmen. The narrative structure – the resourcefulness and unity of the people, the traditional *barrio*, in the face of rapacious modernity – has been a constant in Latin American cinema since the earliest times, but Cabrera offers a fresh and witty inflection which avoids the sentimentality of melodrama or of neo-realism or the triumphalism of sixties and seventies revolutionary optimism. Whether Cabrera offers an example that can be followed by other directors remain an open question.

The same financial setbacks can be seen in Peru, where only a handful of directors were able to make commerically viable films. The most successful was Francisco Lombardi, with *La cuidad y los perros* (The City and the Dogs, 1986) and *Boca de Lobo* (1988). Venezuela, on the other hand, maintained a relative stability despite the contraction of the economy after the mid-1980s. FOCINE offered credits and special incentives for 'quality' films. Exhibitors were also enticed by financial incentives. The support of the public meant that in the early 1980s, the large distribution chains Blancica and MDF had invested in production. The Universidad de los Andes also continued in co-production. In these conditions Diego Rísquez made a trilogy of films on the conquest and history of the New World, Fina Torres won the coveted Caméra d'Ort at Cannes with *Oriana* (1985) and veteran film-maker Román Chalbaud continued to make stylish thrillers up to *Cuchillos de fuego* (Flaming Knives, 1990). Solveig Hoogesteijn's *Macu, la mujer del policía* became a box office hit after its release in 1987. Perhaps the most interesting film on the theme of the *quinto centenario* was Luis Alberto Lamata's *Jericó* (1991), which explored the assimilation of a Dominican friar by an Indian group. Although in the early 1990s it lacked the resources of the early 1980s, Venezuelan cinema continued to have a modest yearly output.

Cuba reorganized the film sector in 1982. Julio García Espinosa became the minister responsible for cinema and he initiated policy changes: a marked increase in production, a reduced shooting budget and the introduction of new directors. As result the veterans allowed space for new film-makers who were more interested in contemporary issues and not afraid of comedy (the 1970s had been a particularly solemn period in film production). Orlando Rojas in *Una novia para David* (A Girl Friend for David, 1985) and *Papeles secundarios* (Secondary Roles, 1989), Rolando Díaz in *Los pájaros tirándole a la escopeta* (Tables Turned, 1984) and in particular Juan Carlos Tabío in *Se permuta* (House Swap, 1984), *Plaff* (1988) and most recently *Fresa y chocolate* (Strawberry and Chocolate, 1993), co-directed with Tomás Gutiérrez Alea, have cast a fresh eye on contemporary issues. Inventive work took place in animation, under the guidance of Juan Padrón, with *Vampiros en la Habana* (Vampires in Havana, 1985) and the series 'Elpidio Valdés' and 'Quinoscopios'. In 1987 these younger directors began to work in decentralized 'creative' groups under the direction of Tomás Gutiérrez Alea, Solás and Manuel Pérez, the most established film-makers in Cuba, who continued to make features throughout the decade. One important result of these 'creative' workshops was the group feature *Mujer Transparente* (Transparent Woman, 1990) which extended the discussions on gender issues in Cuba.

This attempt at decentralization and revival ran up against overwhelming economic pressures as the momentous changes in Eastern Europe undermined the economic (and increasingly the ideological) stability of Cuba. In the 1990s there was little finance available for film-making. Even though it is too early to have the picture clearly in focus it would seem that the 1990s has seen major ideological swings. Directors Sergio Giral and Jesús Díaz – whose *Lejanía* (Parting of the Ways, 1985) had been one of the most thoughtful films of the decade – went into exile, while Daniel Díaz Torres, the maker of *Alicia en el Pueblo de las Maravillas* (Alice in Wonderland, 1991), a mild critique of government policies, was forced into a humiliating recantation. The incident caused the dismissal of García Espinosa and nearly led to the shotgun marriage of ICAIC with the Institute of Radio and Television, (IRT), under the direction of the armed forces. Two years later *Alicia* was shown in international festivals and the Latin American International Film Festival in December 1993, set in Havana, gave its major award to the first ever open treatment of homosexuality in Cuban revolutionary cinema *Fresa y chocolate*. An independent film movement, grouped around the Hermanos Saiz Association, questioned the dominant orthodoxies. But the future remained unpredictable in the extreme.

The exile experience of Cubans – and it is estimated that over 10 per cent of Cuba's current population lives in exile – has received some attention in film. Several exiled film-makers have had successful careers in the United States. These include Orlando Jiménez Leal, one of the directors of the notorious *PM* of the early sixties, and in particular the late Nestor Almendros who became perhaps the world's most successful lighting cameraman. These cineastes and others became increasingly outspoken against the Revolution from the early eighties, especially in the aftermath of the *marielito* wave of exiles, and there appeared a trilogy of explicitly denunciatory documentaries *The Other Cuba* (1983) and *Improper Conduct* (1984), both directed by Jiménez Leal and Almendros and *Nobody Listens* (1988) directed by Almendros and Jorge Ulla, which dealt with the treatment of homosexuality and political prisoners by the regime. Jiménez Leal also directed a fictional comedy *El Super* (1980) on the Cuban American experience, made, as the credits reveal by 'the people who brought you the rhumba, the mambo, Ricky Ricardo, daiquiris, good cigars, Fidel Castro, cha-cha-cha, Cuban-Chinese restaurants plus the Watergate plumbers'. *El Super* follows the trials and tribulations of a Cuban tenement supervisor in Queens who dreams of returning to Cuba and, in the end, has to opt for Miami.

A younger generation of film-makers, born in Cuba but trained in the United States – León Ichaso, Ramón Menéndez, Miñuca Villaverde, Iván Acosta and Orestes Matacena – have tended to work on projects which are not specifically Cuban-American, but have a rather more *latino* focus, such as Menéndez's *Stand and Deliver* (1988). With an increased contact between the United States and Cuba possible in the 1990s, it remains to be seen if the younger generations across the disapora can enter into dialogues that might shake the fixed certainties of their parents' and grandparents' generations.

Cuba had always supported internationalism, giving shelter to exiled Latin American directors, hosting an international film festival and setting up a film school in 1985, but with a bankrupt economy and with little belief left in Latin America that 'new' cinema could be linked to 'revolutionary' or socialist change, this role became increasingly redundant. For a time the republics of Central America, going against the grain of history, picked up the revolutionary mantle from Cuba. The victory of the Frente Sandinista de Liberación Nacional (FSLN) in Nicaragua was captured in moving images by film-makers attached to the FSLN. The Sandinistas in power set up the Nicaraguan Film Institute (INCINE), based on Somoza's film production company, Producine. With scarce resources and with donations from other countries, a rudimentary film production was established in newsreels, documentary film, video and eventually in feature films. Work in video and in super-8 was most widespread due to the cost and difficulty in obtaining 16 and 35 mm film stock and to the need for processing film stock abroad. The then exiled Bolivian film-maker Alfonso Gumucio Dagrón ran a workshop in the techniques of super-8, which could be used by union activists. Longer documentaries included Ramiro Lacayo's *Bananeras* (Banana Workers, 1982) and Iván Arguello's *Teotacacinte 83* (1983) who also made the short feature *Mujeres de la Frontera* (Frontier Women) in 1986. Attempts to produce anything more ambitious, such as full length, co-produced features, largely ended in failure, apart from the Chilean Littin's *Alsino y el condor* (Alsino and the Condor, 1982), and even before the Sandinastas were voted out of power in 1990, INCINE was virtually bankrupt and film-makers were in bitter dispute about the best ways to apportion limited resources.

In El Salvador, the revolutionary struggles were recorded by Radio Venceremos, the communications organization of the FMLN in a series of documentaries, *Carta de Morazán* (Letter from Morazán, 1982), *Tiempo de audacia* (Time of Daring, 1983) and *Tiempo de Victoria* (Time of Victory, 1988), while in Guatemala, a few documentaries followed the vicissitudes of the civil war. In Costa Rica democratic governments supported documentary film-making from the mid-1970s, and independent producers and directors, such as Oscar Castillo could make the occasional feature, such as Castillo's *La Xegua* (1984), a melodrama about the greed and rapaciousness of colonizers. Patricia Howell also produced significant documentaries. In Panama, a state-led company, the Grupo Experimental de

Cine Universitario (GECU), made documentaries in the 1970s under Torrijos, but was forced to cut back under Noriega and after.

In the Caribbean islands, only Puerto Rico had what could be called a film movement. A critical, national documentary movement had been fostered by the Community Education Division of the government of Puerto Rico (DIVEDCO) from the 1950s, with over seventy documentaries, and by the 1980s several directors were working in feature films. The most successful of these was Marcos Zurinaga with *La gran fiesta* (The Gala Ball, 1986) and *Tango bar* (1988), both of which starred the late Raúl Julia, and Jacobo Morales's *Díos los cría* (God Makes Them, 1980) *Nicolás y lo demás* (Nicholas and the Others, 1983) and *Lo que le pasó a Santiago* (What Happened to Santiago, 1989), which portrayed the Puerto Rican middle class, its dilemmas and anxieties. In Haiti, exile film-makers such as Raoul Peck and Arnold Antonin could find occasional funding, whilst the Dominican Republic produced only one major fictional film in the 1980s: *Un pasaje de ida* (One Way Ticket, 1988) by Agliberto Meléndez.

In the wake of democratization in the 1980s, several countries that had suffered under dictatorship had a chance to express new cultural freedoms. Both Ukamau groups could make films in Bolivia in the 1980s. Eguino filmed *Amargo Mar* (Bitter Sea) in 1984 and Jorge Sanjinés followed the documentary *Banderas del amanecer* (Banner at Dawn, 1983) with the fictional *La nación clandestina* (The Secret Nation) in 1989. But funds remain limited and a director as well-known as Sanjinés took on average five years to put together co-production finance to make a feature length film. Other cineastes worked in video. Uruguayan film was slow to recover after the dictatorship, but boasted a very well-stocked and well run Cinemathèque. Chilean exiles continued to work in the 1980s – in particular the prolific Raúl Ruiz – but inside Chile some film-making also became possible in the 1980s, from clandestine documentaries by Littin and Gastón Ancelovici, to feature films by Silvio Caiozzi. After the victory of the democratic parties in November 1989 work slowly began to appear from exiled directors who had returned and from a younger generation brought up under the dictatorship. Whether their work is sustainable remains an open question.

The country to show the strongest revival in film culture after dictatorship was Argentina. The Radical government under Alfonsín (1983–9) abolished censorship and put two well-known film-makers Manuel Antín and Ricardo Wullicher in charge of the INC. Antín's granting of credits to young and established directors and his internationalist strategy had an immediate effect. For several years there was a great flowering of talent, a development that was halted temporarily in 1989 with an economy in ruins and with inflation running at an annual rate of 1,000 per cent. The swingeing neo-liberal reforms of the Menem government in the early nineties restored some confidence and the INC resumed the award of credits, with an income based on a percentage of ticket sales. However, very few films could recoup their costs in the home market and, after a fashionable few years in the mid-1980s – which culminated with the award of an Oscar to *La historia oficial,* directed by Luis Puenzo in 1986 – not many films found a place in international markets. The most visible and successful directors of the period were Luis Puenzo, Fernando Solanas and María Luisa Bemberg while a number of talented directors Sorín, Subiela, Mórtola, Felipelli, Beceyro, Pauls, Barney Finn, Doria, Fischerman, Kamin, Polaco, Pereira, Santiso, Tosso and Stantic made important films, but struggled to maintain a continuity in their work.

There has been a great heterogeneity of styles and themes in Argentine cinema that cannot adequately be surveyed in a brief history. Two general points, however, can be made. After so many years of persecution and censorship, the film-makers showed a great energy and inventiveness in exploring the medium. Secondly, many of the films produced focused directly or obliquely on the traumas of recent history. The conditions that gave rise to a militant cinema in the 1960s no longer existed: new movies were not a call to arms, but rather reflections on society's ills and conflicts. Solanas, for example, realized that films need not simply be didactic weapons, but should also be a source of pleasure, and his *Tangos, el exilio de Gardel* (Tangos, the Exile of Gardel, 1985) and *Sur* (South, 1989) treat political, Peronist, themes through an exciting blend of dance, music, choreography which contain hauntingly evocative images, an effect enhanced by the expert cinematography of Félix Monti, Argentina's most accomplished and innovative lighting cameraman. María Luisa Bemberg, in contrast, has provided Argentina's first sustained feminist viewpoint in a series of intelligent, and commercially viable features: *Señora de nadie* (No One's Woman, 1982), *Camila* (1984), *Miss Mary* (1986), *Yo la peor de todas* (I the Worst of All, 1990) and *De eso no se habla* (We Don't Talk about It, 1993). Her former producer, turned director, Lita Stantic made perhaps the most complex film about the dirty war, *Un muro de silencio* (A Wall of Silence, 1993), a success with the critics, but ignored by the Argentine public who preferred to view politics and repression through a gauze of melodrama and rock music as Marcelo Pineyro's *Tango feroz* (1993). What strategies film-makers should adopt to maintain the viability of their films in a shrinking domestic market is an acutely difficult question to answer.

The only country to reverse the trend towards the withdrawal of state support from the film industry and to resist the chill winds of the neo-liberal market economy has been Mexico. In 1988 Mexican cinema had suffered from over a decade of state neglect and rampant commercialism under the presidencies of José López Portillo (1976–82) and Miguel de la Madrid (1982–8). Some two hundred B-movies on drug trafficking were made in the 1980s, with extreme violence, light pornography or fomulaic comedy as the market leaders. By 1987, Mexican cinema had lost 45 per cent of its national audience and 50 per cent in the United States, which was a major source of income. Independent film-making survived, but the work of Leduc, Ripstein and Hermosillo was confined to university and art house circuits.

President Salinas de Gortari (1988–94) recognized the need to open state enterprises to privatization, as a precondition for entering NAFTA, but was also interested in cultivating the intellectual and artistic community which, for the film sector, implied state investment in cinema. The compromise, put into effect by the head of IMCINE Ignacio Durán, was to mix public and private sector funding. State bodies working in production (CONACINE), distribution (Azteca films) and exhibition (COTSA) were privatized and the closed-shop unions were forced to open up to competition from independent production companies. IMCINE embarked on a policy of co-financing films and the success and prestige of the ensuing films has attracted private Mexican capital and also investment from abroad.

The runaway success of the period was Alfonso Arau's *Como agua para chocolate* (Like Water for Chocolate, 1991) based on the best-selling novel by Arau's then wife, Laura Esquivel, who wrote the script. This became the largest grossing foreign-language film of all time in the United States and was shown throughout the world to similar acclaim.[70] While no other film could match this extraordinary exposure – unique in the history of Latin American cinema – the overall standard remained high and many new directors came to the fore. Six women directors made eight films between 1989 and 1993: the veteran Matilde Landeta, who made a comeback after forty years, Maryse Sistach, Busi Cortés, Dana Rotberg, Guita Schyfter and María Novaro. María Novaro followed *Lola* (1989) with a

[70] See 'An appetite for cinema con salsa', *Newsweek*, 24 January 1994, pp. 44–5.

film that also penetrated the world markets: *Danzón* (1991) which adhered to the 1930s and 1940s successful formulae of combining melodrama with music and dance. Danzón, a Caribbean dance rhythm, experienced, in the wake of the film, a major revival in Mexico City promoting the leading leading actress María Rojo to open a dance club, El Salón Mexico, named after a famous cabaret film of the 1940s. Other directors to capture a mood of popular nostalgia were José Buil in *La leyenda de una máscara* (The Legend of a Mask, 1989) a homage to the masked wrestlers of Mexico, the *lucha libre,* and Carlos García Agraz in *Mi querido Tom Mix* (My Beloved Tom Mix, 1991), where the local cinema, as in *Cinema Paradiso,* becomes the site for memories of a time and place when dreams could be shared by a community. Inside and outside the cinema, an old woman can evoke the cowboy legend of the silent screen, Tom Mix, to redress wrongdoings in the present.

Films have been made on a variety of themes, from historical, *quinto centenario* based works *Retorno a Aztlán* (Return to Aztlan, 1990), directed by Juan Mora Catlett and *Cabeza de Vaca* (1990) directed by Nicolás Echevarría, to post-modern yuppie comedies of manners. A young director, Alfonso Cuarón, for example, has made a modern bedroom farce about a young advertising executive, an energetic Lothario, who is led to believe, through a medical report faked by one of his many rejected conquests, that he has AIDS. *Sólo con tu pareja* (Love in the Time of Hysteria, 1991) manages successfully to make us laugh at our deepest fears. In the period from 1989–93, Mexican cinema was the most dynamic industry in Latin America. Mexico had not solved, however, the perennial problem of guaranteeing distribution and exhibition. The cinemas, in the hands of private capital, still block-booked Hollywood products and there arose the paradoxical situation that it was often easier to see Mexican films of this period in festivals and art cinemas abroad than in Mexico itself.

One hundred years on from the first visits of the Lumière agents to the region, cinema in Latin America retains the resilience that has been the hall-mark of film-makers throughout the region, who made and continue to make films against the odds. In a world of increased globalization, when the concept of national cinema itself is under threat, in a possible deregulated transnational world of signs and electronic impulses, in the current unstable political and cultural environment, there is still a generation of film-makers with an idea in the heads and a camera in their hands. Some still pursue the dream of a Latin American consciousness, others try to work within the nation, which remains the bed-rock for film-making, others still pursue co-productions with European or US companies and institutions as a way of financing an increasingly complex and, some argue, anachronistic endeavour. Gabriel García Márquez encapsulates the optimism for the future in his speech to Latin American film-makers and students in the mid-1980s: 'Between 1952 and 1955, four of us who are [here] studied at the Centro Sperimentale in Rome . . . The fact that this evening we are still talking like madmen about the same thing, after thirty years, and that there are with us so many Latin Americans from all parts and from different generations, also talking about the same thing, I take as one further proof of an indestructible idea.'[71]

[71] Quoted in *Anuario 88*, 1988, p. 1.

# 10

## LATIN AMERICAN BROADCASTING

### INTRODUCTION

On 27 August 1920 four Argentine medical students broadcast Wagner's *Parsifal* from the roof of the Coliseo theatre in Buenos Aires. The next day a newspaper observed that the twenty families who received the opera on their radio sets probably thought Wagner's divine music came directly from heaven. The transmission was one of the most important events in the cultural history of Latin America in the twentieth century. It marked the advent of broadcasting and the modern mass media in the region.

During the 1920s visionary pioneers introduced radio into almost every country in Latin America. Experimental broadcasts began in Mexico in 1921. N. H. Slaughter, a Westinghouse engineer, and two assistants installed the first radio transmitter in Brazil in 1922 on top of the Corcovado mountain overlooking Rio de Janeiro. At the exhibition grounds where the city was celebrating the hundredth anniversary of Brazilian independence, trumpet-shaped loudspeakers blasted out *O Aventureiro* from the performance of Carlos Gomes' opera *O Guarani* at the Teatro Municipal (as well as popular hits like *Yes, We have no Bananas*). Newspapers reported the reception was so good you could hear the audience applaud. A year later the first Brazilian radio station, equipped by Western Electric, went on the air with the motto: 'To work for the culture of those who live in our country and for the progress of Brazil'. Cuba also set up its first radio station in 1922 under the auspices of the International Telephone and Telegraph Company (IT&T). The conductor of the orchestra of the Cuban armed forces became an enthusiast of the new technology, and young literary figures like Alejo Carpentier contributed cultural broadcasts. In 1924 the Colombian government ordered equipment from the German company Telefunken to set up the country's first radio station. It took five years for the equipment to reach Colombia where it was installed in Puente Aranda. President Miguel Abadía Mendez inaugurated the station on 7 August 1929. Four months later a small commercial station began transmitting from the Colombian coastal city of Baranquilla. In Peru, President Augusto B. Leguía inaugurated the first Peruvian radio station, the Peruvian Broadcasting Company – its name was in English – on 20 June 1925. The transmitter was installed and mostly owned by the Marconi Company of England. Two years later the Peruvian Broadcasting Company went bankrupt in spite of an aggressive advertising campaign for the new technology and its own store selling radio receivers. The Marconi Company, also owners of the Peruvian Telegraph and Postal Service, took over the failed station and ran it under government supervision.

The introduction of radio in the 1920s was a turning point in the cultural history of Latin America. It would be a mistake, however, to think that Latin America had no communication media before the advent of radio broadcasting. Argentina, for example, where 345 newspapers were published in 1885, had a large urban audience for popular weekly magazines like *Consejero del Hogar* (1903), *Mundo Argentino* (1911) and *Atlantida* (1918). Other Latin American countries had well-developed domestic newspapers and magazines (as well as, in some cases, nascent film industries) by the turn of the century.

Latin America had not been far behind Europe and the United States in the introduction of the modern printing technologies. By 1889 *O Estado de São Paulo* was using a Marinoni printing press, and before the end of the century the owner of Chile's largest newspaper, *El Mercurio,* had travelled to New York to study the commercial organization, administration, distribution and subscription services of *The New York Herald.* In the first decade of the twentieth century newspapers throughout the continent like Peru's *El Comercio* and *La Prensa* acquired modern printing presses and linotypes allowing them to print large editions quickly and efficiently.

This chapter, however, is mainly about broadcasting, both radio and television, the truly *mass* media. The Latin American newspapers and magazines of the early twentieth century scarcely compared with what by the second half of the century would become the sprawling Latin American radio and television conglomerates with their mass appeal and national audiences. The print media never achieved the audience size or economic weight of radio and television. Their development, moreover, was highly uneven, both within and among countries. Whereas Argentina, for example, had a flourishing newspaper and publishing industry in 1930, Venezuela had only four capital-city newspapers: *La Religion* (1890), *El Universal* (1909), *El Heraldo* (1922) and *La Esfera* (1927). As late as 1935, 90 per cent of the Venezuelan population was illiterate, a situation shared by other, poorer countries of Central and South America. By the Second World War, far less than half of the inhabitants of most Latin American countries could read. Illiteracy slowed the spread of books, newspapers and magazines, just as the lack of electricity and dispersed rural populations in most countries until well after the war slowed the growth of mass audiences for films. The first Latin American films were seen by small publics with access to urban cinemas. Film industries, moreover, were concentrated in the larger, richer countries, notably Mexico, Argentina and Brazil.

Thus, most early Latin American newspapers and magazines can not be considered mass media. They appealed to relatively small, elite audiences. Their sales were direct, without the vast expenditures in advertising that fuelled the growth of commerical broadcasting. At the same time, the early twentieth-century broadcasting media lacked the scales of production, mass marketing and integration with other sectors of the economy that characterize the modern culture industries. They were quantitatively and qualitatively different from the mass media the now occupy so much of the leisure time of Latin Americans.

By the early 1980s, sixty years after the first radio broadcast, Latin America was spending nearly US$4.5 billion annually on advertising. Brazil, Mexico and Argentina were among the twenty largest advertising markets in the world. By 1990 radio had achieved close to 100 per cent coverage of Latin America. It had the largest audience of any communication medium in the region, and every country reported many stations – almost 3,000 in Brazil alone – the vast majority privately owned and commercially operated. In 1991 there were about 164 million radio receivers in Latin America, one for every 2.7 inhabitants. The number of television sets, not introduced until the 1950s, had reached almost 75 million, one for every six inhabitants. Moreover, despite the heterogeneous origins of the Latin American mass media, fifty or so years on it was possible to read the same news, listen to the same music, watch the same soap opera and see the same advertisements for the same products in practically every country of the region.

## RADIO IN THE 1920S AND 1930S: THE ORIGINS OF MASS BROADCASTING

In most Latin American countries the growth of commercial radio coincided with the development of national industries and fulfilled their need for an advertising medium to reach new urban markets, swelled by an influx of migrants from the countryside looking for factory jobs. It was also, as the Colombian scholar Jesús Martín Barbero reminds us, a time of new 'nationalism, based on the idea of a national culture, which would be the synthesis of different cultural realities, and a political unity bringing together cultural, ethnic and regional differences'.[1] Radio provided a vehicle for musicians and entertainers with national appeal and offered both information and amusement to the growing urban workforce. By the end of the 1930s, radio no longer consisted of many small amateur stations, and commercial radio networks had formed all over the region.[2]

Barbero has examined the role of the mass media in the constitution of a national 'imaginary' in Latin America. He identifies a first stage in the development of the media and the constitution of mass culture – from the 1930s to the end of the 1950s – when 'the decisive role of the mass media was their ability to convey the summons of populism, turning the masses into the people and the people into the Nation . . . The cinema in most countries and radio in all gave the people of the different regions and provinces their first taste of the Nation.'[3] The 1930s were a watershed for the decisions on what type of broadcasting system the countries of Latin America would adopt: state-owned or private, educational or commercial. Although some governments at first set up state-owned stations, by the end of the decade, often without an explicit policy formulation, private, commerical broadcasting, in many cases already linked to the growing commercial radio networks in the United States, was firmly established throughout the region.

---

[1] Jesús Martín Barbero, *Communication, Culture and Hegemony: From the Media to Mediations* (London, 1993), p. 153.

[2] A study by Robert W. McChesney shows a similar process in the United States of small non-profit and amateur stations giving way to the commercial radio networks. 'There was little sense prior to 1927, however, that private control meant broadcasting should be dominated by networks, guided solely by the profit motive, and supported by advertising revenues. Indeed, in several important respects, the nature of U.S. broadcasting prior to 1927 was markedly different from the system that would emerge by the end of the decade.' *Telecommunications, Mass Media and Democracy* (Oxford, 1993), p. 14.

[3] Barbero, *Communication, Culture and Hegemony*, p. 164.

*Mexico*

In Mexico the first two decades of media development were a time of considerable state interest in the promotion of national culture and education, the result of the social reforms and nationalist aims of the revolution, including the cultural and economic integration of Mexico's vast Indian populations. After 1910, the Mexican state encouraged the growth of national literature, art, cinema and other forms of expression. The Mexican state used culture and the media to promote a sense of national unity and identity. The state paid for the murals painted on the walls of government buildings and owned the country's principal film studios, most cinemas and the bank financing most films. Despite the revolutionary government's interest in the promotion of national education and culture, however, the Mexican state paid scant attention to the new broadcasting technologies. In 1922 the government authorized the first commercial broadcasting licenses, and Mexican newspaper publishers owned many of the early radio stations. There was, however, some effort to establish a public or state-owned broadcasting sector. In 1924 the Mexican government set up a radio station in the Ministry of Education. By 1931 President General Pascual Ortiz Rubio reported that the Office of Cultural Broadcasting had broadcast 6,785 cultural events and lectures and 726 concerts. President Lázaro Cárdenas (1934–40) donated a radio receiver to every agricultural and workers' community to enable them to listen to the courses, book reviews, and concerts transmitted by three state radio stations – one broadcasting from the Ministry of Education and two from the offices of the Partido National Revolutionario (PNR), the ruling party. Mexican public broadcasting did not survive for long, however. By 1932 there were ten commercial stations in Mexico City and twenty stations in cities in the interior of the country. Many were clustered along the northern border for an audience already accustomed to receiving radio broadcasts from the United States. The private radio stations' substantial advertising revenues allowed them to finance live comedy, dramas, folk music, sports events and the enormously popular radio novelas, the Latin America soap operas. In 1930 Emilio Azcárraga, a distributor of the Radio Corporation of America (RCA) in Mexico had inaugurated the radio station XEW, 'The Voice of Latin America'. The station was affiliated with RCA's radio network, the National Broadcasting Company (NBC). In 1938, XEW had fourteen affiliates. Another of Azcárraga's stations, XEQ, affiliated with the Columbia Broadcasting System (CBS) radio network in the United States, soon expanded to seventeen affiliated stations.

## Argentina

In Argentina, the high levels of print media consumption per capita in the 1920s and 1930s had been the result of the early growth of a literate urban middle class and the economic prosperity of the nation. The urban consolidation of Buenos Aires also facilitated the precocious expansion of private broadcasting, allowing stations to reach the dense urban markets with little investment in transmitters. In 1923 the Ministry of the Navy issued five radio licences to private radio stations in the capital serving an audience of 60,000 radio sets. The administration of the radio licences was passed in 1928 to the Ministry of the Post and Telegraph which enacted the first law regulating private, public and amateur radio stations. Ten years later, there were forty-two radio stations spanning the country, many of them affiliated with one of two commerical radio networks.

## Brazil

The earliest Brazilian radio stations were not commercially operated, although they were privately owned. After the first transmission from the Corcovado mountain, Professor E. Roquette-Pinto and Henry Moritze, the director of the National Observatory, asked the government for one of the two 500 watts Western Electric radio transmitters imported for telegraph services. Their station, Radio Sociedad do Rio de Janeiro, was inaugurated in 1923 as a cultural and educational station set up as a member-supported club. Other early Brazilian radio stations adopted the form of associations or clubs financed by their members. The government, however, taxed the radio stations and their audiences with fees on stations and receivers. Most of the first stations were cultural and educational and directed their broadcasts toward an elite audience. Radio grew slowly under this system. Although stations sometimes used different forms of indirect commercial sponsorship for their programmes, advertising was not allowed until after 1932 when new legislation changed the legal definition of broadcasting to allow for commerical activity. Even after 1932 government regulations hampered radio's commercial expansion, especially that of smaller stations. Only the larger stations were able to comply with the complicated rules and obligations governing their activities.

Despite its slow growth, Brazilian radio played a key role in the political events that changed the country in the early 1930s. By then radio had become an important vehicle for popular recording stars, sports events, comedy shows, news and political debates. The Brazilian stations broadcast the election campaigns of Julio Prestes and Getúlio Vargas in 1929–30. During the Constitutionalist Revolution of 1932 student demonstrators in São Paulo seized the studios of the radio station Record and aired a manifesto in favor of 'Liberty for Brazil and for the Constitution'. The broadcasts of Radio Record became a symbol of the political struggles of the population of São Paulo.

Brazilian radio shed most of its early cultural and educational roots over the first decades of its development. Commercial radio grew, often in association with domestic newspaper chains. By 1938 the radio network owend by Assis Chateaubriand's Diarios e Emmissoras Associadas had five radio stations, twelve newspapers and a magazine. Other early radio chains has been formed by the Carvalho group, Radio Bandeirantes, and Roberto Marinho of the *O Globo* newspaper. Brazil's push towards industrialization and import substitution during the 1930s and 1940s, especially during the Estado Novo (1937–45), stimulated the growth of commerical radio as well as popular entertainment and mass advertising.

*Peru*

Peru, like Mexico a country with a large Indian population, underwent a period of social ferment and national cultural redefinition and reform in the 1920s and 1930s. The Alianza Popular Revolucionaria Americana (APRA) founded by Víctor Raúl Haya de la Torre in 1924, rejected foreign political, cultural and social models. Soon after, José Carlos Mariátegui founded the Peruvian Socialist Party with a programme for Peruvian culture which recognized the central role of indigenous cultural forms in national development and identity. Peruvian radio stations, however, did not take part in the nationalist movements for cultural reform since no Peruvian radio station went on the air until 1935, ten years after the ill-fated establishment of the Peruvian Broadcasting Company by President Leguia in 1925. By 1935, however, the many Peruvians owning radio receivers had turned to foreign shortwave broadcasts like Radio Colonial of the French government, the General Electric station of New York and Spanish and German-language broadcasts from Radio Berlin.

## Colombia

Colombian radio made up for its relatively late birth in 1929 by growing rapidly after 1931 when a Liberal president changed the tax system to make commercial operations of radio stations profitable. Using a formula particular to Colombia, later applied to television, radio became a publi-private hybrid. The Colombian government franchised time slots on state-owned radio stations to private companies who in turn exploited them commercially by selling advertising time. Commercial and amateur radio stations proved useful to the Colombian government in 1932 by providing communication services during Colombia's war with Peru. And stations served the needs of the Colombian economy in the 1930s, a period of rapid industrialization and urbanization. In 1935, for example, Colombian manufacturers of tobacco products, textiles, beer, foodstuffs, and pharmaceutical companies grouped together to set up a large regional radio station on which they could advertise their products. Many owners of Colombian radio station were distributors of foreign-made radio sets like Telefunken, RCA and Philips. Colombia had seventeen stations registered in 1934, forty-four in 1939, and seventy in 1941.

## Chile

Although the Chilean state undertook the expansion of the national education system and supported arts and culture like the national symphony and opera, the government in Chile did not subsidize the nascent mass media during the 1930s. Left on its own without government subsidies or state ownership, Chilean broadcasting developed a commercial character early on, catering to the demands and tastes of the newly forming urban markets. The small Chilean market, however, could not sustain the high costs of national productions and soon turned to the cheaper, imported books, serials and records for its content. Ownership was both domestic and foreign. The foreign mining companies and the national agricultural association owned the largest radio chains. Radio's listeners were consumers, radio's content was banal; neither serious news nor culture was its responsibility.

## Uruguay

In Uruguay, early state interest in the mass media was part of overall national educational and cultural policies. Uruguay was a prosperous, politically stable country in the 1930s, and the state could afford to finance the media and the arts as well as many other public services for its small, urban middle-class population. In 1929 the Uruguayan state set up a non-commercial public broadcasting service, SODRE (Servicio Oficial de Difusión Radio Electrical) with one publicly financed shortwave and two medium-wave frequencies. In addition to broadcasting, SODRE's activities included the National Symphony Orchestra, the Uruguayan National Ballet, and a film club operating in its own cinema. The Uruguayan state, however, did not limit the growth of private commercial media. Economic prosperity and the high educational level of the population made it possible for many small commercial radio stations as well as newspapers to build audiences attractive to advertisers and finance their operations with commercials. There were soon over twenty radio stations in Montevideo supported solely by advertising.

## Cuba

The development of radio in Cuba was limited by presidential decree through most of the 1920s. Until the early 1930s, Cuban radio was run by amateurs with mainly cultural and educational programming. In 1934, however, with the repeal of the Platt Amendment, Cuba's relationship with the United States changed radically. U.S. manufactured products poured into the Cuban markets, and the previous regulations restricting the commerical use of radio were lifted. Radio became an advertising vehicle for the new consumer goods, and its commerical expansion began.

By the end of the 1930s, radio was well established in most of the important cities of Latin America. It had become the main vehicle for the growth of the popular music industry and for radio comedians and entertainers in the major urban areas. Thanks to radio, the recordings of Mexican, Argentine and Caribbean artists were known throughout the continent. In 1935, for example, when Argentine tango idol Carlos Gardel was killed in an air crash in Medellín, Colombia, the same medium that had made him famous broadcast the news of this death direct from the scene of the crash at Las Playas Airport. It was one of the first live radio news programmes in the region.

Latin America radios stations were also beginning seriously to compete with newspapers as a news and advertising medium. Newspaper owners in some countries had tried to stop radio announcers from reading newspapers over the air on their news programmes. In Colombia, for example, Decree 627 of 23 March 1934 (confirmed by Decree 2081 of 28 October 1939) prohibited radio stations from reading the national dailies over the air until twelve hours after their publication. An editorial in *El Tiempo*, one of the leading newspapers, welcomed the measure, calling radio an imbecile invention of the devil that filled the home with cheap ads, old records and bad jokes.[4] Faced with the competition from the new technology, however, newspapers like *O Globo* in Brazil set up their own radio stations, paving the way for the future media conglomerates that would characterize the region.

RADIO COMES OF AGE: THE 1940S AND 1950S

As radio stations grew they inevitably began to come into contact with powerful national and international interests, not the least of which were the U.S. commercial radio networks, advertising agencies and equipment manufactures eager to invest in Latin America and develop markets for their products. In many countries, without state protection and subsidies, the national culture industries were unable to compete with cheaper media imports from larger countries of the region or from the United States. Foreign capital and foreign recorded music and radio programmes flowed into Latin American broadcasting. CBS set up the Cadena de las Americas, NBC operated the Cadena Panamericana with affiliated radio stations in most countries of the region. Other foreign companies also entered Latin American broadcasting. The Sydney Ross pharmaceutical company established one of the earliest radio networks in Colombia; in Chile three U.S. mining companies operated their own commerical radio network.

During the Second World War, U.S. interest in the Latin American media increased. The Office of the Coordinator of Inter-American Affairs (OCIAA) under Nelson Rockefeller, worked to ensure a pro-United States content to Latin American broadcasting and in Latin American newspapers. The Press Division of the OCIAA furnished news and features to over

[4] *El Tiempo*, 24 March 1934.

1,000 Latin American newspapers, magazines and radio stations during the war. News was transmitted by shortwave radio (for the first time the U.S. government set up direct international shortwave broadcasting facilities), by the distribution of feature articles, news photographs, pamphlets and cartoons, and by the publication of a magazine, *En Guardia*. The Radio Division produced its own programmes and worked with private broadcasters to promote the NBC and CBS local affiliate chains in Latin America. The Radio Division brought directors of Latin American radio stations, radio engineers and artists to the United States to study production techniques and dramatic arts. Similarly, the Motion Picture Division production and distributed its own films and co-operated with film companies like Walt Disney Productions to produce and distribute newsreels and films in Latin America. Other OCIAA programmes worked to maintain the level of advertising by U.S. companies in the pro-Allied Latin American media and the supply of newsprint to friendly publishers. The activities had a profound effect on the development of the Latin American media. For the first time U.S. news services became widely used in the region, U.S. motion pictures were broadly available and without competition, and U.S. radio programming and news were routinely aired by local stations.

Latin American governments were also beginning to take a closer look at the growing mass media. With close to 50,000 radio receivers in Rio de Janeiro alone in 1933, Brazilian radio stations had become a force to be reckoned with. By this time private companies operating national radio networks had replaced many of the early radio clubs and associative forms of ownership. During the Civil War of 1932 Brazilian radio had already been subjected to government censorship. The federal government allowed radio stations to report only on the movements and advances of the 'legalistas'. From the first days of the Estado Novo (1937) until 1945, Getúlio Vargas used radio to maintain his power. In 1939 he set up the Department of Information and Press (DIP) in charge of the government information's image, media censorship, and the distribution of public funds to the private media. The activities of the DIP, especially in relation to radio, had the dual purposes of controlling information, news and public opinion; and promoting Brazilian culture, morals and values. The National Radio of Brazil, already the leading radio station in Rio de Janeiro, was taken over by the Vargas government in 1940, and in 1942 it began nationwide shortwave broadcasts. Under Vargas, Radio Nacional received state financing to purchase the latest equipment and provide professional training for its staff. Using music and humorous programmes combined with government propaganda and information programmes like 'Hora do Brasil', the powerful shortwave facilities of the National Radio 'integrated' the enormous, culturally disperse nation and imbued it with a national identity. In addition to its own direct transmissions, daily broadcasts of 'Hora do Brasil' were obligatory for all Brazilian radio stations between 8:00 and 9:00 pm. Radio Nacional co-produced radio programmes with U.S. radio networks CBS, NBC, and the Mutual Broadcasting System under a programme promoted by Roosevelt's Good Neighbor policy.[5] Despite Vargas' authoritarian control of radio through direct ownership and political censorship – in a six-month period between December 1942 and August 1943, the DIP reported 2,256 incidents of censorship of the words of songs and 1,088 incidents of censorship of recordings of radio programmes[6] – there was, however, little regulation of the commercial operations of the new broadcasting technologies. For many years the only legislation governing commercial radio was Decree 20,047 (1931), promulgated almost ten years after the appearance of the first Brazilian radio stations, which gave the state the right to regulate broadcasting services considered in the national interest and Decree 21,111 (1932), which set up a broadcasting licensing procedure defining the rights and responsibilities of licence holders.

In the early 1940s the powerful Argentine commercial radio stations formed three privately owned national networks: Radio El Mundo, Radio Belgrano, and Radio Splendid. The Argentine media, including radio, films, magazines and newspapers, were strongly nationalist and had little of the foreign content and investment that marked the media in many other countries. And they could afford to be so; the Argentine market was big enough to support the domestic media. Moreover, the pro-Axis stand of Argentina during most of the Second World War limited U.S. investment in broadcasting and slowed the flow of Hollywood films and U.S. music to the country. After the war, the populist government of Juan Perón from the mid-1940s determined much of the future course of the Argentine media. Perón protected national media production, defended Argentine national culture, and supported the unions of media workers.

---

[5] During this same period, a daily newscast called 'Reporter Esso,' based on news about the Second World War, was sponsored by Esso Standard Oil and distributed by the United Press. It was aired on many Brazilian radio stations.

[6] Sonia Virgíana Moreira, 'Radio, DIP e Estado Novo: a práctica radiofónica no govêrno Vargas', unpub. paper, 1992.

He also censored films, radio, plays, books, magazines and television. After a period of harassment and censorship, the Perón administration nationalized the three private radio networks by forcing their owners to sell them to the government at reduced prices. (In one case, Perón returned a network to the management of its original owners under close government supervision.) Perón placed much of the Argentine press in the hands of his supporters. In 1951, after a long and bitter struggle with director Alberto Gainza Paz, Perón expropriated *La Prensa,* one of the few remaining independent daily newspapers in the country. Exiled Argentine politicians had to resort to broadcasts to their supporters on radio stations across the border in Uruguay.

The Paraguayan military already controlled the government-owned radio stations when it seized power in 1940. General Higinio Morínigo (1940–47), in clear sympathy with nazi-fascism in Europe, used government radio to advance his authoritarian and nationalist aims and placed drastic curbs on private radio stations. The National Department of Propaganda, created in 1944, heavily censored domestic radio and introduced official government licensing of radio announcers. Under General Adolfo Stroessner after 1954 Radio Nacional del Paraguay became the voice of the presidency and required that all private radio stations broadcast its news programme twice a day.

In other countries of the region also ruled by strong-handed governments like Peru – General Manuel Odría (1948–56) – the commerical expansion of radio was given a free rein. Peruvian Radio suffered government censorship, but its growth was unfettered by an real state intervention affecting its management or ownership. Venezuela, also under military rule except for three years between 1945 and 1948, likewise experienced considerable commercial growth of radio broadcasting with no real state regulation or intervention. In Cuba, unrestricted by state regulation of commercial activities, the domestic broadcasting industry, allied with U.S. investors, brought the number of radio stations in the country by the early 1950s to 156. Cuba had the highest level of radio listenership and national programming of any country in Latin America. Two rival radio chains, RHC Cadena Azul with the support of Procter and Gamble and CMQ, later owned by the Mestre Brothers with support from NBC, dominated the Cuban market. CMQ became one of the first exporters of radio *novelas* to Latin America.

In Colombia, on 9 April 1948, Jorge Eliecer Gaitán, a leading popular Liberal politician, was gunned down in the streets of Bogotá. In the riots that followed, numerous radio stations throughout the country, including the state-owned stations, were taken over by left-wing sympathizers who attempted to direct popular outrage and resentment against the government into a revolutionary movement. They almost succeeded. When the government forces regained control of the country, they imposed a state of siege, revoking all existing radio licences and altering the existing radio legislation to bring commercial radio firmly under government control, restricting news and political reporting. (In 1936, with the support of national industrialists, Colombia's private radio station owners had defeated a bid by President Alfonso Lopez Michelson to nationalize radio.) After 1948 Colombian commercial radio continued to grow, forming networks with close ties with industry, advertising agencies and powerful domestic political groups. It never again, however, played a direct role in popular mobilization or politics.

Despite the considerable government censorship of Latin American radio at the time of its most vigorous commercial expansion, the 1940s and 1950s produced innovative, authentic and widely successful Latin American radio programmes. Latin American radio novellas from Mexico, Argentina and Cuba (for example *El Derecho de Nacer* by the Cuban writer Felix Caignet) and many others mesmerized the growing urban populations. Radio broadcasts of boleros, tangos, and rancheras swept Latin America from the Mexican border to the back streets of Buenos Aires, and radio personalities became famous at home and abroad. In 1941 the sponsor of the first Brazilian soap opera, *Em Busca de Felicidad* received 48,000 letters in the first month of an advertising campaign promising photographs of the stars and a summary of the plot in return for a toothpaste box top.

Pressures from both domestic and foreign industries to use broadcasting as a vehicle to reach mass markets for their products converged to make a docile commercial broadcasting system under the political control of the government attractive both to the private sector and the state. In this respect, the role of broadcasting in the region differed sharply from that of newspapers, which often played a far more polemical political role – and probably less important role as an advertiser – identifying closely with the different political parties and currents.

THE INTRODUCTION OF TELEVISION:
THE 1950S AND 1960S

Latin America in the 1990s has two of the largest private commercial television systems in the world: Mexico's Televisa and Brazil's TV Globo.

Both systems from part of highly diversified multimedia conglomerates. Born soon after the Second World War, the parent companies of both Televisa and TV Globo cover all aspects of production, sales and distribution of television, video, film radio and recordings for their vast domestic markets and considerable foreign sales. The Televisa and TV Globo models are present in practically every country of Latin America with the exception of Cuba. Television's introduction and growth in the region showed a number of similar patterns.

### Mexico

When television technologies appeared on the horizon in Mexico, in contrast with what occurred with radio a quarter of a century earlier, little thought was given to setting up a public or state-owned cultural television system. As early as 1945 the owners of Mexican commercial radio networks XEW, affiliated with NBC, and XEQ, affiliated with CBS, began to push for the introduction and development of commercial television. In 1950 Mexico became the sixth country in the world to establish commercial television. Under President Miguel Alemán Valdés (1946–52), the Mexican government rejected the idea of setting up a state-owned television system modeled after the British Broadcasting Corporation (BBC). President Alemán gave the powerful Mexican private media the first licences to operate commercial television channels and remained an enthusiastic supporter of commercial television, developing personal ties with the television industry. His son later became the president of Televisa.

The first of three channels, Channel 4, was awarded to Rómulo O'Farril, the owner of the daily newspaper *Novedades* in Mexico City. Its first broadcast was President Alemán's state of the union address in 1950. Channel 2 was awarded to Emilio Azcárraga, owner of the two largest radio networks in the country. Channel 5 was given to Gonzalez Camerena, a former engineer of Azcárraga. In 1955, after a brief period of competition, the three channels joined to form one company, Telesistema Mexicano, including a production company to export television programmes to other Latin American countries. By 1959 Telesistema Mexicano operated twenty television channels throughout the country. There was no state or government television channel until 1958 when the Ministry of Education was awarded a small non-commercial channel.

Most of the original equipment for television production and transmission used in Mexico was imported from the United States as were feature films and dubbed U.S. television series. Except for assigning frequencies and limiting direct ownership of television channels to Mexican nationals, there was little government regulation of the new medium. Until 1970 the state made no real attempt to exert any influence over the content or operations of commercial television, although they probably had the leverage to do so as the growth of the commercial television networks was made possible by massive state investments in the national telecommunication infrastructure.

## Brazil

Assis Chateaubriand, a newspaper and radio magnate, was awarded the first licence for a Brazilian television station, TV Tupi in São Paulo, in 1950. The next year he followed with TV Tupi of Rio de Janeiro. Soon after, other companies started TV channels: TV Paulista, TV Continental, TV Rio, and TV Excelsior in Rio and São Paulo. (Channels in Brasília, the new capital from 1960, and in the interior of the country came later.) There was no national plan in the distribution of the channels, and the licences often were awarded as political favours. One of the first television advertisement was produced in 1952 by the U.S. agency J. Walter Thompson for the Ford Motor Company and aired on Telenoticias Panar of TV Tupi in São Paulo. The same agency, working for Ford, sponsored the transmission of the first U.S. television series dubbed into Portuguese.

Despite the rapid growth of the Brazilian economy during the presidency of Juscelino Kubitschek (1956–61) as a result of a programme of import substitution, industrialization and the inflow of foreign capital, television grew slowly. It was considered an urban-based, elite and economically weak medium under considerable foreign influence. Brazilian television services were limited mainly to the urban centres of Rio de Janeiro and São Paulo. There were no facilities for interconnection; each station broadcast a similar fare or mixture of dubbed, imported series and locally produced live programmes. The arrival of video technologies in 1959 enabled the largest television station of the time, Diarios Associados, to film its productions and transmit them on all affiliates. This technological advance ended many of the live, local transmissions and marked the beginning of the national integration of the Brazilian television networks. By then there were 600,000 sets in the country, and the new medium was beginning to attract significant amounts of advertising. Diarios Associados dominated Brazilian television until the mid-1960s. In 1962, however, Globo had signed an agreement with Time-Life which was to provide an injection of capital, technology and professional skills. TV Globo went on the air in January 1965 and quickly became the main force in Brazilian television.

### Argentina

During the administrations of Juan Perón in Argentina between 1946 and 1955, the Peronists achieved an almost total monopoly of newspapers by forcing their owners to sell to supporters of the regime. Likewise, radio owners were obliged to sell their stations to the state to be run commercially by individuals close to the president. Perón introduced television in 1951. The year before he had sent Jaime Yankelevich, a close supporter and former owner of Radio Belgrano, to the United States to purchase equipment for Channel 7. Yankelevich returned with six used cameras, bought at a discount, and promised to get them in working order. There were 7,000 television sets in Argentina in 1951; two years later there were 40,000. Only one Argentine television channel was in operation until the fall of Perón in 1955, when the military regime that overthrew Perón ended the state monopoly of radio and television and tossed the Peronists out of broadcasting. For the next eighteen years all persons who had held positions in Perón's administration or who claimed allegiance to Perón could not appear in any media as producer, technician, writer or actor.

The Argentine military returned newspapers to their former owners but held on to the radio stations. Three years after seizing power and three days before turning it over to an elected government in 1958 the military awarded licences to operate Channel 9, Channel 11, and Channel 13 in Buenos Aires; Channel 7 in Mendoza; and Channel 8 in Mar del Plata. By the time the new private channels went on the air in 1960 there were 850,000 television receivers in Argentina. Argentine law prohibited foreign ownership of television channels; foreign capital, however, entered by forming production companies associated with the private channels. From the start, Goar Mestre, owner of television channels in Cuba before the 1959 revolution, co-owned PROARTEL, the production company of Channel 13, along with CBS and Time-Life. (In addition to PROARTEL, Mestre had other investments in Peruvian and Venezuelan commercial television.) Channel 11 of Buenos Aires had a similar relation with ABC. Channel 9 set up its programming company with NBC. Argentine law also prohibited television networks. The three Buenos Aires stations got around this by affiliating their production companies with stations in the interior of the country. By 1970, PROARTEL had seventeen affiliates.

In order to attract foreign capital the military and civilian governments that followed Perón authorized the free transfer of earnings and capital of foreign companies in Argentina. Between 1958 and 1959 foreign investment in the country jumped from about eight million dollars to over 200 million. Foreign investors and advertisers changed the face of the Argentine media. Television series, magazines and comic books imported from the United States and Mexico replaced Argentine productions, swelling the exodus of Argentine artists and writers which followed the media ban on Perón's supporters.

In 1973 Perón was reelected President of Argentina. His second administration coincided with the expiration of the television licences awarded by the military in 1958 for 15 years. Instead of awarding new licences, or renewing existing ones, Perón nationalized Argentine television. Calling television 'a vital element for Argentine culture and for the spiritual values of the nation', he expropriated the equipment, buildings and furniture of the private production companies and placed new directors in the nationalized channels. Television content, however, continued much the same, and for three years, until a military coup over threw the Peronist administration in 1976, the three government channels broadcast in the midst of economic chaos, uncertainty and corruption.

## Colombia

Colombian television was born in 1954 under the military dictatorship of General Gustavo Rojas Pinilla. The first broadcasting on 13 June 1954 celebrated the General's first year in office. The military dictatorship and the Conservative Party regimes that preceded it has exercised considerable censorship and control over radio and the press. The same period, however, had witnessed the expansion of commercial radio and advertising. The number of Colombian radio stations, now organized in three national radio networks, had doubled. Using public funds, General Rojas was able to buy German and U.S. TV studio and transmission equipment, pay Cuban and German technicians to train Colombian producers and engineers and bring in Argentine artists to coach Colombians actors on the use of television. The Office of Information and Press of the Presidency financed, produced and directed the first television transmissions and supervised the national expansion of television infrastructure. In 1955 General Rojas established a second, state educational television channel. Colombia's first and for many years only broadcasting legislation was enacted by the military dictatorship. It defined television as a public service provided directly by the state and set out a series of national development aims for the new medium.

In 1957 a coalition of military and civilian leaders toppled General Rojas. Falling coffee prices had reduced the country's earnings, making it difficult for the new civilian government to continue financing a noncommercial television system with public funds. The private sector was happy to begin commercial programmes for the rapidly expanding Colombian television audience. At first informally and, after 1963, under the state Institute of Radio and Television, INRAVISION, private companies entered the Colombian television market. INRAVISION rented time to private programming companies for specific types of programmes on the state-owned channels. The programming companies filled their rented slots with original or filmed productions, and sold time to advertisers to finance their operations. INRAVISION owned the television studies and the transmission facilities. In 1965 INRAVISION opened a second channel servicing the area surrounding Bogota. The bid was awarded to Consuelo de Montejo, a former executive in an advertising company. For five years Montejo and her partner, the U.S. network ABC, dominated commercial television in the rich centre region of Colombia, relying mainly on imported U.S. series and telenovelas. In 1970, however, in part as a result of Montejo's criticism of the government, the traditional national media groups operating the first channel were given control of the second channel.

## Venezuela

Venezuelan television went on the air in 1952 under the dictatorship of Marcos Pérez Jiménez. For six months it was the only channel in the country. Early the next year, however, Channel 4 Televisa began broadcasting. Soon after, Channel 2, Radio Caracas Television, founded by a North American, went on the air. Both channels were privately owned and commercially operated, and their licences were of dubious legality. In 1964 a third commercial station, Channel 8, went into operation. In the meantime, the underfinanced state channel survived on inexpensive imported and domestic cultural and educational productions while private commercial television, centralized in wealthy Caracas, rapidly expanded to cover Venezuela's lucrative urban markets. By 1963 one quarter, and in 1968 almost a half of all Venezuelan homes had a television set.

The U.S. television networks were quick to recognize the possibilities of the Venezuelan television market. In 1960 Channel 4 went bankrupt and was bought by the Cuban-Venezuelan industrialist Diego Cisneros. The new owner changed the name of the channel to Venevision. The same year, despite national laws limiting foreign ownership in broadcasting to 20 per cent, ABC-Paramount theatres acquired 42.9 per cent of Venevision's stock. By 1960, NBC had also acquired 20 per cent of Channel 2 Radio Caracas Television, and CBS along with Time-Life had invested in Channel 8, owned by the Vollmer industrial group in association with the exiled Cuban television entrepreneur Goar Mestre. Venezuelan television became a powerful medium of domestic and international advertisers. It operated, however, almost without any laws or government policy. The principal television legislation was a 1940 Telecommunications Law reserving all systems of communication exclusively to state use, which, although revised and improved by successive administrations, did little to protect the wider public interest in the management and content of Venezuelan television.

## Peru

The first Peruvian television broadcast in 1958 was a project of the Peruvian Ministry of Education and UNESCO for an educational channel that could also be used for entertainment. With a loan of US$22,000 the Ministry set up a small studio and transmission facilities for Channel 7 on its top floor. Soon after the first government transmission, President Manuel Prado (1956–62) awarded licences for television channels to the Peruvian commercial radio networks. Channel 4 was given to the Companía Peruana de Radiodifusión. A licence for Channel 9 was given to the Companía de Producción Radiales y Televisión, co-owned by the daily newspaper *El Comercio* and the U.S. network NBC. Channel 13 went to Panamericana Televisión, a Peruvian company with investments from

Goar Mestre and CBS. Channel 2 was awarded to José Eduardo Cavero, the 'Czar of Radio', and in 1962, Channel 11 to Bego Televisión, a radio station.

In 1962 the military removed President Manuel Prado. Under the military, and two years later under civilian president Fernando Belaunde Terry, the government set up a new public administration for broadcasting consisting of the executive, the armed forces, the universities, the National Institute of Planning and the Peruvian Institute of Geophysics. By 1968 Peruvian commercial television received 55 per cent of advertising in Lima, in comparison with only 15 per cent for radio and 25 per cent for newspapers. Some television channels had become very successful financially. Channel 13, Panamericana Telvisión, owned and operated six stations throughout the country and had diversified into publishing, a news agency, real estate and a television production company selling telenoveal hits like *Simplemente Maria* throughout Latin America. In 1968, with the support of the right-wing controlled congress, Belaunde passed a law declaring the commercial activities of the private broadcasters in the public interest. The new law gave the commercial broadcasters special tax privileges, placed them under the protection of the Peruvian government, and reduced broadcasting licence fees.

## Chile

Television was kept out of Chile until long after it was established in most other countries of the region. When television finally began in Chile in the early 1960s, mounting struggles among the political parties of the left, right and centre made state ownership of the new medium unthinkable. The accord between the state and the private sector had broken down and no party trusted state ownership of television when a rival party was in office. The universities were considered independent of government control. Moreover, some believed the university administration of television would guarantee an educational and cultural role for the new technology. Following the Chilean tradition of university management of the performing arts, television channels were finally allowed to develop under the wing of the universities.

The directors of the university channels soon found they were unable to fill all available air time with cultural and educational productions. In the absence of state subsidies or policy guidelines for programming, the universities turned to less expensive, foreign, mainly U.S. programmes and to commercial advertising. As Chilean television's ability to reach voters and influence public opinion increased, the three largest political blocs struggled to impose their mark on the medium. For the Right this meant little regulation, private ownership and commercial freedom. For the Christian Democrats, representing many of the new movements for social and economic reform, this meant a larger state role in the production of programmes for education, modernization and social integration. The parties of the left criticized the foreign-controlled commercial use of television and called for democratization, the end of the private monopoly structure and the incorporation of grassroots participation in television's management.

When the Christian Democrats came to power in 1964 President Eduardo Frei's administration greatly expanded radio and television coverage of the country. The Christian Democrats set up a chain of government radio stations and, in 1970, a government-owned national television network. In the election that year, however, the Christian Democrats lost to the left-wing coalition of Salvador Allende. Fearing control by Allende's Unidad Popular over the newly formed government media, the Christian Democrat-controlled Congress passed laws guaranteeing access by all political parties to the media and limiting the ability of the government to modify ownership or content of the private media. During the Unidad Popular government and until the military coup in 1973, the control of Chilean television was one of many battlegrounds of the different political forces within the country.

## Uruguay

When Uruguayan television began in 1955 economic prosperity was waning. The government authorized three commercial channels associated with the U.S. television networks and reserved a fourth for itself. The government channel, Channel 5, was administered by SODRE, the federal agency in charge of communications. Until 1964 the operations of the government channel were modest; it showed mainly movie reruns and cultural programmes. In 1964 new legislation authorized both public and private advertising on the government channel, and the income derived from advertising allowed Channel 5 to cover its expenses and achieve its modest programming goals. The Uruguayan National Association of

Broadcasters, however, bitterly contested the new law and succeeded in changing it to disallow advertising on government television.

In the 1960s Uruguay began to feel the impact of increased social conflict, the worsening economy and growing authoritarianism. Beginning with the newspaper *Epoca,* the government began routinely to censor and shut down newspapers and magazines and prohibit any news about strikes, political violence, protests or the Tupamaros urban guerrilla movement on radio and television. Owners and reporters who resisted censorship found themselves shut down, jailed and tortured. In other cases, broadcasting and the press became silent partners of government by pliantly accepting the growing government censorship and distortion of events.

By the late 1960s/early 1970s, despite attempts in some countries to set up educational or cultural state-owned television systems, commercially operated broadcasting was firmly established throughout Latin America, and most broadcasting systems had reached accommodations, although at times uneasy, with their governments. The U.S. TV networks had made sizable investments in the Latin American television system, the logical continuation of their earlier investments in Latin American radio stations. Often the U.S. investors simply continued with their same partners as they moved into television. The South American network, LATINO, and Central American Network, CATVN, both associated with the American Broadcasting Company (ABC), included: Channel 11 in Buenos Aires; Channels 13 and 4 in Santiago de Chile; Channel 9 in Bogotá; Channel 7 in San José, Costa Rica; Channel 7 in Santo Domingo, Channels 7, 6, and 3 in Ecuador; Channels 2 and 4 in El Salvador; Channel 3 in Guatemala; Channel 5 in Honduras; Channel 2 in Panama; Channel 12 in Uruguay; and Channel 4 in Caracas. NBC had investments in Channel 2 in Caracas and Channel 9 in Buenos Aires. CBS, in tandem with Time-Life and Goar Mestre had investments in PROARTEL in Argentina, PROVENTEL in Venezuela and PANTEL in Peru.[7]

Time-Life's television investments in the United States and Latin America in the 1950s and 1960s were for their purposes largely unsuccessful, with the exception of TV Globo in Brazil. In response to competition for advertising from commercial television in the United States, Time-Life had tried to establish a beachhead in commercial television by buying

---

[7] In 1971 Mestre purchased CBS's and Time's stock in PROARTEL. Mestre later sold his stock in PANTEL to local investors.

foreign television stations. By 1970, however, Time's management had decided to sell their television stations and concentrate on cable development in the United States. The U.S. networks also reduced their direct investments in Latin America television in the early 1970s, probably as a result of a U.S. government regulation breaking up networks' production and distribution activities and limiting their foreign and domestic syndication sales.

The U.S. television networks, however, influenced Latin American television during a crucial stage of its development. U.S. networks contributed to the establishment of strong commercial broadcasting in all the countries of the region while, at the same time, creating important markets for U.S. exports. According to UNESCO-supported studies, in 1970 an average of 31.4 per cent of the content of Latin American television was imported from the United States, and much of this shown at prime time. Levels of imported programming ranged from a high of 92.7 per cent in Panama to a low of 21.4 per cent in Argentina. Three years later, in 1973, imported programming on domestic television (much of which came from the United States) had reached 84 per cent in Guatemala, 62 per cent in Uruguay, 55 per cent in Chile, 50 per cent in the Dominican Republic, 39 per cent in Mexico and 34 per cent in Colombia.[8]

## DEVELOPMENT AND REFORM: THE 1960S AND 1970S

In the late 1950s and early 1960s Latin American countries were buffeted by severe economic problems, mounting social pressures and growing revolutionary movements. Latin American leaders, often following the lead of the United States, felt the success of the Cuban Revolution was a threat to their own stability and to that of the region, and considered social and economic development a possible defence against revolution. Within the general thinking on development, some of the earlier ideas about the role of cultural expression and communication came back into use. This time, however, the emphasis was placed on the use of the newer audio-visual technologies to provide education, information and modern values to the people.

By now almost every Latin American country had a small government educational radio and television system. The United States and other countries granted Latin American governments large amounts of direct

[8] Tapio Varis, *International Inventory of Television Programme Structure and the Flow of TV Programmes between Nations* (Tampere: Institute of Journalism and Mass Communication, 1973).

economic aid for the purpose of expanding communication systems in the development field. In 1966, for example, Colombian president Carlos Lleras set up an educational television programme in co-ordination with the Ministry of Education as a complement to regular classroom programmes. The same year the president authorized a programme of grassroots integration and rural development for which government television produced an education series for lower-income adults. El Salvador was the first Latin American country to use educational television on a large scale for formal education. In 1967 the U.S. National Board of Educational Broadcasters under contract to the Agency for International Development, AID, conducted a feasibility study for educational television in El Salvador. AID provided US$650,000 for start-up and equipment costs and almost US$2 million for the purchase of additional receivers and transmission facilities. Between 1969 and 1971, 32,000 secondary students and 900 school teachers received training in the project to increase sub-professional employment. In 1968 the Mexican government began an open-circuit educational television system for secondary schools, Telesecundaria. The first year Telesecundaria reached 6,569 registered students. In 1969 the Mexican Ministry of Public Education initiated a pilot project in San Luis Potosi to enable children in rural communities who attended schools of less than six grades to complete primary education in the conventional six-year period.

Private and religious non-profit organizations, operating on a much smaller scale than the private commercial or the state-owned mass media, were many times more successful than governments in setting up media programmes for education and development. The Latin American radio schools are an important example of private media development programmes. The schools, operated by non-profit organizations often under the auspices of the Catholic Church, broadcast educational radio programmes to organize groups under the direction of a monitor. Acción Cultural Popular, ACPO, in Sutatenza, Colombia was one of the earliest experiments in cultural and educational radio. ACPO received its broadcasting licence in 1948 and had begun distributing radio sets with fixed dials to Colombian peasants in the Andean highlands. The Latin American Association of Radio Education (ALER) was set up in 1971 with forty-one member radio schools in seventeen countries and a combined registered audience of approximately 2 million people. The radio schools worked mainly in adult education in rural and lower-income urban areas.

Other experiences with non-commercial or cultural radio were closely connected to specific cultural and ethnic groups like the Aymara Indians in Bolivia, or with specific economic and social groups like the Bolivian tin miners. The radio stations of the tin miners, the Radios Mineras, had begun as early as 1947 when school teachers working in the mining districts installed Radio Sucre. The miners' radio, financed by listeners' contributions under the direction of the miners' union, mushroomed after the Bolivian Revolution in 1952 when the government nationalized the mines, reformed land tenure and allowed universal suffrage. By 1956 nineteen radio stations formed a network of miners radios.[9]

A great deal of the initial research on the mass media in Latin America was related to the experiences of development communication. Communication researches, many of whom were funded by international development agencies and U.S. universities, studied the dissemination of development-orientated messages from the mass media to peasants, children and illiterates. Other studies measured the impact of the media on education, economic modernization, and political participation. The development communication efforts seldom touched on the interests or the activities of the private commercial broadcasters. In fact, the existence of development communication projects often relieved private broadcasters of any obligation to provide educational and cultural services. In some countries, however, partly as a result of the questions raised by the development communications field, for the first time social and political groups were beginning to challenge the commerical media and call for reforms in their operations. Development communication programmes and the relatively small, scattered public broadcasting services did not satisfy the reformers' demands for a more representative public presence in the media's application to larger social and cultural goals.

New political movements, coming to power through free elections or military takeovers, attempted to alter the distribution of wealth and power, including the media, in their societies. These movements gave access and participation in the media to their supporters and decreased the power of the previous, mainly private media owners. The media reformers accused the media owners of ignoring the needs of the majorities and propagating an alienating mass culture that benefited foreign and domestic elites. The work of Latin American communication researchers contrib-

---

[9] In the July 1980 Bolivian military coup 23 miners' radios formed a Chain of Democracy. Five days after the army had taken over the rest of the country, the miners' stations continued on the air broadcasting against the coup until the military defeated the mining communities and captured their stations.

uted to the movements toward media reform in region. Studies by Luis Ramiro Beltrán (Bolivia) and Juan Díaz Bordenave (Paraguay) argued that the uncontrolled growth of commercial media created problems for national development and political democracy. Beltrán and Bordenave championed the formulation of national communication policies and planning measures to counteract these tendencies. Antonio Pasquali (Venezuela) studied the negative impact of mass culture in general on Latin American cultures and societies and worked with his government in the search for institutional structures for more diversified domestic media. Paulo Freire (Brazil) demanded a voice for the poor and oppressed, overwhelmed and suffocated by the mass culture of the media. His theories contributed to educational and cultural programmes throughout Brazil and Latin America. The research of Armand Mattelart in the late 1960s and early 1970s on transnational control of the Latin American media, the class interests in their control, and the role of popular movements supplied a theoretical framework and empirical evidence for debate and reform of the media in Chile and elsewhere. And many more researchers turned their attention to the critical analysis of the content, structure and effects of the commercial mass media in Latin American societies.

The Latin American media reform movements called for more domestic content in the media. The attacked foreign, mainly U.S., films, TV series, wire services, magazines and comic books as forms of cultural imperialism and provided detailed evidence of U.S. presence in the region's media. In fact, by the early 1970s this presence was extensive. U.S. TV series and films accounted for about half of all that was shown on Latin American television and in Latin American cinemas. The U.S. wire services – the Associated Press and United Press International – provided between 60 per cent and 80 per cent of the international news, including news about other Latin American countries, in almost all domestic newspapers.[10] Most media reform movements maintained that an increase in state intervention in the media was the only possible check on foreign influence. Moreover, only the state could control the commercial excesses of the private media and guarantee their role in their country's development.

Awareness about the media in general and especially about inequalities in the international flow of news and entertainment was on the rise throughout

---

[10] Centro International de Estudios Superiores de Comunicación para América Latina (CIESPAL), *Dos semanas de la prensa en América Latina* (Quito, 1967), and Eleázer Díaz Rangel, 'Pueblos subinformados: las agencias de noticias y América Latina,' *Cuadernos de Nuestro Tiempo*, No. 3, Caracas, Universidad Central de Venezuela, 1967.

the Third World in the late 1960s and early 1970s. This awareness permeated the statement and action programmes of the Non-Aligned Movement and fuelled the proposals for a New International Information Order (NIIO). Latin American intellectuals, researchers and policy makers like Gabriel García Márquez, Juan Somavía, Carlos Andrés Pérez, Guido Grooscors, Fernando Reyes Matta, Rafael Roncagliolo and many others made important contributions to the international discussion on NIIO at fora provided by UNESCO and other international organizations.

## Cuba

The earliest and most radical form of long-lasting political change, media reform and state intervention in all forms of communication occurred in Cuba after the 1959 revolution. Fidel Castro took control of one of Latin America's most highly developed media systems with more television sets per capita at that time than any other Latin American country. The Cuban government radically reformed the country's dependent capitalist economy and eliminated private ownership, including that of the media. Before the defeat of Batista, Radio Rebelde, founded by Che Guevara in 1958, could be heard throughout the country. Radio Rebelde played a key role in communications, news and propaganda during the Cuban Revolution. Under the new regime, most of the private media's equipment and infrastructure as well as Radio Rebelde were put at the service of state programmes of health, education and information. The Cuban Film and Art Institute founded in 1959 brought an end to the U.S. domination of film distribution in Cuba and gave new life to the domestic film industry. Television studies and theatres were nationalized as were private radio stations and the six private television channels. Television was consolidated into two nationwide networks, the number of radio stations reduced and reorganized, and in 1962, both radio and television were placed under the Cuban Broadcasting Institute.

As ideology, a deteriorating economy and the hostile attitude of the United States pushed Cuba closer to the Soviet Union, government campaigns against most forms of independent cultural expression followed an initial period of relative cultural autonomy and free speech. The government began to demand ideological purity and persecute artists who supposedly had betrayed the ideals of the revolution. *Granma,* the most important newspapers, practiced an authoritarian style of journalism with strict state control of news. To some these policies made Cuba a symbol of the dangers of state control of the media. To others, Cuba represented the social and educational benefits to be gained from the reform of the private commercial mass media.

## Peru

Following Cuba, the next Latin American media reform movement occurred in Peru. Soon after ousting President Belaunde Terry in 1968, the Revolutionary Government of the Peruvian Armed Forces announced a plan to radically reform the economic, social and political structure of the country and free Peru from foreign capital and influence. The military nationalized most strategic national industries, utilities and services; passed a new Press Law; and set up a National Telecommunications Company. In 1971 the military issued a Telecommunications Law making radio and television stations part of national social and economic development programmes and giving the government the option to expropriate 51 per cent of any television station and 25 per cent of any radio station. The Revolutionary Government established a national film company, a national publishing house, a state-owned advertising agency, a state news agency and a national broadcasting company, ENTEL-Peru. In 1972 ENTEL managed five radio stations and three television channels and represented the government on the boards of 21 radio stations and four television channels.

On 26 July 1974 the military expropriated Peru's national newspapers and announced a plan – never completed – to hand over their management to 'representative bodies of organized sectors of society'. The decree expropriating the papers assigned *El Comercio* to the peasant organizations, *La Prensa* to workers' communities, *Correo* and *Ojo* to professional and cultural organizations, *Ultima Hora* to co-operatives of the service industries and *Expreso* and *Extra* to the universities, teachers organizations and education workers. The military appointed new directors to run the papers for the next year while the transfers to the designated organizations could be completed. As a result of changes within the military regime – on 29 August 1975 General Juan Velasco, the author of the coup was replaced by General Francisco Morales Bermudez – and a host of difficulties setting up the proposed new management, the transfer of newspapers to their new owners never occurred.

The changes in the Peruvian mass media were carried out in the face of fierce opposition from the Peruvian private sector and international associations of private media owners. The reforms attempted, under the tutelage of the military, to integrate Peru's forgotten rural, mainly indigenous, population and urban poor into the national economy and political system and restore their culture. The reforms failed, however, to build a media that either supported the goals of the regime or allowed the genuine participation of the different social groups in their management. In 1980, the military stepped down and Belaunde Terry, once again elected president, returned broadcasting and the newspapers to their former owners.

### Chile

In Chile, although the left had often criticized the mass media and called for their reform as a necessary condition for the democratization of Chilean society, media reforms never got off the ground when the left came to power. Voted into office in 1970, the Unidad Popular government of President Salvador Allende denounced foreign influence in the domestic media and proposed ending the private monopolistic structure of Chilean media. The Unidad Popular, however, did not immediately offer an alternative model for the Chilean mass media but gave first priority to the rapid expansion of state control of industry and agriculture and an immediate increase in the living standards and political participation of low-income groups. In any case, the ability of the coalition to alter the structure of the media was severely limited by the constitutional reforms passed by the opposition-controlled congress, guaranteeing private ownership of the media. The Unidad Popular increased state ownership of some media such as publishing, films, and records and greatly increased grassroots expression in other forms of communication. During the Unidad Popular administration, however, most of the private and, in some cases, the state-owned media were under the control of the opposition.

### Venezuela

In Venezuela, Carlos Andrés Pérez, elected president in 1974, attempted to alter substantially the traditional relationship between the government and the mass media to achieve public service benefits such as wider geographical coverage, more development orientated messages and greater public participation in the selection and elaboration of programmes. Under President Pérez the Venezuelan public sector, rich with petroleum earnings, expanded its activities into wide areas of social and economic development, including the mass media and culture. Soon after taking office, the Pérez government purchased the bankrupt private Channel 8 and set up a presidential commission, the Consejo Nacional de Cultura (CONAC), with representatives of the Church, the military, the universities and other social organizations, to study the Venezuelan media. The task of the commission was to reorganize state expenditures in broadcasting and reform the public administration of cultural institutions to meet the information, education and entertainment needs of all Venezuelans. CONAC met with violent opposition from private television station owners and operators and rival political parties. The commission's opponents questioned the right of the state to place the media under the aegis of a national cultural policy. The CONAC initiatives eventually were abandoned, along with government plans to regulate advertising and the national film industry. In the early 1980s, however, some of the reforms on television advertising and content proposed earlier were enacted into law by President Luis Herrera Campins.

*Mexico*

Two Mexican presidents also attempted in the 1970s to reform the privately owned media and increase the presence of the state in broadcasting, especially in television. The efforts of Presidents Luis Echeverría (1970–76) and José Lopez Portillo (1976–82) to make commercial television comply with national development programmes and constitutional reforms met with enormous opposition from private industry and from factions within the ruling party. Faced with the threat of reforms, in 1973 the two largest private Mexican television networks joined forces, forming the giant Televisa conglomerate and successfully fighting off any real increase in state regulation or control of private industry. The government, however, succeeded in setting up a state-owned television network.[11] The proposed Mexican media reform, including the vaguely defined 'right to information' written into the Mexican Constitution, received extensive public parliamentary debate. The opposition of the private sector, the historical links be-

---

[11] In early 1991, the state-owned television network, IMEVISION, was sold by the Mexican government.

tween members of the ruling party and the private media, and the functional role of the private mass media within the Mexican political system, however, outweighed the government's support for reform. The government backed away from reforms once it realized their potential effectiveness and the impact they could have on its private sector supporters.

## Nicaragua

The reforms in the Nicaraguan media after the overthrow of President Anastasio Somoza by the Sandinistas in 1979 were not as far-reaching as those that occurred in Cuba twenty years earlier. State and private radio continued to exist side-by-side, but television became exclusively state-owned — Channel 6, belonging to Somoza himself, and Channel 2, belonging to private owners close to the Somoza family, became the Sandinista Television System. In 1979 the government set up the Nicaraguan Institute of Cinema that mainly produced documentaries and government newsreels. The newspaper, *La Prensa,* founded in 1926, had been the symbol of resistance to the Somoza dictatorship. The assassination of *La Prensa*'s director, Pedro Joaquim Chamorro, by Somoza loyalists provoked the final successful stage of opposition to the dictatorship. Pedro Joaquim's widow, Violeta Chamorro, was a member of the First Sandinista Junta. She later resigned, breaking with the Sandinistas, after which *La Prensa* became the main opposition to the Sandinista government and the principal target of their censorship. The Sandinista government faced opposition from political parties, the private media, some religious institutions and the growing hostility of the U.S. government. It also faced anti-Sandinista broadcasts from Radio Impacto in Costa Rica and the Contras' September 15 radio station in Honduras. In March 1982, a state of emergency was declared, citing as justification the state of war; under it the Sandinistas initiated strict prior censorship, especially in the press, and from time to time closed down *La Prensa.*

Eleven years after the revolution, in February 1990, the Sandinistas lost power in an election to an opposition coalition, UNO, led by Violeta Chamorro. After the elections, the departing Sandinista government opened a legal avenue for private television channels by repealing the existing broadcasting law. Some radio stations previously operated by the government passed into private hands, and new private radio stations were started. In May 1990 the new government suspended the concession of radio frequencies and licences to operate stations until a new media law was prepared. Opposition and pro-government radio stations were blown up and taken over by opposing sides, and the broadcast facilities of the National Television System and Radio Nicaragua were seized and later released.

By 1976, at the time of the Latin American Intergovernmental Conference on Communication Policies in Latin America and the Caribbean organized by UNESCO in San José, Costa Rica, most Latin American governments were retreating from the attempted reforms of their domestic media. Many countries, however, continued to take an active part in regional movements for reform. And some Latin American governments joined the demands of African and Asian countries for political, economic and cultural sovereignty and a New International Information Order. Several Latin American concepts like participation, a balanced international flow of communication and information and greater public management of the domestic media became key components of international movements for change. Latin American initiatives like a regional feature news service (ALASEI) and a regional government information system (ASIN) were by-products of the movements of the 1970s for domestic reform and cultural autonomy.

As a result of the media reform movements in Latin America, a sharp ideological division developed concerning the role of the state in the mass media. The private commercial media had welcomed state participation in setting up national communication infrastructure such as satellites systems, microwave relays and coaxial cable and in expanding media coverage through educational radio and television. But, they strongly resisted expropriation or state interference in their operations, limitations on their earnings, or regulations of their content and advertising. Reformers supported a wider state role in the media as the only way to allow the media to fulfill their development potential, insure democratic participation and national content and protect national cultures. Memories of the divisive experiences of nationalization and censorship in Cuba, Peru and Nicaragua and the reforms in Chile, Venezuela and Mexico coloured much of the future policy and practice of the Latin American mass media.

## DICTATORSHIP: THE 1970S AND 1980S

By the mid-1970s Argentina, Brazil, Chile and Uruguay were under military dictatorships. (The continued military regimes in Paraguay, Bolivia, and Peru dated from earlier.) The new military rulers and their civilian advisors believed that economic development would be achieved by an autocratic state employing technocrats in increasingly close association with the transnational corporations. In addition to the control of the state and society, the new wave Latin American authoritarian regimes took over education and culture. The military manipulated symbols of nationalism and modernization and, through the mass media, controlled most public and private information and communication.

The military regimes that seized power in Brazil in 1964, Chile in 1973, Uruguay in 1973 and Argentina in 1976 placed television and radio stations under their ownership or strict supervision, censored newspapers and magazines and arrested and killed journalists. The military found the modern media's monolithic organizations, sophisticated new technologies and frequent use of symbols well suited to achieve their goals. At the same time, the ideology of unregulated economic growth under authoritarianism gave a boost to the commercial, often transnational mass media. In many countries state advertising and investment in new communication technologies and infrastructure subsidized the commercial development of the private mass media during the years of dictatorship.

## Brazil

The Brazilian military that took power in 1964 controlled news and information through decrees like the press Law of 1967, Institutional Act No. 5 of 1968, and the National Security Law of 1969. The decrees left private ownership of the media unperturbed but instituted a strict regime of censorship, harassment and even murder of journalists (in 1975 Vladimir Herzog, journalist and film-maker for the state educational television station, died under torture while in the custody of the army). At the same time that the Brazilian military regime controlled and censored the news, it protected and promoted the private domestic media, especially television, by maintaining and reinforcing barriers against foreign investments and imports and encouraging domestic media production. The military initiated a low interest loan programme for the purchase of television sets, built a microwave network to integrate remote regions of Brazil, and indirectly financed the private media through advertising by state-owned corporations and banks.

The military regime found in TV Globo a natural supporter of its policy of national industrialization, foreign investment, and modernization of the Brazilian economy. Globo's advanced technology, imported know-how, and quality mass productions gave the dictatorship an ideal communication system. In turn, Globo's privileged financial position enabled the channel to take full advantage of the military's massive investments in national telecommunications infrastructure and advertising. (In 1970 Brazil invested US\$350 million dollars in advertising; by 1979, advertising investment had grown to US\$1.5 billion dollars.)[12] By 1985, TV Globo, with a audience of 80 million, was the fourth largest television network in the world, producing 90 per cent of its own lively and technically sophisticated programming and exporting *telenovelas* widely throughout Latin America and Europe. Later, as Brazil slowly returned to democracy, TV Globo was able successfully to make the transition from military to civilian rule, adroitly backing in 1984 first the popular campaign for direct elections and then Tancredo Neves' presidency. Globo's power was further demonstrated in the 1989 presidential election which was won by its preferred candidate, Fernando Collor de Mello. The same Globo power that had worked in favour of Collor, however, also worked against him. Brazilians knew their president was in serious trouble when the Globo television network started giving generous coverage to street rallies calling for his impeachment.

## Chile

One of the first measures of the Pinochet regime after the Chilean armed forces overthrew the elected government of President Salvador Allende in 1973 was to dissolve parties of the left and take control of their property and that of their members and sympathizers. With this measure a large portion of the Chilean mass media immediately fell under the control of the dictatorship. The military issued a Law of National Security and related decrees that censored and strictly controlled all the media remaining in private hands. The dictatorship placed military directors in the university television channels and closed down and censored radio stations throughout the country. As many as forty journalists were killed after the coup and many others lost their jobs and went into exile. Likewise, foreign correspondents of U.S. and European newspapers and some news agencies

[12] Ana Maria Fadul, 'The radio and television environment in Brazil', *Intercom* (São Paulo), 1993, p. 12.

were often not allowed to enter the country. Numerous magazines and newspapers were closed, and those that remained open generally were non-political. This change in content was the result of government censorship and control of news as well as the free market economic policies of the Pinochet regime. The withdrawal of state subsidies exposed the Chilean media to foreign competition. The Chilean military made no effort to protect national culture or use nationalist themes as had been the case of their Brazilian counterparts.

Under its free market policy the Chilean military moved to make the government-owned media – the national television network, the national film industry, the government publishing house – financially self-sufficient. The withdrawal of subsidies and the drive toward profits and the bottom line meant that television had to fill most of its time with less expensive foreign series. By 1979, 71.2 per cent of Chilean television programming was imported, compared with 55 per cent in 1973, the year of the coup. Many of those Chilean television and film producers who were not forced into exile made TV commercials in order to survive. The newspaper *El Mercurio,* one of the leaders of the opposition during the Unidad Popular, assumed the role of defender of the free-market, 'neo-liberal' policies of the military regime.

## Uruguay

In Uruguay the military, who came to power in 1973, closed down six newspapers that year, ten in 1974 and eight in 1975. The newspapers that survived did so by buckling to the regime's demands. The military censored television and newspaper – including back editions stored in the national library – shut down many radio stations, and organized a government propaganda department to supply broadcasters with news and pro-government music and entertainment programmes. In 1976 the police chief of Montevideo informed radio stations they could no longer play seven tangos by Carlos Gardel, who had been dead for over forty years, because his songs 'represented a state of mind that had been totally conquered'. The military also censored the 'murgas', informal groups of satirical popular carnival singers, and banned the words freedom, justice, equality and workers from the lyrics of music played on the radio. Censorship of news was tougher than that of popular music and entertainment. Journalists faced enormous dangers in their work. In 1974 the publication in the weekly *Marcha* of a short story that had received a literary prize caused the imprisonment of the author of the story, of the jury for the prize and of the directors of the weekly publication. Subsequently, one director, Carlos Quijano, went into exile in Mexico and another, Julio Castro, died under torture in prison. At the same time, the Uruguayan military's free market policies supported the expansion of the advertising industry and the politically docile commercial media such as television.

### Argentina

In 1976 the Argentine military took control of the country and enacted a series of measure that immediately benefited the private media. The military junta removed the tax on advertising and greatly increased government advertising in the private media – by 60 per cent in the first year. However, in Argentina, as in Brazil, Chile and Uruguay, the military at the same time imposed a regime of terror on the independent media. The junta murdered journalists, closed newspapers, censored publications, blacklisted journalists and artists, and banned foreign and Argentine films, books and magazines. During the dictatorship, seventy-two journalists disappeared and were presumably killed by the military, hundreds were jailed and many others fled into exile. The military expropriated *La Opinion* and jailed and tortured the owner Jacobo Timerman. Soldiers frequently seized and burned entire editions of local magazines and threatened and kidnapped labour leaders from the media industries. With rare exceptions, like the English-language *Buenos Aires Herald,* few newspapers dared give space or time to the leaders of the disbanded political parties and even fewer ran the paid announcements of Argentine human rights groups. The Mothers of the Plaza de Mayo, their white handkerchiefs knotted on their heads, mutely walked around the square in protest. Deprived of any access to the mass media, the mothers invented a new form of communication to denounce the kidnapping of their children.

Despite the Argentine military's declared allegiance to a free market economy, the military maintained tight control over the Buenos Aires television channels, nationalized by Perón in the early 1970s. The military developed a corrupt and complex system of re-sales with advertisers and their clients and used television for lavish advertising campaigns to defend their economic and social policies and attack their enemies. While censorship severely limited the Argentine media during the military regime, the impact on some media of the regime's economic polices had an even worse effect. Newspaper and magazine circulation dropped by almost half, and domestic book publishing and film production registered similar falls.

ALTERNATIVE MEDIA AND THE MOVE TOWARDS
DEMOCRACY

Under the military dictatorships of Brazil, Chile, Uruguay and Argentina, and the older dictatorships in Paraguay and Bolivia and several countries in Central America, people denied access or opposed to the views of the dominant media sometimes developed their own forms of communication like clandestine community radios, underground video productions and comic books, and dissident newspapers and magazines. Likewise, in countries under democratic regimes but with highly monopolized and centralized commercial mass media systems, similar experiences of alternative community and group media appeared. Some of these alternative media were inspired by religious groups, political parties, or labour unions. The Brazilian alternative press was rooted in the popular education movement of the early 1960s. The union newspapers in São Paulo provided a forum and tool for the workers' struggles to regain their political rights. The Catholic Church, influenced by the new streams of thought present in the Second Vatican Council (1962–5) and the Conference of Latin American Bishops at Medellín (1968), was an important actor in many of the experiences of alternative media all over Latin America. In El Salvador, for example, much of the Church's commitment to social change was carried out through its communication resources like the newspaper *Orientación* and the YSAX radio station.

In some cases, the alternative media were both an authentic substitute for the state-controlled mass media and a form of democratic communication that allowed many points of view and gave a voice to different social groups. In others, these media were a filter between the people and the mass media that decoded, interpreted and helped people resist the authoritarian messages. In still others, the alternative media served more traditional community development roles, for example in health and education.

In addition to their political and social role, the popular or alternative media were an important Latin American contribution to communication theory and practice. Many communication theorists hypothesized that the forms of expression contained in the alternative media might eventually replace and enrich the mass media once the authoritarian regimes were removed. Yet, the experiences of popular or alternative communication seldom grew into lasting substitutes for the usual fare of the mass media. The alternative media were hampered by financial, technical and administrative problems, excessively local content, and an inability to go further than dissent. As during the 1980s the military regimes gradually disappeared – by 1990 almost the entire population of Latin America was living under democratically elected regimes – intellectuals and politicians once again turned their attention to the mass media, realizing that lasting changes in communication practices could only be effected through them.

In some countries, this attention took the form of long-delayed reforms in the mass media. In Colombia, for example, although not a recent military dictatorship, most of the broadcasting legislation was written and put into law during the dictatorship of General Gustavo Rojas Pinilla (1953–7). In 1984, as part of a series of reforms giving a greater role to different groups in Colombian society – opposition political parties, local and regional governments, ex-guerrilla movements – President Belisario Betancur signed into law legislation relinquishing presidential control of television. The new law authorized regional television channels and created a decentralized and more participatory administration for national television. In Argentina, Brazil and Uruguay, the leaders of newly elected civilian regimes found it difficult to regulate the commercial operations of the mass media. They were more familiar with the practice of small, alternative dissident media than the complex, new technological and organizational developments of advertising and the mass media. Moreover, the weakness of the Latin American economies during the 1980s made a larger state role in the media difficult. In addition, the strong memories of state control and censorship of the media by the authoritarian regimes made new state regulation anathema to media owners and voters alike. Finally, the new democratic regimes of Latin America needed the private mass media to stay in office. The traditional political parties, emerging from their long exiles, were weak, and the newly elected governments had to rely heavily on the mass media for their public image and popularity. Open elections effectively strengthened the role of the media and made the new democratic leaders reluctant to risk the media's crucial support with talk of reform or regulation.

In Brazil, for example, Globo, with its nationwide television network, radio chain, newspaper, record companies, publishing houses, educational television system, art galleries, electronic industry and theatre agency had become a veritable national ministry of information and culture. After two decades of military rule, debate focused not on the role of the state in the media but on TV Globo's dominant role in shaping public opinion. Independent video and television producers proposed a new system of station licensing, the decentralization and regionalization of media production, and community participation in the selection of cultural programming, but with little success.

In Argentina, the new democratic government found itself the legal owner of media it was unable to understand or regulate because of their size, complexities and corruption. It removed censorship and transferred one state-owned channel to the private sector. Private broadcasters, grown strong under the military, then mounted a campaign against any form of state interference in the media, effectively stopping further policy formulation. In Uruguay, one of the first official acts of the new democratic government was to name a civilian head of the board of directors of the State Broadcasting Service. He immediately presented a plan to modernize the state television channel and raise its audience level to that of the private channels. Pressures from the owners of the private channels, however, forced his resignation and the plan was scrapped. In Bolivia, with the return of a democratically elected regime, pressure from the private sector to privatize public television – eight university channels and one state channel – mounted. In February 1984 the Senate passed a law eliminating the government's monopoly over television and authorizing private channels. Two years later, in 1986, Bolivia had thirty-five new private television channels broadcasting mainly imported television series pirated from the United States and neighbouring countries. A similar expansion of commercial television channels occurred some years later when Chile, too, experienced the return to democracy.

Latin American democratic governments in the 1980s and 1990s faced greatly changed national and international communications industries whose finances and technologies were quantitatively and qualitatively different from the relatively simple print and broadcasting industries of the 1960s and 1970s. Media deregulation in the United States, Europe and Japan, and sales and distribution opportunities made possible by cable, satellite and video combinations had increased the interconnection of media production and distribution and changed the structure of worldwide media ownership. The new technologies – satellites, video, cable – segmented audiences and markets and bypassed domestic regulations and industries. By 1985, for example, foreign television and film producers were selling 30 per cent of their programmes in Latin America directly to the unregulated home video market, and a large black market had formed throughout the region for pre-recorded video tapes. That year Brazil launched the first of two satellites of the Brasilsat system, making it the first Latin American country and the tenth in the world with a domestic satellite system. Some months later, Mexico launched its first satellite, Morelos I.

The relative economic and political stability of the 1990s brought significant growth for domestic broadcasters and the entrance of powerful new foreign investment in domestic entertainment industries, which were themselves undergoing changes in ownership and regulation, as well as the introduction of a host of new services. Radio development, both AM and FM became well established and in most cases concentrated in national radio networks. The growth of television was extremely rapid. Brazil and Mexico, accounting for 54 per cent of the Latin American population, were now home to respectively the world's fourth and fifth largest TV networks: TV Globo and Televisa. Venezuela and Peru now had large domestic private commercial television industries, and Chile, Argentina and Colombia were moving in the same direction, privatizing their state-owned TV stations and authorizing the creation of private radio and television stations.

At the same time, the countries of Latin America had become significant exporters of entertainment and news. Latin American soap operas – *telenovelas* – garnered huge audiences in Poland, China, Russia, Spain and scores of other countries throughout the world. Mexico's ECO news service and Galavision were seen in countries of Europe and North America. On a smaller scale, Brazil, Argentina, Venezuela, Peru, Chile and Colombia became cultural exporters, their radio and television industries filling time on satellite services, cable systems, and radio networks in the region as well as targeting the large Hispanic audiences in the United States.

In 1976, Mexican Televisa had set up Univision to manage its international programming sales. Univision also was in charge of direct and simultaneous television transmissions using satellites and microwave relays to SIN, Televisa's Spanish-language network in the United States. In 1986, SIN affiliated over 400 stations in the United States, including cable systems and UHF channels. That year, however, as a result of a U.S. court decision on foreign ownership, Televisa sold its stations and network to the U.S. company Hallmark. At the time of the sale, Televisa was

producing about 7,000 hours annually for its four national channels, 70
per cent of which was aimed at international sales. Using its enormous
film archives, Televisa was exporting about 20,000 hours of programming
a year.[13] Televisa owned other operations aimed at the U.S.-Hispanic
market: Protele for U.S. and international TV sales, DATEL for te-
lemarketing; Galavision, a U.S. and European basic cable service in Spanish; Videovisa for the production and marketing of video-cassettes;
Fonovisa for the production and marketing of Spanish language records;
and ECO, a Spanish-language news service. Televisa was the world's largest producer of *telenovelas* for the Hispanic networks in the United States,
producing about fifteen telenovellas a year in 1986 and 1987.[14]

Foreign sales of Brazil's TV Globo did not begin until the 1980s.
Although a Globo TV series was sold to neighbouring Uruguay in 1977,
Latin American and European networks were reluctant to buy programmes
from a country whose language and traditions were so different from the
Spanish-speaking world. In 1980, Globo set up an international sales
division and made its first telenovella sale, *Isaura the Slave,* to Swiss TV
Lugano. That year Italian commercial broadcaster Rete-4 took a chance
with *Isaura* and another Globo telenovela, *Dancin'Days,* in an attempt to
make its afternoon television more appealing. The *novelas* took Italian
viewers by storm.[15] Soon, as many as seven *telenovelas* were broadcast at any
given time on Italian television. Globo *novelas* also aired in France, England, Spain, Germany, Hungary, Poland and China. By 1981, Globo
foreign sales were US$3 million; by 1987 they had passed US$14 million.[16] Venezuela's Radio Caracas Television, too, became an exporter of
*telenovelas* throughout Latin America and the United States and diversified
into Miami-based record companies, a television distribution company,
and two Puerto Rican television stations.

## LATIN AMERICAN MASS MEDIA AT THE END OF THE
## TWENTIETH CENTURY

Latin American media entered the 1990s having achieved national coverage
for radio and, in some countries, also for television (see Table 10.1). The
larger domestic broadcasters had weathered attempts at government inter-

[13] 'With 21,000 hours a year, Televisa exports soup to nuts', *Variety,* 25 March 1987, p. 105.
[14] Ibid.
[15] Elizabeth Guider, 'Isaura enslaves viewers worldwide with her special brand of soap', *Variety,* 25 March 1987, p. 131.
[16] 'Brazil TV in Globo's pocket', *Variety,* 25 March 1987, p. 136.

Table 10.1. *Ownership of radio, TV, and VCR receivers in Latin America*
(*1992*)

| Country | Population | Radio sets | TV Sets | VCR's |
|---|---|---|---|---|
| Argentina | 33,200,000 | 22,000,000 | 9,000,000 | 3,250,000 |
| Bolivia | 7,680,000 | 3,000,000 | 900,000 | |
| Brazil | 153,000,000 | 70,000,000 | 40,000,000 | 4,500,000 |
| Chile | 13,360,000 | 4,600,000 | 2,700,000 | 250,000 |
| Colombia | 33,860,000 | 7,000,000 | 4,750,000 | 1,500,000 |
| Costa Rica | 3,250,000 | 800,000 | 250,000 | 50,000 |
| Dominican Republic | 7,440,000 | 1,100,000 | 750,000 | |
| Ecuador | 10,000,000 | 3,500,000 | 2,000,000 | 350,000 |
| El Salvador | 5,000,000 | 2,000,000 | 600,000 | 80,000 |
| Guatemala | 8,600,000 | 2,000,000 | 700,000 | 90,000 |
| Haiti | 6,560,000 | 800,000 | 30,000 | |
| Honduras | 5,000,000 | 1,300,000 | 500,000 | |
| Mexico | 84,420,000 | 30,000,000 | 15,000,000 | 2,500,000 |
| Nicaragua | 3,800,000 | 900,000 | 450,000 | 30,000 |
| Panama | 2,450,000 | 1,000,000 | 560,000 | 200,000 |
| Paraguay | 4,100,000 | 1,000,000 | 600,000 | 45,000 |
| Peru | 22,950,000 | 5,500,000 | 3,500,000 | 750,000 |
| Uruguay | 3,120,000 | 1,800,000 | 750,000 | 80,000 |
| Venezuela | 19,600,000 | 10,500,000 | 3,750,000 | 1,000,000 |
| TOTAL | 438,892,000 | 172,401,000 | 89,330,000 | 14,675,000 |

*Source: World Radio and Television Receivers 1993* (London: BBC International Broadcasting Audience Research, 1993).

vention and the ravages of dictatorship. In a period of economic recession, Latin American broadcasters had embarked on a path of regional and international expansion. New television delivery systems, multi-channel wireless and wired cable systems, often connected to Latin American, U.S. and European satellite channels, multiplied, and the Latin American *telenovela* became ubiquitous on the world's televisions screens.

The countries of Latin America were now on the receiving end of a host of satellite-delivered news and entertainment channels, distributed domestically on cable and pay TV. Portions of satellite-delivered news channels were used on domestic newscasts as well. Most of the signals were carried on PanAmSat, a privately owned satellite, jointly owned by Rene Anselmo (former Chief Executive Officer of Univision) and Emilio Azcarraga of Televisa. PanAmSat put a second Latin American satellite in orbit at the end of 1994 with a capacity for ninety-six channels, most of which was leased to Televisa. The early 1990s witnessed an explosion of satellite growth as ageing systems gave way to new satellites with digital compression, direct-to-home (DTH) capabilities, and longer expected life spans. The gap created by the retirement of Mexico's Morelos 1 and Brasilsat A1 and A2 was filled by Mexico's Solidaridad I and II, Argentina's Nahuel Sat C1/C2, and Brazil's second generation Brasilsat B1 and B2.

In early 1991, the Turner Broadcasting System, parent of CNN, launched two satellite services – CNN International and the tri-lingual TNT Latin America, reaching some 700,000 households in seventeen countries of Latin America and the Caribbean. TNT Latin America transmited mainly films from the Turner library of MGM, RKO and Warner Brothers. CNN International, with a twenty-four hour feed, featured two thirty minute daily newscasts in Spanish. The ESPN sports network began satellite service to Latin America in 1989, although it had been serving Mexico and providing service by tape to other Latin American broadcasters since the mid-1980s. ESPN programming was in English, although some programming was available in both Spanish and English and multi-audio-tracked channels on the satellite transponder had capability for a local language. Telenoticias, an agreement between the U.S. Hispanic TV network Telemundo and Reuters Television, was a twenty-four hour service via satellite to cable and broadcast throughout the region. Other U.S. channels available via satellite in Latin America included HBO Olé, the Discovery Channel, Cinemax, Playboy, NBC Noticias, Fox, MTV and the QVC shopping network.

National broadcasting structures in most of Latin America, continued to change in the early 1990s, mainly in the direction of increased privatization, concentration of ownership and the formation of multi-media conglomerates. There was also some movement towards new broadcasting and media regulation.

### Argentina

In Argentina, in January 1993, in a further move toward privatization following his sale in 1989 of two television channels, President Carlos Menem signed a decree establishing TV Channel 4, dedicated to non-commercial cultural programmes; it replaced the government-owned TV Channel 7 ATC, which was privatized. Ownership of television and radio stations linked to the over 1,000 Argentine cable systems were shifting, and multimedia companies forming with newspapers, TV stations, and radio stations. The *Clarin* newspaper owned and operated Radio Mitre, Channel 13, the news agency Dyn, and the newsprint factory Papel Prensa. Atlantida Publishers (*Gente, Part Ti, El Grafico*) was part owner of Channel 11 and owned Radio Continental. Multimedios America owned the morning financial paper *El Cronista Comercial,* Channel 2, Radio America and the cable TV station Cablevision. The newspaper *La Nacion* purchased Radio del Plata and a cable TV station.

*Brazil*

In Brazil – which in 1994 had 2,917 radio stations and, with the appearance of pay TV and UHF TV, 320 television stations – most of the 286 over-the-air television stations were organized in six national commercial networks. Radio stations were spread over more than 4,000 municipalities, and the building of radio networks was beginning. Satellite access brought with it the possibility of establishing national radio networks similar to the existing television networks. During the early 1990s the Brazilian radio system had undergone a series of technological changes with the introduction of FM, stereo and digital recordings. All of Brazil's large broadcasting and media groups were private – Globo, Bandeirantes, Machete and SBT. TV Globo led the television field with nearly 55 per cent of the total advertising revenue. Machete and SBT each received nearly 13 per cent of total advertising; Bandeirantes 10 per cent, with the rest shared among the smaller stations. Many new television channels began operations. A pay TV system, Abril TV, transmited a Brazilian version of MTV on its UHF station in São Paulo and was expanding to affiliate a VHF station (Channel 9 TV Corcovado) in Rio and at least four other UHF stations in other parts of the country. Another UHF station in São Paulo, TV Jovem Pan specializing in hard news, started broadcasting in February, 1991. Super-Channel, the biggest pay TV channel in Brazil carrying CNN, RAI (Italy), ESPN and a locally produced music channel, had over 20,000 subscribers in São Paulo and 7,000 in Rio, and other smaller cable systems had started up. Satellite dishes proliferated, mainly in Brazil's interior. Dishes permitted better images for traditional channels as well as access to new services of format TV, such as Globosat and PluralSat, the two pay stations that transmit programmes via Direct Broadcast Satellite (DBS) using transponder II of Brasilsat 2. Satellite dishes allowed for nationwide coverage of all national television networks as well as access to foreign channels. International channels were available from Russia, Cuba, Spain, Colombia, Mexico, Italy, Venezuela, England, USA, Chile, Peru, Argentina, Japan, Germany and France.

## Mexico

In Mexico in 1988 the administration of Carlos Salinas Gotari initiated the internationalization of the economy and consolidation of the free-enterprise system. This included new laws governing foreign investment and the 'disincorporation' of hundreds of industries from the powerful and often inefficient state-owned sector, including many related to the broadcasting industry. By the end of the *sexenio* the vast majority of Mexico's broadcasting was privately owned, the Mexican state broadcasting resources was greatly diminished. In 1991, after almost twenty years of operation, the Mexican government privatized the forty stations forming the IMEVISION educational TV network. Channel 11 was one of the few remaining state-owned broadcasting resources. A cultural channel located in Mexico City within the Ministry of Public Education with relay stations in the states of Morelos and Hidalgo, Channel 11 broadcast no advertising but had some commercial sponsorship of its programmes. Governments on the state level throughout the country operated smaller, regional radio and television stations with limited broadcasting schedules.

Mexico in 1994 had 727 AM radio stations, 284 FM radio stations, and twenty-two shortwave stations. Mexico City alone had thirty-two AM, twenty-five FM, and fourteen shortwave stations. Mexican radio was highly developed but less monopolistic than the Mexican television industry, although Televisa, the leading force in Mexican television, had a large radio division, Radiopolis. Televisa consisted of Channels 2, 4, 5, and 9 in Mexico City, affiliated with 209 television stations throughout the country, covering 90 per cent of the national territory. Televisa owned 166 of these stations outright, and had majority interests in another twelve. About thirty-seven privately owned television stations with local or regional coverage were associated with Televisa for the transmission of programming. In Mexico City, Channel 9, owned by Televisa, broadcast to the metropolitan area, with about sixty relay stations throughout the country. Azteca Television owned Channels 7 and 13, the privatized government stations bought by Mexican businessman Ricardo Salinas Pliego. Channel 7 in Mexico City had seventy-seven relay stations throughout the country. Channel 13, also located in Mexico City, had eighty-three relay stations nationwide.

Mexico had over 100 licensed cable systems, with twenty-five year-old Cablevision, part of the Televisa group, and newcomer MVS Multivision the two largest. In 1994, the U.S. company TCI owned 49 per cent stake of Cablevision which had about 200,000 subscribers in Mexico City and carried twenty-two channels. Smaller cable systems operated throughout the country. Multivision which held the exclusive Mexican distribution rights to ESPN, TNT, and CNN and was affiliated with many smaller cable companies in the interior of the country, had about 250,000 subscribers by the end of 1993.

### Chile

The Chilean television system remained a combination of government, university and privately owned stations. In 1994, Channel 13 was owned by the Catholic University in Santiago, UCV by the Catholic University of Valparaiso. Television Nacional de Chile, Channel 7, was government-owned. Megavision, a private station, was 49 per cent owned by Mexico's Televisa. La Red, Channel 4 was private and partly Canadian-owned. Chilevision, Channel 22, was 49 per cent owned by Venezuela's Venevision. All Santiago channels were transmitted to the rest of country via 125 booster stations. Chile ranked fourth among Latin American nations in cable growth with 200,000 subscribers. Its open-door policy to foreign investment attracted television and cable investors from the United States, Argentina, Canada and Mexico, who were competing against local capital for a share in the Chilean cable market. Argentine-based operators had become the most active foreign investors in cable, challenging Chilean operators in some of the country's largest cities. In Santiago, Metropolis, owned by the Argentine multimedia giant *El Clarin,* competed with Intercom, which was controlled by *El Mercurio,* the largest Chilean daily newspaper. U.S.-based United International Holdings, was a 50 per cent partner in Cablevision, a system that counts some 170,000 TV homes in the coastal cities of Viña del Mar.

### Venezuela

In Venezuela two large commercial television networks – Radio Caracas Television RCTV Channel 2 and Venevision Channel 4 – had long dominated television audiences and advertising. RCTV received 57 per cent of the audience share during prime time, Venevisión 36 per cent, and Televen, a commercial station owned by Venevisión, about 4 per cent. All other broadcasters combined reached only a 4 per cent audience share. Radio Caracas Television was owned by the Phelps family group which also owned an AM and an FM radio station in Caracas, the newspaper, *El Diario de Caracas,* a publishing house, a book distributor and a record company. In 1994, other media holdings of the Phelps Group included a production studio, talent agency, record distributor and a chain of record and video stores. The group also owned Coral Pictures Corporation in the United States. Venevisión belonged to the Diego Cisneros Organization, ODC. It owned department stores, supermarket chains, soft drink and manufacturing plants, computer assembly and distribution companies, a radio network, a record company, a home video distributor, a publishing house, a company for talent and live productions and an advertising agency and television company based in Miami for sales and distribution of its television exports in the United States.

In the early 1990s this oligopoly was shaken up by the Government's decision to open up the television market to new stations in Caracas and the provinces. In addition, the appearance of cable (actually microwave transmission systems) gave audiences more alternatives. In 1994 Venezuela was served by two cable networks: Omnivision and Cablevision. Omnivision was partnered with HBO-Olé and Cinemax. Both networks feature U.S.-based film channels such as HBO, news networks such as CNN, and U.S. cable channels such as the Discovery Channel and ESPN. Omnivision subscribers numbered about 500,000 nationwide. Cablevision claimed to attract about 100,000 subscribers.

In 1994, there were over 300 radio stations in Venezuela, almost twice the number in 1985, spread throughout the country and forming a dispersed medium. All growth, however, had been in FM, and the number of AM stations had decreased. About half the country's radio stations were controlled by seven major groups.

*Peru*

In 1994, there were close to 246 television stations in Peru. TV Cable, a UHF system, was Lima's first pay TV company. Owned by Peru's leading private TV network Pan-Americana of the Delgado Parker family, it began operations in the San Isidro district in October 1989. The system served most of San Isidro and planned to extend service to several other up-market Lima neighbourhoods. TV Cable offered eleven channels: CNN, ESPN, Discovery, MTV, RAI (Italy), ECO, Canal 9 (Argentina), Television Chilena (Chile), Televisión Española, O Globo and a local movie channel.

## Colombia

During the early 1990s increasing internationalization and privatization of the domestic economy and provisions of the 1991 Colombian Constitution influenced the course of Colombian broadcasting. Specifically, the evolution of radio and television broadcasting showed a continuation of trends towards the centralization of media ownership in a few groups; the ownership of multimedia groups by large economic conglomerates; the privatization of telecommunications; and the growth of regional television channels and of community-owned radio and television stations. The daily *El Tiempo* was the most notable example of the formation of multimedia groups. It purchased newspapers and publishing houses throughout the country, as well as the cable company TV Cable. Multimedia groups formed in the smaller cities among provincial newspapers, cable systems and TV channels.

In 1994 Colombia had two national channels, four regional channels, pay subscription television services in seven cities, a profusion of parabolic antennas, and a wide use of video cassette recorders and video clubs. Although government-owned the two national channels rented airtime to about thirty programmers who programmed the time and sold advertising. Caracol and Radio Cadena Nacional (RCN) were the two largest programmers. The four regional channels – TeleAntioquia, TeleCaribe, TelePacífico, and TeleCafé – brought audiences a mixture of imported and locally produced programming. The largest pay TV system, Bogota's TV Cable, had a ten-year permit to brodcast on twelve channels using a minimum of 5 per cent Colombian-produced programmes. It used four channels with twenty-four-hour programming: ESPN, Latin (Venezuelan and Mexican television), Movie (Colombian, U.S. and European) and International (CNN, CBS, NBC, Discovery and other U.S. channels). The government had announced intentions to privatize Colombian airwaves. The entire national telecommunications net was expected to be sold to private companies.

## CONCLUSION

Latin America proved fertile soil for radio and television broadcasting in the twentieth century. The music, drama and news of radio and television programmes played to the dreams of the young and consoled the loneliness of the migrants lost in the vast new cities. Growing metropolises and markets drove the expansion of the industry, often with the help of authoritarian leaders and spirited entrepreneurs. At the same time, radio and television helped to link together nations and a continent, joined already by language and religion. Radio and television became important parts of peoples' lives and nations' economies. Latin American broadcasters amassed huge profits, reached large audiences, wielded great power to engage public opinion, and unified the tastes and images of many cultures and peoples.

The economic, social, and political conflicts among the different domestic and foreign actors that occurred around broadcasting defined the ways radio and television developed in each country. Over the almost three-quarters of a century of broadcasting's development in Latin America, wider considerations of broadcasting's rights and obligations, political representation and accountability were largely ignored. The demands of social movements and grassroots organizations for greater political participation and representation proved by and large short-lived. Most reforms led to the development of government and monopolistic private media rather than to democratization. In the mid-1990s Latin American societies faced the challenge of constructing truly democratic media within largely free markets and unregulated economies. This challenge requires attention to the rights as well as the obligations of the increasingly autonomous, powerful and transnational media and culture industries.

# BIBLIOGRAPHICAL ESSAYS

## I. THE MULTIVERSE OF LATIN AMERICAN IDENTITY, C. 1920 – C. 1970

A deeply imaginative reflection on the character of cultural expression in the Americas, presented by historical eras, is *La expresión americana* by the noted Cuban writer José Lezama Lima, first published in Havana in 1957. The sole critical edition is the Portuguese version, *A expressão americana* (São Paulo, 1988), translated with a highly competent introduction and notes by Irlemar Chiampi. In his essays 'Visión de América' and 'Conciencia e identidade de América' in *La novela latinoamericana en vísperas de un nuevo siglo* (Mexico, D.F., 1981), 59–158, Alejo Carpentier addressed continental Americanism. Leopoldo Zea expands the barbarism-civilization theme to global proportions in *Discurso desde la marginación y la barbarie* (Barcelona, 1988). See also his *Filosofía de la historia americana* (Mexico, D.F., 1978). The role of intellectuals is examined in Juan F. Marsal (ed.), *El intelectual latinoamericano* (Buenos Aires, 1970).

Studies of Latin American thought include two classics by the Spanish philosopher José Gaos, *El pensamiento hispanoamericano* (Mexico, D.F., 1944) and *Pensamiento de lengua española* (Mexico, D.F., 1945). Gaos's Mexican disciple Leopoldo Zea produced a volume which, although controversial, remains seminal for the nineteenth century: *The Latin-American Mind*, trans. J. H. Abbott and L. Dunham (Norman, Okla., 1963). See also Harold Eugene Davis, *Latin American Thought: A Historical Introduction*, 2nd ed. (New York, 1974); and W. Rex Crawford, *A Century of Latin-American Thought*, rev. ed. (New York, 1966).

Historical analyses of culture include Germán Arciniegas, *Latin America: A Cultural History* (New York, 1967) and Jean Franco, *The Modern Culture of Latin America: Society and the Artist*, rev. ed. (Harmondsworth,

1970). Two well-illustrated studies of art since independence emphasize historical context: Stanton L. Catlin and Terence Grieder, *Art of Latin America since Independence* (New Haven, Conn., 1966) and Dawn Ades, *Art in Latin America: The Modern Era, 1820–1980* (London, 1989). *La nueva novela hispanoamericana*, 6th ed. (Mexico, D.F., 1980) by the Mexican novelist Carlos Fuentes is a concise study of how modern narrative fiction can 'give form, fix goals, set priorities, and elaborate criticism for a determinate style of life: to say all that cannot otherwise be said.' A study of how language itself yields clues to social experience is the essay 'Language in America' in Richard M. Morse, *New World Soundings* (Baltimore, 1989), 11–60.

Useful for the background of modernism (i.e., Spanish-American vanguardism) are: José Ortega y Gasset, *The Dehumanization of Art and Other Writings on Art and Culture* (New York, 1956); Renato Poggioli, *The Theory of the Avant-garde*, trans. Gerald Fitzgerald (Cambridge, Mass., 1981); Frederick R. Karl, *Modern and Modernism: The Sovereignty of the Artist, 1885–1925* (New York, 1985); R. P. Blackmur, 'Anni Mirabile, 1921–1925: Reason in the madness of letters', in *A Primer of Ignorance* (New York, 1967), 1–80; Malcolm Bradbury and James McFarlane (eds.), *Modernism, 1890–1930* (Harmondsworth, 1976); Richard Kostelanetz (ed.), *The Avant-garde Tradition in Literature* (Buffalo, N.Y., 1982), which acknowledges Brazilian poets; and Meyer Schapiro, *Modern Art, 19th and 20th Centuries* (New York, 1978).

For broad perspectives on Latin American vanguardism, see Guillermo de Torre, *Historia de las literaturas de vanguarda*, 3rd ed., 3 vols. (Madrid, 1974); Oscar Collazos, *Los vanguardismos en la América Latina* (Barcelona, 1977); Saúl Yurkiévich, *A través de la trama: sobre vanguardismos literarios y otras concomitancias* (Barcelona, 1984); Hugo J. Verani et al. (eds.), *Las vanguardas literarias en Hispano-américa* (Rome, 1986); Mário de Andrade, 'O movimento modernista,' in *Aspectos da literatura brasileira*, 4th ed. (São Paulo, 1972), 231–55; and Raúl Antelo, *Na ilha de Marapatá (Mário de Andrade lê os hispano-americanos)* (São Paulo, 1986).

Earlier criticism held that the 'naturalist novels' or 'novels of the land' of the 1930s were derivative, that they fell into the realist or naturalist vein of previous European novels. Since the 1970s, critics have been more tolerant. They no longer draw a sharp line between the esthetically 'elegant' fiction of the 'boom' and the 'worn-out' naturalism and *costumbrismo* of the 1930s and 1940s. They now warn us of 'the dangers of a conception of literary history that perceives progress in literary developments, thereby sanctioning the relegation of certain texts to oblivion.' See Carlos J. Alonso, *The Spanish American Regional Novel, Modernity and Autochthony* (Cambridge, Eng., 1990). For rehabilitation of the fiction of the 1930s, see also Roberto González Echevarría, *Voice of the Masters: Writing and Austerity in Modern Latin American Literature* (Austin, Tex., 1985), and Doris Sommer, *Foundational Fictions, the National Romances of Latin America* (Berkeley, 1991). On the other hand, Flora Süssekind, *Tal Brasil, qual romance?* (Rio de Janeiro, 1984) traces naturalism as a recurrent authorial device of positivist origin from the 1890s to the 1970s, with deeper roots in the eyewitness 'natural history' of the early chroniclers; she makes no resolute attempt to link the Brazilian equivalent to the 'realistic' *novelas de la tierra* with the supposed 'magic' of the narratives that were to follow.

Books that shed light on the transition from the 1930s and 1940s to the 1960s and 1970s include: Emir Rodríguez Monegal, *Narradores de esta América*, 2 vols. (Montevideo, 1969) and *El boom de la novela latinoamericana* (Caracas, 1972); José Donoso, *The Boom in Spanish American Literature* (New York, 1977); Angel Rama, *La novela latinoamericana, 1920–1980* (Bogotá, 1982); and Fernando de Ainsa, *Identidad cultural de Iberoamérica en su narrativa* (Madrid, 1986).

On more specialized subjects, see Antonio Cornejo Polar, *La novela indigenista* (Lima, 1981); Efraín Kristal, *The Andes Viewed from the City: Literal and Political Discourse on the Indian in Peru, 1848–1930* (New York, 1987); Adalbert Dessau, *La novela de la Revolución Mexicana*, trans. Juan José Utrilla (Mexico, D.F., 1972); José Maurício Gomes de Almeida, *A tradição regionalista no romance brasileiro* (Rio de Janeiro, 1981); José Hildebrando Dacanal, *O romance de 30* (Porto Alegre, 1982).

General introductions to identity in Latin America include Martin S. Stabb, *In Quest of Identity: Patterns in the Spanish American Essay of Ideas, 1890–1960* (Chapel Hill, N.C., 1967) and Dante Moreira Leite, *O caráter nacional brasileiro*, 4th ed. (São Paulo, 1983). The following may also be consulted for the national-character essayists: Alberto Zum Felde, *Índice crítico de la literatura hispanoamericana, los ensayistas* (Mexico, D.F., 1954); Juan F. Marsal, *Los ensayistas socio-políticos de Argentina y México* (Buenos Aires, 1969); Peter Earle and Robert Mead, *Historia del ensayo hispanoamericano* (Mexico, D.F., 1973); Isaac J. Lévy and Juan Loveluck (eds.), *El ensayo hispánico* (Columbia, S.C., 1984); and Horacio Cerutti Guldberg (ed.), *El ensayo en nuestra América para una reconceptualización* (Mexico, D.F., 1993).

In the field of philosophy, the Peruvian philosopher Francisco Miró Quesada published two books that follow the technical development of the discipline in Latin America through four generations and stress the regional accents they gave it: *Despertar y proyecto del filosofar latinoamericano* (Mexico, D.F., 1974) and *Proyecto y realización del filosofar latinoamericano* (Mexico, D.F., 1981). Other broad treatments with distinctive emphases include Leopoldo Zea, *El pensamiento latinoamericano* (Barcelona, 1976); Francisco Larroyo, *La filosofía iberoamericana,* 2nd ed. (Mexico, D.F., 1978); Abelardo Villegas, *Panorama de la filosofía iberoamericana actual* (Buenos Aires, 1963); and Arturo A. Roig, *Filosofía, universidad y filósofos en América Latina* (Mexico, D.F., 1981). The Argentine Francisco Romero, one of the region's most distinguished twentieth-century philosophers, outlined his views on New World philosophizing in *Sobre la filosofía en América* (Buenos Aires, 1952). A collection of studies by foremost practitioners that have implications well beyond the book's restrictive title is Luis Recaséns Siches et al., *Latin American Legal Philosophy* (Cambridge, Mass., 1948). For the important impact of exiled Spanish philosophers after 1936, see José Luis Abellán, *Filosofía española en América, 1936–66* (Madrid, 1967), and the chapter 'Filosofía' by Raúl Cardiel Reyes in Salvador Reyes Nevares (ed.), *El exilio español en México, 1939–1982* (Mexico, D.F., 1982), 205–34. A leading interpretation for Brazil is João Cruz Costa, *A History of Ideas in Brazil,* trans. Suzette Macedo (Berkeley, 1964). For an important polemic on the identity question by two leading philosophers, see Augusto Salazar Bondy, *¿Existe una filosofía de nuestra América?* (Mexico, D.F., 1968), and Leopoldo Zea, *La filosofía americana como filosofía sin más* (Mexico, D.F., 1969). A highly competent book of both intellectual and practical interest is Horacio Cerutti Guldberg, *Filosofía de la liberación latinoamericana* (Mexico, D.F., 1983). Anthologies include Aníbal Sánchez Reulet, *La filosofía latinoamericana contemporánea* (Mexico, D.F., 1949); Jorge J. E. Gracia et al. (eds.), *Philosophical Analysis in Latin America* (Dordrecht, 1984); and Jorge J. E. Gracia (ed.), *Latin American Philosophy in the Twentieth Century* (Buffalo, N.Y., 1986).

## 2. LATIN AMERICAN NARRATIVE SINCE C. 1920

The last thirty years have seen an extraordinary transformation in Latin American literature, in the recognition it has achieved internationally and in the scholarly resources available for its study. The most ironic aspect of this remarkable cultural phenomenon is that attention has focused precisely on that contemporary period which historians and critics of literature normally tell us must wait until time has passed and critical

judgements have sedimented. Thus the New Novel and its euphoric culmination, the 'Boom', have received an astonishing amount of concentrated
attention – not only from Latin Americanists – while the colonial period
and the nineteenth century have languished in relative neglect. B. A.
Shaw, *Latin American Literature in English Translation* (New York, 1976)
remains a valuable resource. It can now be supplemented by E. J. Wilson,
*A to Z of Latin American Literature in English Translation* (London, 1991).

## Bibliographies and Dictionaries

Among the most useful bibliographical works are S. M. Bryant, *A Selective
Bibliography of Bibliographies of Latin American Literature* (Austin, Tex.,
1976); P. Ward (ed.), *The Oxford Companion to Spanish Literature* (Oxford,
1978), with good coverage of Spanish American literature despite the
title; W. Rela, *Guía bibliográfica de la literatura hispanoamericana desde el
siglo XIX hasta 1970* (Buenos Aires, 1971); and A. Flores, *Bibliografía de
escritores hispanoamericanos, 1609–1974* (New York, 1975), a very practical
select listing. Indispensable is the remarkable two-volume *Panorama
histórico-literario de nuestra América,* Vol. 1, *1900–1943,* vol. 2, *1944–
1970* (Havana, 1982) which interweaves historical data with literary-
cultural entries. Another valuable resource is N. Klahn and W. F. Corral
(eds.), *Los novelistas como críticos,* 2 vols. (Mexico, D.F., 1991), an anthology of key critical writings by all the leading Latin American novelists of
the last two centuries, with greater emphasis on the recent period.

The indefatigable D. W. Foster has produced a whole series of indispensable listings, including *Mexican Literature: A Bibliography of Secondary
Sources* (Metuchen, N.J., 1983). See also A. M. Ocampo and E. Prado
Velázquez (eds.), *Diccionario de escritores mexicanos* (Mexico, D.F., 1967),
now being updated by Ocampo, the first volume of whose *Diccionario de
escritores mexicanos del siglo XX* appeared in Mexico in 1988.

For the Caribbean area, see D. W. Foster, *Puerto Rican Literature: A
Bibliography of Secondary Sources* (Westport, Conn., 1982), and Instituto de
Literatura y Lingüística de la Academia de Ciencias de Cuba, *Diccionario de
la literatura cubana,* 2 vols. (Havana, 1980), a massive bio-bibliographical
resource.

On Venezuela, see L. Cardoso and J. Pinto, *Diccionario general de la literatura venezolana* (Mérida, Ven., 1974), and on Colombia, J. E. Englekirk and
G. E. Wade, *Bibliografía de la novela colombiana* (Mexico, D.F., 1950).

On the Andean region, see F. and L. Barriga, *Diccionario de la literatura ecuatoriana* (Quito, 1973); G. Jaramillo Buendía et al., *Indice de la narrativa ecuatoriana* (Quito, 1992); J. M. Barnadas and J. J. Coy, *Realidad histórica y expresión literaria en Bolivia* (Cochabamba, 1977); D. W. Foster, *Peruvian Literature: A Bibliography of Secondary Sources* (Metuchen, N.J., 1983) and *Chilean Literature: A Working Bibliography* (Boston, 1978); and E. Szmulewicz, *Diccionario de la literatura chilena* (Santiago, Chile, 1977).

For the River Plate, always well served by bibliographers, see H. J. Becco, *Contribución a la bibliografía de la literatura argentina: bibliografía, antología, historia y crítica general* (Buenos Aires, 1959), vast in scope; P. Orgambide and R. Yahni's businesslike *Enciclopedia de la literatura argentina* (Buenos Aires, 1970); D. W. Foster's indispensable *Argentine Literature: A Research Guide* (New York, 1983); and W. Rela, *Contribución a la bibliografía de la literatura uruguaya* (Montevideo, 1963), now supplemented by A. F. Orreggioni and W. Penco, *Diccionario de literatura uruguaya* (Montevideo, 1987).

Finally, on Brazil, see Instituto Nacional do Livro, *Introdução ao estudo da literatura brasileira* (Rio de Janeiro, 1963), a critical synthesis and bibliography; R. de Menezes, *Dicionário literario brasileiro*, 5 vols. (São Paulo, 1969), with references to 5,000 writers from all periods; A. Brasil, *Dicionário prático de literatura brasileira* (Rio de Janeiro, 1979); and M. Moisés and J. P. Pães (eds.), *Pequeno dicionário de literatura brasileira,* 2nd ed. (São Paulo, 1980)

## General History and Criticism

Probably no scholar will ever again achieve the kind of elegant synthesis produced by Pedro Henríquez Ureña in *Las corrientes literarias en la América hispánica* (Mexico, D.F., 1949), which though it included Brazil appeared first in English as *Literary Currents in Spanish America* (Cambridge, Mass., 1945). It reaches only the first part of the period since 1930, but remains an essential work for preparing the critical terrain. Also invaluable is Luis Alberto Sánchez, *Historia comparada de las literaturas americanas*, 4 vols. (Buenos Aires, 1976), which includes Brazil, Haiti and the United States. Other well-known general histories in English include J. Franco's works, *Society and the Artist: The Modern Culture of Latin America* (London, 1967), mainly literary despite the title, *An Introduction to Spanish American Literature* (Cambridge, Eng., 1969), and *Spanish American Literature since Indepen-*

*dence* (London, 1973), all essential works. The best of the general works in Spanish are E. Anderson Imbert, *Historia de la literatura hispanoamericana,* 2 vols. (Mexico, D.F., 1954), an outstanding synthesis and critical guide, also available in English; A. Zum Felde, *Indice crítico de la literatura hispanoamericana,* 2 vols. (Mexico, D.F., 1959), much admired; and G. Bellini, *Historia de la literatura hispanoamericana* (Madrid, 1985), a solid compendium. Also especially worthy of note is the imaginative collective critical history commissioned by UNESCO and edited by C. Fernández Moreno, *América Latina en su literatura* (Mexico, D.F. and Paris, 1972). Finally, another invaluable contribution is D. W. Foster (ed.), *Handbook of Latin American Literature* (New York, 1987), with individual chapters on national production in each republic.

Specifically on fiction, the best-known traditional works are L. A. Sánchez, *Proceso y contenido de la novela hispanoamericana* (Madrid, 1953); F. Alegría, *Historia de la novela hispanoamericana* (Mexico, D.F., 1959); J. Loveluck (ed.), *La novela hispanoamericana* (Santiago, Chile, 1969), a historic critical anthology which is still an important point of reference for the early part of the period; K. Schwartz, *A New History of Spanish American Fiction,* 2 vols. (Miami, Fla., 1972); and J. Brushwood, *The Spanish American Novel: A Twentieth Century Survey* (Austin, Tex., 1976).

Since the 1970s literary critics have largely lost faith in 'traditional' literary history – usually designed to fix some national or continental identity – as they have in all other 'grand narratives', and there have been few recent attempts at synthesis à la Henríquez Ureña, Sánchez, Torres Ríoseco, Anderson Imbert or Alegría. However, some critics have struggled on in the face of such scepticism, including Gerald Martin, *Journeys through the Labyrinth: Latin American Fiction in the Twentieth Century* (London, 1989), the first panoramic work for some time to attempt a new cartography; G. R. McMurray, *Latin American Writing since 1941* (New York, 1987), and D. Villanueva and J. M. Viña Liste, *Trayectoria de la novela hispanoamericana actual: del 'realismo mágico' a los años ochenta* (Madrid, 1991), a useful guide to recent writers which disproves once and for all the idea that Spanish critics are incapable of writing interestingly about Latin American literature (though the influence of D. L. Shaw's pioneering *Nueva narrativa hispanoamericana* [Madrid, 1981], is plain to see). See also Carlos Fuentes, *Valiente mundo nuevo: épica, utopía y mito en la novela hispanoamericana* (Mexico, D.F., 1990), a characteristic tour d'horizon and tour de force; and, similarly brilliant, R. M. Morse, *New World Soundings: Culture and Ideology in the Americas* (Baltimore,

1989), which includes meditations on literature as well as almost everything else.

Less comprehensive but also valuable are a large number of other works which have appeared since the 1960s: David Gallagher, *Modern Latin American Literature* (Oxford, 1973), much used by undergraduate students; Fernando Aínsa, *Los buscadores de la utopía* (Caracas, 1977) and *Identidad cultural de Iberoamérica en su narrativa* (Madrid, 1986), which trace archetypal themes, as do Rosalba Campra, *América Latina: la identidad y la máscara* (Mexico, D.F., 1987) and the contributors to S. Yurkievich (ed.), *Identidad cultural de América Latina en su literatura* (Madrid, 1986).

On the period of the 'Boom', see Carlos Fuentes, *La nueva novela hispanoamericana* (Mexico, D.F., 1969), José Donoso, *Historia personal del boom* (Barcelona, 1972), E. Rodríguez Monegal, *El boom de la novela latinoamericana* (Caracas, 1972) and, for a retrospective, A. Rama (ed.), *Más allá del boom: literatura y mercado* (Mexico, D.F., 1981). Still indispensable are the interviews of Luis Harss, *Los nuestros* (1966; also in English, with Barbara Dohmann, *Into the Mainstream* [New York, 1967]), carried out at the height of the 1960s euphoria, followed, a few years later by Rita Guibert, with *Seven Voices* (New York, 1973).

Also from this time a series of epoch-making essay anthologies appeared: Mario Benedetti, *Letras del continente mestizo* (Montevideo, 1967); E. Rodríguez Monegal, *Narradores de esta América* (Montevideo, 1969); Julio Ortega, *La contemplación y la fiesta* (Caracas, 1969); Jorge Lafforgue (ed.), *Nueva novela latinoamericana* (Buenos Aires, 1969); Ariel Dorfman, *Imaginación y violencia en América Latina* (Santiago, Chile, 1970); O. Collazos, J. Cortázar and M. Vargas Llosa, *Literatura en la revolución y revolución en la literatura* (Mexico, D.F., 1970), a famous debate; F. Alegría, *Literatura y revolución* (Mexico, D.F., 1971), deceptively titled; G. Brotherston, *The Emergence of the Latin American Novel* (Cambridge, Eng., 1977); A. J. MacAdam, *Modern Latin American Narratives: The Dreams of Reason* (Chicago, 1977); S. Bacarisse (ed.), *Contemporary Latin American Fiction* (Edinburgh, 1980); D. Kadir, *Questing Fictions: Latin America's Family Romances* (Minneapolis, Minn., 1986); J. King (ed.), *Modern Latin American Fiction: A Survey* (London, 1987); P. Swanson (ed.), *Landmarks in Modern Latin American Fiction* (London, 1990); and R. González Echevarría, *The Voice of the Masters: Writing and Authority in Modern Latin American Literature* (Austin, Tex., 1986), and also his very important *Myth and Archive: A Theory of Latin American Narrative* (Cambridge, Eng., 1991). MacAdam, Kadir and González Echevarría are all examples of that

2. *Latin American Narrative since* c.1920      577

curious and disconcerting phenomenon which has seen Latin American fiction treated to the full French poststructuralist treatment, but not from France (nor indeed from Latin America), where very few such studies have been done, but from the United States. The latest studies are now linking the 'Post-Boom' with poststructuralism and postmodernism. Good examples are E. Sklodowska, *La parodia en la nueva novela hispanoamericana, 1960–1985* (Philadelphia and Amsterdam, 1991), and L. Parkinson Zamora, *Writing the Apocalypse* (Cambridge, Eng., 1989).

However, there have also been a large number of studies which, instead of situating Latin American narrative in language or ideology using the template of Barthes, Derrida, Lacan or Foucault, have tried to reinsert it in social history. Much of the impetus for such work has come from Cuba, where Roberto Fernández Retamar's *Calibán* (Havana, 1971) and *Para una teoría de la literatura latinoamericana* (Havana, 1972) were undoubtedly political landmarks. But the acknowledged leader of this movement was the Uruguayan critic Angel Rama, who was taking such studies to new heights at the time of his tragic death in 1983. His most important works were *Diez problemas para el novelista latinoamericano* (Caracas, 1972), *La novela latinoamericana: panoramas, 1920–1980* (Bogotá, 1982), *Transculturación narrativa en América Latina* (Mexico, D.F., 1982) and *La ciudad letrada* (Hanover, N.H., 1984). Rama was also responsible for the precious cultural contribution of editing the Colección Ayacucho of seminal texts of Latin American literature and culture, and he took part in numerous symposia and anthologies relating to Latin American narrative. Others working in a similar tradition are Jorge Ruffinelli (Uruguay), Antonio Cornejo Polar (Peru), Rafael Gutiérrez Girardot (Colombia), Antônio Cándido and Roberto Schwarz (Brazil); also, before his premature death, Alejandro Losada, author of *La literatura en la sociedad de América Latina* (Frankfurt, 1983). For other works in this line, see J. Mejía Duque, *Narrativa y neocolonialismo en América Latina* (Bogotá, 1972); J. Leenhardt (ed.), *Idéologies, littérature et société en Amérique Latine* (Brussels, 1975) and *Littérature latino-américaine d'aujourd'hui* (Paris, 1980); F. Pérus, *Historia y crítica literaria: el realismo social y la crisis de la dominación oligárquica* (Havana, 1982); Julio Rodríguez-Luis, *La literatura hispanoamericana entre compromiso y experimento* (Madrid, 1984); M. Moraña, *Literatura y cultura nacional en Hispanoamérica* (Minneapolis, Minn., 1984); H. Vidal (ed.), *Fascismo y experiencia literaria: reflexiones para una recanonización* (Minneapolis, Minn., 1985); and J. Calviño, *Historia, ideología y mito en la narrativa hispanoamericana contemporánea* (Madrid, 1987). Pathbreaking works attempting to establish a new way of writing Latin American narrative history are Ana Pizarro (ed.), *La literatura latinoamericana como proceso* (Buenos Aires, 1985) and *Hacia una historia de la literatura latinoamericana* (Mexico, D.F., 1987), with contributions from many of the critics mentioned above.

## National Literatures

D. W. Foster's *Handbook of Latin American Literature,* mentioned above, is uneven but useful for all Latin American republics, and will be found invaluable for countries with sparse bibliographical coverage.

On Mexico, Carlos Monsiváis, 'Notas sobre la cultura mexicana en el siglo XX', in *Historia general de México,* vol. 4 (Mexico, D.F., 1976), 283–337, provides a stimulating synthesis. See also J. Brushwood, *Mexico in its Novel* (Austin, Tex., 1966); A. M. Ocampo (ed.), *La crítica de la novela mexicana contemporánea* (Mexico, D.F., 1981), a judicious critical collection; M. Glantz (ed.), *Onda y escritura en México: jóvenes de 20 a 33* (Mexico, D.F., 1971), an epoch-making critical anthology; J. A. Duncan, *Voices, Visions and a New Reality: Mexican Fiction since 1970* (Pittsburgh, Pa., 1986); M. H. Forster and J. Ortega, *De la crónica a la nueva narrativa mexicana* (Mexico, D.F., 1986); S. Sefchovich, *México: país de ideas, país de novelas. Una sociología de la literatura mexicana* (Mexico, D.F., 1987); R. Teichmann, *De la onda en adelante: conversaciones con 21 novelistas mexicanos* (Mexico, D.F., 1987); and Jean Franco, *Plotting Women* (London, 1989), on women writers from the colony to the present day. *Revista Iberoamericana,* no. 148–9 (1990) was entirely devoted to twentieth-century Mexican literature.

The single most useful volume on Central American narrative as a whole is R. L. Acevedo, *La novela centroamericana* (Río Piedras, P.R., 1982), which is judicious and comprehensive, but an important later work is *Literature and Politics in the Central American Revolutions* by J. Beverley and M. Zimmerman (Austin, Tex., 1990). On Honduras, see J. F. Martínez, *La literatura hondureña* (Tegucigalpa, 1987).

For the Caribbean region, see the special number of *Latin American Literary Review,* 16 (1980). On the Dominican Republic, see M. Henríquez Ureña, *Panorama histórico de la literatura dominicana* (Santo Domingo, 1966); D. Sommer, *One Master for Another: Populism as Patriarchal Rhetoric in Dominican Novels* (Santo Domingo, 1983), a book whose perspective is relevant far beyond the Caribbean country on which it is based; and *Revista*

*Iberoamericana*, no. 142 (1988), which has 19 essays on modern Dominican literature. For Haiti, see J. M. Dash, *Literature and Ideology in Haiti*, *1915–1961* (Totowa, N.J., 1981), and for Puerto Rico, J. L. González, *Literatura y sociedad en Puerto Rico* (Mexico, D.F., 1976).

On the special case of Cuba – already prolific beyond its size well before the Revolution – see J. A. Portuondo, *Bosquejo histórico de las letras cubanas* (Havana, 1960) by the critic who set the ideological pace after the Revolution, and R. Lazo, *Historia de la literatura cubana* (Mexico, D.F., 1974). The early years of the Revolution saw a flurry of enthusiastic anthologies, first in France and Britain – for example, J. M. Cohen (ed.), *Writers in the New Cuba* (Harmondsworth, 1967) – and then, especially after the fall of Franco, in Spain: typical examples are M. Benedetti et al., *Literatura y arte nuevo en Cuba* (Barcelona, 1971) and F. M. Laínez, *Palabra cubana* (Madrid, 1975). Crucial background texts are Castro's own 'Words to the Intellectuals' (1961), available in a variety of anthologies of Marxist declarations on literature, and the documents surrounding the Padilla affair of 1971. (See *Libre*, Barcelona, for example, or *Index on Censorship* from this period.) See also J. G. Santana (ed.), *Política cultural de la Revolución Cubana: documentos* (Havana, 1977), which includes statements on the fundamental place of realism in art and literature. On the narrative fiction since the Revolution, see J. Ortega, *Relato de la utopía: notas sobre narrativa cubana de la revolución* (Barcelona, 1973); S. Menton, *Prose Fiction of the Cuban Revolution* (Austin, Tex., 1975) and, for a Cuban view, long delayed, R. Rodríguez Coronel, *La novela de la Revolución Cubana, 1959–1979* (Havana, 1986). Excellent more recent works are G. Pérez Firmat, *The Cuban Condition: Translation and Identity in Modern Cuban Literature* (Cambridge, Eng., 1989), relating Cuban literature to national culture, and W. Luis, *Slavery in Cuban Narrative* (Austin, Tex., 1990). Two essential studies of Cuban pre- and post-revolutionary magazines are L. García Vega, *Los años de 'Orígenes'* (Caracas, 1978) and J. A. Weiss, *'Casa de las Américas': An Intellectual Review in the Cuban Revolution* (Chapel Hill, N.C., 1977).

On Venezuela, see M. Picón Salas, *Formación y proceso de la literatura venezolana* (Caracas, 1940) and J. Liscano, *Panorama de la literatura venezolana actual* (Caracas, 1972). On Colombia, see A. Gómez Restrepo, *Historia de la literatura colombiana* (Bogotá, 1956); D. McGrady, *La novela histórica en Colombia, 1844–1959* (Bogotá, 1962); J. G. Cobo Borda, *La narrativa colombiana después de García Márquez* (Bogotá, 1989); J. Tittler, *Violencia y literatura en Colombia* (Madrid, 1989); A. Pineda, *La novela colombiana a fines del siglo XX* (Bogotá, 1990); and an important if controversial book by R. L. Williams, *Novela y poder en Colombia, 1844–1987* (Bogotá, 1991).

A general treatment of the Andean novel is given by R. Lazo, *La novela andina: pasado y futuro* (Mexico, D.F. 1973). On Ecuador, see A. Rojas, *La novela ecuatoriana* (Mexico, D.F., 1948); J. L. Barrera, *Historia de la literatura ecuatoriana* (Quito, 1960); *Revista Iberoamericana*, no. 144–5 (1988), with 26 essays on Ecuadorean literature; and A. Sacoto, *Novelas claves en la literatura ecuatoriana* (Quito, 1990). On Peru, ravaged by conflict and seemingly insoluble questions of national construction and identity, see L. A. Sánchez, *Introducción a la literatura peruana* (Lima, 1972), and *La literatura peruana: derrotero para una historia cultural del Peru*, 5 vols. (Lima, 1966); J. Higgins, *A History of Peruvian Literature* (London, 1987); more socially oriented, A. Losada, *Creación y praxis: la producción literaria como praxis social en Hispanoamérica y el Perú* (Lima, 1976); J. Rodríguez-Luis, *Hermenéutica y praxis del indigenismo: la novela indigenista de Clorinda Matto a José María Arguedas* (Mexico, D.F., 1980); M. Lauer, *El sitio de la literatura* (Lima, 1988); A. Cornejo Polar, *Literatura y sociedad en el Perú: la novela indigenista* (Lima, 1980) and *La formación de la tradición literaria en el Perú* (Lima, 1989); J. Ortega, *La cultura peruana: experiencia y conciencia* (Mexico, D.F., 1978) and *Crítica de la identidad: la pregunta por el Perú en su literatura* (Mexico, D.F., 1988). On Bolivia, see F. Díez de Medina, *Historia de la literatura boliviana* (Madrid, 1959); E. Finot, *Historia de la literatura boliviana* (La Paz, 1964); A. Guzmán, *Panorama de la novela boliviana* (La Paz, 1973); Evelio Echevarría, *La novela social de Bolivia* (La Paz, 1973); G. Lora, *Ausencia de la gran novela minera* (La Paz, 1979); L. García Pabón and W. Torrico, *El paseo de los sentidos: estudios de literatura boliviana contemporánea* (La Paz, 1983); R. Teixido, *El minero en la novela boliviana* (La Paz, 1988); and C. Castañón, *Literatura de Bolivia* (La Paz, 1989). On Chile, see R. Silva Castro, *Panorama literario de Chile* (Santiago, Chile, 1961); A. Torres Ríoseco, *Breve historia de la literatura chilena* (Mexico, D.F., 1956); F. Alegría, *La literatura chilena del siglo XX*, 2nd ed. (Santiago, Chile, 1967); J. Promis, *Testimonios y documentos de la literatura chilena, 1842–1975* (Santiago, Chile, 1977), M. A. Jofre, *Literatura chilena en el exilio* (Santiago, Chile, 1986); and H. Vidal, *Cultura nacional chilena, crítica literaria y derechos humanos* (Minneapolis, Minn., 1989).

There is profuse coverage of Argentine literature for all periods, though the nineteenth century is better served in terms of synthesis than the twentieth, which is wracked by dissension, personalism and partisanship. The result has been a torrent of political and sociological readings which, on the whole, promise more than they can deliver. The outstanding general history is R. Rojas, *Historia de la literatura argentina: ensayo filosófico sobre la evolución de la cultura en el Plata*, 9 vols. (Buenos Aires, 1957), a continental model. See also A. Prieto, *Literatura y subdesarrollo* (Buenos Aires, 1968); D. Viñas, *Literatura argentina y realidad política: de Sarmiento a Cortázar* (Buenos Aires, 1971); J. Hernández Arregui, *Imperialismo y cultura* (Buenos Aires, 1973); A. Adelach et al., *Argentina: cómo matar la cultura. Testimonios, 1976–1981* (Madrid, 1981), and A. Avellaneda, *Censura, autoritarismo y cultura: Argentina 1960–1983*, 2 vols. (Buenos Aires, 1986), both on the horrifying effects of the military 'process' on culture, not least fiction; K. Kohut, *Literatura argentina de hoy* (Frankfurt, 1989); and N. Lindstrom, *Jewish Issues in Argentine Literature* (Columbia, Mo., 1989). A brilliant recent retrospective, outside this period but an essential preparatory study for it, is B. Sarlo, *Buenos Aires 1920–1930: una modernidad periférica* (Buenos Aires, 1988). As important background sources, see J. King, *'Sur': A Study of the Argentine Literary Journal and Its Role in the Development of a Culture, 1931–1970* (Cambridge, Eng., 1986), and W. H. Katra, *'Contorno': Literary Engagement in Post-Peronist Argentina* (Cranbury, N.J., 1988). On Uruguay, rich beyond its size in novelists and, above all, critics, see A. Zum Felde, *Proceso intelectual del Uruguay*, 3 vols. (1941; 3rd rev. ed., Montevideo, 1967); J. E. Englekirk and M. E. Ramos, *La narrativa uruguaya: estudio crítico bibliográfico* (Berkeley, 1967); A. Rama, *La generación crítica, 1939–1969* (Montevideo, 1972); and J. Ruffinelli, *Palabras en orden* (Buenos Aires, 1974), important interviews. On Paraguay, with no more literary output than Honduras, Panama or Haiti, see H. Rodríguez-Alcalá, *La literatura paraguaya* (Buenos Aires, 1969).

On Brazil, A. Coutinho, *Introdução à literatura no Brasil* (Rio de Janeiro, 1955), Eng. trans. *An Introduction to Literature in Brazil* (New York, 1969), is an outstanding general introduction bringing the reader up to the beginning of this period. S. Putnam's *Marvelous Journey: A Survey of Four Centuries of Brazilian Writing* (New York, 1948) remains a stimulating introduction. See also A. Cândido, *Presença da literatura brasileira* (São Paulo, 1964); A. Bosi, *História concisa da literatura brasileira* (São Paulo, 1972); A. Filho, *O romance brasileiro de 30* (Rio de Janeiro, 1969); H. Alves, *Ficção de 40* (Rio de Janeiro, 1976); A. Brasil, *A nova literatura (O romance)* (Rio de Janeiro, 1973) and *A nova literatura (O conto)* (Rio de Janeiro, 1973); M. Silverman, *Moderna ficção brasileira* (Rio de Janeiro, 1978); J. H. Weber, *Do modernismo à nova narrativa* (Porto Alegre, 1976);

M. C. Lopes, *A situação do escritor e do livro no Brasil* (Rio de Janeiro, 1978);
J. Gaspar Machado, *Os romances brasileiros nos anos 70: fragmentação social e
estética* (Florianopolis, 1981); and A. Cândido, 'Los brasileños y la literatura latinoamericana', *Casa de las Américas*, 136 (1983), 82–92.


### 3/4. LATIN AMERICAN POETRY SINCE C. 1920

An appropriate starting point for any survey of twentieth-century Latin
American poetry is Saúl Yurkievich, *Fundadores de la nueva poesía latinoamericana* (1971; 2nd ed., Barcelona, 1973), which contains essays on César
Vallejo, Vicente Huidobro, Pablo Neruda, Jorge Luis Borges, Octavio Paz
and Oliverio Girondo. Yurkievich, a poet and a perceptive critic, favours
the experimental side of the twentieth-century poetic tradition. Despite its
title, his survey does not include Brazilians. Equally stimulating, and more
wide ranging, is Guillermo Sucre, *La máscara, la transparencia* (Caracas,
1975), with essays on all the principal Hispanic poets from Darío to
Pizarnik and Pacheco; strangely it excludes Pablo Neruda. Another poet-
critic who has written engagingly on Spanish American poets is Julio
Ortega in his *Figuración de la persona* (Madrid, 1970), with essays on Vallejo,
Belli, Parra, Pacheco and many Peruvians. The best survey in English is
Gordon Brotherston, *Latin American Poetry: Origins and Presence* (Cam-
bridge, Eng., 1975), from Darío to Girri and Lihn, and including the
Brazilians. Brotherston's forte is situating the poets in a cultural definition
of American-ness. The most useful academic survey (with bibliographies) is
Merlin Forster, *Historia de la poesía hispanoamericana* (Clear Creek, Ind.,
1981). A sympathetic approach to modern Latin American poets emerges
in Ramón Xirau's *Poesía iberoamericana contemporánea* (Mexico, D.F., 1972).
A chronicle of very recent poetry, arguing for a living avant-garde, is
Eduardo Milán's *Una cierta mirada* (Mexico, D.F., 1989), based on reviews
in Octavio Paz's magazine, *Vuelta*. Pedro Lastra's critical edition of the
special number of *Inti: Revista de Literatura Hispánica*, 18–19 (1983–4),
'Catorce poetas hispanoamericanos de hoy', ranges from Gonzalo Rojas to
Antonio Cisneros. There is also a special number of *Insula*, 'La poesía en
Hispanoamérica, hoy', 512–13 (August–September 1989), edited by Juan
Gustavo Cobo Borda. Also recommended is Tamara Kamenszain, *El texto
silencioso: tradición y vanguardia en la poesía sudamericana* (Mexico, D.F.,
1983), suggesting an alternative tradition in which to ground Latin Ameri-
can poetry. Finally, a recent survey of Latin American poetry by Mike
González and David Treece, *The Gathering of Voices: The Twentieth Century*

*Poetry of Latin America* (London, 1992) is angled socio-politically and reads cumbersomely, but is thorough.

## Monographs

There are many good monographs on individual poets. The early-twentieth-century break with Rubén Darío's cosmopolitan poetics is embodied by Ramó López Velarde and Leopoldo Lugones. Octavio Paz has a key essay on López Velarde in *Cuadrivio* (Mexico, D.F., 1965), while Allen Phillips's *Ramón López Velarde, el poeta y el prosista* (Mexico, D.F., 1962) is more informative. An excellent biography has been written by Guillermo Sheridan, *Un corazón adicto: la vida de Ramón López Velarde* (Mexico, D.F., 1989). Lugones is well covered in Jorge Luis Borges's critical tribute, *Leopoldo Lugones* (Buenos Aires, 1955), and by the more academic Raquel Halty Ferguson, *Laforgue y Lugones: dos poetas de la luna* (London, 1981). The best survey of the break with Rubendarismo is Gwen Kirkpatrick, *The Dissonant Legacy of Modernismo: Lugones, Herrera y Reissig and the Voice of Latin American Poetry* (Berkeley, 1989).

The initiator of the poetic avant-garde is the Chilean Vicente Huidobro. René de Costa has settled many controversial issues surrounding Huidobro's reputation and achievements in his *Vicente Huidobro: The Careers of a Poet* (Oxford, 1984). Pablo Neruda's prolific output is neatly summarized in Manuel Durán and Margaret Safir, *Earth Tones: The Poetry of Pablo Neruda* (Cambridge, Mass., 1981). The detailed study of early Neruda by Jaime Concha, *Neruda: 1904–1936* (Santiago, Chile, 1972) repays study, as does Robert Pring Mill's acute introduction to his *Pablo Neruda: A Basic Anthology* (Oxford, 1975). A stimulating approach is John Felstiner's *Translating Neruda: The Way to Macchu Picchu* (Stanford, Calif., 1980). René de Costa has also surveyed Neruda in *The Poetry of Pablo Neruda* (Cambridge, Mass., 1979), as has Margorie Agosín, *Pablo Neruda* (Boston, 1986). Apart from Neruda's *Memorias* (1974), Emir Rodríguez Monegal's critical biography, *El viajero inmóvil: introducción a Pablo Neruda* (1966; 2nd ed., Buenos Aires, 1977) stands the test of time. Chilean novelist and diplomat Jorge Edwards has written a recent memoir, *Adiós poeta* (Barcelona, 1990). Neruda's late poetry is subtly explored in Christopher Perriam, *The Late Poetry of Pablo Neruda* (Oxford, 1989). Fellow Nobel Prize-winning poet Gabriela Mistral (Lucila Godoy Alcayaga) has been well introduced by Jaime Concha in his anthology, *Gabriela Mistral* (Madrid, 1987).

There has been extensive scholarship on César Vallejo. The best introduction in English is Jean Franco, *César Vallejo: The Dialectics of Poetry and Silence* (Cambridge, Eng., 1976). Juan Larrea's polemical edition of Vallejo's complete poems (Barcelona, 1978) should be counter-balanced by the Archivos edition under Américo Ferrari (Paris, 1988). Ferrari's *El universo poético de César Vallejo* (Caracas, 1971) is elegant and conceptually very clear. Alberto Escobar, *Cómo leer a Vallejo* (Lima, 1973) is also worth reading. Finally, see the introduction to James Higgins, *César Vallejo: A Selection of His Poetry* (Liverpool, 1987).

Jorge Luis Borges's poetry is reviewed by Guillermo Sucre, *Borges el poeta* (Caracas, 1967) and Gerardo Mario Goloboff, *Leer Borges* (Buenos Aires, 1978). See also Emir Rodríguez Monegal, *Jorge Luis Borges: A Literary Biography* (New York, 1978). The American poet Willis Barnstone recalls Borges the poet in *With Borges on an Ordinary Evening in Buenos Aires* (Champaign, Ill., 1993). Octavio Paz has written crucial essays on modern Mexican poets collected in *Generaciones y semblanzas: escritores y letras de México* (Mexico, D.F., 1987). See also by Paz, *Xavier Villaurrutia en persona y en obra* (Mexico, D.F., 1978), *El arco y la lira* (Mexico, D.F., 1956), on poetry in general, and *Los hijos del limo* (Mexico, D.F., 1974), on the decline of the avant-garde. An introduction to Paz's complete works is Jason Wilson, *Octavio Paz* (Boston, 1986). Wilson's earlier *Octavio Paz: A Study of His Poetics* (Cambridge, Eng., 1979) focuses on Paz's debt to surrealism. More recent studies include Alberto Ruy Sánchez, *Una introducción a Octavio Paz* (Mexico, D.F., 1989) and John Fein, *Towards Octavio Paz: A Reading of His Major Poems* (Lexington, Ky., 1986). On the Cuban poet Nicolás Guillén, there is a fascinating essay by Ezequiel Martínez Estrada, *La poesía afrocubana de Nicolás Guillén* (Montevideo, 1966), with a small anthology. For more background information, see Adriana Tous, *La poesía de Nicolás Guillén* (Madrid, 1971) and Keith Ellis, *Cuba's Nicolás Guillén: Poetry and Ideology* (Toronto, 1983).

A clear introduction to a typical Latin American poet of the 1930s and 1940s is Peter Beardsell, *Winds of Exile: The Poetry of Jorge Carrera Andrade* (Oxford, 1977). There are several thorough studies on Mexican poets of the 1920s and 1930s: see, for example, Merlin Forster, *Fire and Ice: The Poetry of Xavier Villaurrutia* (Chapel Hill, N.C., 1976); Edward Mullen, *Carlos Pellicer* (Boston, 1977); Andrew Debicki, *La poesía de José Gorostiza* (Mexico, D.F., 1962); Sonja Karsen, *Jaime Torres Bodet* (Boston, 1971); and Jaime García Terrés, *Poesía y alquimia, los tres mundos de Gilberto Owen* (Mexico, D.F., 1981). The Chilean poet Humberto Díaz-Casanueva's poetry was explored by fellow poet and friend Rosamel del Valle in *La violencia creadora* (Santiago, Chile, 1959), and more briefly by Argentine poet Ricardo Herrera, *La marcas del éxtasis* (Buenos Aires, 1983).

The best introduction to Ernesto Cardenal is Paul Borgeson, *Hacia el hombre nuevo: poesía y pensamiento de Ernesto Cardenal* (London, 1984); it explores Cardenal's work chronologically. There are monographs on the Peruvian poet Carlos Germán Belli by Mario Canepa, *Lenguaje en conflicto: la poesía de Carlos Germán Belli* (Madrid, 1987), and on Alberto Girri by Muriel Slade Pascoe, *La poesía de Alberto Girri* (Buenos Aires, 1986). A subtle critical biography is *Alejandra Pizarnik* (Buenos Aires, 1991), by Cristina Piña. Edith Grossman has written the most informative introduction to Nicanor Parra in English: *The Antipoetry of Nicanor Parra* (New York, 1975). Another general study on Parra is Marlene Gottlieb, *No se termina nunca de nacer: la poesía de Nicanor Parra* (Madrid, 1977). A careful linguistic analysis of the avant-garde poet Oliverio Girondo is Beatriz Nóbile, *El acto experimental* (Buenos Aires, 1968) which should be read with Jorge Schwartz (ed.), *Homenaje a Girondo* (Buenos Aires, 1987).

There are several monographs on individual Brazilian poets. On Drummond de Andrade, John Gledson, *Poesia e poética de Carlos Drummond de Andrade* (São Paulo, 1981), and José Guilherme Merquior, *Verso universo em Drummond* (Rio de Janeiro, 1976). On Manuel Bandeira, see Emanuel de Moraes, *Manuel Bandeira* (Rio de Janeiro, 1962), and a more recent work by Davi Arrigucci, Jr., *Humildade, paixão e morte: A poesia de Manuel Bandeira* (São Paulo, 1990). On João Cabral de Melo Neto, see Marta Peixoto, *Poesia com coisas: uma leitura de João Cabral de Melo Neto* (São Paulo, 1983).

## Surveys of National Poetic Traditions

There are many informative surveys of national poetic traditions, both critical studies and critical anthologies. A chatty, well-documented survey of Brazilian modernism is *The Modernist Movement in Brazil: A Literary Study* (Austin, Tex., 1967), by critic and translator John Nist, complemented by the translation of Wilson Martins, *The Modernist Idea: A Critical Survey of Brazilian Writing in the Twentieth Century* (New York, 1970). Equally comprehensive are Giovanni Pontiero's introduction and notes to his *An Anthology of Brazilian Modernist Poetry* (Oxford, 1969). Manuel Bandeira himself wrote a useful *Apresentação da poesia brasileira* (Rio de

Janeiro, 1967). Luiz Costa Lima sets Brazilian poetry into the Western tradition in his *Lira e antilira: Mário, Drummond, Cabral* (Rio de Janeiro, 1968). A more recent survey, employing critical theory, is Antônio Sérgio Lima Mendonça, *Poesia de vanguarda no Brasil de Oswald de Andrade ao poema visual* (Rio de Janeiro, 1983).

A starting point for Mexican poetry would be Frank Dauster, *Breve historia de la poesía mexicana* (Mexico, D.F., 1956). This should be supplemented by Merlin Forster, *Los contemporáneos, 1920–1932: Perfil de un experimento vanguardista mexicano* (Mexico, D.F., 1964), and Guillermo Sheridan, *Los contemporáneos ayer* (Mexico, D.F., 1985). Andrew P. Debicki's comprehensive *Antología de la poesía mexicana moderna* (London, 1977) contains useful notes and bibliographies. A sensible survey of more recent poetry is Frank Dauster, *The Double Strand: Five Contemporary Mexican Poets* (Lexington, Ky., 1986), with a good bibliography.

The most informative introduction to twentieth-century Colombian poetry is *Poesía colombiana, 1880–1980* (Medellín, 1987) by the poet-critic Juan Gustavo Cobo Borda, who also contributed to Ricardo Herrera's polemical survey of Argentine poetry, *Usos de la imaginación* (Buenos Aires, 1984), supplemented by Herrera's more controversial *La hora epigonal: ensayos sobre poesía argentina contemporánea* (Buenos Aires, 1991). A more conventional study is Juan Carlos Ghiano, *Poesía argentina del siglo XX* (Mexico, D.F., 1957). A politicized view of recent Argentine poetry is Francisco Urondo, *Veinte años de poesía argentina, 1940–1960* (Buenos Aires, 1968), but written before he became a Montonero. A dull but broader academic approach can be found in the first volume of Guillermo Ara's *Suma de poesía argentina* (Buenos Aires, 1969). James Higgins has written a useful introduction in English to Peruvian poetry, *The Poet in Peru* (Liverpool, 1982), with essays on Vallejo, Moro, Belli, Cisneros and others, which can be complemented by Américo Ferrari, *Los sonidos del silencio: poetas peruanos en el siglo XX* (Lima, 1990). Venezuelan poetry is covered in Vilma Vargas, *El devenir de la palabra poética: Venezuela siglo XX* (Caracas, 1980). The Venezuelan poet-critic Juan Liscano has collected his reviews of his country's poets in *Lecturas de poetas y poesías* (Caracas, 1985). An early survey of Chilean poetry is Fernando Alegría's *La poesía chilena* (Santiago, Chile, 1954), updated by Ricardo Yamal, *La poesía chilena actual (1960–1984) y la crítica* (Concepción, Chile, 1988). The best introduction to Puerto Rican poetry available is Cesáreo Rosa-Nieves, *La poesía en Puerto Rico* (San Juan, P.R., 1969). Uruguayan poet Jorge Medina Vidal has surveyed his country's poetry in *Visión de la poesía uruguaya en el siglo* XX (Montevideo, 1967). José Olivio Jiménez covers Cuban poetry in his balanced but academic *Estudios sobre la poesía cubana contemporánea* (New York, 1967). Further studies of national traditions are cited in the section on general anthologies.

*Interviews*

There are a number of collections of interviews with Latin American poets. An amusing start could be made with U.S. poet Selden Rodman, *Tongues of Fallen Angels* (New York, 1974), travelling to interview Neruda, Paz, Cabral, Parra, and others. Hugo Verani collected several interviews with Paz in *Pasión crítica* (Barcelona, 1985); equally stimulating, with more references to poetry, is Paz and Julián Ríos's dialogue, *Solo a dos voces* (Barcelona, 1973). Volumes of interviews with Borges include Georges Charbonnier, *Entretiens avec Jorge Luis Borges* (Paris, 1967), Jean de Mille-ret, *Entrevista con Jorge Luis Borges* (Caracas, 1971), Richard Burgin, *Conversations with Jorge Luis Borges* (New York, 1974), Ernesto Sabato, *Diálogos* (Buenos Aires, 1976) and more recently, Osvaldo Ferrari, *Borges en diálogo* (Buenos Aires, 1985). Mario Benedetti interviewed Fernández Retamar, Gelman, Parra, Rojas, Dalton and others in *Los poetas comunicantes* (Montevideo, 1972). Pedro Lastra has *Conversaciones con Enrique Lihn* (Xalapa, 1980). Juan Gelman talks about his politics as much as his poetry in Roberto Mero, *Conversaciones con Juan Gelman* (Buenos Aires, 1988). Poet Alberto Girri has collected questions asked him in his *Cuestiones y razones* (Buenos Aires, 1978). The philosophically refined Argentine poet Roberto Juarroz published *Poesía y creación: diálogos con Guillermo Boido* (Buenos Aires, 1980). Margaret Randall includes poets in her *Risking a Somersault in the Air: Conversations with Nicaraguan Writers* (San Francisco, 1984). Miguel Angel Zapata has collected interviews with 26 poets in 'Coloquios del oficio mayor', *Inti: Revista de Literatura Hispánica*, 26–7 (1987–8); they include Liscano and Cisneros. Juan Andrés Piña thoroughly inter-views Parra, Anguita, Rojas, Lihn, Hahn and Zurita in *Conversaciones con la poesía chilena* (Santiago, Chile, 1990).

*General Anthologies*

The most comprehensive starting point is José Olivio Jiménez's *Antología de la poesía hispanoamericana contemporánea, 1914–1970* (Madrid, 1971).

Jiménez had earlier combined with Eugenio Florit to produce a critical anthology, *La poesía hispanoamericana desde el modernismo* (New York, 1968), with good bibliographies. A more provocative and influential anthology was created by Argentine surrealist poet Aldo Pellegrini with his *Antología de la poesía viva latinoamericana* (Barcelona, 1966), introducing the Hispanic world to many surrealistic poets. Stefan Baciu has anthologized Spanish American surrealist poetry along orthodox surrealist lines in his *Antología de la poesía surrealista latinoamericana* (Mexico, D.F., 1974). Practising poets make the best anthologists. Mexican poet Homero Aridjis published his *Seis poetas latinoamericanos de hoy* (New York, 1973), ending with Paz and Parra. Two younger poet-critics have attempted to redefine Spanish American poetry. Juan Gustavo Cobo Borda has a poet's catholic tastes, as evidenced in his *Antología de la poesía hispanoamericana* (Mexico, D.F., 1985), with an acute prologue. Julio Ortega, a fine poet-critic, produced the equally wide-ranging *Antología de la poesía hispanoamericana actual* (Madrid, 1987), with prologue and useful notes. José Antonio Escalona-Escalona's uneven anthology, *Muestra de poesía hispanoamericana del siglo XX* (Caracas, 1985) cannot compete with either Cobo Borda's or Ortega's, despite its critical notes on poets in the second volume. The poet-critic Guillermo Sucre has edited a two-volumed anthology *Antología de la poesía hispanoamericana moderna* (Caracas, 1994) which moves from Darío to Cobo Borda. Guerrilla and resistance poetry are well represented in Jorge Alejandro Boccanera and Saúl Ibargoyen Islas, *Poesía rebelde en Latinoamérica* (Mexico, D.F., 1978), with 129 poets, including Brazilians. Boccanera updated his earlier anthology with *La novísima poesía latinoamericana* (Mexico, D.F., 1982), grouping poets nationally. Mario Benedetti has compiled an anthology of guerrilla poets killed in action – Dalton, Heraud, Marighella, etc.–in *Poesía trunca: poesía latinoamericana revolucionaria* (Madrid, 1980). An anthology of Brazilian poetry is Fernando Ferreira de Loanda, *Antologia da nova poesia brasileira* (Rio de Janeiro, 1970). Two Brazilians are included in Jorge Lafforgue's *Poesía latinoamericana contemporánea* (Buenos Aires, 1988), a popular volume that excludes Paz but includes Darío, Agustini, Neruda, Vallejo, Drummond, Bandeira, Cardenal and Parra. Lastly, a young Octavio Paz was involved in the re-issued *Laurel: Antología de la poesía moderna en lengua española* (1941; Mexico, D.F., 1986) with Xavier Villaurrutia, Emilio Prados and Juan Gil-Albert, breaking new ground by combining Spaniards and Spanish Americans.

## National Anthologies

Octavio Paz, with Alí Chumacero, José Emilio Pacheco and Homero Aridjis, edited the stimulating chronologically-reversed anthology, *Poesía en movimiento, 1915–1966* (Mexico, D.F., 1966). For Mexican poetry this could be complemented with Sergio Mondragón's useful *República de poetas* (Mexico, D.F., 1985). For Chilean poetry, see Roque Esteban Scarpa and Hugo Montes, *Antología de la poesía chilena contemporánea* (Madrid, 1968), Alfonso Calderón, *Antología de la poesía chilena contemporánea* (Santiago, Chile, 1970), with a long, useful appendix where the anthologised poets expatiate about poetry, and, more recently, Erwin Díaz, *Poesía chilena de hoy: de Parra a nuestros días* (Santiago, Chile, 1988). A good introduction to Peruvian poetry is Alberto Escobar, *Antología de la poesía peruana* (Lima, 1965). See also Leonidas Cevallos Mesones, *Los nuevos* (Lima, 1967), with Cisneros, Hinostroza, Lauer, and Ortega, among others, also answering questionnaires about their poetry, and critic José Miguel Oviedo, *Estos 13* (Lima, 1973), with a very useful section, 'Documentos', of poets on their poetry. Mirko Lauer and Abelardo Oquendo have grouped together Peru's avant-garde poets in their anthology, *Vuelta a la otra margen* (Lima, 1970). A good anthology of Colombian poetry is Fernando Chary Lara (ed.), *Poesía y poetas colombianos* (Bogotá, 1985).

Argentine poetry has been well served by anthologists. The reader can begin with the well-documented *Antología lineal de la poesía argentina* (Madrid, 1968) by Cesar Fernández Moreno and Horacio Jorge Becco. For a more partisan and lively anthology, see Instituto Di Tella, *Poesía argentina* (Buenos Aires, 1963). Poet Hector Yánover's *Antología consultada de la joven poesía argentina* (Buenos Aires, 1968) is informative, with comments by each selected poet. For the poetry of the 1960s, see Francisco Urondo and Noé Jitrik's *Antología interna* (Buenos Aires, 1965). Leopoldo Castilla has grouped together the more recent, politicized poetry of the last twenty years in *Nueva poesía argentina* (Madrid, 1987). Alejandro Paternain's *36 años de poesía uruguaya* (Montevideo, 1967) has a long introduction to Uruguay's poets of the 1950s and 1960s. For contemporary Cuban poetry, the Spanish poet José Agustín Goytisolo's *Nueva poesía cubana* (Barcelona, 1970) is a good starting point, supplemented by Orlando Rodríguez Sardiñas, *La última poesía cubana* (Madrid, 1973), and Nicaraguan poet Ernesto Cardenal, *Poesía cubana de la revolución* (Mexico, D.F., 1976). For contemporary Nicaraguan poetry, Ernesto Cardenal's *Poesía nicaragüense* (Havana, 1973) is the best, with José Miguel Oviedo's *Musas en guerra: poesía, arte, y cultura en la nueva Nicaragua (1974–1988)* (Mexico, D.F., 1987) very informative. Salvadorean novelist Manlio Argueta has compiled *Poesía de El Salvador* (San José, C.R., 1980). José Antonio Escalona-Escalona has edited *Antología actual de la poesía venezolana (1950–1980)* (Madrid, 1981) in two volumes, with a bibliographical appendix. There is an anthology of Bolivian poetry by Luis Ramiro Beltrán, *Panorama de la poesía boliviana: reseña y antología* (Bogotá, 1982); another on Paraguayan poetry by Roque Vallejos, *Antología crítica de la poesía paraguaya contemporánea* (Asunción, 1968); and one on Honduran poetry by Oscar Acosta, *Poesía hondureña de hoy* (Tegucigalpa, 1971).

Most of the poets alluded to in this bibliographical essay, and in the chapters by Jaime Concha and Jason Wilson in this volume, have been translated into English, both individually, and in several national anthologies. See Jason Wilson, *An A–Z of Modern Latin American Literature in English Translation* (London, 1989).

## Bibliographies

For further bibliography, a comprehensive starting point is Hensley Woodbridge, *Guide to Reference Works for the Study of the Spanish Language and Literature and Spanish American Literature* (New York, 1978), proceeding country by country, excluding Brazil. For Brazil, Irwing Stern (ed.), *Dictionary of Brazilian Literature* (New York, 1988) is rewarding. On women writers, see Diane Marking (ed.), *Women Writers of Spanish America: An Annotated Bio-Bibliographical Guide* (New York, 1987). The most recent bibliography is Jacobo Sefamí, *Contemporary Spanish American Poets: A Bibliography of Primary and Secondary Sources* (New York, 1992). On individual writers, Hugo Verani's *Octavio Paz: bibliografía crítica* (Mexico, D.F., 1983) is judicious and complete; Horacio Jorge Becco, *Jorge Luis Borges: bibliografía total, 1923–1973* (Buenos Aires, 1973) is complete up to its publication date; and Hensley Woodbridge and David Zobatsky, *Pablo Neruda: An Annotated Bibliography of Biographical and Critical Studies* (New York, 1988) is most useful.

## 5. INDIGENOUS LITERATURES AND CULTURES IN
### TWENTIETH-CENTURY LATIN AMERICA

*Sources and Interpretation*

As a succinct introduction to American culture and its place in the world, Claude Lévi-Strauss's essay, 'Race et histoire' (1952), published in translation in *Structural Anthropology*, vol. 2 (Harmondsworth, Eng., 1978), remains unsurpassed; it has the historical underpinning lacking in the four structuralist volumes of his *Mythologiques* (Paris, 1964–71). Joseph H. Greenberg, *Language in the Americas* (Stanford, Calif., 1987) has now laid the foundation for defining American culture in the joint terms of linguistics and genetics. Michael Closs, *Native American Mathematics* (Austin, Tex., 1985) is the first continental account of this subject. In recent years, *América Indígena*, the journal of the Instituto Indigenista Interamericano (Mexico), has increasingly accepted native languages and literatures as a key element in culture and education; see issue 50 (1990). A soundly researched though theoretically naive account of script in Mesoamerica is Joyce Marcus, *Mesoamerican Writing Systems: Propaganda, Myth and History in Four Ancient Civilizations* (Princeton, N.J., 1992). See also, 'Epigraphy', ed. V. Bricker, *Supplement to the Handbook of Middle American Indians,* Vol. 5 (Austin, Tex., 1992); and Elizabeth Boone and Walter Mignolo (eds.), *Writing without Words: Alternative Literacies in Mesoamerica and the Andes* (Durham, N.C., 1994). Facsimiles of nearly all the major codices have been published by the Akademische Druck-und Verlags Anstalt (ADEVA) in Graz. The recent spate of decipherments of Maya hieroglyphic script is reported in Michael Coe, *Breaking the Maya Code* (New York, 1992), and touched on in Miguel León-Portilla, *Time and Reality in the Thought of the Maya* (Norman, Okla., 1987). K. A. Nowotny, *Tlacuilolli: Die mexikanischen Bilderhandschriften, Stil und Inhalt* (Berlin, 1961), remains the lone standard work on the closely-related iconic script, especially in the ritual genre. With respect to the genre of annals, see John B. Glass, 'A census of native Middle American pictorial manuscripts', in *Handbook of Middle American Indians,* vol. 14 (Austin, Tex., 1975), 81–250. The Mixtec tradition is comprehensively treated by Alfonso Caso in *Reyes y reinos de la Mixteca,* 2 vols. (Mexico, D.F., 1977–9); and an update on that of the Chichimec is offered in Gordon Brotherston, *Painted Books from Mexico: Codices in the United Kingdom and the World They Represent* (London,

1995). The sophistication of the Inca quipu, used as a literary source by the mestizo historian Guamán Poma (see below), has been vindicated by Marcia and Robert Ascher, *Code of the Quipu: A Study in Media, Mathematics and Culture* (Ann Arbor, Mich., 1981). Miguel León-Portilla, *Literaturas indígenas de México* (Mexico, D.F., 1992), José Juan Arrom, *Mitología y artes prehispánicas de las Antillas* (Mexico, D.F., 1989), and Gerdt Kutscher, *Nordperuanische Keramik* (Berlin, 1954), are all exemplary in incorporating inscriptions and ancient texts into literary history. Arrom has also newly edited Ramón Pané's *Relación de las antigüedades de las Indias*, 8th rev. ed. (Mexico, D.F. 1988), a unique source for Taino cosmogony.

Within what is often uncritically referred to as 'orality', *Watunna* is a fundamental Carib text encountered as a result of the 1950 expedition described by René Lichy in *Yaku: Expedición franco-venezolana del Alto Orinoco* (Caracas, 1978); it has been edited by Marc de Civrieux in Spanish, *Watunna: Mitología makiritare* (Caracas, 1970), and in English, *Watunna: An Orinoco Creation Cycle*, trans. David M. Guss (San Francisco, 1980). See also David Guss, 'Keeping it oral: a Yekuana ethnology', *American Ethnologist*, 13/3 (1986), 413–29. Little of this critical perception is available in the otherwise standard *Handbook of South American Indians*, 6 vols., ed. J. H. Steward (Washington, D.C., 1946–50). The ideas and practices of the new literary anthropology are set out by exponents in Dell Hymes, *'In Vain I Tried to Tell': Essays in Native American Ethnopoetics* (Philadelphia, 1981); Jerome Rothenberg, *Technicians of the Sacred*, 2nd enlarged edn. (Berkeley, 1985); Dennis Tedlock, *The Spoken Word and the Work of Interpretation* (Philadelphia, 1983); Joel Sherzer and Greg Urban (eds.), *Native South American Discourse* (Berlin, 1986); Joel Sherzer and Anthony C. Woodbury (eds.), *Native American Discourse: Poetics and Rhetoric* (Cambridge, Eng., 1987); and Ellen Basso and Joel Sherzer (eds.), *Las culturas nativas latinoamericanas a través de su discurso* (Quito and Rome, 1990). An analysis that works out from native scripts and texts into political memory and cosmogony is found in Gordon Brotherston, *Book of the Fourth World: Reading the Native Americas through Their Literature* (Cambridge, Eng., 1992), a convenient source for references not otherwise given here.

## World View and Cosmogony

The outstanding example of Mesoamerican cosmogony, the Popol vuh of the Quiché-Maya, was first directly translated into English by Munro

Edmonson, *The Book of Counsel: The Popol vuh of the Quiché Maya of Guatemala* (New Orleans, La., 1971). Edmonson also provided a transcription of the original, in couplet form, and reviewed and compared previous translations into Spanish (Villacorta y Rodas; Recínos), French (Brasseur; Raynaud – the source of the Spanish version made by M. A. González de Mendoza and the Guatemalan novelist Miguel Angel Asturias), and other major languages. His work was followed by Dennis Tedlock's intrepidly entitled *Popol Vuh: The Definitive Edition of the Mayan Book of the Dawn of Life and the Glories of Gods and Kings* (New York, 1985), English text only, which benefits from the author's experience of studying with Quiché shamans in Guatemala. With the lowland Maya books of Chilam Balam, Munro Edmonson again provides direct translations plus original texts, albeit heavily reconstructed, as well as surveys of previous translations; in the case of the Book of Chumayel, *Heaven Born Merida and Its Destiny* (Austin, Tex., 1986), previously known through Gordon's facsimile of 1914 and Ralph Roys's *The Book of Chilam Balam of Chumayel* (Washington, D.C., 1933); and in the case of the Book of Tizimin, *The Ancient Future of the Itza* (Austin, Tex., 1982), rendered as *The Book of the Jaguar Priest* by Maud Makemson (New York, 1951). In their classic study, *El libro de los libros de Chilam Balam* (Mexico, D.F., 1948), Alfredo Barrera Vásquez and Silvia Rendón show the interrelationship between five of the six principal surviving versions of these books (those mentioned above, plus the books of Maní, Kaua, Oxcutzcab and Ixil). Echoes of Yucatec Maya cosmogony are also found in *El ritual de los bacabes,* ed. Ramón Arzápalo Marín (Mexico, D.F., 1987).

In the Nahuatl language tradition, the two cosmogonical texts preserved in the Codex Chimalpopoca, the Cuauhtitlan Annals and the Legend of the Suns, have been translated for the first time directly into English by John Bierhorst, *History and Mythology of the Aztecs* (Tucson, Ariz., 1992). In doubting the integrity of the native year count, which runs unbroken from 1 Reed 635 to 1 Reed 1519 AD and into which the far more ancient story of the Suns is set, this version differs from those in German (Walter Lehmann, *Die Geschichte der Königreiche von Colhuacan und Mexico* [1938; Berlin, 1974] and in Spanish (Primo Feliciano Velázquez, *Códice Chimalpopoca* [Mexico, D.F., 1945]). The pattern of Mesoamerican world ages or Suns is discussed in Jesús Monjarás Ruiz's most useful and informed overview, *Mitos cosmogónicos del México indígena* (Mexico, D.F., 1987), where Mercedes de la Garza notes how in the *Popol vuh* the scheme of four prior Suns has been obscured by translators, among them

Edmonson and Tedlock, who run together the first two distinct creations of mud people and doll people. Garza is also editor of Antonio Médiz Bolio's pioneer 1930 Spanish version of the Chilam Balam Book of Chumayel (Mexico, D.F., 1985). Robert Carmack and James Mondloch have edited papers given at the milestone first international conference devoted to the *Popol vuh: Nuevas perspectivas sobre el Popol vúh* (Guatemala City, 1983). Munro Edmonson (ed.), *Literatures, Supplement to the Handbook of Middle American Indians*, vol. 3 (Austin, Tex., 1985) features modern Mesoamerican creation stories, notably those of the Tzotzil discussed by Gary Gossen; for the Mixe, see Frank Lipp, *The Mixe of Oaxaca: Religion, Ritual and Healing* (Austin, Tex., 1991).

The question of mapping and ritual geography germane to models found in the ancient Mesoamerican books is taken up by, amongst others, Eva Hunt, *The Transformation of the Hummingbird: Cultural Roots of a Zinacantecan Mythical Poem* (Ithaca, N.Y., 1966); Juan Negrín, *The Huichol Creation of the World* (Sacramento, Calif., 1975); Leland C. Wyman, *Southwest Indian Dry Painting* (Albuquerque, N.Mex., 1983); and K. A. Nowotny, *Tlacuilolli*, cited above.

In the Andean area, the key Quechua manuscript of Huarochiri (c. 1608), long neglected, has now been widely edited and translated; see Hermann Trimborn, *Dämonen und Zauber in Inkareich: Fr. de Avila, Tratado de errores* (Leipzig, 1939–41); José María Argüedas, *Dioses y hombres de Huarochirí: Narración quechua* (Lima, 1966); Gérald Taylor, *Ritos y tradiciones de Huarochirí: manuscrito quechua, versión paleográfica* (Lima, 1987); George Urioste, *Hijos de Pariya Qaqa: la tradición oral de Wara Chiri*, 2 vols. (Syracuse, N.Y., 1983); and Frank Salomon and George Urioste, *The Huarochirí Manuscript: A Testament of Ancient and Colonial Andean Religion* (Austin, Tex., 1991). Roswith Hartmann surveys several of these renderings in 'Zur Ueberlieferung indianischer Oraltradition aus dem kolonialzeitlichen Peru: Das Huarochirí Manuscript', in B. Illius and M. Laubscher, *Circumpacifica: Festschrift für Thomas S. Barthel*, vol. 1 (Frankfurt, 1990), 534–61. Felipe Guaman Poma de Ayala's *El primer nueva corónica y buen gobierno*, completed c. 1613 and first published in facsimile as late as 1936 (Paris), has been comprehensively edited and transcribed by John V. Murra and R. Adorno, 3 vols. (Mexico, D.F., 1980). Overall views of Andean cosmogony are presented in J. M. Ossio, *Ideología mesiánica del mundo andino* (Lima, 1973). The Huinkulche and other narratives of Mapuche creation from the southern Andes today are gathered by Bertha Kössler-Ilg in her indispensable *Indianermärchen aus den Kordilleren* (Düsseldorf, 1956); partially available in

Spanish in her *Cuentan los araucanos* (Buenos Aires, 1954), and *Tradiciones araucanas* (La Plata, 1962). Living in San Martín de los Andes, Kössler-Ilg was able to take down directly the recollections of Mapuche born before the military assaults on native territory carried out by Argentina and Chile in the late-nineteenth-century. The link between cosmogony and political consciousness in the Andes today is lucidly described by Malú Sierra in *Mapuche, gente de la tierra* (Santiago, Chile, 1992).

Beside Paul Zolbrod's remarkable reworking of Washington Matthew's late-nineteenth-century texts in *Diné Bahane: The Navajo Creation Story* (Albuquerque, N.Mex., 1984), the most accessible accounts of Anasazi genesis are those found in the dry-painter narratives collected by Gladys Reichard in *Navajo Religion* (New York, 1963), and *Navajo Medicine Men Sandpaintings* (New York, 1977); and in Dennis Tedlock's *Finding the Center: Narrative Poetry of the Zuni Indians* (Lincoln, Nebr., 1972). For the Tatkan Ikala of the Panamanian Cuna, see Erland Nordenskiöld, *An Historical and Ethnographical Survey of the Cuna Indians,* in collaboration with the Cuna Indian Rubén Pérez Kantule, ed. Henry Wassén (Göteborg, 1938); and Fritz Kramer, *Literature among the Cuna Indians* (Göteborg, 1970). Accounts of rain-forest cosmogony are given in Juan Adolfo Vázquez's excellent 'The present state of research in South American mythology', *Numen,* 25 (1970), 240–76; Lawrence Sullivan, *Icanchu's Drum* (New York, 1988), which contains very full notes and bibliography; and John Bierhorst's more popularizing *The Mythology of South America* (New York, 1988). Individual editions and translations of note include: León Cadogan, *Ayvu rapyta* (São Paulo, 1959), and *La literatura de los guaraníes* (Mexico, D.F., 1965); Rubén Bareiro Saguier, *Literatura guaraní del Paraguay* (Caracas, 1980), which includes the early texts of Kurt Onkel-Nimuendajú; Marc de Civrieux, *Watunna: Mitología makiritare* (Eng. trans, *Watunna: An Orinoco Creation Cycle*), cited above; David Guss, 'Medatia' (a companion piece to *Watunna*), in *The Language of Birds* (San Francisco, 1985); Konrad Theodor Preuss, *Die Religion und Mythologie der Uitoto* (Göttingen-Leipzig, 1921); Umusin Panlon Kumu, *Antes o mundo não existia,* trans. Tomalan Kenhiri and Berta Ribeiro (São Paulo, 1980) (a text in the Desana-Tukano tradition also featured in Gerardo Reichel-Dolmatoff, *Amazonian Cosmos* (Chicago, 1971); and Stephen Hugh-Jones, *The Palm and the Pleiades: Initiation and Cosmology in Northwest Amazonia* (Cambridge, Eng., 1979). Shuar-Jivaro texts, in the original language with Spanish translation, are edited by Siro Pellizaro in the Mitología shuar series published in Sucua, Ecuador; the flood story appears in *Tsunki:*

*El mundo del agua y de los poderes fecundantes*, vol. 2 (Sucua, 1979). Mircea Eliade's classic study, *Shamanism: Archaic Techniques of Ecstasy*, trans. W. R. Trask (Princeton, N.J., 1964), is especially illuminating on the epic within American cosmogony.

## Resilience and Medium

Wide-reaching theoretical models of cultural resistance of the kind proposed by Nestor García Canclini, *Culturas híbridas: estrategias para entrar y salir de la modernidad* (Mexico, D.F., 1990), which reflect developments in the global economy, often find themselves modified in specific cases. Examples are Gary Gossen (ed.), *Symbol and Meaning beyond the Closed Community* (Albany, N.Y., 1986); Frank Salomon on Otavalo weaving and lore in David Gross (ed.), *Peoples and Cultures of Native South America* (New York, 1973); Herta Puls, *Textiles of the Kuna Indians of Panama* (Aylesbury, Eng., 1988); Juan Negrín, *Acercamiento histórico y subjectivo al huichol* (Guadalajara, 1985); Alan R. Sandstrom, *Traditional Curing and Crop Fertility Rituals among Otomi Indians (the López manuscripts)* (Bloomington, Ind., 1981), and (with Pamela Effrein), *Traditional Papermaking and Paper Cult Figures of Mexico* (Norman, Okla., 1986); and Catharine Good Eshelman, *Haciendo la lucha: arte y comercio nahuas de Guerrero* (Mexico, D.F., 1988). The theme of specifically literary resistance has been well examined by José María Argüedas, *Canto quechwa* (Lima, 1938), and *Formación de una cultura nacional indoamericana* (Mexico, D.F., 1975) (which includes his seminal 1956 essay on the Inkarrí legend); and Regina Harrison, *Signs, Songs and Memory in the Andes* (Austin, Tex., 1989). Editions of the Náhuatl Tepozteco play are noted in Frances Kartunnen and Gilka Wara Cespedes, 'The dialogue of El Tepozteco and his rivals', *Tlalocan* 9 (1982),115–44; the cycle to which it belongs is treated in Pablo González Casanova's classic *Estudios de linguística y filologías náhuas* (Mexico, D.F., 1977), 209–66. Robert Laughlin, author of the *Great Tzotzil Dictionary of San Lorenzo Zinacantan* (Washington, D.C., 1975), has been a main force in establishing Sna Jtzi'bajom, the writers' center in San Cristobal; see also Neville Stiles, 'Purist tendencies among native Mayan speakers of Guatemala', *Linguist*, 26 (1987), 187–91. Carlos Montemayor's comprehensive *Los escritores indígenas actuales*, 2 vols. (Mexico, D.F., 1992) also deals with computers and 'informants'. See also Juan de Dios Yapita, 'Problemas de traducción de aymara al castellano', *Actas del 3er. Congreso de Lenguas Nacionales* (La Paz, 1976). For observations on the impact of video recorders and other technology, see articles by T. Turner, J. Ruby and others in *Visual Anthropology Review,* 7/2 (1991), and F. Ginsburg, 'Indigenous media: Faustian contract or global village?', *Cultural Anthropology,* 6/1 (1991), 94–114 (noted in Patricia Aufderheide, 'Grassroots video in Latin America', unpub ms. 1992); on the Consejo Regional Indígena del Cauca (CRIC), see Christian Gros, *Colombia indígena: identidad cultural y cambio social* (Bogotá, 1991). The tenacity and adaptability of native lore within modern Latin America are authoritatively detailed by William Rowe and Vivian Schelling in *Memory and Modernity: Popular Culture in Latin America* (London, 1991). The experience of making film out of a Mexican codex is described by Enrique Escalona in *Tlacuilo* (Mexico, D.F., 1989); the *Popol vuh* and *Watunna* have been filmed by PBS and the Museum of the American Indian, New York.

### Modern Authors

No general survey exists of works in native American languages by individually named authors, although Carlos Montemayor's *Los escritores indígenas actuales,* cited above, breaks new ground in providing a common platform for writers in five or six Mesoamerican languages. A general context can be sketched out on the basis of individual publications, as well as collections and scholarly studies relating to particular languages. Among these are counted for Guarani, Julio Correa and Tadeo Zarretea in Antonio Pecci, *Teatro breve del Paraguay* (Asunción, 1981); for Mapudungu/Mapuche, Ivan Carrasco, 'Literatura mapuche', *America Indígena,* 48 (1988), 695–730; Pascual Coña, *Kuifike mapuche yem chumnechi: testimonio de un cacique mapuche,* ed. E. W. Moesbach (1930; Santiago, Chile, 1984); Leonel Lienlaf, *Nepey ñi güñün piuke: se ha despertado el ave de mi corazón* (Santiago, Chile, 1989), with an illuminating prologue by Raúl Zurita; for Quechua, Abdón Yaranga, 'The Wayno in Andean civilization', in G. Brotherston (ed.), *Voices of the First America: Text and Context in the New World* (Santa Barbara, Calif., 1986); Kilku Waraka (Andrés Alencastre), *Yawar Para* (Cuzco, 1972); Carlos Falconi, Eusebio Huamani, Lino Quintanilla and others in Rodrigo Montoya, Edwin Montoya and Luis Montoya, *Urqukunapa yawarnin: la sangre de los cerros* (Lima, 1987); John McDowell, *Sayings of the Ancestors: The Spiritual Life of the Sibundoy Indians* (Lexington, Ky., 1989); Jesús Lara, *Poesía popular quechua* (La Paz, 1947), and *La literatura de los quechuas* (La Paz, 1969); Yuyachkani, in Rodrigo Montoya, 'Quechua theater: History, violence and hope', in *Latin America: Literal Territories,* ed. G. Brotherston (Bloomington, 1993); for Nahuatl, Fausto Hernández Hernández in Joel Martínez Hernández, *Xochitlajtolkoskatl: poesía nauatl contemporánea* (Tlaxcala, 1987); Luis Reyes in Míguel León-Portilla (ed.), 'Yancuic tlahtolli: La nueva palabra: Antología de la literatura náhuatl contemporánea', *Estudios de Cultura Náhuatl,* nos. 18–20 (1988–90); for Maya, Domingo Dzul Poot, *Cuentos mayas,* 2 vols. (Mérida, Mex., 1985–6); Paulino Yama in Allan F. Burns, *An Epoch of Miracles: Oral Literature of the Yucatec Maya* (Austin, Tex., 1983); Asis Ligorred Perramon, *Consideraciones sobre la literatura oral de los mayas modernos* (Mexico, D.F., 1990); and, for Jakaltec Maya, Victor Montejo, *The Bird Who Cleans the World and other Mayan Fables* (Willimantic, Conn., 1992).

### *Impact on Latin American Literature*

Taking the first term of its title from the Cuban ethnomusicologist Fernando Ortiz, Angel Rama's *Transculturación narrativa en América Latina* (Mexico, D.F., 1982), creates the space necessary for any fair discussion of the intertextuality common to native and imported literary traditions in America. Rama also draws heavily on the socio-literary approach of both José María Argüedas and the Brazilians Nunes Pereira, Márcio Souza and Darcy Ribeiro. Under the theme-title 'Proyección de lo indígena en la literatura de la América Hispánica', *Revista Iberoamericana,* 50/127 (1984) deals with native influence on a range of Spanish American authors. Studies with the same focus have been steadily carried by the *Latin American Indian Literatures Journal* from the late 1980s onwards. John Bierhorst's 'Incorporating the native voice: A look back from 1990', in Brian Swann (ed.), *On the Translation of Native American Literatures* (Washington, D.C., 1992), 51–63, has continental scope though the thinness of the data (he totally ignores Asturias, for example) may account for the author's extraordinary opinion that native sources have 'supplied precious little to the formation of English, Spanish, and Portuguese letters in the New World'. José Juan Arrom's analysis of the Modernista Rubén Darío's native debt ("El oro, la pluma y la piedra preciosa: Indagaciones sobre el trasfondo indígena de la poesía de Darío', (1967); reprinted in *Certidumbre de América: estudios de letras, folklore y cultura* (Madrid, 1989), points the way to subsequent case studies.

The veritable network of native texts drawn upon by Asturias, Carpentier, Abreu Gómez, Cardenal and other authors is examined in Gordon Brotherston: 'Gaspar Ilóm en su tierra', in G. Martin (ed.), *M. A. Asturias: Hombres de maíz* (Madrid, 1992), 593–602; 'Pacaraima as destination in Carpentier's *Los pasos perdidos*', in *Latin America: Literal Territories* (Bloomington, Ind., 1993), 154–76; 'The Latin American novel and its indigenous sources', in J. King (ed.), *Modern Latin American Fiction: A Survey* (London, 1987), 60–77; and 'The American Palimpsest', *Book of the Fourth World,* cited above, 341–9. The Andean textual tradition is analysed by Martin Lienhard, *Cultura andina y forma novelesca: Zorros y danzantes en la última novela de Argüedas* (Lima, 1990), and Laura Lee Crumley, 'El intertexto de Huarochirí en Manuel Scorza: Una visión múltiple de la muerte en *Historia de Carabombo el invisible*', *América Indígena,* 44 (1984), 747–55. Telê Porto Ancona López's edition of Mário de Andrade's *Macunaíma* (São Paulo, 1988) superbly reveals the impact of Carib and Tupi texts on that work. Italo Calvino's intuition of the literary wealth of the rain-forest is quoted by Gerald Martin in *Journeys through the Labyrinth* (London, 1989). Garibay's versions of the Cantares mexicanos and their effect on Mexican literature are dealt with in Gordon Brotherston, 'Nezahualcoyotl's Lamentaciones and their Nahuatl origins', *Estudios de Cultura Náhuatl,* 10 (1972), 393–408, and in Sara Castro-Klarén, *Escritura, transgresión y sujeto en la literatura latinoamericana* (Puebla, 1989). For the debate provoked by Bierhorst's translation, *Cantares Mexicanos: Songs of the Aztecs* (Stanford, Calif., 1985), see Amos Segala, *Histoire de la littérature náhuatl: Sources, identités, représentations* (Rome, 1989); and Miguel León-Portilla, '¿Una nueva aportación sobre literatura náhuatl?', *Estudios de Cultura Náhuatl,* 21 (1991), 293–310.

## 6. LATIN AMERICAN MUSIC, C.1920–C.1980

A review of popular music literature, of centres and research collections, and future research on popular music is provided in Gerard Béhague 'Popular music' in *Handbook of Latin American Popular Culture,* edited by Harold E. Hinds, Jr. and Charles M. Tatum (Westport, Conn., 1985), 3–38. Vol. 6/2 (1987) of the journal *Popular Music* is dedicated to Latin America and includes a section on 'sources and resources'. Jan Fairley presents an 'Annotated bibliography of Latin American popular music with particular references to Chile and *nueva canción*', *Popular Music,* 5 (1985), 305–56. John

Schechter provides a good discussion and selected bibliography on popular music in his article 'The current state of bibliographic research in Latin American ethnomusicology', in Dan C. Hazen (ed.), *Latin American Masses and Minorities: Their Images and Realities,* 2 vols. (Madison, Wisc., 1987). For an assessment of studies of Latin American folk and traditional music, see Gerard Béhague, 'Latin America', in Helen Myers (ed.), *Ethnomusicology: Historical and Regional Studies* (London, 1993).

Gilbert Chase, *A Guide to the Music of Latin America* (1955; 2nd ed., Washington, D.C., 1962), remains valuable. For bibliographic references since *c.* 1960, the music section of the *Handbook of Latin American Studies* should be consulted. Gerard Béhague's detailed survey of Latin American art music, *Music in Latin America: An Introduction* (Englewood Cliffs, N.J., 1979; Sp. trans., Caracas, 1983), provides copious bibliographical notes on twentieth-century music. Trends, stylistic development and detailed and updated biographical information concerning Latin American music, musicians and institutions are provided in the twenty volumes of *The New Grove Dictionary of Music and Musicians,* edited by Stanley Sadie (London, 1980). Quite useful, in spite of many factual errors and the lack of updating of the material, is the series *Composers of the Americas/Compositores de las Américas,* published by the OAS (Washington, D.C.), which provides biographical data and catalogues of the works of selected composers from all countries of the Western Hemisphere. For more general and recent research sources, see 'Essay' by Gerard Béhague and 'Bibliography' by John Druesedow in the section on Music in the volume *Latin America and the Caribbean. A Critical Guide to Research Sources,* edited by Paula H. Covington (Wesport, Conn., 1992), 569–88.

Carlos Chávez's life and works have been the subject of numerous studies. Roberto García Morillo, *Carlos Chávez: vida y obra* (Mexico, D.F. 1960) is one of the best analytical studies and includes a catalogue of the composer's works, a bibliography and a discography, brought up to date in *Carlos Chávez, Mexico's Modern-Day Orpheus,* by Robert L. Parker (Boston, 1983). Mexican musical nationalism is well treated in Otto Mayer-Serra's *Panorama de la música mexicana* (Mexico, D.F., 1941), and his study of 'Silvestre Revueltas and musical nationalism in Mexico', *The Musical Quarterly,* 27 (1941), 123–45, is still valuable. Yolanda Moreno Rivas, *Rostros del nacionalismo en la música mexicana* (Mexico, D.F., 1989) is a thought-provoking essay with interesting analyses. Dan Malström, 'Introduction to twentieth-century Mexican music' (unpublished Ph.D dissertation, Uppsala University, 1974) contains good general information, although the musical analyses leave a great deal to be desired. Vol. 5 of *La música de México,* edited by Julio Estrada (Mexico, D.F., 1984) deals with the period 1958–80.

Cuban nationalism and the study of *afrocubanismo* are best treated in Alejo Carpentier, *La música en Cuba* (Mexico, D.F., 1946). Nicolas Slonimsky, 'Caturla of Cuba,' *Modern Music,* 27/2 (1940), 76–80, provides some analytical comments on that composer's works. The early works of Aurelio de la Vega are studied in Alice Ramsay's 'Aurelio de la Vega: His life and his music' (M.A. thesis, California State University, 1963). Ronald Erin wrote on 'Cuban elements in the music of Aurelio de la Vega,' *Latin American Music Review,* 5/1 (1984), 1–32, and Paul Century on 'Leo Brouwer: A portrait of the artist in Socialist Cuba,' *Latin American Music Review,* 8/2 (1987), 151–71, with a detailed bibliography on the composer. For a general assessment of Cuban musical life in the 1980s, see Victoria Elí Rodríguez, 'Apuntes sobre la creación musical actual en Cuba', *Latin American Music Review,* 10/1 (1989), 287–97.

The best and most detailed study of Puerto Rican music in general is Héctor Campos-Parsi's *La música,* which makes up vol. 7 of *La Gran Enciclopedia de Puerto Rico* (Madrid, 1976). Anna Figueroa de Thompson, *An Annotated Bibliography of Writings about Music in Puerto Rico* (Ann Arbor, Mich., 1974) is the best bibliographic reference.

A good general survey of Venezuelan music up to the 1950s is José Antonio Calcaño, *La ciudad y su música* (Caracas, 1958). Colombian music history of the twentieth century is surveyed in José Ignacio Perdomo Escobar, *Historia de la música en Colombia,* 3rd ed. (Bogotá, 1963) and Andrés Pardo Tovar, *La cultura musical en Colombia* (Bogotá, 1966). Studies on Uribe Holguín include Guillermo Rendón's 'Maestros de la música: Guillermo Uribe Holguín (1880–1971),' in *Boletín de Música* (Havana) nos. 50–1 (1975), and Eliana Duque, *Guillermo Uribe Holguín y sus '300 trozos en el sentimiento popular'* (Bogotá, 1980). Segundo Luis Moreno provided a general survey of Ecuadorian music history in 'La música en el Ecuador', in J. Gonzalo Orellana (ed.), *El Ecuador en cien años de independencia,* vol. 2 (Quito, 1930). Peruvian music and musicians have been studied in Rodolfo Barbacci, 'Apuntes para un diccionario biográfico musical peruano', *Fénix,* 6 (1949), Carlos Raygada, 'Guía musical del Perú,' *Fénix,* 12 (1956–7), 13 (1963), and 14 (1964), and Enrique Pinilla, 'La música contemporánea en el Perú,' *Fanal* (Lima), 79 (1966). Four chapters dealing with Peruvian music from 1900 to 1985, written by Enrique Pinilla, form part of the book *La música en el Perú* (Lima, 1985). Bolivian music is surveyed in Atiliano Auza León, *Dinámica musical en Bolivia* (La Paz, 1967).

Numerous articles on Chilean music institutions, composers and their works with catalogues have been published in *Revista Musical Chilena,* a general index of which appears in 98 (1966), 129–30 (1975), and 163 (1985). A general survey of Chilean art music since 1900 is Vicente Salas Viu, *La creación musical en Chile, 1900–1951* (Santiago, Chile, 1952), updated by Samuel Claro V. and Jorge Urrutia B. in their *Historia de la música en Chile* (Santiago, Chile, 1973).

The most relevant studies of Brazilian music are Luiz Heitor Corrêa de Azevedo, *150 anos de música no Brasil (1800–1950)* (Rio de Janeiro, 1956), Mário de Andrade's epoch-making *Ensaio sôbre a música brasileira* (São Paulo, 1928), Renato Almeida, *História da música brasileira,* 2nd ed. (Rio de Janeiro, 1942), Vasco Mariz, *Figuras da música brasileira contemporânea* (Brasília, 1970) and *História da música no Brasil,* 4th ed. (Rio de Janeiro, 1994), and Bruno Kiefer, *História da música brasileira* (Porto Alegre, 1976). *Música contemporânea brasileira,* by José Maria Neves (São Paulo, 1981), brings some updated information on new composers' activities. On the life and works of Heitor Villa-Lobos, see Andrade Muricy, *Villa-Lobos, uma interpretação* (Rio de Janeiro, 1961); Vasco Mariz, *Heitor Villa-Lobos: Life and Work of the Brazilian Composer,* 2nd ed. (Washington, D.C., 1970) (the eleventh edition of this book, much enlarged, appeared in Portuguese translation in 1989 in Belo Horizonte); Lisa M. Peppercorn, *Heitor Villa-Lobos: Leben und Werk des brasilianischen Komponisten* (Zürich, 1972); Bruno Kiefer, *Villa-Lobos e o modernismo na música brasileira* (Porto Alegre, 1981); Luiz Pablo Horta, *Heitor Villa-Lobos* (Rio de Janeiro, 1987); Simon Wright, *Villa-Lobos* (Oxford, 1992); and Gerard Béhague, *Heitor Villa-Lobos: The Search for Brazil's Musical Soul* (Austin, Tex., 1994), the most recent comprehensive examination of the composer's life and work. Specific analytical works include Arnaldo Estrella, *Os quartetos de cordas de Villa-Lobos* (Rio de Janeiro, 1970); Adhemar Nóbrega, *As Bachianas brasileiras de Villa-Lobos* (Rio de Janeiro, 1971) and *Os Choros de Villa-Lobos* (Rio de Janeiro, 1975). Vasco Mariz has written a short biography of Santoro in *Cláudio Santoro* (Rio de Janeiro, 1994).

A general overview of Argentine musical life in the twentieth century is provided in Mario García Acevedo, *La música argentina durante el período de la organización nacional* (Buenos Aires, 1961) and *La música argentina contemporánea* (Buenos Aires, 1963). Opera in Buenos Aires is the subject of Roberto Caamaño (ed.), *La historia del Teatro Colón* (Buenos Aires, 1969). A series of individual biographies of Argentine composers was begun in the early 1960s by the Ministerio de Educación y Justicia in

Buenos Aires, known as the 'Series Ediciones Culturales Argentinas'. It includes biographies on Juan José Castro by Rodolfo Arizaga (1963), on Jacobo Ficher by Boris Zipman (1966), and on Alberto Ginastera by Pola Suárez Urtubey (1967). On Ginastera's life and works, see Gilbert Chase, 'Alberto Ginastera: Argentine composer,' *The Musical Quarterly,* 43/4 (1957), and Malena Kuss, 'Type, derivation, and use of folk idioms in Ginastera's *Don Rodrigo* (1964),' *Latin American Music Review,* 1/2 (1980). Uruguayan music is treated in some detail in Susana Salgado, *Breve historia de la música culta en el Uruguay* (Montevideo, 1971), including comprehensive catalogues of Uruguayan composers' works.

Latin American new, experimental music has not been studied very extensively. For an overview of music since 1950, see Aurelio de la Vega, 'New World composers,' *Inter-American Music Bulletin,* 43 (1964) and 'Avant-garde music at the American Art Biennal of Córdoba', *Yearbook-Anuario* (Inter-American Institute for Musical Research), 3 (1967). See also his review-essay 'A quick encounter with Brazil's art music through some recent recordings', *Latin American Music Review,* 8/1 (1987), 119–31. Juan Orrego-Salas surveyed the contemporary trends and personalities in 'The young generation of Latin American composers: Backgrounds and perspectives', *Inter-American Music Bulletin,* 38 (1963), and Gustavo Becerra Schmidt wrote on 'Modern music south of the Rio Grande', *Inter-American Music Bulletin,* 83 (1972). Orrego-Salas also gave a general appraisal of several Latin American composers' stylistic tendencies in 'Traditions, experiment, and change in contemporary Latin America', *Latin American Music Review,* 6/2 (1985).

## 7/8. LATIN AMERICAN ARCHITECTURE AND ART SINCE C. 1920

There are few reliable general surveys of modern Latin American art and architecture, but see important early contributions by the British professor of literature Jean Franco, *The Modern Culture of Latin America: Society and the Artist* (1967; 2nd ed., London, 1970); the Uruguayan art historian V. Gesualdo (ed.), *Enciclopedia del arte en América,* 5 vols. (Buenos Aires, 1968), a most helpful guide to both art and architecture organized by both country and artist; the U.S. musicologist Gilbert Chase, *Contemporary Art in Latin America* (New York, 1970); and the Argentine art historian and critic Damián Bayón, *Aventura plástica de Hispanoamérica* (1974; Mexico, D.F., 1992). See also Damián Bayón (ed.), *America Latina en sus artes* (Paris and Mexico, D.F., 1974). More recent works include *Historia del arte iberoamericano,* 2 vols. (Madrid, 1988) by the Chilean Leopoldo Castedo, a book that covers art from the pre-Columbian period to the present; Damián Bayón, *Historia del arte hispanoamericano,* Vol. 3, *Siglos XIX y XX* (Madrid, 1988); Damián Bayón (ed.), *Arte moderno en América Latina* (Madrid, 1988), with contributions from J. Romero Brest, Marta Traba, J. A. Manrique and others; Dawn Ades, *Art in Latin America: The Modern Era, 1820–1980* (London, 1989); Oriana Baddeley and Valerie Fraser, *Drawing the Line: Art and Cultural Identity in Contemporary Latin America* (London, 1989) and Edward Lucie-Smith, *Latin American Art of the 20th Century* (London, 1993). Specifically on architecture, see H. R. Hitchcock, *Latin American Architecture since 1945* (New York, 1955); Paul Damaz, *Art in Latin American Architecture* (New York, 1963); Francisco Bullrich, *New Directions in Latin American Architecture* (New York, 1969) and *Arquitectura latinoamericana, 1930–70* (Buenos Aires, 1970); Roberto Segre (ed.), *América Latina en su arquitectura* (Paris, 1973); Damián Bayón, *Panorámica de la arquitectura latinoamericana* (Barcelona, 1977), a useful collection of interviews, illustrated with excellent photographs by Paolo Gasparini; Bayón and Gasparini, *The Changing Shape of Latin American Architecture* (New York, 1979); Ramón Gutiérrez, *Arquitectura y urbanismo en Iberoamérica* (Madrid, 1983); and E. Tejeira-Davis, *Roots of Modern Latin American Architecture* (Heidelberg, 1987).

## Mexico

Works in English on the Mexican muralists include Bertram D. Wolfe, *Portrait of Mexico* (New York, 1937); Bernard Myers, *Mexican Painting in Our Time* (New York, 1956); Alma Reed, *The Mexican Muralists* (New York, 1960); Jaime and Virginia Plenn, *A Guide to Mexican Modern Murals* (Ixtapalapa, 1963); and Desmond Rockfort, *Mexican Muralists: Orozco, Rivera and Siqueiros* (London, 1993). On Rivera, see Desmond Rockfort, *The Murals of Diego Rivera* (London, 1987) and a biography, Bertram D. Wolfe, *The Fabulous Life of Diego Rivera* (New York, 1963). On Orozco, see MacKinley Helm's biography, *Man of Fire: Orozco* (Boston, 1953) and Alma Reed, *José Clemente Orozco* (New York, 1956). On David Alfaro Siqueiros, see Leonard Folgarait, *So Far from Heaven: David Alfaro Siqueiros' 'The March of Humanity' and Mexican Revolutionary Politics* (Cambridge, Eng., 1987). There are several studies of Tamayo: see, in particular, Robert Goldwater, *Tamayo* (New York, 1947) and James B. Lynch, *Tamayo* (Phoenix, Ariz., 1968). Hayden Herrera's *Frida Kahlo* (New York, 1982) contributed to the contemporary fashion for that conflictive woman painter.

In Spanish, the Guatemalan poet and critic Luis Cardoza y Aragón has contributed various luminous studies on Mexican art: see, for example, *La nube y el reloj* (Mexico, D.F., 1940); *México: pintura activa* (Mexico, D.F., 1961) and *México: pintura de hoy* (Mexico, D.F., 1964). Another exceptional figure, Octavio Paz, has written on art, especially Mexican art, with wonderful intuition, from his study of *Tamayo* (Mexico, D.F., 1958) to a more recent collection of essays, *Los privilegios de la vista* (Mexico, D.F., 1987); Eng trans., *Essays on Mexican Art* (New York, 1993). The essayist Samuel Ramos dedicated two of his studies to art: *Diego Rivera* (Mexico, D.F., 1958) and *The Mexican Muralists* (New York, 1960). The 'Three Greats' (Rivera, Orozco, Siqueiros) found the time and energy to write on their own lives and experiences: see by Rivera, *Autobiografía* (Mexico, D.F., 1963) and *Mi arte, mi vida* (Mexico, D.F., 1963); by Orozco, the most literarily endowed of the three, *Autobiografía* (Mexico, D.F., 1942), and *El artista en Nueva York* (Mexico, D.F., 1971); by Siqueiros, *No hay más ruta que la nuestra* (Mexico, D.F., 1945) and, many years later, *A un joven mexicano* (Mexico, D.F., 1967). One of the earliest muralists was the French-born Jean Charlot, who wrote *The Mexican Mural Renaissance, 1920–1925* (New Haven, Conn., 1966) based on his own experiences.

The following works by professional historians and critics are worthy of note: Justino Fernández, *Arte moderno y contemporáneo de México* (Mexico, D.F., 1952) and *La pintura moderna mexicana* (Mexico, D.F., 1964); Raquel Tibol, a dedicated polemist of the left, *Siqueiros, introductor de realidades* (Mexico, D.F., 1961), and *Historia general del arte mexicano: época moderna y contemporánea* (Mexico, D.F., 1964), among others; Juan García Ponce, a novelist who analyses works of art, *Nueve pintores mexicanos* (Mexico, D.F., 1968), and *La aparición de lo invisible* (Mexico, D.F., 1968); Ida Rodríguez Prampolini, a professor at UNAM, *El surrealismo y el arte fantástico de México* (Mexico, D.F., 1969); and Shifra Goldman, *Contemporary Mexican Painting in a Time of Change* (Austin, Tex., 1980). On architecture, Israel Katzman, *La arquitectura moderna mexicana* (Mexico, D.F., 1963) is an important study.

## Central America and the Caribbean

On painting in Cuba, Adelaida de Juan, *Pintura cubana* (Havana, 1980) is an interesting work. On architecture only the works of Roberto Segre, the great specialist on Caribbean architecture, are of real value: see *Diez años de arquitectura revolucionaria en Cuba* (Havana, 1970), and *La vivienda en Cuba: república y revolución* (Havana, 1980).

On the Guatemalan-born painter Mérida, see *Carlos Mérida* (Mexico, D.F., 1961) by the Spanish critic Margarita Nelken. One of the few books on Guatemalan architecture is L. Luján Muñoz, *Síntesis de la arquitectura en Guatemala* (Guatemala City, 1968). See also Lionel Méndez Dávila, *Guatemala* (Washington, D.C., 1966).

On the architecture of Panama, see R. Rodríguez Porcel, *Panorama histórico de la arquitectura de Panamá* (Havana, 1972). A French specialist resident in Santo Domingo, Marianne de Tolentino, has written several works on the art of the Dominican Republic. Holger Escoto, *Historia de la arquitectura dominicana* (Santo Domingo, 1978) is an interesting work on its architecture. On the art and architecture of Puerto Rico, see E. Fernández Méndez, *Historia cultural de Puerto Rico* (San Juan, P.R., 1970).

## Colombia and Venezuela

The Argentine-born Marta Traba was for many years the most important art critic in Colombia. See, for example, a polemical text, *Dos décadas vulnerables en las artes plásticas latinoamericanas* (Mexico, D.F., 1973) and two collections of articles: *Mirar en Bogotá* (Bogotá, 1976) and *Mirar en Caracas* (Bogotá, 1974). On modern Colombian architecture, see Germán Téllez, *Crítica e imagen* (Bogotá, 1977); J. Arango and C. Martínez, *Arquitectura en Colombia, 1538–1951* (Bogotá, 1951) and A. Berty, *Architectures colombiennes* (Paris, 1971). The senior art historian of Venezuela is Alfredo Boulton; see, in particular, his *Historia de la pintura en Venezuela,* 3 vols. (Caracas, 1968). Other distinguished critics are Juan Calzadilla – see, for example, *El arte en Venezuela* (Caracas, 1967) and *El ojo que pasa* (Caracas, 1969), and Roberto Guevara – see, for example, *Arte para una nueva escala* (Caracas, 1977). On architecture, the leading figure remains Italian-born Graziano Gasparini. See, in particular (with J.P. Posani), *Caracas a través de su arquitectura* (Caracas, 1971). There are two volumes in the OAS series on series on Latin American art: Marta Traba, *Colombia* (Washington, D.C., 1959) and Clara Sujo, *Venezuela* (Washington, D.C., 1962).

### Peru, Bolivia and Chile

On Peru, there are valuable contributions by J. M. Ugarte Eléspuru (a painter himself) – see, in particular, *Pintura y escultura en el Perú contemporáneo* (Lima, 1970) – and by Mirko Lauer, *Introducción a la pintura peruana del siglo XX* (Lima, 1976). On Peruvian architecture, see J. García Bryce, 'La arquitectura en el virreinato y la república', in Jose García Bryce, Luis Enrique Tord and Enrique Pinilla (eds.), *Historia del Perú*, vol. 9 (Lima, 1980). For Bolivia, R. Villaroel Claure has contributed two useful volumes: *Pintores, grabadores y escultores bolivianos* (La Paz, 1952), and *Bolivia* (OAS, Washington, D.C., 1963). The country's two leading historians, José de Mesa and his wife, Teresa Gisbert, are primarily specialists on colonial art, but they have contributed important essays on the modern plastic arts, and especially architecture – see, for example, *Emilio Villanueva: hacia una arquitectura nacional* (La Paz, 1984). The classical work on Chilean painting is A. R. Romero, *Historia de la pintura chilena* (Santiago, Chile, 1968). See also Milan Ivelic and Gaspar Galaz, *La pintura chilena* (Valparaiso, 1981). On architecture, above all see O. Ortega, M. Anduaga, C. Miranda, S. Pirotte, F. Riquelme, and A. Sahady: *Guía de la arquitectura en Santiago* (Santiago, Chile, 1976).

### Argentina, Uruguay and Paraguay

A pioneer in the critical approach to the study of art in Argentina was A. Chiabra Acosta ('Atalaya'), *Críticas de arte argentino, 1920–1930* (Buenos Aires, 1934). A contemporary, but more of a historian, was José León Pagano. See his monumental work, *El arte de los argentinos*, 3 vols. (Buenos Aires, 1940). Other distinguished, important – and very different – works are C. Córdova Iturburu, *La pintura argentina del siglo XX* (Buenos Aires, 1958); Aldo Pellegrini, *La pintura argentina contemporánea* (Buenos Aires, 1967); and Romualdo Brughetti, *Geografía plástica argentina* (Buenos Aires, 1958) and *Historia del arte en la Argentina* (Buenos Aires, 1965). The most active and influential author not only in Argentina but in the rest of South America was Jorge Romero Brest. Most of his books are on general subjects, but, on Argentina, see *El arte en la Argentina* (Buenos Aires, 1969). Laura San Martín, *Pintura argentina contemporánea* (Buenos Aires, 1961) is a useful listing of artists. A short book written by a member of a younger generation in collaboration with three other critics is Fermin Févre, *La pintura argentina* (Buenos Aires, 1975), On architecture, see F. Bullrich, *Arquitectura argentina contemporánea* (Buenos Aires, 1963); J. M. Peña and J. X. Martini, *La ornamentación en la arquitectura de Buenos Aires,* 2 vols. (Buenos Aires, 1980); Marina Waisman (ed.), *Documentos para una historia de la arquitectura argentina* (Buenos Aires, 1978); and an important bibliography, *Arquitectura en Argentina* (Buenos Aires, 1980), written by specialists like F. Ortiz, A. de Paula and R. A. Gómez.

On Uruguay there are two fundamental works by J. P. Argul: *Pintura y escultura en el Uruguay* (Montevideo, 1958) and *Las artes plásticas en el Uruguay* (Montevideo, 1966). For a different view, see F. García Esteban, *Panorama de la pintura uruguaya contemporánea* (Montevideo, 1965). The 'pope' of Uruguayan art, Joaquín Torres-García, produced two indispensable books: one on theory, *Universalismo constructivo* (Buenos Aires, 1944), where he preaches his ideas on art, the other – much more intimate – *Autobiografía* (Montevideo, 1939). The great Uruguayan architectural historian was J. Giuría, author of two historical works: *La arquitectura en el Paraguay* (Buenos Aires, 1950), and *La arquitectura en el Uruguay* (Montevideo, 1955). See also L. A. Artucio, *Montevideo y la arquitectura moderna* (Montevideo, 1971). In Paraguay, apart from the book by J. Giuría already mentioned, the literature on art and architecture is scarce. But see J. Báez, *Arte y artistas paraguayos* (Asunción, 1941); and the more recent, and indispensable, book by Ticio Escobar, *Una interpretación de las artes visuales en el Paraguay,* 2 vols. (Asunción, 1984).

## *Brazil*

An early book by Sergio Milliet, *Pintores e pinturas* (São Paulo, 1940) remains valuable. Two theorists of the Antropofagia movement published important works: Mário de Andrade, *0 movimento modernista* (Rio de Janeiro, 1942) and Oswald de Andrade, *Ponta de lança* (1945; Rio de Janeiro, 1972). An early and useful study by the Argentine J. Romero Brest, published in Spanish, is *La pintura brasileña contemporánea* (Buenos Aires, 1945). Like Romero Brest, Mario Pedrosa was a prolific author: see among his general works *Arte, necessidade vital* (Rio de Janeiro, 1949), and *Mundo, homem, arte em crise* (São Paulo, 1975). An Italian resident in Brazil, Pietro Maria Bardi, published two popular books in English: *The Arts in Brazil: A New Museum at São Paulo* (Milan, 1956) and *Profile of the New Brazilian Art* (Rio de Janeiro, 1970). *De Anita ao Museu* (Rio de Janeiro, 1976) by the Paulista writer Paulo Mendes de Almeida, is an interesting work: the title refers to the painter Anita Malfatti and the Museum of Fine Arts in São Paulo. Other interesting works include *O modernismo* (São Paulo, 1975), by Affonso Avila of Belo Horizonte, and *Visconti e as artes decorativas* (Rio de Janeiro, 1983), by an Argentine specialist, Irma Arestizábal.

Three important Brazilian critics belonging, more or less, to the same generation – Aracy Amaral, Frederico Morais, and Roberto Pontual – have made a major contribution to the study of Brazilian art. By Amaral, see in particular *Artes plásticas na Semana de 22* (São Paulo, 1970), and *Arte para quê? A preocupação social no arte brasileira, 1930–1970* (São Paulo, 1984); by Morais, *Artes plásticas: a crise da hora atual* (Rio de Janeiro, 1975) and *As artes plásticas na América latina: do transe ao transitório* (Rio de Janeiro, 1979); by Pontual, *Dicionário das artes plásticas no Brasil* (Rio de Janeiro, 1969) and *Entre dois séculos* (*Arte brasileira do século XX na coleção Gilberto Chateaubriand*) (Rio de Janeiro, 1987) as well as *La peinture de l'Amerique latine au xxe siècle* (Paris, 1990). Other contributions by well-known critics include Ferreira Gullar, *Cultura posta em questão* (Rio de Janeiro, 1965); Clarival do Prado Valladares, *Riscadores de milagres – um estudo sobre arte genuína* (Rio de Janeiro, 1967); and J. R. Teixeira Leite, *Pintura moderna brasileira* (Rio de Janeiro, 1979). An important collective work is *História geral da arte no Brasil*, 2 vols. (São Paulo, 1983), edited by Walter Zanini, former director of the Museum of Fine Arts in Rio de Janeiro.

Three pioneer books on modern Brazilian architecture were Philip Goodwin, *Brazil Builds: Architecture Old and New, 1652–1942* (New York, 1943); Stamo Papadaki, *Works in Progress* (New York, 1950); and Henrique Mindlin, *Modern Architecture in Brazil* (Rio de Janeiro, 1956). Bullrich, *New Directions in Latin American Architecture*, cited above, includes a bright and controversial essay on Brasília. More recent works include Paulo F. Santos, *Quatro séculos de arquitetura* (Rio de Janeiro, 1977); Alberto Xavier, *Brasília e arquitetura moderna brasileira* (São Paulo, 1977); and Carlos Lemos, *Arquitetura brasileira* (São Paulo, 1979). A practical guide is Nestor Goulart Reis, *Quadro da arquitetura no Brasil*, 4th ed. (São Paulo, 1978). See also the useful essay by Julio R. Katinsky, 'Arquitectura y diseño en el Brasil', in D. Bayón, *Arte moderno en América Latina*.

## 9. LATIN AMERICAN CINEMA

### General

Several works cover the development of cinema in Latin America from its inception: see Guy Hennebelle and Alfonso Gumucio Dagrón (eds.), *Les Cinémas de l'Amérique Latine* (Paris, 1981); John King, *Magical Reels: A History of Cinema in Latin America* (London, 1990; Sp. trans., Bogotá, 1994); Jorge A. Schnitman, *Film Industries in Latin America: Dependency and Development* (Norwood, N.J., 1984); Peter B. Schumann, *Historia del cine latinoamericano* (Buenos Aires, 1986); José Agustín Mahieu, *Panorama del cine Iberoamericano* (Madrid, 1990); Paulo Paranagua, *Cinema na América Latina: longe de Deus e perto de Hollywood* (Porto Alegre, 1984); and John King, Ana López and Manuel Alvarado (eds.), *Mediating Two Worlds: Cinematic Encounters in the Americas* (London, 1993). See also Ana López, 'Towards a "Third" and "Imperfect" Cinema: A theoretical and historical study of film-making in Latin America' (unpublished Ph.D. dissertation, University of Iowa, 1986).

Two books focus on early cinema: XI Festival del Nuevo Cine Latinoamericano, *Cine latinoamericano: años 30–40–50* (Mexico, D.F., 1990) and Silvia Oroz, *Melodrama: O cinema de lágrimas da América Latina* (Rio de Janeiro, 1992). In the main, however, general works have focused in particular on the 'new' cinema movements of the last thirty years. See, in particular, Julianne Burton (ed.), *Cinema and Social Change in Latin America: Conversations with Filmmakers* (Austin, Tex., 1986). See also Burton (ed.), *The Social Documentary in Latin America* (Pittsburgh, Pa., 1990) and *The New Latin American Cinema: An Annotated Bibliography, 1960–1980* (New York, 1983). Other books/catalogues concentrating on the modern period include: Pat Aufderheide (ed.), *Latin American Visions: Catalogue,* (Philadelphia, Pa., 1989); Zuzana M. Pick, *The New Latin American Cinema: A Continental Project* (Austin, Tex., 1993); E. Bradford Burns, *Latin American Cinema: Film and History* (Los Angeles, 1975); Michael Chanan (ed.), *Twenty-five Years of the New Latin American Cinema* (London, 1983); Isaac León Frias (ed.), *Los años de la conmoción, 1967–1973* (Mexico, D.F., 1979); Coco Fusco (ed.), *Reviewing Histories: Selections from New Latin American Cinema* (Buffalo, N.Y., 1987); Octavio Getino, *Cine latinoamericano: economía y nuevas tecnologías audiovisuales* (Havana and Merida, Ven., 1987); Alfonso Gumucio Dagrón, *Cine, censura y exilio en América Latina* (La Paz,

1979); *Hojas de cine: testimonios y documentos del nuevo cine latinoamericano*, 3 vols. (Mexico, D.F., 1988); Augusto Torres Martínez and Manuel Pérez Estremera, *Nuevo cine latinoamericano* (Barcelona, 1973); Teresa Toledo, *Diez años de un festival* (Madrid, 1990); Luis Trelles Plazaola, *Cine y mujer en América Latina* (Río Piedras, P.R., 1991), *South American Cinema: Dictionary of Filmmakers* (Río Piedras, P.R., 1989) and *Nostalgias y rebeldías: 5 directoras latinoamericanas de cine en Europa* (Río Piedras, 1992).

Several critics have explored Latin American cinema within the broader context of Third Cinema/Third World debates. For the seminal essay on 'Third Cinema', see Fernando Solanas and Octavio Getino, *Cine, cultura y descolonización* (Mexico, D.F., 1973) and Getino's further comments in *A diez años de 'Hacia un tercer cine'* (Mexico, D.F., 1982). General studies include Roy Armes, *Third World Filmmaking and the West* (Berkeley, 1987); John H. Downing (ed.), *Film and Politics in the Third World* (New York, 1987); Teshome Gabriel, *Third Cinema in the Third World: The Aesthetics of Liberation* (Ann Arbor, Mich., 1982); Zuzana Pick (ed.), *Latin American Filmmakers and the Third Cinema* (Ottawa, 1978); and Jim Pines and Paul Willemen (eds.), *Questions of Third Cinema* (London, 1990). Certain film journals, in particular *Cineaste, Framework, Jump Cut* and *Positif,* carry regular articles on Latin American cinema. See, for example, 'Latin American Film', *Jump Cut,* 30 (March 1985); 'Latin American Dossier', Parts 1 and 2, *Framework,* 10 (Spring 1979), 11–39 and 11 (Autumn 1979), 18–27; 'Latin American Militant Cinema', special issue, *Cineaste,* 4/3 (1970–1).

## Argentina and Uruguay

The literature tends to paint the picture in broad brush-strokes, with only one or two works concentrating on particular directors or genres. See Tim Barnard (ed.), *Argentine Cinema* (Toronto, 1986); Fernando Birri, *La escuela documental de Santa Fe* (Santa Fe, Arg., 1964); Jose Miguel Couselo, *El negro Ferreyra: un cine por instinto* (Buenos Aires, 1969); Couselo et al., *Historia del cine argentino* (Buenos Aires, 1984); Domingo Di Núbila, *Historia del cine argentino,* 2 vols. (Buenos Aires, 1971); Estela Dos Santos, *El cine nacional* (Buenos Aires, 1971); Claudio España, *Medio siglo de cine: Argentina Sono Films* (Buenos Aires, 1984); Octavio Getino, *Notas sobre el cine argentino* (Mexico, D.F., 1984); John King and Nissa Torrents (eds.), *The Garden of Forking Paths: Argentine Cinema* (London, 1988); Agustín Mahieu, *Breve historia del cine argentino* (Buenos Aires, 1966) and *Breve historia del cine nacional:* 1896–1974 (Buenos Aires, 1974); Jorge Abel Martin, *Los filmes de Leopoldo Torre Nilsson* (Buenos Aires, 1980); Instituto Nacional de Cinematografía, *Diccionario de realizadores contemporáneos* (Buenos Aires, 1987); Daniel López, *Catálogo del nuevo cine argentino* (Buenos Aires, 1987); Tomás Eloy Martínez, *La obra de Ayala y Torre Nilsson* (Buenos Aires, 1961); Juan José Rossi (ed.), *El cine documental etnobiográfico de Jorge Prelorán* (Buenos Aires, 1985); and Fernando Solanas, *La mirada: reflexiones sobre cine y cultura* (Buenos Aires, 1989); see also Robert Stam, 'Hour of the Furnaces and the two avant-gardes', *Millenium Film Journal,* 7–9 (1980–1). On Argentine cinema in the 1980s, see David William Foster, *Contemporary Argentine Cinema* (Columbia, Mo., 1992). See also Claudio España (comp.), *Cine argentino en democracia, 1983–1993* (Buenos Aires, 1994).

On Uruguay, see Eugenio Hintz (ed.), *Historia y filmografía del cine uruguayo* (Montevideo, 1988). There are interviews with Mario Handler and Walter Achugar in Burton (ed.), *Cinema and Social Change.* See also Walter Achugar et al., 'El cine en el Uruguay', in *Hojas de cine,* Vol. 1.

## Brazil

The most complete one-volume guide to Brazilian cinema, with the most comprehensive bibliography, is Paulo Antonio Paranagua (ed.), *Le Cinéma brésilien* (Paris, 1987). In English, the main reference works are Randal Johnson, *Cinema Novo x 5: Masters of Contemporary Brazilian Film* (Austin, Tex., 1984) and *The Film Industry in Brazil: Culture and the State* (Pittsburgh, Pa., 1987), and Randal Johnson and Robert Stam (eds.), *Brazilian Cinema* (Rutherford, N.J., 1982). In Brazil, there are major works on all the different periods of cinema development. See, in particular, on the silent period, Vicente de Paulo Araujo, *A bela época do cinema brasileiro* (São Paulo, 1976) and *Salões, circos e cinema de São Paulo* (São Paulo, 1981). See also Jean-Claude Bernadet, *Filmografia do cinema brasileiro, 1900–1935* (São Paulo, 1979). Bernadet is one of Brazil's most important critics. His work, which spans the silent period to the present day, includes: *Cinema brasileiro: propostas para uma história* (Rio de Janeiro, 1979); *Trajetória crítica* (São Paulo, 1978); *Brasil em tempo de cinema* (Rio de Janeiro, 1967); *Piranha no Mar de Rosas* (São Paulo, 1982); *Cineastas e imagens do povo* (São Paulo, 1985); and *O vôo dos anjos: Bressane, Sganzerla* (São Paulo, 1990). Other general works which include the silent period are Paulo Emilio Salles

Gomes, *Cinema: trajetoria no subdesenvolvimento* (Rio de Janeiro, 1980) and Gomes and Adhemar Gonzaga, *70 anos de cinema brasileiro* (Rio de Janeiro, 1966). Gomes has also studied Brazil's most important early director, Humberto Mauro, in his *Humberto Mauro, Cataguases, Cinearte* (São Paulo, 1974). See also Ismail Xavier, *Sétima Arte: um culto moderno* (São Paulo, 1978) and Jose Carlos Avellar, *Imagem e som: imagem e ação* (Rio de Janeiro, 1982). On the early talkies, in particular the *chanchada,* see Afrânio M. Catani and José de Melo Souza, *A chanchada no cinema brasileiro* (São Paulo, 1983) and Sérgio Augusto, *Este mundo é um pandeiro: a chanchada de Getúlio a JK* (São Paulo, 1989). The attempted 'modernization' of cinema in the 1940s and 50s is charted in Maria Rita Galvão, *Burguesia e cinema: o caso Vera Cruz* (Rio de Janeiro, 1981).

Perhaps the most acute analyst of the Cinema Novo period is one of its major practitioners, Glauber Rocha: see, *Revisão crítica do cinema brasileiro* (Rio de Janeiro, 1963) and *O século do cinema* (Rio de Janeiro, 1983). Other works include Ismail Xavier, *Sertão mar: Glauber Rocha e a estética da fome* (São Paulo, 1983) and Xavier's 'Allegories of underdevelopment: From the "Aesthetics of Hunger" to the "Aesthetics of Garbage" (unpublished Ph.D. thesis, New York University, 1982); Michel Estève (ed.), *Le 'cinema novo' brésilien,* Etudes cinématographiques, no. 93–6 (Paris, 1972) and *Le 'cinema novo' bresilien 2: Glauber Rocha,* Etudes cinématographiques, no. 97–9 (Paris, 1973); Sylvie Pierre, *Glauber Rocha* (Paris, 1987); José Gatti, *Barravento: a estréia do Glauber* (Florianópolis, 1987); Raquel Gerber, *O cinema brasileiro e o processo político e cultural (de 1950 a 1978)* (Rio de Janeiro, 1982); José Maria Ortiz Ramos, *Cinema, estado e lutas culturais: Anos 50/60/70* (Rio de Janeiro, 1983); Fernão Ramos, *Cinema marginal (1968–1973)* (Rio de Janeiro, 1987); and José Carlos Avellar, *O cinema dilacerado* (Rio de Janeiro, 1986). On more recent movements, see 'Brazil: Post Cinema Novo', *Framework,* 28 (1985).

## Mexico

As with Brazil, the most up-to-date book on Mexican cinema, and the most useful introductory guide, has been edited by Paulo Antonio Paranagua: *Le Cinéma mexicain* (Paris, 1992).

Mexican scholars have developed an extensive bibliography. The most widely published film critic is Emilio García Riera, whose most comprehensive work is the *Historia documental del cine mexicano, Epoca sonora* (Mexico, D.F., 1969–93), 12 vols. to date. Other titles by García Riera include: *El cine mexicano* (Mexico, D.F., 1963); *Historia del cine mexicano* (Mexico, D.F., 1986); *El cine y su público* (Mexico, D.F., 1974); *Filmografía mexicana de medio y largo metrajes, 1906–1940* (Mexico, D.F., 1985); *Fernando de Fuentes* (Mexico, D.F., 1984); *Emilio Fernández* (Guadalajara and Mexico, D.F., 1987); *Los hermanos Soler* (Guadalajara, 1990); *Julio Bracho* (Guadalajara, 1986); and *Arturo Ripstein habla de su cine* (Guadalajara, 1988). Another stimulating critic to cover the history of cinema is Jorge Ayala Blanco. See his *La aventura del cine mexicano* (Mexico, D.F., 1968); *La búsqueda del cine mexicano* (Mexico, D.F., 1974); *La condición del cine mexicano* (Mexico, D.F., 1986); *La disolvencia del cine mexicano, entre lo popular y lo exquisito* (Mexico, D.F., 1991). With María Luisa Amador, Ayala Blanco has published the *cartelera* of four decades of cinema in Mexico: *Cartelera cinematográfica 1930–1939* (Mexico, D.F., 1982), *1950–1959* (Mexico, D.F., 1985); *1960–1969* (Mexico, D.F., 1986); and *1970–1979* (Mexico, D.F., 1988). Other general works include Aurelio de los Reyes, *Medio siglo de cine mexicano (1896–1947)* (Mexico, D.F., 1987); Carl J. Mora, *Mexican Cinema: Reflections of a Society, 1896–1980* (Berkeley, 1982); Beatriz Reyes Nevares, *Trece directores del cine mexicano* (Mexico, D.F., 1974), Eng. trans. *The Mexican Cinema: Interviews with Thirteen Directors* (Albuquerque, N.Mex., 1976); and Alberto Ruy Sánchez, *Mitología de un cine en crisis* (Mexico, D.F., 1981). Ruy Sánchez is the editor of the magazine *Artes de México,* which has published two beautifully-illustrated numbers on Mexican cinema: 'El arte de Gabriel Figueroa', *Artes de México,* 2 (Winter 1988) and 'Revisión del cine mexicano', *Artes de México,* 10 (Winter 1990). The cultural critic Carlos Monsiváis has written extensively on Mexican cinema in witty and trenchant style: for selections of these essays see his *Amor perdido* (Mexico, D.F., 1977), *Escenas de pudor y liviandad* (Mexico, D.F., 1988), and *Rostros del cine mexicano* (Mexico, D.F., 1993).

On the origins of Mexican cinema, see Gustavo García, *El cine mudo mexicano* (Mexico, D.F., 1982); Manuel González Casanova, *Crónica del cine silente en México* (Mexico, D.F., 1989); Andrés de Luna, *La batalla y su sombra (La revolución en el cine mexicano)* (Mexico, D.F., 1984); Aurelio de los Reyes, *Los orígenes del cine en México (1896–1900)* (Mexico, D.F., 1973). See also de los Reyes, *Cine y sociedad en México, 1896–1930:* Vol. 1, *Vivir de sueños (1896–1920)* (Mexico, D.F., 1983). On early talkies and the 'Golden Age' of Mexican cinema, see the studies of individual directors by García Riera, already mentioned. See also Juan Bustillo Oro, *Vida cin-*

*ematográfica* (Mexico, D.F., 1984); Henry Burdin, *La mexicaine María Felix, le roman d'une vie* (Paris, 1982); Adela Fernández, *El indio Fernández, vida y mito* (Mexico, D.F., 1988); Alejandro Galindo, *Verdad y mentira del cine mexicano* (Mexico, D.F., 1981); Diana Negrete, *Jorge Negrete: biografía autorizada* (Mexico, D.F., 1987); Miguel Angel Morales, *Cómicos de México* (Mexico, D.F., 1987); Tomás Pérez Turrent, *La fábrica de sueños: Estudios Churubusco, 1945–1985* (Mexico, D.F., 1985); Gabriel Ramírez, *Lupe Vélez: la mexicana que escupía fuego* (Mexico, D.F., 1986); David Ramón, *Sensualidad: las películas de Ninón Sevilla* (Mexico, D.F., 1989); Paco Ignacio Taibo, *La música de Agustín Lara en el cine* (Mexico, D.F., 1984), *Siempre Dolores* (Mexico, D.F., 1984), *María Félix, 47 pasos por el cine* (Mexico, D.F., 1985), and *El indio Fernández: el cine por mis pistolas* (Mexico, D.F., 1986); Eduardo de la Vega Alfaro, *El cine de Juan Orol* (Mexico, D.F., 1985) and *Arcady Boytler* (Guadalajara, 1992); Ariel Zuñiga, *Vasos comunicantes en la obra de Roberto Gavaldón* (Mexico, D.F., 1990).

Work on modern cinema includes: Paola Costa, *La 'apertura' cinematográfica, México, 1970–1976* (Puebla, 1988); Klaus Eder, *Arturo Ripstein: Filmemacher aus Mexico* (Munich, 1989); Marcela Fernández Violante, *La docencia y el fenómeno fílmico: Memoria de los XXV años del CUEC, 1963–88* (Mexico, D.F., 1988); Vicente Leñero, *Tres guiones cinematográficos: Magnicidio, los Albañiles, Cadena Perpetua* (Mexico, D.F., 1982); Tomás Pérez Turrent, *Canoa: memoria de un hecho vergonzoso* (Puebla, 1984); Pérez Turrent et al., *Rafael Corkidi* (Mexico, D.F., 1978); Florencio Sánchez, *Crónica antisolemne del cine mexicano* (Xalapa, 1989) and *Hermosillo: pasión por la libertad* (Mexico, D.F., 1989); Nelson Carro Rodríguez, *El cine de luchadores* (Mexico, D.F., 1984); Charles Ramírez Berg, *Cinema of Solitude: A Critical Study of Mexican Film, 1967–1983* (Austin, Tex., 1992). Chon A. Noriega and Steven Ricci (eds.), *The Mexican Cinema Project* (Los Angeles: UCLA Film and Television Archive, 1994) introduces the new, major archive of Mexican films at the University of California, Los Angeles (a joint project with the Mexican Institute of Cinematography, IMCINE).

## Chile

Few works cover Chilean cinema before the 1960s. There are two general studies: Carlos Ossa Coo, *Historia del cine chileno* (Santiago, 1971) and Alicia Vega, *Re-visión del cine chileno* (Santiago, 1979). On 'new cinema' from the 1960s and 'exile' cinema, see Francesco Bolzoni, *El cine de*

*Allende* (Valencia, Spain, 1975); Michael Chanan (ed.), *Chilean Cinema* (London, 1976); Gabriel García Márquez, *La aventura de Miguel Littín, clandestino en Chile* (Mexico, D.F., 1986), Eng. trans., *Clandestine in Chile* (Cambridge, Eng., 1989). For further criticism on Littín, see Ana López, 'Towards a "Third" and "Imperfect" Cinema', mentioned above. (Almost all the survey books cited at the beginning of this essay contain essays on Littín and on the two other best-known directors of the period, Raoul Ruíz and Patricio Guzmán.) See also Patricio Guzmán and Pedro Sempere, *Chile: el cine contra el fascismo* (Valencia, 1977); *Literatura Chilena, Creación y Crítica*, 27 (January–March 1984), special issue on Chilean cinema; and Jacqueline Mouesca, *Plano secuencia de la memoria de Chile* (Madrid, 1988). Raoul Ruíz has received concentrated critical attention in the past decade. See the sections in *Afterimage*, 10 (1982) and in particular the special editions of two eminent French film journals dedicated to his work: *Cahiers du Cinéma*, 345 (March 1983) and *Positif*, 274 (December 1983).

## Cuba

Two stimulating general studies are Michael Chanan, *The Cuban Image: Cinema and Cultural Politics in Cuba* (London, 1985) and Paulo Antonio Paranagua (ed.), *Le Cinéma cubain* (Paris, 1990). See also Arturo Agramonte, *Cronología del cine cubano* (Havana, 1966). On cinema after the revolution, see Néstor Almendros, *A Man with a Camera* (London, 1985); Santiago Alvarez et al., *Cine y revolución en Cuba* (Barcelona, 1975); Michael Chanan, *Santiago Alvarez* (London, 1980); María Eulalia Douglas, *Diccionario de cineastas cubanos, 1959–1987* (Mérida, Ven., 1989); Ambrosio Fornet, *Cine, literatura y sociedad* (Havana, 1982); Fornet (ed.), *Alea: Una retrospectiva crítica* (Havana, 1987); Julio García Espinosa, *Una imagen recorre el mundo* (Havana, 1979); Tomás Gutiérrez Alea, *Dialéctica del espectador* (Mexico, D.F., 1983), Eng. trans. first published in *Jump Cut* 29 and 30 (1984–5) and in book form as *The Viewer's Dialectic* (Havana, 1988); and Michael Myerson (ed.), *Memories of Underdevelopment: The Revolutionary Films of Cuba* (New York, 1973). The development of cinema from 1959 is charted in the journal *Cine Cubano*. See also the special dossier on Cuban cinema in *Jump Cut*, 19 (December 1978), 20 (May 1979) and 22 (May 1980).

## Bolivia and Peru

Bolivia has produced several interesting works of criticism. See, in particular, Alfonso Gumucio Dagrón, *Historia del cine en Bolivia* (La Paz, 1982); Carlos D. Mesa, *La aventura del cine boliviano, 1952–1985* (La Paz, 1985) and *El cine boliviano según Luis Espinal* (La Paz, 1982); Beatriz Palacios Mesa, Jorge Sanjinés et al., *Cine boliviano: del realizador al crítico* (La Paz, 1979); and Jorge Sanjinés and El Grupo Ukamau, *Teoría y práctica de un cine junto al pueblo* (Mexico, D.F., 1979). Sanjinés is included in all the major general studies of new Latin American cinema.

Surprisingly, there is no general reference work on Peruvian cinema. See, however, the articles in *Hablemos de Cine;* for example, Isaac León Frías, 'Hacia una historia de cine peruano', 50–1 (1970); various authors, 'Diccionario del cortometraje peruano', 70 (1979) and 71 (1980); and 'Encuentro con Federico García', 75 (1982). On Francisco Lombardi, Peru's best-known director, see Paulo Antonio Paranagua, 'Francisco Lombardi et le nouveau cinéma péruvien', *Positif,* 338 (April 1989).

## Colombia and Venezuela

For general reference on the Colombian cinema, see Hernando Martínez Pardo, *Historia del cine colombiano* (Bogotá, 1978); Umberto Valverde, *Reportaje crítico al cine colombiano* (Bogotá, 1978); and Hernando Salcedo Silva, *Crónicas del cine colombiano, 1897–1950* (Bogotá, 1981). The Bogotá-based magazine, *Cuadernos de Cine Colombiano,* produced a series of studies of individual directors in the early 1980s: see 2 (1981) on Ciro Durán; 3 (1981) on Francisco Norden; 4 (1981) on Lizaro Tarco Tulio; 7 (1982) on Jorge Silva and Marta Rodríguez; 10 (1983) on Luis Ospina; and 11 (1983) on Camila Loboguerrero. On cinema of the 1980s, see Orlando Mora and Sandro Romero Rey, 'Cine colombiano, 1977–1987: Dos opiniones', *Boletín Cultural y Bibliográfico,* 25/5 (1988), 31–49, and various authors, 'Colombia: En busca de un cine perdido', *Gaceta* (July–August 1989), 21–33. Finally, see Carlos Alvarez, *Sobre el cine colombiano y latinoamericano* (Bogotá, 1989).

Studies of Venezuela concentrate on recent cinema. See Jesús M. Aguirre and Marcelino Bisbal, *El nuevo cine venezolano* (Caracas, 1980); Edmundo Aray, *Cine venezolano: producción cinematográfica de la ULA* (Mérida, Ven., 1986); Rodolfo Izaguirre, *El cine en Venezuela,* 2nd ed.

(Caracas, 1981) and *Cine venezolano: largometrajes* (Caracas, 1983); R. Grazione et al., *Clemente de la Cerda* (Caracas, n.d.); Alvaro N. P. Naranjo, *Román Chalbaud: un cine de autor* (Caracas, 1984); and Ricardo Tirado, *Memoria y notas del cine venezolano*, 2 vols. (Caracas, 1988).

### The Caribbean and Central America

On Caribbean cinema, see Arnold Antonin, *Material para una pre-historia del cine haitiano* (Caracas, 1983); Kino García, *Breve historia del cine puertorriqueño*, 2nd rev. ed. (Bayamón, P.R., 1989); José Luis Sáez, *Historia de un sueño importado, ensayos sobre el cine en Santo Domingo* (Santo Domingo, 1982). See also *Hojas de cine,* Vol. 3, cited above.

Central America has received critical attention mainly in the last fifteen years as a result of revolutionary/guerrilla cinema. On Nicaragua, see Alfonso Gumucio Dagrón, *El cine de los trabajadores* (Managua, 1981), as well as *Hojas de cine,* vol. 3, cited above; Armand Mattelart (ed.), *Communicating in Popular Nicaragua* (New York, 1986); and John Ramírez, 'Introduction to the Sandinista documentary cinema', *Areito,* 37 (1984). Essays on the cinemas of the remaining Central American republics are found in *Hojas de cine,* vol. 3, cited above. See also the special edition of *Jump Cut* on the revolutionary cinema in El Salvador: *Jump Cut,* 26 (1981). On Panama, see Pedro Rivera, 'Apuntes para una historia del cine en Panamá,' *Formato* 16, 3 (1977).

## 10. LATIN AMERICAN BROADCASTING

The historical literature on the Latin American mass media from the 1920s to the late 1960s – most of it published in small editions, often by the pioneers of broadcasting – is not abundant. The extensive literature on development communications in Latin America was written mainly in the United States. There is a significant Latin American body of critical work around media reforms and the New International Information Order, much of which is contained in Fernando Reyes Matta (ed.), *La Información en el Nuevo Orden Internacional* (Mexico, D.F., 1977) and in UNESCO Reports and Papers on Mass Communication: 70 Television Traffic – A One-Way Street?; 92, Transnational Communication and Cultural Industries; 93, Foreign News in the Media: International Reporting in 29 Countries; 98, The New International Economic Order: Links

Between Economics and Communication; and 99, International Flow of Information: A Global Report and Analysis, There have been some studies on the media under the military dictatorships of the 1970s and early 1980s, such as G. Munizaga, *El discurso público de Pinochet* (Buenos Aires, 1983) and the studies cited below on Brazil and Argentina. Finally, there is extensive descriptive and applied literature on the experiences of alternative communications.

There have been important efforts to collect and analyse the literature on Latin American communications. Several annotated bibliographies of national communication research have been published: P. Anzola and P. Cooper, *La investigación en comunicación social en Colombia* (Lima, 1985); G. Munizaga and A. Rivera, *La investigación en comunicación social en Chile* (Lima, 1983); O. Peirano and T. Kudo, *La investigación en comunicación social en el Perú* (Lima, 1982); J. B. Rivera, *La investigación en comunicación social en Argentina* (Lima, 1986); Enrique Sánchez Ruiz, *Tendencias en la investigación sobre televisión en México* (Guadalajara, 1992); and Luis Ramiro Beltran, et al., *Bibliografía de estudios sobre comunicación en Bolivia* (La Paz, 1990). R. Atwood and E. McAnany (eds.), *Communication and Latin American Society* (Madison, Wis., 1986), is a book by Latin American and U.S. scholars on the trends in critical research in Latin America. Statistics on the private media industries can be found in the trade newspaper *Variety* Once a year, *Variety* dedicates a special issue to the Latin American communication industries. See, for example, '11th Focus on Latin America and U. S. Hispanic Markets' (March 12, 1986); '12th Focus on Latin American and U. S. Hispanic Markets' (March 25, 1987); and 'Global Report: The Latin Americas' (March 25, 1991).

For the history of the media in Argentina, see A. Ford, J. B. Rivera, and E. Romano, *Medios de comunicación y cultura popular* (Buenos Aires, 1985), and J. Noguer, *Radiodifusión en la Argentina* (Buenos Aires, 1985). For the history of the Brazilian media, M. E. Bonavita Federico, *História da comunicação radio e TV no Brasil* (Petrópolis, 1982) and M. Ferraz Sampaio, *História do radio e da televisão no Brasil e no mundo* (Rio de Janeiro, 1984) are useful. See also S. V. Moreira, *O Radio no Brasil* (Rio de Janeiro, 1991). For the history of the Chilean media, see M. de la L. Hurtado, 'Sistemas de televisión proyectos estatales en Chile', *Opciones,* (January–April 1987), D. Portales, *La dificultad de inovar: un estudio sobre las empresas de televisión en América Latina* (Santiago, Chile, 1987), and M.de la L. Hurtado, *Historia de la TV en Chile, 1958–1973* (Santiago, 1989).

There is considerable literature on the history of the media in Colombia: see, in particular, H. Martínez, *Qué es la televisión?* (Bogotá, 1978); R. Pareja, *Historia de la radio en Colombia, 1929–1980* (Bogotá, 1984); B. H. Tellez, *Cincuenta años de radiodifusión colombiana* (Medellín, 1974) and *25 años de television colombiana* (Bogotá, 1975). For the history of the media in Mexico, see Nestor García Canclini, *Las culturas populares en el capitalismo* (Mexico, D.F., 1982); F. Fernández, *Los medios de difusión masiva en México* (Mexico, D.F., 1982); L. A. Noriega and F. Leach, *Broadcasting in Mexico* (London, 1979); and C. G. Mont, *El desafío de los nuevos medios de comuniación en México* (Mexico, D.F., 1992).

The history of the Peruvian mass media has been chronicled in J. Gargurevich, *Mitos y verdad de los diarios de Lima* (Lima, 1972) and *Prensa, radio y TV: historia crítica* (Lima, 1987). See also C. Ortega and C. Romero, *Las políticas de comunicación en el Perú* (Paris, 1976).

For Venezuela, see O. Capriles, *El estado y los medios de comunicación en Venezuela* (Caracas, 1980); A. Pasquali, *Comunicación y cultura de masas*, 5th ed. (Caracas, 1980) and *El aparato singular: Análisis de un día de TV en Caracas* (Caracas, 1967); and *Proyecto Ratelve (diseño para una nueva política de radiodifusión del estado venezolano)* (Caracas, 1977). The historical information on the development of broadcasting in Cuba can be found in R. Infants, 'Le XXVe anniversaire de L'Institut Cubain pour la Radio et la Television', in *CEMEDIM, 6* (1987), and for Bolivia in R. Rivadeneira and N. Tirado, *La televisión en Bolivia* (La Paz, 1986).

On the role of the United States in the Latin American media, see L. R. Beltran, and E. Fox, *Comunicación dominada: Estados Unidos en los medios de América Latina* (Mexico, D.F., 1982); A. Mattelart, *Multinacionales y sistemas de comunicación: los aparatos ideológicos del imperialismo* (Mexico, D.F., 1977); J. Schnitman, *Film Industries in Latin America: Dependency and Development* (Norwood, N.J., 1984); A. Wells, *Picture Tube Imperialism? The Impact of US Television on Latin America* (New York, 1972). An interesting study of the role of the United States during the Second World War is David Rowland, *History of the Office of the Coordinator of Inter-American Affairs* (Washington, D.C., 1947).

There are a number of interesting recent studies of the *telenovela:* Renato Ortiz, *Telenovela: história e produção* (São Paulo, 1989); J. Martín Barbero and S. Muñoz (eds.), *Televisión y melodrama* (Bogotá, 1992); A. M. Fadul, *Ficção seriada na TV: as telenovelas latinoamericanas/Serial Fiction in TV: The Latin American telenovelas* (São Paulo, 1993).

On television development and reform in Latin America, see CIESPAL, *Política nacional de comunicación* (Quito, 1981) and Elizabeth Fox et al.,

*Comunicación y democracia en América Latina* (Lima, 1982). In the case of Argentina, see O. Landi (comp.), *Medios, transformación cultural y política* (Buenos Aires, 1987), and for Brazil, see S. Mattos, *The Impact of the 1964 Revolution on Brazilian Television* (San Antonio, Tex., 1982); M. O. Sodre, *Monopólio da fala* (Petrópolis, 1981). For the reforms in Peru, see S. Mattos, *The Development of Communication Policies under the Peruvian Military Government* (San Antonio, Tex., 1981); L. Peirano et al., *Prensa: apertura y límites* (Lima, 1978). For Nicaragua, see A. Mattelart (ed.), *Communicating in Popular Nicaragua* (New York, 1986).

The literature on alternative communication in Latin American is extensive. See, in particular, the collections by R. Reyes Matta (comp.), *Comunicación alternativa y búsquedas democráticas* (Mexico, D.F., 1983); M. Simpson Grinberg (comp.), *Comunicación alternativa y cambio social: I, América Latina* (Mexico, D.F., 1981); Regina Festa et al., *Comunicación popular y alternativa* (Buenos Aires, 1986); and R. M. Alfaro et al., *Cultura de masas y cultura popular en la radio peruana* (Lima, 1990). For Central America, see R. Sol, *Medios masivos y comunicación popular* (San José, C.R., 1984). For information on developments in communication technology, see A. Mattelart and H. Schmucler, *Communication and Information Technologies: Freedom of Choice for Latin America?* (Norwood, N.J., 1985); and Instituto para América Latina, Sistema Económico Latinoamericano (IPAL/SELA), *Comunicación, tecnología y desarrollo* (Buenos Aires, 1987).

Finally, see two important books on communication theory by J. Martín Barbero: *De los medios a las mediaciones: comunicación, cultura y hegemonía* (Barcelona, 1987), and *Procesos de comunicación y matrices de cultura: itenerario para salir de la razón dualista* (Mexico, D.F., 1989).

# INDEX

# Index